KOUROI

ARCHAIC GREEK YOUTHS

BY G·M·A·RICHTER

PHAIDON

KOUROI

ARCHAIC GREEK YOUTHS

A STUDY OF THE DEVELOPMENT OF THE KOUROS TYPE IN GREEK SCULPTURE

BY GISELA M·A·RICHTER
IN COLLABORATION WITH IRMA A·RICHTER

WITH FIVE HUNDRED AND NINETY-ONE ILLUSTRATIONS
INCLUDING ONE HUNDRED AND SEVENTY-NINE FROM
PHOTOGRAPHS BY GERARD MACKWORTH-YOUNG

THE PHAIDON PRESS·LONDON·MCMLX

MADE IN GREAT BRITAIN
TEXT PRINTED AT THE UNIVERSITY PRESS · ABERDEEN

PLATES PRINTED BY ROBERT MACLEHOSE & CO · LTD
THE UNIVERSITY PRESS · GLASGOW

CONTENTS

PREFACE TO THE FIRST EDITION

THE incentive to write this book came from the acquisition by the Metropolitan Museum of the kouros or 'archaic Apollo' illustrated in figures 25-32. The lively discussions which centred round this statue revealed the necessity of a detailed study of the kouros type. The result was first an article in *Metropolitan Museum Studies*[1] in 1934, and then the Ryerson Memorial Lectures given at the invitation of the School of Fine Arts, Yale University, in January and February of 1938. The text of the present book, which is an enlargement of these lectures, was completed and ready for the press in the summer of 1939. The outbreak of the war made it seem desirable to postpone the publication, particularly since the photography was not completed. This has been undertaken by Gerard M. Young, whose beautiful photographs of the sculptures in the Akropolis Museum have become famous. After a delay of more than two years, it now seems best to proceed with the available material. Fortunately Mr. Young had taken the photographs of practically all the kouroi in Greece, except those in Delos and Delphi (which had not yet been mounted), and those in Samos and Rhodes (for which other good views were obtainable). He had also photographed the important contingent in the Louvre. For the rest we have made the best substitutions possible in the circumstances. Where no adequate illustrations were procurable, the reader is referred to illustrations in other books. However, the original plan of illustrating in several views every kouros which is included in the descriptions has, to some extent at least, been carried out.

The publication of this book was made possible by grants from the Associates in Fine Arts of Yale University, the American Council of Learned Societies, and the Metropolitan Museum of Art. I take this opportunity of expressing to these institutions and to their committees my appreciation of and gratitude for their help. My thanks are also due to the Metropolitan Museum for facilitating my researches in every way, including a free use of its excellent and constantly expanding collection of photographs. I owe much to the encouragement of Maitland Griggs, trustee of the Metropolitan Museum and chairman of the Associates in Fine Arts of Yale University, and to the generous aid of Francis H. Taylor. Theodore Sizer of Yale University proved throughout a resourceful friend in need.

It is a pleasure to acknowledge also the assistance of my colleagues. In studying the anatomy of the kouroi I have had the advantage of professional aid from my sister, Irma A. Richter. Indeed, without her co-operation this book could not have been written. Part of the chapter on Procedure is hers (pp. 11-12). As usual, I am particularly beholden to my friend J. D. Beazley, who took the time to read my manuscript and made many important suggestions. I also want to express my thanks to Marjorie J. Milne, who has checked, corrected, and supplemented my historical introductions and discussions of inscriptions.[2] I have profited from stimulating discussions with B. Ashmole, E. S. G. Robinson, Agnes B. Brett, and the late E. T. Newell, on intricate numismatic problems; and with M. N. Tod and A. E. Raubitschek on the often elusive epigraphical evidence. Several questions connected with Egyptian history have been elucidated by L. A. Bull. Throughout, valuable assistance has been given me by A. Fieldman, particularly in the checking of references

[1] v, 1934, pp. 20-56. A German translation of this article appeared in Brunn-Bruckmann-Arndt, *Denkmäler griechischer und römischer Skulptur*, nos. 751-5.

[2] In the inscriptions we have mostly followed the standard publications.

and in the preparation of the indices. C. A. Waterhouse of the British Museum has lettered the anatomical figs. 1 and 2; and L. F. Hall has drawn the illustrations on pp. 17, 42, 45, 54.

To many other colleagues I am indebted for help and information, especially of course to the directors and curators of the museums in which the kouroi reside. Not only was I able to examine their kouroi many times—when necessary, on chairs and ladders—but requests for information were always cheerfully answered; and permission to use unpublished material was freely given. I should like to mention with special gratitude in this connection B. Ashmole, C. W. Blegen, Elizabeth Blegen, E. Buschor, L. D. Caskey, J. Charbonneaux, P. de la Coste-Messelière, P. Devambez, H. Diepolder, W. B. Dinsmoor, E. J. Forsdyke, F. R. Grace, G. Hanfmann, Ida T. Hill, R. Hinks, E. Homann-Wedeking, G. Karo, C. Karouzos, Semni P. Karouzou, S. Konstantinou, K. Kouroniotes, N. I. Kyparissis, E. Langlotz, D. Levi, G. Libertini, S. Marinatos, B. D. Meritt, A. Merlin, A. Minto, V. Müller, G. P. Oikonomos, E. Paribeni, A. Philadelpheus, F. Poulsen, F. N. Pryce, M. Robertson, M. I. Rostovtzeff, Mary H. Swindler, A. J. B. Wace, C. Weickert, J. H. Young, R. Zahn.

G. M. A. Richter

PREFACE TO THE SECOND EDITION

Kouroi, first published by the Oxford University Press of New York in 1942, soon went out of print. A new edition seemed desirable, thoroughly revised, with new material added to text and plates. Thanks to the generosity of the Phaidon Press I have been able to do this, and moreover to improve on the illustrations. The plates, originally somewhat grey collotypes, have been replaced by halftones, which do better justice particularly to Mr. Young's fine photographs.

In the years that have passed since the appearance of the first edition, the scheme there evolved has proved its worth. 'The detailed analysis of the consecutive development of anatomical knowledge along naturalistic lines, not only in general structure, but in the rendering of each and every part' has been of use both in dating the kouroi themselves and for the chronology of related works.

In this new presentation the six classes of kouroi adopted in the first edition have been retained, and so has the order of the kouroi themselves; but the insertion of about forty more kouroi in their respective places, and the addition of new illustrations have made a renumbering and repaging necessary. Moreover, the title of the book has been slightly changed, in accordance with the publisher's suggestion.

The principal additions are: The statue of Aristodikos (no. 165); the torso from Markopoulo (no. 32); the fragments unearthed in the Agora (no. 7); a head from Thera in Leyden (no. 19); a head said to be from Naxos in Copenhagen (no. 50); a head from near Naupaktos in Delphi (no. 46); a head perhaps from Athens in the Louvre, on loan from the Museum of Amiens (no. 141); a torso from Megara in the Eleusis Museum (no. 93); a fragmentary torso perhaps belonging to the well known head from Epidauros (no. 91); a torso in Geneva (no. 90); a head perhaps from Athens in Kansas City (no. 164); an unfinished head of unknown provenance in Munich (no. 71); a wooden head from a statuette found in Samos (no. 20); a bronze statuette in the Walter C. Baker collection (no. 158); a head said to be from Greece, in New York (no. 172); two bronze statuettes, one from Dodona, the other from Crete, in Berlin (nos. 45, 53); a lead statuette from Samos, in Florence (no. 21); another lead statuette in the Stathatos Collection (no. 13); a terracotta statuette from Perachora (no. 44); a fragmentary torso from Gortyna; (no. 177); one of the kouroi from Cyrene (no. 133); heads from Keramos, Miletos, and Kalymnos (nos. 130, 132, 129); a statue from Cyprus (no. 180); and several examples from Italy—a torso from Metapontum in Potenza (no. 187); a head from Marzabotto (no. 189); the fine statue from Megara Hyblaia in Syracuse (no. 134); a bronze statuette from Selinus in Palermo (no. 30 bis); and a terracotta statuette from Taranto in Oxford (no. 62). With the generous permission of Mr. Papadimitriou I have also been able to add, as no. 159 bis, the almost intact bronze statue found in July 1959 in the Piraeus. A number of other pieces—including the recently discovered kouros from near Pergamon and one from Miletos—I have grouped with their near relatives, without detailed analysis or illustrations. All these newcomers fitted neatly into their various categories.

I have also added illustrations that were missing before (for instance those of the important early kouroi in Santorin, no. 18, now published by Mr. Kondoleon, and of the two kouroi in Florence, nos. 70, 169, published by Minto); and have improved others. My Epilogue has been considerably expanded, now constituting what amounts to a seventh class of kouroi; for I felt that the final chapter in the evolution of the kouros type (from about 485 to 460 B.C.) needed a more adequate treatment than I had given it.

I have been able to profit from several new interpretations, especially in the reading of inscriptions, those, for instance of Kleobis and Biton (no. 12) and of the Akropolis Torso 665 (no. 137). I have taken into consideration the evidence presented against taking literally the passage in Herodotos V, 62, regarding the archaic temple of Apollo at Delphi. Throughout I have inserted references to Buschor's *Frühgriechische Jünglinge* (1950), where the same theme as in my *Kouroi* is treated in a more general way; and in a few instances I have been able to refer to his forthcoming *Altsamische Standbilder IV*, of which he has kindly sent me the proof of the List of Illustrations.

In the 'absolute chronology' of the kouros type little that is new has happened in the last eighteen years. We still have no specific confirmation of the supposed beginning of Greek monumental sculpture at about 660-650 B.C., nor any definite evidence for the upper limit of the Sounion group. What little has happened, however, strengthens former suppositions (cf. pp. 38 f.). One of the major discoveries of our time—that the Mycenaeans were, it seems, early Greeks—does not affect us here, for the Mycenaeans did not forestall their descendants in trying to understand the complicated anatomy of the human form. Their artistic interests lay elsewhere.

My thanks are due to many friends, especially in the sometimes arduous task of procuring photographs. I want to mention in particular E. Kunze, H. Herrmann, H. A. Thompson, A. Frantz, L. Talcott, E. Harrison, N. Kondoleon, C. and S. Karouzos, S. Marinatos, S. Threpsiadis, J. Papadimitriou, N. Platon, D. Levi, Mrs. Stathatos, P. Dikaios, D. E. L. Haynes, J. Boardman, H. Diepolder, E. Buschor, D. von Bothmer, J. Marcadé, J. Charbonneaux, P. Devambez, G. Daux, P. Levèque, E. Sollberger, V. Poulsen, M. G. Gjödesen, W. Deonna, H. Brunsting, P. E. Arias, L. Barnabò Brea, G. Caputo, W. D. Wungaerden, C. Blümel, H. Hoffmann, and the director of the Museum in Istanbul. Mrs. G. U. S. Corbett has drawn the Delos Colossus with head (cf. p. 52), from the seventeenth-century sketch published by S. Reinach in *B.C.H.* XVII, 1893, pl. V.

G. M. A. R.

FOREWORD

MORE than fifty years have passed since the appearance of Deonna's '*Apollons archaïques*'. In that time a number of new 'Apollos'—or kouroi, i.e. youths, as we now call them*—have been found, several of great importance; our knowledge of archaic Greek sculpture has advanced considerably; and the arts of photography and reproduction have been improved. But Deonna's work has not been superseded. Everyone who has worked in that field will appreciate the admirable collection of material there assembled. Our aim in this book has been not to present a comprehensive corpus of kouroi, since that had already been accomplished, requiring only the addition of the recently discovered examples; but to trace the development of the kouros type in greater detail than has been done before, from its first appearance in the seventh century to its final dissolution during the first half of the fifth century B.C. During this long period we shall find a consecutive, systematic development along naturalistic lines, not only in general structure, but in the rendering of every part, down to such details as the tragus and antitragus of the ear, and the alignment of the toes. Nowhere else can this development be observed so clearly. A detailed analysis, therefore, will serve as a key to the relative chronology of the whole of archaic Greek sculpture.

In tracing this development we have chosen for treatment about 200 kouroi,[1] including the majority of the extant stone and bronze statues in fair condition and a selection of stone, bronze, and terracotta statuettes—enough, it would seem, to draw a representative picture.[2] We have given an anatomical analysis of each kouros and the salient facts regarding its provenance, condition, material, and dimensions, as well as references to the chief publications.[3] We have divided these kouroi into six groups, each composed of members showing the same degree of anatomical knowledge, and we have named each group after the best preserved examples with a known provenance—Sounion, Orchomenos-Thera, Tenea-Volomandra, Melos, Anavysos-Ptoon 12, Ptoon 20. The antecedents and successors of these groups have been discussed in a prologue and an epilogue.

Since in the majority of cases the assignment of individual kouroi to specific 'schools' seems to me precarious, at least in the present state of our knowledge (cf. pp. 5 f.), I have classified our material within the respective groups merely according to the place of discovery, whenever known, and, for convenience, have followed a geographical route from mainland Greece to the Islands, East Greece, North Africa, and west to Italy and Sicily. It is obvious, of course, that a statue was not necessarily made where it was found, especially when it comes from an international sanctuary, like Delphi; though when a statue is of a local stone and the locality from which it is derived has a long artistic tradition, or the dedicator comes from that locality, the probability is that the statue is

* The Greek word *κοῦρος* (Epic and Ionic form of *κόρος, κῶρος*), is used in general for boy, youth (specifically for *Διὸς κοῦροι*, Dioskouroi; cf. e.g. E. Castagnoli, *Studi e Materiali di Storia delle Religioni*, XXX, 1959, p. 5), but not for the statues here considered.

1 In cases where only the head is preserved, it is of course not always certain that the subject was a kouros. Since these heads, however, are excellent examples of their periods and help to clarify the development of the kouros type, it seemed to us useful to include them.

2 I have personally examined the originals of all these kouroi except nos. 8, 19, 21, 26, 45, 53, 54, 58, 61, 81, 82, 107, 115, 130–133, 175, 178, 184, 189, for which I have had to rely on photographs and of which the descriptions and assignments must therefore be accepted with reserve.

3 Preference has been given to official catalogues and accounts of the discoveries of the statues; but Deonna is cited in each case and the chief publications of the inscriptions are included. Dimensions and material are taken from Deonna or the official publications. I have not tried to remeasure each kouros or re-examine its material, except in a few cases which called for discussion.

'home made'. Certainty comes only in those rare instances when the sculptor's origin is actually given in an inscription. Nevertheless, from our geographical classification a number of interesting relations emerge, based on the broad divisions of East and West. And, quite apart from the question of origin, the fact that a statue was found in a certain place reflects on the artistic importance of that place. For in days when transport was difficult and costly (cf. p. 31) the importation of large marble blocks, worked or unworked, presupposes a certain amount of wealth and culture. And so, since our records of seventh- and sixth-century history are scanty, and comparatively little of the literature of that period has survived, this continuous series of statues from the most varied parts of Greece is a precious relic. It sheds new light on the activities of this early age, on its artistic leaders, on the relation of the Greek states to one another.

I have tried, therefore, to present our groups of kouroi, with other significant works which can be related to them, against the background of their time. In so doing, I have picked up what shreds of information are available from ancient literature, but have utilized above all the evidence which the kouroi themselves supply. With their help we have been able to present what in some respects is a new picture of ancient Greece.

In the drawing of this picture there is one major difficulty. Though the relative chronology seems assured, at least along general lines, the absolute chronology is necessarily tentative, as will be seen by our short summaries of the evidence. The monuments which can be definitely dated are lamentably few—not enough to ensure precision for the series, especially in the early groups. And yet, taken in conjunction with the most important evidence—the progressive development of archaic art—our skeleton supplies a good working basis. But to be too precise and assign a definite date to each statue would seem to be premature. We have therefore given a fairly long period to each group, a full quarter of a century or so, and have sometimes made the dates of adjoining groups overlap, to show their tentative nature. Only so can we hope to approximate accuracy. Occasionally it has proved possible to place a specific work early or late in its group.

Since the same anatomical development took place not only in the kouroi but in all archaic Greek sculpture, our findings will help to assign other works to their respective periods. Thus sculptures of which the date has been in dispute may through their relation to certain kouroi be dated with more confidence.

But the most important result of our studies will be, I hope, a more intimate acquaintance with the Greek kouroi themselves—with those early manifestations of the Greek genius produced while Greece was still young. Many of these kouroi are great works of art and so repay abundantly the time spent with them. Together they make us realize how the Greek mind worked—not in brilliant flashes only, but in a continuous, concentrated effort.

N.B.—In transliterating Greek names, I have followed the customary usage of retaining the Greek form except when this would render a familiar name like Croesus unrecognizable to the non-professional reader.

LIST OF CHIEF ABBREVIATIONS

A.J.A.—American Journal of Archaeology
ARCH. CL.—Archeologia classica
ANNALI—Annali dell' Instituto di corrispondenza archeologica
ANNUARIO—Annuario della Regia Scuola Archeologica di Atene e delle Missioni Italiane in Oriente
ARCH. ANZ.—Archäologischer Anzeiger. Beiblatt zum Jahrbuch des deutschen archäologischen Instituts
ARCH. ZTG.—Archäologische Zeitung
ARNDT, EINZELAUFNAHMEN—P. Arndt, W. Amelung, and F. Bruckmann, Photographische Einzelaufnahmen antiker Skulpturen
ATH. MITT.—Mitteilungen des deutschen archäologischen Instituts, Athenische Abteilung
B.C.H.—Bulletin de correspondance hellénique
B.S.A.—The Annual of the British School at Athens
BABELON, TRAITÉ—J. Babelon, Traité des monnaies grecques et romaines, 1901
BEAZLEY, DEVELOPMENT—J. D. Beazley, The Development of Attic Black-Figure, 1951
BEAZLEY, *ABV*.—J. D. Beazley, Attic Black-Figure Vase-Painters, 1956
BLÜMEL, *Kat*.—C. Blümel, Katalog der Sammlungen antiker Skulpturen, Berlin, II, I, 1940
BRUNN-BRUCKMANN, DENKMÄLER—Brunn-Bruckmann's, Denkmäler griechischer und römischer Sculptur (continued by P. Arndt and G. Lippold)
BUSCHOR, ALT. ST.—E. Buschor, Altsamische Standbilder, I–III, 1934; IV, 1960
BUSCHOR, FR. J.—E. Buschor, Frühgriechische Jünglinge, 1950
C.A.H.—The Cambridge Ancient History
C.V.—Corpus vasorum antiquorum
Δελτ. 'Αρχ.—Δελτίον 'Αρχαιολογικόν
DEONNA—W. Deonna, Les 'Apollons Archaïques', étude sur le type masculin de la statuaire grecque au VIme siècle avant notre ère, 1909
DICKINS, CATALOGUE—G. Dickins, Archaic Sculpture (Catalogue of the Acropolis Museum, vol. I), 1912
DINSMOOR, ARCHITECTURE—W. B. Dinsmoor, The Architecture of Ancient Greece, 1950
'Εφ. 'Αρχ.—'Εφημερὶς 'Αρχαιολογική
F.d.D.—Fouilles de Delphes (École Française d'Athènes)
HOMANN-WEDEKING, ANFÄNGE—E. Homann-Wedeking, Die Anfänge der griechischen Plastik, 1950
I.G.—Inscriptiones Graecae
JAHRBUCH—Jahrbuch des deutschen archäologischen Instituts
J.H.S.—The Journal of Hellenic Studies
KAROUZOS, *'Οδηγός—Χ. Καρούζου, Τὸ Μουσεῖο τῆς Θήβας, ὁδηγὸς μὲ* 46 *εἰκόνες*, 1934
KASTRIOTES, *Γλυπτά—Π. Καστριώτου, Γλυπτὰ τοῦ 'Εθνικοῦ Μουσείου Κατάλογος Περιγραφικός*, 1908
KAVVADIAS, *Γλυπτά—Π. Καββαδία, Γλυπτὰ τοῦ 'Εθνικοῦ Μουσείου Κατάλογος Περιγραφικός*, 1892
KERN, INSCR. GR.—O. Kern, Inscriptiones Grecae, 1913
LANGLOTZ, BILDHAUERSCHULEN—E. Langlotz, Frühgriechiche Bildhauerschulen, 1927
LANGLOTZ, ZEITBESTIMMUNG—E. Langlotz, Zur Zeitbestimmung der strengrotfigurigen Vasenmalerei und der gleichzeitigen Plastik, 1920
MARCADÉ, SIGNATURES—J. Marcadé, Recueil des signatures de sculpteurs grecs, I, 1953, II, 1958
M.F.A. BULLETIN—Bulletin of the Museum of Fine Arts (Boston)
M.M.A. BULLETIN—Bulletin of the Metropolitan Museum of Art (New York)
MET. MUS. STUDIES—Metropolitan Museum Studies
MON. DELL' INST.—Monumenti inediti pubblicati dall' Instituto di corrispondenza archeologica
MON. LINC.—Monumenti antichi pubblicati per cura della Reale Accademia dei Lincei
MON. PIOT—Monuments et mémoires publiés par l'Académie des inscriptions et belles-lettres (Fondation Eugène Piot)
NOTIZIE d. SC.—Notizie degli scavi di antichità, communicate alla R. Accademia dei Lincei
ÖST. JAHR.—Jahreshefte des österreichischen archäologischen Institutes in Wien

PAULY-WISSOWA, R. E.—Paulys Real-Encyclopädie der classischen Altertumswissenschaft, new edition begun by G. Wissowa

PAYNE AND YOUNG, ACROPOLIS—H. Payne and G. M. Young, Archaic Marble Sculpture from the Acropolis, 2nd ed. 1951

PRYCE, CATALOGUE—F. N. Pryce, Catalogue of Sculpture in the Department of Greek and Roman Antiquities of the British Museum, vol I, part I: Prehellenic and Early Greek, 1928

REV. ARCH.—Revue archéologique

RICHTER, ARCH. GK. ART—G. M. A. Richter, Archaic Greek Art against its historical background, 1949.

RICHTER, CAT. OF GK. SC.—G. M. A. Richter, Catalogue of Greek Sculptures in the Metropolitan Museum, 1954

RÖM. MITT.—Mitteilungen des deutschen archäologischen Instituts, Römische Abteilung

SCHRADER, AKROPOLIS—H. Schrader, Die archaischen Marmorbildwerke der Akropolis, 1939

S.G.D.I.—Sammlung der griechischen Dialekt-Inschriften

KOUROI

I. THE KOUROS TYPE

THE kouros type of a standing youth—the so-called archaic Apollo—runs through archaic Greek sculpture like a chief theme in music. He makes his appearance with the beginnings of Greek monumental sculpture and continues through the whole history of archaic Greek art. We find him in Asia Minor, in the Islands, in continental Greece, in North Africa, and in the west, throughout the length and breadth of the Greek world. Wherever Greek sculptors were active, wherever Greek culture flourished, the Greek kouros appears.

The scheme adopted was always the same—a nude youth, generally broad-shouldered and narrow-waisted, standing erect in a frontal pose, one leg, usually the left, advanced,[1] the weight evenly distributed, the arms, at least in the earlier marble statues, hanging by the sides, the hands either clenched or, more rarely, laid flat against the thighs.

What was the meaning of this type, whence was it derived, when and where does it make its first appearance? It used to be assumed that every statue in this primitive scheme represented Apollo —hence the popular name of 'archaic Apollo'. That the type was sometimes used to represent this god there can be no doubt, for Apollo appears in the kouros scheme in a vase painting in the British Museum[2] (opp. p. 16), where the presence of a suppliant, perhaps Kassandra, perhaps Helen, definitely identifies him; in a relief from Miletos in Berlin, with the attributes of bow and deer (cf. p. 132), and in the bronze statue recently found at the Piraeus (no. 159 bis). Moreover Diodoros'[3] description of the statue of the Pythian Apollo at Samos as resembling 'Egyptian works, with his arms hanging by his sides and his legs parted', clearly applies to a figure of the kouros type.

But that all kouroi do not represent Apollo is also certain. Many have been discovered in cemeteries where they must have served as tombstones representing human beings. The type was used in archaic times for victors in the games; Pausanias[4] describes a statue of Arrhichion, a pankratiast who won three Olympic victories, as in the kouros scheme—'archaic in attitude, with the feet not much separated, and the arms hanging down by the side to the buttocks' (cf. p. 77). A number of kouroi have been found not in sanctuaries of Apollo, but in those of other deities, for instance, on the Akropolis at Athens, in the precinct of Poseidon at Sounion, and in the temenos of Hera at Samos. These—whatever their meaning—were hardly intended to represent Apollo. Furthermore, some kouroi, even when found in a sanctuary of Apollo, are inscribed with the name not of the god but of a mortal. The 'Delphi Twins' do not represent Apollo, but, as the inscription informs us, the Argive youths Kleobis and Biton, honoured for a pious deed by commemorative statues. Even a dedication to Apollo is not sufficient to show that the statue represented the god, but merely that it was offered as a gift to that god.

[1] For a possible reason for this stance, cf. F. Poulsen, *Delphi*, pp. 92f., quoting Aristotle, *De incessu animalium*, 4 (706a).

[2] E 336, *C.V.*, British Museum, fasc. 5, III. I. c, pl. LXV, 2a; by the Dwarf Painter, cf. Beazley, *Attic Red-Figure Vase-Painters*, p. 651, no. 4; Schefold, *Jahrubuch*, LII, 1937, p. 44, fig. 7.

[3] I.98.9: *εἶναι δ' αὐτὸ λέγουσι κατὰ τὸ πλεῖστον παρεμφερὲς τοῖς Αἰγυπτίοις, ὡς ἂν τὰς μὲν χεῖρας ἔχον παρατεταμένας, τὰ δὲ σκέλη διαβεβηκότα.*

[4] VIII.40.I. On the corruptions of the name in the MSS. see Hitzig's critical note. *Ἀρριχίων* (Philostratos Maior, *Imag.* 347 K. ff. etc., see Jüthner on Philostratos *Gymnasticus* 21) is the proper form, cf. Bechtel, *Historische Personennamen*, p. 77. For the theory—first put forth by Furtwängler, *Ath. Mitt.* V, 1880, p. 26 f.—that Akropolis 698 (figs. 564-569) represents a victorious athlete, cf. Schuchhardt in Schrader, *Akropolis*, p. 195, and especially Raubitschek, *Hesperia*, VIII, 1939, p. 156, where the whole subject of such dedications is discussed.

It is clear, therefore, that the kouros type was not confined to Apollo but was a favourite expression of the early Greek sculptor, with a variety of meanings. It may represent a god or, more frequently, a mortal—a victorious athlete or a youth who died before his time. The colossal scale is no indication that a deity is intended, for Kleobis and Biton are over life size. Nor is it likely that the Sounion giants, which were found in the sanctuary of Poseidon, represent that deity, since the archaic Poseidon is bearded. That the same type was used for Apollo and mortals is natural when we remember that to the Greeks Apollo was in appearance simply a glorified young man. This is the guise he is apt to assume. 'Like to a man, lusty and powerful, in his first bloom, his hair spread over his broad shoulders' is a description of Apollo in the Hymn to the Pythian Apollo (ll. 449-50) written about 600-590 B.C., the very time of our early kouroi.[5]

That the kouros type derived inspiration from Egypt there can be no doubt. The resemblance in general posture and structure between the early Greek kouroi and the Egyptian statues is too striking to be accidental. And such identical details as the clenched hand with a bit of stone left inside it, and the wig-like headdress with separate tresses bound at the ends,[6] are unmistakable proof of relationship. Besides, we have Diodoros' specific statements[7] that the products of the Greek sculptor Daidalos had the same shape (ῥυθμός)[8] as the old Egyptian statues; and that the statue of Apollo at Samos which was in the kouros scheme 'resembled Egyptian works'. Nor is there anything surprising in this influence of Egypt on Greece, since we hear of Greeks in Egypt from the middle of the seventh century on, and they were probably there even earlier (cf. pp. 27 f., 37).

Besides the influence of Egypt, one can discern that of Mesopotamia—especially in the tendency to interpret the muscles of the human body as decorative patterns. This tendency reveals itself also in the elaboration of the hair, with its little spiral curls arranged symmetrically to right and left. And perhaps the Greeks borrowed from Assyria such specific stylizations as the outlining of the calf by a curving groove, the marking of the peroneal muscles and the fibula by two long ridges, the occasional ridge surrounding the elbow, and the downward inclination of the parallel toes.[9] The stylization of the ear, with the tragus as an excrescence from the lobe, and the abnormally large eyes are traits common to both Egyptian and Assyrian sculptures. Assyrian influence in early Greek sculpture is, of course, not surprising; for we hear of contacts between Greeks and Mesopotamians

[5] Schmid and Stählin, *Geschichte der griechischen Literatur*, I, p. 235 f.

[6] Cf. p. 50, note 66 and e.g. Winlock, M.M.A. *Bulletin*, XXVIII, 1933, pp. 156 ff., figs. 1-3; *The Treasure of El Lahun*, 1934, pl. III. For a general study of the much debated question of Oriental influence on early Greek art cf. F. R. Grace, *A.J.A.* XLVI, 1942, pp. 341 ff. In my discussions I have confined myself to the specific renderings that may be traceable to foreign contacts.

[7] I.97.6 and I.98.9.

[8] M. J. Milne supplies me with the following note on ῥυθμός = shape: 'ῥυθμός = rhythm is of course common in literary criticism and that the word could be used in a transferred sense for "proportions" seems to be shown by Xenophon, *Mem.* III, 10.10. If Diodoros' observation were original with him the sense "proportions" would seem extremely likely. But in Ionic ῥυθμός means "shape" (cf. Herodotos v. 58, Hippokrates περὶ ἄρθρων 62, and its use for σχῆμα by the Abderite philosophers, for which see references given by Kranz in Diels, *Fragmente der Vorsokratiker* III[5], p. 388). It occurs also in that sense perhaps in Pindar (*Oxyrhynchus Papyri* XV, No. 1791, l.5) and Alexis (Athenaios 125 f.). That this sense survived in the κοινή is indicated by the Septuagint version of 2 Kings 16, 10. Since we know that Diodoros took this part of his work (on famous Greeks who visited Egypt and on the Egyptian source of Greek science, philosophy, art, etc.) from Hekataios, since Hekataios came from Abdera, since earlier Abderites used ῥυθμός for "shape" and since this use continued in the κοινή for a hundred years or so after the time of Hekataios, it is extremely likely that Diodoros found the word in Hekataios and took it directly over, quite possibly misunderstanding it and giving it some such sense as "proportion" or "style". 'Ρυθμός coupled with συμμετρία is used of a sculptor's work in Diog. Laert. VIII.47. In modern Greek it is commonly applied to style, e.g. ὁ Γοτθικὸς ῥυθμός.'

[9] For all these features cf. the reliefs from Khorsabad in the Louvre, Paterson, *Assyrian Sculptures*, pls. V, VII, VIII. In Egyptian sculpture peroneal muscles and fibula are sometimes indicated by two ridges on the outer side of the lower leg, and the calf is sometimes shown as a modelled shape, but no groove is used to outline it.

as early as the reign of Sennacherib (705-681 B.C.). And about a century later a brother of the poet Alkaios was in Nebuchadnezzar's service.[10] Moreover, the Phoenician traders who acted as intermediaries between East and West doubtless familiarized the Greeks with Oriental designs. And Syria, the early importance of which we are beginning to realize, must also have contributed its share of oriental culture.

Naturally, in addition, the Greeks added much of their own; for instance, the complete nudity which served best their purpose of anatomical study and which corresponded to their athletic ideal; the free stance without any support at the back; and, above all, a new sense of freshness and life. They rejuvenated an old, practically worn-out scheme. Moreover their own past played its part. The geometric element in the earliest kouroi, the marked feeling for abstraction, are a direct inheritance of the Greek geometric age. Actually, the earliest Greek statues are less naturalistic than the Egyptian, closer to the geometric conception. For instance, whereas in Egyptian statues, even those of the Early Kingdom, we find renderings based on direct observations of nature—eyes, mouth, and ears conceived in the round, a spherical skull, forearms correctly semi-pronated, the inner malleolus higher than the outer—in the earlier Greek kouroi eyes, mouth, and ears are flat and stylized, the skull is undeveloped, the forearms unnaturally twisted, the malleoli level. However, within one hundred years the Greeks from their more primitive beginnings mastered the rendering of anatomical structure; whereas the Egyptians in two thousand and more years show no development along these lines. The Greek effort was concerted, each generation building on the attainment of the preceding one, and never losing an inch of the ground gained. Egyptian art has no such systematic growth. It would be difficult to date an Egyptian statue merely from the knowledge of anatomy displayed.[11]

But the adherence of the Egyptians to one scheme, their satisfaction in the grandiose figures which they had produced, left their mark also on the Greeks. The Greek sculptor saw at the beginning of his career the value of confining himself to a few types. The scheme of the Greek kouros remains the same throughout its long development during a period of over a century. It differs somewhat in appearance according to whether it comes from the East or the West, each period brings its modifications, each statue is the expression of a different artist, but the general type persists. Only when the anatomy of the human body was finally understood and the way made clear for the broaching of new problems was the scheme dissolved.

This phenomenon of concentration is peculiarly Greek. If we want to understand the Greek mind, its desire for clarity and order, its joy in the grappling with problems, we shall find this struggle with one major task singularly illuminating. The artists of Egypt and Mesopotamia, whose magnificent works inspired the Greeks, had, as we saw, no such ambitions; they were content to produce their

[10] Hogarth in *C.A.H.* III, p. 248.

[11] To mention only one seemingly insignificant instance: The ear appears in Egyptian art usually without antitragus, but occasionally an antitragus is represented. (Cf. e.g. the head of a granite statue of the god Amūn, late XVII to early XIX dynasty, Metropolitan Museum 07.228.34; the upper part of a limestone statue of King Amen-hetep III of the XVIII dynasty from western Thebes in the British Museum; and the limestone statue of Amen-hetep I in the form of Osiris, XVIII dynasty, in the British Museum.) The same is true of Assyrian art; in the majority of cases the ear has no antitragus, but now and then the antitragus appears, even as early as the ninth century B.C. (Cf. e.g. figures on the slabs 21, 25, of the frieze of Ashur-Nasir-pal in the British Museum; Budge, *Assyrian Sculptures in the British Museum, reign of Ashur-Nasir-pal, 885-860* B.C. pls. XXX, XXXIV; and the slab 17.19.2081 in the Metropolitan Museum.) How significant this variation is we realize when we compare Greek art in this respect. In the earliest kouroi the antitragus is never represented (cf. pp. 17, 40); somewhat later it is tentatively, incorrectly rendered (cf. pp. 62, 95); in the course of the third quarter of the sixth century it appears in correct form and is then never omitted (cf. pp. 117, 133).

masterpieces with the same conventions generation after generation. But the inquisitive Greek reached out continually for greater knowledge and precision. And so we owe to him, among a multitude of other things, the discovery of naturalistic art.

We who are used to naturalism in art from childhood on, who learn anatomy and drawing from life as a matter of course, find it hard to realize how arduous was the struggle to achieve it, how deeply rooted were the conventions which had passed unchallenged for centuries. In our own modernistic age it has often been questioned whether this realism was a gain. But though it is true that some of the monumental early statues are more impressive works of art than some of the later naturalistic ones, no one will deny that Greece, with her search after natural form, opened wide the doors for new developments. The art of fifth-century Greece, of Rome and the Italian Renaissance, of eighteenth- and ninteenth-century France, are all founded on the achievements of early Greece.

The laboratory, so to speak, in which the Greek sculptor worked out this naturalistic art was the kouros type. Its careful analysis is therefore infinitely important. We can here study in a large number of examples the gradual evolution of Greek art during the archaic period. We can see developing before our eyes the conception of the figure as a whole and of its various parts—the skull, ear, eye, mouth, collar-bones, chest, abdomen, shoulder-blades, arm, knee, foot, etc. For in Greek art each part of the human body, each feature of the head, each lock of hair is viewed independently as a shape in itself as well as part of a co-ordinate whole. It is a fascinating study to watch the large, flat, almond-shaped eyes which occupy the whole width of the face gradually diminish and assume volume and individual life; to watch the formal, big, flat spirals of hair contract into shapely locks; to see the sharply cut, flat lips assume modelled shapes; to observe how the geometric patterns of the ear become gradually naturalistic. And the same applies to the body and limbs. But even at the end of the period, when naturalism was achieved, each form retains its individuality, while contributing by its proportions and shape to the scheme of the whole. It is this "architectural" quality which is distinctive of Greek sculpture.

But how can we assume, someone will ask, that artists progressed along similar lines everywhere in Greece at the same time? Today some artists lag behind, working in their old age as they did in their youth, refusing to adopt new ways. Surely in Greece it must have been the same. Our answer is that in some cases it undoubtedly was[12]—but probably not nearly so often as now. The Greeks were a people full of curiosity. They were marching along a new path which interested them profoundly. They were making new discoveries in the artistic field, comparable in import to those made in science and philosophy. And they were the immediate descendants of people who had sailed in little boats to discover and colonize the Greek world. Surely there would be few among them who would refuse to share in the new venture. Nor is this merely a guess. We shall see in our subsequent studies that the progression in anatomical knowledge was amazingly uniform. The different parts developed together. A statue with a primitive and stylized skull and ear and eye will

[12] For instance, some coins with identical obverse dies show on their reverses earlier and later styles. The late Edward T. Newell, who called this interesting fact to my attention, cited as examples some of the coins of Olympia, contrasting especially Seltman, *Temple Coins of Olympia*, plate III, *βθ* and *βκ*, *βν* and *βκ*. In Renaissance art the same circumstances holds, as shown, for instance, by such approximately contemporary artists as Sandro Botticelli and Luca Signorelli—one a conservative, the other a progressive; or Il Borgognone and Leonardo da Vinci, both active in Milan at the same time, but one carrying on the old Lombard tradition, the other starting a new era. On the problem of different generations as it affects art history, cf. W. Pinder, *Das Problem der Generation in der Kunstgeschichte Europas* (a reference I owe to Professor R. Krautheimer).

be found to have also a primitive and stylized chest and back and knee. A statue with a more naturalistic skull and ear will also have a more naturalistic back and knee. Naturally there are transitional works between one group and the next. Here and there a progressive artist anticipates, occasionally a conservative lingers. We shall find that bronze figures differ in some respects, for instance in the rendering of the arms, from those of stone, indicating that technical considerations play a part (cf. pp. 12, 40). On statuettes the anatomical renderings are often abbreviated, owing to the small space at the disposal of the artist.[13] There are enough slight exceptions to remind us that the makers of our statues were human beings, not machines. But human nature, we shall find, was incalculable only within narrow limits. We can present no case in which an artist anticipates or harks back more than a short space of time. In no instance do we find really late features in a really early scheme (in spite of the fact that a completely naturalistic model was continuously present in every human being). The great majority of sculptures show a uniform progression. At least this is true of pure Greek art, not—and this too is significant—of such mixed and imitative arts as Cypriote and Etruscan (cf. p. 93).

The only possible explanation of this phenomenon is that progression along naturalistic lines occupied sculptors throughout the Greek world, that new discoveries were welcomed and shared,[14] and that communications between Greek states were constant and speedy.[15] If there were exceptions, people who preferred the old ways and did not march with the times, we must place them with their real contemporaries. If they were living, let us say, about 530 B.C., and elected to work in the style of their youth, the middle of the century, we must group their work as characteristic of the middle. It is the style, not the individual that counts.

The close similarity in anatomical structure among the members of each group of kouroi of whatever provenance throws light also on one of the most discussed questions of our day—the characteristics of the various schools in early Greek sculpture. The picture presented by our kouroi, of a uniform and universal progression towards naturalism, presupposes constant intercourse. And this intercommunication would tend to obliterate local characteristics.

As a result of our findings we suggest that regional distinctions became merged in a common progression. The broad divisions of East and West indeed remain.[16] One can distinguish the soft, fleshy kouroi of Asia Minor and Samos from the harder, more athletic versions of Argos; and when there are a number of examples, as for instance from Attica at certain periods, it is possible, perhaps, to segregate the Attic statues; though even here one cannot always be certain, as these statues may be merely the product of one artist or workshop (cf. p. 30). To go further and set up Parian, Naxian, Chian, Spartan, Sikyonian, etc., schools, when often we have no certain examples of such schools, would seem, at least at present, to be going beyond the evidence. The fact that some statues share specific anatomical renderings is not sufficient reason for ascribing them to the same school. Such common renderings help to date rather than to localize a statue. And the differences among

[13] The representations especially of ears and feet do not therefore always tally with those on the larger statuettes and the statues.

[14] The readiness to share observations and accept common conventional renderings may also partly be due to the fact that the early Greeks derived their knowledge of anatomy not from dissecting the human body, but from observing it from without (cf. p. 11).

[15] As Mrs. D. O. Robbins has suggested to me, we may even surmise that at the periodic meetings of Greeks from every quarter at the festivals of Olympia, Delphi, Delos, etc., the latest observations in anatomy were eagerly discussed.

[16] This is, however, not a racial distinction, based on Dorians and Ionians, but rather a regional difference, dependent on environment. It will be seen, for instance, that the art of the Dorian Hexapolis is not, as is often claimed, Dorian but Eastern (cf. p. 36). Here environment evidently obliterated racial differences.

contemporary kouroi, which of course exist, may be due to individual, not to regional taste. For every work of art is primarily the expression of its maker. Perhaps if our material were more plentiful we could see more clearly and segregate certain groups more convincingly. But at present the only safe criterion seems to be the chronological one based on the general advance towards naturalism. At least that is the picture which is presented by our groups of kouroi.

Moreover, this picture coincides with the evidence which we obtain from ancient writers. In Homer's time, craftsmen were in demand everywhere and moved from place to place.[17] And this practice evidently continued; for we learn that sculptors during the sixth century travelled extensively, received orders from near and distant places, and intermingled constantly.[18] We hear of Theodoros of Samos working for Sparta[19] and advising on a temple at Ephesos;[20] of Endoios of Athens working for Tegea[21] and Ephesos;[22] of Smilis of Aegina working for Samos,[23] Argos,[24] and Olympia;[25] of Dipoinos and Skyllis, Cretans by birth, going to Sikyon,[26] proceeding to Aitolia,[27] working for Ambracia,[28] Argos,[29] Kleonai,[30] and Tiryns.[31] We are told of works by the Lacedaemonians Theokles[32] and Dorykleidas[33] at Olympia. We learn that the Lacedaemonian Medon worked for the Megarians,[34] Bathykles of Magnesia at Amyklai,[35] Cheirisophos of Crete at Tegea.[36] And inscriptions teach the same lesson. Signatures of artists from various localities are found all over Greece. With such intercourse—East, West, North, and South—native differences would tend to disappear in a common progression. Viewed against this background the similarities and differences in our kouroi can be properly understood.

[17] Cf. *Odyssey* XVII.382-6.

[18] Cf. on this subject the excellent remarks by Picard, *Manuel d'archéologie grecque, La Sculpture*, I, pp. 438 ff.

[19] Pausanias II.12.10.

[20] Diog. Laert. II.103.

[21] Pausanias VIII.46. 1,5.

[22] Athenag. *Libellus pro christianis* 17, p. 19 (ed. Schwartz).

[23] Pausanias VII.4.4.

[24] Athenag. *Libellus pro christianis* 17, p. 19 (ed. Schwartz).

[25] Pausanias V.17.1.

[26] Pliny, *N.H.* XXXVI.9.

[27] Ibid.

[28] Pliny, *N.H.* XXXVI,14.

[29] Ibid. and Pausanias II.22.5.

[30] Pliny, *N.H.* XXXVI.14 and Pausanias II.5.1.

[31] Clem. Al. *Protr.* IV.42.

[32] Pausanias V.17.2 and VI.19.8.

[33] Pausanias V.17.1.

[34] Pausanias V.17.2 and VI. 19.12.14. See Robert, *Archäologische Märchen*, 111 ff.

[35] Pausanias III.18.9.

[36] Pausanias VIII.53.8.

II. THE TECHNIQUE

(a) Materials

STONE. The favourite material for the early kouroi was marble, to judge at least by those now extant. Since Greek quarries often vary from layer to layer, it is frequently difficult to determine accurately a specific marble[1] (see p. xi). Speaking generally, however, the Island marbles were popular during the whole of the archaic period throughout the Greek world—especially the coarse-grained Naxian and the transparent Parian. In addition, local marbles were employed here and there—for instance, the blue-veined Boeotian for some of the kouroi from Mount Ptoon. Attica presents a varied picture. The early Athenian kouroi—the Sounion, New York, and Dipylon statues—are of coarse-grained, apparently Naxian, marble. During the second quarter and the middle of the sixth century, the blue-veined Hymettian marble appears to have been in favour—as indicated by the Moschophoros, the Phaidimos base, and several other monuments of that period.[2] However, no kouros of this local marble has so far come to light. Pentelic marble was evidently in use from the second quarter of the sixth century; the korai nos. 582, 583, 586, 589, and 593[3] found on the Akropolis are in that material, as well as the fragmentary kouros no. 66 of the Volomandra group, and the kouroi nos. 89 and 101 of the Melos group. The kouros no. 137 of the Anavysos-Ptoon 12 group is of Island marble, but is set into a base of Pentelic marble. These sculptures, however, are exceptions. Speaking generally, Pentelic marble does not seem to have been commonly employed for sculpture until about 500 B.C.[4]—perhaps because its calcareous veins made it unpopular and the better layers had not yet been quarried.

Besides marble, softer limestone was of course used (cf. nos. 10, 11, 27, 56, 57, 58), though not nearly so often as one would think, considering the advantages its greater softness offered to the sculptor. It is indeed remarkable that such great achievements as the Dipylon-New York-Sounion group of statues, the Delos Colossus, the Samian and Theraean colossi, the Thasos Kriophoros, and Kleobis and Biton had apparently no important limestone predecessors in which the problems of stone carving on a large scale were tried out in an easier medium. Naturally this circumstance may be due to chance, and any day may bring forth a colossal early limestone kouros. We must remember that we owe the survival of the sixth-century architectural sculptures in limestone (πώρινος λίθος) of the Athenian Akropolis to the accident of the Persian destruction. On the other hand, the ambition of the seventh-century Greek sculptors to carve hard stone may be directly due to inspiration from Egypt and Mesopotamia (cf. p. 2), where the carving of very hard stone was thoroughly understood. Greece, however, while borrowing what she needed and liked, went her own way. She preferred her own white marbles to the Oriental coloured stones. There are no early Greek sculptures in basalt, porphyry, and granite. Only after Rome took Egypt into her orbit do classical sculptures in coloured stone make their appearance.

[1] Cf. Lepsius, *Griechische Marmorstudien*, Berlin, 1890; Henry S. Washington, *A.J.A.* II, 1898, pp. 1 ff. An up-to-date study of Greek marbles based on modern scientific methods is much needed. Recent investigations, however, have shown the complexity of the task.

[2] Cf. Winter, *Ath. Mitt.* XIII, 1888, p. 117.

[3] So described by Dickins in his *Catalogue of the Acropolis Museum*, and Casson, *Technique*, p. 88.

[4] Cf. Winter, op. cit. p. 116; Dinsmoor in *Studies in the History of Culture* (1942), p. 188.

Even at Naukratis the early Greek sculptors abstained from using coloured stones for their statuettes and preferred the native white alabaster and sandstone—which approximated more closely the appearance of marble (cf. nos. 28, 29, 59-61, 82-5).

WOOD. Wood must have been a common material in Greece, just as it was in Egypt. The once popular theory that the carving of wood preceded that of stone has recently gained some support from discoveries of Greek temples of the geometric period.[5] For it is argued that since a temple presumably housed an image of the deity, and since no geometric cult statues have survived, the latter must have been of wood, which easily disintegrates in the climate of Greece. Of course these wooden images may have been comparatively small, and not to be classed in the category of monumental sculpture.

In addition to these possible primitive wooden statues or statuettes we may visualize wooden statues in Greece at all times. Pausanias' frequent references to wooden statues during his travels in Greece are in no way confined to primitive xoana. They belonged to both early and late periods.[6] We are told by ancient writers that Hegylos, Theokles, 'Dontas', Smilis, Endoios, Kanachos, Pheidias, Patrokles, Timarchos, and Kephisodotos made wooden statues.[7] In the inventories made at Delos after 166 B.C. of the contents of the sanctuaries there, numerous wooden statues and statuettes are listed, among them 'twenty-three archaic wooden Apollos' and 'ten wooden Artemises' in the temple of Apollo,[8] and 'fifteen damaged archaic wooden statues' in the building of the Andrians. Athenaios[9] mentions 'innumerable' gilt statues carried in the procession of Ptolemy Philadelphos (283-247 B.C.), of which at least some were presumably of wood. In a procession at Rome during the war with Hannibal in 207 B.C. two wooden Junos were carried.[10] And this testimony is borne out by the few surviving wooden sculptures, for they comprise both early and late examples.[11] For a wooden statuette probably of a kouros cf. no. 20 and figs. 17-19.

BRONZE. Though few bronze statues of kouroi now remain (cf. nos. 159 bis, 181, 195), in antiquity there must have been many; for bronze was a favourite material in Greece. Unfortunately its intrinsic value caused it to be melted down and only an infinitesimal proportion of ancient bronze statues have survived. Many bronze statuettes of kouroi, however, of all periods, have been preserved.

Though the well-known passage in Pausanias[12] cannot be taken literally as meaning that casting of statues was not practised in Greece before the middle of the sixth century, it is evident that at first bronze statues and colossal ones had to be made by the cumbrous method of fastening hammered

[5] Cf. especially V. Müller, *Met. Mus. Studies*, v, 1934-6, pp. 159 ff.

[6] Cf. the list given by Frazer, *Pausanias*, IV, pp. 245 f., and the summary of the evidence presented by Alexander, *M.M.A. Bulletin*, XXXIV, 1939, p. 273 f., and *A.J.A.* LIV, 1940, pp. 293 ff., from which I have freely borrowed in my account above.

[7] Cf. Overbeck, *Schriftquellen*, nos. 328, 342, 351, 403, 635, 1041, 1333.

[8] Durrbach and Roussel, *Inscriptions de Délos*, III, 1935, no. 1428, col. II, 50, 51.

[9] 197c.

[10] Livy XXVI.37.

[11] Cf. e.g. the early statuettes from Samos (Ohly, *Ath. Mitt.*, LXVIII, 1953, pp. 77 ff.); the early statuette of a bearded man from Klazomenai in Munich (*Arch. Anz.* 1938, cols. 423 ff., figs. 3, 4); the three statuettes of the late seventh and early sixth century B.C. found in 1934 at Palma di Montechiaro in Sicily (Zanotti-Bianco, *J.H.S.* LVIII, 1938, p. 249, fig. 2, and Caputo, *Mon. ant. dei Lincei*, XXXVII, 1938, pp. 587 ff.); the Hellenistic Hekate from Alexandria in the Metropolitan Museum (*A.J.A.* XLIV, 1940, pp. 294 ff., fig. 3), and that in the Alexandria Museum (Breccia, *Monuments de l'Egypte*, I, 1926, p. 110, pl. LXXIV); the statuette of Alexander the Great in the Louvre, MND 1396, (Richter, *Handbook of Greek Art*, fig. 290); and an archaistic head of Dionysos in the Walters Collection, Baltimore. The wooden sarcophagi found in Crimean and Alexandrian tombs sometimes have sculptural decorations (Watzinger, *Griechische Holzsarkophage*, and *Compte-rendu de la Commission archéologique*, 1882-8, pp. 48 ff., pls. III-IV).

[12] VIII.14.8: *διέχεαν δὲ χαλκὸν πρῶτοι καὶ ἀγάλματα ἐχωνεύσαντο Ῥοῖκός τε Φιλαίου καὶ Θεόδωρος Τηλεκλέους Σάμιοι.*

sheets of bronze onto a wooden core. Pausanias mentions an image of Zeus made by this σφυρήλατον process,[13] without, however, stating the size; and a few, comparatively small examples have survived to our day; for instance, the Dreros kouros (figs. 12, 13) and a statuette found at Samos.[14]

The invention of hollow casting is now attested for the early seventh century B.C. by extant examples in that technique.[15] It doubtless gave a great impetus to the making of bronze statues. How well understood this technique was in the Greek world in the sixth century is shown by the mould for a bronze statue found in the Athenian Agora,[16] as well as by the Piraeus and Piombino kouroi (nos. 159 bis, 180) and other bronze originals of the late archaic period. As a consequence, from about 500 B.C. for over a century, bronze became the favourite material of many Greek sculptors.[17] Naturally statuettes were cast solid before and after the introduction of hollow casting; for the small amount of bronze there involved made the simpler process of solid casting desirable. Statuettes of kouroi in solid bronze are therefore common from the seventh to the early fifth century.

TERRACOTTA. Since clay was abundant in Greece it is perhaps strange that so few free-standing terracotta archaic sculptures from Greece are known. Though architectural and votive examples have been unearthed at Kalydon,[18] Thermon,[19] and Olympia,[20] and the head of a warrior has been found in the Agora at Athens,[21] no terracotta statues of kouroi have so far come to light, and only occasionally a statuette (cf. nos. 44, 177). And in South Italy and Sicily—where clay sculptures seem to have been more common—the only important representatives so far found are a statuette from Taranto (no. 62) and a head from Agrigento (cf. p. 112). It is clear that the interest of the early Greek sculptor centred in stone carving and bronze work.

OTHER MATERIALS. Ivory statuettes of the eighth to seventh century have survived and it is likely that statuettes of kouroi were also made in this material, though no significant Greek example is extant.[22] There is no allusion in literature to chryselephantine kouroi, but that the technique was practised in the archaic period we learn from references to such statues in ancient literature[23] and from the recent discoveries at Delphi.[24] No Greek kouroi of gold, silver, or amber[25] seem to be known; but lead statuettes of kouroi have been discovered at Sounion[26], Samos (cf. no. 21) and supposedly Phigaleia (cf. no. 13).

[13] III.17.6.

[14] Buschor, *Alt. St.* p. 24, figs. 74, 77.

[15] Cf. e.g. Jantzen, *Griechische Greifenkessel* (1955), pp. 54 ff.

[16] Cf. *Hesperia*, VI, 1937, pp. 82 f. (Thompson), and p. 343 f. (Shear).

[17] Wace, *An Approach to Greek Sculpture*, p. 18 f.; Raubitschek, *Bulletin de l'Institut archéologique bulgare*, XII, 1938, p. 139.

[18] Poulsen and Rhomaios, *Erster Vorläufiger Bericht über die dänisch-griechischen Ausgrabungen von Kalydon*. pls. XXX ff.

[19] Koch, *Röm. Mitt.*, XXX, 1915, pp. 51 ff.; E. D. Van Buren, *Greek Fictile Revetments*, pls. 34 ff.

[20] Kunze, *Hundertstes Winckelmannsprogramm*, Berlin, 1940, pp. 27 ff.; V. *Olympia Bericht*, pp. 103 ff., pls. 54-74; VI. *Olympia Bericht*, pp. 169 ff.

[21] Cf. H. A. Thompson, *Hesperia* XXIII, 1954, p. 61 f., pl. 14, a; Richter, *Handbook of Greek Art*, fig. 112.

[22] The small ivory statuette, no. 68.8-10.1 in the British Museum, is probably Etruscan, not Greek, as indicated by the moulded, altar-like base which occurs, as A. Raubitschek informs me, in Italic monuments (cf. Studniczka, *Öst. Jahr.*, VI, 1903, p. 142 f.). A magnificent ivory statuette of a kneeling figure of which the upper part is in the kouros scheme has been found in Samos and will be published by Buschor in *Alt. St.* IV. Its date should be around 630 B.C.

[23] Cf. Overbeck, *Schriftquellen*, nos. 328 ff.

[24] *Illustrated London News*, 1939, p. 202 f.; Amandry, *B.C.H.* LXIII, 1939, pp. 86 ff., pls. 19-42.

[25] For an Italic statuette of a kouros in amber cf. p. 93.

[26] Staïs, *'Εφ.'Αρχ.* 1917, p. 202, fig. 13. The right instead of the left leg is advanced.

(b) Colour

Undoubtedly colour was extensively used on stone kouroi, as in other Greek sculptures. Traces of colour on fillets, hair, lips, eyes, inside nostrils, and around nipples attest this polychromy (cf. e.g. nos. 1, 6, 58, 136). What treatment the nude parts received is a moot question.[27] That they were toned in some way and not left uncompromisingly white seems likely, considering the glare of white marble in the brilliant Greek sunlight and the universal Egyptian practice of painting nude parts of white limestone figures brown and yellow. Since Greek sculptors used colour on eyes and lips to approximate a naturalistic effect, they probably also toned their kouroi to suggest the sunburnt skin of Greek youths. No actual traces of this original toning have survived on Greek kouroi; but the much admired reddish-brown colour of the New York kouros—due to the stain left by the earth of Attica—may perhaps give an idea of the original effect.

(c) Tools

The tools used by the carvers of marble kouroi were of course identical with those employed in the making of other early Greek sculptures[28]: first, perhaps, the hammer, for the preliminary blocking out; and then successively the point (i.e. punch) and the claw chisel; the flat chisel and the gouge; the rasp and other abrasives.

Marks of the point are visible on the earliest kouroi—especially on unfinished portions, foot-plinths, and bases—and it is evident that this tool was universally used at all periods. How soon the claw chisel was introduced is still uncertain.[29] The appearance of claw-chisel marks on the back of the Akropolis kore no. 593[30] and on a head in Munich (cf. no. 71) shows that this tool must have been part of the sculptor's equipment by 570 B.C. or so.[31] How much earlier we do not know; for, whereas the presence of a tool mark is positive proof that the tool was used at a given period, its absence is not proof to the contrary. We must remember that since the sculptor endeavoured to obliterate tool marks in his finished product, the presence of such marks is more or less accidental; also that comparatively few Greek sculptures of the seventh and early sixth centuries have survived. On the other hand, whereas Egyptian points and flat chisels have been found,[32] there is no evidence that the claw chisel was known in Egypt. It seems to have been a Greek invention. Whatever was the time of its introduction, by the third quarter of the sixth century its use was widespread, for claw marks are frequent on sculptures from that period on.

It has been claimed that, in the archaic period, the flat chisel and the gouge were used only on hair and drapery, and that other surfaces were worked entirely with the point and sometimes the claw chisel, except for the final smoothing with abrasives;[33] and that to this extensive use of the

[27] Cf. Richter, *Met. Mus. Studies*, I, 1928–9, pp. 25 ff., and the references there cited.

[28] On this subject cf. Blümner, *Gewerbe u. Künste*, II, 1879, p. 194 and III, 1884, p. 192; Blümel, *Griechische Bildhauerarbeit*, 1927, pp. 3 ff., pl. 1; Richter, *Sculpture and Sculptors of the Greeks*, 1950, pp. 143 ff.; Casson, *Technique*, 1933, pp. 169 ff.; Blümel, *Griechische Bildhauer an der Arbeit*, 1940.

[29] Casson, *A.J.A.* XLI, 1937, p. 107 f.

[30] Ibid. fig. 1.

[31] Payne in Payne and Young, *Acropolis*, p. 9, dated the statue 'well before the middle of the sixth century'; Langlotz in Schrader, *Akropolis*, p. 44, about 580 B.C.

[32] Petrie, *Tools and Weapons*, p. 20, pls. XXI, XXII; Clarke and Engelbach, *Ancient Egyptian Masonry*, p. 224, fig. 263.

[33] Blümel, *Bildhauerarbeit*, pp. 6 ff.; *Bildhauer*, pp. 21 ff.

point is due the 'velvety' surface of early Greek sculpture as against the smoother surface of later sculpture. A number of unfinished archaic statues seem to bear out this theory.[34] In reliefs, however, marks of the narrow flat chisel are sometimes visible on the backgrounds, and of the broad flat chisel (the drove) on backgrounds, backs, and sides.[35]

(*d*) *Procedure*

Several half-worked marble blocks, evidently intended for statues of kouroi, have been found in the quarries of Attica and Naxos.[36] Two of the Naxian examples and one of the Attic ones are of colossal size (5½ metres, 2 metres without head and legs, and 2.10 metres, respectively). Another Attic example, found near the first one, is only 47 cm. high. An enormous, roughly trimmed block, over 10 metres long, still lies in the quarries of Naxos, apparently intended for a bearded draped statue, perhaps a Dionysos.[37]

From this evidence we may deduce that Greek sculptors had large blocks trimmed in the quarries prior to transportation. This would be a natural proceeding when transport was difficult and costly (cf. p. 31), and a decrease in weight desirable. The compactness of the kouros type made a preliminary trimming comparatively easy.

'The early kouroi retain a close connection with the blocks out of which they were hewn and reveal the procedure of their makers. The figure was obviously first mapped out on a smoothened surface of the stone. Proportions of height and width could be determined at the start. The composition was simple and compact, the arms adhering closely to the flanks. From this two-dimensional sketch on the front plane the sculptor carved his way into the stone and gradually detached the three-dimensional figure from the block wherein it was embedded. When it emerged it at first resembled a rectangular pillar into whose surfaces geometrical shapes had been carved. Only by slow degrees was it freed from this obvious connection with its rectangular framework and its geometric foundations and did it assume the varied and many-sided forms of nature.

'It is important to remember that in his study of human anatomy the early Greek sculptor did not take recourse to the dissector's knife.[38] The artist could but surmise the underlying causes of the complicated shapes which he wished to represent, and had to rely on observation from without—for which ample opportunities were afforded in the gymnasiums and at the athletic festivals. The early Greek sculptor's approach to the human form was therefore in accordance with the action of his chisel—from without inward. The study of anatomy did not constitute an end in itself apart from the problem of representation in stone. He started with geometric traditions, with patterns decorative rather than true, and groped his way, intent on a truthful representation of nature. His conception of form and the development of his art were conditioned by his technique.

'The closer the figure approached to nature the more were its geometric foundations concealed, and finally a perfect interpretation of the anatomical structure made its appearance, embodying a

[34] Cf. Blümel, *Bildhauerarbeit*, p. 5 f., pls. 7-9; *Bildhauer*, figs. 2 ff.

[35] Cf. Casson, *Technique*, p. 182 f., fig. 66; *J.H.S.* LIV. 1934, p. 78 f.; also Richter, 'The Drove', *A.J.A.*, LVII, 1943, pp. 188 ff.

[36] Deonna, nos. 17, 18, 116, 120, 121; Blümel, *Bildhauer*, figs. 2 ff.

[37] Deonna, p. 22; Blümel, *Bildhauer*, figs. 2-4.

[38] On the history of anatomy cf. the article by Dr. Craigie in the ninth and eleventh editions of the *Encyclopædia Britannica* s.v. Anatomy. Apparently it was not until the time of the Ptolemies that the Greeks acquired anatomical knowledge derived from dissecting the human body.

new kind of unity such as is inherent in organic nature and life. Yet that other kind of unity, which is imposed by the block and its spatial relations and is inherent in the stone-worker's technique, continued to assert itself automatically as the tool worked its way from the front plane into the stone. Thereby all shapes were ranged and related to each other according to their proportions in a preconceived three-dimensional space.[39] The way in which this conception of space was brought into play is seen more clearly in relief carving, which constituted so prominent a feature of Greek art. For here the arrangement of forms in a series of receding vertical planes, and the contrast between the dimensions of height and width as against the dimension of depth were obviously displayed.[40] Sculpture in relief may be said to stand half way between sculpture in the round and drawing on a plane surface. All three aimed at the representation of the human figure; but while sculpture in the round rendered the third dimension as it is, relief and drawing suggested it by various degrees of foreshortening.

'These two kinds of unity, organic and spatial, were interrelated and combined. As in music a melody is set in measured time, so in Greek sculpture the composition of the figure is set in proportioned space.

'Works in bronze entailed a different technique from those in stone and engendered a different conception; for here a model was first set up in clay from which the bronze was cast. There was no block of stone at the start to enforce compactness and frontality or to suggest a rectangular conception of form. Instead of working inward from without by hewing away the superfluous material wherein the form lay hidden, the artist, starting with nothing, built up his figure by adding on clay and outlining it against space in clear and telling silhouette, without being tied to a strictly frontal pose. The figure grew from within outward, like a plant. This technique obviously lent itself to the expression of movement, action, gesture, and consequently stimulated the study of the structure and function of bones and muscles. Thereby it encouraged the development towards naturalism. Even the earliest statuettes cast in bronze display more freedom in the action of the limbs and more roundness of form than their contemporaries in stone. And gradually the naturalistic conception influenced work in stone also.

'However, as we have seen (cf. p. 7), stone was the principal material at least to the middle of the sixth century, before the general adoption of hollow casting, and it was by carving rather than by modelling that the Greek sculptor developed his sense of form. In stone carving he conformed to a three-dimensional conception of space that was adhered to also by the later, more naturalistic Greek artist and that has since become an established principle in the representation of objects in space. On this conception, for instance, the Renaissance artist founded his science of perspective for securing the relative position of objects in space in pictorial representation. The picture plane whereon he traced, as through a pane of glass, the objects receding into space may be considered the equivalent and direct descendant of the smoothed surface of the block of marble whereon the early Greek sculptor drew the outline of the shapes he wished to carve. It may therefore justly be said that the Greeks by their achievement in this field have determined the course of the visual arts in Europe.' (Irma A. Richter.)

[39] Cf. Hildebrand, *Das Problem der Form*. The chapter on sculpture in stone explains the emancipation of the figure from the block, beginning with early Egyptian sculpture.

[40] Cf. Hildebrand, op. cit., chapter on the conception of relief.

(e) Mounting: Plinths, Bases, and Inscriptions

To visualize the kouroi in their sanctuaries and cemeteries we must know how they were mounted. Unfortunately few plinths and fewer bases of stone kouroi are extant. The reason is obvious. The most vulnerable parts of a stone kouros are the knees and ankles. A great many kouroi, therefore, have been broken at these joints and have become separated from their feet and bases. Since statues were generally considered more valuable than bases (even when the latter were inscribed), the former found their way into museums, whereas the latter have in many cases disappeared, or perhaps are still underground. Nevertheless, by good fortune, a few bases of stone kouroi of different periods have survived—enough to show the ancient practice in a general way.[41]

We may examine the bases of our kouroi,[42] group by group, and then summarize the results.

Sounion Group. The bases found with the Sounion statues (nos. 2, 5) are exceptionally well preserved and show the normal practice. The foot-plinth is carved in one piece with the figure and is approximately oval in shape. It is inserted into a corresponding depression on the upper face of a rectangular marble base. The contours of foot-plinth and depression in base correspond only roughly, for there had to be room for the molten lead, which was poured into the interstices and which kept the plinth firmly embedded in the base. Whether, in addition, a marble tenon or metal dowel secured plinth to base, as was, for instance, the case in some seventh- and sixth-century female statues,[43] cannot now be determined, for that portion is not visible; but, to judge from other early plinths which are no longer inside their ancient bases (cf. nos. 1, 14, 145), this was not the case. The lead, which was often allowed to run beyond the edges of the plinth, was evidently as a rule considered a sufficiently strong fastening. Occasionally there may have been other devices. It has been suggested that the holes on the sides of the plinth of the Delos Colossus (no. 15) were made so that the molten lead might penetrate into them and give additional support[44] (cf. p. 53).

The plinth was often higher than the depression in the base,[45] protruding sometimes as much as 2-2.5 cm. above the upper plane of the base. The shape of the plinth varied. It was either oval (nos. 2, 14, 145), or hexagonal (nos. 15, 16), or followed the contours of the feet (no. 1); occasionally it was rectangular (cf. no. 12).[46] The upper plane of the plinth in the Sounion and New York kouroi is not level, being highest in the middle and sloping downwards to rounded edges.

The base is generally, but not always, rectangular; for instance, that of the kouros dedicated by Euthykartides (no. 16) is triangular, with decorated corners. The lower portion of the base, which was inserted into the ground and so was not seen, was often left rough (cf. nos. 2, 5, 16). Thereby

[41] On this subject cf. especially the excellent article by Raubitschek, 'Zur Technik und Form der altattischen Statuenbasen', in *Bulletin de l'Institut archéologique bulgare*, XII, 1938, pp. 139-48; also Deonna, *Dédale*, I, pp. 108 ff., and the earlier articles cited by them. Dr. Raubitschek kindly read my account in MS. and made many valuable suggestions.

[42] I have included only those bases of kouroi which can be roughly dated and which have been published or are exhibited in the well-known museums—either in galleries or store-rooms. There must be many other bases found in old excavations, the present location of which seems to be no longer known (cf. e.g. Deonna, p. 174).

[43] E.g. Nikandre's statue (p. 27), the statue found at Samos (Buschor, *Alt. St.* II, fig. 75), and the Antenor Kore (Heberdey, *Ath. Mitt.* XV, 1890, p. 130 f.; Raubitschek, op. cit. p. 141, note 6).

[44] Raubitschek, op. cit. p. 143.

[45] E.g. in the Sounion base no. 2 (at the back) and in the Calf Bearer, Akropolis Museum, no. 624; Kirchner, *Imagines Inscriptionum Atticarum*, pl. 2, no. 5; Schuchhardt in Schrader, *Akropolis* p. 278 f., fig. 324.

[46] For a theory that the two plinths of Kleobis and Biton were inserted into a common base, since they have a common inscription, cf. Raubitschek, op. cit. p. 140, note 8. For another instance of a rectangular plinth cf. the little base from Laconia; Wace and Hasluck, *B.S.A.* XI, p. 87, fig. 8. (I owe this reference to Dr. Raubitschek.)

we can determine how much of the base protruded above ground. The two larger Sounion bases protruded only about 11 cm., though they are 25 and 24 cm. high; the base of the statue dedicated by Euthykartides (no. 16), which is 58 cm. high, protruded about 25 cm.[47] The earliest kouroi were evidently mounted low.

Since the kouroi were generally either dedicatory offerings or memorials for the dead, an inscription was in order. In the Delos Colossus (no. 15), the inscription was carved on the front face of the base; in Euthykartides' statue (no. 16) on the upper surface and front face of the base; in Kleobis and Biton (no. 12), on the upper surface of the foot-plinths; in Dermys and Kittylos (no. 11), on the front face and right side of the base and the names of the figures were added near the lower legs. It is noteworthy that in the Sounion kouroi (nos. 2-5) there are no inscriptions on bases, plinths, or preserved portions of the figures (cf. pp. 42-46). Perhaps the inscriptions happened to be on the missing portions of the legs, or they were added in colour, as on the Siphnian frieze, and have disappeared.[48]

The bronze statuette of a kouros (no. 22) from Samos has most of its foot-plinth preserved. The latter is cast in one piece with the figure, and was perhaps roughly rectangular in shape.

Orchomenos-Thera Group. Several plinths, with feet of stone kouroi belonging probably to the Orchomenos group, have been found in the Ptoan Sanctuary (nos. 36-8). The shape is either hexagonal or follows roughly the contours of the feet. Their bases have apparently not survived.[49] The plinth of a limestone statuette from Knidos (no. 57) is rectangular; it was not made for insertion into a base, for an inscription runs partly along its side. Two bronze statuettes, one dedicated by Polykrates (no. 54), the other from Samos (no. 51), have their rectangular foot-plinths preserved—the former with an inscription engraved on the sides. Both plinths are cast in one piece with the figure.

Tenea-Volomandra Group. Two plinths of stone kouroi, both from Samos, belong to the Tenea-Volomandra group. One is hexagonal (no. 79); the other, a mere fragment (no. 80), was perhaps oval. The plinth of the Tenea kouros (no. 73) is preserved in part, but its original shape is uncertain.

None of the extant stone kouroi belonging to this period have their bases preserved; but the Calf-Bearer shows that the practice of inserting a foot-plinth of a shape roughly following the contours of the feet into a rectangular base persists. Though this base is 44.5 cm. high, its lower half is left rough, indicating that only the upper half protruded above the ground.[50] The bases of the Geneleos group[51] and of the female statue dedicated by Phaidimos[52] are in step formation. The former is of limestone, about 51 cm. high; in the latter the top block is of marble, the three lower ones are of limestone, and the whole is about 1.18 m. high (part of the lowest block is roughly finished). That occasionally dedications were mounted on high columns in the first half of the sixth century is indicated by the Naxian Sphinx at Delphi. In the kouros dedicated by Leukios (no. 77) the dedicatory inscription was carved on the upper leg.

[47] Homolle, *B.C.H.* xii, 1888, p. 464.

[48] This suggestion was made to me by Professor J. C. Sloane.

[49] A number of bases with remnants of feet found in the Ptoan Sanctuary are mentioned by Holleaux, *B.C.H.* xi, 1887, pp. 195 ff.; but no distinction is made between base and foot-plinth, and their present whereabouts is not known (cf. Deonna, p. 174). One has an inscription on the 'face supérieure' (Holleaux. op. cit. p. 197, no. xxxvi).

[50] Schuchhardt in Schrader, *Akropolis*, p. 281.

[51] Schede, *Abhandlungen der preussischen Akademie der Wissenschaften*, 1929, phil.-hist. Klasse no. 3, fig. 14, pls. xi, xii; Buschor, *Alt. St.* ii, figs. 90-101.

[52] Eichler, *Öst. Jahr.* xvi, p. 86, note 1.

A bronze statuette in Boston (no. 76) has a rectangular foot-plinth with two holes at opposite corners for fastening, presumably to a small marble base.[53]

MELOS GROUP. For the Melos group we have a stone witness in the kouros dedicated by the sons of Charopinos, of which the marble foot-plinth and base are preserved (no. 105). The plinth, which roughly follows the contours of the feet, is inserted into an oblong base, 40 cm. high, with rounded corners. The lower portion of the base is only roughly finished with the point, from which we must infer that only the smoothed portion, about 15 cm. high, protruded from the ground. The dedicatory inscription was carved on the upper surface of the base. The foot-plinth of the Melos kouros (no. 86) also roughly follows the contours of the feet. A bronze statuette from Olympia[54] has a long rectangular plinth with holes for fastening to a base. The statue from Megara Hyblaia (no. 134) has an inscription on the right leg.

ANAVYSOS-PTOON 12 GROUP. Two stone kouroi of the Anavysos-Ptoon 12 group have their foot-plinths preserved (nos. 137, 145). Both plinths are oval, but wider than those of the early statues.[55] One (no. 137) is still inserted into a rectangular base, which is 33.5 cm. high and has been smoothed on its sides except for a small portion at the bottom. In this case, therefore, a considerable portion of the base, perhaps about 30 cm., presumably protruded from the ground. At the top of the front face of the base are remains of an inscription. Enough is preserved of the foot-plinth of the Munich kouros (no. 135) to indicate that its shape roughly followed the contours of the feet. A rectangular, inscribed block, said to have been found near the kouros from Anavysos (no. 136) is supposedly the middle portion of its three-stepped base; it is of Parian marble, 24 cm. high. Part of a dedicatory inscription is preserved on a piece of a leg[56] which evidently belonged to a colossal kouros of this period.

PTOON 20 GROUP. In the last group (Ptoon 20) the kouros no. 165 retains its hexagonal foot-plinth and rectangular base. The latter is inscribed on its front face 'Aristodikos', in the genitive; it is 28.7 cm. high and smoothed down to the bottom. A pair of feet found at Delos,[57] with foot-plinth still inside its base, probably belongs to this period; for the base is shaped like a capital, which is one of the several forms current at this time for other statues.[58] Two rectangular bases, from the Themistoklean wall (cf. p. 138), probably of this period, are respectively 22.5 and 31.5 cm. high.

Several dedicatory inscriptions have survived. On a kouros from the Ptoan Sanctuary (no. 155) the inscription is carved on the left thigh; on the bronze kouros from Piombino (no. 180), on the right foot; on a bronze statuette from the Ptoan Sanctuary (no. 157), on the left leg.

A bronze statuette of this period, in New York (no. 172), has the usual rectangular foot-plinth cast in one piece with the figure, with holes for fastening to a base. In one from Naxos, now in Berlin (no. 174), the soles are provided with tangs which pass into a plinth and are fastened with iron bolts; the plinth is rectangular, hollow, and has thick walls. A bronze statuette of Apollo (?) from Sparta, now in Athens has a rectangular, box-like plinth, with two extensions, front and back, on which are holes for fastening to a base.[59]

[53] Raubitschek, op. cit. p. 132.

[54] Inv. B2400. Kunze, v. *Olympiabericht*, 1956, pls. 52, 53.

[55] In the fourth century, the oval plinths are still wider, as Dr. Raubitschek pointed out to me; cf. Will, *B.C.H.* LXII, 1938, pp. 289 ff.

[56] Buschor, *Alt. St.* p. 12, figs. 17, 18 and in *Festschrift Bernhard Schweitzer*, pp. 98 ff. See my p. 114.

[57] Deonna, no. 107, fig. 143.

[58] Raubitschek, op. cit. pp. 148 ff.

[59] C. Karousos, *Charites*, pp. 33 ff.

Summing up these data, one can say that, judging from the few stone kouroi which have survived with foot-plinths, bases, and dedicatory inscriptions, similar methods of mounting prevail throughout most of the archaic period. The foot-plinth was carved in one piece with the statue. It varied in shape, the earlier ones generally following more or less closely the contours of the feet, though there are oval examples, both early and late. The plinth was inserted into a marble or limestone base, which was generally but not always rectangular and which had a depression on its upper surface, roughly corresponding to the form of the plinth. It was held secure in its bedding by the lead which was poured into the interstices between it and the base, and was allowed to overflow on the upper surface. The early bases were low, protruding only a few inches above the ground. Later they gradually became higher, and are of varied shapes, including columns and rectangular shafts, like those of other contemporary statues; for at least one base in the form of a capital, with feet evidently of a kouros of this period, is known.[60] Occasionally a three- or four-stepped base was used (cf. no. 136), as in Phaidimos kore (Athens, National Museum, no. 81).

The dedicatory inscriptions were carved on the base, on the plinth, or on the statue itself, instances of all three occurring early and late.

The foot-plinths of bronze statuettes of kouroi were regularly rectangular, sometimes in step formation.[61] They were either cast in one piece with the figure, in which case they often had holes for fastening to a base;[62] or they had tangs under the feet, which passed into a plinth and were fastened by rivets. Presumably—as was the case in other statuettes—the plinths were inserted into little stone bases, fitting into depressions, and fastened with molten lead; sometimes tangs on the under side of the plinths fitted into corresponding holes in the bases.[63]

Knowing how the kouroi were mounted, can one go further and visualize them as they stood in sanctuaries and cemeteries? The evidence as above presented shows that the majority of the kouroi were set up singly, each on its own base, which often was partly let into the ground. Only occasionally, for some special reason, as in the case of Kleobis and Biton (no. 12) and of Dermys and Kittylos (no. 11), were two kouroi combined. (Whether the Sounion kouroi, nos. 2-5, constituted a group is not known.) As dedications, therefore, the kouroi did not differ from other statues. Those which commemorated the dead were presumably erected in the family plots of the aristocratic Eupatrids (cf. p. 31), and were likewise placed directly on the ground. The high platforms of the Athenian Kerameikos belong to a later age.

(*f*) *Proportions*

On the proportions of the kouroi cf. the analyses of the 'Apollo of Tenea' (no. 73) by L. D. Caskey, *A.J.A.* XXVIII, 1924, p. 358 ff., and of the New York statue (no. 1) by I. A. Richter, *Met. Mus. Studies*, V, 1, 1934, pp. 51 ff., and Brunn-Bruckmann-Arndt, *Denkmäler*, text to nos. 751-5, pp. 27 ff. It is clear that they were carefully designed with parts interrelated according to a fixed scheme.

[60] From Delos, A4327. Cf. Deonna, no. 107, fig. 143.

[61] Cf. e.g. the kouros from Samos, Buschor, op. cit. fig. 36, with which we may compare the kore in Boston (Caskey in *Master Bronzes selected from Museums and Collections in America* [Exhibition in Buffalo, February, 1937], no. 66).

[62] Generally, but not always at opposite corners of the plinth. For an instance with holes in the middle of the front and back cf. *F.d.D.* V. p. 39, fig. 121.

[63] Cf. the clear description by Raubitschek, op. cit. p. 132 f.

Fig. 1. Suppliant at a statue of Apollo. From a red-figured vase in the British Museum (E. 336).

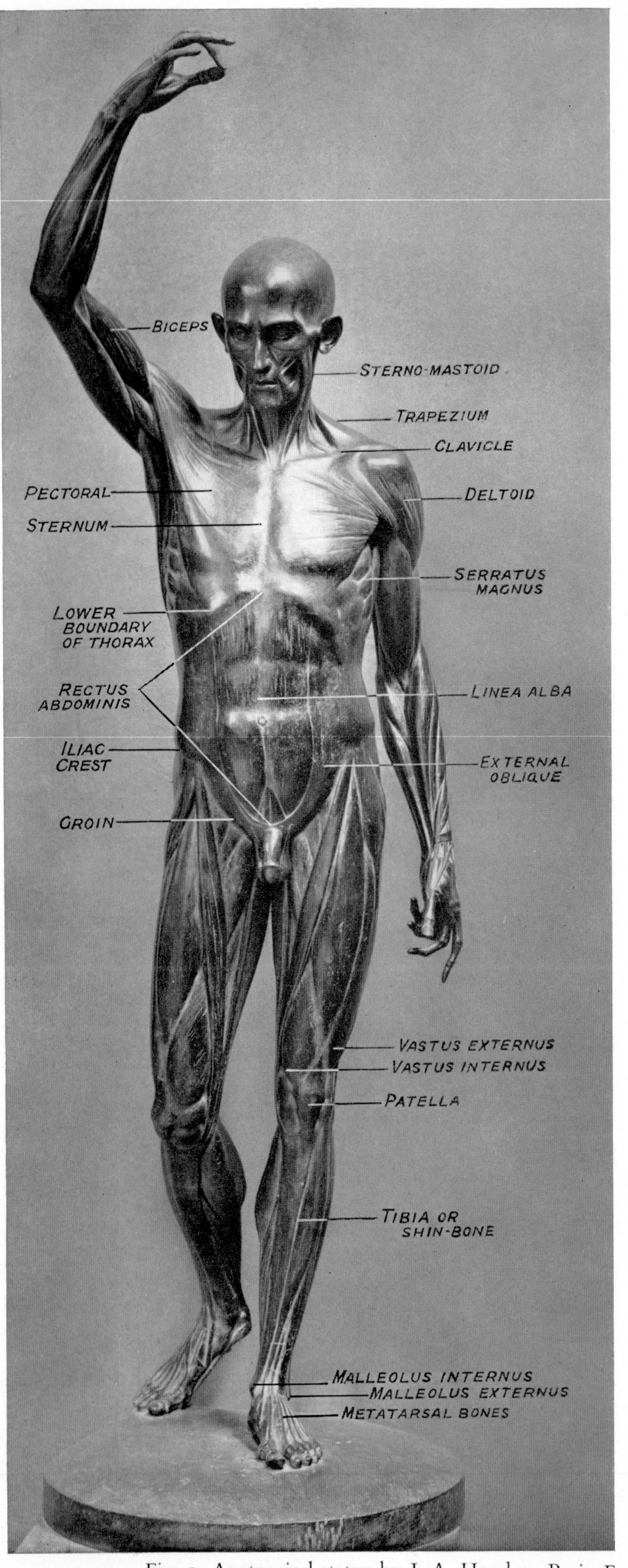

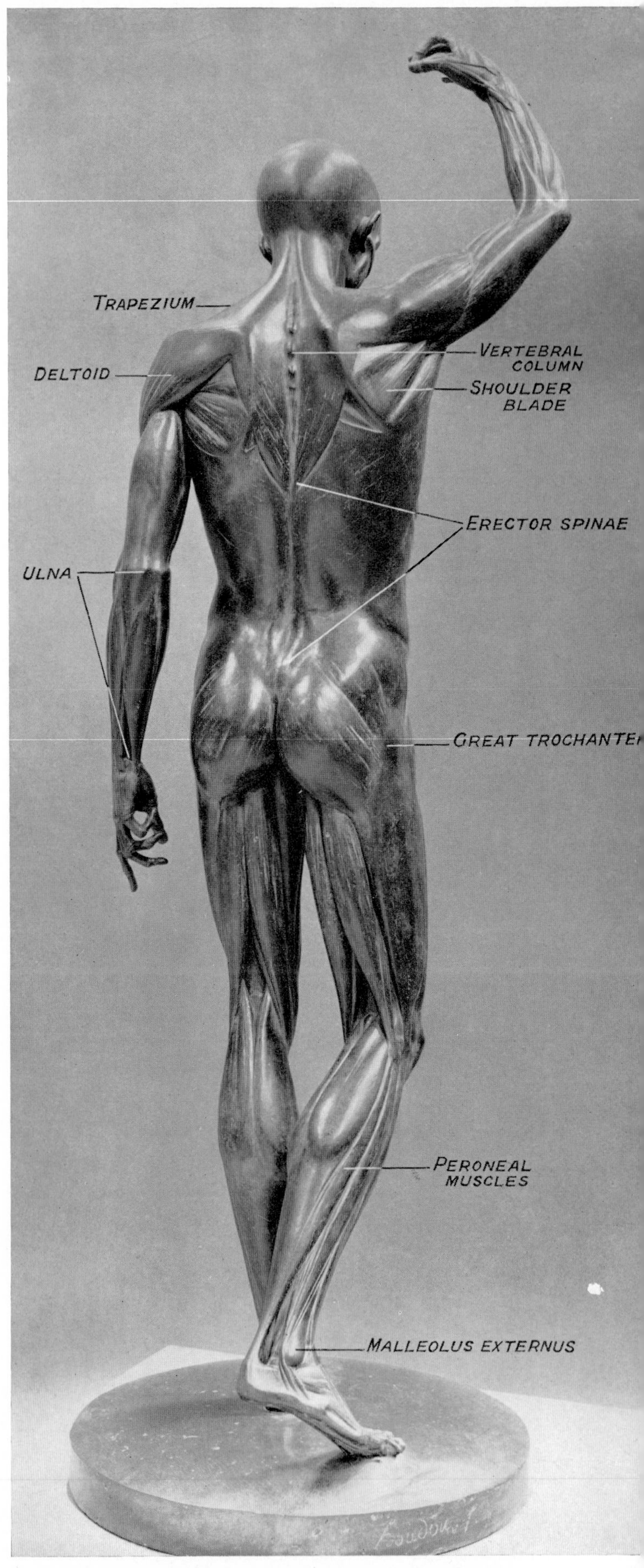

Fig. 2. Anatomical statue by J. A. Houdon. Paris, Ecole des Beaux-Arts. (With lettering by C. A. Waterhouse)

III. SUMMARY OF ANATOMICAL ANALYSES

IN tracing the development of the kouros type in Greek sculpture, we have here taken account of the proportions and structures of the figure in general, and of certain salient anatomical landmarks the representation of which underwent evolution. It will be found that they serve as useful clues for determining the particular period to which a statue belongs.

Beginning with a straight and stiff-limbed structure of often abnormal proportions, the artist gradually worked towards a more relaxed stance and natural proportions. At first grooves, ridges, and knobs on the surface were used to indicate anatomical detail, of which the real purport was not understood. They were composed in a series of patterns, each distinct and separate from the other. Only gradually did the Greek artists comprehend the significance of the human shape and learn to model and interrelate its various anatomical parts. When they had once mastered this, the road was open to depart from the strictly frontal stance.

HEAD. In the head special interest attaches to the formation of the skull, the ear, the eye, and the mouth, both in their constructions and their relative sizes and positions. (The nose is unfortunately usually missing.)

Skull. At first the skull is undeveloped, being flat at the back, though occasionally somewhat rounded at the top. Gradually it becomes more rounded, until in the latest periods (Anavysos-Ptoon 12, Ptoon 20) it assumes its characteristic spherical shape.

Ear. In the ear the points stressed are its construction in one or more planes and its various component parts, especially the helix (external rim), the lobe, and the two little flaps above it, known as tragus and antitragus. At first the ear is schematized and usually carved in one plane; gradually it assumes a more natural shape. The tragus is at first (Sounion to Tenea-Volomandra) knob-like, and forms either a separate protuberance on the cheek or an excrescence from the lobe; by Anavysos-Ptoon 12 it has assumed a natural form. The antitragus is regularly observed in the later periods, from Ptoon 12 on (only exceptionally and tentatively earlier). See illustration below.

Eye. In the eye the points brought out are the gradual realization of the roundness of the eyeball and of the recess at the inner corner, called canthus, and the final appearance (in Ptoon 20) of the lachrymal caruncle (see below).

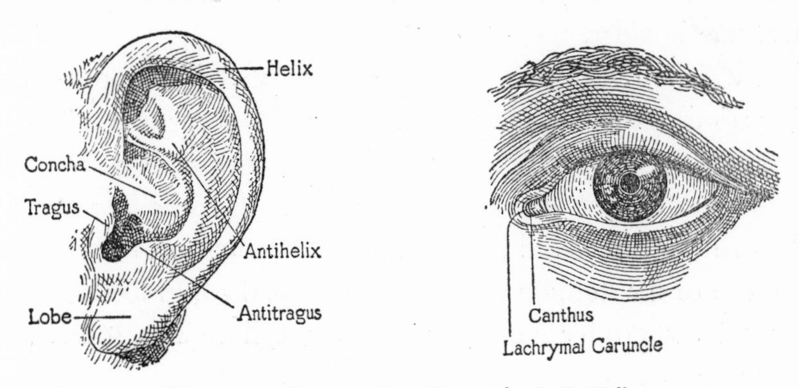

DETAILS OF EAR AND EYE. Drawn by L. F. Hall.

Mouth. In the mouth emphasis is laid on the relative position of the lips, their shape, and the formation of the corners.

Hair. The hair is represented at first in a highly stylized manner, almost as a wig. The tresses start from the forehead and descend more or less parallel to one another. The fact that the hair radiates from a place near the vertex of the skull, though sometimes partially observed in the earliest period (cf. nos. 12, 14), becomes a general observation only in the latest periods (Ptoon 20, exceptionally Anavysos-Ptoon 12). The fashion of wearing the hair also changes. At first it is always long. In the Anavysos-Ptoon 12 period it occasionally descends only as far as the nape of the neck. In the Ptoon 20 period it is usually short or rolled up behind. Various conventions are adopted for suggesting the strands of curly hair. Globules forming beaded tresses are in vogue from the Sounion to the Ptoon 12 group, the solid, boardlike mass, however, becoming gradually looser; finally, in Ptoon 20, wavy strands become popular. Spiral curls distinguish the hair along forehead and temples from Sounion to Ptoon 20.

NECK. The chief features of the neck are the powerful sterno-mastoid muscles, so called because they run from the mastoid process behind the ear to the top of the sternum (breastbone) and to the inner part of the clavicles (collar-bones); they divide the anterior triangle of the neck from the posterior part. In the earliest examples (Sounion and Orchomenos-Thera) their attachment to the clavicles and sternum is indicated in stylized fashion. Somewhat later (Tenea-Volomandra) the construction of the neck is often generalized; the sterno-mastoid muscles, when marked, are indicated by slightly modelled shapes.[1] The anterior triangle of the neck is better understood in the Melos group. In the Anavysos-Ptoon 12 group the sterno-mastoids are modelled, but their attachment to the sternum is often not shown, with the result that sometimes a continuous groove or hollow runs above the clavicles. Not until the latest group (Ptoon 20) is the structure of the neck correctly indicated. Laterally the outward slope of the neck to the shoulder is formed by the bulging trapezium muscle. This is not observed in the early periods, when the outline of the neck from ear to shoulder forms a concave curve. It is only in the latest period (Ptoon 20) that the bulge of the trapezium is indicated.

TORSO, FRONT. In the front part of the trunk the determining parts observed by the early sculptor are:

(1) The *clavicles* (collar-bones)—their shape and position. At first they are represented as flat ridges protruding along their whole course from the top of the sternum to the shoulder; only later (Anavysos-Ptoon 12, Ptoon 20) do they assume their characteristic curve: convex near the sternum, concave near the shoulder.

(2) The *median line*, which divides the front of the torso lengthwise into two symmetrical parts. This line in the early periods (Sounion, Orchomenos-Thera) is sometimes marked by a continuous groove extending from the sternal notch to the navel; at other times it is divided into two sections, corresponding to the sternum (breastbone) and the linea alba (middle line of the abdomen). Soon the groove along the sternum is replaced by modelled shapes, and only the groove along the linea alba—from the lower end of the sternum to the navel—is marked. In the latest periods (Anavysos-Ptoon 12 and Ptoon 20) the groove corresponding to the linea alba sometimes continues for a short distance below the navel.

[1] Throughout our analyses we shall use the word model with the meaning 'to assume the appearance of natural relief' (*Webster's Dictionary*). We are quite aware that the narrower sense of the word 'to fashion in a plastic material' does not apply to our kouroi, since they were carved directly in stone. But we have not been able to think of a more appropriate word which avoids this confusion and still conveys our meaning. 'Rounded' is hardly specific enough.

(3) The *thorax* (chest). In the earlier works its lower boundary takes the form of a pointed (or only slightly rounded) arch, in accordance with the subcostal margin formed by the cartilages of the false ribs, but later the arch becomes well rounded (generally Anavysos-Ptoon 12) and finally (Ptoon 20) semicircular, taking account of the upper boundary of the rectus abdominis. In the Ptoon 20 period there is sometimes observable at the lower end of the sternum a small raised plane caused by the projection of the xiphoid appendage.

(4) The *rectus abdominis* (the flat muscle lying on either side of the middle line of the abdomen [linea alba], which stretches from the lower end of the thorax to the pubes). Its transverse divisions above the navel, when marked, at first number from three upward and are suggested by mere incisions, but gradually (from Orchomenos on) they assume modelled shapes, and in the last period (Ptoon 20) they are reduced to two, the top, or third, division being incorporated into the semicircular arch which forms the lower boundary of the thorax.[2] In the later periods (exceptionally in Melos, oftener in Anavysos-Ptoon 12 and in Ptoon 20) the lower boundary of the rectus abdominis is indicated by grooves, one on each side of the abdomen.

(5) The *navel*. At first it is rendered as a knob surrounded by a circular groove, then (from Melos on) often as a depression, and finally (Ptoon 20) often with a fold of skin above—though this also occurs exceptionally earlier (e.g. nos. 70, 92).

(6) The *serratus magnus* muscle on the side of the chest, arising by serrations or digitations from the ribs and interlocked with the digitations of the *external oblique muscle*. This is observed only in the latest period (Ptoon 20). While the serratus magnus travels backwards from these digitations towards the shoulder-blades, and its course is hidden from view, the external oblique travels downward and forward to the pelvis and abdomen.

(7) The *flanks*. In the early period they are variously rendered. At first there is either no protrusion to mark the iliac crest (upper end of pelvis), or there is a continuous girdle-like ridge round the waist (Sounion, sometimes Orchomenos-Thera). A knob sometimes marks the anterior spine of the iliac crest. Gradually (from Tenea-Volomandra on) the external oblique muscle assumes its characteristic bulge over the iliac crest.

(8) The *lower boundary of the abdomen* (groin). In the earlier works it descends with straight sides towards the genitals, but later it assumes the form first (generally Anavysos-Ptoon 12) of a small, then (generally Ptoon 20) of a large semicircle—a counterpart to the semicircle of the lower boundary of the thorax. The convexity downward corresponds to the tendon of the external oblique muscle named 'Poupart's ligament', which runs from the anterior spine of the ilium to the spine of the pubic bone. The pubes, when marked, has at first a straight upper edge, to judge at least by the few extant early examples (cf. nos. 12, 15, 41). From Tenea-Volomandra on, examples occur with the upper edge in the form of two concave curves with a raised central point (cf. nos. 82, 106, 156, 168), but the straight upper edge is retained also later in some instances (cf. no. 92).

TORSO, BACK. In the back of the trunk the determining factors are:

(1) The *vertebral column* (spine), descending all the way down the middle line of the back. At first it is straight (Sounion, Orchomenos-Thera), gradually it assumes a gentle curve (some examples in Orchomenos-Thera, Tenea-Volomandra, Melos), and finally (Anavysos-Ptoon 12, Ptoon 20) its characteristic *S*-shaped curve, bringing the greatest protrusion of the back, when seen in profile,

[2] Richer, *Le Nu dans l'art*, pp. 39 ff., points out that archaeologists have often misunderstood this important fact—as if in nature there were only two transverse divisions above the navel; cf. also his *Anatomie artistique*, p. 174 f.

level with that of the chest. In the earlier periods—Sounion, Orchomenos-Thera, Tenea-Volomandra—the greatest protrusion of the back, seen in profile, is higher than that of the chest.

(2) The *spinal furrow*, caused by the prominences of the *erector spinae* muscles on either side of the vertebral column. The attachment of these muscles to the posterior part of the iliac crest in the lumbar region is at first only occasionally observed and marked by grooves; later it is indicated by modelled shapes. Occasionally the muscle is indicated along its whole course on both sides of the spinal furrow.

(3) The *shoulder-blades* with their muscular covering. At first they are outlined by grooves, then they are indicated as separate, raised planes, and later (from Tenea-Volomandra on) as modelled shapes. Their complicated construction is not fully realized until the later period (occasionally Anavysos-Ptoon 12 [cf. no. 144], generally Ptoon 20).

ARM. In the arm the *deltoid, biceps,* and *elbow* (upper end of ulna) are of course salient features. The rotation of the radius round the ulna, which carries the hand with it, determines the appearance of the *forearm*. When the arm is in the so-called supine position the two bones of the forearm lie parallel to each other, the radius being the more external bone, and the palm of the hand being directed forward; in the other or 'prone' position, the radius crosses obliquely in front of the ulna, and the palm of the hand is directed backward. This complicated action is not at first understood. Instead, the forearm is supinated, that is, directed forward, whereas the palm of the hand is directed towards the body (at least in the stone examples). This gives the arm, when seen from the front, a broad and flat appearance and makes an unnatural transition from the forearm to the wrist. Later (from Melos on), however, the action is understood and the forearm and hand are correctly semi-pronated (there are a few transitional examples). In bronze statuettes the forearm is generally turned towards the body, even in the early periods, and is not always held close to the thigh.

LEG. The chief anatomical features of the leg of which we have studied the developments are:

(1) The *buttocks* and the *great trochanter* (external process of the thigh bone), the position of which is marked by a slight hollow, while the surrounding muscles form a pronounced general convexity in this region. This depression over the great trochanter is at first (Sounion) sometimes suggested by a small incised curve, then (Orchomenos-Thera, Tenea-Volomandra) generally omitted, and in the subsequent periods (occasionally Melos, regularly later) rendered by a modelled depression.

(2) The construction of the knee, with the patella (kneecap) and the two *vasti muscles*, one on each side. The vastus internus at first (Sounion, most of Orchomenos-Thera) descends to about the same level as the vastus externus; later (occasionally Orchomenos-Thera, regularly from Volomandra on) it descends lower; and gradually (from Anavysos-Ptoon 12 on) the bulge above the inner side of the knee increases.

(3) The *tibia* (shin-bone), with its rounded lateral prominence at the ankle, known as internal *malleolus*, and the *fibula* ending in the external malleolus. At first the shin descends almost vertically and the two malleoli are level; later (from Tenea-Volomandra on) the sharp anterior edge of the shin describes the characteristic inward curve and the external malleolus is placed lower and further back than the internal one.

(4) The two *peroneal* muscles, rising from the outer side of the fibula and causing a furrow down the outer side of the lower leg.

(5) The *foot*, its arch, and the relative positions of the toes, their relative length and direction. At first (Sounion, Orchomenos-Thera, Volomandra), the toes are more or less parallel and their

ends as they touch the ground recede along a continuous curve, the big toe projecting further than the second toe; moreover the four smaller toes curve downwards with nails pointing towards the ground; the metatarsal bones begin to be lightly indicated in the Tenea-Volomandra period. Later (Melos) the second and big toes sometimes have about the same projection, and the four smaller toes no longer point sharply downwards, but form a gentle curve. Finally (Anavysos-Ptoon 12, Ptoon 20) the second toe projects further than the big toe, and the small toe curves markedly inwards, so that the toes are no longer all parallel nor do they recede along one continuous line; the nails point forwards and the articulation of the joints, as well as the metatarsal bones, are well rendered. It is noteworthy that in the classical period of Greek sculpture the second toe tip regularly projects further than big toe. In nature, however, this is not always the case.[3] Sometimes the tip of the big toe, sometimes that of the second toe projects further. The big toe is usually the longest from base to tip, in spite of having only two phalanges, whereas the other toes have three; but the second toe may project further, for its root is further forward.

STANCE. Though the stance of the statue remains strictly frontal, with the weight evenly distributed on both legs, until the very end of the period under consideration, nevertheless, as time went on, the artist tried to suggest the asymmetry of the two sides of the figure arising from the forward position of the left leg. Even as early as Orchomenos-Thera, the left hip is sometimes placed slightly forward, in sympathy with the advanced leg (cf. no. 40). From Ptoon 12 on, the hips are no longer always level, that of the advanced leg being sometimes higher than that of the receding leg; later (occasionally early Ptoon 20, regularly late Ptoon 20) hip and buttock of the supporting leg rise, foreshadowing the rhythmic movement of the body in the Polykleitan era, when the weight is poised on this leg.

To make this development clear we present herewith the most tangible of these findings in tabular form. Further details are noted in the anatomical summaries of each group and in the analyses of the individual statues.

[3] F. G. Parsons in *Encyclopaedia Britannica*, 14th ed., I, s.v. Anatomy, p. 884, says, for instance, that it is 'seldom seen in Englishmen'.

TABLE OF ANATOMICAL ANALYSES

	SOUNION	ORCHOMENOS-THERA	TENEA-VOLOMANDRA	MELOS	ANAVYSOS-PTOON 12	PTOON 20
GENERAL STRUCTURE	Proportions often abnormal	Proportions more or less normal		. . . .	Proportions normal .	. . . .
	Greatest protrusion of back, viewed in profile, higher than that of chest (a few Eastern exceptions in Volomandra period)			Greatest protrusion of back level with that of chest . . .		
	Vertebral column more or less straight	Vertebral column assumes curve, sometimes gentle, sometimes more pronounced			Curve of vertebral column *S*-shaped . . .	
	Anatomical details indicated by grooves, ridges, and knobs on surface	Forms generally more modelled	Forms more modelled	. . . .	Forms modelled . .	. . . .

	SOUNION	ORCHOMENOS-THERA	TENEA-VOLOMANDRA	MELOS	ANAVYSOS-PTOON 12	PTOON 20
HEAD						
Skull	Undeveloped; flat at back and often at top				Spherical; well developed	
Ear	Stylized and usually carved in one flat plane	Carved in one plane, but less stylized	Carved in more than one plane			
	Tragus knob-like; either separate protuberance on cheek or excrescence from lobe			Tragus sometimes assumes more natural form. Anterior part of helix, which is directed backward (crus helicis), is often prominent, joining upper end of tragus	Tragus assumes natural form	
	Antitragus regularly not indicated			Antitragus sometimes tentatively indicated, though wrongly placed	Antitragus indicated . . .	
Eye	Large and flat	Not so large and seen more in the round	Roundness of eyeball indicated			
	Recess at inner corner (canthus) not marked	Recess at inner corner occasionally marked by groove	Recess at inner corner indicated by loop			
	Lachrymal caruncle not indicated					Lachrymal caru sometimes indi
Mouth	Horizontal. Both lips generally on same plane. Corners of mouth form triangular depressions	Generally horizontal; no longer always in one plane; triangular depressions often at corners	Lips generally curve upward and meet more or less at corners. Upper lip protrudes over lower			Lips curve upw. only in early ex amples. Upper protrudes mark over lower and are well shaped
Hair	Long and falls down back . . . . In some examples bulges beneath fillet over shoulder and back				Ocasionally descends only as far as nape of neck	Generally short rolled up behind
	Arranged in parallel beaded tresses . . . . Exceptionally hair radiates at back from point near vertex of skull					Hair generally r ates from point vertex of skull a carved in wavy strands

	SOUNION	ORCHOMENOS-THERA	TENEA-VOLOMANDRA	MELOS	ANAVYSOS-PTOON 12	PTOON 20
CK	Sterno-mastoids, when marked, are indicated by grooves running to sternal notch		Construction of neck often generalized. Sterno-mastoids, when marked, indicated by slightly modelled shapes	Anterior triangle of neck better understood	Sterno-mastoids, when marked, indicated by modelled shapes. Their attachment to clavicles and sternum often not indicated, with result that continuous groove or hollow runs above clavicles	Structure of neck correctly indicated
	No indication of swelling of trapezium on outline of shoulder					Indication of swelling of trapezium on outline of shoulder, slight in early examples, more developed in later ones
RSO, FRONT Clavicles	Represented as flat ridges protruding along whole course to shoulders				Attempt made to indicate backward curve	Assume *S*-shaped curve and lose themselves in shoulders
Median Line	Sometimes marked by continuous groove from sternal notch to navel, sometimes divided into two sections		Groove along sternum generally replaced by modelled shapes and only groove along linea alba is marked			
					Groove along linea alba sometimes continued for short distance below navel	
ower Boundary f Thorax	Has shape of pointed or only slightly rounded arch			Often assumes shape of somewhat rounded arch	Arch rounded	Arch semicircular
ectus Abdominis	Transverse divisions above navel, when marked, number from three upward					Number reduced to two, top one being incorporated into lower boundary of thorax. Small raised plane caused by projection of xiphoid appendage sometimes observable at lower end of sternum
				Lower boundary occasionally marked by grooves, one on each side of the abdomen		
avel	Generally rendered as knob surrounded by circular groove			Generally modelled as depression		
			In a few examples with fold of skin above			In most examples with fold of skin above
erratus Magnus	Not indicated					Generally indicated
lanks	Either no protrusion to mark iliac crest, or continuous girdle-like ridge round waist	Slight protrusion at flanks (sometimes prolonged into girdle-like ridge) occasionally marks anterior spine of iliac crest	Slight indication of external oblique bulging over iliac crest	Indication of external oblique bulging over iliac crest	Swelling of external oblique over iliac crest well developed	

Torso, front (*continued*)	Sounion	Orchomenos-Thera	Tenea-Volomandra	Melos	Anavysos-Ptoon 12	Ptoon 20
Lower Boundary of Abdomen	Generally descends with straight sides towards genitals				Assumes shape of small semicircle or deep curve	Assumes shape o semicircle
				Occasionally forms deep curve		
					In a few cases the straight sides are ret (e.g. Nos. 175, 179, 181)	
	Pubes has straight upper edge					
			In a few examples upper edge is in form of two concave curves with raised central point			Upper edge witl concave curves comes regular f
Torso, back *Shoulder Blades*	Outlined by grooves on surface of back	Indicated as separate, raised planes	Indicated as modelled shapes			
					Occasionally construction well understood	Construction we understood
Erector Spinae	Attachment to posterior part of iliac crest sometimes indicated by grooves in lumbar region	Sometimes indicated as raised planes	Sometimes indicated as modelled shapes		Indicated as modelled shapes	
Arm	Forearm supinated, that is, directed forward, whereas palm of hand is directed towards body (in stone examples); cf. p. 12			Forearm and hand sometimes correctly semi-pronated; that is, both are directed towards body; at other times still turned forward in supine position but with inward twist	Generally forearm and hand semi-pronated; only occasionally forearm still in an intermediate position between supination and semi-pronation	Forearm and ha correctly semi-p nated
	Arms often separated from body along considerable way between armpit and hand	Generally joined to body along considerable way		Sometimes attached to body only below armpit and at hand	Hands generally no longer attached to body but joined to it by short supports	Arms somet held f from even i stone figure
	In bronze statuettes arms are often held from body in relatively free positions					
Hand	Thumb often large		Size of thumb normal			
					Metacarpal bones sometimes indicated	
Leg	Depression over great trochanter sometimes suggested by small incised curve	Depression over great trochanter generally omitted		Depression over great trochanter rendered by mo depression		
	Vastus internus descends to about same level as vastus externus		Vastus internus descends lower than vastus externus			
					Bulge of vastus internus increases	
	Shin almost vertical	Shin sometimes curves inward	Shin curves inward			
	Malleoli level		External malleolus lower and further back than internal one			

LEG (*continued*)	SOUNION	ORCHOMENOS-THERA	TENEA-VOLOMANDRA	MELOS	ANAVYSOS-PTOON 12	PTOON 20
Foot	Toes more or less parallel and their ends as they touch the ground recede along continuous curve, the big toe projecting further than the second toe			Big toe projects a little further than or is about the same length as second toe, and little toe slants inward	Toes no longer all parallel and do not recede along continuous curve; second toe projects further than big toe and small toe curves markedly inward	
			Little toe slants inward			
	Four smaller toes curve downward with nails generally pointing towards ground, either sharply or gently			Four smaller toes and toe nails curve gently downward	Toes and nails point forward	
			Metatarsal bones occasionally lightly indicated		Articulation of joints well rendered. Metatarsal bones indicated	
STANCE	Weight evenly distributed on both legs and flanks level				Sometimes flank of advanced leg placed forward and higher than that of receding leg	At first occasionally, later regularly, flank and buttock of supporting leg rise in conformity with action
		Left flank occasionally placed slightly forward				

IV. PROLOGUE: THE FORERUNNERS

OUR study of the kouros type properly begins with the Sounion group and its contemporaries, which may be dated, provisionally at least, in the late seventh and early sixth century (cf. pp. 38 f.); for only of this group enough examples have survived for detailed examination. But these impressive statues naturally had antecedents. Let us briefly review these in order to understand better the achievement of the sculptors of the Sounion group.

Already in the geometric period of the eighth century B.C., there appear bronze statuettes of standing male figures in frontal pose, with broad shoulders and narrow waist and with left leg advanced—though, as they are of metal, not carved out of blocks of stone, their arms are not attached to their sides (figs. 3-5).[1] The forms are generalized, the structure is simplified, there is practically no anatomical detail; and the proportions are abnormal, the trunk being generally very short and flattened out, the legs long and rounded, and the face flattened out and turned upwards.

Following these summary renderings, we meet during the first half of the seventh century statuettes of a more formalized character. Good examples are several warriors from Olympia[2] (figs. 6-8) in which, though the structure is still generalized, a new life and elasticity are apparent. In the famous bronze statuette in Boston[3] (figs. 9-11), inscribed with a dedication to Apollo by Mantiklos, the geometric scheme persists in so far as the chest is flat, the shoulders broad, the waist narrow, the legs rounded, the proportions abnormal; but for the first time each part is given a distinct shape and a three-dimensional value.

A more developed stage is reached in the statuette (made of hammered bronze plates over a wooden core) found at Dreros in Crete[4] (figs. 12, 13). Here the human figure has assumed a more natural shape, and attempts at anatomical construction may be observed. Thus, there are indications of the clavicles, the lower boundary of the thorax, the groin, the spinal furrow, the knee, the outline of the calf, the inward curve of the shin. On the other hand, the proportions remain abnormal, the head being large and the trunk short. We may perhaps date the statuette round the middle of the seventh century B.C.

In the well-known statuette from Delphi[5] (figs. 14-16) a somewhat more advanced stage is reached, in that the proportions are more normal and the stance more natural; but the form is generalized and little anatomical detail is given. The broad belt round the waist is a feature which is met with in male and female figures throughout the middle and second half of the seventh century (cf. p. 52, note 68). From the resemblance of this statuette to Protocorinthian paintings, for instance the spruce, neat figures on the Chigi vase,[6] it may be tentatively dated in the third quarter of the seventh century. To the same stage of development belongs the remarkable wooden statuette of a youth from

[1] M.M.A. *Bulletin*, XXXII, 1937, p. 37 f., figs. 1-3. Cf. also the many similar statuettes found at Olympia, Athens, and Delphi (Furtwängler, *Olympia*, IV, pl. 16, and Kunze, IV. *Olympia Bericht*, p. 113, pl. 36; de Ridder, *Bronzes de l'Acropole*, no. 692; Perdrizet, *F.d.D.* V. pls. I, II, passim). For Oriental forerunners cf. V. Müller, *Frühgriechische Plastik*, pls. XXXVII ff.

[2] Cf. Kunze, *op. cit.*, pp. 120 ff., pls. 38 ff.

[3] Caskey in *Master Bronzes in America* (Exhibition in Buffalo, February 1937), no. 65.

[4] Marinatos, *Arch. Anz.* 1936, cols. 217 ff., figs. 2, 3; *B.C.H.* LX, 1936, pl. LXIII, p. 485.

[5] Perdrizet, *F.d.D.* V, pl. III, pp. 34 ff.

[6] Cf. Payne, *Protokorinthische Vasenmalerei*, pls. 27-9.

Samos, with hair dressed in Daedalid fashion and wearing a short, girded chiton[7] (figs. 17-19), as well as the terracotta kouros from Gortyna (only the upper part is preserved).[8]

We have, then, in these statuettes—the geometric and sub-geometric warriors, the figure dedicated by Mantiklos, the one found at Dreros, and the ones from Delphi, Samos, and Gortyna—four distinct stages preceding the Sounion group. But they are mere statuettes of bronze, wood, and terracotta. Can we also find life-size stone predecessors? For they must have existed. Such a consummate work as the New York kouros, such bold dedicatory offerings as the Sounion group and the Delos Colossus cannot have been first attempts in the field.

We may claim as such forerunners two approximately life-size marble kouroi from Delos.[9] One, unfortunately now a mere fragment (figs. 20, 21), is very flat front and back, and obviously very early; it may be contemporary with the statue dedicated by Nikandre (*c.*650 B.C.).[10] The other kouros, preserved down to the waist, but with its face sadly battered and the arms missing (figs. 22-4), displays rather more developed forms than Nikandre's statue; the chest and the hair have more volume and the line of the armpit has a more natural curve. If the commonly accepted dating of Nikandre's statue, around the middle of the seventh century, is correct, then the kouros with head (figs. 22-4) should date perhaps in the third quarter, preceding the Sounion group by some decades.

It would seem then that the earliest extant stone kouroi come from the island of Delos, an Ionic sanctuary.

The emergence of this important fact throws a new ray of light on the much discussed question, where and when did monumental sculpture in stone start in Greece? Was it in the East, was it in Crete? Though evidence is accumulating that there may have been fairly large sculptures as early as the eighth century[11] (for temples of the geometric period have been found in Samos,[12] Sparta,[13] Eleusis,[14] and Perachora,[15] and a temple presupposes a cult figure), the fact remains that nothing of that time has survived except diminutive bronzes, terracottas, ivories—and these in abundance. The geometric and early seventh-century cult statues—if they existed—were therefore presumably of wood and so have left no trace. So far the earliest extant free-standing stone statue appears to be the statue dedicated by Nikandre, found at Delos, and probably a product of Naxos; for it is inscribed: 'Nikandre, distinguished among women, the daughter of Deinodikes of Naxos, sister of Deinomenes, and wife of Phraxos, dedicated me to the far-darter, the shooter of arrows.' Its probable date, about 660-650 B.C., and that of the earliest stone kouros (figs. 20, 21) synchronize with the opening up of Egypt to the Greeks;[16] for though there is evidence that the Greeks had intercourse with Egypt as early as the second half of the eighth century B.C., this was confined to piratical

[7] Ohly, *Ath. Mitt.* LXVIII, 1953, pp. 86 ff., no. 5.

[8] D. Levi, *Annuario*, XVII-XVIII, 1955-6, p. 79, fig. 62, b (on p. 51).

[9] Deonna, nos. 93 (A. 4085), 82 (A. 334).

[10] N. M., Athens, no. 1. Cf. Jenkins, *Dedalica*, pp. 68-70. The dating is borne out by a comparison with (1) a Protocorinthian lekythos in the Louvre, assigned to the middle of the seventh century (Payne, *Necrocorinthia*, pp. 11, 94, pl. 1, 7-11, pl. XLVII, 4, 5); and (2) the statuettes of sphinxes and a mourner from the Kerameikos, assigned to about 670-650 B.C. (cf. *Arch. Anz.* 1933, cols. 271 ff., figs. 6-8).

[11] Cf. the excellent summary by V. Müller, *Met Mus. Studies*, V, 2, 1936, pp. 157 ff.

[12] Buschor, *Ath. Mitt.* LV, 1930, pp. 13 ff.

[13] Dawkins in *Artemis Orthia*, pp. 9 ff.

[14] Kourouniotes, *'Ελευσίς, 'Οδηγός*, 1934, p. 8; *Eleusis* (English ed.), 1936, p. 14 (tr. by Broneer).

[15] Payne, *Perachora*, pp. 27 ff.

[16] Meyer, *Geschichte des Altertums*, III^2, p. 149, note 1.

raids and sporadic trading ventures.[17] In the seventh century we hear of actual settlements. Herodotos informs us that Psammetichos I, king of Egypt from about 660 to 609 B.C., gave the Ionians and Carians 'places to dwell in called the Camps, opposite to each other on either side of the Nile', and that, owing to intercourse with these settlers, who 'were the first men of alien speech to settle in Egypt', the Greeks had 'exact knowledge of the history of Egypt from the reign of Psammetichos onwards'.[18] We also know that the Greeks had relations with Mesopotamia and the Near East at this time and earlier (cf. p. 2). What more natural than that the eager young Greeks who came in contact with these old, artistic civilizations should borrow freely from them? The Greek traders and travellers must have opened their eyes wide when they saw the colossal stone sculptures of the Orient. They must have bethought themselves of the material that was ready to their hand, that was superior to the hard, coloured stones of Egypt and Mesopotamia, their own glistening white marbles from Naxos and Paros and the other Greek islands. And so the stimulus was given, we may conjecture, to the rise of monumental stone sculpture in Greece.

Now, since Ionian Delos provides us with several very early statues not far removed from the beginning of stone sculpture in Greece,[19] and since the Ionians were the first Greeks to come into intimate contact with Egypt, cannot East Greece and the Cyclades put in as good a claim to have initiated stone sculpture as Crete, which has been the favourite candidate for this role with many archaeologists? For the seventh-century limestone sculptures from Crete—the seated and standing female figures from Prinias[20] and Gortyna[21] and the figure from Eleutherna[22]—are not demonstrably earlier than the statue dedicated by Nikandre; and the same applies to the large terracotta head from Archanes.[23] The extant early stone sculptures from the Peloponnese and northern Greece—for instance, the reliefs from Mycenae,[24] the stele from Malessina, the statue formerly at Skimatari now in Thebes, the seated statue from Tegea—have been dated in the third and last quarters of the seventh century.[25] The same applies to the Auxerre figure of unknown provenance, generally attributed to Crete on account of its resemblance to the standing figures from Prinias,[26] but also related to the fragments found in Samos.[27]

But what about the literary tradition? Have we not the specific statements of ancient writers that the great Daidalos[28] worked in Crete and that 'the first to win fame as sculptors in marble were Dipoinos and Skyllis, who were born in Crete', and who were the pupils or sons of Daidalos?[29] Yes, but this tradition is confused, for no clear distinction is drawn between the Daidalos mentioned by

[17] H. R. Hall, *C.A.H.* III, pp. 252, 269, 276 f.

[18] II.154 (tr. A. D. Godley). See also my p. 37.

[19] Besides Nikandre's statue and the two kouroi above mentioned cf. the female figure from Delos, Homolle, *De antiquiss. Dianae simul.* pl. V, and Löwy, *Öst. Jahr.* XII, 1909, p. 250, fig. 126, and that from Samos, Buschor, *Alt. St.* II, figs. 72, 73, 75, p. 23 f. On the importance of the Cycladic islands in early archaic Greek art cf. Kondoleon, *Κυκλαδικά*, II, 1956, pp. 1 ff.

[20] Pernier, *Annuario*, I, 1914, pp. 21 ff.

[21] Cf. D. Levi, *Boll. d'Arte*, XLI, 1956, p. 272 f., fig. 58, and *La Parola del Passato*, XLIX, 1956, figs. 6–9.

[22] Jenkins, *Dedalica*, p. 51, pl. VIII, 1, 1a.

[23] Cf. Jenkins, op. cit. pl. VI, 1, 1a.

[24] Rodenwaldt in *Corolla Curtius*, 1937, pp. 63 ff., pls. 7–10; Wace, *J.H.S.* LIX, 1939, p. 210.

[25] Cf. Jenkins, op. cit. pp. 70 ff.; Payne, *Necrocorinthia*, p. 234 f., pl. XLVII, 10, 11.

[26] Löwy, *Öst. Jahr.* XII, 1909, p. 246, fig. 123.

[27] Cf. Buschor, *Alt. St.* II, figs. 72, 73, 75, p. 23 f.

[28] For recent discussions of Daidalos cf. Rumpf, *Bonner Jahrbücher*, Heft 135, 1930, pp. 74 ff.; Schweitzer, *Xenokrates*, 1932; Richter, *Met. Mus. Studies*, v. 1, 1934, pp. 48–50; Hanfmann, *A.J.A.* XXXIX, 1935, pp. 189 ff.; Homann-Wedeking, *Anfänge*, pp. 42 ff.; Becatti, *Röm. Mitt.* LX–LXI, 1953–54, pp. 22 ff.

[29] Pliny, *N.H.* XXXVI.9; Pausanias II.15.1.

Homer and associated with king Minos,[30] and a later historical one. But even if there actually was such a historical Daidalos, his connection with Crete is only part of the story. We have also a tradition that Daidalos was an Athenian by birth and that he worked in Athens before he went to Crete,[31] being distinguished among other things for his work in stone.[32] And Daidalos' descendants were identified with the Attic School: 'This Onatas, though the style of his sculpture is that of Aegina, I should place second to none of Daidalos' successors and the Attic School.'[33] Athens, therefore, as well as Crete, can lay claim to Daidalos.[34] Moreover Daidalos' origin is not a decisive factor; for he cannot have been the earliest sculptor of life-size figures, since it is his innovations in the pose of his statues—the parting of the legs and the freeing of the arms—and the life-like quality which he imparted to his figures that won him applause. Besides, what little is said of the chronology of the 'historical' Daidalos would place him at the earliest in the late seventh century. At least Pausanias[35] dates him three generations earlier than Kallon, and Kallon is placed by an inscription[36] around 500. So Daidalos cannot very well have initiated monumental Greek sculpture. Furthermore, regarding the priority of Dipoinos and Skyllis, Pliny himself records that *before* their time 'the sculptor Melas had already lived on the island of Chios', suggesting that there was an earlier, East Greek school.[37] And the date he assigns to the birth of Dipoinos and Skyllis—about the 50th Olympiad, or 580-577 B.C., 'while the empire of the Medes still lasted, and before Cyrus became king of Persia'—should certainly place them later than the earliest Greek stone sculptures. Furthermore, we are specifically told that, though Dipoinos and Skyllis were born in Crete, they worked in the Peloponnese.

From all these arguments it would seem to follow that though Crete was undoubtedly a great artistic centre in the seventh century, as we know from the limestone sculptures and the numerous terracottas, vases, and bronzes found there, the theory that stone sculpture had its birth there cannot be considered proved. To judge by the evidence as just outlined, it was perhaps rather from the Islands and East Greece that the first impetus came—especially in the carving of marble statues. But wherever this epoch-making venture began, it soon became widespread. The primitive figures from Delos of the middle of the seventh century are presently followed by slightly more advanced works from a larger area, and then, at the end of the century, by a host of impressive works from all over Greece. It is this fine flowering all over the Greek world, as a result of the preliminary efforts which we have reviewed above, that we shall consider in our first, the Sounion group.

[30] *Iliad* XVIII.591 f.

[31] Pausanias VII.4.5, IX.3.2; Diodoros IV.76-7.1.

[32] Diodoros, IV.76.1.

[33] Pausanias, V.25.13: *τὸν δὲ 'Ονάταν τοῦτον ὅμως, καὶ τέχνης ἐς τὰ ἀγάλματα ὄντα Αἰγιναίας, οὐδενὸς ὕστερον θήσομεν τῶν ἀπὸ Δαιδάλου τε καὶ ἐργαστηρίου τοῦ 'Αττικοῦ*. As Stuart Jones points out in *Select Passages from Ancient Writers*, p. 44, 'the words *τε καί* are clearly not disjunctive, but serve to identify the descendants of Daidalos with the *ἐργαστήριον 'Αττικόν*'.

[34] On the Attic origin of Daidalos see especially Töpffer, *Attische Genealogie*, pp. 165 ff., who besides quoting the various Attic genealogies of Daidalos refers to the pertinent statements that there was a sanctuary of Daidalos' sister Perdix beside the Akropolis (Suidas s.v. *Πέρδικος ἱερόν· παρὰ τῇ ἀκροπόλει*), and that the grave of his nephew Kalos was situated at the foot of the Akropolis (Pausanias I.21.4).

[35] II.32.5 and II.51.I.

[36] *I.G.* I², 501.

[37] *N.H.* XXXVI. 11; unless, as has been suggested, the Melas here mentioned is really the hero Melas. But since Melas occurs as a personal name in the historical period, there is no objection to a sculptor named Melas.

V. THE SOUNION GROUP

(*c.* 615-590 B.C.)

General Survey and Historical Background *

THE Greek kouroi of the Sounion group do not, as we saw, represent the beginning of Greek sculpture. That we have tried to picture in the tentative and unsatisfactory way that our meagre evidence makes possible (cf. pp. 26 ff.). The end of the seventh century was no longer the dawn, it was the bright morning of Greek art; and it produced some of the masterpieces of European sculpture.

One of the most remarkable features of this period—as we now come to realize it—is the widespread activity in the artistic field. At a time when our extant historical and literary records are few and fragmentary, the sculptures reveal to us an era of general splendour—especially in Attica, Argos, the Corinthian colony of Corcyra, Thasos, Naxos, Delos, Thera, Samos.

ATTICA. Particularly imposing is the group from Attica. It includes the four (or more) dedicatory statues found near the temple of Poseidon at Sounion (nos. 2-5); the tomb statue from the Dipylon, of which the head and the right hand are preserved (no. 6); the fragments of a statue found in the area of the Athenian Agora (no. 7); the practically complete statue in New York (no. 1); the statue in the collection of Mr. Kalliga in Athens (no. 8), of which only the right hand survives; and a statue from the Kerameikos (no. 9). The Dipylon, Agora, New York, and Sounion statues—and the Kalliga one, as far as one can judge from the hand—are so similar, and share so many anatomical peculiarities not found elsewhere, that one may surmise that they were the products of one distinguished workshop.[1]

The statue from the Kerameikos, on the other hand, is an average product of slightly later date. The flat ear with a single uniformly broad groove separating the helix from the antihelix, and the stylization of the rectus abdominis with horizontal cuts marking its divisions relate it to the New York-Dipylon-Sounion figures; but the slight rounding of some of the shapes, for instance, the shoulder-blades, points to a rather more developed stage. It must be earlier, however, than the statue no. 31, in which the rounding of the forms has progressed still further.

Other marble works of this early period from Attica are the sphinx no. 24.97.87 in New York[2]

* In my *Arch. Gk. Art* (1949) I somewhat expanded the short historical resumés at the beginning of each chapter in this book.

[1] Cf. my analysis in *Met. Mus. Studies*, v, 1, 1934, pp. 34 ff. I there thought that one might see a slight progression along naturalistic lines from the Dipylon to the New York to the Sounion kouroi. Buschor, *Fr. J.*, pp. 15 ff., placed the three figures in the same order. Miss Evelyn Harrison, *Hesperia*, xxiv, 1955, pp. 298 ff., has argued that it is likely that certain fragments found in the Athenian Agora (cf. my no. 7) belong to the Dipylon kouros, and that, since the anatomical renderings on these fragments are closely related to the Sounion kouroi, the latter should not be the last in the series. Though it is not certain that the Agora fragments belonged to the Dipylon kouros, it seems on the whole best—since all these statues form a remarkably homogeneous group—simply to regard them as approximately contemporary, as indeed I did in my *Archaic Greek Art* (1949), p. 9. Budde, *Die attischen Kuroi* (Diss. 1939), exaggerated, I think, the differences between the Sounion statue and the Sounion torso, claiming for the latter a greater softness and roundness. The illustrations are here perhaps misleading. The only real differences I have been able to note on the originals are: (1) the width of the shoulders is greater in the Sounion statue than in the torso; (2) the additional groove in the region of the shoulder-blades, which appears in the Sounion statue, is absent in the torso; (3) the arrangement of the hair is different in statue and torso. Otherwise the scheme is identical. The two statues therefore differ only in unimportant details. L. Politis (*'Εφ. 'Αρχ.*, 1937, p. 750) placed the Kalliga hand between the New York and Sounion kouroi.

[2] Richter, *Archaic Attic Gravestones*, pp. 14 ff., figs. 30-2.

and the superb head of a Gorgon in the Akropolis Museum, no. 701.[3] In the latter, the renderings of the ear (which is carved in one flat plane and strongly stylized, with a single, uniformly broad groove separating the helix from the antihelix), and of the eye (which is flat and has a deep depression under it) relate it to the Dipylon and New York kouroi. In the New York sphinx the quadrangular structure, the flat ear, and the rendering of the hair recall the New York kouros. The earliest poros pedimental sculptures found on the Athenian Akropolis—the lioness with a calf in her claws, for instance—must also belong here. Furthermore, Athenian pottery of this period is remarkably distinguished. It is the time of the earliest Attic black-figure, when the wild, sprawling figures of the preceding decades became systematized to form a powerful, orderly decoration.

From the study of these sculptures there arises out of the obscurity of the past a new picture of aristocratic, pre-Solonic and early Solonic Athens. Instead of being subservient to continental Greece or Ionia, she is leading in the arts, erecting splendid funerary memorials and colossal dedications. We can only dimly envisage the extraordinary courage and enterprise which the production of these large statues implied—the importation from the Islands of huge blocks of marble, the encouragement of pioneer sculptors to carve the statues, and the erection of the completed figures. No wonder there is an echo in literature of a great sculptor 'Daidalos' active in Athens at this period and distinguished among other things for his work in stone (see p. 29).

How great a feat it was merely to transport large blocks of stone in ancient times we may realize from an inscription tentatively dated 327-326 B.C., which lists the expenditures in bringing column drums from the quarries of Mount Pentelikon to the stone yards of Eleusis,[4] a distance of about 41 kilometers of which 700 metres were down the steep slopes of the mountain. The transport, we learn, was done by teams of oxen, and the price was computed for each pair of oxen per day, at the average rate of a little over four drachmas. For each separate drum, weighing about $5\frac{1}{2}$ tons, a team of thirty-odd pairs of oxen was required for three days, costing in the aggregate almost four hundred drachmas. For the twenty-three drums listed in the inscription the total would therefore have been approximately 9,200 drachmas—a formidable sum, especially when we consider that the daily wage of a workman in the fourth century was from one to two and a half drachmas a day.[5] Transport facilities two or three centuries earlier were certainly no better.

From the writings of Solon (archon in 594), who is our chief literary source of this period,[6] we have thought of the time which preceded his reforms as one of acute distress for the majority of the population, of violent dissension between the wealthy few and the enslaved many. But the Eupatrids, 'the mighty who shone in pride of wealth', as Solon describes them, were, we now learn, astonishingly enlightened from another point of view. They used their riches not merely for material ends but on artistic projects of great magnitude. For it is only they who could have financed these undertakings, only they who had the power and wealth to accomplish these feats. Probably the silver mines of Laurion, which Xenophon[7] states were worked from 'a very early time', at least partly financed these ambitious projects. That this was a time of special activity in Attica is also indicated

[3] Payne and Young, *Acropolis*, p. 10, pl. 1. Payne there dates it in the second quarter of the sixth century—too late, I think, for ears in the Volomandra group are no longer so flat and stylized; Schuchhardt in Schrader, *Die archaischen Marmorbildwerke der Akropolis*, p. 319 f., no. 441, rightly connects it with the Dipylon head, and dates it 'beginning of the sixth century'.

[4] *I.G.* II-III^2, 1673 ff.; Glotz, *Le Travail dans la Grèce ancienne*, 1920, p. 348, and *Revue des études grecques*, XXXVI, 1923, pp. 26 ff.

[5] Glotz, *Le Travail dans la Grèce ancienne*, p. 338.

[6] Cf. K. Freeman, *The Work and Life of Solon* (1926); Richter, *Met. Mus. Studies*, V, I, 1934, p. 44, note 71.

[7] *Πόροι* IV.2; cf. Richter, *Met. Mus. Studies*, V, I, 1934, p. 44, note 71.

by the fact that, apparently around 600, Athens embarked for the first time on a vigorous foreign policy, taking Salamis from Megara and wresting Sigeion in the Troad from Lesbos.[8]

BOEOTIA. From Boeotia come two products, the group of Dermys and Kittylos (no. 11), from a cemetery at Tanagra, and a head from the Ptoan Sanctuary (no. 10). Both are of a limestone which is presumably local, and are therefore perhaps of Boeotian workmanship. In conception they are related to the Attic statues, but cruder. In the Dermys and Kittylos the rendering of the vasti muscles above the knee with grooves above recalls that of the New York statue, but it is less elegantly executed. In the head no. 10 the features are similar in structure to those of the Sounion group. Note the large, almond-shaped eye, with the lower lid forming a shallow curve, the upper a pronounced arch; the broad groove separating the upper lid from the eyebrow and the deep depression separating the lower eyelid from the cheek; the flat ear carved all in one plane; the flat skull front and back. The head, therefore, seems to be best explained as a provincial work of this period.[9]

That Boeotia played an important part artistically as early as the seventh century B.C. is suggested by her distinctive pottery of that period, her terracotta statuettes, and her magnificent pithoi with reliefs.[10] We now learn that she apparently made her contribution also in sculpture as early as the late seventh or early sixth century. The fact that one of these pieces comes from the Ptoan Sanctuary is specially significant, for it perhaps supplies evidence for the dating of the earliest Ptoan temple.[11]

ARGOS. Though Kleobis and Biton (no. 12) were found at Delphi, we know from the signature of the artist, (. . . .)medes of Argos, that they are Argive works. Moreover, Herodotos (I, 31), ends his famous account of the exploit of Kleobis and Biton and their subsequent death with the remark: 'Then the Argives made and set up statues of them at Delphi.' The accentuated muscular development and thick-set proportions of the Delphian statues bear out Herodotos' statement that Kleobis and Biton were prize-winners (*ἀεθλοφόροι*) and had great strength of body (*ῥώμη σώματος*). They exemplify in fact the athletic ideal of the Peloponnese. The four-sided shape of the torso, the cubic form of the head, the purely linear rendering of the lower boundary of the thorax place these statues definitely in the Sounion group; but the fact that some of the forms are already seen somewhat in the round (note especially the shoulder-blades, some of the muscles of the arms and legs, the ear) suggests a date a little later than the Sounion statues, perhaps the beginning of the sixth century. The rendering of the hair is closely related to that of the Tegea statue (cf. no. 18); in both, the tresses are brought over the shoulder to fall on the chest and bulge from beneath the fillet over the shoulder and back, and both have three cords (or a triple ring, cf. p. 49) tied at the bottom of each tress.[12] Noteworthy also is the fact that the tresses at the back of the skull radiate from a point

[8] Cf. Adcock, *C.A.H.* IV, p. 32.

[9] Lullies, *Jahrbuch*, LI, 1936, pp. 138 ff., calls the style archaizing and dates the head in the third quarter of the sixth century. The ear, which Lullies mentions specifically as a late rendering, would, according to our findings, be impossible even in the second quarter of the sixth century. The modelling of ears in the Volomandra group already shows considerable depth (cf. p. 79). Grace, *Archaic Sculpture in Boeotia*, 1939, p. 59, dates the head in the early part of the second quarter of the sixth century.

[10] Hampe, *Frühe griechische Sagenbilder*, pp. 56 ff., pls. 36-9. Fragments of similar pithoi have been found at Tenos, cf. *B.C.H.* LXII, 1938, p. 479 f., fig. 34.

[11] No trace of this temple has been preserved. The present foundations date from the fourth century, but have been thought to follow those of an earlier temple, because of the long, narrow cella with deep pronaos and no optisthodomos. The only remnants of an archaic temple are pieces of terracotta revetments of the second half of the sixth century. It has been suggested that the earliest temple was of wood, for which limestone was gradually substituted (cf. Orlandos, *Δελτ. Ἀρχ.* I, 1915, p. 96 f.; Karo, *Arch. Anz.*, 1915, col. 182; Dinsmoor, *Architecture*, p. 218).

[12] One may also compare the similar rendering in the seated statue from Arcadia (National Museum, Athens, no. 57) and in the ivory kneeling figure from Samos (cf. p. 9, note 22).

near the vertex of the skull, as in the Thasos and Thera colossi (nos. 14, 18). In all other known archaic kouroi—until the Ptoon 20 group—the tresses start from the forehead and hang down more or less parallel to one another (cf. p. 18).

We know little of the history of Argos at this time. Under King Pheidon (perhaps early seventh century) she had been the most flourishing state in the Peloponnese. Then Sparta rose as a menace to her neighbours, and a long protracted struggle ensued, of which few details are known except that by about 550 Argos had lost the whole coast strip of Kynouria, and that about 494 she suffered a crushing defeat at the hands of the Spartan king Kleomenes. That in the early sixth century Argos was still powerful may be deducted from the anti-Argive policy of Kleisthenes, tyrant of Sikyon.[13] Kleobis and Biton reinforce this evidence. They show us that about the beginning of the sixth century, Argos was rich enough to make this splendid dedicatory offering, carved out of Island marble, artistically one of the finest creations of early Greece.

It is also interesting to remember that Sakadas, the world-renowned Argive musician, won the prize for flute-playing three successive times at the Pythian games at Delphi in 590,[14] 582, and 578. If our dating of Kleobis and Biton is correct, they stood erect in the Delphian Sanctuary, still fairly fresh and unweathered, when Sakadas won his musical victories there.

CORINTH. Corinth at this period was at the height of her prosperity under the great tyrant Periander (*c.*625-585[15]), and was a leader in commerce, the arts, and literature. The elaborate Kypselos chest, mentioned by Pausanias[16] as a dedication by the Kypselids, was adorning Olympia,[17] Corinthian vases were exported to the ends of the world, the great poet Arion was resident in Corinth. We should expect important Corinthian representatives of the kouros type. But the extensive American excavations in Corinth have not as yet yielded a single kouros contemporary with the Sounion group, or any other major sculpture of that period.[18] Unfortunately the destruction of Corinth under the Roman consul L. Mummius in 146 B.C. was a thorough piece of work. Nevertheless, we may gain a conception of early Corinthian sculpture from the products of one of her colonies. The pedimental sculptures from Korkyra,[19] the modern Corfu, show a kinship with the Argive Kleobis and Biton. They have the same bold monumental style and similar anatomical construction.[20] They too are products of the early Dorian school.

[13] Wade-Gery, *C.A.H.*, III, p. 555 f.

[14] Pausanias X.7.4, gives 586, but 590, given by the Marmor Parium and the Pindar scholia, is to be preferred. See Busolt, *Griechische Geschichte*, I, p. 697, note 1; Beloch, *Griechische Geschichte*, I, 2, pp. 143 ff.

[15] For controversy on the dates of Kypselos and Periander cf. Wade-Gery, *C.A.H.* III, pp. 764 ff., who gives good resumés of the evidence and decides for the early dating. Beloch, *Griechische Geschichte*, I, 2, pp. 274 ff., and Lenschau in Pauly-Wissowa, *R. E.* Supplement IV, s.v. *Korinthos*, cols. 1015 ff., favour a later date, assigning to the Kypselids the period 610-540 B.C. The later date is also ably sponsored by H. R. W. Smith, *Univ. of Cal. Pub. in Classical Arch.* I, no. 10, pp. 254 ff.

[16] Pausanias V.17.5.

[17] For the probable date of the chest cf. von Massow, *Ath. Mitt.* XLI, 1916, pp. 13 ff.

[18] The date now assigned to the early temple of Corinth is about 540 B.C. For a fragment of what may have been a metope of the temple, cf. B. H. Hill, *A.J.A.* XXX, 1926 p. 48, fig. 3.

[19] Cf. the beautiful illustrations in Rodenwaldt, 'Altdorische Bildwerke in Korfu', in *Bilderhefte antiker Kunst*, V, figs. 10 ff.; and *Korkyra* II, pls. 1 ff.

[20] Anatomically the Corfu figures tally in every respect with the Sounion group, as borne out by the following anatomical osbervations: The greatest protrusion of the back seen in profile is higher than that of the chest (Chrysaor). Anatomical details are indicated by grooves, ridges, and knobs. The ear, though worked in more than one plane, is stylized; the tragus is an extension of the lobe; there is no antitragus. The eye is flat; the recess at the inner corner is not marked. The hair bulges forward over the shoulder. The sterno-mastoids are indicated by grooves and there is no indication of the swelling of the trapezium. The clavicles protrude as flat ridges along their whole course to the shoulders. The lower boundary of the thorax has the shape of a slightly rounded arch (Zeus). The lower boundary of the abdomen descends with straight sides towards the genitals. The depression over the great trochanter on

THASOS. The great Kriophoros of Thasos (no. 14) is unfortunately not finished, so the details of construction are not clear. Only the hair is carved in detail; as in Kleobis and Biton and in the Thera colossi, the tresses radiate from a point near the vertex of the skull—an exceptional rendering in early archaic art (cf. p. 18). Charles Picard, who found this statue in a medieval wall, speaks of the great feat it was to bring it down the steep hill with no roads.[21] The feat of bringing it up, 2,500 years ago, must have been even greater. Where it stood and why it was never completed we do not know. Perhaps it was intended for the temple of Apollo on top of the hill overlooking the sea; perhaps it represented Hermes, and stood in a sanctuary of that god.

The statue is eloquent testimony to the wealth and enterprise of Thasos at this period. And the little that we know of the early history of Thasos bears this out. We are told that Thasos was perhaps colonized at an early date by the Phoenicians, who were probably attracted by its gold mines,[22] that towards the end of the eighth century it received a colony from Paros;[23] that these Greek colonists extended their power to the mainland, where they owned gold mines, and that from these sources they gradually grew very wealthy. It was during a war between the Parian colonists and the Thracians of the mainland that the poet Archilochos threw away his shield.[24]

Archilochos[25] describes life in Thasos as primitive ('thrice-miserable Thasos',[26] where 'the misery of all Greece gathered'[27]). Conditions in the interval between his stay there, presumably in the middle of the seventh century, and the wealthy community implied by the Kriophoros must have improved.

NAXOS. Two kouroi found at Delos can be connected with Naxos. The Delos Colossus (no. 13) has on its base an inscription (of perhaps the fourth century B.C.) stating that the statue was dedicated by Naxians. Its remarkable history is given on p. 52. A distinctive feature is the bulging out of the thighs from the waist—which we shall meet again in the Thera colossi (no. 18). Of the other kouros, only the feet and the base are preserved (no. 16), the latter with an inscription: 'Euthykartides the Naxian made me and dedicated me.'[28] It is interesting to find at this early age a sculptor rich enough to dedicate an important statue at Delos and signing his name conspicuously on the front of the base.[29] It seems to bear out the contention that in the seventh and sixth centuries the manual trades were in high standing.[30]

What little we know about the early history of Naxos suggests that she played a prominent role. It was under her protectorate, it would seem, that Delos became the religious centre of an

the side of the buttock is not shown. The vasti are level. The toes are parallel, including the little one, and their ends as they touch the ground recede along a continuous curve, the big toe projecting further than the second one; they slope downward (in the feet of Zeus; only slightly so in those of the giant and of the seated figure). A knob on the outer side of the left foot of the giant probably represents a metatarsal bone (as in the New York and Sounion statues).

[21] *B.C.H.* XLV, 1921, p. 113.

[22] Herodotos, II.44, VI.47; Busolt, *Griechische Geschichte*, I, p. 270; Beloch, *Griechische Geschichte*, I, 2, p. 74; Picard, *B.C.H.*, XLVII, 1923, p. 266 f.

[23] Thucydides, IV, 104, 4. According to Dionysios of Halikarnassos in 720/716, according to the Lydian Xanthos in 708/4.

[24] Frgt. 6, Diehl.

[25] On the dating of Archilochos to *c.* 680-640 B.C., cf. Jacoby, *Classical Quarterly*, 1941, pp. 97 ff.

[26] Frgt. 129, Bergk: *Θάσον δὲ τὴν τρισοιζυρὴν πόλιν.*

[27] Frgt. 52, Bergk: *ὡς Πανελλήνων ὀιζὺς ἐς Θάσον συνέδραμεν.*

[28] Homolle, *B.C.H.* XII, 1888, p. 464; Durrbach, *Choix d'inscriptions de Délos*, p. 2, no. 1 ; Marcadé, *Signatures*, II, 45.

[29] For other instances cf. e.g. Löwy, *Inschriften griechischer Bildhauer*, nos. 1 (Mikkiades and Archermos of Chios), 5 (Ekphantos).

[30] On the position of the artist in ancient times cf. P. N. Ure, *Origin of Tyranny*, pp. 13 ff.; Schweitzer, *Der bildende Künstler und der Begriff des Künstlerischen in der Antike*, 1925, p. p. 45; and especially Guarducci, *Arch. cl.* X, 1958, pp. 138 ff.

amphictyony of island Ionians. One report has it that she was the first to make coins.[31] She was a rival of Paros, as indicated by the bitter feud between them.[32]

These scanty notices in ancient writers are eloquently reinforced by our two sculptures. Only a rich and powerful state could have erected so impressive a dedication as the Delos Colossus. The splendour of the periodic reunions of Ionians on Delos during the festival of Apollo is reflected in the famous description in the Hymn to the Delian Apollo (written perhaps in the seventh century):[33] 'There the Ionians with trailing robes gather in thy honour with their children and modest wives; mindful of thee they delight thee with boxing and dancing and song, whenever they hold their gathering. A man would say that they were deathless and unageing if he came upon the Ionians so met together, beholding them so graceful, and he would be glad at heart looking at the men and well-girded women with their swift ships and great wealth.' The Naxian Colossus, towering in the midst of the other dedications, was doubtless much admired by these Ionians and a source of pride to the dedicators.

DELOS. The fragmentary torso from Delos (no. 17), with belt and with thighs bulging out from the waist, is related to the Delos colossus. The comparatively round forms and soft modelling point to an Eastern origin. We may note particularly the bulge of the vastus internus over the knee; it is not yet placed lower than that of the vastus externus, for the difference in the relative positions of the two vasti was not observed until the period of the Volomandra kouros. The rendering of the pubes as a stylized plane, with straight upper edge, occurs also on Kleobis and Biton.[34]

THERA. Parts of two colossal kouroi and fragments of two others (no. 18) have been found in Santorin, not far from the excavated portion of ancient Thera. In some important features, such as the bulge of the hips and thighs from the waist, the oval shape of the head, the rather soft and generalized forms, these statues are related to the colossus of Delos; whereas in the arrangement of the hair and in the square shoulders, they resemble Kleobis and Biton (no. 12). In other words—as far as our limited repertoire allows us to judge—they show both Ionian and Dorian connections. And that is what we might expect; for we are told that Thera was colonized by Dorians from Sparta (along with Aegids and Minyans[35]), and yet influence from the neighbouring Cyclades must have been strong (cf. p. 34). Where these stupendous statues originally stood we do not know, but they reveal to us a glimpse of the early importance of Thera.

SAMOS. During the recent excavations at the Heraion by the German Archaeological Institute under the able leadership of Dr. Buschor, fragments of about thirty archaic kouroi ranging through the sixth century have been found. Of these about ten were colossi one and a half to three times life size. One, three times life size, of which only part of a leg and perhaps a hand survive (nos. 24, 25), can be related to the Sounion group as a slightly later product (for the forms are somewhat modelled),

[31] Aglaosthenes in Pollux, *Onomastikon*, IX. 83; but E. G. S. Robinson kindly supplies me with the following note: 'The earliest coins certainly attributed to Naxos, with a kantharos (cf. Babelon, *Traité* III, pl. LXII, 5 and 6) can hardly have been struck before 550 B.C.; but a coin with a Satyr's head (cf. *Traité* III, pl. LXIII, no. 4), which has with some probability been attributed to Naxos, might well date from the first quarter of the sixth century.'

[32] *I.G.* XII, 5 test. 1220.

[33] On the date cf. especially Jacoby, *Sitzungsberichte, Berlin*, 1933, p. 717 and note 3; Drerup, *Mnemosyne*, V, 1937, p. 107 f., 133; and on the relation of the Delian to the Pythian hymn, the brilliant analysis by Deubner in *Sitzungsberichte, Berlin*, 1938, pp. 248 ff.

[34] For a later form with upper edge in the form of two concave curves cf. nos. 82, 106, 156, 160, 167, 175, 176; for parallels on vases cf. C. M. Robertson, *J.H.S.* LVIII, 1938, p. 49.

[35] Herodotos IV.147 ff.; Pindar, *Pyth.* V. 74 ff.; IV. 257 ff.

perhaps belonging to the early years of the sixth century. Three statuettes, one of lead (no. 21) and two of bronze (nos. 22, 23), give an idea of the treatment of the whole figure. The rendering of form reveals a softer and more generalized conception than that of the Attic or Peloponnesian kouroi. The vertebral column is more curved than in the stone examples, and the arms are detached from the body and held in relatively free postures (cf. p. 12). A small head of wood (no. 20) may also have belonged to a kouros of this period. Furthermore, the remarkable ivory statuette (datable *c.*630 B.C.) which in its upper part resembles the kouros type testifies to the high standard of workmanship in early Samos (cf. p. 9, note 22).

Of the early history of Samos we know little, except that during the seventh century she became a leading commercial centre of Ionia, with a foothold on the mainland, colonies in Amorgos, Perinthos, and in Cilicia, and active trade relations with the West, Egypt, and Cyrene.[36] We hear of enterprising sailors who, about 610 B.C., grew rich on the voyage to Tartessos and dedicated in the Heraion 'a bronze krater supported by three bronze colossi seven cubits (10½ feet) high'.[37] As was the case in most Greek states at this time, the most influential section of the community was the landed gentry. The remains we have considered show us that these *geomoroi*, as they were called, were active in the artistic field, just as were the Athenian aristocrats in Attica.

RHODES. From Rhodes, where a Doric dialect was spoken,[38] one might expect Dorian kouroi, comparable perhaps to Kleobis and Biton. But the little example which stands as witness of the Rhodian style of this time—a limestone statuette in the British Museum—shows strong Egyptian influence (no. 27). It is a striking instance of the influence of association as against that of heredity. And this is true also of the later kouroi from Rhodes (nos. 124-7, 154).[39]

CRETE. Limestone sculptures dating from the second half of the seventh century B.C. have been found at Prinias, Eleuthernai, and Gortyna; and many seventh-century bronze and terracotta statuettes have come to light on various Cretan sites. The statuettes include the kouros from Dreros of about 650 B.C. (see figs. 12, 13) and the upper part of a terracotta kouros from Gortyna (see p. 27), both earlier than the Sounion group.

UNKNOWN PROVENANCE. A bronze statuette in Stockholm (no. 26)[40] is of unknown provenance but markedly Eastern in type. It should be noted that the forearms, instead of being in the supine position, as they are regularly in stone statues, are semi-pronated (cf. p. 40). The same observation applies to other early bronze statuettes (cf. nos. 22, 23). The material evidently was a determining factor.

NAUKRATIS. In 1888 the British Museum acquired an alabaster statuette through Sir Flinders Petrie, who had purchased it from a peasant at Naukratis (no. 28). It is not known definitely whether the figure came from the temple of Apollo, but it clearly belongs to the Sounion group. Similar headless statuettes from Naukratis (cf. no. 29) may be assigned to this period. And a limestone head

[36] Beloch, *Griechische Geschichte*, I, I, pp. 211, 256, 261 f.

[37] Herodotos IV.152. On the date of this Samian expedition cf. my *Arch. Gk. Art*, p. 39, note 109.

[38] Rhodes is called an Argive colony; cf. Pindar, *Ol.* VII.19; Thucydides VII.57.6; Herodotos I.144; II.178. But the colonization took place at a very early period; cf. *Iliad* II. 653 ff.

[39] It follows that we can hardly claim the 'Daedalic' statuettes found in Rhodes as exclusively *Dorian* in style.

[40] Jacobsthal, *J.H.S.* LXXI, 1951, p. 92, called this statuette a twin brother of the ivory 'hawk-priestess' from Ephesos, which is now dated in the second half of the sixth century. In style, however, the bronze seems to me definitely earlier; at least its anatomical renderings tally with those of the Sounion group; the well organized face of the priestess may be contrasted with the more primitive features of the youth. Both, however, have the East Greek spirit; so, to use Jacobsthal's apt phrase, the likeness is not one of style but of physiognomy.

of cubic shape with large, almond-shaped eyes (no. 30) is related to the Sounion and Dipylon kouroi.

The date of the foundation of Naukratis has been much disputed. The literary evidence is confusing. Herodotos (II.178) says that Amasis, king of Egypt (569-526), 'gave the city of Naukratis to Greeks who came to Egypt to live in'. This statement can be interpreted to mean either that Naukratis was not colonized by the Greeks before the time of Amasis, or that Amasis conceded a definite colony to the Greeks, who had already lived there for some time. Strabo (XVII.801) makes the Milesians build a fort under Psammetichos (663-609) at the Bolbitic mouth of the Nile, and later sail up to the Saite nome, conquer Inaros, and found Naukratis. As Inaros belongs to the fifth century, this evidence is hardly satisfactory. On the other hand, the presence at Naukratis of some Corinthian pottery, datable in the late seventh century[41] and of early Athenian pottery, datable in the late seventh and early sixth century[42]—in addition to a quantity of Rhodian and early 'Naukratite'[43] vases—indicates that Greeks must have settled at Naukratis before Amasis' reign.

If our dating of the alabaster statuettes and the limestone head in London is correct, it furnishes additional evidence for the early dating of Naukratis.

These small statuettes can give us only a faint idea of the artistic trends in East Greece at this period. We gain a better picture of its importance in the cultural life of Greece when we remember that about this time lived the poets Sappho and Alkaios of Lesbos and the philosopher Thales of Miletos. There is no better way to appreciate and understand early Greek sculptures than to read the writings of their actual contemporaries. The same directness that distinguishes early Greek lyric poetry characterizes these kouroi; they are the products of the same young and gifted people. When we read Sappho's lines 'Around the fair moon the stars hide their bright beauty',[44] or 'When the moon spreads her light over the salt sea and the flowery field and the dew lies so fair on the ground and the roses bloom',[45] we feel that something of the same radiant clarity has passed into our kouroi. And when we remember the sayings attributed to Thales: 'The oldest of all things is God, for he is uncreated. The most beautiful is the universe, for it is God's handiwork';[46] we feel that the same simple grandeur has been expressed in the sturdy kouroi.

ITALY. Though no marble kouros of the Sounion group has as yet been found in the West, the type was evidently known there at that time, as shown by a few survivals in other materials; for instance, a bronze statuette from Selinus (no. 30 bis) in the Palermo Museum (inv. S 905—no. 73; P. Marconi, *Itinerario*, no. 11, pl. 55, 1), and a bronze statuette from Majorca now in Barcelona (cf. my *Arch. Gk. Art*, fig. 83); furthermore, a primitive limestone head, supposedly from Megara Hyblaia and evidently Sikel work, shows Greek influence in the rendering of its stylized ears, which resemble those in the Sounion group (cf. Barnabò Brea, *Annuario*, XXIV-XXVI (new series VIII-X), 1946-8, p. 65, fig. 4).

[41] Cf. Payne, *Necrocorinthia*, p. 25; Cook, *J.H.S.* LVII, 1937, p. 228. We must remember that there was evidently little trade between Miletos and Corinth before this time (hardly any Corinthian pottery has been found at Miletos, Wiegand, *Abh. Berl. Akad.*, 1908, Anhang Abh. I, p. 8), and that therefore the date of the Corinthian pottery we happen to find at Naukratis cannot be taken as an upper limit for the Greek settlement on that site.

[42] Beazley and Payne, *J.H.S.* XLIX, 1929, p. 253 f.

[43] E. R. Price, *J.H.S.* XLIV, 1924, pp. 180 ff.; R. M. Cook, *B.S.A.* XLIV, 1949, pp. 154 ff.; Boardman, *B.S.A.* LI, 1956, pp. 55 ff.

[44] Frgt. 4, Diehl.

[45] Frgt. 98, 9 ff., Diehl.

[46] Quoted by Diogenes Laertios 1.35.

Absolute Chronology

In computing the absolute chronology of our groups of kouroi we must remember that the dates assigned apply to the style, not to a specific work. For, as we have said, there must have been progressives and conservatives among Greek artists as there are today, though probably the conservatives were fewer and less strongly entrenched than now (cf. p. 4 f.). Therefore, when we try to place a work in relation to a dated historical event we must allow a certain leeway. To give sufficient time for one group of kouroi to develop into the next, and to allow for a certain development within the group, it seems best to give a range of twenty to twenty-five years for the members of each group. And this is the span indicated on external grounds for the later groups (cf. pp. 76 ff., 114 ff.).

The tentative date assigned to the Sounion group of kouroi—late seventh and early sixth century B.C., perhaps about 615-590—is based primarily on the necessity of allowing sufficient time for the successive stages of development from the kouroi of this period to the later ones, some of which are dated by external evidence. Working backward from the Tenea-Volomandra group, which is placed on external grounds in the second quarter of the sixth century, through the Orchomenos-Thera group, we arrive at the period around 600 for the Sounion group.

Additional support for this assignment is derived from a comparison with vase paintings. Several of the statues of the Sounion group show a marked resemblance to the figures on early Athenian pottery, for instance, the Nessos amphora[47] and the human heads on the horse amphorae.[48] They display the same grand and vigorous style and similar renderings of details—a flat skull, large eyes, a stylized, volute-shaped ear, hair bulging forward beneath the fillet, a large thumb. The Nessos amphora and the earliest horse amphorae have been dated, independently of the sculpture, in the last decades of the seventh century[49] and around 600 B.C.[50] respectively.

When we compare the New York-Sounion kouroi with plastic heads on Corinthian pottery we find that they closely resemble those on an early Corinthian pyxis in Berlin.[51] The heads show the same bold and angular style, they have the same large eyes, the hair curves round the forehead in a similar fashion, and they have about the same degree of depth. If Payne's assignment of Early Corinthian pottery to the last quarter of the seventh century[52] is approximately correct, we should have here a most welcome fixed point within the late seventy century for the Sounion group. It is true that the foundation of Selinus can no longer (as Payne, following Thucydides, thought) be confidently assigned to *c.*628 B.C.,[53] but this does not affect the dating of Early Corinthian

[47] *Antike Denkmäler*, I, pl. 57, p. 46; Beazley, *Development*, pp. 14 ff.

[48] Lullies, *C.V.* Munich, fasc. I, pls. I-II.

[49] Payne, *Necrocorinthia*, p. 344 = between 620-600. J. M. Cook, *B.S.A.* XXXV, 1934-5 (published in 1938), p. 200 f., proposed a slightly earlier date 'about the time of the beginning of Early Corinthian, that is 625'; but the difference in style between the Kynosarges amphora, which he dates *c.*640 B.C. (p. 201), and the Nessos amphora is so great that an interval of more than 15 years between the two seems called for. R. S. Young in *A.J.A.* XLVI, 1942, p. 57, went back to the later dating: *c.*630-600 for the Piraeus amphora and the works of the Nessos Painter. Beazley, *Development*, pp. 13 ff., puts the Piraeus amphora and the works of the Nessos Painter in the last decades of the seventh century.

[50] Lullies, op. cit. p. 7; Beazley, *A.B.V.*, pp. 15 ff.

[51] Payne, *Necrocorinthia*, p. 293, pl. 47, 7-9.

[52] Cf. Payne, op. cit. pp. 55 ff. and passim.

[53] Cf. Vallet and Villard, *B.C.H.* LXXXII, 1958, pp. 16 ff., who point out that the recent rearrangement of the material from the sanctuary of Demeter Malophoros at Selinus has brought to light a number of Proto-Corinthian and Transitional vases, so that the dating of the foundation of Selinus must be pushed up to *c.*650 B.C., that is, to the date given by Diodoros, XIII, 59, 4, as well as by Synkellos and Hieronymos. For the literary evidence cf. Vallet and Villard, *B.C.H.* LXXVI, 1952, pp. 318 ff., and the references there cited.

pottery in the last quarter of the seventh century; for it is confirmed by excavations at Massalia (Marseilles), which is said to have been founded *c.*600 B.C.[54] and where hardly any Early Corinthian vases were found, only Middle and Late Corinthian, as well as by the preliminary excavation of Kamarina, founded in 598 B.C., where so far only Middle Corinthian ware has come to light[55].

If the earliest coins of Attica with the head of Athena[56] could after all, be assigned to the time of Solon's reform of the currency, they would give us profile heads dated in Solon's archonship, 594 B.C.[57] The flat cheeks, large eyes, thick lips, stylized ears, and the bold, rather *farouche* character of these heads tally well with the general style of our Sounion group.

Anatomical Analysis

The conception of form in these statues is abstract and geometrical, with the emphasis on the architectural shape and the interrelation of parts. The shape of the figure as a whole displays the four separate faces of the rectangular block from which it is carved. On the surface of this cubic form, anatomical details are indicated by grooves and ridges, delicately carved with a fine sense of the composition as a whole. The proportions of the figure display many obvious deviations from nature, and the anatomy is only partially understood. The ideal of the art of the time was not realism, but a simplified conception of the human figure, a solid, harmonious structure in which essentials were emphasized and generalized into expressive patterns. In the New York statue, which happily is preserved almost complete, we can appreciate the beauty of these interrelations. On the body, the shallow upward curves of the clavicles are contrasted with the deep downward curves of the pectorals; the pointed arch beneath the thorax is counterbalanced by the pointed pelvic arch; at the back the swing of the shoulder-blades makes a design with the girdle of the pelvis and the perpendicular groove of the spine. The limbs are rendered with the same decorative sense. The indications of the bones and muscles on the legs form effective patterns; the foot, with its massive heel and gripping toes, supplies a firm base; viewed from the back, the volumes of buttocks, thighs, calves, and feet have finely undulating contours. The arms show similar contrast of masses, and a similar accentuation of salient parts; the clenched hands with their angular outlines make a pleasing design. And crowning the figure, set on a long slender neck, is the massive head, carved in large, simple planes, with almond-shaped eyes, patterned ears, and schematized hair. This architectural conception, based on keen though naïve observance of nature, gives to these early statues their distinctive character. In the words which Pausanias[58] used of the works of Daidalos: 'there is something inspired in their appearance.'

[54] Cf. Wackernagel, Pauly-Wissowa, *R.E.*, XIV, 2, 1930, s. v. Massalia, cols. 2130 f.

[55] Cf. Villard, *Mélanges d'archéologie et d'histoire de l'École française de Rome*, IX, 1948, pp. 29 f.; Vallet and Villard, *B.C.H.*, LXXXII, 1958, p. 24.

[56] Regling, *Die Griechischen Münzen der Sammlung Warren*, no. 804, pl. XIX.

[57] I repeat here my note in *Arch. Gk. Art*, p. 7: 'The date of these coins is disputed. Head, in his *B.M.C. Attica*, 1888, pp. xiii ff., and in his first edition of *Historia Numorum*, 1887, pp. 309 ff., had placed them in the time of Solon. In 1897 von Fritze, *Zeitschrift für Numismatik*, XX, p. 142, assigned them to Peisistratos, and this date was almost universally adopted by numismatists; see Regling, *Gr. Münzen der Sammlung Warren*, 1906, p. 132, and *Phil. Woch.*, 45, 1925, col. 222; Babelon, *Traité*, I, cols. 732 ff.; Seltman, *Athens, Its History and Coinage*, pp. 6 ff., 40 ff.; E. S. G. Robinson, *B.M.C. Cyrenaica*, p. xxviii, note 4. Recently H. A. Cahn, *Museum Helveticum*, III, 1946, pp. 133 ff., reassigned them to the period of Solon, to which stylistically they—in my opinion—belong. See also Casson, *J.H.S.* XLII, 1922, pp. 214 ff. The style certainly does not seem Peisistratid and the interpretation of these coins as barbaric offers many difficulties.' At all events the question of date is not yet settled by numismatists (cf. Schwabacher, *Gnomon*, XXIX, 1957, p. 10).

[58] II.4.5.

STRUCTURE IN GENERAL. Torso foursided and flat front and back, with broad shoulders and long, narrow waist. Head cubic. In some examples (cf. nos. 15, 17, 18) thighs bulge out from waist. Proportions often abnormal, especially head, thighs, thumb. Greatest protrusion of back, seen in profile, higher than that of chest. Vertical column in most examples more or less straight (for an occasional exception cf. no. 22). Anatomical details indicated by grooves, ridges, and knobs on surface. Only in a few examples are some forms seen somewhat in the round (cf. nos. 12, 17); they may be placed late in group.

HEAD. *Skull.* Undeveloped at back and generally rather flat on top (in some bronze and wooden statuettes [nos. 20, 26, 28] skull is more rounded).

Ear. Usually placed high; stylized, and carved in one plane (for exceptions cf. nos. 12, 27). Tragus knob-like; either separate protuberance on cheek or excrescence from lobe. No antitragus.

Eye. Large and flat. Lower eyelid forms shallow curve, upper eyelid a pronounced arch. Recess at inner corner not marked.

Mouth. Horizontal. Outlines of lips form sharp edges, and corners of mouth are sharply cut, forming a triangular depression; both lips generally on same plane. Sometimes sharp-edged fold above lip.

Hair. Resembles a wig; separate tresses divided into globules or parallelograms. Fillet generally tied behind, with ends stylized. In some examples (cf. nos. 11, 12) hair bulges beneath fillet over shoulder and back. In a few cases (cf. nos. 12, 14, 18) hair radiates at back from point near vertex of skull.

NECK. Sterno-mastoids indicated by grooves forming a triangle with apex at sternum. Outline of neck forms concave curve running from ear to shoulder, without indication of swelling of trapezium.

TORSO, FRONT. Clavicles, when marked, travel upward from sternal notch as flat ridges, protruding all along their course as far as deltoid. Lower boundary of thorax marked by grooves forming obtuse angle (rarely a narrow arch, cf. Kleobis and Biton) some distance below pectorals. Three or more divisions of rectus abdominis above navel marked by grooves (sometimes omitted). No protuberance at flanks for anterior part of iliac crest; but in some examples (nos. 1, 2, 3) a ridge runs round flanks like a girdle, with sometimes a knob below it on either side. Navel shaped like round button surrounded by circular groove. Lower boundary of abdomen (Poupart's ligament) descends with straight sides towards genitals (except in statuette from Rhodes, no. 27, where it is rounded). Pubes, when represented, has straight upper edge (nos. 12, 17).

TORSO, BACK. Spinal furrow, shoulder-blades, and sometimes erector spinae and ribs (cf. no. 2) indicated by grooves.

ARM. Generally separated from body along considerable way between armpit and hand. In stone statues forearm, viewed from front, is turned forward in supine position, but palm of hand, instead of being directed forward, is twisted towards body in semi-pronated position. In bronze statuettes, however, forearm is often correctly semi-pronated in relatively free postures. A ridge or groove sometimes surrounds upper and lower ends of ulna (at elbow and wrist, respectively). Hand clenched and angular in outline. Thumb often large.

LEG. Hollow over great trochanter sometimes marked by ridge or groove. Patella indicated as rounded or squarish block, with the two vasti muscles descending to almost the same level. Shin sharp and only slightly curved. Malleoli level.

Foot. Generally highly arched. Toes more or less parallel, and their ends as they touch the ground recede along one continuous line, the big toe projecting further than the second toe and the little toe being only slightly curved. Four smaller toes generally curve downward, with nails pointing towards ground, while big toe points forward.

FOOT-PLINTH. Upper plane generally uneven and higher at back than in front. Its shape follows approximately contours of soles.

Kouroi Nos. 1-30 bis

1 : Figs. 25-32, 60-62

NEW YORK, METROPOLITAN MUSEUM, no. 32. 11. 1. From Attica (?).

Statue, from head to foot-plinth. The only restorations are the missing slivers at fractures (at waist and knees, above ankles, at wrists, at left elbow, above and below right elbow, at left thumb), part of upper knuckle of right index finger, small piece on third joint of that finger. Besides these slivers and numerous surface chips there are missing only a few small pieces—on nose, lips, chin, knot of neckband, outer side of right arm, right thumb, tip of left thumb.

Island marble.
Height 1.843 m.; of head to bottom of chin, 30.8 cm.
Said to be from Attica.
G. M. A. Richter, *Met. Mus. Studies*, v, 1, 1934, pp. 20 ff; I. A. Richter, Ibid. pp. 51 ff. (on proportions of statue).
G. M. A. and I. A. Richter in Brunn-Bruckmann-Arndt, *Denkmäler*, nos. 751-5.
Buschor, *Fr. J.* pp. 17 ff., figs. 15-20.
Homann-Wedeking, *Anfänge*, pp. 77 ff., fig. 36.
Richter, *Cat. of Gk. Sc.*, no. 1.

GENERAL STRUCTURE. Body four-sided, flat front and back, with broad shoulders and long, narrow waist. Proportions abnormal, head being too large for body (its height is about one sixth of total height), neck too long, thighs too short, first phalanxes of hand too long. Greatest protrusion of back, seen in profile, higher than that of chest. Vertebral column more or less straight. Anatomical details indicated by grooves, ridges, and knobs on surface.

HEAD. General shape of head retains rectangular character of block of marble. Face long and oval, broader above than below.

Skull. Top, a flattened dome; back flat.

Ear. Placed high and slants towards line of jaw, so that neck shows behind it. Carved in one flat plane and form stylized, with single, uniformly broad groove separating helix from antihelix. Plain lobe. Tragus knob-like and disconnected. No indication of antitragus.

Eye. Position horizontal, large and almond-shaped, lower eyelid forming shallow curve, upper a pronounced arch. No indication of recess at inner corner. Broad, well-defined groove separates upper lid from eyebrow, and deep depression separates lower eyelid from cheek; consequently, roundness of eyeball not suggested. Iris was painted, and differentiation of surface noticeable, though colour has disappeared. At outer corners of eyes front and side planes of head meet in sharp edge.

Nose. Root formed by sharp edges of eyebrows. Shape long and narrow. Nostril indicated on side by arched groove and below by narrow slit, painted red (of right nostril only bit of opening remains with traces of red).

Mouth. Corners sharply cut to form triangular depressions. Sharp edges along upper and lower lips. Short, sharp-edged fold runs upward from each corner of mouth above upper lip. Both lips on same plane.

Hair. Hangs down behind in fourteen beaded tresses produced by dividing mass vertically and then carving beads along these lines in approximately horizontal alignment. Each tress ends in a member of triangular outline with apex pointing downward, and is tied above with a band or ring,[59] painted red. Fillet encircles head, cutting across second row of beads in front; at back it is tied in reef knot, and long ends, after following encircling band for some distance, hang loosely down. Band in passing behind ear changes somewhat in direction. Impression fillet makes in hair at back marked.

NECK. Sterno-mastoid muscles marked by two delicate grooves sloping inward to meet clavicles on either side of sternum. Outline of neck forms concave curve running from ear to shoulder, with no indication of muscular development of shoulder, swelling of trapezium being omitted. Neckband tied in front, with reef knot.

TORSO, FRONT. Clavicles rise abruptly from median line and sweep in shallow curve towards shoulder; they project evenly all along their course, becoming gradually narrower. Median line shown by groove running from clavicles to navel. Nipples marked as

[59] Cf. p. 50, note 66.

round knobs placed rather far apart; each surrounded first by red circle, then by incised radiating lines, slightly curving, each area being bounded by lightly incised circles. Lower boundary of thorax indicated by groove making obtuse angle some distance below pectorals, and ending on either side midway between chest and flanks. Transverse divisions of rectus abdominis above navel not indicated. Contour of waist forms slender inward curve. Navel shaped like a round button. Lower boundary of abdomen marked by broad ridge, with straight sides in front, which travels all the way round the waist like a girdle, protruding more on sides than front and back, and forming angle at back. A knob below this girdle on either side in front is probably erroneous indication of anterior spine of iliac crest, placed here too low. Neat, sharp cuts indicate junctions between genitals and legs. Ridge marks root of penis; transverse ridge divides scrotum; pubes was perhaps painted.

TORSO, BACK. Perpendicular groove marks spinal furrow, on either side of which a curved groove indicates shoulder-blades. No indication of erector spinae.

ARM. On deltoid are three grooves marking its divisions. Transition between deltoid and pectorals indicated by wide furrow. Elbow outlined by ridge curving round upper end of ulna, with ends extending downward. Course of ulna indicated by sharp straight ridge, and its lower end, at wrist, is indicated by knob round which a ridge is carved on side towards thumb. Forearm, viewed from front, is turned forward in what is called the 'supine' position, but palm of hand, instead of being directed forward, is twisted towards body. This gives arm, seen from front, broad and flat appearance and makes unnatural transition from forearm to wrist.

Hand. Clenched and angular in outline. Thumb is very thick from front to back and faces front way; last joint of index finger very long and rests against side of thigh; little finger likewise touches thigh at back. Marble left adhering between thumb and forefinger and at back inside bend of little finger; also above fingers to a height of 11.5 cm., separating palm and wrist from thigh.

LEG. Curving groove on side of buttock marks position of great trochanter. Groove travels down outer side of thigh corresponding to ilio-tibial band. Vasti muscles bulge above knee cap, vastus internus descending only slightly lower than vastus externus; grooves running above and parallel to this double curve suggest bulging flesh. Patella is solid block, broader above than below, from which shin bone starts on its downward course with straight, sharp edge. On outer side of shin, just below patella, is knob indicating head of fibula. On outer side of lower leg, two grooves indicate peroneal muscles; on inner side, ridge marks upper edge of shin-bone; at back, lower boundary of calf shown by incised arc. Outer and inner malleoli of ankle level.

Foot. Highly arched. Heel forms square block. In front of external malleolus small protrusion indicates a tarsal bone. Toes recede along one continuous line, the second toe being shorter than the big toe; little toe only slightly curved inward. The four small toes curve gently downward, with nails pointing towards ground, while big toe points forward. Little toe bulges outward on upper, that is, first joint. Toe-nails marked by single groove.

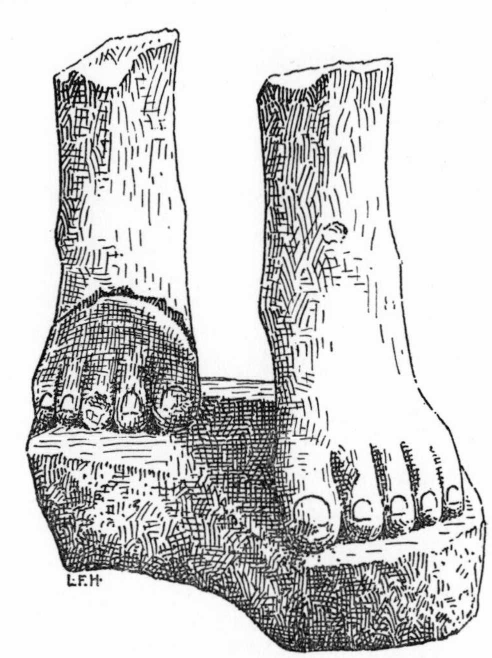

FEET AND PLINTH OF NO. 1, NEW YORK.
Drawing by L. F. Hall.

FOOT-PLINTH. Worked in one piece with statue. Form irregular, roughly following contours of soles. Upper plane is not horizontal, but slopes gently downward, being higher at back than in front; edge rounded; surface left rough.

2 : Figs. 33–39

ATHENS, NATIONAL MUSEUM, no. 2720. From Sounion. Figs. 36–38 are from a cast, without restorations. Figs. 33–34 show the head with the piece of hair added in 1958 (cf. Burn, *J.H.S.* LXXVIII, 1958, p. 13, pls. III, IV.)

Statue, from head to base. Restorations: Whole left arm from a little below shoulder and including hand; outer part of right arm from middle of upper arm to middle of forearm; left leg including most of thigh and back part of foot; right leg from under kneecap to above ankle; large part of face including left eye (except outer corner) with eyebrow and part of forehead above it, nose, mouth (except right corner), chin, and adjacent part of left cheek (except piece under left eye). Base with plinth and feet does not certainly belong to this statue (see below).

Island marble.

Height of statue as restored 3.05 m. (originally probably higher, for reconstructed lower legs are short compared to those of New York kouros and Sounion fragments, cf. nos. 1, 4).

Height of base *c.*25 cm.; width 80 cm.; length 98 cm.

Found in 1906, in a deep pit east of the temple of Poseidon at Sounion, together with a torso (no. 3), fragments of arms, legs, and hair (no. 4), and three bases with feet (no. 5) in addition to the base on which the statue is now mounted.

Staïs, *'Εφ. Ἀρχ.*, 1917, pp. 189 ff.
Rhomaios, *Antike Denkmäler*, IV, 1931, pp. 91–105, pls. 47–56.
Budde, *Die attischen Kuroi* (Diss. 1939), pp. 9–11.
Buschor, *Fr. J.*, pp. 22 ff., figs. 22–8.
Homann-Wedeking, *Anfänge*, p. 79, fig. 37.
Deonna, no. 7, figs. 16–17.

The dimensions of the statues found in the pit vary. The feet of base *b* (cf. p. 45 f.) are approximately the same length as those now reconstructed as part of the statue, indicating that they must have belonged to another colossal figure of about the same size as this one. As the torso no. 3 was approximately the same height as the statue, though somewhat slenderer (cf. p. 44), base *b* may have belonged to it. Some of the fragments (no. 4) are of about the same scale as these two statues, and may be assigned to one or both of them. Others are smaller and must have formed part of a smaller statue, or statues, which perhaps stood on the smaller third and fourth bases. It is noteworthy that the plinths of the statues were inserted obliquely into their bases; that is, the statues are turned a little to the (spectator's) left.[60] Staïs and Rhomaios (loc. cit.) surmised that these statues stood together as one votive offering on a levelled rock, SE. of the temple façade. But only the two large statues (nos. 2, 3) come into consideration, for only they are of approximately the same size. A group of statues of different scale would have made a strange looking ensemble. Moreover, the kouroi found scattered over the Heraion at Samos indicate that the Sounion statues could also have been single dedicatory offerings. In the absence of a dedicatory inscription (cf. p. 14) one can only make guesses. On the other hand, the preserved fragments are so similar in style that they must be about contemporary, and may even be the work of the same sculptor, or at least workshop.

The considerable weathering of the statues and fragments suggests that they were exposed in the open air for a long time. The fact that they were found all broken up together in a pit makes it probable that the statues were destroyed by the Persians in 480 or 479 B.C. and were stowed away afterwards, like the 'Persian debris' on the Akropolis.

GENERAL STRUCTURE. Body four-sided, flat front and back, with broad shoulders and long, narrow waist. Head and neck in more normal proportions to body than in New York statue. Proportion of thighs to lower legs not known, since latter are restored. First phalanxes of hand abnormally long. Greatest protrusion of back, seen in profile, higher than that of chest. Vertebral column more or less straight. Anatomical details indicated by grooves, ridges, and knobs on surface.

HEAD. Cubic.

Skull. Top a flattened dome; back flat.

Ear. Abnormally large. Placed high and almost vertical. Carved in one flat plane, and form stylized, with single, uniformly broad groove separating helix from antihelix; antihelix divides above into two curving ridges. Lobe decorated with two concentric grooves, one broad, one narrow; knob-shaped tragus projects directly from it. No indication of antitragus.

Eye. Large and almond-shaped, lower eyelid forming shallow curve, upper pronounced arch. Broad, deep groove separates upper lid from eyebrow, and deep depression separates lower eyelid from cheek; consequently, roundness of eyeball not suggested. Iris was painted, and differentiation of surface is noticeable. At outer corners of eyes, front and side planes of head meet, forming sharp edge. No indication of recess at inner corner.

Nose. Whole of original nose missing.

Mouth. Only right corner of mouth preserved, with triangular depression.

Hair. Hangs down behind in fourteen tresses. Mass was divided first vertically, then horizontally, into grooves and ridges. Each tress ends in an elongated member and is tied by a band or ring.[61] Fillet becomes double in front, framing row of spiral curls; below it, on each side, are tresses of wavy hair; behind, fillet is tied in reef knot, and its ends, after following for short distance encircling band, hang loosely down, forking at tips. Slight suggestion of impression made by fillet in hair at back.

NECK. Sterno-mastoid muscles indicated by grooves forming triangle with apex at sternum. Outline forms convex curve running from ear to shoulder, without indication of swelling of trapezium.

TORSO, FRONT. Clavicles indicated by two upward-curving ridges, protruding all along their course as far as deltoid. Median line marked by groove running from clavicles to navel. Nipples marked by knobs surrounded by incised, straight, radiating lines. Lower boundary of thorax indicated by groove making obtuse angle some

[60] Rhomaios, op. cit. p. 92; Raubitschek, 'Zur Technik und Form der altattischen Statuenbasen' in *Bulletin de l'Institut archéologique bulgare*, XII, 1938, p. 145.

[61] Cf. p. 50, note 66.

distance below pectorals. Four horizontal grooves indicate transverse divisions of abdominal muscle. Contour of waist forms inward curve. Navel shaped like round button surrounded by circular groove. Lower boundary of abdomen marked by broad ridge (with straight sides in front) which travels all way round like a girdle, forming angle at back. A knob below this girdle on either side in front is probably erroneous indication of anterior spine of iliac crest placed here too low. Neat, sharp cuts indicate junctions between genitals and legs. Ridge marks root of penis; transverse ridge divides scrotum.

TORSO, BACK. Right and left of spinal furrow, region of shoulder-blades is indicated by pair of curved grooves (of which the upper continues along back of upper arm as far as elbow). Beneath them four straight grooves slant downward and outward, perhaps to indicate ribs. Perpendicular groove on each side of spine in lumbar region marks attachment of erector spinae.

ARM. On deltoid are three grooves marking its divisions. Transition between deltoid and pectorals indicated by groove. Elbow outlined by curving ridge above upper end of ulna, from which, on preserved inner side, groove travels downward; doubtless a second groove was on missing outer side, as in New York statue. Enough remains of right forearm to show that it was turned forward, as in New York statue, in supine position, whereas hand is twisted towards body. No straight ridge at back of forearm to indicate ulna. Knob which marks lower end of ulna at wrist is surrounded by semicircular ridge on side towards thumb.

Hand (only right preserved). Clenched, with thumb facing front and index finger bent, with last joint very long and resting against side of thigh; little finger likewise touches thigh at back. Ridges mark two joints of thumb. Marble left adhering between thumb and forefinger, and at back inside bend of little finger; also above fingers for several inches, separating palm and wrist from thigh.

LEG (only upper right leg preserved). Curving groove on side of buttock marks position of great trochanter. Two grooves of unequal lengths travel down outer side of thigh corresponding to ilio-tibial band. Divisions of vasti marked on thigh by two grooves, which meet some distance above knee and then continue, to join top of patella. Vasti muscles bulge quasi-symmetrically over kneecap; upper groove suggesting bulging flesh very shallow. Patella is solid, quadrangular block, slightly broader above than below; beneath it on outer side is knob indicating head of fibula. Malleoli level.

Foot. Highly arched. Heel forms square block. In front of external malleolus small protrusion indicates a tarsal bone. Toes recede along one continuous line, the second toe being shorter than the big toe; little toe only slightly curved inward. The four small toes curve downward and make sharp angle after first joint, while big toe points forward. Big toe very broad and its two joints marked by ridges. Little toe bulges outward on its upper, that is, first joint.

FOOT-PLINTH. Worked in one piece with statue. Its form about oval, following roughly contours of soles. Let into ancient base and leaded. Upper plane slopes forward, being higher at back than in front; edge protrudes *c.*2.5 cm. at back, with rounded contour, but is level with base in front.

BASE. Rectangular. Smoothed on upper surface and on upper part of sides (for *c.*11.5 cm.), whereas on lower part surface is left rough. Lower half was therefore evidently not intended to be seen, and must have been covered with earth. Distance between base and foot-plinth at back (where lead is partly missing) is as much as 3.5 cm. This shows that depression made in base for insertion of plinth was sometimes only roughly calculated.[62] Direction of feet does not tally with front of base (cf. p. 43).

3 : Figs. 40-41

ATHENS, NATIONAL MUSEUM, no. 3645. From Sounion. Figs. 40-41 show the torso with the pieces of arms added in 1957-8 by Mr. Papathenasupoulos.

Torso, from neck to above left knee. Restorations: Right leg and both knees.

Island marble.
Height as preserved *c.*1.65 cm.
Distance from sternal notch to top of navel 39.2 cm., whereas in Sounion statue it is 39.5 cm.; width between armpits 51.3 cm., whereas in Sounion statue it is 60.8 cm. The heights, therefore, of the two figures were probably about the same, but the Sounion statue was broader than the torso.
Found in 1906 in same pit as the statue no. 2.
Staïs, *'Εφ. 'Αρχ.* 1917, pp. 189 ff.
Rhomaios, *Antike Denkmäler*, IV, 1931, pp. 91 ff., pls. 55, 56.
L. Budde, *Die attischen Kuroi* (Diss. 1939), p. 11 f.
Buschor, *Fr. J.*, pp. 53 ff., figs. 54, 55.
Homann-Wedeking, *Anfänge*, pp. 79 ff., figs. 38, 39.
Deonna, no. 8.

GENERAL STRUCTURE. Body four-sided, flat front and back, with broad shoulders and long, narrow waist. Seen in profile, greatest protrusion of back higher than

[62] On the Charopinos base (no. 105) the distance between edges of plinth and depression in base is 3.2 cm. I do not therefore think that the 2.8 cm. width left for the lead filling in the Antenor statue (cf. Payne and Young, *Acropolis*, p. 31, note 2) can be used as an argument against statue and base belonging together; cf. also Langlotz in Schrader, *Akropolis*, p. 83.

that of chest. Vertebral column more or less straight. Anatomical details indicated by grooves and ridges on surface.

HAIR. Hangs down behind in fourteen tresses, each ending in spiral, arranged symmetrically to right and left of centre; ridges zigzag horizontally across mass of hair.

NECK. Only small part preserved. Grooves of sterno-mastoids marked on either side of sternum. Swelling of trapezium not indicated.

TORSO, FRONT. Clavicles, median line, nipples, lower boundary of thorax, divisions of rectus abdominis, navel, knob for anterior spine of iliac crest, lower boundary of abdomen, and genitals as in Sounion statue.

TORSO, BACK. Grooves for spinal furrow, ribs, erector spinae as in Sounion statue, but region of shoulder-blades marked by single instead of double groove.

ARM. Divisions of deltoid marked by three grooves, as in Sounion statue; transition between deltoid and pectorals indicated by groove.

LEG. Only upper left leg and small piece of right preserved. On these, anatomical details same as in Sounion statue: curving groove on side of buttock marks position of great trochanter. On front of thigh, divisions of vasti muscles marked by two grooves which meet some distance above knee and then continue, to join top of patella. Vasti bulge quasi-symmetrically over kneecap; shallow upper groove suggests bulging flesh. Grooves on outer side of thigh mark leg muscles.

4 : Figs. 42–47

ATHENS, NATIONAL MUSEUM, no. 3863. From Sounion.

Fragments of legs, arms, and hair.

Island marble.
Found in 1906 in same pit as nos. 2, 3, 5.
Richter, *Met. Mus. Studies*, v. 1, 1934, pp. 31 ff., figs. 26–34.
Richter in Brunn-Bruckmann-Arndt, *Denkmäler*, nos. 751–5, pp. 13 ff., figs. 21–4.

a Piece of lower left leg from above ankle to about middle of calf (height 37.1 cm.; figs. 42–44 and illustration below). Shows same scheme as that used on shank of New York statue: sharp front edge of shin-bone, two grooves on outer side for peroneal muscles, ridge on inner side for edge of shin-bone, and incised arc at back for lower boundary of calf.

b Piece of lower right leg, from below patella to part way down calf (height *c.*40 cm.; cf. fig. 45). Shows sharp front edge of shin-bone, two grooves on outer side for peroneal muscles, and knob below patella for head of fibula, as in New York statue. Side of calf battered.

c Piece of front upper right leg, with two grooves for vasti muscles (height 30.5 cm.; cf. *Met. Mus. Studies*, v. 1934, p. 47, fig. 33).

d Piece of left arm at elbow, which is outlined by ridge curving round upper end of ulna, as in New York statue (height 21.9 cm.; cf. fig. 46).

e Fragment of hair (height 12.5 cm.; cf. fig. 47) from right side of head, showing parts of three tresses and hanging end of fillet. Tresses arranged as in Sounion statue, with mass divided vertically and horizontally, not obliquely as in Sounion torso. Ridges distinctly smaller than in Sounion statue, the distance from middle of one horizontal ridge to next being 2 cm., whereas in Sounion statue it is 3 to 4 cm.

f–n Nine miscellaneous pieces of legs or arms and one piece with no outside surface.

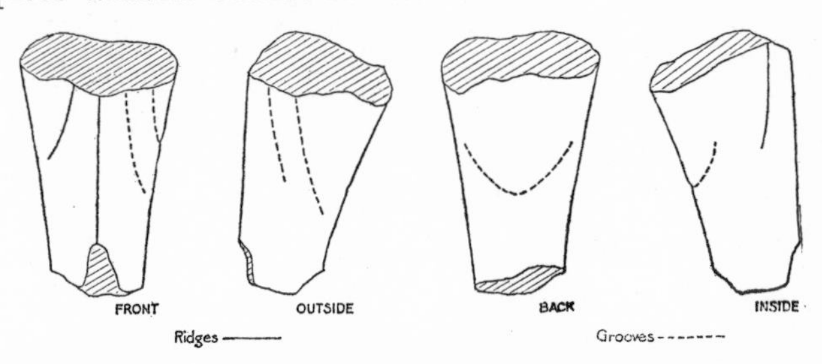

FRAGMENT OF LOWER LEFT LEG OF STATUE FROM SOUNION (no. 4a). Drawing by L. F. Hall.

To judge by the measurements, the fragments *a* and *b* could belong to either the Sounion statue or the Sounion torso, and fragment *c* could belong to the Sounion torso (the Sounion statue has an upper right leg); fragments *d* and *e*, on the other hand, are considerably smaller in scale and may perhaps have formed part of the statue which stood on base *c* or *d* (cf. p. 43).

5 : Figs. 48–49

ATHENS, NATIONAL MUSEUM, no. 2720 (base *a*); no. 3645 (base *b*); no. 3939 (bases *c*, *d*).

Bases of four statues. In addition to the base with plinth and feet which has been tentatively reconstructed as part of the Sounion statue (base *a*, cf. p. 44), three other bases (*b*, *c*, *d*) have been found. One (*d*) is only a fragment, with no trace of the plinth save for the cutting; the other two retain foot-plinths and parts of feet.

Marble.
Base *a*. Reconstructed as part of statue no. 2. Height 25 cm.; width 80 cm.; length 98 cm.; length of foot 41 cm. (cf. figs. 33–35).
Base *b*. In the National Museum, Athens. Height 24 cm.; width *c.*84 cm.; length 97 cm.; length of foot 42 cm. (fig. 48).
Base *c*. Height 20.5 cm. (of which *c.*13 cm. are smoothed); width 72 cm.; length 97.5 cm.; approximate length of feet 32 cm. (fig. 49).
Base *d*. Only about half is preserved. Width 65 cm.; length 85 cm.
The feet of base *b* are approximately the same length as those of

base *a*; that is, they are 42 cm. long, whereas the right foot of base *a* is 43 cm. long. Since the Sounion statue and torso were originally about the same height (cf. p. 44) base *b* may very well have belonged to the torso. The feet of base *c* are considerably smaller, that is, about 32 cm. long; they may have belonged to a statue—of which several fragments are preserved—of a scale smaller than the others (cf. p. 45).

Found in 1906 in the same pit as nos. 2-4.
Staïs, *'Eφ. 'Apχ.*, 1917, p. 190.
Rhomaios, *Antike Denkmäler*, IV, 1931, pp. 91, 102, figs. 15-19.

Bases *a*, *b*, and *c*. Upper surface smoothed, also upper part of sides, whereas lower part is only roughly finished with point. Lower part of base was evidently not intended to be seen, and only *c*.12 cm. protruded.
Foot-plinth is roughly oval in shape, let into a rectangular base, and leaded; upper plane of foot-plinth slopes towards edge; latter rounded in places.
To judge by the preserved fragments, the feet of bases *b* and *c* are similar in style to those of base *a*. Malleoli are level. Heel formed square block. Toes recede along one continuous line, the big toe projecting further than the second toe; four small toes curve downward. Little toe bulges outward on its upper, that is, first joint; big toe is very broad and its two joints are marked by ridges. As in base *a*, the direction of the feet does not tally with the front of the base; that is, the statues must have been turned to the (spectator's) left.

6 : Figs. 50-53, 65-67

ATHENS, NATIONAL MUSEUM, no. 3372 (head), no. 3965 (hand). From the Dipylon.

Head, part of neck, and right hand.

Island marble.
Height of head 44 cm.; length of hand *c*.29.2 cm.
Found near the Dipylon: head in 1916, hand in 1930.
Buschor, *Ath. Mitt.* LII, 1927, pp. 205 ff. (head), pls. XXVIII, XXIX.
Ibid. LV, 1930, pp. 163 ff. (hand).
Richter, *Met. Mus. Studies*, v. 1, 1934, pp. 32 ff.
Richter in Brunn-Bruckmann-Arndt, *Denkmäler*, nos. 751-5, pp. 15 ff.
Politis, *'Eφ. 'Apχ.*, 1937 (published in 1939), pp. 747 ff.
Budde, *Die attischen Kuroi* (Diss. 1939), pp. 3 ff.
Buschor, *Fr. J.*, pp. 15 ff. figs. 11-14.
Homann-Wedeking, *Anfänge*, p. 75.

GENERAL STRUCTURE. Since body is missing, proportion of head to figure not known but since hand and head are in same proportion to each other as are those of New York statue,[63] head was probably also abnormally large. Direction of grooves for sterno-mastoids more as in New York statue than as in Sounion one, indicating that neck must have been abnormally long, for lines would have to be produced to same length before meeting clavicles or sternum.

[63] Width of four fingers at upper joint (measured at widest point of knuckles) of New York hand, 8.1 cm.; of Dipylon hand, 9.6 cm. If we take these two measurements and the height of the New York head (measured to juncture at neck) as three members of an equation, we obtain for *x*, that is, for the height of the Dipylon head, 36.5 cm. This approximates within 2 mm. the actual height of the Dipylon head, which is 36.7 cm. (measured to juncture at neck).

HEAD. Face long and narrow.
Skull. Recedes abruptly from forehead.
Ear. Placed high and slants towards line of jaw, showing neck behind it. Carved in one flat plane and stylized, with single, uniformly broad groove separating helix from antihelix. Antihelix divides above into two curving ridges. Lobe decorated with circular groove; tragus projects directly from it. No indication of antitragus.
Eye. Large and almond-shaped, lower eyelid forming shallow curve, upper pronounced arch. Broad, well-defined groove separates upper lid from eyebrow, and deep depression separates lower eyelid from cheek; consequently, roundness of eyeball not suggested. At outer corners of eyes front and side planes of head meet in sharp edges. No indication of recess at inner corners.
Nose. Mostly missing, but preserved contour indicates long, narrow bridge. Traces of red at openings of nostrils.
Mouth. Only small parts preserved at both corners of mouth, which are sharply cut, forming triangular depression. Short, sharp-edged fold above upper lip preserved on right side.
Hair. Hangs down behind in twelve tresses and was tied at back with ribbon of which only small piece now visible. Mass of hair first divided vertically, and then beads carved along vertical lines, but not in horizontal alignment. Fillet round head tied in reef knot, and its ends, after following encircling band for considerable distance, hang loosely down (ends shorter than in Sounion and New York statues). Fillet makes no impression on hair behind. Traces of second fillet, indicated in paint with lower outline incised, visible beneath front row of beads.
NECK. Only upper part preserved. Sterno-mastoid muscles indicated by grooves starting from jaw in direction of sternum. Deep groove running down on each side below ear, evidently intended to represent upper portion of sterno-mastoid muscles. Two parallel lines incised round neck to indicate neckband.
RIGHT HAND. Clenched and angular in outline. Thumb mostly missing; last joint of index finger missing. Little finger touches thigh at back. Above it, some of marble preserved that was left adhering between thumb and forefinger, and at back, inside bend of little finger. Lower end of ulna, at wrist, indicated by knob, round which ridge is carved on side towards thumb.

7 : Figs. 54-59, 68

ATHENS, Agora Museum, no. S530 (forearm); S287 (back); S1739 (knee); S 1908 (shoulder).

Four fragments of a statue.

Island marble.
Found, separately, in the area of the Agora excavations, 1933-55.
E. Harrison, *Hesperia*, xxiv, 1955, pp. 290 ff.

a Part of left forearm and hand (in two pieces, joined).
Length 32 cm.
Clenched and angular in outline. Marble left adhering between bend of little finger and strip separating palm and wrist from thigh. Lower end of ulna, at wrist, indicated by knob, round which ridge is carved on side toward thumb.
b Parts of back and advanced left leg (in two pieces joined).
Length 55.5 cm.
Perpendicular grooves mark spinal furrow and erector spinae. Horizontal ridge at waist. Remains of diagonal groove at upper right edge, evidently to indicate a rib (cf. Sounion kouros, no. 2). Diagonal groove on side of buttock marks position of great trochanter. A long groove running down outer side of thigh corresponds to ilio-tibial band.
c Right knee and back of thigh.
Height 35 cm.
Vasti muscles bulge quasi-symmetrically over kneecap. Inner vastus slightly lower than outer. The patella tapers downward. On the outer side of leg are three grooves.
d Left shoulder extending to back.
Maximum dimension 24.4 cm.
Groove at back evidently one of the three that in the Sounion and New York kouroi mark divisions of deltoid muscle.
Similarity of marble, texture, and scale (between three-fourth and four-fifth that of the Sounion statue) show that the four fragments, though found in different localities, must have belonged to the same statue (cf. Harrison, loc. cit.).
Miss Harrison (loc. cit.) has further suggested that these fragments may have belonged to the same statue as did the Dipylon head and hand (no. 6). The two hands are indeed very similar (cf. figs. 65, 68). There are, however, also differences; for instance, the form of the bit of marble left adhering between the bend of the little finger varies in the two hands, being five-sided in the Agora example, four-sided in the Dipylon; and the ridge round the upper end of the ulna makes a deeper curve in the Agora example than in the Dipylon. (In the New York kouros, in which both hands are preserved, these designs are very close to each other (cf. figs. 60, 62). Moreover, judging from the measurements that Mr. Homer Thompson and I took on the Agora and Dipylon hands, the Agora one seems to be slightly smaller than the Dipylon. In view, therefore, of the similarity of scheme used in several statues of this group (cf. figs. 60-68), the question whether the Agora fragments belonged to the Dipylon kouros must for the present remain open.

8 : Figs. 63-64

ATHENS, Coll. of Mr. Marinos Kalliga. Probably from the Mesogaia.

Right hand and small piece from side of thigh. Part of thumb missing.

Marble.
Length 16.5 cm.
Found very probably (πιθανώτατα) in the Mesogaia, Attica.
Politis, *'Εφ. 'Αρχ.*, 1937 (published in 1939), pp. 747 ff.

Clenched and angular in outline. Marble left adhering between bend of little finger; also above fingers, separating palm from thigh. Lower end of ulna, at wrist, indicated by knob, round which ridge is carved on side towards thumb.

9 : Figs. 69-71

ATHENS, National Museum, no. 71. From the Kerameikos.

Statue, from top of head to upper thighs. Restorations: Most of face, pieces at neck and waist, parts of hair.

Island marble.
Height 75 cm.
Found in the Kerameikos, Athens, in 1887, and therefore a tomb figure.
Staïs, *'Εφ.'Αρχ.*, 1887, cols. 35 ff., pl. 1.
Buschor, *Fr. J.*, pp. 53 f., fig. 56.
Deonna, no. 3, figs. 4-6.
Staïs and Deonna, locc. citt., thought that the feet also existed; but in the museum inventory, I am told, only pieces of head and body are mentioned.

General Structure. Broad shoulders and narrow waist. Head large in proportion. Seen in profile, greatest protrusion of back higher than that of chest. Vertebral column more or less straight.
Head. *Skull.* Flat at back.
Ear. Enough preserved to show that it resembled that of New York and Dipylon heads; that is, it is flat and stylized, with single, uniformly broad groove separating helix and antihelix. Position vertical.
Mouth. Preserved left corner of mouth sharply cut, forming triangular depression.

Hair. Hangs down behind in (apparently) fourteen tresses. Mass divided first vertically, then horizontally, into grooves and ridges; each tress ends below in a more or less pointed member. Round forehead and temples arranged in short strands. Fillet encircles head; was tied at back, and one end remains, which hangs loosely down, forking at tip.

NECK. Much broken but traces survive of grooves for sterno-mastoids. No indication of swelling of trapezium.

TORSO, FRONT. Clavicles rise abruptly from median line in shallow curve towards shoulders, without indication of sternal notch; they project evenly all along their course, becoming gradually narrower. Median line indicated by groove in two sections, one along sternum, the other along linea alba. Nipples marked by knobs. Lower boundary of thorax indicated by grooves forming obtuse angle, with apex well below pectorals. Three horizontal grooves cross median line above navel, perhaps to indicate transverse divisions of abdominal muscle. Contour of waist forms slender inward curve. Navel marked by knob surrounded by circular groove. Lower boundary of abdomen marked by broad ridge, which apparently travelled all the way round, like a girdle.

TORSO, BACK. Deep groove indicates spinal furrow. Shoulder-blades indicated by slightly raised planes, bounded below by two curving grooves.

ARM. Mostly missing. Was separated from body for about same distance as in New York and Sounion statues.

10 : Figs. 72-75

ATHENS, NATIONAL MUSEUM, no. 15. From the Ptoan Sanctuary.

Head and part of neck.

Whitish limestone, probably Boeotian.
Height 33 cm.
Found in the Ptoan Sanctuary, at Perdikovrysi, Boeotia, in 1885.
Holleaux, *B.C.H.* x, 1886, pp. 98 ff., pl. v.
Kastriotes, *Γλυπτά*, no. 15.
Deonna, no. 35.

GENERAL STRUCTURE. Four-sided.

HEAD. *Skull.* Top and back flat.

Ear. Slants towards line of jaw. Carved in one plane. Tragus shown as excrescence from lobe. No indication of antitragus.

Eye. Large and almond-shaped; lower lid forms shallow curve, upper a pronounced arch. Broad groove separates upper lid from eyebrow and deep depression separates lower eyelid from cheek; consequently, roundness of eyeball not suggested. No indication of recess at inner corner.

Nose. Narrow at bridge and broad at bottom; front and side planes meet in sharp edges, and sharp grooves separate sides from cheek. Nostrils indicated below by narrow slits.

Mouth. Thin lips, placed horizontally.

Chin. Prominent; partly missing.

Hair. Hangs down behind in beaded tresses, produced by dividing mass vertically and horizontally by shallow grooves; beads not in horizontal alignment. Fillet encircles head, but has no loose hanging ends. Over forehead and temples hair arranged in short strands, symmetrically to right and left.

NECK. No indication of sterno-mastoids on preserved part.

11 : Figs. 76-77

ATHENS, NATIONAL MUSEUM, no. 56. Dermys and Kittylos,[64] from Tanagra.

Grave stele. Figures worked in high relief.

Limestone.
Height of figures 1.47 m.; total height *c.*2 m.
Found at Tanagra, in 1887, in necropolis of Kokali.
Körte, *Ath. Mitt.* III, 1878, pp. 309 ff.
Kastriotes, *Γλυπτά*, no. 56.
Papaspiridi, *Guide du Musée National*, p. 22.
Buschor, *Fr. J.*, pp. 32 ff., figs. 37, 38.
I.G., VII, 579.
S.G.D.I., 875.
P. Friedländer, *Epigrammata*, no. 4.

Inscription on base: *'Αμφαλκες [ἐσ̣]τασ' ἐπι Κιτυλοι ἐ|δ' ἐπι Δερμυι*; on stele, near legs: *Δερμυς, Κιτυλος*

GENERAL STRUCTURE. Torso four-sided, flat in front, with broad shoulders and narrow waist. Head not abnormally large. Dermys puts the left leg forward, Kittylos the right.

HEAD. Face so battered that little detail is visible.

Ear. Slants backward in Dermys, is vertical in Kittylos. Carved in one flat plane and stylized. Tragus knob-shaped. No indication of antitragus.

Hair. Hangs down behind in long mass, divided by curving, quasihorizontal grooves; a somewhat shorter mass, also divided by horizontal grooves, is brought forward and hangs over each shoulder.

[64] As Beazley has pointed out to me, the name is Kittylos, not Kitylos; cf. Wilamowitz-Möllendorff, *Hermes*, XXI, 1886, p. 111. The name is derived from *κισσός*, with Boeotian *ττ* for *σσ* and a single consonant written for a double one. For names from *κισσός* cf. Bechtel, *Die Personennamen des Griechischen*, p. 593, and for the ending cf. *Κροκύλος*, Theokritos V.11. The meter confirms this derivation as the first syllable of *Κίτυλος* must be long.

NECK. Lower boundary marked by sharp edge. No indication of sterno-mastoids. Hair hides region of trapezium.

TORSO, FRONT. No indication now visible of clavicles, median line, lower boundary of thorax, divisions of rectus abdominis. No protrusion at flanks to indicate anterior part of iliac crest. Lower boundary of abdomen marked by short straight lines descending towards genitals.

ARM. Outer arm of each figure is laid against side, with lower part of forearm and clenched hand in relief, and with thumb facing front. Each inner arm is laid round back of companion and is visible only at side; placed much too high.

LEG. Lower ends of vasti level; grooves running above this double curve suggest bulging flesh (as in New York kouros). Shin has sharp edge and is almost straight. Malleoli level.

Foot. Toes battered, but appear to have receded along one continuous line, big toe being longer than second toe. Not clear whether toes pointed downward.

FOOT-PLINTH. Base rectangular; upper side slopes down from back to front.

12 *A* and *B* : Figs. 78-83, 91, 92

DELPHI MUSEUM, nos. 467, 1524 (statues), 980, 4672 (plinths). Kleobis and Biton, from Delphi.

Statues, from head to plinth.[65] Restorations in *A* (no. 467, the better preserved one): Ankles and most of feet except small parts adhering to foot-plinth; in *B*: Left leg from below knee, left foot except small part in front, right knee, ankle, and foot with back part of plinth. *B* is badly battered, especially face. Modern rectangular hole towards top of spinal furrow in both *A* and *B* was made for support of statues. Figs. 78, 79 show the statues as now exhibited, standing on their plinths, with no attachment to wall. The base into which the two plinths were inserted has not been found.

Island marble.

Height of *A*, as restored, with plinth 2.16 m.; without plinth 1.97 m. Height of *B*, as restored, with plinth 2.18 m.; as preserved without plinth 1.58 m.

Length from top of sternum (at junction of clavicles) to lower end of sternum (along statue) in *A* 27.2 cm., in *B* 26.2 cm.; to top of navel in *A* 44.3 cm., in *B* 43.3 cm.; to top of pubes in A 57 cm., in *B* 55 cm. Width across pectorals in *A* 40 cm., in *B* 41 cm. Width of outer ends of front tresses in A 40.5 cm., in *B* 38.5 cm. The dimensions of the two statues are therefore not absolutely identical, *A* being in places slightly longer, *B* in places somewhat wider; but these differences need not have been intentional, as the statues were carved free-hand, and exact duplication was therefore out of the question. If a real difference had been intended it would presumably have been made more marked.

Found in Delphi, *A* in 1893, N.W. of the Treasury of the Athenians; *B* in 1894 about 10 metres W of *A*; plinth of *A* in 1893 near the statues, of *B* in 1907, in walls of Roman bath near eastern gate of temenos.

Homolle, *F.d.D.* IV, fasc. 1, pp. 5 ff., pls. I-II.
Buschor, *Fr. J.*, pp. 35 ff., figs. 39-41.
Deonna, no. 66, figs. 67-9.
A publication by Rhomaios is in preparation.

The inscription starts on the upper face of the plinth of *B*, running from left to right in two lines, and is continued on the upper face of the plinth of *A*, running from right to left, again in two lines. Much is missing and the surface is much weathered. There have been several readings (cf. Tod, *Greek Historical Inscriptions*² (1946), no. 3). The following is that proposed by Premerstein (*Oest. Jahr.* XIII, 1910, p. 45), and followed, with the addition of line 2, by Daux, *B.C.H.* LXI, 1937, p. 66; de La Coste-Messelière *B.C.H.* LXXVII, 1953, p. 178; Marcadé, *Signatures*, I, 115 (on pl. XXIV the inscriptions are reproduced from photographs).

[Κλεοβις και Βι]τον ⁝ ταν ματαρα
– – – – s hι/ – – –
continued an base of *A*:
εαγαγον τοιδ'υιοι
[– – – –] μεδες εποιεε hαργειος·

Which of the two statues was intended for Kleobis, which for Biton, is not definitely known. Rhomaios and Marcadé (locc. citt.), however, have pointed out that since the inscription starts on the plinth of the less well preserved statue, it is this one that presumably represents Kleobis. I have called the better preserved statue A, since anatomically it is the important one.

A. GENERAL STRUCTURE. Shape four-sided, especially torso, head, and thighs, whereas arms and lower legs more rounded. Broad shoulders and short waist. Upper arm short and thigh long, compared to those of New York kouros. As now reconstructed, statue contains head about seven times. Greatest protrusion of back, seen in profile, higher than that of chest. Vertebral column slightly curved. Some anatomical details still indicated by grooves (lower boundary of thorax, peroneal muscles), but other shapes seen in the round, though still co-ordinated into patterns.

HEAD. Cubic. Forehead low and receding. Face broad.

Skull. Top and back flat.

Ear. Placed about correct height, slanting towards line of jaw; lies against hair. Helix and antihelix carved in

[65] J. D. Beazley called my attention to the fact that the statues, as restored, appear to lean too far back, whereas in the cast of Kleobis in the Ashmolean Museum the pose is about right. He surmises that the statue when first restored was poised correctly, but that later the modern dowels in the shanks gave, and the statue fell back. In the New York cast, Kleobis also leans forward.

one plane, whereas concha (inside of ear) is deeper. Lobe flat. Tragus modelled separately as a flat form adhering to cheek. No indication of antitragus.

Eye. Position horizontal. Eyebrows indicated by broad ridges; deep groove separates them from upper eyelids. Upper eyelid has considerable depth and is shaped to indicate roundness of ball; along its edge is a narrow ridge, perhaps an attempt to indicate eyelashes; a narrow groove along the middle seems to indicate a crease. Lower eyelid distinctly further back than upper, and almost level with cheekbone. Recess at inner corner not marked.

Nose. Root of nose formed by edges of eyebrows. Broad and short, compared to that of New York kouros.

Mouth. Placed horizontally. Corners sharply cut to form triangular depressions. Sharp edges along upper and lower lips. No sharp-edged fold above upper lip.

Hair. Falls down back in mass divided vertically and horizontally into quasi-rectangular members, each of which is further differentiated by curving ridges to indicate texture of hair. Thereby its fluffiness is effectively suggested. Six tresses fall down back and three in front on each side. At back of skull, strands radiate from crown, but towards front they are carved horizontally and vertically from side to side and front to back. Double fillet circles round back of head and stops abruptly behind ears; beneath it, hair bulges forward over shoulder and back; strands are then tied together further down by a second double fillet; and each strand is further tied separately near bottom by triple cord, spiral, or moulded ring.[66] Over forehead are eight spiral locks, with holes in centres, arranged symmetrically to right and left; over each temple is a loop.

NECK. Short and straight. Groove separates head from neck. Sterno-mastoid muscles marked by two grooves, which descend to head of sternum. Hair falling over chest hides line between neck and shoulders.

TORSO, FRONT. Clavicles indicated by two ridges, which travel upward until hidden by hair. Heads of clavicles do not meet, but depression between them marks head of sternum. Course of sternum between pectorals shown by modelled depression instead of groove. Groove travels from lower end of thorax to almond-shaped navel. Nipples button-like and placed far apart. Lower boundary of thorax indicated by groove forming narrow arch some distance below pectorals. Transverse divisions of rectus abdominis not indicated. No indication of protuberance at flanks for anterior part of iliac crest. Lower boundary of abdomen descends with straight sides towards genitals. Pubes carved as stylized form in relief (with straight upper edge), which is divided into rhomboids with similar striations as on hair of head.

TORSO, BACK. Broad groove indicates spinal furrow. Shoulder-blades marked by raised planes. Triangular shape in lumbar region marks attachment of erector spinae.

ARM. Slightly bent at elbow and brought forward. Free from body from somewhat below armpit to hand. Shape of arm well rounded. Muscles of upper arm—deltoid, biceps, triceps—differentiated; similarly muscles of lower arm. Upper end of ulna (elbow) modelled; no ridge round it. Lower end of ulna at wrist, indicated by groove which surrounds its lower edge and travels upward on one side. Forearm, viewed from front, is turned forward (though not so markedly as in New York statue), whereas palm of hand is twisted towards body.

LEG. Buttocks well developed; no indication of depression above great trochanter. Thick thighs; muscles indicated on outer sides by two broad grooves. Vasti muscles descend to about same level; their bulge indicated by slight groove above. Patella more rounded than in New York statue, and pads of fat beneath it marked; below, surrounded by two curious, broad ridges. Front edge of tibia (shin-bone) fairly sharp and curves slightly inward. Two grooves indicate peroneal muscles. Form of calf modelled.

Foot. As Rhomaios observed, both *A* and *B* wore boots, like nos. 22, 23 (figs. 117-122). The incised, deeply scalloped upper boundary is clearly visible on the right leg of *B* (fig. 92). This also explains why the remains of feet show no differentiation of toes. Outlines of soles indicate that big toe projects further than second toe and that toes receded along one continuous curve.

FOOT-PLINTH. Roughly rectangular (front corners broken). Upper surface fairly level.

B. The forms in *B* are the same as in *A*, but there is a deviation in the rendering of the hair. In *A* eight spiral locks are carved above forehead and temples, in *B* only six; in *A* there are six tresses at the back, in *B* eight.

That in modelling *B* appears somewhat softer than *A* is due, I think, not to Ionian workmanship, as suggested by some, but to extensive weathering.

13 : Figs. 114-116

ATHENS, NATIONAL MUSEUM, COLLECTION OF MRS. HELÈNE STATHATOS.

[66] The spiral is J. D. Beazley's suggestion, the ring Lady Beazley's. The objection to a cord or a spiral is that the ends are not indicated. Lady Beazley showed me that a ring would keep strands of her own thick, fluffy hair nicely in place. But then how explain the many bands of different widths in the hair of the Polledrara kore?

Statuette from head to knees. Broken in two pieces at waist and reattached. Surface has suffered.

Lead.
Said to have been found near the temple of Apollo Epikourios at Phigaleia.
Height 3.7 cm.
Not before published.

GENERAL STRUCTURE. Flat front and back. Worked in two pieces; seams visible at sides.
HEAD. *Ear.* Large; not differentiated.
Eye. Indicated by round protuberance under arched brow.
Mouth. Not now visible.
Hair. Falls down back in six tresses, ending in curving line at bottom; two more tresses fall down chest in front.
TORSO, FRONT. Clavicles indicated by protrusions at sternal notch; rest hidden by hair. Pectorals marked by raised planes, on which nipples are indicated. Lower boundary of thorax forms acute angle. No divisions now visible on rectus abdominis. No indication of protuberance at flanks; instead, hips bulge out from narrow waist. Lower boundary of abdomen marked by grooves descending to genitals.
TORSO, BACK. Undifferentiated. Spinal column and erector spinae not marked; also not shoulder-blades. Buttocks level.
ARM. Was separated from body.
LEG. Patella marked by knob. Vasti level.

14 : Figs. 84-86, 106

THASOS, MUSEUM. Kriophoros (Ram-bearer), from Thasos.

Statue, from head to foot-plinth. Was never finished, parts only roughly blocked out; only hair more or less completed. Was broken across chest, at knees, and above ankles. Restorations: areas at fractures, part of right arm from below biceps to above wrist, and a piece of left elbow.

White marble, perhaps Parian (Picard).
Height, as restored, 3.50 m.; with plinth 3.60 m.
Found built into a medieval wall on the akropolis of Thasos, during excavations of 1914-20.
Picard, *B.C.H.* XLV, 1921, pp. 88, 113 ff.
Zervos, *L'Art en Grèce* (2nd. ed.), figs. 108-10.
Buschor, *Fr. J.*, pp. 31 ff., figs. 32-4.

GENERAL STRUCTURE. Head small in proportion (goes about $7\frac{1}{2}$ to 8 times into height of body); thighs short; lower legs long. Greatest protrusion of back, seen in profile, higher than that of chest. Vertebral column more or less straight.

HEAD. Face roughly blocked out; nose in one line with forehead; sides receding and flat.
Skull. Flat at top and undeveloped at back.
Ear. Large, flat, and laid on hair; details not carved.
Hair. Arranged in tresses, which radiate from crown and of which eight fall down back and four on either side in front; each tress divided horizontally into beads, and ends below in triangular member. Fillet forms large flat knot at back, with ends hanging down immediately after knot, forming double curve.
NECK AND TORSO, FRONT. In present unfinished state, no sternomastoids, clavicles, or median line marked. No indication of protuberance at flanks for anterior part of iliac crest. No divisions of rectus abdominis.
TORSO, BACK. Spinal furrow marked by groove. Shoulders somewhat rounded.
ARM. Cannot tell whether forearm was turned forward in supine position, as that part is missing.
Hand. Thumb laid on thigh. Left hand grasped hind legs of ram.
LEG. Perhaps indication of patella and vasti on left, but uncertain.
Foot. Roughly blocked out; toes recede more or less along one line; cannot tell whether toes curved downward.
FOOT-PLINTH. Oval; higher at back than in front.

15 : Figs. 87-90

DELOS AND LONDON, BRITISH MUSEUM, B 322.

Fragments of a colossal statue:
a Torso in two pieces. Temenos of Apollo, Delos. Figs. 87-89.
b Part of left hand. Delos Museum, A 4094.
c Part of left foot together with part of plinth. British Museum, B 322. Fig. 90.
d Base with inscription. Temenos of Apollo, Delos.

Island marble.
About four times life size (circumference round waist 2.76 m.).
Deonna, no. 81 (with long bibliography); no. 105 (hand).
Pryce, *Catalogue*, B 322, p. 152 f., fig. 192 (with part of plinth).
Picard and Replat, *B.C.H.*, XLVIII, 1924, pp. 217 ff. (base).
Raubitschek, *Bulletin de l'Institut archéologique bulgare*, XII, 1938, p. 143 (base).
Buschor, *Fr. J.*, pp. 27 ff., figs. 29, 30.
Pfeiffer, *Journal of the Warburg and Courtland Institute*, XV, 1952, pp. 20 ff.
I.G. XII, 5 test. 1425 c.
S.G.D.I. 5421.
Homolle, *B.C.H.* III, 1879, p. 2 (inscription).
Durrbach, *Choix d'inscriptions de Délos*, I, p. 3 f., no. 3.

Plutarch (Nikias 3) states that 'the great statue of the Naxians'—presumably this statue—was knocked down by a palm tree which Nikias had dedicated in 417 [67] B.C. When this fall occurred is not known; but the statue was apparently re-erected and stood perhaps upright during the whole of antiquity. 'The first modern traveller who saw the statue was Bondelmonte (about A.D. 1420), who found it prostrate, and says that he made an unsuccessful attempt to set it up (*Liber Insularum Archipelagi*, ed. Sinner, p. 92, and see *Rev. Arch.* 1883, I, p. 79). In 1445 Cyriac of Ancona sketched the base with one foot still in position (*Bull d'Inst.* 1861, p. 182). The head was still intact in 1655 when Thévenot saw it (*Voyages*, Paris, 1689, I, p. 332), but had disappeared by 1675, when Spon heard that a little time previously a *proveditore* of Tinos had sawn the face away (*Voyage de Dalmatie*, etc., Lyon, 1678, I, p. 179), and Wheler in the same year recorded a tradition that head, hands, and feet had been carried off by an Englishman of the name of Mr. Simon, in 1672, and that previous to this the statue was upright on its base (*Journey*, p. 56); this last detail is obviously a fiction. Tournefort in 1700 found only the fragments extant at present (English ed. of 1740, vol I, pl. facing p. 303); they were seen by Leake in 1806, afterwards lost to view, and finally recovered by L. Ross in 1835' (quoted from Pryce, *Catalogue*, p. 153; cf. also S. Reinarch, *B.C.H.* XVII, 1893, pp. 129 ff., and Picard and Replat, *B.C.H.* XLVIII, 1924, pp. 221 ff.).

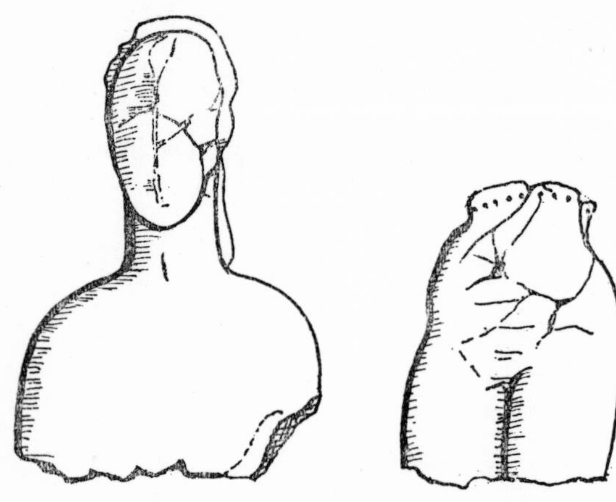

COLOSSAL STATUE. DELOS. No. 15(a). (Drawn by Mrs. G. U. S. Corbett from *B.C.H.* XVI, 1893, pl. V.)

a Torso in two pieces.

(1) from neck to waist, height 2.20 m., (2) from waist to below buttocks, height 1.20 m. On surface are names and marks made by modern travellers.

GENERAL STRUCTURE. Torso flat front and back. Broad, sloping shoulders and narrow waist; thighs bulge out from waist. To judge from an old drawing (see below), head was abnormally large and neck abnormally long. Greatest protrusion of back, seen in profile, higher than that of chest. Vertebral column more or less straight.

HAIR. Arranged in eight strands which fall down back along horizontal line; each ends in a spiral curl, arranged symmetrically to right and left from centre. In front apparently four metal locks came down on each side, to judge by four holes on left side above chest, and remains of two on right side.

NECK. Sterno-mastoids and sternal notch indicated by slightly modelled forms.

TORSO, FRONT. Clavicles appear to travel slightly upward. Median line indicated by slight depression. Pectorals summarily modelled. No certain trace now of lower boundary of thorax or of divisions of rectus abdominis. At waist above break are remains of ridge, and row of eight small holes, evidently for fastening of metal belt.[68] On sides, a little above waist, are dowel holes, perhaps for support of arms. At waist, ridge and small holes for belt.

TORSO, BACK. Deep groove marks spinal furrow, and vertical groove on either side of this indicates erector spinae; curving grooves mark shoulder-blades.

LEG (only upper thighs preserved). Badly damaged, especially back, which has large quadrangular holes, vertically arranged, perhaps made for transportation. Dowel hole on right side, perhaps for attachment of hand (explained by Deonna as another hole like the four for transportation).

b Part of left hand (third, fourth, and little fingers), clenched, with hole passing through it; probably held bow.

Preserved greatest length 60 cm., width 40 cm.

Deonna (op. cit. no. 104, fig. 141) thought that proportions were different from those of colossus; but size is about four times life size;[69] that is, the same as that of the colossus.

Lower end of ulna, at wrist, marked. Metatarsal bones very lightly indicated.

c Fragment of foot-plinth with parts of four toes of left foot.

Height of plinth 64 cm.; width of front side *c.*58 cm.; length of big toe 35 cm.; width of four toes *c.*59 cm.

Presented to British Museum by Captain J. Murray of H.M. Sloop Satellite, 1819.

[67] On the date cf. Courby, *B.C.H.* XLV, 1921, pp. 179 ff., and especially 185.

[68] Belts are of course common for both nude male and draped female statues in the seventh century; cf. e.g. the bronze warriors from Olympia (figs. 6-8), the kouroi found at Delphi and Delos (figs. 14-16, 22-24), the Polledrara kore (Pryce, *Catalogue*, I, 2, p. 156 f., no. D1, pl. I), the statue from Arcadia (National Museum, Athens, no. 57), and the ivory statuette from Samos (cf. p. 9, note 22).

[69] Another fragment of a hand in the Delos Museum (Deonna, no. 105, fig. 142) is too small to come into consideration.

Toes parallel to one another; their ends recede along one continuous line, big toe projecting further than second toe. As far as one can tell in present poor preservation, toes curved downward. Left (spectator's) side of plinth is at right angles, right side at an obtuse angle with the front for insertion in hexagonal base (see below). There is a large dowel hole on each side.[70]

d Base.

Quadrangular, 3.47 × 5.15 × .70 m.
Deep impression in upper surface for insertion of plinth was apparently hexagonal.
Naxian marble.
On the surface many marks made by modern travellers.

There are two inscriptions on opposite sides: one, of a later date, which states that the statue was dedicated by the Naxians (probably added after the statue had fallen and was re-erected); and an early one, evidently made when it was first set up, which reads (in a trimeter): [*τ*]*ο ἀϝυτο λιθο ἐμι ἀνδριας και το σφελας*, 'I am of the same stone both statue and base.'
This has been interpreted as meaning that the statue and plinth were made in one piece. But this is the rule in archaic sculpture, and so not worth recording. On the other hand, the fact that the rectangular base is of the same Naxian marble as the statue is worthy of note, for sometimes the base is of limestone; cf. Durrbach, loc. cit. *Σφέλας*, base of a statue, may be a development of the meaning footstool;[71] for a plain, rectangular base is one of the forms of the Greek footstool.[72]
The missing portion above this inscription probably contained the original dedication.

16 (not illustrated)

DELOS, Museum, no. A728. From Delos.

Triangular base with heads of ram, lion, and a Gorgon at the three corners (ram and Gorgon apparently left unfinished). Foot-plinth, with remains of two feet evidently of a kouros, inserted in hexagonal depression in upper part of base. Now only part of left foot and tips of big and second toes of right foot preserved, but photograph published in 1888 (see below) shows that considerable part of right foot was then extant. Lower part of base only roughly blocked out; was evidently intended to be covered by ground.

Naxian marble.
Approximate dimensions of base: 90 by 80 cm., height 58 cm.
Height of plinth without foot *c.*11 cm.; with foot *c.*19 cm. Upper surface of plinth about level with upper surface of base.
Found in Delos in temenos of Apollo, in 1885.
Kavvadias, *Ath. Mitt.* x, 1885, p. 287.
Homolle, *B.C.H.* xii, 1888, pp. 463 ff., pl. xiii.
Durrbach, *Choix d'inscriptions de Délos*, i, p. 2, no. 1.
Deonna, no. 106.
I.G. xii.5, 1425.
S.G.D.I. 5419.
Kern, *Inscr. Gr.*, pl. 6.
Marcadé, *Signatures*, ii, 45.

Base inscribed (boustrophedon): *Εὐ̣θ̣υκαρτιδης* ⁝|*μ' ἀ* ⁝ *νεθεκε* ⁝ ho:| *Nahσιος* ⁝ *πο|ιεσας*, 'Euthykartides the Naxian made me and dedicated me.' For the name Euthykartides in Naxos, cf. Naupliotes and Hiller von Gaertringen, *Ath. Mitt.* xxxvi, 1911, p. 282, line 28.
Along the grooves of the letters small holes are visible. Evidently the letterer, before proceeding with the cutting of his letters, made an outline of them with his point.[73]
Foot. Toes of left foot much battered and tip of big toe missing; but enough remains to show that toes were parallel and that the four smaller toes apparently curved gently downward. In right foot, big toe longer than second toe.

17 : Figs. 94-95

DELOS, Museum, no. A333. From Delos.

Torso, from waist to below right knee.

Naxian marble.
Height 85 cm.
Found in Delos, in 1906.
Deonna, no. 83.

General Structure. Thighs bulge out from waist below belt, which is indicated in relief. Suggestion of softness of flesh in modelling.
Torso, front. No protrusion at flanks for anterior part of iliac crest. Very short groins. Pubes shown as stylized form in relief, with straight upper edge, and hair carved in small ringlets. Penis was carved separately and is missing. Vertical groove divides scrotum.

[70] Made either for fastening plinth to base (Raubitschek, loc. cit.) or for extraction of plinth when it was removed from its base (Picard and Replat, op. cit. p. 223 f., note 3).
[71] 'Liddell and Scott quote Nikandros, *Theriaka* 644 for the meaning, a hollow block of wood for putting anything into, but this is unwarranted as it is drawn from the reading of the scholion given by the Aldine edition, which is untrustworthy; cf. Keil in Schneider, *Nicandrea*, pp. iv and 51' (M. J. Milne).
[72] Richter, *Ancient Furniture*, p. 17, fig. 35.
[73] Cf. the similar holes in the inscription of the 'Megakles' stele in the Metropolitan Museum, Casson, *A.J.A.* xxxix, 1935, p. 516, fig. 5. It should be noted that also there the holes are not confined to the Os as Casson thought, but are visible along the grooves of some of the other letters. A preliminary point-cut outline of all the letters was evidently made as a guide for the cutting. In some cases the grooves obliterated the holes, in others not. The holes are particularly conspicuous in the Os, for they were more difficult to cut neatly than the other letters. Cf. Richter, *Cat. of Gk. Sc.*, no. 15, pl. xvi.

ARM. Was held against side at hand, with comparatively small area of attachment.

LEG. Buttocks rounded but not pronounced. Depression over great trochanter indicated by flat plane. Thighs rounded with indication of muscles at side. Vastus internus bulges over knee, but vastus externus hardly indicated. Patella rounded.

18 : A–D Figs. 97-102

SANTORIN, MUSEUM. From Thera.

Fragmentary colossal statues:

A. Statue, in two pieces, from head (face missing) to below buttocks. Height 1.68 m.; of head 39 cm. Figs. 97-99 and drawings below.

B. Upper part of statue (face also missing). Much weathered. Height 1.03 m.; of head 37 cm. Figs. 100-102.

In addition, two battered fragments belonging to two further kouroi (*C, D*) were found: part of a torso with belt, and a piece with upper legs.

All are of Island marble and were found not far from the ancient city of Thera, in 1931.

DeWaele, *Arch. Anz.*, 1931, cols. 102-5, fig. 2.
Kontoleon, *'Αρχ.'Εφ.*, 1939-41, pp. 1 ff., figs. 1-6 (*A*); figs. 9-11 (*B*); figs. 12-14 (*C,D*).
Buschor, *Fr J.*, p. 60 f., figs. 66, 67.
Homann-Wedeking, *Anfänge*, p. 67 f., figs. 24, 25.

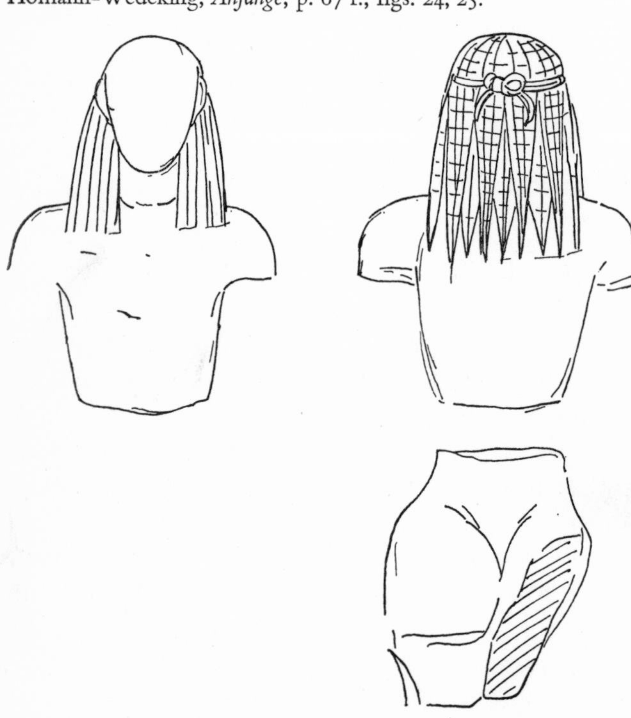

FRAGMENTS OF COLOSSAL STATUE. No. 18 A.

GENERAL STRUCTURE. Torso flat front and back. Broad shoulders and narrow waist. Greatest protrusion of back, seen in profile, higher than that of chest. Vertebral column more or less straight. Head large in proportion.

HEAD. *Skull*. Flat at back.

Ear. Laid on hair.

Hair. Carved in tresses which radiate from crown and fall down back and over each shoulder in front. At back, tresses arranged in two layers, one in front of other. Strands divided horizontally by shallower grooves; at ends each was perhaps tied by cord or ring (cf. p. 50, note 66). Fillet encircles head and is tied at back in reef knot, with short curving ends hanging down immediately after knot.

TORSO, FRONT. Little anatomical detail now visible. Some trace of clavicles. No belt visible.

TORSO, BACK. Groove for spinal furrow. No indication of shoulder-blades.

19 : Figs. 103-105

LEYDEN, RIJKSMUSEUM, no. Ro III. 49.

Head with neck. Battered. Large hole passes through mouth to back.

It has been suggested that the head belonged to the fragmentary kouros from Thera (Kondoleon, *'Εφ.'Αρχ.*, 1939-41, p. 7, figs. 12, 13; my no. 18 C). To judge from the illustrations it might fit.

Island marble, perhaps Naxian.
Bought in Santorin by Colonel Rottiers in 1827, and said to have been found in the ancient city of Thera.
Height 47 cm.; of face 30 cm.
Janssen, *De Griekse, Romeinse, en Etrurische Monumenten van het Museum van Oudheden te Leyden*, 1843-8, p. 20, no. 152.
Pleyte and Jesse, *Catalogue*, 1897, p. 94, pl. IV.
Guide of Museum, 1951, p. 9, fig. 4.

HEAD. *Skull*. Somewhat rounded at top, flat at back. Face oval.

Ear. Flat and stylized. Slants towards line of jaw. Tragus indicated but not antitragus.

Eye. Elongated. Eyeball protrudes.

Hair. Falls down back in mass which is divided vertically and horizontally into beaded tresses, with five tresses falling on each shoulder. Over forehead and temples arranged in large spiral curls, directed upward and symmetrically to right and left of centre.

NECK. Sterno-mastoids and throat not marked.

20 : Figs. 107-108

ATHENS, NATIONAL MUSEUM, no. 18809. From Samos.

Head with tang.

Wood.
Height 3.5 cm.
Found in the Heraion, Samos.
Ohly, *Ath. Mitt.*, LVIII, 1953, p. 83 f., no. 2 (there thought to be either male or female).
Buschor, *Fr. J.*, p. 32.

Skull. Top and back only slightly rounded.
Ear. Slants towards line of jaw. Carved in one plane and stylized. Tragus knoblike. No indication of antitragus.
Eye. Large and almond-shaped. Both lids strongly curved. Eyeball protrudes. No indication of recess at inner corner. Groove separates upper lid from eyebrow and lower lid from cheek.
Nose. Narrow at bridge, broad at bottom. Nostrils missing.
Mouth. Full lips, placed horizontally; do not meet at outer corners.
Chin. Prominent.
Hair. Hung down in mass, divided vertically into strands, with deep horizontal grooves and ridges at back. In front bulges over shoulder in so-called Daedalid fashion. Over forehead and temples two horizontal ridges.

21 : Figs. 111-113

FLORENCE, MUSEO ARCHEOLOGICO.

Statuette, from head to right foot. A very early member of this group (or a forerunner?).

Lead.
Height 11.5 cm.
From Tigani, Samos. Gift of C. J. Forsyth Major, 1889.
Minto, *Critica d'Arte*, VIII, 1943, pp. 17 ff.

GENERAL STRUCTURE. Flat front and back. Seen in profile, greatest protrusion of back higher than that of chest. Vertebral column straight.
HEAD. *Skull.* Somewhat rounded top and back. Face triangular.
Ear. Large and flat; laid against hair.
Eye. Large, with curving lids and protruding iris.
Mouth. Straight.
Chin. Prominent.
Hair. Falls down back in broad mass, divided vertically on skull, and both vertically and horizontally below, ending in ten separate tresses; further tresses are directed to front, three on each shoulder, in 'Daedalid' fashion.
NECK. No indication of sterno-mastoids or of throat.
TORSO, FRONT. Clavicles hidden by hair. Pectorals indicated by protruding planes and placed high. No indication of divisions of rectus abdominis or of lower boundary of thorax. Navel incised. Lower boundary of abdomen descends towards genitals with straight sides pointing sharply downward. No protrusion at hips.
TORSO, BACK. Groove marks spinal column. Shoulder-blades marked by separate planes corresponding to those of pectorals. No indication of erector spinae.
ARM. Joined to body only at armpit, but connected with top of thigh by support (extant only on left side). Forearm turned forward in supine position, with hand held open.
LEG. Prominent thighs and buttocks. Two ridges travel down outer side of thigh. Broken at knees with pieces missing; but vasti and malleoli were apparently level. Shin straight. Ridges mark lower leg muscles. Toes missing.

22 : Figs. 117-119

VATHY, MUSEUM. From Samos.

Statuette, from head to foot-plinth.

Bronze.
Height 19 cm.
Found in the Heraion, Samos.
Buschor, *Alt. St.* I, p. 9, figs. 5, 7, 8; *Fr. J.*, p. 74 f., figs. 84, 85.

GENERAL STRUCTURE. Trunk four-sided. Head abnormally large; goes a little more than five times into total height. Greatest protrusion of back, seen in profile, higher than that of chest. Vertebral column somewhat curved.
HEAD. *Skull.* Flat at top, but well developed at back above fillet.
Ear. Large and flat, placed vertically.
Eye. Large; placed somewhat obliquely. No recess at inner corner.
Mouth. Horizontal; upper lip protrudes over lower.
Hair. Falls in mass behind ending in slightly curving line, with one tress in front on either side, and roll over forehead and temples. Strands of hair indicated by incised lines, wavy at back.
NECK. No indication of sterno-mastoids. Transition between neck and shoulders hidden by tresses.
TORSO, FRONT. Clavicles protrude prominently and travel upward. Median line, lower boundary of thorax and divisions of rectus abdominis not marked. No indication of protrusion at flanks for anterior part of iliac crest. Lower boundary of abdomen descends with straight sides towards genitals.
TORSO, BACK. Groove marks spinal furrow. Slight indication of shoulder-blades. Erector spinae not indicated.
ARM. Held away from body; bent and brought forward. Forearm turned towards body.
Hand. Perhaps held attribute.
LEG. Well developed. Knee marked by incised rhomboids without differentiation of vasti. Front edge of

shin-bone curves slightly inward. Malleoli more or less level. Boots on feet (like nos. 12, 23).
FOOT-PLINTH. In one piece with statuette.

23 : Figs. 120-122

VATHY, MUSEUM. From Samos.

Statuette, from head to ankles.

Bronze.
Height 20 cm.
Found in the Heraion, Samos.
Buschor, *Alt. St.*, p. 9, figs. 6, 9, 10.

GENERAL STRUCTURE. Flat front and back. Sloping shoulders. Very long thighs. Height of head goes about seven times into total height of body. Seen in profile, greatest protrusion of back higher than that of chest. Vertebral column more or less straight.
HEAD. *Skull.* Domed on top and well developed behind.
Ear. Large and flat, with lobes sloping backward.
Eye. Hollow; one has original inlay preserved.
Mouth. Horizontal.
Hair. Falls in mass behind, ending in practically straight line; divided behind into horizontal grooves and ridges; on skull indicated by incised lines.
NECK. No indication of sterno-mastoids or swelling of trapezium.
TORSO, FRONT. Clavicles and median line not indicated. Knobs for nipples. Lower boundary of thorax placed very low; marked by two straight lines forming obtuse angle. No divisions of rectus abdominis. No indication at flanks of protrusion of anterior part of iliac crest. Navel marked as incised circle. Lower boundary of abdomen descends towards genitals with straight sides pointing sharply downward.
TORSO, BACK. Flat, with no indication of spinal furrow or of shoulder-blades.
ARM. Held away from body; preserved left elbow bent.
LEG. Knee marked as incised oval without differentiation of vasti. Had boots, of which upper incised parts remain (cf. nos. 12, 22).

24 : Fig. 96

VATHY, MUSEUM. From Samos.

Upper left leg to knee.

Marble.
Height 1.32 m. Three times life size.
Found in the Heraion, Samos, between the temple and the Southern Colonnade.
Buschor, *Alt. St.* I, p. 8, figs. 3-4, 19.

Vasti bulge with slight indication of upper boundary of bulging flesh. Broad furrow, somewhat modelled, on outer thigh.

25 : Fig. 93

VATHY, MUSEUM. From Samos.

Right hand of a colossal statue.

Marble.
Buschor, *Alt. St.* I, p. 8, figs. 1, 2.

Index finger next to thigh. No indication of metatarsal bones. Skin of thumb marked.
As it was found not far from the upper left leg, no. 24, and the sizes fit, Buschor believes the two may have belonged to the same statue. For further fragments apparently belonging to this statue cf. Buschor, *Alt. St.* IV, figs. 253 ff.

26 : Figs. 123-125

STOCKHOLM, NATIONAL MUSEUM, no. 314.

Statuette, from head to above ankles.

Bronze.
Height 16 cm.
Provenance not known. Gift of Queen Josephine of Sweden, 1868.
Brising, *Antik Konst i Nationalmuseum*, pl. XIV.
Langlotz, *Bildhauerschulen*, pl. 59, c.
Kjellberg, *Konst-historisk Tidscrift*, VI, 1937, p. 33 f.
V. H. Poulsen, *From the Collections of the Ny Carlsberg Glyptothek*, II, 1932, p. 102 f. (there considered Etruscan, but the parallels cited seem to me different).[74]

GENERAL STRUCTURE. Flat front and back. Sloping shoulders. Head large in proportion. Greatest protrusion of back, seen in profile, higher than that of chest. Vertebral column more or less straight.
HEAD. Round face.
Skull. Somewhat rounded at top, flat at back.
Ear. Large, flat, and placed vertically. Antihelix indicated by engraved line.
Eye. Long, narrow, and obliquely set. No recess at inner corner.
Mouth. Large and more or less horizontal.
Hair. Falls down behind in broad mass, ending in horizontal line, with engraved wavy lines descending vertically from skull.
NECK. No indication of sterno-mastoids or of swelling of trapezium.
TORSO, FRONT. No indication of clavicles or of median line. Lower boundary of thorax marked by incised, pointed arch. Similar incised line across abdomen. Divisions of rectus abdominis not marked. Navel marked by incised circle. No indication of anterior part of

[74] And when I referred the question to Valentin Müller, Doro Levi, and George Hanfmann, they all agreed that the statuette had no place in Etruscan art.

iliac crest at flanks. Lower boundary of abdomen descends towards genitals with straight sides pointing sharply downward.
TORSO, BACK. Groove marks spinal furrow. No indication of shoulder-blades or erector spinae.
ARM. Attached to body most of way. Forearm turned to body in semi-pronated position.
Hand. Not clenched; palm and fingers laid against side.
LEG. No indication of depression above great trochanter. Long thighs. Knees marked by incisions without differentiation of vasti.

27 : Figs. 126-128

LONDON, BRITISH MUSEUM, B 330. From Rhodes.

Statuette from head to knees. The restorations shown in former publications have now been removed.

Light grey limestone.
Height 25.4 cm.
Found at Kamiros, Rhodes, probably in 1864.
Pryce, *Catalogue*, B 330, p. 160 f., pl. XXXV.

GENERAL STRUCTURE. Broad shoulders and slim waist; flat chest and back, but slightly protruding abdomen. Head large in proportion to torso. Seen in profile, greatest protrusion of back rather higher than that of chest. Little indication of anatomical detail; different elements conceived rather as volumes. Traces of red paint indicate that the figure wore a short chiton.
HEAD. *Skull.* Flat at top and back.
Ear. Carved in more than one plane, but large in proportion. Tragus indicated but no antitragus.
Eye. Injured.
Nose. Lower part missing, broad at base.
Mouth. Small; lips do not meet at corners.
Hair. Resembles an Egyptian headdress, without indication of individual strands.
NECK. Planes of neck and chest meet at sharply marked angle. No indication of sterno-mastoid muscles or of swelling of trapezium.
TORSO, FRONT. Clavicles, median line, lower boundary of thorax, and divisions of rectus abdominis not marked. Navel marked by short, vertical groove. No indication of anterior part of iliac crest at flanks. Lower boundary of abdomen rounded.
TORSO, BACK. Broad, shallow groove for spinal furrow. No indication of shoulder-blades or erector spinae.
ARM. Mostly missing.
Hand. Not clenched; palm and fingers laid against thigh.
LEG. Small buttocks. No differentiation of vasti.

28 : Figs. 129-130

LONDON, BRITISH MUSEUM, B 438. From Naukratis.

Statuette, from head to below knees. Was broken in several pieces, which have been put together with some restorations at junctures; of these the most important are: part of neck, small portion of hair, and part of left buttock. The restorations shown in former publications have now been removed.

Alabaster.
Height 25.7 cm.
From Naukratis. Acquired by the British Museum in 1888 through Flinders Petrie, who purchased it from a peasant at Naukratis.
Pryce, *Catalogue*, B 438, p. 183 f., pl. XXXIX.
Deonna, no. 148, figs. 168-9.

GENERAL STRUCTURE. Flat and plank-like (therefore one cannot speak of greatest protrusion of back), but abdomen protrudes slightly. Vertebral column straight. Sloping shoulders. Head large, neck long, upper arm short.
HEAD. *Skull.* Rounded above, not developed at back.
Ear. Large and thick, slanting towards line of jaw. Upper part more or less in one plane. Lobe protrudes.
Eye. Large and almond-shaped, with sharp-edged groove above upper lid and below lower lid. No recess at inner corner.
Nose. Partly missing. Broad at base.
Mouth. Lips do not meet at corners, and curve slightly upward. Some red preserved.
Chin. Pointed.
Hair. Falls down back in mass, divided horizontally and vertically into tresses of rectangular members. On each side four such tresses are brought over shoulder to fall on chest. Thick fillet (with traces of red) encircles forehead.
NECK. Partly restored. No indication of sterno-mastoids. Line of neck to shoulders hidden by hair.
TORSO, FRONT. Clavicles and median line not marked. Lower boundary of thorax indicated by groove forming acute angle, placed very high, the apex just below nipples. Each nipple formed by knob encircled by groove. No divisions marked of rectus abdominis. Navel formed by knob encircled by groove. No protrusion at flanks marks anterior part of iliac crest.
TORSO, BACK. Groove marks spinal furrow. No indication of shoulder-blades or erector spinae.
ARM. Adheres to body most of way. Upper arm short. Forearm in supine position (as shown by transverse groove at bend of arm), whereas palm is twisted towards body.
Hand. Clenched, with thumb, which is very long, next to thigh. Stone left adhering between thumb and forefinger and, at back, inside bend of little finger.

LEG. Small buttocks. No indication of hollow formed above trochanter on sides of buttocks. Knees marked as incised rhomboids, without differentiation of vasti.

29 : Fig. 131

LONDON, BRITISH MUSEUM, B 444. From Naukratis.

Statuette, from below neck to below knees. Part of right arm missing.

Sandstone.
Height 10 cm.
From Naukratis. Excavated by Flinders Petrie, in 1884.
Petrie, *Naukratis*, I, pl. 1, 4.
Pryce, *Catalogue*, B 444, p. 187 f., fig. 225.

GENERAL STRUCTURE. Broad shoulders. Flat back. Vertebral column straight.
HAIR. Falls down back to shoulders in mass ending in curved line.
TORSO, FRONT. Anatomy generalized. No protrusion at flanks. Lower boundary of abdomen descends with short straight sides towards genitals.
TORSO, BACK. Groove marks spinal furrow. No indication of shoulder-blades or erector spinae.
ARM. Adheres to sides along whole way. Forearm held in supine position.
Hand. Clenched, with thumb next to thigh. Stone left adhering between thumb and forefinger.
LEG. Patella and vasti indicated by incisions, but vasti not differentiated.

30 (not illustrated)

LONDON, BRITISH MUSEUM, 1934.3-8.5. From Naukratis.

Head and part of neck from a large statuette.

Greyish limestone.
Height *c*.14.8 cm.
Found in the temenos of Aphrodite, Naukratis.
E. A. Gardner, *Naukratis*, II, pl. XIII, 4.

GENERAL STRUCTURE. Shape quadrangular; flat at top and back; back cut smooth.
HEAD. *Ear*. Much injured; was apparently placed vertically and high.
Eye. Large, flat, and almond-shaped; slopes slightly upward. Sharp-edged groove above upper lid and below lower lid. No recess at inner corner.
Nose. Fairly narrow. Nostril indicated on side by incised, arched groove, below by round hole.
Mouth. Lips protruding and placed horizontally. Incised grooves travel from above corners downward to point of chin.
Hair. Not indicated at back, but hangs down sides. On skull and on sides mass not differentiated.

In this group belongs also a bronze statuette in MAJORCA, not strictly a kouros for he shoulders a quiver, but related to the type in stance and anatomical renderings (cf. Garcia y Bellido, *Archivo Español de Arqueologia*, 45, 1941, p. 524 f., fig. 10; Richter, *Arch. Gk. Art*, p. 58, fig. 83.

30 bis : Figs. 108-109

PALERMO, NATIONAL MUSEUM, S 905—no. 73.

Statuette, from head to foot-plinth. No restorations, but surface puckered.

Bronze.
Height *c*.11.3 cm.
Found at Selinus.
P. Marconi, *Itinerari*, no. 11, p. 55, 1.

GENERAL STRUCTURE. Broad shoulders; flat front and back; narrow waist. Vertebral column straight.
HEAD. *Skull*. Well developed behind; wears polos.
Ear. Large. Placed more or less vertically.
Eye. Protruding eyeballs. Alert expression.
Nose. Large.
Mouth. More or less horizontal.
Hair. Falls down back in broad mass, ending in horizontal line; mass divided on sides and at back into horizontal ridges, but smooth on skull. Over forehead and temples large spiral curls.
TORSO, FRONT. Clavicles marked by ridges travelling upward. Median line indicated by groove along sternum. Lower boundary of thorax marked by two straight lines forming acute angle; placed low. No divisions of rectus abdominis shown. No protrusion at flanks. Lower boundary of abdomen descends with short, straight sides towards genitals.
TORSO, BACK. Flat and generalized.
ARM. Held away from body, with hand clenched and laid against thigh.
LEGS. Shapely and placed about parallel. Patella indicated by round knob. No differentiation of vasti muscles.
Foot. Toes recede along one continuous line, the second toe being shorter than the big toe.
FOOT-PLINTH. Rectangular; in one piece with statuette.

VI. THE ORCHOMENOS-THERA GROUP

(*c.* 590-570 B.C.)

General Survey and Historical Background

ATTICA. We saw that the preceding period was one of remarkable achievement. In Attica that brilliant epoch was succeeded by a lull. At least the only kouroi from Attica which may be assigned to this time are the statue formerly in the 'Theseion' (no. 31) and a much battered and fragmentary torso from Markopoulo (no. 32). Then, in the second quarter of the century, material becomes again more plentiful (cf. p. 75). One might suppose that this difference was owing merely to the chances of excavation, except for the fact that the evidence of the kouroi is reinforced by that of the other remains. Comparatively few distinguished sculptures from Attica are assignable to the early part of the sixth century, whereas from 575 or so a number of masterpieces again appear (cf. p. 75). This lull and reawakening in the artistic world of Attica may therefore be a reflection of political events. Solon was elected archon in 594. His revolutionary reforms were naturally accompanied by great unrest. The aristocrats, who had been the patrons of art, found their freedom of action curbed, their wealth impaired. A law seems to have been enacted even restricting the extravagance of private funerals.[1] At such a time it would not be surprising if there were few artistic activities.

BOEOTIA. From Boeotia come two crude, vigorous kouroi, one found perhaps at Orchomenos, the other in the Ptoan Sanctuary (nos. 33, 34). They are the immediate successors of the large-eyed, angular example of the preceding period (no. 10). Several pairs of feet, evidently from statues of kouroi, also come from the Ptoan Sanctuary (nos. 36-8). The kouros in the British Museum (no. 39), for which a Boeotian provenance is claimed, may be a decade or so later.

The famous oracle connected with the Ptoan Sanctuary[2] is now silent, but the statues dedicated in the sanctuary have become peculiarly eloquent. For Boeotia, after the great legendary period of *Oedipus* and *The Seven Against Thebes*, hardly figures in history before the late sixth century. All we know of her earlier activities is the rising power of Thebes and the gradual formation of a Boeotian League under her suzerainty.[3] The Hesiodic school of poets shows that she was an important literary centre. We can extract some slight information from early pottery and terracotta statuettes from Boeotia, as well as from her coinage (e.g. of Thebes, Tanagra, and Haliartos), which perhaps started soon after 600 B.C. and which suggests that during the first half of the sixth century the Boeotian League was of some consequence.[4] The happy chance of the discovery of the Ptoan Sanctuary with its impressive statues eloquently bears out this surmise, at least if these figures are Boeotian products, as is likely; for several are of Boeotian marble, and we have no evidence that the rather remote Ptoan Sanctuary attracted offerings from other localities at this early period,

[1] Cf. Adcock, *C.A.H.* IV, p. 44; Richter, *Met. Mus. Studies*, v. I, 1934, p. 46 f., note 80.

[2] Herodotos VIII.135; Pausanias IX.23.6.

[3] Cf. Cary, *C.A.H.* III, pp. 608 ff.

[4] Hampe, *Frühe griechische Sagenbilder in Böotien*; Head, *Historia Numorum*,[2] p. 348 f.; Babelon, *Traité*, II, pp. 939 ff., 951 ff., 963 ff., pl. XII.

though we know of instances later (cf. p. 113). And even if the statues were not made in Boeotia, the fact that they were dedicated there suggests a certain prominence for Boeotia.

CORINTHIA. A fragmentary terracotta statuette of a kouros from Perachora[5] (no. 44) may be dated about 590-580 B.C., by the resemblance of the head to those on Middle Corinthian pyxides.[6] As the statuette was presumably a local product we probably have here a specimen—though an insignificant one—of Corinthian manufacture.

ACTIUM. One of the most distinguished examples of this period, no. 40 (unfortunately headless), was found at Actium in Acarnania. It is a finely proportioned figure, to be dated perhaps 580-570. It probably belongs to the famous sanctuary of Apollo of which traces have been found—perched on a hill, just as Strabo[7] described it. Since Actium belonged to the territory of Anaktorion,[8] which is said to have been founded by Corinthians at the time of Kypselos, it seems legitimate to associate its early products with Corinth. On the other hand, since the statue comes from a sanctuary, there is the possibility that it is an offering of another state.

ARCADIA. The kouros from Phigaleia (no. 41 and p. 77) appears to belong to this period, when the cities of Arcadia were still powerful, fighting the increasing menace of Sparta.

DELPHI. The bronze statuette from Delphi (no. 42), with broad shoulders and a flat, sharp-edged chest, recalls the kouros of Orchomenos (no. 33).

DODONA. A bronze statuette from Dodona, in Berlin (no. 45) appears to be a provincial product of this period.

Also from the North, from near NAUPAKTOS, comes a fine head (no. 46), evidently of a kouros.

TRAPEZIA. The diminutive bronze statuette from Trapezia[9] (no. 43) in the British Museum also belongs here.

DELOS. Of the continuous series of kouroi from Delos, two fragmentary examples (nos. 47, 48) may be assigned to this group. Delos, throughout the sixth century, continued to be the centre for the Ionian festival in honour of Apollo. Athens, always proud of her Ionian connection, took part in this festival from an early period.[10] We may expect, then, the early statues from Delos to be Ionian or Attic dedications.

THERA. The kouros from Thera (no. 49) is a distinguished product of this time. It was found as long ago as 1836, opposite the rock tombs of Cape Exomyti, and was therefore probably a tomb statue. What we noted in the colossi of the preceding period (cf. no. 18) applies also to this statue. Though Thera was a Dorian colony (cf. p. 35), a comparison between this product and its contemporaries shows that the style is more Ionian than Western. The sloping shoulders and soft forms make a striking contrast with the muscular figures from Actium and Boeotia. Environment evidently exercised here too a determining influence. Noteworthy also is a certain similarity between this kouros and the statue no. 677 from the Athenian Akropolis,[11] especially in the rendering of the eye,

[5] Jenkins in Payne, *Perachora*, p. 207, pl. 91, no. 42.

[6] Cf., as Payne points out, especially the one in Oxford, *Necrocorinthia*, p. 47, no. 14; *C.V.* Oxford, fasc. 2, III c, pl. VII, 7.

[7] VII.325.

[8] Thucydides I.29.3.

[9] In the inventory of the British Museum, the statuette is entered as 'from Trapezia', and nothing further is known regarding its provenance. I have not been able to track down a Trapezia in Greece. Trapeza is the modern Greek name of a mountain near Parnassos, and of a cave in the plain of Lasithi, Crete (*B.S.A.* XXXVI, 1935-6, p. 13); Pape, *Wörterbuch der griechischen Eigennamen*³, p. 1546, lists Trapeza as a town in Arcadia mentioned by Stephanus of Byzantium, and as a promontory in the Troad mentioned by Pliny.

[10] The 'Deliastai' are mentioned in Solon's laws (*Athenaios* VI.234 e); cf. also Cary, *C.A.H.* III, p. 576.

[11] Buschor, *Alt. St.*, figs. 80-83; dated by him 580-570.

with the groove or ridge marking the upper boundary of the upper lid. The Akropolis statue has by some been connected with Samos on account of its similarity to the figure from the Heraion dedicated by Cheramyes, now in the Louvre.[12]

NAXOS. The famous Sphinx at Delphi (perhaps 580-570[13]), a dedication of Naxos, throws light on her importance about this time; and this is borne out by a colossal head (no. 50), said to be from Naxos, which must have belonged to a kouros of this epoch.

SAMOS. From Samos come two lively bronze statuettes, one of stocky proportions and with large head (no. 52), the other more elongated (no. 51). If our dating is correct, they are contemporaries of the famous young boxer Pythagoras of Samos, 'with long hair and purple robe', who won renown at Olympia in 588 B.C.[14]

A fine bronze statuette (no. 54) from the Pourtalès Collection, now in the Hermitage, has an inscription 'Polykrates dedicated it' in Argive letters (note form of lamda). The style of the statuette is earlier than the time of the tyrant Polykrates and the name Polykrates is a common one. The type, however, with its rounded forms is Eastern rather than Argive.

CRETE. A somewhat farouche statuette in Berlin (no. 53) is said to have been found in Crete.

MILETOS. A bronze statuette (no. 55) of rounded forms, with sloping shoulders, is said to come from Miletos, another great power in the East Greek world. In the early sixth century lived her famous tyrant Thrasyboulos, who advised his friend Periander, tyrant of Corinth, to get rid of all prominent citizens. To about the same period as the small bronze kouros we may perhaps assign the earliest of the seated statues which lined the Sacred Way at Didyma, a few miles south of Miletos[15] (cf. p. 92).

KNIDOS. From Knidos comes a limestone statuette, now in the British Museum (no. 56). Again this product from a Dorian outpost in the East belongs stylistically to the Eastern not to the Western world. The heavy, fleshy body with its soft, rounded contours has its counterparts in Milesian and Samian sculptures rather than in those of the Peloponnese.

UNKNOWN PROVENANCE. A limestone statuette in Leipzig of unknown provenance (no. 58) must be an East Greek product of about this period, with strong Egyptian influence.

NAUKRATIS. From Naukratis we have a few minor statuettes which may perhaps be dated in the period under consideration (nos. 59-61). They carry on the tradition of the slightly more angular and flatter examples (nos. 28, 29) of the preceding group.

ITALY. A terracotta statuette of a thickset male figure, now in Oxford (no. 62) comes from Taranto.

Absolute Chronology

If the dates assigned to the Sounion and Volomandra groups are about correct—and in both cases we have at least some external evidence—the members of the intermediate Orchomenos-Thera group should occupy the decades 590-570 B.C.

A comparison with heads on Corinthian pottery is again useful. The closest resemblance is with

[12] Ibid. figs. 86-9; dated by him 570-560.
[13] Note its similarity to the kore no. 677 from the Athenian Akropolis.
[14] Diogenes Laertios VIII.47-8.
[15] Pryce, *Catalogue*, B 271, p. 106, pl. VI.

those on Middle Corinthian vases (dated about 600-575). The heads on the vases in Berlin[16] and the Louvre,[17] for instance, have the same stolid expression, comparatively flat skull, large eyes, and horizontal mouth as the Orchomenos-Thera kouroi.

A comparison with vase paintings shows that some of the figures on vases which have been assigned to about 590-570[18] often have thick-set, heavy forms, like many of the kouroi of the Orchomenos-Thera group.

Anatomical Analysis

In general the figures look like inferior descendants of the preceding group. None of them display the monumental quality and impressive bearing of the former generation. The forms are less abstract and architectural. The majority of the figures are thick-set and somewhat awkward. Instead of the elegant curves of the former period, they often have a clumsy appearance. Though the origin from the four-sided block is still evident, and much of the anatomy is indicated by grooves, the artist is now more intent on the corporeal quality of the figure. More details are seen in the round. In the Boeotian kouroi, for instance, the divisions of the rectus abdominis and the flanks are modelled, whereas other anatomical renderings are still purely linear. In other words, a new conception is slowly being injected into the geometrical scheme; a step forward is taken towards the naturalistic ideal.

STRUCTURE IN GENERAL. Body tends to be less plank-like than before. Proportions more normal, but head sometimes very large. Greatest protrusion of back, seen in profile, higher than that of chest. Vertebral column more or less straight. Anatomical detail still often indicated by grooves, but forms on the whole more modelled and seen in the round than in Sounion group.

HEAD. *Skull*. Tends to be higher, but back still undeveloped.

Ear. Still placed high. Carved in one plane (in marble statues), but less stylized. Tragus generally an excrescence of lobe. No antitragus (but see no. 50).

Eye. Not so large as in preceding group and seen more in the round. Recess at inner corner occasionally marked by groove. Upper eyelid occasionally has groove.

Mouth. Generally horizontal. Edges of lips no longer so sharp; corners of mouth sometimes still form triangular depressions, at other times slope upward. No longer always in one plane.

Hair. Less like a wig, and tresses less rigid.

NECK. Sterno-mastoids indicated by grooves. No indication of swelling of trapezium.

TORSO, FRONT. Clavicles protrude as flat ridges all along their course as far as deltoid. Lower boundary of thorax marked by grooves generally forming an acute angle, sometimes a narrow arch. Transverse divisions of rectus abdominis above navel, when marked, number three or more and are indicated by modelled forms. Navel shaped as button surrounded by groove, occasionally with horizontal cut at each side. Generally slight protrusion at flanks (sometimes prolonged into girdle-like ridge) marks anterior part of iliac crest. Lower boundary of abdomen descends with straight sides towards genitals (except no. 56 where it is rounded). Pubes, when represented, has straight upper edge (cf. no. 41).

[16] Payne, *Necrocorinthia*, pl. 48, nos. 1-4.

[17] Ibid. pl. 47, nos. 12, 13; pl. 48, nos. 13, 14.

[18] Cf. e.g. the vases attributed by S. Papaspyridi-Karouzou to the earlier Sophilos, *Ath. Mitt.* LXII, 1937, p. 132 f.

TORSO, BACK. Spinal furrow marked by groove. Shoulder-blades indicated as separate raised planes outlined by grooves. Occasional attempt to model erector spinae.

ARM. Joined to body along considerable distance. In stone statues forearm is turned forward in supine position, but palm of hand, instead of being directed forward, is twisted towards body. In bronze and terracotta statuettes forearm is often correctly semi-pronated. Thumb still sometimes large. Occasionally ridge surrounds elbow (cf. no. 33).

LEG. No indication of hollow over great trochanter. Lower ends of vasti muscles sometimes slightly differentiated, at other times almost level. Malleoli level.

Foot. Flatter than in Sounion group. Toes more or less parallel and their ends as they touch the ground recede along one continuous line, the big toe projecting further than the second toe. The four smaller toes generally curve downward (either gently or sharply), with nails pointing towards ground. Little toe slants inward.

FOOT-PLINTH. Foot-plinth uneven; shape follows roughly outlines of soles.

Kouroi Nos. 31-62

31 : Figs. 132-133, 136-137

ATHENS, NATIONAL MUSEUM, no. 3858. From New Phaleron.

Upper part of statue, to waist.

Island marble, large grained.
Height 70 cm.
Found in Moschato, New Phaleron, near Piraeus Street. Formerly in the 'Theseion'.
Kyparissis and Homann-Wedeking, *Ath. Mitt.*, LXIII/LXIV, 1938-9, pp. 156 ff., pls. 49-54.
Langlotz in Schrader, *Akropolis*, p. 41.
Buschor, *Fr. J.*, pp. 55 ff., figs. 57-9.
Homann-Wedeking, *Anfänge*, pp. 87 f., fig. 46.
C. Karousos, *Εἰς Μνήμην Οἰκονόμου*, III, 1953-4, pp. 19 ff.

GENERAL STRUCTURE. Flat front and back. Seen in profile, greatest protrusion of back higher than that of chest. Vertebral column straight. Head and neck disproportionately long compared to small chest.
HEAD. *Skull.* Top and back flat. Remains of meniskos at top.
Ear. Large; placed high and vertical; slight differentiation of planes. No antitragus.
Eye. In about same plane with eyebrow and cheek bones; placed horizontally.
Mouth. Horizontal.
Hair. Hangs down back in mass divided into tresses. Over forehead and temples arranged in spiral curls, symmetrically to right and left from centre. Fillet passes below these curls and is tied behind in a loose knot, with ends hanging down obliquely along furrows which determine direction of strands of hair. Mass ends below in horizontal line.
NECK. No sterno-mastoids marked. No indication of swelling of trapezium.
TORSO, FRONT. Clavicles travel upward (partly coincide with break). Median line marked by depression below sternum only. Lower boundary of thorax indicated by groove making acute angle, slightly rounded at apex. No transverse divisions of rectus abdominis above navel. Navel marked as round button. Down each side of torso, along area originally covered by arms, are horizontal tool marks (cf. no. 116).
TORSO, BACK. Large groove for spinal furrow. Shoulder-blades indicated by raised planes.

32 : Figs. 134-135

ATHENS, NATIONAL MUSEUM, no. 4181.

Torso, from neck to above waist. Battered.

Marble.
Height 30 cm. (smaller than life size).
Found in Markopoulo, Attica. Formerly in the Museum at Markopoulo.
Kyparissis and Homann-Wedeking, *Ath. Mitt.*, 63/64, 1938/9, p. 158, pls. 55-7.

GENERAL STRUCTURE. Seen in profile, greatest protrusion of back higher than that of chest.
Hair. Hangs down to top of shoulders; arranged in tresses travelling obliquely towards middle and ending below in horizontal line.
NECK. Necklace indicated by double incised line. No indication of swelling of trapezium.

TORSO. Little anatomical detail. Clavicles, lower boundary of thorax not marked. Broad groove indicates spinal furrow. Shoulder-blades shown as modelled shapes. No indication of erector spinae.

33 : Figs. 138-140

ATHENS, NATIONAL MUSEUM, no. 9. Once at Orchomenos.

Statue, from head to above knees.

Bluish, presumably Boeotian, marble.
Height 1.27 m.
In 1860 was in court of convent at Skripou near Orchomenos. Place of discovery not known. May have come from Ptoan Sanctuary.
Kastriotes, *Γλυπτά*, no. 9.
Conze and Michaelis, *Annali*, 1861, p. 79 f., pl. E, 1.
Deonna, no. 26, figs. 25-7.

GENERAL STRUCTURE. Plank-like and thick-set. Broad shoulders, short thorax. Head large in proportion. Highest protrusion of back, seen in profile, above that of chest. Vertebral column more or less straight. Anatomy indicated by ridges and grooves, but there are attempts at modelling roundness of form, for instance in rectus abdominis, flanks, and erector spinae.
HEAD. *Skull.* Forms pronounced arch, but is flat at back.
Ear. Placed high and vertical. Carved in one plane, with knob-shaped tragus shown as a separate protuberance. No indication of antitragus.
Eye. Almond-shaped. Carved in a flat, frontal plane and surrounded by shallow ridges indicating eyelids. No indication of recess at inner corner.
Nose. Mostly missing.
Mouth. Region of mouth carved in the round.
Chin. Strong and protruding.
Hair. Hangs down back, mass being divided vertically and horizontally into rectangular members, and terminating below in slightly curving line. Above forehead and temples large spiral locks arranged symmetrically to right and left. Fillet encircles head and crosses behind (no knot is indicated), with ends travelling obliquely down.
NECK. Sterno-mastoids shown by two grooves forming acute angle above sternum. Swelling of trapezium not indicated.
TORSO, FRONT. Clavicles indicated by sharp horizontal edge outlining plane of shoulder all along their course towards deltoid. Median line marked by shallow groove travelling from sternal notch to navel. Pectorals placed high. Nipples marked as round buttons placed far apart. Lower boundary of thorax indicated by grooves forming acute angle, with apex above nipples. Four transverse divisions of rectus abdominis above navel. Navel marked as round button. Slight protrusion at flanks indicates anterior part of iliac crest. Lower boundary of abdomen descends with straight sides towards genitals. Transition from abdominal region to flanks, where side and front planes meet, is outlined on either side by a curved edge, running from iliac crest to lower rib of thorax. Contour of waist forms inward curve.
TORSO, BACK. Spinal furrow marked by deep groove. Shoulder-blades indicated as separate planes outlined by grooves. Erector spinae shown in the round along its entire course.
ARM. Separated from body from below armpit to some distance below elbow. Elbow marked by curved ridge which, however, does not continue downward as it does in New York statue and Sounion fragment (cf. figs. 28, 46). Forearm, viewed from front, is turned forward in supine position, but palm of hand instead of being directed forward is twisted toward body.
Hand. Clenched, with thumb placed next to thigh. Thumb long and protrudes below other fingers.
LEG. Pronounced thigh. No indication of depression over great trochanter or of muscles on outer side of thigh.

34 : Figs. 141-143

THEBES, MUSEUM, no. 1. From the Ptoan Sanctuary.

Statue, from top of head to above right knee. Most of face missing, but back of head preserved. Feet and foot-plinth perhaps preserved (cf. no. 36). Back of right leg, from buttock to above knee, restored.

Bluish, presumably Boeotian, marble.
Height 1.42 m.
Found in Ptoan Sanctuary in 1903.
Mendel, *B.C.H.* XXXI, 1907, p. 191, no. 2, figs. 2-4 (reproduced in our figs. 141-143). Front part of left thigh and parts of left buttock added since Mendel's publication.
Karouzos, *'Οδηγός*, p. 12, no. 1.
Deonna, no. 42.

GENERAL STRUCTURE. Four-sided and angular, except for rectus abdominis, which is rounded. Greatest protrusion of back, seen in profile, higher than that of chest. Vertebral column straight.
HEAD. *Skull.* Flat behind, but bulges at top.
Ear. High and vertical. Divisions carved in one flat plane, with antihelix slightly more prominent than helix. Tragus forms excrescence of lobe. No antitragus.
Hair. Hangs down behind; mass divided horizontally and vertically into tresses of rectangular members. Each tress ends below in triangular member with apex pointing

downward. Plain fillet, without knot or loose ends, encircles hair. Spiral curls above temples.
NECK. Sterno-mastoids not indicated. No indication of swelling of trapezium.
TORSO, FRONT. Clavicles indicated by sharp horizontal edge outlining plane of shoulder all along their course towards deltoid (as in no. 33). Median line hardly indicated. Thorax carved in flat planes, its lower boundary marked by grooves forming an acute angle placed just below pectorals. Five transverse divisions of rectus abdominis indicated above navel by modelled forms. Navel shown as a rounded protrusion. Slight protrusion at flanks indicates anterior part of iliac crest. Lower boundary of abdomen descends with straight sides towards genitals.
TORSO, BACK. Deep groove marks spinal furrow. Shoulder-blades indicated by separate planes outlined by grooves. Erector spinae not indicated.
ARM. Attached to side along whole way, except for short distance at elbow. Upper arm short. Curved ridge above elbow. Lower end of ulna indicated by knob at wrist. Forearm, viewed from front, turned forward in supine position, but palm of hand, instead of being directed forward, is twisted towards body.
Hand. Clenched, with index finger next to thigh.
LEG. Depression over great trochanter not indicated.

35 (not illustrated)

THEBES, MUSEUM, no. 5. From the Ptoan Sanctuary.

Small torso, from pectorals to knees.

Island marble.
Height 50 cm.
Found in Ptoan Sanctuary, in 1903.
Mendel, *B.C.H.* 1907, p. 199, no. 6, fig. 10.
Karouzos, *'Οδηγός*, p. 12, no. 5.
Deonna, no. 46, figs. 54, 55.

GENERAL STRUCTURE. Seen in profile, greatest protrusion of back higher than that of chest. Vertebral column more or less straight.
TORSO, FRONT. Lower boundary of thorax not clearly distinguishable. No indication of divisions of rectus abdominis. Flanks only very slightly developed. Lower boundary of abdomen descends with straight sides towards genitals.
TORSO, BACK. Back rather well shaped, but only vertical groove for spinal furrow marked.
ARM. Only slightly separated from body at elbow. Forearm turned forward in supine position, whereas palm of hand is directed towards body.
LEG. No indication of depression over great trochanter. Vasti level.

36 : Fig. 148

THEBES, MUSEUM. From the Ptoan Sanctuary.

Foot-plinth with feet.

Island marble.
Length of plinth 45 cm.; length of foot 23 cm.
From Ptoan Sanctuary.
Deonna, no. 56, fig. 61 (who thought that it might belong to the kouros no. 34).

LEG. Malleoli level.
Foot. Metatarsal bones not indicated. Toes parallel, but small one slants slightly inward. Recede along one line, big toe projecting somewhat further than second toe. Big toe points forward; four smaller toes point downward, but not sharply.
FOOT-PLINTH. Shape of plinth follows more or less outlines of soles. Upper side uneven.

37 : Fig. 149

THEBES, MUSEUM. From the Ptoan Sanctuary.

Fragment of foot-plinth, with left foot and front part of right foot.

Boeotian marble.
Length of plinth 30 cm.; length of left foot 17 cm.
Found in Ptoan Sanctuary.
Deonna, no. 58, fig. 63.

FOOT. Metatarsal bones not indicated. In left foot toes curve gently downward, in right foot sharply so.
FOOT-PLINTH. Shape, where preserved, follows outlines of soles.

38 : Fig. 147

ATHENS, NATIONAL MUSEUM, no. 2325. From the Ptoan Sanctuary.

Foot-plinth with pair of feet, evidently of a kouros.

Marble.
Total length *c.*45 cm.; preserved height, with foot, *c.*29 cm.; height of plinth *c.*12 cm.
Found in Ptoan Sanctuary.
Kastriotes, *Γλυπτά*, no. 2325.
Deonna, no. 40.

LEG. Outer and inner malleolus of ankle level.
Foot. Metatarsal bones not indicated. Toes parallel and slope gently downward. Recede along one continuous line, big toe projecting further than second toe.
FOOT-PLINTH. Hexagonal. Not quite level at top.

39 : Figs. 151-153

LONDON, British Museum, B 474.

Statue, from head to left knee.

Coarse-grained white marble, with black stains or veins (Boeotian?).
Height 77 cm.
From Greece, probably from Boeotia. Acquired by British Museum in 1878.
Pryce, *Catalogue*, B 474, pp. 202 ff., pl. xlii.
Deonna, no. 25, figs. 22-4.

General Structure. Shape four-sided, but here and there attempts at rendering roundness of forms. Broad shoulders, narrow waist. Proportions more or less normal. Seen in profile, greatest protrusion of back higher than that of chest. Vertebral column fairly straight.
Head. Sides of face slope backward.
Skull. Flat at top and at back.
Ear. Placed vertically; left ear slightly higher than right. Carved in one flat plane. Tragus projects directly from lobe. No indications of antitragus.
Eye. Set obliquely. Incised line marks upper boundary of upper eyelid. No indication of recess at inner corner.
Nose. Fairly narrow. Nostril indicated on side by arched groove and below by narrow slit.
Mouth. Corners slope upward. Lower lip recedes slightly behind upper. No deep depression at corners of mouth. Groove outlines upper lip at corners.
Hair. Hangs down back in solid mass, which ends below in a practically horizontal line; divided vertically and horizontally into squares. Over forehead arranged in roll with vertical divisions. No fillet.
Neck. Sterno-mastoid muscles indicated by two shallow grooves which meet at sternum. No indication of swelling of trapezium.
Torso, front. Clavicles indicated by ridges, which travel upward in one curve and protrude all along their course until they reach top of shoulder. Median line marked by shallow groove which travels from bottom of sternum to a little above navel. It slants slightly on its downward course from (spectator's) right to left. Nipples far apart. Lower boundary of thorax indicated by grooves forming a right angle, with apex just under line of pectorals. No transverse divisions of rectus abdominis shown. Navel marked as small round button, surrounded by shallow circular groove. Slight protrusion at flanks indicates iliac crest, which continues like a girdle as a prominent ridge round flank, becoming shallower at back and disappearing at lower end of spinal furrow. Lower boundary of abdomen descends with straight sides towards genitals.
Torso, back. Broad, shallow depression marks spinal furrow. Shoulder-blades indicated by raised planes. No indication of erector spinae.
Arm. Both missing. Was attached to side along considerable distance.
Leg. Buttocks well developed. No indication of depression over great trochanter. Two grooves, travelling down outer side of thigh and meeting at acute angle, indicate thigh muscles. Vasti (preserved on left leg) level; upper boundary indicated by shallow depression.

Here too belongs the marble head, 10·2 cm. high, from Tanagra, now in BERLIN. (Blümel, *Kat.*, A 3).

40 : Figs. 154-156

PARIS, Louvre, no. MNB 767. From Actium.

Torso from neck to knees. Surface somewhat corroded. Modern hole at back (made presumably for fastening to wall) now filled with plaster. Some plaster additions at fractures of legs for mounting. As at present mounted leans a little too far back.[19]

Naxian marble.
Height 1 m.
Found at Actium, in Acarnania, in 1867 (by Monsieur Champoiseau, French consul at Janina). Probably from a sanctuary of Apollo, of which traces have been found.
Collignon, *Gazette archéologique*, xi, 1886, pp. 235 ff., pl. 29, left.
Louvre, *Catalogue sommaire*, 1922, p. 41, no. 688.
Buschor, *Fr. J.*, p. 43 f., figs. 45, 46.
Deonna, no. 1, fig. 1.

General Structure. Form still somewhat rectangular. Viewed in profile, greatest protrusion of back higher than that of chest. Upper portion of vertebral column more or less straight. Indication of anatomical detail by grooves and ridges survives, but there are attempts at modelling roundness of form.
Hair. Hangs down back in tresses of rectangular members, mass being divided vertically by deep grooves and horizontally by shallow grooves, and terminating below in practically horizontal line.
Neck. Grooves which indicate sterno-mastoids end in an acute angle at sternal notch. No indication of swelling of trapezium.
Torso, front. Clavicles indicated by modelled ridges protruding all along their course and placed more or less horizontally. Nipples indistinct. Lower boundary of thorax forms grooved, rounded arch, with apex well below pectorals. Median line marked by broad, shallow groove from this arch to navel. No divisions now seen

[19] An exact copy of this kouros appeared some time ago on the antiquity market and is now exhibited as a study piece in the Museum of Archaeology, Cambridge. For a similar example, cf. Blanco, Catalogo de la Escultura, Museo del Prado, no. 437E). Though ancient kouroi are all of the same type, none are exact duplicates (not even Kleobis and Biton).

of rectus abdominis. Navel indistinct. Protrusion at flanks indicating iliac crest continues like a girdle round flank, becoming shallower at back and disappearing at lower end of spinal furrow. Left flank placed slightly forward but at same height as right flank. Lower boundary of abdomen descends with short, straight sides towards genitals.

TORSO, BACK. Spinal furrow marked by shallow depression. Shoulder-blades indicated by raised planes, placed very far apart. No indication of erector spinae.

ARM. Joined to side along most of course. Upper arm short. Elbow outlined by curving ridge above upper end of ulna. Forearm, viewed from front, turned forward in supine position, but palm of hand, instead of being directed forward, is twisted towards body.

Hand. Clenched, with thumb placed next to thigh; marble left adhering between thumb and forefinger, and at back within bend of small finger.

LEG. No indication of depression over great trochanter. Pronounced thigh. Broad groove on outer side indicates thigh muscle. On right leg vastus internus descends lower than vastus externus, but on left leg vasti are about level.

41 : Figs. 144-146

OLYMPIA, MUSEUM. From Phigaleia.

Torso from neck to right knee. Broken in two at waist. Surface battered.

Marble, greyish and fairly fine grained.
Height 1.045 m.
Found at Phigaleia.
Hyde, *Olympic Victor Monuments*, pp. 327, 332 f., fig. 79.
Frazer, *Pausanias*, III, p. 40 f., IV, p. 391 f.
L. Budde, *Die attischen Kuroi* (Diss. 1939), p. 54, pl. 1.
Buschor, *Fr. J.*, p. 12 f., fig. 9.
Deonna, no. 79.

For inscription on chest, [π]εταλια Δ, cf. p. 77, and Hiller von Gaertringen, *I.G.* V,2, 424, who considered it not earlier than the fourth century B.C.

GENERAL STRUCTURE. Flat front and back. Seen in profile, greatest protrusion of back higher than that of chest. Vertebral column more or less straight.

HAIR. Falls in tresses down back and in front on either side of chest.

TORSO, FRONT. No indication of clavicles visible. Lower boundary of thorax placed abnormally high. Apparently three divisions of rectus abdominis above navel. No protrusion at flanks visible. Short groins. Pubes carved as stylized form in relief, with straight upper edge.

TORSO, BACK. Broad depression marks spinal furrow. Shoulder-blades indicated as raised planes. No indication of attachment of erector spinae.

ARM. Right upper arm was attached to side and slopes slightly backward; as there is no indication of attachment of hand on thigh, arm must have been bent and forearm brought forward. Same applies to left arm.

LEG. Left leg only slightly advanced. Buttocks developed. Depression over great trochanter not marked. Ridge on outer side of thigh. Vasti level.

42 : Figs. 157-159

DELPHI, MUSEUM, no. 2846. From Delphi.

Statuette, from head to above ankles. Left lower leg bent out of shape. Surface much weathered.

Bronze.
Height 15.5 cm.
Found at Delphi, in 1895, outside Sanctuary.
Perdrizet, *F.d.D.* V, p. 29, pl. 1, 6.

GENERAL STRUCTURE. Broad shoulders, large head, short neck. Seen in profile, greatest protrusion of back higher than that of chest. Vertebral column more or less straight.

HEAD. *Skull.* Fairly flat at top, somewhat rounded at back.

Ear. Large, and placed vertically. Was apparently carved in more than one plane.

Eye. Flat and set slightly obliquely. No recess at inner corner.

Mouth. Lips curve slightly upward.

Hair. Falls down back in mass divided horizontally by grooves; smooth on skull.

NECK. No indication of sterno-mastoids or of swelling of trapezium.

TORSO, FRONT. Clavicles indicated by sharp horizontal edge outlining plane of shoulder all along their course towards deltoid (as in no. 33). No median line discernible. Chest flat. Lower boundary of thorax marked by grooves forming acute angle below pectorals. No divisions of rectus abdominis. No protrusion at flanks. Lower boundary of abdomen descends towards genitals, with straight sides pointing sharply downward.

TORSO, BACK. Groove marks spinal furrow. Shoulder-blades indicated as raised planes. No indication of erector spinae.

ARM. Joined to side most of way, except for short distance above elbow. Forearm cursorily modelled.

Hand. Clenched, with thumb placed against thigh.

LEG. No indication of depression over great trochanter. Knees marked as rhomboids with vasti level on either side.

43 : Figs. 160-162

LONDON, BRITISH MUSEUM, 1905.6-10.1. From Trapezia (?).

Statuette, from head to plinth.

Bronze.
Height, with base, *c.* 7 cm.
Said to be from Trapezia (see p. 60, note 9).

GENERAL STRUCTURE. Back flat. Stands with feet level; left leg not advanced. Sloping shoulders; narrow waist. Head large in proportion; its height goes about $5\frac{1}{2}$ times into height of whole figure.
HEAD. *Skull.* Flat at top and back.
Ear. Consists of protruding helix ending in lobe. No tragus or antitragus marked.
Eye. Set horizontally. Iris protrudes. No recess at inner corner.
Mouth. Lips curve upward.
Hair. Falls down back in mass, which is divided horizontally and vertically into beaded tresses, with two tresses falling on each side of chest. No fillet.
NECK. Sterno-mastoids and swelling of trapezium not indicated.
TORSO, FRONT. No clavicles marked; only notch for sternum. No median line indicated. Pectorals outlined by curving grooves. Lower boundary of thorax marked by grooves which form acute angle, with apex well below pectorals, and continue to flanks. Divisions of rectus abdominis suggested by two horizontal incisions above navel. Navel is round button, surrounded by circular groove. Slight protrusion at flanks. Short groins.
TORSO, BACK. No spinal furrow or erector spinae marked. Shoulder-blades hidden by hair.
ARM. Forearm joined to side and turned towards body in semipronated position.
Hand. Clenched, with thumb next to thigh.
LEG. No indication of depression over great trochanter. Vasti not differentiated. Patella forms raised knob. Shin curves slightly inward. Malleoli not indicated.
Foot. Toes recede along continuous line, big toe being slightly longer than second toe, and small toe being practically parallel to others (in left foot; not clearly distinguishable in right foot).
FOOT-PLINTH. In one piece with statuette. Rectangular. Upper surface not quite level. Has two holes for fastening at opposite corners.

44 : Figs. 163-165

ATHENS, NATIONAL MUSEUM, no. 16503.

Statuette, from head to left foot. Restorations: The right leg, the left leg from below waist to above knee, the left arm from above elbow.

Terracotta.
Height, as restored 23.3 cm.; trunk with head 13.3 cm.; left leg as preserved 7.3 cm.
Found at Perachora, in the temenos of Hera limneia.
Jenkins in Payne, *Perachora*, pl. 91, no. 42a. The right leg there shown turned out to be a second left leg and so must have belonged to another, similar statuette (no. 16503a) ; height 5.6 cm.

GENERAL STRUCTURE. Short trunk, broad shoulders, short upper arms, developed legs, back flat. Anatomy summary. Not much detail given.
HEAD. *Skull.* Flat at back; somewhat rounded on top.
Ear. Flat; laid over hair.
Eye. Large, with curving lids.
Mouth. Mostly missing; lips do not meet at corners.
Chin. Protruding.
Hair. Falls down back in tresses, with three tresses brought forward to each shoulder. Tresses bandlike and divided horizontally into small rectangles. Over forehead and temples wavy tresses.
NECK. No indication of throat or sterno-mastoids.
TORSO. No indication of lower boundary of thorax, of pectorals, or of rectus abdominis. No protrusion at flanks. Navel incised as small circle.
ARM. Extended, with hand clenched.
LEG. Patella marked as round knob. Vasti and malleoli level.

45 : Figs. 166-168

BERLIN, STAATLICHE MUSEEN, no. 7976.

Statuette from head to feet. Lower left leg bent somewhat out of shape.

Bronze.
Height 18 cm.
From Dodona. Acquired by Staatliche Museen in 1887.
Neugebauer, *Katalog, Staatliche Museen, Berlin* I, no. 213, pl. 38.
Berlin *Führer*, Bronzen, p. 37, no. 7976.
Furtwängler, *Kleine Schriften*, II, p. 435.
Buschor, *Fr. J.*, pp. 40 ff.

GENERAL STRUCTURE. Flat front and back. Greatest protrusion of back, seen in profile, higher than that of chest. Vertebral column straight. Head rather large.
HEAD. *Skull.* Somewhat rounded at top, flat at back.
Ear. Large, flat, placed vertically.
Eye. Large; placed horizontally; both lids strongly curving; no indication of recess at inner corner. Irises were inlaid and are missing.
Mouth. Lips more or less horizontal.
Hair. Parted in middle and hangs down back, where it is tied two-thirds way down.
Chin. Prominent.
Neck. No indication of sterno-mastoids or of swelling of trazepium.

TORSO, FRONT. Clavicles protrude all the way to shoulders. Median line indicated by groove from sternal notch to navel. Lower boundary of thorax marked by arched groove well below pectorals. Slight protrusion at flanks marks anterior part of iliac crest. Three horizontal divisions of rectus abdominis above navel. Short groins.
TORSO, BACK. Groove marks spinal furrow. No indication of shoulder blades or of erector spinae.
ARM. Held away from body, and bent at elbow, right more sharply than left. Forearm turned towards body. Hands held attributes.
LEG. No indication of depression caused by great trochanter. No differentiation of vasti. Shin slightly curved. Malleoli level on right leg; on left leg inner malleolus is above outer, perhaps due to distortion of leg.
FOOT. Toes recede along continuous line, second toe being shorter than big toe.

46 : Figs. 169-171

DELPHI, MUSEUM, no. 7534.

Head and neck. Face battered. Piece missing on left side.

Island marble.
Height 22.8 cm.
Found at Trikorgon, near Naupaktos, in 1938.
Lerat, *Les Locriens de l'Ouest*, 1952, p. 157.
Daux, *B.C.H.* LXXX, 1956, p. 297, figs. 10-12.

GENERAL STRUCTURE. Forehead somewhat receding
Ear. Large and flat. Only frame marked, without interior divisions. Slants towards line of jaw. Tragus shown as excrescence from lobe. No antitragus.
Eye. Placed horizontally. Eyeball protrudes. Depression under lower lid.
Nose. Broad.
Mouth. Lips do not meet at corners.
Hair. On skull bandlike tresses travel obliquely downward to right and left from a central division as far as fillet, below which they become horizontal. Fillet encircling head outlines skull at back; ends cross at back, travelling obliquely down; no knot indicated. Over forehead and temples, instead of the usual spiral curls, is a broad diadem decorated with lotus buds and circles, arranged symmetrically to right and left from centre.
NECK. Sterno-mastoids marked by two incised grooves, with convex plane between indicating throat.

47 : Figs. 174-175

DELOS, MUSEUM, A 3997. From Delos.

Upper part of statue, from head to below pectorals.

Naxian marble.
Height 59 cm.
From the temenos of Apollo, Delos.
Deonna, no. 84, figs. 97-9.

GENERAL STRUCTURE. Seen in profile, highest protrusion of back higher than that of chest. Vertebral column straight.
HEAD. Face much weathered and details indistinct.
Skull. Flat at back.
Ear. Placed rather high. Large and flat.
Mouth. Lips curve upward.
Hair. Falls down back, with four strands brought over each shoulder hiding clavicles. Front strands divided horizontally and end in pointed members.
NECK. No indication of sternal notch or of sterno-mastoids.
TORSO, FRONT. Pectorals somewhat modelled.
TORSO, BACK. Battered. Little detail now discernible.
ARM. Lower part of right arm has been recently added.

48 : Figs. 176-177

DELOS, MUSEUM, 4045. From Delos.

Torso, from neck to above knees.

Island marble.
Height *c.*51.5 cm.
Found at Delos.
Deonna, no. 86.

GENERAL STRUCTURE. Similar to no. 47. Seen in profile, greatest protrusion of back higher than that of chest. Vertebral column straight.
HAIR. Mass falls down back and is divided vertically and horizontally into beaded tresses, ending in pointed members and forming a horizontal line. Three similar tresses fall down front on each side of chest.
TORSO, FRONT. Little anatomical detail visible. Pectorals somewhat modelled. No apparent protrusion of flanks. Lower boundary of abdomen descends with straight sides towards genitals.
TORSO, BACK. Broad groove marks spinal furrow.
LEG. Depression over great trochanter not indicated.

49 : Figs. 178-183

ATHENS, NATIONAL MUSEUM, no. 8. From Thera.

Statue, from head to right knee. Large piece of neck with an adjoining portion of hair restored; also small piece of right jaw along fracture. Some plaster additions at fractures of legs for mounting.

Island marble.
Height 1.24 m.
Found in 1836 at Thera, opposite rock tombs of Cape Exomyti; perhaps was tomb statue.

Schrader in Hiller von Gaertringen, *Thera*, III, p. 285, pls. 7, 12, 13, 14.
Kastriotes, *Γλυπτά*, no. 8.
Buschor, *Fr. J.*, pp. 67 ff., figs. 79, 80.
Deonna, no. 129.

GENERAL STRUCTURE. Flat front and back; sloping shoulders; neck tilted forward. Greatest protrusion of back, seen in profile, higher than that of chest. Vertebral column more or less straight.
HEAD. *Skull.* Slightly developed at back.
Ear. Placed high and slants towards line of jaw. Carved in one plane, with elongated tragus shown as separate protuberance. No indication of antitragus.
Eye. Almond-shaped; surrounded by grooves; narrow ridge models upper boundary of upper eyelid. Outer corner of eye placed higher than inner and lower lid curves elegantly upward. At inner corner groove indicates recess.
Nose. Narrow slits indicate nostrils.
Mouth. Triangular depression at corners of mouth. Sharp, short fold curves round upper lip. Corners slope upward.
Hair. Hangs down behind in massed beaded tresses, with pointed ends forming a curve. Over forehead and temples arranged in large spiral curls, symmetrically to right and left from centre. Fillet encircles head; has no hanging ends.
NECK. Mostly restored. No grooves for sterno-mastoids preserved. No indication of swelling of trapezium.
TORSO, FRONT. Clavicles only slightly indicated. Median line marked by groove running from sternum to navel, sloping slightly to right. Rounded, arched groove for lower boundary of thorax placed well below pectorals. No divisions of rectus abdominis discernible. Navel indicated by circular groove, with short, horizontal incision on each side. Slight protrusion at flanks indicates anterior part of iliac crest. Lower boundary of abdomen descends with straight sides sharply towards genitals.
TORSO, BACK. Broad groove indicates spinal furrow. No detailed muscular construction.
ARM. Joined to side except for small portion at elbow. Forearm, viewed from front, turned forward in supine position, but palm of hand, instead of being directed forward, is twisted towards body.
Hand. Clenched, with thumb next to thigh. Thumb short and carved in flat relief on hand. Joint above nail indicated by two incised curving lines.
LEG. No indication of depression over great trochanter. Broad furrow travels down outer side of thigh corresponding to ilio-tibial band.

50 : Figs. 172-173

COPENHAGEN, NY CARLSBERG GLYPTOTHEK, no. 2821.

Head.

Naxian marble.
Height 41 cm.
Said to have been found in Naxos.
V. H. Poulsen, *From the Collections of the Ny-Carlsberg Glyptotek*, II, 1938, pp. 65 ff.
Buschor, *Fr. J.*, pp. 61 ff., figs. 68-70.
F. Poulsen, *Catalogue*, no. 11 a.
Homann-Wedeking, *Anfänge*, p. 87 f., fig. 47.

GENERAL STRUCTURE. Four-sided.
HEAD. *Skull.* Top rounded, back flat.
Ear. Large, placed high and more or less vertically. Slight differentiation of planes. Slight thickening on antihelix suggests a tentative rendering of antitragus.
Eye. Placed horizontally; upper eyelid arched.
Mouth. Triangular depression at corners. Sharp, short fold curves round upper lip.
Nose. Was narrow at bridge and broad below.
Hair. Fell down back in mass, divided horizontally and vertically to form beaded tresses. Over forehead and temples large spiral curls—arranged in upward direction and symmetrically to right and left from centre—are laid on fillet; the latter is broad in front and at sides, but narrow at back, where it is tied in reef knot with ends hanging loosely down. For such decorated fillets cf. nos. 63, 64, 70, 72.

Here should belong the much weathered head from Melos, National Museum, ATHENS, no. 1586 (Deonna, no. 115; Kondoleon, *Ἐπιστημονικὴ ἐπετηρὶς τῆς φιλοσοφικῆς σχολῆς τοῦ Πανεπιστημίου Ἀθηνῶν*, 1957-8, pp. 220 ff.).

51 : Figs. 184-186

VATHY, MUSEUM. From Samos.

Statuette, from head to plinth.

Bronze.
Height 11 cm.
From the Heraion, Samos.
Buschor, *Alt. St.* I, p. 11, figs. 29, 31, 32.

GENERAL STRUCTURE. Broad shoulders, slim waist, heavy calves. Seen in profile, greatest protrusion of back higher than that of chest. Vertebral column more or less straight. Head large (height goes about $4\frac{1}{2}$ times into total).

HEAD. Receding forehead.
Skull. Somewhat rounded at top, flat behind.
Ear. Large and laid against hair.
Eye. Horizontal. No recess at inner corner.
Mouth. More or less straight.
Hair. Falls behind in mass, which is divided horizontally into grooves and ridges, and ends below in slightly curving line; two tresses are brought to front on either side.
TORSO, FRONT. Little anatomical detail. Median line marked from sternal notch to navel. Slight protrusion at flanks.
TORSO, BACK. No anatomical detail marked.
ARM. Held to side, with thumb touching thigh. Forearm semi-pronated, that is, turned towards body.
LEG. Ends of vasti level. Malleoli level.
Foot. Toes parallel and recede along one continuous line, big toe projecting further than second toe.
FOOT-PLINTH. Rectangular and in one piece with statuette.

52 : Figs. 187-189

VATHY, MUSEUM. From Samos.

Statuette, from head to above right ankle.

Bronze.
Height 19 cm.
From the Heraion, Samos.
Buschor, *Alt. St.* I, p. 13, figs. 35, 37, 38.

GENERAL STRUCTURE. Viewed in profile, greatest protrusion of back higher than that of chest. Vertebral column forms slight curve.
HEAD. Receding forehead.
Skull. Somewhat rounded at top, flat behind.
Ear. Placed high and slopes backward; laid against hair.
Eye. Large.
Mouth. Lips slope upward.
Hair. Falls on back in mass divided horizontally; ends below in straight line. Fillet across forehead not continued behind.
NECK. No indication of sterno-mastoids or of swelling of trapezium.
TORSO, FRONT. Grooves mark clavicles, travelling upward. Median line not indicated. Lower boundary of thorax not clearly marked. No divisions of rectus abdominis. Flanks only slightly developed. Lower boundary of abdomen descends towards genitals with straight sides, sloping sharply downward.
TORSO, BACK. Upper part of back covered by hair; little anatomical construction.
ARM. Right arm slightly bent at elbow, left arm sharply.
LEG. No hollow to show depression over great trochanter. Lower ends of vasti level.

53 : Figs. 190-192

BERLIN, STAATLICHE MUSEEN, no. 10556. From Crete.

Statuette, from head to plinth.

Bronze.
Height 17.3 cm.
Said to be from Crete.
Neugebauer, *Katalog, Staatliche Museen, Berlin*, I, no. 159, pl. 20.

GENERAL STRUCTURE. Viewed in profile, greatest protrusion of back higher than that of chest. Vertebral column more or less straight.
HEAD. *Skull.* Somewhat rounded at top.
Ear. Flat. Laid on hair.
Eye. Large and protruding.
Mouth. Horizontal.
Nose. Large.
Hair. Falls down back and on shoulders in triangular mass, divided into vertical tresses by incised lines. Groove delineates back of skull, as if by fillet. In front, mass divided horizontally, in 'Daedalid' fashion.
TORSO. Anatomy generalized. Little detail indicated. No protrusion at flanks. Short groins. Small buttocks. Nipples, navel, and lower boundary of thorax incised; latter placed immediately below pectorals.
ARMS. Lowered and hands attached to sides of body. Forearm turned inward in semi-pronated position. Hands clenched and perforated for holding of objects.
LEGS. Anatomy generalized.
PLINTH. Quadrangular. Two small holes for attachment to a base (in front of right foot and behind left).

54 : Figs. 193-195

LENINGRAD, HERMITAGE.

Statuette. At the top of the head is a hole for attachment. Surface apparently worn.

Bronze.
Height 13 cm.
Formerly in the Pourtalès Collection.
Catalogue de la vente Pourtalès-Gorgier, 6 février, 1865, p. 110, no. 546.
Panofka, *Antiques du cabinet Pourtalès*, pp. 42 ff., pl. XIII.
Deonna, p. 265, no. 64.
I.G. IV. 565.
Roberts, *Greek Epigraphy*, part I, p. 110, no. 74.

Inscribed on three sides of foot-plinth in Argive letters (note form of λ): *Πολυκρατες* | *ἀνεθε* | *κε*, 'Polykrates dedicated (it).' The style of the statuette is earlier than the time of the tyrant Polykrates. Polykrates is of course quite a common name and occurs frequently, for instance, in inscriptions from the Argolid, see index of *I.G.* IV, p. 395.

General Structure. Sloping shoulders; rounded forms; large head. Viewed in profile, greatest protrusion of back higher than that of chest. Vertebral column forms a slight curve.
Head. *Skull.* Flat at top and back.
Ear. Flat.
Eye. Slopes upward.
Mouth. Horizontal.
Hair. Falls down back in mass divided into stylized tresses, which are indicated by incised lines and dots; near bottom, hair is tied by a fillet and another fillet encircles head; at top of head hair left plain.
Neck. No sterno-mastoids discernible on photograph. No indication of swelling of trapezium.
Torso, front. Few anatomical details discernible. Lower boundary of thorax indicated by incised arch. No transverse divisions of rectus abdominis marked above navel. Navel indicated by small circular depression. No protrusion at flanks. Lower boundary of abdomen descends with straight sides towards genitals. Pubes marked by incised triangle, with straight upper edge.
Torso, back. Spinal furrow marked by groove. Shoulder-blades not separately indicated. No indication of erector spinae.
Arm. Held against body and separated from it only for small distance at elbow. Forearm appears to be semi-pronated.
Hand. Clenched.
Leg. Depression over great trochanter not indicated. Knee marked as incised rhomboid with no differentiation of vasti. Shin slopes only slightly inward. Outer malleolus marked as an incised semicircle.
Foot. Toes recede along one curve, big toe projecting further than second toe. Toes more or less parallel.
Foot-plinth. Rectangular and in one piece with statuette.

55 : Figs. 196-197

PARIS, Cabinet des Médailles. From near Miletos (?).

Statuette, from head to above left ankle.

Bronze.
Height 16 cm.
Said to have been found near Miletos (Scala Nova). Gift of M. Clerget, 1843.
Babelon and Blanchet, *Catalogue des bronzes antiques de la Bibliothèque Nationale*, no. 96.
Langlotz, *Bildhauerschulen*, pl. 59, 1.

General Structure. Rounded forms, but some still indicated by incisions. Sloping shoulders. Flat back; its greatest protrusion seen in profile higher than that of chest.
Head. *Skull.* Flat at top and back.
Ear. In about correct position, but slopes backward. No details discernible.
Eye. Outline and iris incised. Slopes upward.
Hair. Falls down back in mass forming horizontal line below; on it are incised wavy lines flowing downward. Above forehead and temples two masses of hair meet in centre, forming tiara-like frame.
Neck. No indication of sterno-mastoids or of bulge of trapezium.
Torso, front. Little anatomical detail. Clavicles not indicated. Nipples shown as incised circle. Lower boundary of thorax not marked. No transverse divisions of rectus abdominis above navel. Navel marked as incised circle. Protrusion at flanks hidden by arms. Lower boundary of abdomen descends towards genitals with short, straight lines.
Torso, back. Groove marks spinal furrow. Shoulder-blades and erector spinae not indicated.
Arm. Attached to side as far as elbow; bent at elbow and held forward.
Leg. Knee incised. Vasti not differentiated. Shin perpendicular.

56 : Figs. 200-201

LONDON, British Museum, B 320. From Knidos.

Statuette, from head to knees.

Yellowish limestone.
Height 17 cm.
From Knidos. Acquired by British Museum in 1893.
Pryce, *Catalogue*, B 320, p. 150 f., fig. 189.

General Structure. Thick-set, with rounded forms. Anatomical structure generalized. Right leg advanced instead of left one. Head turns slightly to right; otherwise frontal. Greatest protrusion of back, seen in profile, hidden by headdress. Vertebral column straight. Upper legs very short.
Head. *Skull.* Developed at top but not at back.
Ear. Slants slightly towards line of jaw; flat, but lobe protrudes; placed high; large in proportion. No antitragus.
Eye. Long, narrow, and slightly oblique. No recess at inner corner.
Nose. Rather small; red traces inside nostrils.
Mouth. Small. Lips retain red traces.
Chin. Prominent.
Hair. Resembles Egyptian headdress, without indication of individual strands. Fillet encircles forehead and is tied behind in knot, with short, hanging ends.

NECK. No indication of sterno-mastoids or of swelling of trapezium. Lower boundary of neck marked by groove.
TORSO, FRONT. Rounded, sloping shoulders. Clavicles not indicated. Lower boundary of pectorals marked, but not lower boundary of thorax or median line. No divisions of rectus abdominis above navel. No protrusion at flanks. Slightly protruding abdomen; lower boundary rounded.
TORSO, BACK. No anatomical details of back marked, not even spinal furrow.
ARM. Short; joined to body along entire length. Forearm in supine position (as indicated by transverse groove at bend of arm).
Hand. Palm clenched, twisted towards body. Thumb disproportionately large and placed next to thigh.
LEG. Short thigh. Ends of vasti level.

57 : Fig. 150

LONDON, BRITISH MUSEUM, B 321. From Knidos.

Foot-plinth and feet, broken from a statuette. Right foot very slightly drawn back. The feet cannot, therefore. belong to the statuette no. 56,[20] where the right leg is advanced; moreover the feet are too large for the figure.

Grey limestone.
Height *c.*5 cm. Length of left foot *c.*6 cm.
From Knidos. Acquired by British Museum in 1893.
Pryce, *Catalogue*, B 321, p. 151, fig. 190.

Inscribed (on upper surface of plinth and along left edge) in archaic Melian alphabet: *Εὔαρχος με ἀνεθ|ηκε τοισι Διοσ|κοροισιν*, 'Euarchos dedicated me to the Dioskouroi.' Traces of red colour in letters.
LEG. Malleoli level.
Foot. Toes parallel, including little one. Recede along continuous curve, big toe projecting further than others; latter point downward, but not sharply.
FOOT-PLINTH. Irregularly rounded. Upper surface uneven; is highest in middle and slopes towards edge.

58 : Figs. 198-199

LEIPZIG, UNIVERSITY MUSEUM.

Statuette, from head to above knees. Traces of red colour on lips, inside nostrils, on lobes of ears, across forehead (for fillet); perhaps traces of black on hair and left eyebrow (cf. Rumpf, loc. cit.).

White limestone.
Height 33.5 cm.
Purchased in Italy. Provenance not known. Gift of E. P. Warren, 1908.
Rumpf, in *Antike Plastik, Walther Amelung zum 60ten Geburtstag*, pp. 217 ff., figs. 1-3.

GENERAL STRUCTURE. Greatest protrusion of back, seen in profile, higher than that of chest. Rounded, sloping shoulders. Vertebral column straight. Abdomen slightly protruding.
HEAD. *Skull.* Flat at back.
Ear. Large and vertical. Carved in more than one plane.
Eye. Details not clear.
Mouth. Details of mouth not clear.
Hair. Resembles an Egyptian headdress; parted in middle, with grooves running vertically down back to indicate individual tresses.
NECK. Groove separates planes of neck and chest. No indication of sterno-mastoids or of swelling of trapezium.
TORSO, FRONT. Little anatomical detail. Little, if any, protrusion at flanks. Abdomen protrudes slightly; its lower boundary descends with short sides towards genitals.
TORSO, BACK. Broad, shallow groove for spinal furrow. Little muscular construction.
ARM. Forearm in supine position.
Hand. Twisted towards body and clenched. Thumb laid against thigh.
LEG. No indication of depression over great trochanter.

59 : Fig. 206

LONDON, BRITISH MUSEUM, B 442. From Naukratis.

Statuette, from neck to above knees. White stains.

Alabaster.
Height 15.2 cm.
Found in temenos of Aphrodite, Naukratis, in 1886.
Gardner, *Naukratis*, II, pl. XIV, 13.
Pryce, *Catalogue*, B 442, p. 186 f., pl. XI.

GENERAL STRUCTURE. Rounded forms, sloping shoulders. Flat back.
HAIR. Falls down back in solid mass ending in horizontal line; three tresses descend to chest on either side.
TORSO, FRONT. Little anatomical detail. No protrusion at flanks. Line of pectorals marked, but not lower boundary of thorax. Nipples and navel indicated.
TORSO, BACK. Depression marks spinal furrow. No indication of shoulder-blades or of erector spinae.
ARM. Adheres to body most of way; right is bent at elbow with hand brought to front; left lowered with forearm in supine position and hand twisted towards body.

[20] Cf. Pryce, *Catalogue*, B 321, p. 151, note.

60 : Fig. 207

LONDON, BRITISH MUSEUM, B 441. From Naukratis.

Statuette, from below neck to above knees. Part of right arm, at elbow, missing.

Alabaster.
Height 12 cm.
From the temenos of Apollo, Naukratis; excavated 1884.
Petrie, *Naukratis*, I, pl. I, 3.
Pryce, *Catalogue*, B 441, p. 185 f., fig. 223.

GENERAL STRUCTURE. Rounded forms, sloping shoulders. Flat back. Vertebral column straight.
HAIR. Falls down back in mass, ending below in zigzag line.
TORSO, FRONT. Anatomy generalized. Line of pectorals marked, but not lower boundary of thorax. Nipples and median line not indicated. No divisions marked of rectus abdominis. Navel formed by depression with knob in centre. No protrusion at flanks. Lower boundary of abdomen descends with short, straight sides towards genitals.
TORSO, BACK. Groove marks spinal furrow. No indication of shoulder-blades or erector spinae.
ARM. Adheres to body most of way. Right is bent at elbow, with forearm laid on chest; left is lowered, with forearm turned forward in supine position (as shown by transverse groove at bent of arm), whereas palm of hand is twisted towards body.
Hand. Clenched. Long thumb.
LEG. Small buttocks. No indication of depression over great trochanter.

61 : Figs. 204-205

CAIRO, MUSEUM, no. 27426. From Naukratis.

Statuette, from below neck to above knees.

Alabaster.
Height 15.2 cm.
From Naukratis.
Edgar, *Catalogue du Musée de Caire, Greek Sculpture*, pp. v, 1, no. 27426, pl. I.
Deonna, no. 143.

GENERAL STRUCTURE. Forms slightly more rounded than in no. 28. Highest protrusion of back, seen in profile, higher than that of chest. Vertebral column straight.
TORSO. Anatomy generalized. No protrusion at flanks. Abdomen protrudes slightly; its lower boundary descends with short, straight sides towards genitals.
ARM. Adheres to side along whole way, except for smallish bit from below armpit to elbow.
Hand. Clenched.

62 : Figs. 202-203

OXFORD, ASHMOLEAN MUSEUM, no. 1886-744.

Statuette, from head to footplinth.

Pale greyish terracotta, low fired.
Height *c*.15 cm.
From Taranto.
A. J. Evans, *J.H.S.* VII, 1886, p. 25, fig. 3, p. 27, no. 8.
Winter, *Die Typen figürlicher Terrakotten*, I, p. 177, no. 4.

GENERAL STRUCTURE. Large head; goes about 3½ times into body. Flat at back; made from mould.
HEAD. *Ear*. Placed low. Modelled in different planes; no tragus or antitragus indicated.
Eye. Set obliquely downward. Large in proportion. No recess at inner corner.
Mouth. Lips horizontal; do not meet at corners.
Hair. Arranged in spiral curls over forehead and temples; falls down back in undifferentiated mass; two beaded tresses brought down in front over each shoulder, reaching to waist.
NECK. Two deep grooves indicate sterno-mastoids.
TORSO, FRONT. Clavicles marked by ridges travelling upward. Lower boundary of thorax marked by pointed arch. Slight protrusion at flanks. Small depression indicates navel. Lower boundary of abdomen descends with straight sides to genitals.
ARM. Held against body entire way, with palm of hand open and laid on thigh. Deltoid and biceps developed.
LEG. Vasti level. Patella rectangular. Shin vertical.
FOOT. Large in proportion. Toes parallel, except little one, which curves slightly inward.
FOOT-PLINTH. Rectangular.

Here too, or in the Sounion group, should belong the limestone statuette, from below neck to knees, from Naukratis, in the Ashmolean Museum, OXFORD (Hogarth *B.S.A.* V, 1898-9, pl. XIV, 7; Deonna, no. 153); and perhaps late in this group the curious little terracotta figure (13.5 cm. high as preserved) given by H. Seyrig to the LOUVRE (Mollard-Besques, *Revue des Arts*, 1956, pp. 250 ff.).

VII. THE TENEA-VOLOMANDRA GROUP
(*c.* 575-550 B.C.)

General Survey and Historical Background

ATTICA. The second quarter of the sixth century appears to have been one of remarkable activity and achievement, especially in Attica. It produced not only a number of fine kouroi, but also a host of other masterpieces—the Berlin Standing Kore, the Moschophoros, the Diskophoros Relief, the Rampin Horseman, the Bluebeard Pediment. Athenian pottery was conquering the world market, and magnificent Attic pots, like the François vase, were being made for far-away Etruria.

Of the kouroi from Attica assignable to this period only one—that found at Volomandra (Kalyvia)—is well preserved; of several others only fragments remain and we cannot even be sure in all cases that they were male statues; one (no. 66) consists of a head, hand, and part of a leg, all in Pentelic marble—a rare material for sculpture at this early time (cf. p. 7).

It is difficult not to connect this flourishing period with historical events. Though the revolutionary reforms of Solon had caused widespread discontent, they had laid the foundation of a prosperous state. They were followed by an era of increase in production, trade, and foreign intercourse. And so the arts again flourished.

CORINTH. Tenea, the modern Athikia, is seven miles distant from Corinth. The statue, which was found there in 1846 in a cemetery (no. 73), may be a Corinthian product.[1] It is one of the finest kouroi extant, and fortunately almost complete. The Greek feeling for life and movement finds here an early expression. Though the derivation of the type from the Orient is still apparent, the limbs and joints have a new elasticity; in an extraordinary way the figure combines a monumental quality with youthful vigour.

Corinth at this time was one of the foremost cities of Greece. If the dating of Periander about 625-585 is correct (cf. p. 33), the statue may date comparatively soon after his death, when an oligarchy had seized the power. That the second quarter of the sixth century was still a period of wealth and power in Corinth is indicated by the widespread popularity of Late Corinthian pottery (*c.*575-550 B.C.) over the whole ancient world. The kouros of Tenea stands as a distinguished witness of Corinthian appreciation of sculpture at that time.

As several authorities have pointed out (e.g. Furtwängler and Langlotz, locc. citt.) the bronze statuette in Boston (no. 76), probably from Olympia, is stylistically related to the Tenea kouros.

ACTIUM. Perhaps also to be connected with Corinthian art is the second kouros from Actium (no. 74), for, as we saw, that territory was colonized by Corinthians (cf. p. 60). Like its predecessor (no. 40) it is a vigorous, finely modelled work.

BOEOTIA. The continued importance of Boeotia at this time is suggested by the head of a kouros (no. 75) from the Ptoan Sanctuary, and by three important kouroi (nos. 94-96) which we have placed with the Melos group, but which really are transitional between the Volomandra and Melos periods.

[1] Cf. Payne, *Necrocorinthia*, pp. 233, 237.

UNKNOWN PROVENANCE. Our knowledge of this period has recently been enlarged by a splendid kouros (no. 70), which was formerly in the possession of Signor Milani, one-time director of the Archaeological Museum in Florence. It is a typical product—full of life and yet retaining the old monumental quality. The accentuation of the muscles indicates the prevalent interest in construction.

SAMOS. To judge from the results of excavations, there was great artistic activity in Samos at this time. A lower right leg and part of a left foot (nos. 78, 79), both perhaps from a colossus three times life size, belong to this period. Of another kouros, which formed part of a group of three, only the feet on the hexagonal foot-plinth have been preserved (no. 80). A statue dedicated to Apollo by Leukios (no. 77) is a rather elegant product, in good condition but headless; though in all other respects it tallies with other examples of this group, the greatest protrusion of its back, seen in profile, is level with, not higher than that of the chest, as is the case in two statuettes from Naukratis (nos. 84, 85). We have here early instances of a realization of the shape of the thorax, which became current only in the next period. And it is noteworthy that all three figures are Eastern.

We may relate to these Samian youths several female figures found in the Heraion—the famous figure in the Louvre dedicated to Hera by Cheramyes,[2] and the group by the sculptor Geneleos dedicated to Hera by . . . oche.[3] The similarity of the side views of the hands of Philippe[4] and of the Leukios statue (no. 77) is noteworthy.

What is the historical background of these statues? Again our records are scanty. There is some evidence of early tyrannies in Samos about 600 or later, but they are doubtful.[5] The rich landowners, the Geomoroi, and enterprising merchants seem to have wielded their power until early in the second half of the century, when Polykrates became tyrant. The poet Asios, who may have lived about this time, gives us a graphic description of Samians as they went to the Heraion, 'their snowy chitons sweeping the ground,' 'their flowing hair bound with gold', 'on their arms finely wrought bracelets'.[6] This picture of wealth and luxury is borne out by the statues we have mentioned. Their distinction, their delicate workmanship, the enterprise and technical knowledge implied by the colossus three times life size and the life-size group of five standing, seated, and reclining figures are eloquent testimony of the pre-eminence of Samos. She was clearly a leader in the Ionian world.

NAUKRATIS. Finally, several alabaster statuettes from Egypt (nos. 82-85) probably belong here, notably the Golenischeff figure in Moscow (no. 82). They are more rounded in structure than the foregoing examples (nos. 59-61). By this time Amasis, the philhellenic king, had come to the throne (569-526 B.C.); cf. p. 37.

Absolute Chronology

An important landmark for the absolute dating of this group is perhaps provided by the observation[7] that the dedication by Rhombos belongs to about the same time as a decree which

[2] Buschor, *Alt. St.*, figs. 86-9, and in *Schweitzer Festschrift*, pp. 96 f. Note the downward curving toes.
[3] Buschor, *Alt. St.* I, figs. 90-95, 99-101, and in *Schweitzer Festschrift*, pp. 95 f.
[4] Ibid. fig. 95.
[5] Cf. P. N. Ure, *Origin of Tyranny*, p. 69, note 5.
[6] In Athenaios XII.525e. f.
[7] Raubitschek, *Öst. Jahr.* XXXI, 1938, Beiblatt, col. 33 f.

may refer to the Panathenaia dated in 566 B.C.[8] As Rhombos' Moschophoros belongs stylistically early in this group, we may—if the decree has been properly interpreted—take 570 as an approximate upper limit for the group.

Another landmark would have been supplied by the statue formerly at Phigaleia, now at Olympia (no. 41), if—as some thought[9]—it could be identified with the statue of Arrhichion, the pankratiast who won three victories in the pankration, Olympiads 52-4 (572-564 B.C.). For that statue was described by Pausanias (VIII.40.1) as 'archaic, especially in its attitude, with feet not much separated and arms hanging down by the side as far as the buttocks', that is, as being of the kouros type, and as 'having an inscription ... which had disappeared (*ἠφάνιστο*)[10] in the course of time'; and both these requirements at first glance seem to be met by the statue at Phigaleia, since it is a kouros and has an inscription across the chest.[11] But unfortunately there are several stumbling-blocks. The inscription on the Phigaleia statue is still surprisingly clear, and could not therefore have 'disappeared' almost 2,000 years ago. The chief argument, therefore, for the connection between the Phigaleia statue and Arrhichion loses its force; for there must have been many kouroi at Phigaleia, and there is no reason to think that the one that happens to have been found is the one which Pausanias saw. Furthermore, the Phigaleia kouros is stylistically earlier than the time of Arrhichion; it belongs to the Orchomenos-Thera rather than the Volomandra group.

As in the two earlier groups,[12] the little heads in the round which sometimes occur on Corinthian pottery supply a useful comparison, however limited in scope. We may note a certain degree of resemblance between late Corinthian heads, for instance those on a pyxis in St. Louis[13] and the kouros from Tenea (no. 73). They have the same wide-awake, rather intense look, accentuated features, and hair arranged in small scallops round the forehead. If the dates *c.*575-550 B.C. assigned to Late Corinthian pottery are correct, the placing of the Tenea kouros and its contemporaries in this period would be further substantiated.

The terracotta Kneeling Boy from the Agora[14] was found in a well in a fill which contained no red-figured pottery, only black-figure of the third quarter of the sixth century, including 'little-master' lip-cups and band-cups of about 540 B.C. As its surface is fairly fresh, it was probably not made very long before it was broken and thrown into the well—presumably not more than ten or fifteen years. If we analyse its anatomical structure—as far as its broken condition allows—we can make the following observations: the skull is domed at the top but flat at the back; the ear is modelled in more than one plane, but no antitragus is indicated; the eye is large, flat, almond-shaped,

[8] See p. 78, note 27.

[9] Frazer, *Pausanias*, IV, pp. 391-2, III, pp. 40-41; Hyde, *Olympic Victor Monuments*, p. 333.

[10] '*ἀφανίζω* normally refers to complete disappearance; see passages cited in Liddell and Scott. The object which has disappeared may be (1) *in situ* but hidden by the obtrusion of some other object, (2) removed to another place, or (3) destroyed (e.g. Xenophon, *Anabasis*, III.2.11), gone without leaving a trace (e.g. Herodotos III.126; Thucydides IV.80.4; Menander, *Epitrep.* 208 ff.; Euripides, *Phoen.* 1041 f.). Had the inscription been partly effaced Pausanias would presumably have used some such phrase as "*ἀμυδρὰ γράμματα*"; cf. Thucydides VI. 54.6-7. *ὑπὸ τοῦ χρόνου* refers not necessarily to attrition, but to the many accidents and actions that may occur in a long period of time' (M. J. Milne). For the form of the name see p. 1.

[11] Hiller von Gaertringen *I.G.* V,2,424 read *ΕΤΛΛΙΛΔ* = [*π*]*ετάλια Δ'* 'ten leaves', and considered the letters to be of the fourth century B.C. or later. Some have thought them perhaps modern (Kourouniotes, in Hyde, op. cit. p. 333, note 1, and A. W. Parsons, in a letter to Alan Wace: 'The letters on the chest are both meaningless and modern.').

[12] Cf. pp. 38, 61 f.

[13] Cf. Payne, *Necrocorinthia*, pl. 35, nos. 1, 4. Payne, op. cit. p. 237, related the Tenea kouros to the heads of the late Middle Corinthian pyxis 73.10-12.1 in the British Museum (cf. his plate XLVIII, 12, 15), dated by him *c.*580-570, but saw that the kouros must be later than the heads.

[14] Vanderpool, *Hesperia*, VI, 1937, p. 434, pl. X, figs. 1-7, and VII, 1938, p. 394, fig. 30.

and set obliquely; the upper eyelid is separated from the brow by a broad, well-defined groove; the lips do not meet at the corners; the construction of the neck is generalized; there is no indication of the swelling of the trapezium on the outline of the shoulder; the clavicles are represented as flat, straight ridges; the lower boundary of the thorax has the shape of a pointed arch; there are three transverse divisions above the navel in the rectus abdominis; the swelling of the external oblique over the iliac crest is not developed, but a protrusion at the flanks marks the anterior spine of the iliac crest. We shall find kouroi corresponding to this anatomical structure among the late members of the Tenea-Volomandra group, for instance Actium 2 (no. 74). We thereby obtain a tentative date round the middle of the sixth century for the lower limit of that group.

The resemblance between the figures on the François vase by Kleitias[15] and the Moschophoros[16] has often been remarked; notably in the rendering of the himation with straight inner and curved outer edges.[17] It has also been pointed out that the inscriptions on the two monuments are similar and that both resemble that of a decree which may refer to the Panathenaia, dated in 566.[18] The Kleitias vase has been dated—independently of the sculpture—in the second quarter of the sixth century.[19] Since the Moschophoros shows the same anatomical development as the early members of our Tenea-Volomandra group, we obtain another corroboration of the dating of our group.

The figures on the Burgon[20] and Halle[21] vases—the earliest extant fairly well-preserved Panathenaic amphorae—may be dated round 566,[22] the year of the archon Hippokleides.[23] Rumpf[24] and Ashmole[25] recently reminded us that the Burgon vase *may* be earlier, for the Panathenaia was a very old festival,[26] which, we are told, was merely enlarged in 566 to comprise gymnastic contests;[27] and the Burgon amphora has a chariot race. On the other hand, the Panathenaic amphora in Halle has runners and so cannot date before 566, and it is of the same general type as the Burgon one, perhaps slightly later. We can therefore hardly move up the Burgon amphora many years. It has also been pointed out that the inscription on the Burgon amphora resembles that of the decree which may refer to the Panathenaia.[28] We therefore obtain a date in the decade 570-560 for the thick-set Athena and charioteer on the Burgon amphora. Their stockiness and broad arms relate them to the Moschophoros, which retains something of the heavy proportions of the Orchomenos group, rather than

[15] Furtwängler and Reichhold, *Griechische Vasenmalerei*, I, pls. I-III, XI-XIII.

[16] Payne and Young, *Acropolis*, pls. 2-4; Schuchhardt in Schrader, *Die archaischen Marmorbildwerke der Akropolis*, p. 278, no. 409, pls. 153-4.

[17] Payne and Young, *Acropolis*, p. 3, note 1.

[18] Raubitschek, loc. cit.

[19] Payne, *Necrocorinthia*, p. 345 ('early in the sixties'). Langlotz in Schrader, *Die archaischen Marmorbildwerke der Akropolis*, p. 16 ('um 570'). Beazley, *Development*, p. 26 ('about 570').

[20] British Museum B 130; *C.V.* British Museum, fasc. I, III H e. pl. 1, 1a-b; *Mon. dell' Inst.* x, pl. 48, i, k; Brauchitsch, *Die Panathenäischen Preisamphoren*, pp. 6 ff.; Smets, 'Groupes chronologiques des amphores panathénaïques inscrites,' *L'Antiquité classique* v, 1936, p. 87; Beazley, *Development*, p. 89 f., and *A.B.V.*, pp. 89, 120.

[21] Langlotz, *Zeitbestimmung*, p. 9, pl. 1, 1.

[22] Brauchitsch, op. cit. p. 79 (*c.*560); Langlotz, op. cit. p. 9 (*c.*566).

[23] Pherekydes, *Frgt.* 2, Jacoby.

[24] *Sakonides*, p. 21, note 51.

[25] *Transactions of the International Numismatic Congress*, London, 30 June-6 July 1936, p. 21, note 2.

[26] Cf. references collected by Michaelis, *Parthenon*, p. 318.

[27] Eusebios, *Chron. Ol.* 53, 3. 'We must remember, however, that this statement may be in origin merely an ancient theory, the purpose of which was to reconcile the tradition that the Panathenaia were founded by Erichthonios with the historical fact of the founding in 566' (M. J. Milne).

[28] Raubitschek, loc. cit.

to the Tenea and Volomandra kouroi, which are slender and elongated. The latter should then be late members of our group, and may be dated perhaps 560-550 B.C.

It has been suggested that the Volomandra kouros may be connected with an inscription which has been identified as a signature of Aristion of Paros and which has been dated not earlier than 555 B.C. But the evidence that the inscription belongs to the statue consists merely of a report that the two were found in the same cemetery; and of the name of 'Aristion of Paros' only the final sigma (of *Πάριος*) is preserved—though the hand that carved the inscription resembles that of a signature of Aristion.[29] The upper limit of the date proposed—555—tallies, however, fairly well with the rest of the archaeological evidence. For since the Volomandra kouros is distinctly later than the Moschophoros and the latter may perhaps be dated 570-560, the former could be assigned to 560-550.

Anatomical Analysis

This period marks a great development. The artist is more alive than before to correct anatomical construction. His figures become more rounded, his forms more modelled; and so intent is he on the rendering of the individual bones and muscles that he tends to emphasize them. But the feeling for design, inherited from the past, is still strong. The kouros from Tenea (no. 73) is, like the earlier kouros in New York (no. 1), a masterpiece of correlation; but instead of linear patterns, volumes are co-ordinated. The shoulders, pectorals, flanks, thighs, arms, form beautifully contrasting shapes; so do the knee, the curving shin, the articulated feet; while the head, with its undulating mass of hair and its scalloped edge along temples and forehead, makes an effective crowning feature.

STRUCTURE IN GENERAL. Greatest protrusion of back, seen in profile, higher than that of chest. (For exceptions cf. nos. 77, 84, 85). Vertebral column assumes slight curve, but stance still stiff.

HEAD. *Skull.* More domed than before, but back mostly undeveloped.

Ear. Sometimes placed lower than before (cf. no. 73), but usually still high. Carved in more than one plane. Tragus indicated by a separate protrusion on cheek or as extension from lobe. No anti-tragus.

Eye. Occasionally outer corner considerably higher than inner. Recess at inner corner is sometimes indicated but not caruncle.

Mouth. Lips generally curve upward and meet more or less at corners. Upper lip protrudes over lower.

Hair. Mass often arranged in horizontal undulations or in globules, with flame-like diadem or scalloped edge framing forehead.

NECK. Construction of neck often generalized. When sterno-mastoids are shown they are indicated by slightly modelled shapes. No indication of swelling of trapezium.

TORSO, FRONT. Clavicles protrude all along their course as far as deltoid. Thorax more modelled than before, and lower boundary indicated by arched instead of pointed groove. Three or four transverse divisions of rectus abdominis above navel generally shown as modelled forms. Navel shaped as button surrounded by groove, often with horizontal cut at each side; occasionally fold of skin indicated above it (cf. no. 70). Slight indication of external oblique bulging over iliac crest.

[29] Raubitschek, *Öst. Jahr.* xxxi, 1938, cols. 58 ff.

Lower boundary of abdomen descends with straight sides towards genitals. Pubes, when represented, has sometimes upper edge in the form of two concave curves rising to a central point (cf. no. 82).

TORSO, BACK. Spinal furrow, shoulder-blades, and sometimes erector spinae indicated by modelled shapes.

ARM. Generally joined to body along considerable distance. Forearm, viewed from front, is turned forward in supine position, but palm of hand is twisted towards body. Thumb no longer abnormally large, and hand less tightly clenched than before.

LEG. Depression over great trochanter occasionally indicated by slight modelling. Inner vastus descends markedly lower than outer. Patella more modelled. Anterior edge of shin-bone forms decided curve and is no longer sharp. Inner malleolus higher than outer.

Foot. Arched. Occasional suggestion of metatarsal bones. Ends of toes as they touch the ground recede along one curve, the big toe projecting somewhat further than the second toe and the little toe slanting inward. The four small toes point downward either gently or sharply, with nails pointing towards ground.

FOOT-PLINTH. Uneven; shape follows roughly outlines of soles (cf. no. 73).

Kouroi Nos. 63-85

63 : Figs. 208-216

ATHENS, NATIONAL MUSEUM, no. 1906. From Volomandra.

Statue from head to heels. Was broken across neck, thighs, knees, and ankles, and has been put together with some plaster restorations at fractures. Front parts of both feet also restored.

Parian marble.
Height 1.79 m.
Found in 1900 during illicit excavations at Kouvara-Kalyvia, in the district of Volomandra, Attica, in what was apparently an ancient cemetery. The exact spot was afterwards located by the discovery of further fragments belonging to the statue (Kavvadias, loc. cit.). The cemetery appears to have been long in use.
Kavvadias, *'Εφ. 'Αρχ.* 1902, cols. 43 ff., pls. 3-4.
Kastriotes, *Γλυπτά*, no. 1906.
Papaspiridi, *Guide du Musée National*, p. 27.
Budde, *Die attischen Kuroi* (Diss. 1939), pp. 12 ff.
Buschor, *Fr. J.*, pp. 57 ff., figs. 61-3.
Homann-Wedeking, *Anfänge*, p. 90, fig. 48.
Deonna, no. 5, figs. 10-12.

GENERAL STRUCTURE. Broad shoulders, narrow waist, long thighs, broad arms. Whole more rounded and less plank-like than before. Stands very erect with neck almost perpendicular. Attempt to accentuate individual muscles, such as roundness of deltoid, biceps, calf. Intensive study of individual parts. Viewed in profile, greatest protrusion of back higher than that of chest. Vertebral column somewhat curved.

HEAD. *Skull.* Back flat.

Ear. Vertical and placed rather high. Concha carved in deeper plane than helix. Lobe relatively smaller than in Sounion statue and not circular, with prolongation above, meeting knob-shaped tragus, which is separately indicated. No antitragus.

Eye. Almond-shaped and set obliquely, with upper eyelid protruding over lower one; roundness of eyeball indicated by curving plane of upper lid; upper eyelid separated from brow by incised line; eyebrow rounded without sharp edge. Recess at inner corner indicated by groove.

Nose. Openings of nostrils viewed from below are shaped as slits. Point of nose a rounded lobe. Wings of nostrils well developed.

Mouth. Lower lip carved in deeper plane than upper. Lips slope upward; corners more modelled than before and grooves separate them from cheeks; no sharp fold above upper lip. Upper lip forms obtuse-angled triangle. Under lip slightly cleft.

Chin. Strong and prominent.

Hair. Falls down back in undulating mass ending in slightly curving line; divided horizontally and vertically into rounded globules; each tress ends below in triangular member. In front flame-like members, suggesting locks of hair, rise from forehead and temples to cover fillet. They may be either decorations of fillet or tufts of hair (cf. the mane of the Perachora lion [30]), but in view of arrangement on no. 70, the former is more probable (cf. also nos. 50, 64, 72). Fillet has no hanging ends; makes impression on hair, shaping back of head.

NECK. Short and comparatively undeveloped. Sternomastoids not visible. No indication of muscular development of trapezium.

TORSO, FRONT. Clavicles turn upward from sternum. Nipples shaped like little buttons and placed far apart. Median line marked by shallow depression from bottom of sternum to navel. Thorax well developed; its lower boundary seems to be indicated by rounded arch below pectorals. Three modelled transverse divisions of rectus abdominis above navel, which is placed relatively low. Flanks lean, with only slight indication of oblique muscle over iliac crest. Lower boundary of abdomen descends with straight sides to genitals, forming acute angle. Ridge at upper end of penis.

TORSO, BACK. Spinal furrow, shoulder-blades, and erector spinae indicated by slightly modelled shapes. On either side of spinal furrow, and below grooves outlining shoulder-blades, a shallow groove travels downward and outward.

ARM. Separated from torso only for short distance at elbow. Upper end of ulna (elbow) surrounded above by folds of flesh (less stylized than in New York statue, no. 1). Forearm, viewed from front, is turned forward in supine position, whereas palm of hand is twisted towards body.

Hand. Only part of right remains. Clenched. Index finger (small portion preserved) next to thigh.

LEG. Great trochanter forms slight, modelled depression. Broad depression on outer side of thigh corresponds to ilio-tibial band. Two vasti differentiated, vastus internus descending lower than vastus externus. Patella less block-like than before, assuming a more oval shape. Anterior ridge of shin-bone has pronounced curve inward and is rounded. On the lower leg, both peroneal muscles and calf well developed and modelled, instead of being indicated by grooves and ridges. Inner malleolus higher than outer.

Foot. Heel is narrow and tapers upward. Toes missing.

64 : Figs. 217-218

NEW YORK, METROPOLITAN MUSEUM, no. 21.88.16. From near Sounion (?).

Head and part of neck. Surface has suffered from cleaning; incrustation, which originally covered surface and of which strongly adhering traces remain, was removed by acid, which has imparted a sheen to surface. Nose, upper lip, and ear battered.

Island marble.
Height 21.9 cm.
Said to be from near Sounion.
Richter, in Brunn-Bruckmann-Arndt, *Denkmäler*, 1929, no. 721; *Cat. of Gk. Sc.*, no. 2.
Buschor, *Fr. J.*, pp. 57 f., figs. 64, 65.

HEAD. *Skull.* Rounded.

Ear. Slants towards line of jaw. Carved in several planes. Tragus separately indicated. No antitragus.

Eye. Set obliquely; upper and lower eyelids of about equal depth, with rounded eyeball protruding; upper boundary of upper eyelid marked by ridge; groove surrounds lower eyelid. Recess at inner corner not indicated.

Mouth. Lips have sharp edges and curl upward, meeting at corners. Cheeks form concave curve with chin (cf. no. 73), which is cleft in middle.

Hair. Fell on back in mass which is divided horizontally and vertically into beaded tresses; beads aligned horizontally and decrease in size towards front. Fillet plain behind, without hanging ends. Over forehead and temples is a broad band with grooved flame- or leaf-like members, and with a second, narrower band laid over them; the latter was probably once decorated with rosettes, as the three holes for attachment suggest. Whether the flame-like members are part of an ornamented fillet or represent ends of hair is not clear; probably the former (cf. nos. 50, 63, 70, 72). Fillet cuts into hair behind.

65 : Figs. 219-220

ATHENS, AKROPOLIS MUSEUM, no. 617. From the Akropolis.

Head, perhaps of a kouros.

Island marble.
Height 17.5 cm.
Found SE. of Erechtheion, in 1887.
Dickins, *Catalogue*, p. 147, no. 617.
Payne and Young, *Acropolis*, p. 3, pl. 9, 3; pl. 10, 1-4.
Langlotz in Schrader, *Akropolis*, p. 127 f., no. 86, pl. 95.
Budde, *Die attischen Kuroi* (Diss. 1939), p. 18.
Deonna, no. 14.

HEAD. *Skull.* Rounded.

Ear. Slants slightly towards line of jaw. Carved in several planes, but kept rather flat. Tragus forms separate, rounded protuberance. No indication of antitragus.

[30] Caskey, *Catalogue of Greek and Roman Sculpture*, no. 10.

Eye. Set obliquely. No indication of recess at inner corner.
Mouth. Lips slope upward and do not meet at corners.
Hair. Simple fillet encircles hair. Hair falls down in mass which on skull is left smooth, at back is divided horizontally by grooves, and on sides (in front) is divided horizontally and vertically into beaded tresses; above forehead and temples, mass is wavy with scalloped contour.

66 : Figs. 221-225

PARIS, LOUVRE, no. MNC 748. From Athens.

Head, left leg, left hand. Face battered.

Pentelic marble.
Height of head 20 cm.; height of hand *c.* 11 cm.; height of preserved fragment of leg 32 cm. All three are somewhat smaller than life.
Found in Athens, in 1887.
Collignon, *Gazette archéologique* XII, 1887, pp. 88 ff., pl. 11; *Les Statues funéraires*, pp. 56-7, figs. 29-30.
Winter, *Ath. Mitt*, XIII, 1888, p. 120.
Budde, *Die attischen Kuroi* (Diss. 1939), pp. 16 ff.
Buschor, *Fr. J.*, p. 57 f., fig. 60.
Homann-Wedeking, *Anfänge*, p. 83 f., fig. 40.
Deonna, no. 23.

Since all three pieces are of the same scale (a little smaller than life), and are of Pentelic marble, which is an unusual material in this period, it is probable that they belong to the same statue.
HEAD. *Skull.* At back only slightly developed, but rounded at top.
Ear. Placed rather low; slants towards line of jaw. Carved more or less in one plane. Tragus forms extension from lobe, passing into cheek. No indication of antitragus.
Eye. Almond-shaped and rather flat; lower eyelid almost straight, upper forms pronounced arch. No indication of recess at inner corner discernible. Broad, well-defined groove separates upper lid from eyebrow. Iris and pupil incised on preserved left eye.
Nose. Mostly missing.
Mouth. Mostly missing; downward furrow at each corner.
Hair. Fell on back in mass; is left plain on skull and at back, but is carved in beaded tresses on sides (in front). Encircling fillet is tied in a reef knot with ends hanging down in a curve immediately after knot. Above forehead and beneath fillet, mass of hair is divided vertically into series of waves of scalloped contour, with parting in middle; this parting is continued as a groove along skull, stopping somewhat before crown.

LEFT HAND. Loosely clenched. Tips of fingers missing. Thumb not abnormally long.
LEFT LEG. Anterior ridge of shin-bone has pronounced curve inward and is fairly sharp. Peroneal muscles indicated by two somewhat modelled ridges.

67 : Figs. 226-227

LONDON, BRITISH MUSEUM, B 473. From Athens (?).

Head and part of neck. Probably not of a kouros but of a sphinx, for the sterno-mastoid muscle on right side bulges more than that on left, and this seems to indicate that head was turned towards left.[31] Nevertheless included here since it is an excellent and well preserved example of this period.

Parian marble.
Height 22 cm.
From the Elgin Collection; therefore presumably from Athens, perhaps from the Akropolis.
Pryce, *Catalogue*, B 473, p. 201 f., fig. 245.
Deonna, p. 144.

HEAD. *Skull.* Fairly rounded at top and back.
Ear. Placed correctly. Slants towards line of jaw. Carved more or less in one plane, with large, flat lobe, and tragus projecting directly from it. No antitragus.
Eye. Placed obliquely, with inner corner sloping down to form recess. Incised line marks upper boundary of upper eyelid.
Mouth. Lips slope upward and are more or less on one plane.
Hair. Fell down back in mass, which is divided horizontally by grooves; round forehead mass has scalloped contour. Incised fillet encircles hair without knot or falling ends.

68 : Figs. 228-229

ATHENS, NATIONAL MUSEUM, no. 3860.

Torso from neck to thighs. Battered, especially at back. Evidently an early member of this group or a late one of the preceding.

Island marble, apparently Naxian.
Height 75 cm.
Provenance not known. Formerly in a private collection in Athens, then in the 'Theseion'.
Kyparissis and Homann-Wedeking, *Ath. Mitt.* 63/64, 1938/39, p. 159 f., pls. 58-61.

GENERAL STRUCTURE. Viewed in profile greatest protrusion of back higher than that of chest. Vertebral column somewhat curved.

[31] I owe this observation to B. Ashmole. Cf. Lechat, *Au Musée de l'Acropole*, p. 386.

Hair. Fell behind in mass, divided vertically and horizontally into beaded tresses, and terminating in pointed members along straight line.

TORSO, FRONT. Generalized. Clavicles only slightly marked. Median line indicated by shallow depression. No transverse divisions above navel shown in rectus abdominis. Slight protrusion at flanks. Lower boundary of abdomen descends with straight sides towards genitals; groove is continued along sides of waist.

TORSO, BACK. Broad depression marks spinal furrow. Shoulder-blades not much differentiated (but surface is here battered).

ARM. Was detached from body below armpit and above wrist.

LEG. Slight depression indicates hollow made by great trochanter. Buttocks level.

69 : Figs. 230-233

BOSTON, MUSEUM OF FINE ARTS, no. 39.552. From Attica (?).

Torso, from neck to waist. Copious remains of red colour on hair.

Island marble, 'seemingly Parian'.
Height 40.5 cm.
Said to come from Attica.
Caskey, M.F.A. *Bulletin*, XXXVIII, 1940, pp. 75 ff.
Buschor, *Fr. J.*, p. 72 f., figs. 82, 83.

GENERAL STRUCTURE. Broad shoulders, narrow waist. Viewed in profile, greatest protrusion of back higher than that of chest. Vertebral column forms curve.

HAIR. Falls down back in nine separate wavy tresses, of which ends form curving line. The tresses are alternately smooth and subdivided lengthwise by undulating grooves into four narrow strands. Three similar tresses in front on either side are subdivided each into three strands. Holes along neck on left side caused by chisel working at back of tresses.

NECK. Comparatively undeveloped. Sterno-mastoids not indicated. No indication of muscular development of trapezium.

TORSO, FRONT. Clavicles turn upward from sternum; sternal notch hardly indicated; continuous depression above clavicle. Median line indicated by shallow, modelled depression from lower end of sternum to region of navel (fracture comes just above navel). Nipples shaped like little buttons and placed far apart. Each nipple surrounded by circle of small holes. Shoulders well developed. Four shallow depressions mark divisions of deltoid (see no. 1). Lower boundary of thorax indicated by narrow, rounded arch below pectorals. Four modelled transverse divisions of rectus abdominis above region of navel.

TORSO, BACK. Broad groove indicates spinal furrow, and shallower groove on either side marks erector spinae muscles. Shoulder-blades indicated by slightly modelled shapes.

ARM. Attached to side for some distance below armpit.

70 : Figs. 239-244

FLORENCE, MUSEO ARCHEOLOGICO. From Greece (?).

Statue, from head to below knees. Chin and end of nose with openings of nostrils restored. Statue broken across neck, but neck ancient.

Island marble.
Height 1.39 m.
Acquired by Professor Milani in 1902 from Sig. F. Briganti-Bellini[32] at Osimo (Ancona).
Minto, *Critica d'Arte*, VIII, 1943, pp. 1 ff.

GENERAL STRUCTURE. Broad shoulders, narrow waist, broad arms, small hands. Viewed in profile, greatest protrusion of back higher than that of chest. Vertebral column forms gentle curve.

HEAD. *Skull.* Rounded above, rather flat behind.

Ear. Placed high and vertical. Carved in more than one plane. Tragus separate protuberance. No antitragus. Flat lobe.

Eye. Outer corner rather higher than inner. No recess at inner corner indicated. Eyeball protrudes and iris and pupil incised.

Nose. Long and rather narrow.

Mouth. Lips curve upward. Under lip has vertical cleft.

Hair. Falls down back in beaded tresses, each ending in pointed member; mass divided vertically by sharp grooves, and horizontally by shallower depressions; on skull, divisions run from side to side. Round forehead and temples, two rows of spiral locks arranged symmetrically to right and left from centre. Broad fillet encircling head is tied behind in reef knot, and its ends fall perpendicularly down; on its front are flame-like members with rosette in middle and ridge along bottom. Presence of spiral curls suggests that in this case flame-like members are not ends of hair but, like the rosette, decorations of fillet. If that is the case, the similar flame-like members on nos. 50, 63, 64, 72, may also be decorative motifs, not ends of hair.

NECK. Sterno-mastoids indicated by slightly modelled shapes. Throat indicated, but not swelling of trapezium on shoulder.

[32] In whose palace it and no. 169 are said to have been for over a century (cf. Minto, op. cit., p. 1).

TORSO, FRONT. Clavicles travel upward towards deltoid. Median line marked along sternum and linea alba. Nipples shaped like little buttons, each surrounded by an incised circle. Thorax well developed; its lower boundary forms rounded arch. Three transverse divisions of rectus abdominis above navel. Navel indicated by button-like knob, with creased fold above it. Protrusion at flanks indicates bulge of external oblique over iliac crest. Lower boundary of abdomen descends with straight sides towards genitals. Penis mostly missing; ridge marks its root.

TORSO, BACK. Spinal furrow, shoulder-blades, and erector spinae indicated by slightly modelled shapes.

ARM. Joined to body below armpit and at hand. Fold of flesh above and on outer side of ulna indicated by ridge. Course of ulna indicated by straight ridge, and its lower end, at wrist, is marked by knob. Forearm turned forward in supine position, whereas palm of hand turned towards body.

Hand. Clenched; thumb rather short. Joint above nail indicated by two incised lines. Marble left adhering between thumb and forefinger.

LEG. No indication of depression over great trochanter. Inner vastus descends lower than outer and is divided from it by groove, which travels some distance upward from patella and then bifurcates. This is an unusual attempt to indicate upper part of vasti, without however leaving room for attachment of rectus femoris to patella. Patella forms rounded block with a knob beneath to indicate the pads of fat or perhaps the ligament of the patella; a third knob is evidently intended for the tubercle of the shin-bone (tibia).

71 : Figs. 251-252

MUNICH, GLYPTOTHEK, no. 48.

Head and part of neck. Unfinished; features merely blocked out. Marks of point and of claw chisel visible. Piece at top missing.

Parian marble.
Height 14.2 cm.
Provenance not definitely known; 'perhaps from the Greek Islands'.
Furtwängler, *Beschreibung der Glyptothek*, no. 48.
Mendel, *B.C.H.* XXXI, 1907, p. 203.
Blümel, *Griechische Bildhauerarbeit*, p. 51, no. 6.
Deonna, no. 160.

HEAD. *Skull.* Back of head flat.

Work on ear and hair started on one side, on the other only roughly blocked out. Ear vertical. Carved in more than one plane, but still fairly flat. Tragus excrescence from lobe.

Eye. Horizontal. Each blocked out as protruding mass.

Mouth. Lips horizontal. Do not meet at corners. Lower lip recedes only slightly.

Hair. Falls down back, and tresses brought over shoulders; on left shoulder three tresses indicated; at back only roughly blocked out.

72 : Fig. 253

ATHENS, NATIONAL MUSEUM, no. 48. From Aegina (?).

Front part of head. Eyes much battered.

Parian marble.
Height 32 cm.
Said to have been found in Aegina.
Furtwängler, *Ath. Mitt.* VIII, 1883, pl. XVII, pp. 373 ff.
Deonna, no. 73.

HEAD. Face oval.

Ear. Both missing.

Eye. Slants upward. Apparently no recess at inner corner.

Mouth. Lips slope upward and do not meet at corners.

Chin. Broad and prominent.

Hair. Over forehead and temples arranged in wavy mass with scalloped edge; above this mass is a fillet from which rise flame-like members; the latter may be either ends of hair or decorations of the fillet (cf. nos. 50, 63, 64, 70); since they do not align with the scallops, it is perhaps more likely that they are parts of the fillet.

73 : Figs. 245-250

MUNICH, GLYPTOTHEK, no. 168. From Tenea.

Statue, from head to back of foot-plinth. Restorations: Slivers at fractures and middle of right arm.

Parian marble.
Height 1.53 m.
Found in 1846 in an ancient cemetery at Athikia (the ancient Tenea), about seven miles distant from Corinth.
Furtwängler, *Beschreibung der Glyptothek*, no. 47.
Sieveking and Weickert, *Fünfzig Meisterwerke der Glyptothek*, 1928, pls. 4, 5.
Caskey, 'The Proportions of the Apollo of Tenea,' *A.J.A.* XXVIII, 1924, pp. 358 ff.
Buschor, *Fr. J.*, p. 49, figs. 50-3.
De Luca, 'Il Kouros di Tenea,' *Arch. Cl.* XI, 1959, pp. 1 ff.
Deonna, no. 80.

GENERAL STRUCTURE. Form seen as a whole; parts harmoniously inter-related. Sloping shoulders, narrow waist, long thighs. Seen in profile, greatest protrusion of back higher than that of chest. Vertebral column slightly curved.

HEAD. *Skull.* Top developed, but back flat.
Ear. Slants towards line of jaw. Placed in approximately correct position. Concha carved in deeper plane than helix. Lobe flat with prolongation above forming tragus. No indication of antitragus.
Eye. Set horizontally with lower eyelid only slightly receding. Broad, shallow depression separates upper eyelid from eyebrow. Roundness of eyeball hardly indicated. Recess at inner corner marked by groove.
Nose. Sharp and long. Wings of nostrils well developed; openings viewed from below indicated by slits.
Mouth. Lips slope slightly upward and do not meet at corners; vertical furrow at each corner.
Chin. Broad and strong. Cheeks form concave curve, but not so markedly as in New York head, no. 64.
Hair. Falls down back in undulating mass, divided horizontally and ending below in curving line; above forehead and temples divisions are vertical with scalloped edge. One fillet encircles head on front and sides and meets second fillet, which circles round back of head and stops abruptly behind ears.
NECK. Long and comparatively undeveloped. Sterno-mastoid muscles not indicated. No indication of swelling of trapezium.
TORSO, FRONT. Clavicles indicated by horizontal ridges which protrude all along their course, becoming flatter as they reach shoulders. Median line marked by shallow groove from a little below lower end of sternum to a little above navel. Nipples carved as small round buttons. Lower boundary of thorax indicated by shallow depression forming irregular arch some distance below pectorals. No transverse divisions marked of rectus abdominis above navel. Navel carved as small round button, with horizontal incision on either side. Slight protrusion at flanks indicates external oblique descending over iliac crest. Flanks about level. Lower boundary of abdomen descends towards genitals with straight sides, which if continued would form an acute angle. Ridge marks root of penis.
TORSO, BACK. Spinal furrow and shoulders indicated by shallow grooves. On either side of spinal furrow a groove travels downward and outward. No indication of erector spinae.
ARM. Attached to side from considerably below armpit to above wrist. Muscles (deltoid, biceps) indicated by rounded forms. Upper end of ulna (elbow) marked by protrusion. Forearm, viewed from front, is turned forward in supine position, whereas palm of hand is twisted towards body.
Hand. Loosely clenched. In right hand, all fingers are carved, four in front and little finger behind; in left hand, only thumb and forefinger are indicated for front view. Skin around nail marked in left hand but not in right. In each hand little finger touches thigh at back. Between hands and thighs marble left adhering for about four inches.
LEG. No indication of depression over great trochanter. Vasti differentiated, the vastus internus descending lower than the vastus externus. Patella less block-like than before, assuming a more oval shape. Anterior ridge of shin-bone has pronounced curve inward and is rounded. Peroneal muscles and calf, instead of being indicated by grooves and ridges, are more modelled. Inner malleolus higher than outer.
Foot. Heel narrow and tapers upward. Metatarsal bones slightly indicated. Toes recede along one curve, second toe being only slightly shorter than or about same length as big toe, and little toe slanting inward. The four small toes slant downward with nails pointing towards ground, but not sharply.
FOOT-PLINTH. Partly missing. Embedded in modern base; original outline not quite clear, but apparently followed roughly contours of soles of feet; its upper surface is uneven.

74 : Figs. 255-257

PARIS, LOUVRE, no. MNB 766. From Actium.

Torso, from neck to knees. Surface much corroded. Modern hole at back (now filled with plaster) made presumably for fastening to wall. Some plaster additions made at fractures of legs for mounting.

Probably Island marble.
Height 1 m.
Found at Actium, Acarnania, in 1867, with no. 40; probably from a sanctuary of Apollo, of which traces have been found.
Collignon, *Gazette archéologique*, xl, 1886, pp. 235 ff., pl. 29.
Louvre, *Catalogue sommaire*, p. 41, no. 687.
Buschor, *Fr. J.*, p. 43 f., figs. 45, 46.
Deonna, no. 2.

GENERAL STRUCTURE. Viewed in profile, greatest protrusion of back a little higher than that of chest. Vertebral column curved.
HAIR. Hangs down back, mass being divided vertically and horizontally into beaded tresses, which are gathered by a double band allowing ends to descend over back in fan-like formation.
NECK. Lower ends of sterno-mastoids indicated by two ridges meeting at sternal notch. No indication of swelling of trapezium.
TORSO, FRONT. Clavicles indicated by modelled ridges protruding along whole course in an elegant curve until they reach shoulders; placed more or less horizontal. Median line, somewhat obliterated, travels from end of sternum to navel. Nipples indistinct. Lower boundary of

thorax forms grooved, pointed arch with apex about height of lower end of pectorals. Four transverse divisions of rectus abdominis discernible above navel. Navel indistinct. Protrusion at flanks indicates external oblique descending over iliac crest. Flanks level. Lower boundary of abdomen descends with straight sides towards genitals.

TORSO, BACK. Spinal furrow indicated by broad, deep groove; on either side of it, and running parallel to it, a narrower, shallower groove marks erector spinae along its whole course. Shoulder-blades shown by raised planes.

ARM. Free from body except under armpit and at hand. Upper arm short. Forearm, viewed from front, is turned forward in supine position, whereas palm of hand is twisted towards body.

Hand. Loosely clasped with second finger next to thigh. Marble between thigh and hand left adhering.

LEG. Slight indication of depression over great trochanter. Lower end of vastus internus slightly lower and more protruding than that of vastus externus.

75 : Fig. 254

THEBES, MUSEUM, no. 14. From the Ptoan Sanctuary.

Upper part of head.

Island marble.
Height 16 cm.
Found in the Ptoan Sanctuary, in 1903.
Mendel, *B.C.H.* XXXI, 1907, p. 210 f., no. 8, fig. 11.
Grace, *Archaic Sculpture in Boeotia*, p. 64 f., fig. 75.
Deonna, no. 52.

HEAD. *Skull.* Fairly flat at top and back.

Ear. Slants towards line of jaw. Carved in more than one plane, but still fairly flat. Tragus indicated, but no antitragus.

Eye. Slopes upward. Inner recess indicated by groove.

Hair. Top of head smooth. At back, mass divided into beaded tresses. Above forehead and temples large, flat, lozenge-shaped members.

76 : Figs. 261-263

BOSTON, MUSEUM OF FINE ARTS, no. 03.996. From Olympia (?).

Statuette. Left forearm bent slightly out of position.

Bronze.
Height 16.6 cm.
Said to be from Olympia.
Furtwängler, *Kleine Schriften*, II, pp. 433 ff., pl. 44, 1.
Langlotz, *Bildhauerschulen*, p. 74, pl. 35 a.
Buschor, *Fr. J.*, pp. 86 ff., figs. 101, 102.
Deonna, p. 272, no. 93.

GENERAL STRUCTURE. Sloping shoulders, narrow waist, thick neck. Viewed in profile, greatest protrusion of back higher than that of chest. Vertebral column forms curve.

HEAD. *Skull.* Top of head rounded, but back undeveloped.

Ear. Large; placed vertically and in approximately correct position. Concha carved in deeper plane than helix. Tragus excrescence from lobe. No indication of antitragus.

Eye. Set horizontally.

Mouth. Horizontal.

Chin. Broad and prominent.

Hair. Falls down back in thick mass divided vertically into tresses, which are subdivided horizontally by short grooves. Three such tresses travel horizontally above forehead and temples beneath thick, notched fillet.

NECK. Sterno-mastoids not indicated. No indication of swelling of trapezium.

TORSO, FRONT. Clavicles indicated as flat ridges travelling upward to shoulders. Median line indicated from lower end of sternum to region of navel. Lower boundary of thorax forms arch below pectorals. Three transverse divisions of rectus abdominis marked above navel. Navel almond-shaped. Slight protrusion at flanks indicates external oblique descending over iliac crest. Short groins.

TORSO, BACK. Spinal furrow indicated by broad depression. Shoulder-blades mostly hidden by hair.

ARM. Held away from body and brought forward. Forearm, viewed from front, turned forward in supine position, whereas palm of hand is twisted towards body.

Hand. Clenched; originally grasped object.

LEG. Depression over great trochanter marked by flat plane. Vastus internus descends slightly lower than vastus externus. Shin slopes inward. Inner malleolus higher than outer.

Foot. Toes recede along one curve, big toe projecting further than second toe.

FOOT-PLINTH. Rectangular and in one piece with statuette; has two holes with rivets for fastening near opposite corners.

77 : Figs. 258-260

VATHY, MUSEUM. From Samos.

Torso from neck to knees.

Grey, coarse-grained marble.
Height 1.00 m.
Found at the Glyphada near Tigani, Samos, in 1890.
Wiegand, *Ath. Mitt.* XXV, 1900, p. 149 f., pl. XII.
Buschor, *Alt. St.* I, p. 17 f., figs. 57, 59, 60; *Fr. J.*, p. 77 f., figs. 86, 87.
Deonna, no. 137.

Inscribed on left upper leg: *Λευκιος ἀνεθηκεν τωι Ἀπολωνι*, 'Leukios dedicated it to Apollo.'

GENERAL STRUCTURE. Viewed in profile, greatest protrusion of back level with that of chest. Vertebral column slightly curved.

HAIR. Fell behind in mass which was divided vertically and horizontally into beaded tresses terminating in triangular members along straight line.

TORSO, FRONT. Clavicles only indicated at sternum. Median line marked by shallow depression along linea alba. Lower boundary of thorax modelled. No transverse divisions of rectus abdominis marked above navel. Slight protrusion at flanks indicates anterior part of iliac crest. Lower boundary of abdomen descends with straight sides towards genitals.

TORSO, BACK. Hollow between shoulders marks spinal furrow. Shoulder-blades not much differentiated. Big hollow over buttocks. No indication of erector spinae.

ARM. Detached from body from below armpit to above wrist. Upper arm short. Forearm, viewed from front, turned forward in supine position, whereas palm of hand is twisted towards body.

Hand. Clenched; index finger laid against thigh.

LEG. No indication of hollow over great trochanter. Lower ends of vasti almost level.

Here also belongs the lower part of a torso, from waist to left knee, height 60 cm., i.e. about life size, from Mysilmos, SAMOS, Buschor, *Alt. St.*; p. 18 f., figs. 55, 56.

78 : Figs. 234-235

SAMOS, APOTHEKE OF THE HERAION.

Lower right leg from knee to above ankle. Destroyed during the last war, so Dr. Buschor informs me.

Marble.
Height 1.30 m. Three times life size.
From the Heraion, Samos. Found outside early temenos.
Buschor, *Alt. St.* 1, p. 10, figs. 15, 16; *Fr. J.*, p. 79, fig. 92.

Inner vastus descends lower than outer and upper boundary of cushion indicated. Region of patella modelled with attachment to shin-bone. Head of tibia shown on outer side as elongated protuberance connecting below with ridge sloping towards shin-bone. Shin sharp and curved. Separation of inner edge of tibia from calf indicated by modelling.

79 : Fig. 236

SAMOS, APOTHEKE OF THE HERAION.

Front of left foot with plinth.

Marble.
Three times life size.
Found near no. 78, and the two may belong together.
Buschor, *Alt. St.* 1, p. 10, figs. 13, 14.

FOOT. Toes parallel to one another (except small one which turns slightly inward), and their ends recede along one line. Curve downward as if gripping ground, with nails pointing sharply downward. Big toe separated from others by broad groove.

FOOT-PLINTH. Rounded. Sides worked with point, upper surface smoothed.

80 : Figs. 237-238

SAMOS, APOTHEKE OF THE HERAION.

Pair of feet on hexagonal plinth.

Samian marble.
Length of feet 34 cm. Width of plinth 14.5 cm. Height of plinth 8 cm.
Found in the Heraion of Samos, *in situ*, at north end of Sacred Way, west of Geneleos group. Formed part of a group of three.
Buschor, *Alt. St.* 1, p. 10, figs. 11, 12; *Ath. Mitt.* LV, 1930, p. 43.
Schede, *Abhandlung der preussischen Akademie der Wissenschaft*, 1929, phil.-hist. Klasse, no. 3, p. 24, pl. XIII.

FOOT. Inner malleolus higher than outer. Toes parallel and point downward, but not as sharply as in no. 79. Recede along one line, big toe projecting further than second toe; small toe turns slightly inward. Big toe separated from others by deep groove.

FOOT-PLINTH. Hexagonal. Sides worked with point, upper surface smoothed. Was inserted in limestone base.

Here should belong the unfinished torso from Naxos, National Museum, ATHENS, no. 14 (Deonna, no. 116; Blümel, *Griechische Bildhauerarbiet*, pls. 5, 6).

81 : Figs. 267-269

CAIRO, MUSEUM, no. 27425. From Sa el-Hagav.

Statuette, from head to above knees. Traces of red on lips.

Alabaster.
Height 11 cm.
From Sa el-Hagav (Saïs).
Edgar, *Catalogue du Musée de Caire, Greek Sculpture*, p. 1, no. 27425, pl. 1.
Deonna, no. 142.

GENERAL STRUCTURE. Forms rounded. Sloping shoulders. Greatest protrusion of back, seen in profile, hidden by hair. Vertebral column forms slight curve.

HEAD. *Skull.* Flat at back.
Ear. Large; parts not differentiated.
Eye. Slants slightly upward.
Mouth. Lips curve upward at corners; upper lip protrudes.
Hair. Falls down back in smooth mass.
NECK. Sterno-mastoids and swelling of trapezium not marked.
TORSO, FRONT. Little anatomical detail. Clavicles, lower boundary of thorax, and divisions of rectus abdominis not discernible. Slight protrusion at flanks. Lower boundary of abdomen descends with straight sides towards genitals.
TORSO, BACK. Depression marks spinal furrow. No detailed muscular construction.
ARM. Attached to body along much of course. Forearm, viewed from front, turned forward in supine position, whereas hand is twisted towards body.
Hand. Clenched.

82 : Figs. 264-266

MOSCOW, MUSEUM OF FINE ARTS, no. NI I.a. 3000. From Naukratis (?).

Statuette, from head to above knees. Traces of black colour on eyebrows, eyelids, pupils, moustache, imperial, curls on forehead below fillet, pubes; red on fillet and lips. Parts of lips and chin missing.

Alabaster.
Height 17.5 cm.
Perhaps from Naukratis. In 1887, was in the collection of Dr. Oikonomopoulos in Cairo. Later in the Golenischeff Collection.
Kieseritzky, *Jahrbuch*, VII, 1892, p. 179 f., pl. VI.
Deonna, no. 144.

GENERAL STRUCTURE. Forms rounded. Sloping shoulders. Greatest protrusion of back, seen in profile, level with that of chest. Vertebral column forms slight curve.
HEAD. *Skull.* Flat at back.
Ear. Modelled in more than one plane. No indication of antitragus.
Eye. Narrow and more or less horizontal.
Mouth. More or less horizontal.
Hair. Falls down back and on sides in notched tresses. Fillet across forehead. On front part of skull tresses pass from side to side.
NECK. Sterno-mastoids not discernible.
TORSO, FRONT. Little anatomical detail. Clavicles, lower boundary of thorax, and divisions of rectus abdominis not discernible. Slight protrusion at flanks. Lower boundary of abdomen descends with straight sides towards genitals. Pubes has upper edge in the form of two concave curves rising to a central point.[33]
TORSO, BACK. Depression marks spinal furrow. No detailed muscular construction.
ARM. Attached to body along much of course. Forearm, viewed from front, turned forward in supine position, whereas hand is twisted towards body.
Hand. Clenched.
LEG. No indication of depression over great trochanter.

83 : Fig. 270

LONDON, BRITISH MUSEUM, B 446. From Naukratis.

Statuette, from neck to above right knee. Surface much damaged.

Alabaster, burnt.
Height 7.05 cm.
Found in the temenos of Apollo, Naukratis, in 1884.
Petrie, *Naukratis*, I, pl. I, 9.
Pryce, *Catalogue*, B 446, p. 188 f., fig. 226.

GENERAL STRUCTURE. Rounded forms. Greatest protrusion of back seen in profile hidden by mass of hair.
HAIR. Falls down back in mass divided by vertical grooves, and on shoulders in tresses.
TORSO, FRONT. Little anatomical detail. Little if any protrusion at flanks.
TORSO, BACK. Depression marks spinal furrow.
ARM. Adheres to side along most of way. Forearm, seen from front, in supine position, whereas hand is twisted towards body.

84 : Fig. 271

LONDON, BRITISH MUSEUM, B 443. From Naukratis.

Statuette, from neck to above knees. Back of right arm missing.

Alabaster.
Height 10.2 cm.
From Naukratis. Excavated 1884.
Pryce, *Catalogue*, B 443, p. 187, fig. 224.
Deonna, no. 149.

GENERAL STRUCTURE. Forms rounded. Sloping shoulders. Greatest protrusion of back, seen in profile, about level with that of chest. Vertebral column forms slight curve.
HAIR. Falls down back in mass divided by vertical grooves, ending in approximately horizontal line.
TORSO, FRONT. Little anatomical detail. Clavicles, median line, lower boundary of thorax, and divisions

[33] For a parallel at this early period cf. no. 106.

of rectus abdominis not marked. Pectorals slightly modelled. Very slight protrusion at flanks to mark iliac crest. Lower boundary of abdomen descends with short, straight sides towards genitals.
TORSO, BACK. No indication of spinal furrow, shoulder-blades, and erector spinae.
ARM. Attached to body along most of way. Forearm, viewed from front, held in supine position (as indicated by transverse line at bend of arm), whereas hand is twisted towards body.
Hand. Clenched.
LEG. No indication of depression over great trochanter.

85 : Fig. 272

BOSTON, MUSEUM OF FINE ARTS, no. 88.734. From Naukratis.

Statuette, from neck to above left knee.

Alabaster.
Height 14.5 cm.
From the temenos of Aphrodite, Naukratis.
Caskey, *Catalogue of Greek and Roman Sculpture*, p. 3 f., no. 1 (ill.).
Deonna, no. 150.

GENERAL STRUCTURE. Forms rounded. Sloping shoulders. Back flat. Vertebral column straight.
HAIR. Falls down back and shoulder in tresses.
TORSO, FRONT. Anatomy generalized. Slight protrusion at flanks. Lower boundary of abdomen descends with short, straight sides towards genitals.
TORSO, BACK. Groove for spinal furrow. No detailed muscular structure.
ARM. Joined to side except for small portion above elbow. Forearm, viewed from front, turned forward in supine position, but palm of hand twisted towards body.
Hand. Clenched, but outline rounded, not angular as in Sounion group.

Here also belong the alabaster head from Naukratis in the Museum of Fine Arts, BOSTON (Caskey, *Catalogue of Sculpture*, no. 2; Deonna, no. 151), and the limestone heads, also from Naukratis, in the BRITISH MUSEUM (Pryce, *Catalogue*, B 439, 440, figs. 221, 222).
If the head from CYRENE (E. Paribeni, *Catalogo delle sculture di Cirene*, 1959, no. 5; Chamoux, *Cyrène*, pl. XXI, 1, 2) belonged to a kouros, it should be a member of this group.

VIII. THE MELOS GROUP

(*c.* 555-540 B.C.)

General Survey and Historical Background

THE style of the kouroi of the Melos group is astonishingly uniform. Similar slender, graceful, generalized products have been discovered throughout Greece and the Islands, and, to judge from the large number of extant examples, the output was active. As the best preserved statue comes from Melos (it is complete except for part of the right leg and a piece of the plinth), we have named this group after it. Melos, we are told,[1] was a very early Lacedaemonian settlement, but there is nothing tangible that one might call Peloponnesian in the style of this figure.

Many of the preserved statues of this period are torsos without heads, or heads without bodies. Their provenances comprise Attica, Boeotia, Epidauros, Megara, Euboea, Delphi, Perinthos (?), Delos, Thasos, Naxos, Paros, Andros, Thera, Samos, Didyma, Keramos, Kalymnos, Miletos, Rhodes, Olbia, Cyrene, and Sicily.

ATTICA. The Attic contingent is meagre. In addition to no. 87, from Eleusis, and no. 89 from Keratea, perhaps the torso no. 68, National Museum, Athens, no. 3860, formerly in the 'Theseion,' may come from Attica (cf. Kyparissis and Homann-Wedeking, *Ath. Mitt.* LXIII-LXIV, 1938-9, pls. 58-61; p. 159 f.: 'Fundort unbekannt). As far as one can tell from what is preserved, it belongs either late in the preceding group or early in the Melos one.

MEGARA. From the mass of rather second-rate works a few masterpieces stand out; for instance, the colossal kouros from Megara (no. 92)—an impressive work of individual style. It dates from a time when Megara—which had been one of the leading Greek states in the seventh and early sixth centuries, the founder of Selinus, Byzantion, and Chalkedon—was still strong; before her strength was broken by her neighbours and rivals—Corinth and Athens.[2] We may picture her as a leader in engineering,[3] famous for the aqueduct built by her tyrant Theagenes,[4] and resplendent with buildings like the fountain which, Pausanias[5] tells us, was worth seeing for its size, its decorations, and the number of its columns. How important her interest in the arts was at this time is shown by the torso, one of the finest works of the period. A slighter work from Megara is a recently found torso, in the Eleusis Museum (no. 93).

ARGOLID. A fine head, over life-size, comes from Epidauros, and to it may belong a recently found fragment of a torso (no. 91).

[1] Thucydides v.84.2; 112.2 ('several hundred years' before the Athenians took it in 416 B.C.); Herodotos VIII.48; Busolt, *Griechische Geschichte*, I, p. 352.

[2] Cf. Meyer, Pauly-Wissowa, *R.E.* XV, I, s.v. Megara, cols. 183 ff.

[3] Eupalinos, who built the aqueduct at Samos, was a Megarian.

[4] Dated by his connection with his son-in-law Kylon, the would-be tyrant of Athens, probably about 632 B.C.; cf. Wade-Gery, *C.A.H.* III, p. 554. For a later dating cf. Beloch, *Griechische Geschichte*, I, 2, pp. 302 ff. Cf. also Schachermeyr in Pauly-Wissowa *R.E.* V a, s.v. Theagenes (2), cols. 1342-3.

[5] I. 40.1. Remains of this fountain have long been known, cf. Delbrück and Vollmöller, *Ath. Mitt.* XXV, 1900, pp. 23 ff.; Elderkin, *A.J.A.* XIV, 1910, pp. 47 ff.; Dunkley, *B.S.A.* XXXVI, 1935-6, pp. 145 f.; and in 1957, during excavations conducted by Mr. Papadimitriou, much of the imposing building has come to light, cf. Daux, *B.C.H.* LXXXII, 1958, p. 688 f. figs. 35, a, b.

BOEOTIA. From Boeotia comes an important contingent, including several examples (nos. 94-96) transitional between the Volomandra and the Melos groups. It is interesting to note that the kouros once at Orchomenos, now at Chaironeia (no. 99), bears a marked resemblance to one from Thasos in Istanbul (no. 108).

EUBOEA. A fine, though badly preserved head at Chalkis (no. 86) reminds us of the early importance of Euboea, the founder—in the eighth century B.C.—of colonies in Thrace (Chalkidike), Southern Italy, and Sicily.

Other noteworthy products are several torsos from DELOS (nos. 110-112), of delicate workmanship; the torso from NAXOS in Berlin (no. 115); the statue from PAROS in the Louvre (no. 116); the bronze statuette from DELPHI (no. 106) and a group from SAMOS (no. 123). Furthermore a limestone torso, of unknown provenance, now in Geneva (no. 90), appears to be an early example of this group.

PAROS. The torsos from Delphi (nos. 103, 104), Paros (nos. 117, 118) and Thasos (no. 108) have been grouped by Langlotz[6] and others as belonging to a Parian school. The alleged chief characteristic of this school is the form of the abdomen, of which the lower boundary forms a 'deep curve' with an additional, more pronounced curve over each hip.[7] But this same form appears on a number of other kouroi in this and the succeeding periods, for instance, on no. 99 at Chaironeia, no. 120 from Samos, no. 114 from Thera, no. 151 from Delos, no. 154 from Rhodes, and on two kouroi from Cyrene (cf. p. 112). Moreover, on the kouros from Paros in the Louvre (no. 116), presumably a Parian work, the abdomen is not particularly deep and the curve at the hips does not appear; and in another kouros from Paros (no. 118) the abdomen is also not markedly deep. In fact, there are only two kouroi from Paros in which the required form occurs—the torso in Copenhagen (no. 117) and one recently discovered.[8]

It would seem therefore that this 'chief characteristic' of the Parian School is neither exclusively nor universally Parian. As a matter of fact, a deep or a shallow abdomen cannot be considered a characteristic of any special locality, for both forms appear concurrently at different times in different places. Judging from the extant examples, abdomens with short sides are the rule in the earlier periods, whereas in the later periods abdomens with long sides are about as frequent as those with short sides.[9] What is important, however, is the development of the shape of the lower boundary of the abdomen. During the early periods, this lower boundary descends with straight sides towards the genitals; beginning with the Melos group each side sometimes assumes a curved, outwardly convex outline; during the Ptoon 12 period this becomes a regular feature; and when the period of Ptoon 20 is reached, the lower boundary becomes semicircular.

Thus, what has been considered by the supporters of the Parian school as a local characteristic is merely a chronological one. And the same applies to the additional curve over each hip, which is due to the swelling of the external oblique muscle over the iliac crest. The Parian statue in the Louvre (no. 116), being an early example of the Melos group, does not have it in pronounced form,

[6] *Bildhauerschulen*, p. 132, and in Schrader, *Akropolis*, p. 34, note 31.

[7] Rösch, *Altertümliche Marmorwerke von Paros*, p. 42: 'Für die Gestaltung des Bauches lässt sich als übereinstimmender Zug feststellen, dasz das Bauchdreieck lang ausgezogen ist'; Homann-Wedeking, *Ath. Mitt.* 60/61, 1935/6, p. 206: '. . . der Knick in der Leistenbeuge, die Art wie sich der Bauch gegen die Schenkel absetzt, ein Leitmotiv in der plastischen Gestaltung parischer Jünglingsbilder.'

[8] So Mr. Karouzos informs me. I have not seen either the original or a photograph.

[9] For early long-drawn-out abdomens cf. e.g. nos. 63, 73.

whereas the statues from Paros in Copenhagen (no. 117) and those from Samos (no. 120), from Boeotia (no. 99), and from Rhodes (no. 154), being later, show a more developed form.

An argument used by the supporters of the Parian school is based on the supposition that one or the other of two fragmentary kouroi found at Delphi (nos. 103, 104) belongs to the base on which is inscribed a dedication of 'the children of Charopinos the Parian'[10] (no. 105); for both these kouroi have long-drawn-out abdomens, and one has the additional curve over the hip. But we must remember that (1) neither torso is known to have been found in the vicinity of the inscribed base; (2) the letters on the base are not in the Parian but in the Delphian alphabet, so that we have no evidence that the statue which surmounted it was a Parian work; (3) there are many instances of commissions to artists who were not compatriots of their clients (cf. p. 6).

An interesting group of bronze statuettes of nude female figures which served as mirror supports, can be assigned to this period.[11] They are comparable to the kouroi in structure as well as attitude. As several of them are complete, with even the feet extant, they supplement in welcome fashion our comparatively meagre store of well-preserved statues from Greece and the Cyclades. Their feet, it should be noted, show the same scheme as do the other kouroi of this epoch (nos. 86, 106, 123); the big toe projects a little further than or is about the same length as the second toe, and the toes form a gentle downward curve.

Samos, Rhodes, Asia Minor, Egypt, Olbia. The Eastern contribution of this period —when the East Greek cities came under the suzerainty of Croesus, king of Lydia—may be gauged by a number of heads found in Samos (no. 122), Didyma (no. 128), Rhodes (nos. 125, 126) Keramos, near Halikarnassos (no. 130), Çandarh, the ancient Pitane, near Pergamon (see p. 111), Kalymnos (no. 129), Miletos (no. 132), and Olbia[12] (a Milesian colony). All have the soft modelling which we associate with Eastern workmanship, and the skull in each is rather more developed than in the contemporary Western examples. Several have a distinctive coiffure: a second, short layer of tresses reaching from forehead to ears, is laid over longer tresses, on each side of a central parting, and sometimes each short tress terminates in a spiral curl. It is possible that this coiffure was an Eastern fashion; it occurs also on the head of the seated statue from Didyma in the British Museum, B 271, which is somewhat earlier than the figures of the Melos group (cf. p. 61).

On two of the heads from Rhodes (nos. 125, 126) there is an early, tentative rendering of the antitragus, which occurs in similar fashion on the head formerly associated with the karyatid of the Knidian Treasury at Delphi (cf. p. 95).

Cyrene. Three torsos of kouroi from Cyrene (cf. no. 133 and p. 112) have the generalized structure characteristic of this period. Two have the deep abdomen that has been associated with Paros, but which, as we saw, is found also in kouroi from other localities (cf. p. 91).

Sicily. A kouros found at Megara Hyblaia (no. 134) is the earliest marble kouros so far found in Sicily or South Italy. It is of Island marble, and either it or the block out of which it was carved must have been imported. That fine archaic sculpture was produced in the West as early as the first

[10] Homolle, *F.d.D.* iv, fasc. 1, p. 57; Langlotz, *Bildhauerschulen*, p. 132; De La Coste-Messelière, *Au Musée de Delphes*, p. 16, n. 1; Marcadé, *Signatures*, 1, 21. An identical inscription appears on a votive column also from Delphi (Marcadé, op. cit., under 1, 26).

[11] Praschniker, *Öst. Jahr.* xv, 1912, pp. 219 ff., xviii, 1915, pp. 57 ff.; Langlotz, op. cit. pp. 86–7, nos. 11, 12, 13, 16, 17, 18; Richter, *M.M.A. Bulletin*, xxxiii, 1938, pp. 130 ff., and *A.J.A.* xlii, 1938, pp. 337 ff.

[12] Cf. Waldhauer, *J.H.S.* xliv, 1924, p. 46, fig. 1 (now in the Moscow Historical Museum), and *Die antiken Skulpturen der Ermitage*, ii, p. 1, no. 84, and p. 3, figs. 3, 4 (fragment of a head).

half and the middle of the sixth century B.C. is shown by the many examples in terracotta and local limestone that have come to light in various localities, notably the metopes from Selinus and Foce del Sele.[13] A terracotta head of a kouros recently found at Agrigento also belongs here (cf. p. 112).

ETRURIA. Two Etruscan bronze kouroi worked in repoussé relief (cf. fig. 364) probably belong to this period; for they form part of the decorations of an Etruscan chariot which was found in the same tomb as two Athenian 'little-master' cups, 'datable about 550–530, possibly about 540 B.C.' (Beazley). Their anatomical development does not show the same organic progression as that of the Greek kouroi. In many respects the anatomy is still primitive. The head is large in proportion; the ears are flat; the lower boundary of the thorax forms an angle far below the pectorals; there is no protrusion at the flanks; the vasti are not differentiated.

The same mixture of early and late features is found in other Etruscan sculptures, for instance in a bronze statuette in the Guglielmi Collection of the Vatican,[14] (where a comparatively advanced rendering of the head is combined with such early characteristics as the absence of protrusion at the flanks, the placing of the lower boundary of the thorax far below the pectorals, and the lack of differentiation in the vasti muscles); likewise in an amber statuette in the British Museum[15] (where again a comparatively advanced rendering of the face is combined with a primitive body), and in a late archaic terracotta torso from Veii[16] (which has an early rendering of the rectus abdominis, with three divisions above the navel). It is evident that the Etruscans had not the same interest in the construction of the human body as the Greeks, and did not make a consistent advance in their knowledge of it. In Cypriote art we find the same story. An advanced head is often combined with a primitive body. In a limestone statue from the Cesnola Collection (no. 1356), for instance, dated by E. Gjerstadt *c.*525 B.C., the arms are still joined to the body for most of the way, the forearms are not yet correctly semi-pronated, the neck shows no indication of sterno-mastoids, and the ear has no antitragus. It is only in Greek art that a uniform progression in the knowledge of anatomy may be observed, suggesting a prolonged and widespread interest in this subject.

Absolute Chronology

We shall see that for the following (Ptoon 12) group we have a reliable landmark in the Siphnian Treasury, which is dated by external evidence a little earlier than 525 B.C. (cf. p. 114 f.). The Melos group, therefore, which shows throughout a somewhat earlier anatomical structure, must immediately precede it.

A comparison with Corinthian pottery brings out a certain relation between kouroi of the Melos group and late examples of Late Corinthian ware dated round 550[17]. The moulded heads on these vases show a generalized conception similar to that of the kouroi, their features are no longer individually accentuated, and they are worked with about the same degree of naturalism.

The sculptures from the columns of the temple of Artemis at Ephesos had been thought to provide

[13] Cf. Zancani Montuoro and Zanotti-Bianco, *Heraion alla Foce del Sele*.

[14] Cf. Magi in Beazley and Magi, *Raccolta Guglielmi*, II, pp. 165 ff., pls. 47–9.

[15] No. W.T. 1456. From Armento di Basilicata. Height *c.*6 cm. *Synopsis of Contents of the British Museum, Department of Greek and Roman Antiquities*, Second Vase Room, pt. I (London 1878), p. 27, no. 23.

[16] *Le Arti*, II, I, 1939, pl. IX, 4.

[17] Cf. e.g. Myres, *Handbook of the Cesnola Collection*, p. 292 f., no. 1724; Payne, *Necrocorinthia*, p. 322, no. 1309; M. J. Milne, *A.J.A.* XLVI, 1942, pp. 217 ff., figs. 1, 2.

a definite landmark for mid-sixth-century sculpture; for most of these columns are said by Herodotos[18] to have been furnished by Croesus (561-547).[19] Several pieces of his dedicatory inscription (perhaps from several columns) have been preserved,[20] but they cannot be definitely associated with any of the fragments of sculptures which have been found. Moreover, the sculptures themselves are of different styles and evidently do not all date from one period.[21] The work on the columns must have covered a considerable time.[22] These observations of course invalidate the importance of the Ephesos columns as a definite landmark for absolute chronology.

Nevertheless there are certain considerations which help to reinstate at least some of the Ephesos sculptures as chronological evidence. The fact that the dedication by Croesus was inscribed on the astragal directly under the sculptured drum (and in one piece with it)[23] suggests that Croesus' columns were actually sculptured during his lifetime. Herodotos' statement that Croesus gave the *majority* of the columns makes it likely that among the sculptured drums that have survived at least some were dedicated by Croesus. It is probable therefore that those sculptures which are earliest in style[24] belong to Croesus' reign. And they should date not earlier than the end of Croesus' siege of Ephesos, which took place soon after his accession[25] and not later than his fall in 547.[26] A date round 550 is therefore indicated for the earliest of the Ephesian sculptures.

Now, if we examine the early sculptures from the point of view of their anatomical development, we shall find that they have the same forms as our Melos group. For instance, in the man B 90 the protrusion of the back, seen in profile, is a very little higher than that of the chest; his skull is flat at the back, though domed on top; of his ear just enough remains to show that it is still of the primitive form without antitragus (the tragus is broken off). In the lower part of the man B 121, the foot has the big toe projecting further than the second toe.[27] We shall see that in the succeeding group of kouroi the second toe projects further than the big toe, and this is the rule in all subsequent Greek art. We may therefore claim also the fragment B 121 as not later than our Melos group.[28] And that period is suggested also by the flat, curving folds in the drapery of B 121, which correlate with the renderings of Exekias.[29]

[18] I.92: *Κροίσῳ δὲ ἐστὶ ἄλλα ἀναθήματα ... ἐν δὲ Ἐφέσῳ αἵ τε βόες αἱ χρύσεαι καὶ τῶν κιόνων αἱ πολλαί.*

[19] Croesus' dates are not absolutely certain. If the passage in the Nabonidus Chronicle (II.16 ff.) has been rightly interpreted as referring to Lydia (cf. Sidney Smith, *Babylonian Historical Texts*, pp. 101 ff.; Lehmann-Haupt, *Wiener Studien*, XLVI, 1928, pp. 123 ff.) then the fall of Sardes would have taken place in 547. This date is substantially supported by Eusebios, Hieronymus, etc., and contradicted only by the Marmor Parium—a not very good source—which according to Jacoby's probable restoration gives 541 B.C. On the subject of Croesus' dates cf. Weissbach in Pauly-Wissowa, *R.E.* Supplement V, s.v. Kroisos, col. 457, and in Supplement IV, s.v. Kyros, cols. 1144 f.

[20] Pryce, *Catalogue*, I, I, p. 38.

[21] A. H. Smith in Hogarth, *Excavations at Ephesos*, The Archaic Artemisia, pp. 294-5; Pryce, *Catalogue*, I, I, p. 47 f.

[22] A temple of Artemis is referred to by Macrobius, *Saturnalia*, V.22.4-5, as having been dedicated within the lifetime of Timotheos (*c.*450-366 B.C.), but Wilamowitz (Timotheos, *Die Perser*, p. 107) has pointed out that this must be a misunderstanding. The temple referred to by Pliny, *N.H.* XXXVI.95 as having taken 120 years to build is perhaps not, as Pryce (op. cit. p. 36) thought, the Croesus temple, but the fourth-century one, though we cannot be certain, as the passage is confused, Skopas, the sculptor of the later temple, and Chersiphron, the architect of the Croesus temple, both being mentioned.

[23] As W. B. Dinsmoor has pointed out to me.

[24] Pryce, op. cit. p. 48.

[25] Herodotos I.26. We do not know when the Artemision was actually begun, but since it was a large building and involved difficult engineering feats (Vitruvius VII, pr. 16, and X.2.12-13; Pliny *N.H.* XXXVI.96-7) it must have been under construction for some time before Croesus dedicated his columns.

[26] For this date see above, note 19.

[27] Though the foot is in relief, it is in high relief, and we may therefore expect the differentiation of the toes to correspond to the renderings of works in the round (cf. p. 117, note 27).

[28] Pryce, op. cit. p. 59, considered this fragment as later in style than B 90; but he gives no specific reasons.

[29] Cf. Langlotz's excellent analysis in *Zeitbestimmung*, p. 12 f.

Our anatomical findings, therefore, and the date furnished by Croesus help to place the Melos group round the middle of the sixth century, that is, from a little before to a little after 550.

Since the karyatid head formerly associated with the Knidian Treasury at Delphi has been shown not to belong,[30] it can no longer serve as a landmark for absolute chronology. Stylistically, however, this head tallies with the kouroi of the Melos group—in its structure, the forms of its features, and the renderings of the drapery of the figures on the polos (we may note especially the treatment of the lower part of Hermes' short chiton; also the curious formation of the ear, similar to that in the Rhodian kouroi nos. 125, 126).[31]

Anatomical Analysis

The conception of the whole figure is simpler than before, in that the muscles are no longer separately accentuated. The forms, especially of the thorax and arm, are more true to nature. There is a tendency to generalization and flowing contour, and the effect of the whole is more graceful, but also tamer, than in the preceding group. In several examples we can see transitional forms between the earlier and later renderings. We have instances of forearms neither in the supine nor in the semi-pronated positions, but in an intermediary stage—turned slightly forward, though with an inward turn corresponding to the twist of the palm of the hand towards the body (cf. 94, 95, 96, 112, 116, 124). We have examples in which the greatest protrusion of the back, seen in profile, is still slightly higher than that of the chest. Though the lower boundary of the abdomen generally has straight sides, it sometimes forms a deep curve. And in some ears we see a tentative rendering of the antitragus. The Melos group, in other words, forms a transition between the earlier Volomandra-Tenea group and the later Anavysos-Ptoon 12 group.

STRUCTURE IN GENERAL. Greatest protrusion of back, seen in profile, level with or only slightly higher than that of chest. This is an advance on the earlier rendering, when the greatest protrusion of the back was placed definitely higher and the back had a more plank-like shape. Vertebral column slightly curved.

HEAD. *Skull.* Still generally flat at back, though sometimes well developed (for instance in no. 101 and in Eastern group, nos. 122, 125, 126, 127, 128).

Ear. Still generally placed high. Carved in more than one plane. Tragus sometimes assumes a more natural form. No indication of antitragus except tentatively here and there (cf. nos. 125-6). Anterior part of helix, which is directed backward (crus helicis), often prominent, joining upper end of tragus.

Eye. Sometimes outer corner considerably higher than inner. Recess at inner corner indicated, but not caruncle.

Mouth. Lips generally curve upward, and meet more or less at corners. Upper lip protrudes over lower.

Hair. Mass of hair generally arranged in beaded tresses, of which the globules are generally rather smaller than before. Large spiral curls often frame forehead.

NECK. Sterno-mastoids, when shown, indicated by slightly modelled shapes, but form is generalized. Occasionally throat is modelled for first time. No indication of swelling of trapezium.

[30] Cf. De La Coste-Messelière, *B.C.H.* LXII, 1938, pp. 285 ff., LXXVII, 1953, pp. 346 ff.

[31] Cf. Richter, *B.C.H.* LXXXII, 1958, pp. 92 ff.

TORSO, FRONT. Clavicles still generally protrude as flat ridges along whole course. Thorax better constructed than before; its lower boundary marked by rounded or pointed arch. Navel usually indicated as depression; no longer button-like. Three or four transverse divisions of rectus abdominis above navel generally indicated as modelled forms. Indication of external oblique bulging over iliac crest. Lower boundary of abdomen descends generally with straight, sometimes with curving sides towards genitals. Pubes, when represented, has upper edge either straight or in the form of two concave curves rising to a central point (cf. nos. 92, 106).

TORSO, BACK. Spinal furrow, shoulder-blades, and erector spinae often carved in the round.

ARM. Still attached to body below armpit and at hand. Forearm, viewed from front, no longer always turned forward in supine position, but sometimes assumes natural semi-pronated position conforming with palm of hand. (In several examples a transition between the two positions is observable.)

LEG. Depression over great trochanter sometimes indicated. Vastus internus descends below vastus externus. Junction of patella to shin-bone now more natural. Curve of shin-bone not as accentuated as before.

Foot. Few kouroi of this period with feet have been preserved. To judge from the extant feet of the kouros from Melos (no. 86) and of several bronze statuettes, the toes curve gently downward and still recede along one curve as they touch the ground, the big toe projecting a little further or being about the same length as the second toe, and the little toe slanting inward.

Kouroi Nos. 86-134

86 : Figs. 273-279

ATHENS, NATIONAL MUSEUM, no. 1558. From Melos.

Statue from head to plinth. Restorations: Right leg from just below knee to above ankle. Plinth broken in three pieces, but almost complete. Surface much weathered.

Naxian marble.
Height 2.14 m.
Found in Melos, in 1891. Feet and plinth found subsequently (after the last war, I am told).
Holleaux, *B.C.H.* XVI, 1892, pp. 560 ff., pl. XVI.
Kastriotes, *Γλυπτά*, no. 1558.
Δελτ. Ἀρχ., VII, 1891, p. 90 (circumstances of discovery of statue).
Buschor, *Fr. J.*, p. 64, figs. 76, 77.
Homann-Wedeking, *Anfänge*, p. 90, fig. 49.
Deonna, no. 114.

GENERAL STRUCTURE. Long and slender. Carved more in the round than no. 63. Muscles no longer separately accentuated. Seen in profile, greatest protrusion of back only slightly higher than that of chest. Vertebral column curved.

HEAD. *Skull.* Flat at back.

Ear. Long and placed high and vertical. Lobe flat with prolongation above, meeting tragus. No indication of antitragus.

Eye. Set obliquely. Carved more in the round than in nos. 63, 73, with feeling for eyeball. Recess at inner corner indicated.

Nose. Long and slender.

Mouth. Lips curve upward; meet at corners.

Hair. Falls down back in solid mass, which ends below in a horizontal line. Both at back and in front divided horizontally and vertically into squares. Over forehead and temples arranged in eight large spirals symmetrically to right and left from centre. No fillet.

NECK. Tilts slightly forward; long and rounded. No indication of sterno-mastoids now visible; construction of neck generalized; throat indicated. No swelling of trapezium.

TORSO, FRONT. Only heads of clavicles near sternum clearly visible. Median line only faintly visible. Thorax rather flat; arch indicating its lower boundary rises to level of pectorals. Four transverse divisions of rectus abdominis above navel. Navel marked by circular groove. Slight protrusion at slender flanks indicates swelling of external oblique over iliac crest. Lower boundary of abdomen descends with straight sides towards genitals.

TORSO, BACK. Broad, deep groove marks spinal furrow. Shoulder-blades indicated by slightly raised rounded planes, outlined by grooves; below these, similar grooves, one on each side, travel from spine downward and outward (cf. nos. 63, 120, 135). Slight indication of erector spinae.

ARM. Detached from side from a little below armpit to a little above wrist. Long and slender. Not bent at elbow. Forearm no longer in supine position, but turned inward in correct semi-pronated position; transition from forearm to wrist consequently natural.

Hand. Clenched, with thumb next to thigh but separated from it by deep groove. Little finger touches thigh at back. Lower head of ulna at wrist indicated by protrusion.

LEG. Depression over great trochanter not indicated. Internal vastus descends slightly lower than external one. Front edge of shin-bone is rounded and has not same decided inward curve as in nos. 63, 73. Patella has triangular shape, and attachments of muscles at side of knee better understood than in nos. 63, 73. Junction of patella with shin-bone now natural. Inner malleolus higher than outer.

Foot. Big toe directed forward; four others move gently downward and recede along one curve as they touch the ground, the big toe projecting a little further than the second one, and the little toe slanting slightly inward.

FOOT-PLINTH. Roughly oval in shape, following more or less contours of feet.

87 : Figs. 280-284

ELEUSIS, MUSEUM, no. 61. From Eleusis.

Statue, from top of head to knees. Face missing. Broken at neck; restoration at fracture.

Island marble.
Height 1.05 m.
Found at Eleusis, before 1896.
Kourouniotes, *'Ελευσίς, 'Οδηγός*, 1934, p. 71, no. 61.
Deonna, no. 19.

GENERAL STRUCTURE. Long and slender. Viewed in profile, greatest protrusion of back slightly higher than that of chest. Vertebral column straight.

HEAD. *Skull.* Somewhat rounded.

Ear. Has little depth and slants towards line of jaw. Antihelix forks into two ridges. Tragus projects from lobe. No antitragus indicated.

Hair. Falls down back in mass, which is divided horizontally by grooves and ends below in pointed members along horizontal line. On sides (in front) mass divided both horizontally and vertically. Above temples mass has scalloped edge. Simple fillet makes impress on hair.

NECK. Upper ends of sterno-mastoids slightly modelled; lower ends missing. No swelling of trapezium indicated.

TORSO, FRONT. Clavicles travel upward to shoulders. Median line indicated by depression from bottom of sternum to navel. Lower boundary of thorax not discernible. Divisions of rectus abdominis not clear. Navel marked by a depression. External oblique bulges a little over iliac crest. Lower boundary of abdomen descends with straight sides sharply towards genitals.

TORSO, BACK. Spinal furrow formed by broad groove. Shoulder-blades rather flat and not separately indicated. Erector spinae slightly modelled.

ARM. Separated from body from above elbow to hand. Forearm turned towards body in semi-pronated position.

Hand. Joined to thigh, but separated from it by groove.

LEG. Depression over great trochanter indicated. Inner vastus descends slightly lower than outer.

88 : Figs. 285-287

ATHENS, NATIONAL MUSEUM, no. 72.

Small torso from below neck to above knees. Either an early member of this group or a late one of the preceding.

Parian marble.
Height 44 cm.
According to Deonna, loc cit., this torso was found in the Kerameikos, but in the Museum inventory all that is said about its provenance is that in 1885 it was in the Museum basement (cf. also Kavvadias, *Γλυπτά*, 1890-92, p. 103). Deonna surmises that the torso is identical with one referred to by Furtwängler, *Arch. Ztg.* XL, 1882, col. 323, note 3, as being in the storeroom of the Archaeological Society in Athens.
Kavvadias, *Γλυπτά*, no. 72.
Kastriotes, *Γλυπτά*, no. 72.
Deonna, no. 4.

GENERAL STRUCTURE. Viewed in profile, greatest protrusion of back slightly higher than that of chest. Vertebral column somewhat curved.

TORSO, FRONT. Median line marked along linea alba. Lower boundary of thorax not discernible. Three

transverse divisions of rectus abdominis above navel are indicated by horizontal grooves. Navel marked by button-like protuberance within deep depression. Slight protrusion at flanks indicates swelling of external oblique over iliac crest. Lower boundary of abdomen descends towards genitals with straight sides.
TORSO, BACK. Right shoulder-blade (only one preserved) outlined by shallow groove. Erector spinae slightly indicated. Deep groove marks spinal furrow.
ARM. Separated from body from well below armpit to above wrist. Forearm turned towards body in semi-pronated position.
Hand. Clenched, with index finger placed against thigh.
LEG. No depression over great trochanter indicated. Preserved left knee oval shaped.

89 : Figs. 291-292

ATHENS, NATIONAL MUSEUM, no. 1904. From Keratea.

Statue, from head to below right knee. Unfinished: face and neck only roughly blocked out with point.

Pentelic marble.
Height 1.43 m.
Found in a cemetery at Keratea, Attica, in 1893.
Leonardos, *'Εφ. 'Αρχ.* 1895, cols. 75 ff., pl. VI.
Kastriotes, *Γλυπτά*, no. 1904.
Deonna, no. 6.

GENERAL STRUCTURE. Seen in profile, greatest protrusion of back level with that of chest. Vertebral column forms gentle curve.
HEAD. *Skull.* Rounded. Features unfinished and battered.
Ear. Placed high.
Eye. Large and rather flat, placed horizontally.
Hair. Falls down back in mass, which is divided into beaded tresses. Simple fillet without hanging ends.
NECK. Sterno-mastoids not discernible. Slight indication of swelling of trapezium.
TORSO, FRONT. Clavicles, lower boundary of thorax, divisions of rectus abdominis above navel not discernible. External oblique swells slightly over iliac crest. Lower boundary of abdomen descends with straight sides towards genitals.
TORSO, BACK. Much battered. Spinal furrow indicated by depression. Shoulder-blades not indicated. Too worn to determine whether erector spinae was marked.
ARM. Was joined to body for considerable way below armpit and at hand.
LEG. Apparently no indication of depression over great trochanter. As far as one can judge from battered state of right knee, inner vastus slightly lower than outer.

90 : Figs. 288-290

GENEVA, MUSÉE DE GENÈVE, no. 19175.

Torso from neck to middle of thighs. Surface battered.

Shell limestone.
Height 39 cm.
Provenance not known.
Deonna, *B.C.H.* LXXV, 1951, pp. 38 ff.

GENERAL STRUCTURE. Right leg, not left, slightly advanced. Viewed in profile, greatest protrusion of back higher than that of chest. Vertebral column only slightly curved.
TORSO, FRONT. Clavicles indicated by horizontal ridges. Median line marked. Lower boundary of thorax forms pointed arch. Four transverse divisions shown above navel in rectus abdominis. Slight protrusion at flanks to indicate swelling of external oblique over iliac crest. Lower boundary of abdomen descends with straight lines towards genitals.
TORSO, BACK. Short, deep, broad groove marks spinal furrow. Shoulder-blades not separately indicated. Buttocks about level.
ARM. Detached from side from somewhat below armpit to above thigh. Not bent at elbow. Forearm turned forward in supine position, whereas palm of hand is turned toward body.
HAND. Right held some object. Left arm missing from above elbow.

91 : Figs. 293-296

ATHENS, NATIONAL MUSEUM, no. 63. From Epidauros.

Head with part of neck, to which probably belongs the lower part of a torso, from below waist to below knees, found by Mr. Papadimitriou in 1956 in the same general locality in which the head came to light; marble and scale (a little over life size) are the same in both. Either an early member of this group or a late one of the preceding.

Island marble.
Height of head 34 cm.; of fragment of torso *c.*86 cm.
Found in the ruins of ancient city of Epidauros.
Kastriotes, *Γλυπτά*, no. 63.
Δελτ. 'Αρχ., 1888, pp. 153, 158.
Buschor, *Fr. J.*, p. 49, fig. 49.
Deonna, no. 75.

HEAD. Face oval.
Skull. Rounded at top, but flat at back.
Ear. Vertical, fairly flat. Tragus formed by excrescence from upper end of lobe. No antitragus marked.
Eye. Set obliquely. Groove marks upper boundary of

upper eyelid. Recess at inner corner of eye marked by downward cut.
Mouth. Lips curve upward and do not meet at corners.
Hair. Fell down back in mass. On skull simply blocked out; but below fillet divided horizontally and vertically into rectangular members; over forehead and temples arranged in large spiral curls symmetrically to right and left from centre.
ARM. Both arms were lowered to thighs, where traces of attachments remain.
LEG. Slight indication of depression over great trochanter. On outer side of thighs a broad groove travels downward. Buttocks level.

92 : Figs. 297-299

ATHENS, NATIONAL MUSEUM, no. 13. From Megara.

Torso, from neck to above right knee.

Island marble.
Height 2 m.
Found in Megara, in 1860.
Kavvadias, *Γλυπτά*, no. 13.
Pervanoglu, *Φιλίστωρ* I, 1861, p. 366 f.
Buschor, *Fr. J.*, p. 86, figs. 97, 98.
Homann-Wedeking, in Brunn-Bruckmann, *Denkmäler*, pls. 791-2.
Deonna, no. 77.

GENERAL STRUCTURE. Colossal. Elongated. Vertebral column slightly curved. Since back is injured in region of shoulder-blades, it is not possible to say where greatest protrusion was.
HAIR. Hangs down back; mass is divided horizontally and vertically into rectangular shapes, and ends below in curving line.
NECK. Attachments of sterno-mastoids to sternum indicated by modelled forms. No indication of swelling of trapezium.
TORSO, FRONT. Clavicles horizontal and protrude along whole course. Median line vertical along sternum but turns towards advanced leg from bottom of sternum to navel, tilt of genitals conforming. Ridges across sternum probably suggest articulation of the upper ribs. Lower boundary of thorax indicated by an arched groove far below pectorals. Rectus abdominis has three transverse divisions modelled above navel. Navel modelled with considerable depth and fold of flesh indicated above it. Flanks slender. Protuberance which indicates external oblique descending over iliac crest continues like a girdle as a prominent ridge round back, forming an angle at vertebral column. Lower boundary of abdomen descends with short, straight sides toward genitals. Pubes indicated as raised plane with straight, horizontal upper edge. Down each side of torso, where front and back meet, is a prominent ridge; for sides were not carved properly in the round where they were hidden by arms.
TORSO, BACK. Spinal furrow marked by broad depression. Shoulder-blades battered. Erector spinae not discernible.
ARM. Was separated from body except at hand; traces of attachments on both thighs. The quadrangular hole on right side near attachment of hand with remains of dowel, and another large hole on right side below armpit were perhaps due to an ancient repair.
LEG. Slight indication of depression over great trochanter. On outer side of thigh a broad groove travels downward.

93 : Figs. 300-301

ELEUSIS, MUSEUM.

Torso from below neck to middle of thighs. Broken in two pieces horizontally. Lower part battered.

Height *c.*86 cm.
Found at Megara.
Not published (here reproduced with the permission of Mr. Papadimitriou).

GENERAL STRUCTURE. Seen in profile, highest protrusion of back higher than that of chest.
Hair. Descends in parallel tresses.
TORSO, FRONT. Clavicles form curve. Lower boundary of thorax arched. Three horizontal divisions in rectus abdominis above navel. Protrusion at flanks not well developed. Lower boundary of abdomen descends to genitals with slightly curving lines.
TORSO, BACK. Battered. Spinal furrow marked by groove veering to (spectator's) right. Shoulder-blades marked by raised planes.
ARM. Was attached to body below armpit and probably at thighs in front.
LEG. Depression over great trochanter marked. Buttocks about level; left advanced.

94 : Figs. 302-305

THEBES, MUSEUM, no. 3. From the Ptoan Sanctuary.

Statue, from head to below right kneecap.

Boeotian(?) marble.
Height 1.37 m.
Found in Ptoan Sanctuary, in 1903.
Mendel, *B.C.H.* XXXI, 1907, pp. 193 ff., no. 3, pl. XX, figs. 5-6.

Karouzos, Ὁδηγός, p. 12, no. 3, figs. 8, 9.
Buschor, *Fr. J.*, p. 66 f., fig. 78.
Deonna, no. 43.

General Structure. Seen in profile, greatest protrusion of back higher than that of chest. Vertebral column forms slight curve.
Head. *Skull.* Rounded at top, but flat at back.
Ear. Slants slightly towards line of jaw; carved in several planes, but still fairly flat. Tragus attached to lobe. Antitragus not indicated.
Eye. Upper eyelid highly arched; groove marks its upper outline. No indication of recess at inner corner.
Mouth. Lips curve upward; perpendicular groove travels downward at each corner.
Hair. Falls down back in beaded tresses, ending in pointed members along horizontal line. Fillet knotted, with ends hanging down immediately after knot. Above forehead and temples hair arranged in series of curls, each of which is made up of three strands.
Neck. Sterno-mastoids indicated by slightly modelled shapes. No swelling of trapezium shown.
Torso, front. Clavicles horizontal and protruding all the way to shoulder. Deep groove marks median line from bottom of sternum to navel. Lower boundary of thorax indicated by groove forming acute angle just below pectorals. Four transverse divisions of rectus abdominis above navel, which is placed low. Navel marked as small, round button, with horizontal incision on either side. External oblique muscle bulges somewhat over iliac crest. Lower boundary of abdomen descends with straight sides towards genitals. Pubes carved as stylized form in relief, with straight upper edge.
Torso, back. Spinal furrow indicated by deep groove. Shoulder-blades marked by curving grooves. Slight indication of erector spinae along its whole course.
Arm. Only right preserved. Attached to body except for considerable portion at elbow. Forearm turned slightly forward in supine position, but with inward turn corresponding to twist of palm of hand towards body. Curving ridge above upper end of ulna (elbow).
Hand. Index finger was carved next to thigh.
Leg. No indication of depression over great trochanter. Inner vastus descends lower than outer and is more developed.

95 : Figs. 306-311

ATHENS, National Museum, no. 10. From the Ptoan Sanctuary.

Statue, from head to below knees.

Naxian marble.
Height 1.30 m.
Found in Ptoan Sanctuary, Boeotia, in 1885, about 20 m. distant from temple of Ptoan Apollo.
Holleaux, *B.C.H.* x, 1886, pp. 66 ff., pl. iv.
Kastriotes, Γλυπτά, no. 10.
Papaspiridi, *Guide du Musée National*, p. 26.
Grace, *Archaic Sculpture in Boeotia*, p. 65 f., figs. 76-7.
Buschor, *Fr. J.*, p. 63, figs. 74, 75.
Deonna, no. 28.

General Structure. Slender torso, well-developed arms, long waist. Little muscular development. Seen in profile, greatest protrusion of back somewhat higher than that of chest. Vertebral column forms slight curve.
Head. *Skull.* Gentle protrusion at back.
Ear. Small; slants towards line of jaw; carved more or less in one plane, but more naturalistic in shape than in Volomandra kouros, no. 63. Tragus slightly curved. No antitragus.
Eye. Eyeball flat. No indication of recess at inner corner.
Mouth. Triangular depressions at corners. Lips carved without detail.
Hair. Falls down back with ends forming curve; mass divided on skull into strands, but below fillet divided horizontally and vertically into rectangular shapes. Above forehead and temples divisions are vertical, with scalloped edge. Fillet, which encircles head without hanging ends, makes no impression on hair at back.
Neck. Slight indication of sterno-mastoids by modelled shapes. No indication of swelling of trapezium.
Torso, front. Slight indication of clavicles. Transition from chest to neck confused. Median line marked by shallow groove from below sternum to navel. Lower boundary of thorax not discernible. Divisions of rectus abdominis not discernible. Navel marked by depression and placed very low. Slight protrusion at flanks indicates swelling of external oblique over iliac crest. Lower boundary of abdomen descends with short, straight sides towards genitals.
Torso, back. Groove marks spinal furrow. No detailed indication of shoulder-blades or erector spinae.
Arm. Attached to torso along whole way, except for small distance at elbow. Forearm turned slightly forward in supine position, but with inward turn corresponding to twist of palm of hand towards body.
Hand. Thumb placed on thigh, and forefinger curves up behind it.
Leg. No indication of depression over great trochanter. Broad groove travels downward on outer side of thigh. Inner vastus descends lower than outer.

96 : Figs. 312-314

THEBES, MUSEUM, no. 6. From the Ptoan Sanctuary.

Torso, from neck to knees.

White, coarse-grained marble, probably Island.
Height 62 cm. Under life-size.
Found in Ptoan Sanctuary, in 1903.
Mendel, *B.C.H.* XXXI, 1907, pp. 196 ff., figs. 7, 8.
Karouzos, *'Οδηγός*, p. 12, no. 6.
Deonna, no. 44.

GENERAL STRUCTURE. Viewed in profile, greatest protrusion of back slightly higher than that of chest. Vertebral column forms gentle curve.
HAIR. Falls on back in pointed mass which is divided by grooves horizontally and vertically.
NECK. No indication of swelling of trapezium.
TORSO, FRONT. Clavicles travel upward and protrude all the way to deltoid. Median line marked by groove from bottom of sternum to navel. Thorax well developed; lower boundary formed by arched groove. Three transverse divisions of rectus abdominis above navel. Navel marked as small round button, with horizontal incision on either side. External oblique bulges a little over iliac crest. Flanks symmetrical. Lower boundary of abdomen descends with straight sides towards genitals.
TORSO, BACK. Spinal furrow marked by fairly deep depression. Shoulder-blades not separately indicated. Erector spinae not separately indicated.
ARM. Lower forearm very slightly turned to front.
Hand. Palm turned to body. Forefinger next to thigh.
LEG. No indication of depression over great trochanter. Inner vastus descends slightly lower than outer.

97 : Fig. 315

THEBES, MUSEUM, no. 4. From the Ptoan Sanctuary.

Torso, from lower part of head to right thigh.

Local blue marble.
Height 73 cm.
Found in the Ptoan Sanctuary, in 1903.
Mendel, *B.C.H.* XXXI, 1907, p. 198 f., no. 5, fig. 9.
Karouzos, *'Οδηγός*, p. 12, no. 4.
Deonna, no. 45.

GENERAL STRUCTURE. Viewed in profile, greatest protrusion of back level with that of chest. Vertebral column slightly curved.
HAIR. Hangs down in beaded tresses, each tress ending in pointed member; ends form curving line. Lower part undulating, following curve of shoulder.
NECK. No indication of sterno-mastoids or of swelling of trapezium.
TORSO, FRONT. Clavicles horizontal; disappear into shoulders. Median line hardly indicated. Well-developed chest; lower boundary of thorax indicated by arched groove placed below pectorals. Three transverse divisions of rectus abdominis above navel. External oblique bulges over iliac crest. Lower boundary of abdomen (preserved on one side) descends with straight sides towards genitals.
TORSO, BACK. Spinal furrow marked by broad groove. No indication of shoulder-blades or of erector spinae.
ARM. Was separated from body for good distance above and below elbow.

98 : Not illustrated

THEBES, MUSEUM, no. 2. From the Ptoan Sanctuary.

Statue, from back of head to below knees. Considerably restored in places.

Bluish, presumably Boeotian marble.
Height 1.48 m.
From Ptoan Sanctuary.
Karouzos, *'Οδηγός*, p. 12, no. 2.
Mentioned by Mendel, *B.C.H.* XXXI, 1907, p. 191 (*débris d'un grand Apollon*).
Deonna, no. 47, figs. 56, 57 (there shown in two fragments—torso and upper legs; since then reconstructed with head and additional fragments).

GENERAL STRUCTURE. Viewed in profile, greatest protrusion of back level with that of chest. Vertebral column curved.
TORSO, FRONT. Clavicles travel upward and lose themselves in shoulders backward. Median line hardly indicated. Lower boundary of thorax indicated by arch placed well below pectorals. Pectorals placed high. Divisions of rectus abdominis above navel not clear, because of damage to surface. External oblique muscle—preserved on right side—bulges over iliac crest.
TORSO, BACK. Depression marks spinal furrow. No separate indication of shoulder-blades or of erector spinae.
ARM. Attached to body except near elbow. Forearm turned towards body in semi-pronated position.
LEG. No indication of depression over great trochanter. Vastus internus descends below vastus externus.

99 : Figs. 316-318

CHAIRONEIA, MUSEUM. Once at Orchomenos.

Torso, from below neck to above right knee. Broken at waist; restorations at fracture.

Parian marble.
Height 77 cm.
Seen by Conze and Michaelis in 1860 in the court of the convent at Skripou near Orchomenos; afterwards lost; then refound.
Körte, *Ath. Mitt.* III, 1878, p. 307 f., no. 2.
Lullies, *Jahrbuch*, II, 1936, p. 149 f., figs. 10-12.
Buschor, *Fr. J.*, p. 141, figs. 160, 161.
Deonna, no. 27.

GENERAL STRUCTURE. Viewed in profile, greatest protrusion of back slightly higher than that of chest. Vertebral column curved.
HAIR. Hangs down back in mass divided into beaded tresses, with beads aligned horizontally, and each tress ending below in pointed member. Ends form slightly curving line. Vertical bands in middle evidently represent the two hanging ends of fillet.
TORSO, FRONT. Clavicles travel upward. Lower boundary of thorax and median line not clearly discernible. Transverse divisions of rectus abdominis above navel not clearly discernible, but its lower boundary is indicated by two grooves, one on either side of the abdomen, descending towards the genitals. External oblique bulging over iliac crest was probably more developed than present restoration. Two groins descend towards genitals, forming deep curve.
TORSO, BACK. Broad groove indicates spinal furrow; a shallower groove along each side of this furrow marks erector spinae along its entire length. Region of shoulder-blades damaged.
ARM. Was attached to side well below armpit and at hand.

100 : Figs. 319-321

ATHENS, NATIONAL MUSEUM, no. 11. From the Ptoan Sanctuary.

Torso, from neck to middle of thighs.

Island marble.
Height 80 cm.
Found in Ptoan Sanctuary, in 1885.
Kastriotes, *Γλυπτά*, no. 11.
Holleaux, *B.C.H.*, XI, 1887, p. 184, no. VII.
Buschor, *Fr. J.*, p. 61, fig. 71.
Deonna, no. 29.

GENERAL STRUCTURE. Viewed in profile, greatest protrusion of back about level with that of chest. Vertebral column slightly curved.
HEAD. *Hair.* Falls down back in mass, divided horizontally and vertically into rectangular members, and ending below in pointed members aligned horizontally.
NECK. Sterno-mastoids indicated by broad, shallow grooves meeting in a point over sternal notch. No indication of swelling of trapezium.
TORSO, FRONT. Clavicles horizontal and protrude all the way to shoulders. Median line marked by groove which runs from sternum to navel. Lower boundary of thorax indicated by shallow grooves forming arch. No transverse divisions of rectus abdominis above navel now visible. Navel indicated by incised circle. Slender flanks. Slight indication of external oblique bulging over iliac crest. Lower boundary of abdomen descends gently with straight sides towards genitals.
TORSO, BACK. Groove marks spinal furrow.
ARM. Was attached to side below armpit and at thigh.
LEG. Slight indication of depression over great trochanter.

101 : Figs. 322-323

ATHENS, NATIONAL MUSEUM, no. 16. From the Ptoan Sanctuary.

Head and neck. Surface much encrusted and weathered.

Pentelic marble.
Height 24 cm.
Found in Ptoan Sanctuary, in 1885.
Holleaux, *B.C.H.* X, 1886, pp. 74 ff., pl. VII.
Kastriotes, *Γλυπτά*, no. 16.
Deonna, no. 36.

HEAD. *Skull.* Well shaped.
Ear. Modelled in different planes. Tragus connected with lobe. No antitragus.
Eye. No recess at inner corner discernible.
Mouth. Lips curve slightly upward at corners.
Hair. Fell down back in mass, which is only roughly blocked out on skull and at back, but is divided into beaded tresses on front of sides; above forehead and temples mass is carved in waves with scalloped edge; two short straight tresses in front of each ear.
NECK. Sterno-mastoids marked.

Another head from the Ptoan Sanctuary (National Museum, Athens, no. 19; Deonna, no. 38; F. R. Grace, *Archaic Sculpture in Boeotia*, p. 68, fig. 78) also belongs here, as an early member of the Melos group, transitional between Tenea-Volomandra and Melos.

102 : Figs. 324-325

CHALKIS, MUSEUM, no. 44.

Head and part of neck.

Island marble.
Height *c.*25 cm.
Provenance unknown, but probably Euboea. Acquired from old private collection.

Homann-Wedeking, *Ath. Mitt.* 60/61, 1935/6, p. 216, pls. 82,2 and 83,2.
Buschor, *Fr. J.*, pp. 133 ff., fig. 152.

HEAD. *Skull.* Back mostly missing.
Ear. Slants towards line of jaw. Placed approximately in right position. Modelled in different planes. Tragus marked, but no antitragus.
Eye. Recess at inner corner indicated by narrow groove. Other details obliterated.
Mouth. Rather short. Lips curve slightly upward and do not meet at corners.
Chin. Broad and prominent.
Hair. Hangs down back. Mass divided horizontally and vertically into beaded tresses. Single row of large spiral curls over forehead, with tresses arranged in arcs of concentric circles over temple. Part of simple fillet preserved.

103 : Fig. 339

DELPHI, MUSEUM, no. 2696. From Delphi.

Torso, from neck to below genitals. Broken across waist. Since the photograph reproduced in fig. 280 of the 1st edition was taken, a piece from the top of the left arm has been found and attached (cf. Marcadé, *B.C.H.* LXXVII, 1953, p. 272, fig. 65, and our present fig. 339).

Parian marble.
Height 80 cm.
Found in 1895 at Delphi, above the SE. gate of the temenos.
Homolle, *B.C.H.* XXIV, 1900, p. 459, fig. 2.
Homolle, *F.d.D.* IV, fasc. 1, p. 56, no. 24, fig. 26 (Homolle thought that either this torso or the fragment no. 104 perhaps belonged to the base no. 105; cf. p. 92).
Buschor, *Fr. J.*, p. 150, fig. 173.
Deonna, no. 67, figs. 70, 71.

GENERAL STRUCTURE. Viewed in profile, greatest protrusion of back about level with that of front. Vertebral column forms curve.
HAIR. Fell down back in beaded tresses, with ends forming curve.
TORSO, FRONT. Clavicles travel upward. Thorax well developed. Vertical furrow marks median line from lower end of sternum to navel. Transverse divisions of rectus abdominis above navel not clearly discernible. Slight indication of swelling of external oblique over iliac crest. Lower boundary of abdomen descends towards genitals, forming deep curve.
TORSO, BACK. Much battered. Spinal furrow and erector spinae modelled.
ARM. Was attached to side until well below armpit.
LEG. Depression over great trochanter indicated.

104 : Fig. 340

DELPHI, MUSEUM, no. 4859. From Delphi.

Fragment from above flanks to middle of thigh. Back much battered.

Parian marble.
Height 40 cm.
Found at Delphi, inside Sanctuary, but exact place is not known.
Homolle, *B.C.H.* XXIV, 1900, pp. 459 f., fig. 3.
Homolle, *F.d.D.* IV, fasc. 1, p. 57 f., no. 25, fig. 27 (Homolle thought that either this fragment or no. 103 perhaps belonged to the base no. 105; cf. p. 92).
Deonna, no. 68.

TORSO, FRONT. Protrusion at flanks shallow. Lower boundary of abdomen descends towards genitals with more or less straight sides, pointing sharply downward.
ARM. Fractures at sides show that arms were held closely to sides from below waist.
LEG. Depression over trochanter marked.

105 : Fig. 335

DELPHI, MUSEUM, no. 2278. From Delphi.

Plinth, with parts of feet inserted into base and leaded.

Parian marble.
Right foot: length 29 cm.
Height of base: 20.5 cm.; length: 65 cm.
Found at Delphi, in 1880, between Naxian column and portico of the Athenians.
Homolle, *F.d.D.* IV, fasc. 1, pp. 54 ff., no. 23, fig. 24.
Haussoullier, *B.C.H.* VI, 1882, p. 445 f. (ill.).
Deonna, no. 69.
Marcadé, *Signatures*, I, 26.

Inscribed on upper side of base: *τοι Χ̣αροπ̣ινο π̣αιδες ἀνεθεσαν το Παριο*, 'The children of Charopinos the Parian dedicated it.'
The letters are not in the Parian but the Delphian alphabet. There is therefore no evidence furnished by the base that the statue which surmounted it was a Parian work (cf. p. 92).
FOOT. Enough remains of toes to show that they were well articulated, that they sloped gently downward, and that the big toe apparently projected a little further than the second toe.
Base. Corners rounded. At bottom of all four sides surface left roughly finished with point; above that smoothed. Presumably therefore only about 15 cm. of base protruded above ground. Space filled by lead between edges of plinth and of depression in base at one point as much as 3.2 cm.; both edges at this point clearly visible; cf. p. 44.

106 : Figs. 330-333

DELPHI, MUSEUM, no. 1663. From Delphi.

Statuette, from head to feet. Cast hollow; walls thick. Rectangular repairs for faults in casting. Surface considerably worn.

Bronze.
Height 41 cm.
Found at Delphi, in 1894.
Perdrizet, *F.d.D.* v, p. 35 f., no. 39, pl. IV.
Deonna, p. 271, no. 87.

GENERAL STRUCTURE. Sloping shoulders, long thighs. Seen in profile, greatest protrusion of back about level with that of chest. Vertebral column slightly curved.
HEAD. *Skull.* Back mostly missing.
Ear. Placed high; modelled in more than one plane; slants towards line of jaw. Apparently no antitragus marked.
Eye. Large and placed horizontally. Prominent lids; upper lid arches over eyeball.
Mouth. Lips curve upward.
Hair. Falls down back, shoulders, and chest in tresses. Notched fillet surrounds hair; under it is a diadem which is ornamented with rosettes and reaches to ears.
NECK. Sterno-mastoids marked by grooves meeting at sternal notch. Hair hides line of neck at shoulders. Necklace with pendant indicated in relief.
TORSO, FRONT. Median line travels from end of sternum to navel. Lower boundary of thorax not clear. Apparently three transverse divisions above navel in rectus abdominis. Navel marked by knob with apparently fold of flesh over it. Protrusion at flanks marks swelling of external oblique over iliac crest. Lower boundary of abdomen descends with short, straight sides gently towards genitals. Pubes indicated by raised, stylized plane, with upper edge in the form of two concave curves rising to central point (cf. no. 82).
TORSO, BACK. Spinal furrow marked by depression. Shoulder-blades slightly modelled. No indication of erector spinae.
ARM. Right arm bent at elbow and held away from body.
LEG. No indication of depression over great trochanter. Inner vastus descends lower and is more developed than outer. Inner malleolus higher than outer.
Foot. Shod with sandal. Toes recede along continuous line, big toe projecting further than second toe and little toe slanting inward. Toes not strongly articulated. Smaller toes and nails of left foot point gently downward; those of right foot point forward.

107 : Figs. 326-327

BERLIN, STAATLICHE MUSEEN, no. 538.

Head and part of neck, perhaps of kouros. Battered.

Coarse-grained white marble.
Height 35 cm.
Acquired by Berlin Museum in 1871 in Istanbul. Formerly in the collection of M. Déthier, who said that it was found at Perinthos; but this has turned out to be a mistake (cf. Blümel, *loc. cit.*). Some have thought that it must come from Asia Minor (cf. remarks of Deonna, p. 186, note 1, and Heuzey, *B.C.H.* VIII, 1884, p. 335 f.); but this is only a surmise.
Beschreibung der antiken Skulpturen, p. 210, no. 538.
Blümel, *Kat.*, A 20.
Deonna, no. 78.

GENERAL STRUCTURE. Modelling soft and fleshy.
HEAD. *Skull.* Back well developed.
Ear. Slants towards line of jaw. Carved in different planes. No indication of antitragus.
Hair. Falls in mass behind, divided horizontally and vertically into beaded tresses. Three tresses brought to front on each side.
NECK. No indication of sterno-mastoids.

108 : Figs. 336-338

ISTANBUL, MUSEUM, no. 374. From Thasos.

Torso, from below neck to knees. Surface has much suffered.

Thasian marble.
Height 1.34 m.
Found in Thasos. Exact finding place not certain.
Mendel, *B.C.H.* XXVI, 1902, pp. 467 ff., pl. IV.
Mendel, *Catalogue des sculptures*, II, no. 517.
Buschor, *Fr. J.*, p. 141, fig. 159.
Deonna, no. 127.

GENERAL STRUCTURE. Viewed in profile, greatest protrusion of back higher than that of chest, for, though back is well developed, chest is flat. Vertebral column forms curve.
HAIR. Hangs down back in beaded tresses.
TORSO, FRONT. Clavicles not clear. Lower boundary of thorax forms rounded arch. Three transverse divisions of rectus abdominis above navel. Slight indication of external oblique bulging over iliac crest. Lower boundary of abdomen descends towards genitals, forming deep curve.
TORSO, BACK. Spinal furrow marked by broad depression. Shoulder-blades indicated by raised planes. Erector spinae indicated.
LEG. Slight indication of depression over great trochanter. Muscles on outside of thigh marked by grooves. Inner vastus descends a little lower than outer.

109 : Figs. 328-329, 334

COPENHAGEN, NY CARLSBERG GLYPTOTHEK, no. 2823. From Thasos.

Head and neck. Part of back missing. Dowel hole for meniskos on top of skull.

Thasian marble.
Height 27.7 cm.
From Thasos. In a private collection there before 1906; later in the collection of A. Wix.
Sitte, *Öst. Jahr.* XI, 1908, pp. 142 ff., figs. 36-8, 40, pls. I, II.
V. H. Poulsen, *From the Collections of the Ny Carlsberg Glyptothek*, II, 1938, pp. 70 ff.
Buschor, *Fr. J.*, p. 71 f., fig. 81.
F. Poulsen, *Catalogue of Ancient Sculpture*, no. 18a.
Deonna, no. 128.

HEAD. *Ear.* Slants sharply in direction of jaw. Carved in several planes. Flat lobe. Tragus indicated but no antitragus.
Eye. Upper eyelid forms pronounced arch, lower slight curve. Recess at inner corner indicated.
Mouth. Lips curve slightly upward.
Chin. Pronounced.
Hair. Fell down back in mass, which was divided horizontally and vertically into beaded tresses. Arranged above forehead and temples in wavy tresses passing from side to side. Fillet encircles head. At back, above break, curves outward; this has been thought to indicate that the body was that of a sphinx. But also in kouroi hair sometimes curves outward, following curve of shoulders (cf. e.g. nos. 116, 117, 128, 144, 145, 147).

110 : Figs. 341, 344

DELOS, MUSEUM, no. A 4051. From Delos.

Torso, from neck to below knees.

Island marble.
Height 76 cm.
Found in 1904 at western terrace of temenos in Delos, where it had been used as building material.
Holleaux, *Comptes rendus de l'Académie des Inscriptions et Belles-Lettres*, II, 1904, p. 730.
Deonna, no. 89.

GENERAL STRUCTURE. Well proportioned and slender. Viewed in profile, greatest protrusion of back level with that of chest. Vertebral column slightly curved.
HAIR. Falls down back in beaded tresses, ending in pointed members along horizontal line.
NECK. No indication of swelling of trapezium.
TORSO, FRONT. Clavicles indicated by horizontal ridges. Median line marked by groove from bottom of sternum to navel. Lower boundary of thorax marked by shallow groove which forms nearly flat arch well below pectorals. Apparently three transverse divisions of rectus abdominis above navel. Navel is button-like protuberance within slight depression. External oblique bulges slightly over iliac crest. Lower boundary of abdomen descends with straight sides towards genitals.
TORSO, BACK. Spinal furrow marked by groove. Shoulder-blades marked by grooves. No indication of erector spinae.
ARM. Separated from body except at hand. Forearm turned towards body in semi-pronated position.
LEG. Buttocks and thighs well developed. Groove on outer thigh marks the ilio-tibial band. Inner vastus descends lower than outer.

111 : Figs. 342, 345

DELOS, MUSEUM, no. A 4083. From Delos.

Torso, from neck to below knees. Partly unfinished. Second-rate work.

Island marble.
Height 1.20 m.
Found in 1904 at western terrace of temenos in Delos, where it had been used as building material.
Holleaux, *Comptes rendus de l'Académie des Inscriptions et Belles-Lettres*, II, 1904, p. 730.
Deonna, no. 87.

GENERAL STRUCTURE. Seen in profile, greatest protrusion of back level with that of chest. Vertebral column slightly curved.
HAIR. Falls down back in a smooth, undifferentiated mass, which ends below in horizontal line.
NECK. No indication of swelling of trapezium.
TORSO, FRONT. Clavicles indicated by horizontal ridges which protrude along their whole course to deltoid. Pectorals placed high. Median line marked by broad groove from bottom of sternum to navel. Lower boundary of thorax almost obliterated. Rectus abdominis modelled as separate form but its divisions obliterated. Navel placed low and marked by depression. Slight indication of external oblique bulging over iliac crest. Lower boundary of abdomen descends with straight sides towards genitals. Genitals unfinished.
TORSO, BACK. Spinal furrow marked by broad groove. Shoulder-blades indicated by raised planes placed rather far apart. No indication of erector spinae.
ARM. Attached to body most of way except at elbow; intervening marble would perhaps have been partly removed if statue had been completed. Biceps well developed. Above protrusion of elbow a fold of flesh is indicated. Forearm turned towards body in semi-pronated position.
Hand. Unfinished; separate fingers not indicated.
LEG. No indication of depression over great trochanter. Muscles on outer thigh modelled. Inner vastus descends lower than outer.

112 : Figs. 343, 346

DELOS, MUSEUM, A 4048. From Delos.

Torso, from above pectorals to below kneecap.

Island marble.
Height 1 m.
Found at Delos, in 1885-6.
Deonna, no. 91.

GENERAL STRUCTURE. Seen in profile, greatest protrusion of back about level with that of chest. Vertebral column curved.
HAIR. Falls down back in beaded tresses, which form horizontal line below.
TORSO, FRONT. Median line marked by groove which descends to navel. Lower boundary of thorax marked by arched groove. Three transverse divisions of rectus abdominis indicated above navel. Navel marked as slight depression. Slight indication of external oblique bulging over iliac crest. Lower boundary of abdomen descends with straight sides towards genitals.
TORSO, BACK. Spinal furrow marked by groove. Shoulder-blades mostly missing. Erector spinae not marked.
ARM. Detached from body from a little above elbow to wrist. Rounded edge along sides where front and back planes meet (cf. nos. 92, 116). Forearm held in supine position, but with slight inward twist.
Hand. Index finger placed next to thigh.
LEG. No indication of depression over great trochanter. Groove on outer thigh marks leg muscles. Inner vastus descends a little lower than outer. Two grooves marking upper boundary of vasti descend towards kneecap.

113 : Not illustrated

DELOS, MUSEUM, no. A 1742. From Delos.

Torso, from neck to below knees. Surface much battered.

Island marble.
Height *c*.1.21 m.
Found in Delos, 27 May, 1908.
Holleaux, *Comptes rendus de l'Académie des Inscriptions et Belles-lettres*, 1908, p. 259 f., fig. 9.

GENERAL STRUCTURE. Slender and well shaped. Seen in profile, greatest protrusion of back a little higher than that of chest. Vertebral column slightly curved.
HAIR. Falls down back, but tresses no longer distinguishable.
NECK. No indication of swelling of trapezium.
TORSO, FRONT. Clavicles, lower boundary of thorax, divisions of rectus abdominis above navel not now discernible. Slight indication of external oblique swelling over iliac crest. Lower boundary of abdomen descends with straight sides towards genitals.
TORSO, BACK. Little anatomical detail now discernible.
ARM. Separated from body most of way. Forearm turned towards body in semi-pronated position.
Hand. Index finger next to thigh.
LEG. Depression over great trochanter not indicated. Inner vastus descends slightly lower than outer.

114 : Fig. 362

SANTORIN, MUSEUM. From Thera.

Torso, from below neck to above left knee. Much weathered.

Parian marble.
Height 94 cm.
Found in Thera, in 1902, beneath the terrace of the temple of Apollo Karneios.
Hiller von Gaertringen, *Thera*, III, p. 65, pls. 6, 15.
Deonna, no. 130.

GENERAL STRUCTURE. Greatest protrusion of back, seen in profile, level with that of chest. Vertebral column forms curve.
TORSO, FRONT. Little anatomical detail discernible. Protrusion at flanks marks iliac crest. Lower boundary of abdomen descends with straight sides towards genitals.
TORSO, BACK. Broad depression for spinal furrow.

115 : Figs. 353-355

BERLIN, STAATLICHE MUSEEN, no. 1555. From Naxos.

Torso, from neck to below left knee.

Naxian marble.
Height 1.12 m.
From Naxos. In 1892 was in the house of the physician Damiralis in Naxos and was said to have been found in the city in 1875.
Sauer, *Ath. Mitt.* XVII, 1892, p. 44, no. 44.
Buschor, *Fr. J.*, p. 63, figs. 72, 73.
Homann-Wedeking, *Anfänge*, p. 90 f., fig. 51.
Blümel, *Kat.*, A 18.
Deonna, no. 117.

GENERAL STRUCTURE. Greatest protrusion of back, viewed in profile, slightly higher than that of chest. Vertebral column slightly curved.
HAIR. Falls behind in mass divided horizontally and vertically into rectangular members, and terminating below in horizontal line.
NECK. No indication of swelling of trapezium.
TORSO, FRONT. Clavicles indicated by horizontal ridges

which protrude all along their course until they reach shoulders. Lower boundary of thorax indicated by rounded arch with apex well below pectorals. Median line marked by shallow groove from this arch to navel. No divisions now seen of rectus abdominis. Slight protuberance at flanks indicates external oblique descending over iliac crest, which continues as a prominent ridge round back, forming an angle at vertebral column. Flanks about level.

TORSO, BACK. Spinal furrow marked by shallow depression. Shoulder-blades indicated by raised rounded planes.

ARM. Attached to side below armpit and at hand from above wrist. Not bent at elbow. Forearm turned towards body in semi-pronated position.

Hand. Clenched, with thumb towards front and placed next to thigh, but separated from it by deep groove. Little finger touches thigh at back. Lower end of ulna, at wrist, indicated by protrusion.

LEG. Depression over great trochanter not indicated. Internal vastus descends slightly lower than external one.

116 : Figs. 356-358

PARIS, LOUVRE, no. MND 888. From Paros.

Statue, from head to knees. Two pieces broken from left arm refitted, with slight restorations at fractures. Slight plaster additions at fractures of legs for mounting.

Parian marble.
Height 1.035 m.
Found in the Asklepieion, Paros.
Rubensohn, *Ath. Mitt.* XXVII, 1902, pp. 230 ff., pl. XI.
Louvre, *Catalogue sommaire*, p. 41, no. 3101.
Buschor, *Fr. J.*, p. 123 f., figs. 142, 143.
Deonna, no. 122.

GENERAL STRUCTURE. Modelling soft and rounded. Greatest protrusion of back, seen in profile, level with that of chest. Vertebral column forms curve.

HEAD. *Skull.* Rounded at top, but only slightly developed at back.

Ear. Placed high and far back; right ear vertical, left ear slants backward. Modelled in different planes. No tragus or antitragus marked.

Eye. Slopes slightly upward. Groove outlines upper boundary of upper eyelid. Other details obliterated.

Mouth. Lips curve upward at corners.

Hair. Hangs down back; mass divided horizontally and vertically into beaded tresses, ending below in pointed members forming downward curve. Over forehead single row of large spiral curls arranged symmetrically to right and left from centre: loop over each temple. Simple fillet encircles hair showing somewhat formation of skull behind.

NECK. No indication of sterno-mastoids or of swelling of trapezium.

TORSO, FRONT. No indication of clavicles. Median line marked by shallow groove which travels from bottom of sternum to navel and curves slightly towards side of advanced leg. Pectorals placed high. Nipples not distinguishable. Thorax well developed. Its lower boundary forms a somewhat irregular rounded arch. Three transverse divisions of rectus abdominis above navel faintly indicated. Navel marked as rounded knob surrounded by groove. Slight protrusion at flanks indicates iliac crest. Flanks level. Lower boundary of abdomen descends with straight sides towards genitals. Down each side of torso, where front and back meet, is a ridge, the flanks not having been carved properly in the round, since they were covered by the arms. Some of the grooves and holes made by the tool as it tried to reach this area can still be seen.

TORSO, BACK. Spinal furrow indicated by shallow depression. Slight indication of shoulder-blades as raised planes. No indication of erector spinae.

ARM. Attached to side for considerable way below armpit and at hand. Slightly bent and well developed. Forearm turned slightly forward in supine position, but with inward turn corresponding to twist of palm of hand towards body.

Hand. Loosely clenched with second finger next to thigh.

LEG. Buttocks rather flat. No indication of depression over great trochanter. On outer side of thigh, groove travels downward. On right leg vastus internus descends lower than vastus externus; on left leg ends of vasti almost level.

117 : Figs. 347-349

COPENHAGEN, NY CARLSBERG GLYPTOTHEK, no. 2030. From Paros.

Torso, from neck to above right knee. Large hole in front of thorax.

Parian marble.
Height 81 cm.
From Paros.
Löwy, *Archäologisch-epigraphische Mittheilungen aus Oesterreich-Ungarn*, XI, 1887, p. 160 f., figs. 14, 15.
Ny Carlsberg Glyptothek, *Billedtavler*, pl. I, Ia.
Buschor, *Fr. J.*, pp. 126 f., figs. 146, 147.
F. Poulsen, *Catalogue of Ancient Sculpture*, no. Ia.
Deonna, no. 123.

GENERAL STRUCTURE. Soft modelling. Seen in profile, greatest protrusion of back somewhat higher than that of chest. Vertebral column curved.

Hair. Hangs down back in undulating strands, which end below in spiral curls, forming curving line. In front, four such strands fall over clavicles on each side of chest.
Neck. No indication of sterno-mastoids or of swelling of trapezium.
Torso, front. Sternal notch indicated by gentle depression between heads of clavicles. Median line not discernible. Lower boundary of thorax forms arch. Three transverse divisions of rectus abdominis faintly marked above navel. Protrusion at flanks indicates swelling of external oblique above iliac crest. Lower boundary of abdomen descends towards genitals, forming deep, narrow curve. Genitals were carved separately and are missing.
Torso, back. Broad groove for spinal furrow. Shoulder-blades modelled as separate slightly raised planes. Lumbar region modelled with indication of erector spinae.
Arm. Right arm was brought forward, as indicated by traces on right side.
Leg. Buttocks rather flat. Depression over great trochanter indicated by slight depression. Broad groove marks ilio-tibial band on side of thigh.

118 : Figs. 350-351

PAROS, Museum. From Paros.

Torso, from below neck to above knees. Surface much weathered.

Island marble.
Height 56 cm.
Found in Paros.
Sieveking in Arndt, *Einzelaufnahmen*, Serie v, p. 54, nos. 1330, 1331.
Buschor, *Fr. J.*, p. 123, figs. 144, 145.
Deonna, no. 125.

General Structure. Soft modelling. Greatest protrusion of back, viewed in profile, about level with that of chest. Vertebral column slightly curved.
Hair. Falls behind in mass, which is divided into tresses, terminating below in horizontal line.
Torso, front. Few anatomical details discernible. No divisions seen of rectus abdominis. Protrusion at flanks indicates iliac crest. Flanks level. Lower boundary of abdomen descends with straight sides towards genitals.
Torso, back. Spinal furrow marked as broad depression. No indication of erector spinae.
Leg. Rather flat buttocks. No indication apparent of depression over great trochanter.

119 : Fig. 352

ANDROS, Museum. From Andros.

Torso, from below neck to knees.

White, coarse-grained marble.
Height 82 cm.
Found in Andros.
Theophil Sauciuc, *Andros*, 1914, p. 42 f., fig. 51.

General Structure. Seen in profile, greatest protrusion of back a little higher than that of chest. Vertebral column slightly curved.
Torso, front. Little anatomical detail discernible. Clavicles fairly horizontal. Slight protrusion at flanks. Lower boundary of abdomen descends with straight sides towards genitals.
Torso, back. Spinal furrow marked by shallow depression. Shoulder-blades indicated as separate planes. Erector spinae not marked.
Arm. Was attached to body below armpit and at hand.

120 : Figs. 359-361

VATHY, Museum. From Samos.

Torso, from neck to above left knee.

Island marble.
Height 1.05 m.
From Misokampos, Samos.
Buschor, *Alt. St.* I, p. 18 f., figs. 58, 61, 62; *Fr. J.*, p. 142, figs. 162, 163.

General Structure. Seen in profile, greatest protrusion of back above that of chest. Vertebral column curved.
Hair. Hangs down back in beaded tresses, with ends forming curve.
Torso, front. Clavicles slant upward; groove above sternal notch. Depression marks median line. Lower boundary of thorax forms grooved arch. Three transverse divisions of rectus abdominis marked above navel. Slight protuberance at flanks shows swelling of external oblique above iliac crest. Flanks symmetrical. Lower boundary of abdomen descends towards genitals, forming a deep curve.
Torso, back. Spinal furrow marked by deep groove. Shoulder-blades marked by curving grooves; beneath, on each side, a groove travels downward and outward perhaps to indicate ribs (cf. nos. 63, 86, 135). Erector spinae shown as modelled shape.
Arm. (Mostly missing.) Was attached to body for considerable way below armpit and then separated until juncture at hand.
Leg. Slight hollow over great trochanter.

121 : Not illustrated

VATHY, Museum. From Samos.

Torso, from neck to middle of thighs.

Grey marble.
Height 85 cm.
Found in the northern cemetery, Samos.
Wiegand, *Ath. Mitt.* xxv, 1900, p. 151.
Buschor, *Alt. St.* I, p. 19, figs. 65, 66.
Deonna, no. 138.

General Structure. Seen in profile, greatest protrusion of back about level with that of chest. Vertebral column forms slight curve.
Hair. Hangs down back in beaded tresses, with ends forming curve.
Torso, front. Clavicles slant upward. Depression marks median line. Lower boundary of thorax forms pointed arch, placed well below pectorals. Divisions of rectus abdominis not clear. Navel marked as button surrounded by circular groove within depression. Slight protrusion at flanks shows swelling of external oblique above iliac crest. Lower boundary of abdomen descends towards genitals, forming deep curve.
Torso, back. Deep groove marks spinal furrow. Shoulder-blades not discernible.
Arm. Was attached to body below armpit and at hand.

122 : Figs. 377-378

VATHY, Museum. From Samos.

Head and neck. Face battered.

Marble.
Height 39 cm. About 1½ life size.
Found East of the Heraion, Samos.
Buschor, *Alt. St.* I, p. 14, figs. 42-4.

General Structure. Modelling soft and fleshy.
Head. *Skull.* Well developed.
Ear. Carved in different planes; placed about correctly; slants towards line of jaw.
Mouth. Vertical groove at corners of lips.
Hair. Hangs down back in mass divided into beaded tresses. Shorter tresses brushed back on sides are similarly subdivided; each tress ends in a spiral curl. No fillet.
Neck. No sterno-mastoids marked.

123 : Fig. 363

VATHY, Museum. From Samos.

Youth from group of two youths and female draped figure.

Bronze.
Height 13 cm.
Found in the Heraion, Samos.
Buschor, *Alt. St.* I, p. 12, figs. 33, 34.

General Structure. Viewed in profile, greatest protrusion of back a little higher than that of chest. Cursory workmanship; details indistinct.
Hair. Falls down in mass behind, ending in approximately horizontal line.
Torso, front. Clavicles travel upward. Lower boundary of thorax indicated as an arch below pectorals. No divisions of rectus abdominis marked. Slight protrusion at flanks. Lower boundary of abdomen forms shallow curve.
Arm. Attached to side all the way down. Forearm turned towards body.

124 : Figs. 365-368

RHODES, Museo Archeologico. From Rhodes.

Torso, from neck to knees.[32]

Island marble.
Height 1.15 m.
Found with no. 154 on the akropolis of Kamiros, Rhodes, leaning against an altar of Helios.
Jacopi, *Clara Rhodos*, vi-vii, I, p. 256, fig. 44; pp. 274 ff., no. 6, figs. 62-5, pl. x.

General Structure. Sloping shoulders. Soft, rounded modelling. Greatest protrusion of back, seen in profile, level with that of chest. Vertebral column forms slight curve.
Hair. Hangs down back as far as shoulders in mass divided horizontally and vertically, with ends ending in horizontal line.
Neck. No indication of swelling of trapezium.
Torso, front. Clavicles slant slightly upward, protruding along their whole course. Median line marked from lower end of sternum to navel. Lower boundary of thorax not discernible. Divisions of rectus abdominis above navel not now discernible. Slight protrusion at flanks indicates external oblique descending over iliac crest. Lower boundary of abdomen descends with straight sides towards genitals.
Torso, back. Fairly flat. Groove marks spinal furrow. Shoulder-blades shown by slightly raised planes. Likewise erector spinae.
Arm. Free from body except under armpit and at hand. Forearm turned forward in supine position, but with inward turn corresponding to twist of hand towards body.
Hand. Clenched, with thumb and little finger next to thigh. Marble left adhering between thumb and index finger.

[32] L. Laurenzi showed me (in 1938) a very battered head in two pieces (height 31 cm., height of face from forehead to chin 20.5 cm.) which he thought might belong to this statue. It was found by him near where the statue was discovered.

LEG. No indication of depression over great trochanter. Vastus internus descends slightly lower and is more developed than vastus externus.

125 : Figs. 373-375

RHODES, MUSEO ARCHEOLOGICO. From Rhodes.

Head and neck. Surface very worn, especially face.

Grey marble with white veins.
Height 33 cm.
Found in 1931-2 at Kamiros, Rhodes.
Jacopi, *Clara Rhodos*, VI-VII, I, pp. 265, 268, figs. 50-54.

GENERAL STRUCTURE. Heavy, rounded forms. Eastern type.
HEAD. Receding forehead.
Skull. Flat at top and back.
Ear. Large; slants towards line of jaw. Construction similar to that of no. 126; that is, ear is carved in several planes, with an attempt at indication of antitragus; but latter is wrongly placed; instead of being at root of antihelix it joins on to helix (cf. no. 126 and p. 95.)
Eye. Almost horizontal. Recess at inner corner no longer discernible.
Mouth. Lips more or less horizontal.
Hair. Falls down at back in mass of undulating strands, mass being divided horizontally and vertically into rectangular members.
NECK. Sterno-mastoids not indicated.

126 : Fig. 376

RHODES, MUSEO ARCHEOLOGICO, no. 13650. From Rhodes.

Left side of head and neck.

Island marble.
Height 26 cm.
Found in 1931-2 at Kamiros, Rhodes.
Jacopi, *Clara Rhodos*, V, I, pp. 78 ff., fig. 50.

GENERAL STRUCTURE. Soft forms.
HEAD. *Skull.* Well developed.
Ear. Carved in different planes; inner portion of antihelix in much lower plane than helix. Attempt to indicate antitragus, but it is wrongly placed. Instead of being at root of antihelix, it joins on to the helix, cutting across the antihelix (cf. no. 125 and p. 95).
Eye. Recess at inner corner indicated.
Hair. Falls down behind in solid mass; divided horizontally and vertically by grooves forming beads, which are not horizontally aligned. Shorter tresses, similarly subdivided, extend backward on either side of broad parting in middle, each tress ending in spiral curl. No fillet.

127 : Figs. 369-370

ISTANBUL, MUSEUM, no. 1645. From Rhodes (?).

Head and neck.

White-blue marble with blackish veins.
Height 47 cm.; larger than life-size.
Provenance not certain, but supposed to be Rhodes (cf. Mendel, loc. cit.).
Heuzey, *B.C.H.* VIII, 1884, pp. 333 ff., pl. X.
Mendel, *Catalogue des sculptures*, II, no. 530.
Schede, *Meisterwerke der türkischen Museen*, I, pl. I.
Buschor, *Fr. J.*, pp. 80 ff., figs. 90, 91.
Guide to the Istanbul Museum, p. 38, pl. I.
Deonna, no. 134.

GENERAL STRUCTURE. Modelling soft and fleshy.
HEAD. *Skull.* Rounded at top, rather flat at back.
Ear. Slants towards line of jaw. Carved in different planes.
Eye. Set obliquely.
Mouth. Lips curve slightly upward.
Hair. Falls in mass behind, divided first vertically, and then horizontally to form tresses. Shorter tresses, similarly subdivided, extend backward from forehead to temples, reaching to behind ears. Above forehead small vertical ridges and above temples oblique ones.

128 : Figs. 371-372

LONDON, BRITISH MUSEUM, B 283. From Didyma.

Head and left shoulder.

Island marble.
Height 31 cm.
From Didyma.
Pryce, *Catalogue*, B 283, p. 114, f., fig. 174.
Deonna, no. 131.

GENERAL STRUCTURE. Modelling soft and fleshy. Shoulders sloping and rounded.
HEAD. *Skull.* Top and back well developed.
Ear. Placed correctly; slants slightly towards line of jaw; carved in different planes. Tragus indicated, but apparently no antitragus.
Eye. Set more or less horizontally with eyeball protruding; details not clear.
Mouth. Horizontal. Lips meet at corners.
Hair. Falls down back in solid mass, which ends below in slightly curving line; divided horizontally by broad, shallow grooves and vertically by deeper, narrower ones; shorter tresses, similarly subdivided, extend backward on either side of parting in middle of front (cf. nos. 122, 126, 127, 129, 130). No fillet.
NECK. No indication of sterno-mastoids or of swelling of trapezium.

TORSO, FRONT. Clavicle marked by shallow ridge, which loses itself on shoulder.

129 : Figs. 379-380

LONDON, BRITISH MUSEUM, B 323.

Front of a head. Surface much weathered. Battered. Back missing.

Coarse-grained marble.
Height 22 cm.
From the Temple of Apollo, Kalymnos. Excavated by C. T. Newton, 1855.
Newton, *Travels and Discoveries*, I, p. 307.
Pryce, *Catalogue*, B 323.

GENERAL STRUCTURE. Modelling soft and fleshy.
HEAD. *Skull.* Top well developed.
Eye. Set more or less horizontally, with eyeball protruding. Details not clear.
Mouth. Lips full and curving; meet at the corners.
Nose. Broad at base.
Hair. Was evidently divided vertically and horizontally into tresses (only small part remains), with shorter, similarly subdivided tresses extending backward from forehead and left temple (as in nos. 122, 126, 127, 128, 130, 132.

130 : Figs. 381-383

SMYRNA, MUSEUM, no. 1022.

Head and part of neck.

Marble.
Height 24 cm.
Found at Keramos, near Halikarnassos.
Picard, *Rev. des études grecques*, XLVI, 1933, p. 106.
Devambez, *A.J.A.*, XXXIX, 1935, pp. 344 ff.
Brommer, *Arch. Anz.* 1952, cols. 55 f., figs. 7, 8.
Buschor, *Fr. J.*, p. 142, fig. 164.

GENERAL STRUCTURE. Modelling soft and fleshy.
HEAD. *Skull.* Rounded at top, rather flat at back.
Ear. Slants towards line of jaw. Carved in different planes.
Eye. Set more or less horizontally. Inner corner directed downward.
Hair. Falls down behind in mass, divided vertically and horizontally into beaded tresses, some of which fall on shoulder. Above forehead and temples vertical, undulating, shorter ridges extend backward to above ears.
Chin. Strong.
Neck. Thick.

Here should also be placed a similar head in Cairo, found in Egypt (Bissing, *Arch. Anz.* 1901, p. 99, no. 3, fig. 9; Edgar, *Catalogue général des antiquités egyptiennes*, no. 27428, pl. I; Deonna, no. 146; Brommer, *Arch. Anz.* 1952, cols. 48 ff., figs. 1-4); the height is 6.5 cm.

131 : Fig. 384

SMYRNA, MUSEUM.

Back of head.

Fine-grained, greyish marble.
Height 24.5 cm.
Provenance not known.

SKULL. Rounded at top, somewhat flat behind.
Ear. Slants towards line of jaw. Carved in different planes.
Hair. Falls in mass behind, divided vertically and horizontally by grooves forming rounded beads. Shorter tresses, similarly subdivided into elongated beads, extend backward on either side, reaching to behind ears.

132 : Figs. 385-386

SMYRNA, MUSEUM, no. EN 508.

Back of head.

Marble.
Height *c.*23 cm.
From Miletos.

SKULL. Rounded at top, flat at back.
Ear. Slants towards line of jaw. Carved in different planes.
Hair. Falls behind in mass divided vertically into grooves forming undulating tresses. Similar, shorter tresses extend backward from temple to behind ear (cf. no. 129).

From Didyma come also two torsos belonging to the Melos group, now in the Museum of SMYRNA: (1) no. 470: 98 cm. high, preserved from below neck to middle of left thigh. (2) no. 520: 68 cm. high, preserved from below neck to upper thighs; it has a deep abdomen (see p. 91), and a ridge travels at its sides from protuberance at shanks to back.

Here too belongs the limestone statue of a kouros, with a mantle hanging from the left shoulder, found in 1958 in a necropolis at Çandarh, and now in the Museum at PERGAMON. It is 1.62 m. high, practically complete, with plinth and base preserved, but with the surface much weathered. (Boehringer, in *Neue Deutsche Ausgrabungen, Deutsches Archäologisches Institut*, 1959, p. 167 f., figs. 34, 35.)

To judge by a small photograph kindly sent me by C. Blümel, a kouros from Miletos in BERLIN should also belong here; height as preserved, from head to right knee, 1.646 m. It is shortly to be published by C. Blümel.

Likewise here should belong the fine, battered head, of unknown provenance, now in the collection of Dr. E. Borowsky, BASLE. Height 18 cm. Cf. *Mostra di Sculture antiche*, Bergamo, 1958, p. 6, no. VII. Also the torso in CLEVELANA, Inv. no. 53.125, height 62·5 cm.; cf. Cahn, *Antike Kunst* I, 1958, pp. 75 f., pl. 32; Schefold, *Meisterwerke griechischer Kunst* (1960), no. 163.

133 : Fig. 387

CYRENE, MUSEUM, no. 14.002.

Torso, from below neck to knees.

Coarse-grained marble.
Height 1.18 m.
Found at Cyrene, near the Strategeion.
Homann-Wedeking, in Brunn-Bruckmann, *Denkmäler*, text to pls. 791, 792, fig. 2.
Chamoux, *Cyrène*, pp. 246 ff., pl. XXI, 3.
E. Paribeni, *Catalogo delle sculture di Cirene*, no. 4, pls. 6, 7.

GENERAL STRUCTURE. Greatest protrusion of back, seen in profile, higher than that of chest. Vertebral column slightly curved.
Hair. Falls down back in mass divided horizontally and vertically into rectangular shapes and ending below in pointed members along horizontal line.
TORSO, FRONT. No indication of swelling of trapezium on line of shoulder. Lower boundary of thorax forms pointed arch with apex well below pectorals. Median line marked by shallow groove. No divisions discernible in rectus abdominis. Protuberance at flanks, that indicates external oblique descending over iliac crest, continues as a ridge round back to vertebral column and in front to genitals, marking lower boundary of abdomen. Navel indicated by incision. Flanks level.
TORSO, BACK. Spinal furrow marked by broad depression.
ARM. Was attached to side for some distance below armpit and at hand from above wrist (as indicated by fractures on both sides).
LEG. Internal vastus about level with external one. Buttocks rather flat and level.

Here too should belong two other torsos of kouroi from CYRENE and now in the Museum there, nos. 14000, 14001 (Olivero, *Africa Italica*, II, p. 29, figs. 19, 22; Chamoux, *Cyrène*, pp. 348 f., pl. XXI, 4, 5; E. Paribeni, *Catalogo delle sculture di Cirene*, nos. 2, 3, pls. 2-5).

134 : Figs. 388-390

SYRACUSE, NATIONAL MUSEUM. From Megara Hyblaia.

Torso from neck to below knees. Inscription on right leg (see below). An early member of this group or a late one of the preceding.

Island marble.
Height 1.19 m.
Found in 1940 south of the ancient city of Megara Hyblaia; perhaps from a cemetery.
Bernabò Brea, *Annuario*, XXIV-VI (new series VIII-X), 1946-8, pp. 59 ff., pls. VII-X.

GENERAL STRUCTURE. Viewed in profile, greatest protrusion of back a little higher than that of chest. Vertebral column curved.
Hair. Hangs down back in thick mass, divided into beaded tresses and tied with fillet near bottom.
TORSO, FRONT. Clavicles marked by ridges from sternal notch to shoulders. Lower boundary of thorax forms narrow arch with apex well below pectorals. No divisions visible in rectus abdominis. Linea alba marked by slight depression. Slight protuberance at flanks indicates external oblique descending over iliac crest. Flanks about level. Lower boundary of abdomen descends with straight sides towards genitals. Navel indicated by oval knob within depression.
TORSO, BACK. Deep groove marks spinal column. Shoulder-blades indicated by slightly raised, rounded planes.
ARM. Attached to side for considerable way from below armpit and at hand above wrist. Not bent at elbow. Forearm turned toward body in semi-pronated position.
HAND. Clenched, with thumb turned toward front and placed next to thigh. Little finger touches thigh at back.
LEG. Buttocks rather flat and about level. Depression caused by great trochanter indicated. On outer side of thigh groove travels downward. Internal vastus descends only slightly lower than external one.
Inscribed, right to left, on right leg: *Σομροτίδα: τô hιατρô: τô Μανδροκλέος*:; "Of Sombrotidas, the physician, son Mandrokles". The alphabet is that of the majority of archaic inscriptions found in Megara Hyblaia; cf. Carrabelli, *Annuario*, XXIV-VI (new series VIII-X), p. 67 f.; there dated middle of sixth century B.C.

Here too should belong the terracotta head found at AGRIGENTO and now in the Antiquario there (Griffo, *Agrigento, Guida*, 1955, p. 108, fig. 24); Bernabò Brea, Musei e Monumenti di Sicilia, 1958, p. 137, left.

IX. THE ANAVYSOS-PTOON 12 GROUP
(*c.* 540–520 B.C.)

General Survey and Historical Background

ATTICA. The period of the Anavysos-Ptoon 12 group is again one of great development. The most notable kouroi come from Attica, the near-by island of Keos, and Boeotia. The yield from Attica is indeed impressive—the Munich kouros (no. 135), the statue recently found at Anavysos (no. 136), the Akropolis torso (no. 137), the Rayet head (no. 138), and several heads, in the Akropolis Museum (no. 139, 140), the Louvre (nos. 141, 142), and Boston (no. 143). The three first are closely related, though hardly the work of the same artist, for there are fundamental differences. In point of time they must belong early in the group, the Munich kouros being perhaps the earliest, if we may judge by the linear rendering of some of the muscles.

One can understand the high distinction of these and other works of this epoch, like the Peplos kore 689 and her 'twin' 688, when one remembers that their historical background is the time of Peisistratos and his sons, when Athens became one of the leading Greek states, the centre of the artistic life of the time.

KEOS. The statue which was found in Keos (no. 144) is one of the finest products of the time, comparable to the Attic kouroi nos. 135-137, though probably a little later; for the anatomical rendering especially of the back is more advanced. It is of course likely that Keos, being so close to Athens, was artistically under Attic influence at this time. Since the famous lyric poet Simonides was born at Keos in 556 B.C., he might have seen this statue—surely one of the most distinguished products of his home—when he was perhaps about 30 years old.[1]

BOEOTIA. The Ptoan Sanctuary supplies the attractive statue Ptoon 12 (no. 145) and heads from two other kouroi (nos. 146, 147). Ptoon 12 resembles the Attic and Keos kouroi (nos. 135-7, 144), but is softer, less sturdy. In point of development it is more advanced than the Attic statues, perhaps a little earlier than the Keos one. It has often been considered a product of Attica. That prominent Athenians made dedicatory offerings at the Ptoan Sanctuary in the sixth and early fifth centuries is shown by two inscriptions found there, one by Alkmeonides in celebration of a victory in the Panathenaic games, datable in the decade 566-556,[2] the other by Hipparchos, perhaps a son of the younger Peisistratos,[3] datable about 497-496. It is therefore quite possible that Ptoon 12 was an Attic dedication. On the other hand, there is no reason why it should not be Boeotian. The different members of the Boeotian League were at this time issuing a flourishing coinage. We hear of Boeotia joining Megara in the colonization of Herakleia on the Pontos.[4] And there was in Boeotia, as we have seen, a long sculptural tradition (cf. pp. 32, 59, 75, 90 f.). Moreover, the style is sufficiently unlike that of the three extant kouroi from Attica of this period to indicate perhaps a different origin.

[1] Cf. Geffcken, Pauly-Wissowa, *R.E.*, 2. Reihe, III, A, 1, 1927, cols. 186 f.

[2] Bizard, *B.C.H.* XLIV, 1920, pp. 227 ff. Bizard dated it 554-539; Raubitschek, on the style of the letters, has suggested the date given above.

[3] Cf. Bizard, op. cit. pp. 237 ff., who assigned it to Hipparchos the tyrant, and so dated it 520-514. For the date above given cf. Meritt, *Hesperia*, VIII, 1939, pp. 64 ff.

[4] Ephoros, frgt. 44, Jacoby; Ap. Rhod. II, 874; Promathidas of Herakleia, frgt. 3.

EUBOEA. A head in the Museum at Chalkis (no. 148) was probably found, like no. 102, in Euboea, but its exact provenance is not known, for it entered the Museum from an old, private collection. It must once have been a fine example of this period, but is now badly battered.

DELOS. A torso from Delos (no. 151) has a markedly long-drawn-out abdomen, of the form by some considered Parian (cf. p. 91), but observable on kouroi of different provenance belonging to this and the preceding period (cf. e.g. nos. 103, 104, 108, 117, 118, 120, 154).

NAXOS. As we saw, the mid-sixth-century torso in Berlin (no. 115) is our only example from Naxos of about the time of her great tyrant Lygdamis, the friend of Peisistratos and Polykrates. We have reason to believe that she played her part in the artistic activity of the second half of the sixth century, especially as Herodotos[5] informs us that a little later—at the beginning of the Ionian revolt—she 'surpassed all the other islands in prosperity'. That there is so little sculpture from Naxos —no worthy successors of the Naxian Colossus, and the Naxian Sphinx—may very well be due to chance; for Naxos has as yet been inadequately excavated.[6] Or perhaps the reason is that interest in bronze casting—associated especially with Rhoikos and Theodoros in the neighbouring Samos at just about this time (cf. p. 8)—diverted interest from work in marble to that in bronze. In that case, the disappearance of contemporary statues would be sufficiently explained by the fact that bronze, being intrinsically valuable, was melted down.

SAMOS. At all events, when we turn to Samos we find that a similar circumstance holds. We have reached the time of the tyrant Polykrates (537-*c.*522), when Samos 'ruled the waves', undertook great building operations, entertained the poet Anakreon, produced her own great philosopher Pythagoras. We should have expected many splendid Samian works of this prosperous epoch. Instead, it is of just this period that the extensive excavations in Samos have yielded little sculpture. The best examples of kouroi are the sadly mutilated torso from near Chora (no. 153), where a number of graves have been found, and two pieces of the left leg of a colossus (1½ to 1⅔ times life size) from the Heraion, inscribed [Χηρα]μύης *μάνέθηκ*[*ε θεῆι περικαλλ*]*ὲς ἄγαλμα*, datable c. 540 B.C.[7] The few other kouroi of this period are minor works in an even more mutilated state.[8] Perhaps the popularity of bronze for the sculpture of this period would give a plausible explanation (cf. p. 9).

Absolute Chronology

For this group we have a valuable landmark for absolute chronology in the Siphnian Treasury at Delphi, which can be definitely dated before 525 B.C. on external evidence. For Herodotos speaks of an adverse oracle which was given to the Siphnians while they were building their Treasury at Delphi, and which was afterwards fulfilled in a Samian attack[9]—dated in 525 by its connection with Kambyses' attack on Egypt.[10] In the present state of the text, Herodotos seems to imply that the

[5] v.28.

[6] For a temple dating from 'the last third of the sixth century' see Welter, *Ath. Mitt.* XLIX, 1924, pp. 17 ff.; *Arch. Anz.* 1930, cols. 132 ff.

[7] Cf. Buschor, *Alt. St.* I, p. 12, figs. 17-18; in *Schweitzer Festschrift*, 1954, pp. 97 ff., fig. 3, pl. 13; and *Alt. St.* IV, figs. 262, 263.

[8] Buschor, *Alt. St.* I, figs. 63, 64, 70, 71.

[9] III.57, 58. For a different version of the story cf. Pausanias X.11.2: 'But when out of greed they ceased to bring the tribute, the sea flooded and obliterated the mines.'

[10] The Egyptian campaign took place in the fifth year of Kambyses' reign (= spring of 525 B.C.), cf. Gauthier, *Le Livre des rois d'Egypte*, IV, pp. 135 ff.

attack followed soon after the oracle, the *τότε* in the sentence: *τοῖσι δὲ Σιφνίοισι ἦν τότε ἡ ἀγορὴ καὶ τὸ πρυτανήιον Παρίῳ λίθῳ ἠσκημένα* seeming to refer to the time the oracle was given. And archaeologists[11] have accordingly dated the Siphnian Treasury about 525 B.C.[12]

On the sculptures of the Siphnian Treasury[13]—frieze, pediment, and parts of two Karyatids—we find the following anatomical characteristics:

(1) The highest protrusion of the back is level with that of the chest.

(2) The skull is spherical and rounded at the back.

(3) The ear is well developed, with tragus and antitragus correctly rendered, as can be seen especially on the well preserved ears of one of the Karyatids, and of Hephaistos and Leto on the frieze.[14]

(4) The forearms are correctly semi-pronated.

(5) The muscles of the lower leg are accentuated.

(6) In the feet, the second toe projects further than the big toe. The joints of the toes are strongly articulated. The metatarsal bones are indicated. The small toe is turned inward. The toes and nails all point forward.

All these characteristics may be observed in the kouroi of the Ptoon 12 group.[15] The latter, therefore, can be assigned approximately to the time of the Siphnian Treasury, the early examples—for instance, the Munich, Anavysos, and Akropolis kouroi (nos. 135-137)—may then antedate the Siphnian sculptures by a decade or so, and the more developed examples—for instance, the Keos and Ptoon 12 kouroi (nos. 144, 145)—may be about contemporary with the Siphnian sculptures.

If the epitaph inscribed on a base belonged to the Anavysos kouros (no. 136), as seems likely[16], one might hope to derive from it some evidence for absolute chronology. The inscription reads: *στε̃θι: καὶ οἴκτιρον: Κροίσο[υ] παρὰ σε̃μα θανόντος: ὅν ποτ' ἐνὶ προμάχοις: ὤλεσε θο̃ρος Ἄρες*, 'stay and mourn at the monument of dead Croesus, whom furious Ares destroyed one day as he fought in the front ranks'. To judge by the forms of the letters the date might be in the second or third quarter of the sixth century. Arvanitopoulos suggested that the youth Croesus here commemorated was so named after Croesus, king of Lydia. But this is not necessary, for the name may have been a common Lydian one, in which case, if the youth was born in East Greece, neither the date of King Croesus' birth (596 B.C.) nor that of his reign (561-547) would furnish a criterion. Foreign names were fairly common in East Greece in the archaic period. Arvanitopoulos further suggested that the battle in which furious Ares destroyed Croesus must have been either that in which Peisistratos took Nisaia from the Megarians,[17] not long before 561 B.C., or that of Pallene, somewhat between

[11] Cf. Langlotz, *Zeitbestimmung*, p. 17 f., and de La Coste-Messelière, *Au Musée de Delphes*, p. 242, note 5.

[12] J. E. Powell, *The Classical Quarterly*, XXIX, 1935, p. 151 f., suggested, however, that the sentence in question might be out of place and originally came after *καὶ ἦν τοῦτο τὸ ἡ Πυθίη προηγόρευε τοῖσι Σιφνίοισι, φυλάξασθαι τὸν ξύλινον λόχον κελεύουσα καὶ κήρυκα ἐρυθρόν*, and that its displacement in the text was caused by the occurrence of the words *κήρυκα ἐρυθρόν* also at the end of the oracle. In that case the *τότε* would refer to the time of the Samian attack, and there would be no definite indication of how long the interval was between the oracle and the attack.

[13] Picard and de La Coste-Messelière, *F.d.D.* IV, fasc. 2, pp. 57 ff., pls. VII ff.

[14] *F.d.D.* IV, pls. XX, XV, XI.

[15] On the few figures of the Siphnian frieze on which the rectus abdominis is indicated, the transverse divisions above the navel are not marked.

[16] Arvanitopoulos, *Polemon*, II, 1938, pp. 81 ff.; *Revue des études grecques*, LII, 1939, p. 463 f., no. 105; P. Friedländer, *Epigrammata*, p. 86, no. 82; Stevens and Vanderpool, *Hesperia*, Supplement, VIII, 1949, pp. 361 ff.; D. M. Robinson, *ibid.* pp. 363 f. Cf. also my p. 119.

[17] Herodotos I.59.

541 and 537,[18] in which the Athenians 'of the city' fought the followers of Peisistratos.[19] The first one, though favoured by Arvanitopoulos, seems too early for the style of the statue—unless we assume with Wade-Gery[20] and Arvanitopoulos that *ποτέ* indicates an interval between death and monument—an assumption incapable of proof.[21] The date of the battle of Pallene, on the other hand, fits the style of the statue admirably (cf. note 18). Moreover, since Lygdamis, the Naxian noble, furnished a contingent to Peisistratos in this battle,[22] we might expect among the combatants a youth with an Eastern name.[23] And if the youth was an Easterner—possibly a refugee from Ionia[24]—this might help to explain the unusual fleshiness of the Anavysos kouros. At least only among the Eastern kouroi do we find a comparable physique (cf. for instance, the kouros from Samos, no. 176).

The bronze rider from the North slope of the Akropolis[25] was found in a well which was filled up during the last quarter of the sixth century. Assuming that it was not immediately thrown away after it was dedicated, its date should be before about 525 B.C. Though the anatomical construction of the rider is generalized, we can make two observations which place it in the Ptoon 12 group: the greatest protrusion of the back, seen in profile, is level with that of the chest; the skull is rounded at the top, but rather flat at the back. The curious proportions of the horse may be due to the individual taste of the artist.

The lower limit of the group is perhaps given by the sculptures of the temple of Apollo at Delphi, (cf. p. 129 f.), which anatomically belong early in the succeeding, Ptoon 20, group (cf. no. 166).

A comparison with anatomical renderings on Athenian vase paintings bears out our findings in a general way. They are discussed on p. 132.

Anatomical Analysis

The form is rendered with greater freedom and sureness than ever before and the stance is less rigid. The various parts are well shaped and conceived in the round; chest and back are well developed.

STRUCTURE IN GENERAL. Greatest protrusion of back, seen in profile, corresponds to that of chest; more depth is given to thorax, and vertebral column assumes its characteristic *S*-shaped curve.

[18] 'In the text of Aristotle, *'Αθηναίων Πολιτεία* 14-15, on which we depend for the date of the battle of Pallene, there are corruptions. A further difficulty is that we cannot be sure whether the archonship of Komeas, in which Peisistratos' first tyranny began, belongs to 561-560 or to 560-559. Of the emendations proposed for the text of Aristotle those of Wilamowitz (*Aristoteles und Athen*, I, pp. 21 ff.), which would date the battle of Pallene in 541-540 (or 540-539 if Komeas is dated 560-559), and of Bauer (*Forschungen zu Aristoteles*, pp. 50 ff.) and Schachermeyr (in Pauly-Wissowa, *R.E.* XIX, cols. 164 ff.), which would date it 539-538 (or 538-537, depending on Komeas), seem the more likely' (M. J. Milne).

[19] 'Of course, though the two battles above mentioned are the only ones recorded as taking place in or near Attica between *c.*565 and 525, we must remember that we have no connected military history of this period. Moreover if the monument was a cenotaph, Croesus might have died fighting at Sigeion or in the Chersonnese' (M. J. Milne).

[20] *J.H.S.* LIII, 1933, pp. 71 ff.

[21] 'Wade-Gery himself cites objections raised by Gilbert Murray, Syme, and Beazley—that passages such as *Iliad* VI. 459 ff., VII. 87 ff. etc. clearly show that the Greeks as a matter of fact often played "an imaginative game with time" and were capable of projecting themselves into the mind of the future reader. That the writer of Croesus' epitaph did so is rendered likely by the phrase *στῆθι καὶ οἴκτιρον*' (M. J. Milne).

[22] Herodotos 1.61: *κομίσας καὶ χρήματα καὶ ἄνδρας.*

[23] This plausible suggestion I owe to Marjorie Milne.

[24] At this time, of course, Naxos was still independent (Thuc. 1.16).

[25] Broneer, *Hesperia*, VII, 1938, pp. 203 ff.

Distinction in action of two flanks occasionally observed. The flanks are no longer symmetrical, but sometimes vary, the flank over the advanced leg being placed more forward and higher, as if the body were leaning on this leg. We have here the first harbinger of the dissolution of the frontality and the symmetrical construction which had characterized not only all archaic Greek art, but Egyptian and Mesopotamian for thousands of years. We shall see how this initial observation was developed in the succeeding periods (cf. pp. 133, 148).

HEAD. *Ear.* Assumes more natural form and is generally correctly placed. Both tragus and antitragus indicated.

Eye. Generally horizontal. Roundness of eyeball indicated. Recess at inner corner marked by loop, but not lachrymal caruncle.

Mouth. Lips still curve upward. Upper lip protrudes markedly over lower.

Hair. No longer a rigid mass but sometimes follows curve of shoulder, suggesting its soft and supple quality. Occasionally shorter than before, reaching down only to nape of neck.

NECK. Sterno-mastoids, when shown, indicated by modelled shapes. Their attachment to sternum and clavicles generally not indicated, with the result that a continuous groove or hollow runs above clavicles. No indication of swelling of trapezium.

TORSO, FRONT. Attempt made to indicate backward curve of clavicles. Lower boundary of thorax now forms a well-rounded arch at about correct distance below pectorals. Three transverse divisions of rectus abdominis modelled above navel. Groove over linea alba occasionally continues for a short distance below navel. Navel sometimes has fold of flesh above it. Swelling of external oblique over iliac crest well developed. Lower boundary of abdomen descends towards genitals, with sides which are generally no longer straight but outwardly slightly convex.

TORSO, BACK. Spinal furrow, shoulder blades, and erector spinae carved in the round.

ARM. Bent slightly at elbow; hand no longer adheres to body but is joined to it by short supports. Forearm, viewed from front, no longer turned forward in supine position, but assumes natural, semi-pronated position with palm of hand directed towards body. In some transitional cases, though the attempt is made to show correct formation in semi-pronated position, the forearm is still broad (cf. nos. 136, 137). In hand, metacarpal bones sometimes indicated.

LEG. Depression over great trochanter modelled. Vasti, patella, and shin-bone well shaped. Vastus internus descends below vastus externus. Inner malleolus higher than outer.

Foot. Toes no longer recede along one line, the second toe projecting further than the big toe and the small being short and turned inward.[26] Toes and nails point forward instead of downward. Joints of toes strongly articulated, and metatarsal bones indicated.

FOOT-PLINTH. Sometimes oval (nos. 137, 145), at other times follows more or less outlines of soles (no. 135); upper surface sometimes level (nos. 137, 145), sometimes not (no. 135).

[26] This applies of course only to works in the round, or to high reliefs where the foot is practically worked in the round (as in the Siphnian frieze). In low reliefs (and in vase paintings) the difficulty of representing all five toes next to one another made it sometimes necessary to carve them as receding along one line.

Kouroi Nos. 135-154

135 : Figs. 391-394, 399

MUNICH, GLYPTOTHEK, no. 169. From Attica.

Statue, from head to foot-plinth. Restorations: Some slivers round breaks at base of neck, at waist (front and back), on arms, below knee, at ankles.The restored lower part of the nose and left side of lips (shown in former publications) were removed in 1939. Surface much encrusted.

Parian marble.
Height with plinth 2.11 m.; without plinth 2.08 m.
Said to have been found in Attica. Acquired by the Glyptothek in 1910.
Arch. Anz. 1912, col. 114.
Wolters in Brunn-Bruckmann, *Denkmäler*, nos. 661-2 (there with restorations on nose and lips).
Wolters, *Führer durch die Glyptothek*, no. 169.
L. Budde, *Die attischen Kuroi* (Diss. 1939), pp. 231 ff.
Buschor, *Fr. J.*, pp. 99 ff., figs. 113-17.

GENERAL STRUCTURE. Easy stance. Greatest protrusion of back, seen in profile, corresponds to that of chest. Vertebral column *S*-shaped. Back rounded.
HEAD. *Skull.* Back spherical and well developed.
Ear. Placed in correct position with reference to eye, but vertical. Carved in different planes. Both tragus and antitragus shown.
Eye. Set almost horizontally; recess at inner corner indicated by small loop.
Mouth. Lips curve upward and appear to meet at corners.
Hair. Descends behind only to middle of neck; arranged in short ringlets on skull, and in longer ringlets round neck and forehead, symmetrically from centre to right and left. Plain fillet without hanging ends.
NECK. Sterno-mastoids modelled. No indication of swelling of trapezium.
TORSO, FRONT. Attempt made to indicate backward curve of clavicles which, however, protrude all the way to shoulders. Shallow groove marks median line from lower end of sternum to navel. Lower boundary of thorax indicated by shallow depression forming arch well below pectorals. Three transverse divisions of rectus abdominis above navel. Navel marked by depression. Distinct swelling of external oblique over iliac crest. Left flank slightly higher than right. Lower boundary of abdomen forms small semicircular arch above genitals.
TORSO, BACK. Spinal furrow marked by rather shallow depression forming *S*-shaped curve. Shoulder-blades marked by shallow grooves. Similar grooves, two on either side, travel from middle of spine downward and outward, with their concavity upward; they are either an unusual attempt to denote the latissimus dorsi muscles or perhaps two lower ribs (cf. nos. 63, 86, 120). Tendons at base of erector spinae slightly modelled (at this point surface is partly restored).
ARM. Separated completely from side, except for small distance below armpit and for support at hand. Well formed, with deltoid and biceps developed. Slightly bent at elbow. Upper arm short. Forearm broad, but attempt made to show correct formation in semi-pronated position; a groove denotes muscle at back of forearm.
Hand. Clenched. Separated from body. Metacarpal bones indicated. Thumbs mostly missing.
LEG. Depression over great trochanter indicated. Powerful thighs. Vastus internus descends well below vastus externus. Patella indicated as rounded block. Shin curves sharply inward. Pronounced calves. Groove on outer side of thigh indicates thigh muscle. Grooves on outer side of lower leg indicate peroneal muscles. Inner malleolus higher than outer.
Foot. Joints of toes strongly articulated and metatarsal bones indicated. Length of big toe in relation to first not certain, as big toe of left foot and first toe of right foot are chipped. Small toe turned somewhat inward. All toes and nails point forward.
FOOT-PLINTH. Embedded in modern base. Original contour at back follows more or less outlines of soles. Upper surface not quite level; rises towards middle.

136 : Figs. 395-398, 400-401

ATHENS, NATIONAL MUSEUM, no. 3851. From Anavysos.

Statue, from head to heels. Restorations: Pieces at left biceps and above left ankle, lower part of left patella, outer malleolus of right foot, and small slivers at modern fractures—where statue was sawn for export (at waist, knees, ankles, wrists, above left elbow, at supports). Fracture of right foot is ancient. Surface remarkably fresh. Traces of red colour on hair, fillet, iris, and pubes. Strongly adhering rootmarks on surface. Foot-plinth missing. Since photographs for figs. 395-396 were taken, most of the missing parts of left hand have been added (cf. fig. 397).

Parian marble.
Height 1.94 m.
Found at Anavysos, Attica, in 1936. Seized by Greek police in Paris and returned to Greece in 1937.[27]
Philadelpheus, *B.S.A.* XXXVI, 1935-6, pp. 1 ff., pls. I-V, and *'Εφ.'Αρχ.* 1937, 2, pp. 668 ff.
Von Buttlar, *Neue Jahrbücher für Antike*, II, 1939, pp. 358 ff. (with photographs by H. Wagner).
Buschor, *Fr. J.*, pp. 106 ff., figs. 124-6.
Homann-Wedeking, *Anfänge*, p. 85 f., fig. 43.
Picard in *Revue des études grecques* LI, 1938, p. 93, expressed doubts about the authenticity of the statue. But, quite apart from the story of its discovery, export, and return (what Greek would face imprisonment and exile for the smuggling of a forgery?), the genuineness of the statue is borne out by its style, which is consistently of one comparatively short period—transitional between the Melos and Ptoon 12 statues. It seems unlikely that a forger would have had enough detailed knowledge of the development of the kouros type to carve, for instance, the forearms in this transitional form (broad, but with an inward twist to show formation in semi-pronated position); to indicate the curious grooves on each side of the spinal furrow running downward and outward (reminiscent of the renderings in nos. 63, 73); to omit the attachment of the sterno-mastoids to the sternum resulting in a continuous groove above the clavicles; to omit the indication of the swelling of the trapezium; and to place the left flank slightly forward and higher than the right, instead of level with the right as in the earlier periods, or lower than the right or supporting leg, as in the later periods and in nature.

The statue is now mounted on a three-stepped base, of which only the front of the middle, inscribed portion is ancient (no. 4754, 24 cm. high, Parian marble). The dimensions of the upper and lower portions have been deduced from dowel cuttings. The extant portion was found in 1938, supposedly near the place where the statue was discovered. It was presented to the National Museum in 1954 by 'a friend of Greek antiquities'. For the inscription and publications see p. 115 f.

GENERAL STRUCTURE. Figure rounded and fleshy; bulging muscles. Viewed in profile, greatest protrusion of back level with that of chest. Vertebral column forms *S*-shaped curve.

HEAD. *Skull.* Back of skull spherical and well developed, fillet which encircles hair bringing out shape at back.
Ear. Carved in different planes. Tragus shown as excrescence of lobe. Only very slight swelling at region of antitragus.
Eye. Set horizontally; upper eyelid arched round eyeball. Recess at inner corner indicated, but not lachrymal caruncle. Iris and pupil incised.
Mouth. Lips broad at corners.
Chin. Prominent. Grooves at corners, travelling downward.

[27] *The Illustrated London News*, 9 October 1937, p. 626.

Hair. Falls down back in undulating mass following curve of shoulders; on skull above fillet carved in waves running from side to side; below fillet at back divided vertically and obliquely into beaded tresses; ends form curving line. Above forehead and temples arranged in two groups of spiral curls, symmetrically to right and left of centre and decreasing in size from ear to forehead. Plain fillet without hanging ends.

NECK. Sterno-mastoids indicated by two grooves, but not throat between. Attachment of sterno-mastoids to sternum not marked, with result that continuous groove runs above clavicles. No indication of swelling of trapezium.

TORSO, FRONT. Clavicles placed horizontally and are rather shallow; attempt made to indicate backward curve. Median line marked by groove from bottom of sternum to a short distance below navel. Nipples marked by knobs. Lower boundary of thorax forms deep arch indicated by shallow groove. Three transverse divisions of rectus abdominis above navel; its lower boundary marked by arched groove. Navel indicated by knob with fold of flesh above. Distinct swelling of external oblique over iliac crest. Left flank placed slightly forward and higher than right, conforming with advanced leg. Lower boundary of abdomen forms small semicircular arch beneath genitals. Pubes was indicated in colour. Ridge marks root of penis.

TORSO, BACK. Well developed but curiously constructed. On either side of deep groove which marks spinal furrow, another shallower groove travels downward and outward. Shoulder-blades not indicated. Tendons at base of erector spinae modelled.

ARM. Separated completely from side except for small distance below armpit and for support of hand. Slightly bent at elbow. Deltoid and biceps developed. Forearm broad, but attempt made to show correct formation in semi-pronated position. Wrist slender, forming marked contrast with broad forearm in front view.
Hand. Clenched; separated from body. Metacarpal bones lightly indicated. Nail of right thumb marked, not that of index finger. Four-sided prop connects palm of hand with thigh. Little finger rests against thigh.

LEG. Depression over great trochanter indicated by modelled shape. Powerful thigh. Vastus internus descends well below vastus externus. Anterior edge of shin curves sharply inward. Patella indicated as rounded block. Pronounced calf. Modelled ridges on outer side of lower leg indicate peroneal muscles. Inner malleolus higher than outer.
Foot. Heel broad and tapers upward. Toes and plinth missing.

137 : Figs. 406-408, 436, 442

ATHENS, AKROPOLIS MUSEUM, nos. 665, 596.

Torso, from neck to right knee (no. 665); base with plinth and feet (no. 596). The left hand and pieces of missing left arm and of left lower leg have been identified (cf. Schuchhardt, op. cit. figs. 178-81). Front much corroded.

Statue and plinth of Island marble; base of Pentelic marble.
Height of torso 96 cm.; height of base 33.5 cm.
Torso found in 1887, east of Erechtheion; base soon afterwards.
Dickins, *Catalogue*, pp. 103 f., 200 ff., nos. 665, 596.
Schrader, *Auswahl archaischer Marmorskulpturen*, pp. 53 ff., pls. XVI-XVII.
Payne and Young, *Acropolis*, p. 43, pls. 97, 98, 123, no. 3 (the base is there called limestone by mistake).
Schuchhardt in Schrader, *Akropolis*, p. 189 f., no. 298, pls. 115, 116.
L. Budde, *Die attischen Kuroi* (Diss. 1939), p. 19 f.
Buschor, *Fr. J.*, pp. 97 ff., figs. 109-12.
Homann-Wedeking, *Anfänge*, p. 91, fig. 50.
I.G., I², 724.
Deonna, no. 13.
Raubitschek, *Bulletin de l'Institut archéologique bulgare*, XII, 1938, p. 145 (base); *Dedications from the Athenian Akropolis*, no. 62.

Traces of letters of an inscription visible on front of base. In *I.G.* I², 724, the reading is given as [.]ε̣λ̣ι̣ος ε̣ - - ; Schuchhardt, loc cit. tentatively reads κετιος; Raubitschek, *Dedications*, reads ε̣τ̣ιος ἀ[νέθεκε - - - (c. 6)].[28]

GENERAL STRUCTURE. Viewed in profile, greatest protrusion of back level with that of chest. Vertebral column forms *S*-shaped curve.
HAIR. Falls down in mass to top of shoulders.
NECK. Attachment of sterno-mastoids to sternum not indicated; continuous groove above clavicles. No indication of swelling of trapezium.
TORSO, FRONT. On account of battered condition some anatomical details not clear. Clavicles more or less horizontal, but attempt made to indicate backward curve. Lower boundary of thorax not discernible. Rectus abdominis not discernible. Distinct swelling of external oblique over iliac crest. Lower boundary of abdomen not clear.
TORSO, BACK. Well developed. On either side of deep groove indicating spinal furrow, another shallower groove travels downward and outward (cf. nos. 63, 135, 144).

[28] With the following comment: 'The reading and restoration of the inscription are uncertain; instead of [.]ε̣τ̣ιος, [.]ει̣τ̣ος could equally well be read, and the first letter of the second word can also be read as μ. The preserved letters presumably belong to the first and only line of the inscription; they contain, therefore, part of the dedicator's name, which may have been Geitos.'

ARM. Separated completely from side, except for small distance below armpit and for support at hand. Slightly bent at elbow. Deltoid and biceps developed. Forearm broad, but attempt made to show correct formation in semi-pronated position. Elbow and wrist modelled.
Hand. Clenched. Separated from body. Support for left hand slightly higher and further forward than that of right hand. Metacarpal bones indicated.
LEG. No depression at head of great trochanter. Inner vastus descends lower than outer and is more developed. Inner malleolus higher than outer.
Foot. Joints of toes strongly articulated; metatarsal bones indicated. Little toe slants inward. Toes do not recede along continuous line, second toe being about same length as big toe.
FOOT-PLINTH. Oval. Upper side level. Let into rectangular base and fastened with lead. On base numerous traces of claw chisel.

138 : Figs. 409-410

COPENHAGEN, NY CARLSBERG GLYPTOTHEK, no. 418. From Athens (?).

Head and part of neck. A foot is said to have been found with the head, but its whereabouts are not now known.

Parian marble.
Height 31.5 cm.
Said to be from Athens.
Rayet, *Monuments grecs*, 1877, pl. I, no. 6, pp. 1 ff., pl. I.
Arndt, *La Glyptothèque Ny Carlsberg*, pp. 1-2, pls. I, II.
V. H. Poulsen, *From the Collections of the Ny Carlsberg Glytothek*, II, 1938, pp. 94 ff., figs. 20-23.
Budde, *Die attischen Kuroi* (Diss. 1939), p. 262 f.
Buschor, *Fr. J.*, p. 105 f., figs. 122, 123.
F. Poulsen, *Catalogue*, no. 11.

HEAD. *Skull.* Spherical.
Ear. In correct position. Both tragus and antitragus indicated.
Eye. Large and bulging. Upper eyelid arched round eyeball; groove round lower end of lid; inner recess indicated but not caruncle.
Mouth. Lips well shaped and meet in deep recess at corners. Cleft lower lip. Chin broad, with depression in centre.
Nose. Mostly missing.
Hair. Short. Mass differentiated into shallow circular waves on which are carved rows of curls radiating from crown; above forehead and temples, hair arranged in short tufts symmetrically to right and left of centre.
NECK. Sterno-mastoids modelled with throat between.

139 : Figs. 402-403

ATHENS, AKROPOLIS MUSEUM, no. 663. From the Akropolis.

Head and neck. The forward tilt suggests that the statue was perhaps not a kouros (but see no. 49). Part of meniskos preserved. Traces of red on hair and eyes.

Island marble.
Height 17 cm.
Found on the Akropolis.
Dickins, *Catalogue*, p. 199, no. 663.
Payne and Young, *Acropolis*, p. 46, pl. 100, 1-4.
Schuchhardt in Schrader, *Akropolis*, p. 245, no. 322, pl. 151.
Budde, *Die attischen Kuroi* (Diss. 1939), p. 31 f.
Buschor, *Fr. J.*, p. 134, fig. 153.
Deonna, no. 15.

HEAD. *Skull.* Domed.
Ear. Slants towards line of jaw. Tragus and antitragus marked.
Eye. Narrow, with broad upper lids arching over eyeball. Recess at inner corner indicated.
Mouth. Lips curve upward and meet at corners.
Hair. Arranged in horizontal ridges on skull; in front, beneath simple fillet which encircles head, fringe of corkscrew locks; at back, below fillet, are wavy ridges ending in spiral curls at nape of neck.

140 : Fig. 415

ATHENS, AKROPOLIS MUSEUM, no. 653.

Head and part of neck, perhaps of kouros. Surface damaged (by fire?). Hole on top of skull for meniskos.

Island marble.
Height 13.5 cm.
Found on the Akropolis.
Dickins, *Catalogue*, p. 191, no. 653.
Payne and Young, *Acropolis*, p. 46, pl. 99.
Schuchhardt, in Schrader, *Akropolis*, p. 245 ff., no. 323, pl. 163.
Deonna, no. 16.

HEAD. *Skull.* Rounded at top, rather undeveloped at back.
Ear. Carved in several planes, but kept fairly flat. Tragus and antitragus marked. Very small lobe. No recess at inner corner.
Mouth. Lips more or less straight. Vertical grooves at corners.
Hair. On skull blocked out in broad waves running from side to side. Rounded fillet encircles head. Beneath it, in front, are corkscrew curls. Mass behind is divided into tresses by vertical grooves, and each tress is further subdivided by oblique grooves.

141 : Figs. 404-405

PARIS, LOUVRE. On loan from Museum of Amiens (no. 171).

Head and neck. Surface cleaned with acid. Battered. Former plaster restorations have been removed.

Parian marble.
Height 32 cm.
Perhaps from Athens. It was presented to the city of Amiens by Théodore de Lagrenée, who was minister at Athens from 1835.
Besques, *Mélanges Charles Picard*, 1949, pp. 89 ff.

HEAD. *Skull.* Spherical and well developed. Simple fillet encircles head.
Ear. Slants slightly in direction of jaw. Carved in different planes and laid against hair. Tragus and antitragus indicated.
Eye. Recess at inner corner marked by loop directed downward. No indication of lachrymal caruncle.
Mouth. Lips more or less horizontal; do not meet at corners.
Hair. Falls down back and sides in straight mass, subdivided into ribbon-like, wavy tresses below fillet, but left smooth on skull. Above forehead and temples arranged in spiral curls, symmetrically to right and left of centre.
Neck. Forms fine curve. Sterno-mastoid muscles and throat very lightly modelled.
The four holes in region of fillet at top of head are not ancient; also not those in nose, upper lip, lower lip, and on each side of fillet. (They have now been filled with plaster.)

142 : Figs. 411-412

PARIS, LOUVRE, no. MNC 1357. From Attica (?).

Head and neck. Surface has apparently been cleaned with acid.

Parian marble.
Height 27 cm.
Said to be from Attica.
Collignon, *B.C.H.* XVI, 1892, pp. 447 ff., pl. V.
Louvre, *Catalogue sommaire* (1922), p. 42, no. 695.
Budde, *Die attischen Kuroi* (Diss. 1939), p. 25 f.
Buschor, *Fr. J.*, p. 104, figs. 118, 119.
Deonna, no. 24.

HEAD. *Skull.* Spherical and well developed, fillet which encircles hair bringing out shape at back.
Ear. Slants slightly in direction of jaw. Carved in different planes. Tragus and antitragus indicated.
Eye. Upper eyelid arched around eyeball. Recess at inner corner marked by small loop. Caruncle not marked.
Nose. Missing.
Mouth. Lips well shaped; vertical cleft in middle of lower lip.
Hair. Falls down to height of shoulders in mass which is divided into shallow horizontal waves; below plain fillet hair further differentiated by vertical wavy strands

ending in spiral curls. Round forehead and temples, two rows of spiral curls arranged symmetrically to right and left from centre.
NECK. Sterno-mastoids modelled.

143 : Figs. 413-414

BOSTON, MUSEUM OF FINE ARTS, no. 34.169. From Attica (?).

Head and part of neck. Only left part of face preserved. Traces of red colour on iris and hair (on spirals and skull). Part of meniskos left in apex of head.

Island marble.
Height 25 cm.
Perhaps from Attica.
Caskey, *M.F.A. Bulletin*, XXXIV, 1936, p. 6 f., and *A.J.A.* XL, 1936, p. 307, figs. 1A-C.
Budde, *Die attischen Kuroi*, p. 28 f., no. 58.
Buschor, *Fr. J.*, p. 105, figs. 120, 121.

HEAD. *Skull.* Rounded.
Ear. Though surface is battered, enough remains to show that it was carved in several planes and that both tragus and antitragus were indicated.
Eye. Eyebrow and contours of eyeball, iris, and pupil incised.
Mouth. Only left corner preserved.
Hair. Two rows of spiral curls round forehead and temple. Surface of skull left rough, showing claw chisel marks. At back, hair is short and ends in double row of spirals, which were left partly unfinished.

144 : Figs. 419-424

ATHENS, NATIONAL MUSEUM, no. 3686. From Keos.

Statue, from head to below right calf.

Island marble.
Over life-size.
Found in a cemetery at Livadi, in the island of Keos, 1930.
Karo, *Arch. Anz.* 1930, col. 129.
Stavropoulos, *'Εφ. 'Αρχ.*, 1937, pp. 687 ff.
Buschor, *Fr. J.*, p. 132 f., figs. 148-51.

GENERAL STRUCTURE. Torso forms correlated whole, with harmonious lines. Viewed in profile, greatest protrusion of back level with that of chest. Vertebral column forms *S*-shaped curve.
HEAD. *Skull.* Spherical and well developed.
Ear. Modelled in different planes, with correctly formed tragus and antitragus.
Eye. Horizontal. Upper eyelid arches over eyeball. Recess at inner corner indicated by small loop.
Mouth. Broad lips curve slightly upward. Vertical groove at corners.
Hair. Falls down back in undulating mass following curve of shoulders. Mass divided vertically and horizontally into beaded tresses; ends form curving line. Over forehead and temples are two groups of three large spiral curls arranged symmetrically to right and left from centre. Simple fillet surrounds hair.
NECK. Sterno-mastoids and throat between indicated by modelling, but their attachment to sternum not marked, with result that continuous groove runs above clavicles. No indication of swelling of trapezium.
TORSO, FRONT. Clavicles curve backward. Median line indicated by groove from lower end of sternum to a little below navel. Chest well developed. Lower boundary of thorax forms fine arch, with feeling of bulging form beneath. Three transverse divisions above navel in rectus abdominis. Navel marked by knob surrounded by circular groove. Flanks well developed, with oblique muscle bulging over iliac crest. Left flank placed very slightly forward and very little higher than right, conforming with advanced left leg. This gives pelvis slight twist. Lower boundary of abdomen forms deep curve. At root of penis, shallow horizontal ridge.
TORSO, BACK. Spinal furrow, shoulder-blades, erector spinae modelled.
ARM. Largely missing. To judge from what is preserved and from traces of supports for hands on thighs, they were separated from sides along entire way.
LEG. Depression on side of buttock marking position of great trochanter indicated by modelling. Buttocks and thighs powerful and well developed. Various muscles differentiated. Vasti bulge over patella; inner vastus descends markedly lower than outer. Patella in right proportion. Junction of patella with shin natural. Anterior border of shin curves inward with rounded edge.

145 : Figs. 425-429, 437

ATHENS, NATIONAL MUSEUM, no. 12. From the Ptoan Sanctuary.

Statue, from head to foot-plinth; but legs from below knees to above ankles missing, so feet not joined to body. The fragment of a right calf mentioned by Holleaux, *B.C.H.* XI, 1887, p. 185, note 2, and Deonna, p. 156, note 2, as perhaps belonging to this statue cannot now be found.[29] Supports joining hands to sides restored in plaster, but traces of original, quasi-cylindrical supports preserved.

Island marble.
Height of statue to knees 1.60 m.
Found in Ptoan Sanctuary: torso in 1885; feet and plinth in 1886; head in 1903; all distant from one another.

[29] So S. Konstantinou kindly informed me.

Holleaux, *B.C.H.* XI, 1887, pp. 185 ff., pl. VIII (torso).
Mendel, *B.C.H.* XXXI, 1907, pp. 187 ff., pls. XVII-XIX (head and statue).
Papaspiridi, *Guide du Musée National*, p. 28, no. 12, pl. II.
Budde, *Die attischen Kuroi* (Diss. 1939), pp. 20 ff.
Buschor, *Fr. J.*, pp. 115 ff., figs. 134, 135.
Deonna, no. 30.

GENERAL STRUCTURE. Figure rounded and slim; slender waist; modelled in the round. Viewed in profile, greatest protrusion of back level with that of chest. Vertebral column forms *S*-shaped curve.

HEAD. *Skull.* Spherical and well developed, fillet which encircles hair bringing out shape at back.

Ear. Placed in correct position with reference to eye, but vertical. Carved in different planes. Tragus and antitragus shown.

Eye. Set almost horizontally. Upper eyelid arched round eyeball. Inner recess indicated by small loop, but not lachrymal caruncle.

Mouth. Lips broad at corners; curve slightly upward.

Hair. Falls down in undulating mass, divided vertically into tresses with shallow horizontal grooves; ends form curving line. Above forehead and temples two groups of five spirals are arranged symmetrically to right and left of centre, with loop at each ear. Plain fillet without hanging ends.

NECK. No indication of attachment of sterno-mastoids; continuous groove runs above clavicles. No swelling of trapezium.

TORSO, FRONT. Clavicles placed horizontally; attempt made to indicate backward curve. Median line marked by groove from lower end of sternum to a little below navel. Lower boundary of thorax forms deep arch indicated by a shallow groove. Three transverse divisions of rectus abdominis above navel. Navel marked by knob surrounded by circular groove. Distinct swelling of external oblique over iliac crest. Left flank is placed slightly forward and higher than right, conforming with advanced left leg. Lower boundary of abdomen descends with straight sides towards genitals.

TORSO, BACK. Considerably weathered. Spinal furrow, shoulder-blades, and erector spinae modelled.

ARM. Separated from side along entire way. Bent at elbow. Well formed and broad. Forearm turned towards body in correct, semi-pronated position.

Hand. Was fastened to sides by support; held, however, in same clenched position as before, with fingers bent and thumb placed across joint of forefinger. Metacarpal bones indicated.

LEG. Slight indication of depression over great trochanter. Vastus internus descends well below vastus externus, and both bulge over patella. Inner malleolus higher than outer.

Foot. Well shaped, long, and slender, with tapering heel. Joints of toes strongly articulated and metatarsal bones indicated. Toes do not recede along one line, second toe projecting further than big toe, and small toe short and turned inward. Nails elongated, like foot, and arched at root.

FOOT-PLINTH. Oval. Level at top, left rough at sides.

146 : Figs. 430-431, 434

THEBES, MUSEUM, no. 15. From the Ptoan Sanctuary.

Head and neck.

Island marble.
Height 19 cm.
Found in the Ptoan Sanctuary, in 1903.
Mendel, *B.C.H.* XXXI, 1907, p. 200, no. 7, pl. XXI.
Karouzos, *'Οδηγός*, p. 13, no. 15, figs. 4-6.
Deonna, no. 51.

HEAD. *Skull.* Spherical and well developed.

Ear. Vertical. Carved in different planes. Tragus indicated. Part missing where antitragus would be.

Eye. Wide open. Horizontally placed, but inner corner dips. Recess at inner corner indicated by loop. Surface injured at region where lachrymal caruncle would be. Iris marked by incised circle, and pupil by incised dot.

Mouth. Lips horizontal.

Hair. Mass divided horizontally and vertically into beaded tresses, which terminate at nape of neck in elongated members along curving line. Fillet without knot or hanging ends encircles head; makes deep impression on hair; groove runs along middle of fillet. Round forehead and temples beaded strands.

147 : Figs. 432, 433, 435

ATHENS, NATIONAL MUSEUM, no. 18. From the Ptoan Sanctuary.

Head and neck.

Limestone.
Height 26 cm.
Found in the Ptoan Sanctuary, in 1886.
Δελτ. 'Αρχ, 1886, p. 9, 17.
Kastriotes, *Γλυπτά*, no. 18.
Deonna, no. 37.

HEAD. *Skull.* Rounded.

Ear. Well constructed, with tragus carved in correct form. Antitragus apparently indicated on right ear; that region missing on left ear.

Eye. Almond-shaped. Horizontally placed.

Mouth. Lips curve upward at corners.

Hair. Falls behind in mass; divided into quasi-horizontal waves, with scalloped edge above forehead and temples.

NECK. Sterno-mastoids modelled.

148 : Figs. 416-418

CHALKIS, MUSEUM, no. 45. From Euboea (?).

Head and neck.

Island marble.
Height c.30 cm.
Provenance unknown, but probably Euboea. Entered museum from old private collection.

HEAD. *Skull.* Rounded.
Ear. Slants towards line of jaw. Modelled in different planes, with inside shell much deeper than helix. Both tragus and antitragus indicated.
Eye. Slopes upward. Recess at inner corner indicated; lachrymal caruncle not discernible in present condition.
Mouth. Lips curve upward and meet at corners.
Chin. Broad.
Hair. Hangs down to top of shoulders. Mass divided vertically into tresses and each tress subdivided by oblique grooves. Above forehead and temples, three rows of spiral curls.

149 : Fig. 440

DELPHI, MUSEUM, no. 2557. From Delphi.

Torso, from neck to right knee.

Parian marble.
Height 1.07 m.
Found in 1895 in a Byzantine structure outside gate of temenos.
Homolle, *F.d.D.* IV, fasc. 1, p. 58 f., no. 25, fig. 28.
Buschor, *Fr. J.*, pp. 90 f., figs. 103, 104.
Deonna, no. 70.

GENERAL STRUCTURE. Greatest protrusion of back, seen in profile, level with that of chest. Vertebral column forms *S*-shaped curve.
HAIR. Falls down back in mass, divided vertically and horizontally into beaded tresses.
NECK. Sterno-mastoids indicated by modelled forms.
TORSO, FRONT. Clavicles travel upward to shoulders and attempt made to indicate their backward curve. They are not attached to sterno-mastoids, with result that a continuous groove runs above them. Median line marked by shallow groove from lower end of sternum to navel. Lower boundary of thorax indicated by groove forming arch. Apparently three transverse divisions of rectus abdominis above navel. External oblique bulges markedly over iliac crest. Lower boundary of abdomen descends towards genitals, forming deep curve (cf. p. 91).
TORSO, BACK. Battered, especially in region of left shoulder-blade. Attachment of erector spinae in lumbar region not indicated.
ARM. Was separated from body from somewhat below armpit; traces of supports for hands on thighs.
LEG. Depression over great trochanter indicated. Inner vastus descends lower and is more developed than outer.

150 : Figs. 438-439

ATHENS, NATIONAL MUSEUM, no. 64. From Delphi.

Head and part of neck. Top of head missing. Battered.

White limestone (turned reddish on surface).
Height 23 cm.
Found at Delphi.
Kastriotes, *Γλυπτά*, no. 64.
Conze and Michaelis, *Annali*, 1861, p. 65, no. 3 (apparently refers to this head, cf. Deonna, loc. cit.).
Deonna, no. 72.

HEAD. *Skull.* Developed at back.
Ear. Well constructed. Both tragus and antitragus marked.
Eye. Recess at inner corner indicated, but no lachrymal caruncle.
Mouth. Lips curve upward at corners.
Hair. Short; arranged in spiral curls over skull.

151 : Figs. 443-444

DELOS, MUSEUM, A 4047. From Delos.

Torso, from below neck to below knees. Surface much battered.

Island marble.
Height c.93 cm.
Found at Delos, in 1904.
Deonna, no. 90.

GENERAL STRUCTURE. Large part of front of thorax missing; cannot therefore tell relation of its greatest protrusion to that of back. Vertebral column forms curve.
HAIR. Not visible on preserved part of back. Must have been fairly short.
TORSO, FRONT. Clavicles, median line, lower boundary of thorax, and divisions of rectus abdominis not now discernible. Slight indication of external oblique swelling over iliac crest. Lower boundary of abdomen forms deep curve (cf. p. 91).
TORSO, BACK. Spinal furrow and erector spinae modelled. Shoulder-blades battered.
ARM. Was separated from body from below armpit to hand.
LEG. Apparently no indication of depression over great trochanter. Inner vastus descends lower than outer and is more developed. Thigh muscles modelled.

152 : Figs. 445-446

DELOS, MUSEUM, no. A 1741. From Delos.

Statue, from head to above ankles. Head and lower parts of legs have been recently added. Head much battered and does not certainly belong.

Island marble.
Height 1.60 m.
Found in Delos, in 1907, west of the hypostyle hall. Finding place of head not known.
Marcadé, *B.C.H.* LXXIV, 1950, p. 374. To be published by P. Levêque in his book *Sculptures archaïques de Délos*.

GENERAL STRUCTURE. Seen in profile, greatest protrusion of back level with that of chest. Vertebral column forms *S*-shaped curve.
NECK. Apparently no indication of swelling of trapezium.
TORSO, FRONT. Details obliterated, but clavicles appear to slope backward. Well-developed thorax; lower boundary obliterated. No transverse divisions of rectus abdominis discernible. External oblique swells over iliac crest. Left hip a little further forward than right. Lower boundary of abdomen descends to genitals, forming deep curve (cf. p. 91).
TORSO, BACK. Spinal furrow and erector spinae modelled. Surface of shoulders obliterated.
ARM. Must have been free from body; traces of supports uncertain.
LEG. No indication of swelling over great trochanter. Inner vastus descends lower than outer. Shin-bone curves inward. Buttocks level.

153 : Fig. 441

VATHY, MUSEUM. From Chora, Samos.

Torso, from neck to above knees.

Marble.
Height (from neck to pubes) 61 cm.
Found at Chora, Samos.
Buschor, *Alt. St.* I, p. 20, figs. 76-9; *Fr. J.*, p. 148, fig. 174.

GENERAL STRUCTURE. Seen in profile, greatest protrusion of back level with that of chest. Vertebral column makes *S*-shaped curve. Soft, indistinct forms.
HAIR. Falls down back in beaded tresses.
TORSO, FRONT. Lower boundary of thorax indicated by modelled arch. Median line marked by broad furrow reaching down a little below navel. Divisions of rectus abdominis above navel not clear. Navel indicated by depression. Flanks developed. Lower boundary of abdomen forms curve; two transverse grooves on abdomen and two grooves below groins mark bulging flesh.
TORSO, BACK. Spinal furrow indicated by broad groove.
ARM. Was attached to side.
LEG. Buttocks level. Depression over great trochanter indicated by modelled form.

For a leg of a colossal kouros from SAMOS dedicated by [Chera]myes cf. p. 114.

154 : Figs. 447-449

RHODES, MUSEO ARCHEOLOGICO. From Rhodes.

Torso, from below neck to knees.

Island marble.
Height 1.16 m.
Found with no. 124 on the akropolis of Kamiros, Rhodes, leaning against an altar of Helios.
Jacopi, *Clara Rhodos*, VI-VII, I, p. 256, fig. 44, pp. 276 ff., no. 7, figs. 66-7, pls. XI, XII.
Buschor, *Fr. J.*, p. 150, figs. 171, 172.

GENERAL STRUCTURE. Greatest protrusion of back, seen in profile, level with that of chest. Vertebral column form *S*-shaped curve.
HAIR. Hangs down in tresses, with ends forming slight curve following line of shoulders.
TORSO, FRONT. Clavicles slope backward from sternum. Median line marked by groove from lower end of sternum to navel. Chest was well developed (large piece now missing). Lower boundary of thorax forms deep arch. Three transverse divisions marked above navel in rectus abdominis. Flanks well developed, with external oblique muscle bulging over iliac crest. Left flank placed very slightly forward, conforming with advanced leg. Lower boundary of abdomen forms deep curve (cf. p. 91). Pubes and penis were attached separately and are missing.
TORSO, BACK. Spinal furrow, shoulder-blades, and erector spinae indicated by modelled forms.
ARM. To judge from what is preserved and from traces of supports on thighs, arms were separated from sides along entire way. On right side, four holes, perhaps from an ancient repair.
LEG. Depression over great trochanter on side of buttock indicated. Buttocks and thighs well developed. Vasti bulge over patella; inner vastus descends lower than outer. Patella small and rounded. Modelled groove on outer side of thigh denotes ilio-tibial band.

X. THE PTOON 20 GROUP
(*c.* 520–485 B.C.)

General Survey and Historical Background

WITH the Ptoon 20 group we have reached the last chapter of our drama, the consummation in the development of the kouros type. During this period the Greek sculptor attained full knowledge of the structure of the human figure. The forms which had been gradually developed during more than a century he now learned to combine into a harmoniously proportioned whole.

In our old histories of Greek sculpture, this gradual evolution from stylization to naturalism was described as a progress from rude beginnings to perfect development. We should hardly use such words today; for we have learned to appreciate more than before the inherent beauty of the early works. 'Rude beginnings' is no longer the expression used to evaluate the Sounion and Tenea statues. But even the present generation must acknowledge that the mastery over anatomical structure which the Greek sculptor attained after a sustained effort of more than a century was an admirable feat; admirable and fraught with consequences for all subsequent European art.

The chief historical events of this epoch are first the expulsion of the Peisistratids in 510, with the subsequent establishment of the Athenian democracy; then the Persian invasion. The attack on Naxos in 499 started the trouble with Persia. The Ionian revolt began soon after and spread; but it was finally put down in 493 with the subjection of the Greeks of Asia and most of the Islands. The expedition against Thrace and Macedonia took place in 492. Then came the fateful battles of Marathon (490), Salamis (480), Plataea (479) and Mykale (479). In the West, the defeat of Carthage at Himera (480) marked a turning point. It is therefore against a background of stress, fear, and exaltation that the art of this period was produced.

BOEOTIA. The kouros Ptoon 20 (no. 155), after which we have named this group, comes from the Ptoan Sanctuary. The inscription which is engraved on the two thighs states that Pythias of Akraiphia and Aischrion dedicated it to the Ptoan Apollo of the silver bow. We know that Akraiphia was a city in Boeotia, situated at the foot of the Ptoan mountain, on the northeast shore of Lake Kopaïs. Though Pausanias[1] says that Akraiphia belonged to Thebes from early times, at the period at which Ptoon 20 was made Akraiphia must have been an independent member of the Boeotian League; for there are coins preserved, datable about 510 B.C., with the familiar Boeotian shield and the letter *A*.[2] Since a Boeotian dedicated the statue in a Boeotian sanctuary, it would seem at least possible that it is a Boeotian work—though archaeologists have pronounced it Peloponnesian, Ionic, Attic, Aeginetan, Sikyonian, Chian.[3] A bronze statuette in Athens (no. 157), also from the Ptoan Sanctuary, is inscribed 'Eueitias dedicated it, property of the Ptoan'.

An excellent work of this period from Boeotia is the kouros found in the excavations at Eutresis, 1924–6 (no. 156). The material is white marble, fine-grained, with slightly bluish veins, perhaps Boeotian. The statue was therefore presumably made in Boeotia.

[1] IX.23.5.

[2] Head, *Historia Numorum*², p. 344; Babelon, *Traité*, II, p. 947 f., pl. XLI, 16. The date about 510 was suggested to me by E. S. G. Robinson.

[3] Cf. Deonna, pp. 158 f.

We have then in these statues, it would seem, distinguished Boeotian representatives of the last phase of archaic sculpture. They carry on a long tradition, traceable, as we have seen, from the seventh century on. One of the surprising results of the excavations of the Ptoan Sanctuary is this revelation of the important part which Boeotia played in the field of sculpture through the whole of the archaic period. And of all these products none equal or at least surpass these late examples. It is perhaps significant that at this very period Boeotia made a distinguished contribution also in literature. Pindar, Korinna, Myrtis were all Boeotians active around 500. (Pindar's 10th Pythian, his earliest extant ode, is dated 498 B.C.) So it would seem that the contemptuous attitude of the Athenians towards the Boeotians, which we note in literature (they are referred to as 'dense and stupid and witless'[4] and are nicknamed ὗς[5]), was due at least partly to political enmity and neighbourly jealousy.[6]

ATTICA. Several kouroi from Attica are datable shortly before and shortly after 500 B.C.: from the Akropolis a delicate marble torso (no. 160) and a beautifully preserved bronze statuette, a masterpiece on a small scale (no. 162); from near Athens a good, but fragmentary torso (no. 161), considerably more developed than the other two pieces. A head in Kansas City (no. 164), thought to have come from Athens, is a fine, fairly early example of this group; whereas the well preserved statue of Aristodikos (no. 165)—one of the finest of the later kouroi—should date from *c.*500 B.C. Here also belong a fragment of a torso and parts of two legs found in the Themistoklean wall (cf. no. 161 bis). The bronze Apollo from the Piraeus (no. 159 bis) is an early example of the group.

The large number of other late sixth-century Attic sculptures—korai, grave monuments, the Athenian Treasury at Delphi, and perhaps the sculptures of the temple of Apollo at Delphi furnished by the Alkmeonidai (cf. p. 129 f.)—show that the late sixth century was an active time for artistic Attica. By way of contrast the supply of Attic sculptures during the first decade or two of the fifth century is scanty. The circumstance may perhaps be explained by the preoccupation with the Persian danger. The important war memorials erected to commemorate the victory at Marathon—the bronze 'Athena Promachos' on the Akropolis and the group of Attic heroes at Delphi—were by Pheidias and cannot be earlier than the second quarter of the century.[7] The Nike, Akropolis 690, is a fine but comparatively minor work (cf. p. 131 f.).

AEGINA. Aegina, on the other hand, just at this time produced the pediments of the temple of Aphaia (*c.*500-480, cf. p. 131). She was still at the height of her prosperity, carrying on successful engagements against Athens and Sparta, and even daring to take the side of Persia part of the time. It is not surprising, therefore, that her artistic contribution was of the finest.

SPARTA. A distinguished bronze statuette found in Sparta shortly before 1949 is now in the National Museum, Athens.[8] Its date should be near that of the Aigina sculptures.

EUBOEA. Two kouroi of this period come from Euboea—one fairly early, found at Metochi (no. 166), the other, perhaps a couple of decades later (no. 167), an outstanding work from Eretria. We know that exceptionally fine sculpture was being produced round this time by or for Euboea, since the pedimental group of the temple of Apollo Daphnephoros at Eretria[9] is one of the most

[4] Plutarch, *De esu carnium*, I.6; but see Gildersleeve, *Pindar*, p. viii.
[5] Plutarch, loc. cit.; Pindar, *Ol.* VI.90 and scholia.
[6] On this question cf. W. R. Roberts, *Ancient Boeotians*, passim.
[7] Pausanias I.28.2; X.10.1.
[8] Cf. C. Karousos, *Charites*, pp. 33 ff., pls. V, VI.
[9] Kourouniotes, *Antike Denkmäler*, III, pls. 27-8.

distinguished works of the late sixth century. The prosperity of Eretria came to an abrupt end in 490, when she was sacked by Persia and her inhabitants were transferred deep into Asia. Chalkis received a crippling blow from Athens in 506 B.C.

DELPHI. The three standing youths of the East pediment of the sixth-century temple of Apollo at Delphi (no. 165) are of the kouros type. To judge by their anatomy, they belong very early in the Ptoon 20 group (see p. 130).

UNKNOWN PROVENANCE. A head in Berlin (no. 169), of unknown provenance, which was bought in Trieste in 1877, appears to be an early example of this group. Two heads, one in New York (no. 172), the other in Copenhagen (no. 171), likewise of unknown provenance, also belong here.

ANAPHE (?). The finding place of the Strangford kouros in the British Museum (no. 159) is not definitely known, but is perhaps Anaphe, a small island east of Thera. The statue is relatively well-preserved, is worked in a dry, precise manner, and is datable in the late sixth century.

DELOS. In Delos has been found a fragmentary torso of what must once have been a fine statue (no. 174). It is the latest representative from Delos of the long series of archaic kouroi which began with the Delos colossus.

NAXOS. The bronze statuette from Naxos in Berlin (no. 175)—a dedication by Deinagores to Apollo—is an early example of this group, to judge at least by such an early feature as the straight sides of the lower boundary of the abdomen. It was therefore probably produced before the Ionian revolt and before the subjugation of Naxos by Persia (cf. p. 126).

SAMOS. From Samos comes an interesting, fleshy version (no. 176), suggesting Eastern connections. It belongs to the era after the tyrannies of Polykrates and his brother Syloson, when Aiakes, the son of Syloson, was reigning[10] and Samos was a favoured vassal of Persia.

CRETE. A small fragment of a kouros of this period (no. 177) has been found at Gortyn, Crete,[11] showing that the type was known there, as elsewhere. The fact that the fragment came to light in the pronaos of a temple of Apollo is of special interest.

CYPRUS. An example from Cyprus, in the British Museum (no. 179 and p. 131), combines such late features as the indication of the swelling of the trapezium on the line from neck to shoulder and the marking of two divisions of the rectus abdominis above the navel with such early traits as a groove above the clavicles, straight sides of the lower boundary of the abdomen, and the use of grooves to indicate the shoulder-blades. It may therefore be placed at the beginning of the Ptoon 20 group, and is perhaps the work of an artist who stood somewhat outside the circle of his contemporaries. A small limestone kouros also from Cyprus (no. 180) is an attractive but summary work of about 500 B.C.

The fact that we have comparatively few examples from East Greece and the Islands is probably owing to political events, for the Ionian revolt against Persia (500–494 B.C.) must have overshadowed all activities. But that important work was still undertaken in Asia Minor is shown by such sculptures as the 'Harpy Tomb' from Xanthos[12] and several pieces from Ephesos.[13]

CYRENE. An attractive little head of a kouros belonging to this period came to light in Cyrene, during the Italian excavations there (cf. p. 144).

10 Aiakes' tyranny was not continuous; cf. Herodotos IV.138, VI.13,25 ; Judeisch, Pauly-Wissowa, *R.E.* I, 1, s.v. Aiakes (2).
11 Savignoni, *Mon. Linc.* XVIII, 1907, cols. 248 ff., fig. 30.
12 Pryce, *Catalogue*, I, 1, B 287, pp. 122 ff., pls. XXI–XXIV.
13 Cf. e.g. Pryce, op. cit. B 178 ff.

RUSSIA. We may also mention a small marble kouros found in Southern Russia on the site of the ancient Olbia, and now in the Museum at Olbia[14] (no. 178). Only the upper part of the torso is preserved, but enough to show that it belongs to the Ptoon 20 group. Olbia, it will be remembered, was a Milesian colony, and two heads found there, evidently of kouroi of the Melos group (cf. p. 92), are of the Eastern type. The soft modelling of the Olbia torso also suggests Eastern connections. It was a time, indeed, when the south Russian colonies kept up close intercourse with their parent cities, before the Attic penetration.

ITALY. A number of excellent kouroi of this period have been found in Italy and Sicily—Agrigento, Leontinoi, Grammichele, Megara Hyblaia, Metapontum, Marzabotto (nos. 181-9). It used to be thought that they were the only marble kouroi that have survived from the West.[14a] The example recently found at Megara Hyblaia (no. 134) shows that such marble kouroi were either made in or imported into Sicily as early as or before the mid-sixth century.

Absolute Chronology

The upper limit of this group may perhaps be fixed by the sculptures of the temple of Apollo at Delphi. For the dating of this temple we have important, though somewhat confused, literary evidence. Herodotos[15] and Aristotle[16] both state that the Alkmeonidai undertook the building of the temple after the battle of Leipsydrion—which took place after the death of Hipparchos (514 B.C.), probably in 513; and this testimony is reiterated by other writers (Isokrates,[17] Demosthenes,[18] Philochoros,[19] Themistios[20]), who all state that the Alkmeonidai were exiled by the Peisistratidai or the *τύραννοι*. Moreover, the scholiast on Aristeides, *Panathenaikos*,[21] expressly tells us that it was after the death of Hipparchos [514 B.C.] that the Alkmeonidai went into exile.[22]

Furthermore, Herodotos[23] informs us that the Alkmeonidai 'finished the temple in finer fashion than was stipulated by the model; in particular, whereas they had contracted to build the temple of poros stone, they made its front of Parian marble'.

According to this evidence, the sculptures of the temple should date after the battle of Leipsydrion, that is, after 513.[24] It has been pointed out, however, that Herodotos may have been misled and that

[14] I owe my knowledge of this figure to Professor M. Rostovtzeff; cf. also p. 152.

[14a] For a nude female statue of marble from Orvieto cf. Körte, in *Studien für H. Brunn dargebracht*, pp. 1 ff.; Santangelo, *Musei e Monumenti etruschi*, pl. 38.

[15] v.62.

[16] *Constitution of Athens* 19.3-4.

[17] xv.232.

[18] *Against Meidias*, 144.

[19] Scholiast on Pindar, *Pyth.* vii.9. who says, furthermore, that the Alkmeonidai finished the temple after the expulsion of the Peisistratids, that is, after 510 B.C.

[20] iv.53a, reading *φυγόντες* with Dindorf.

[21] Dindorf. vol. iii, p. 118.

[22] There must, therefore, have been a second exile of the Alkmeonidai at this time (the first having taken place at the beginning of Peisistratos' third tyranny). This literary evidence, which was examined by Homolle with great acumen in 1902, has recently been confirmed by the discovery of a fragment of an archon list found in the Athenian Agora, which makes a Kleisthenes the archon of 525-524; for it is unlikely, as Meritt (*Hesperia* viii, 1939, pp. 59 ff.) has pointed out, that this Kleisthenes is any other than the famous member of the Alkmeonid family who carried out the reforms of 507 B.C.

[23] v.62 *τόν τε νηὸν ἐξεργάσαντο τοῦ παραδείγματος κάλλιον τά τε ἄλλα καὶ συγκειμένου σφι πωρίνου λίθου ποιέειν τὸν νηόν, Παρίου τὰ ἔμπροσθε αὐτοῦ ἐξεποίησαν.*

[24] Homolle, *B.C.H.*, xxvi, 1902, pp. 587 ff.; De La Coste-Messelière, *B.C.H.* lxxvii, 1946, pp. 271 ff.

his statement was then repeated by all later writers;[25] for it seems unlikely that the great Delphian temple, which was burnt down in 548 B.C., should have stood in ruins for over thirty years, especially as Herodotos[26] himself says that Amasis (who died in 526 B.C.), contributed a large sum toward its rebuilding. It seems more likely that work started earlier, though it naturally continued for a considerable time. Furthermore, architecturally the temple has been dated earlier than the 'Hekatompedon' of Athens, that is, earlier than *c.*520–510 B.C.[27] So if we assign a date of *c.*520 to the Delphian pedimental sculptures we should not go far wrong.

Anatomically the kouroi from the pediment of this temple[28] (cf. no. 139) bear out this earlier dating. They belong in the Ptoon 20 group; for they have such advanced renderings as a slight swelling of the trapezium on the slope of the neck to the shoulder, a semicircular lower boundary of the abdomen, and indications of the serratus magnus and of the xiphoid appendage at the lower end of the sternum. But they must belong *early* in the group, for the lower boundary of the thorax is rendered as a grooved, fairly narrow, and only slightly modelled arch, and the flanks are still level.

On this evidence the upper limit of the Ptoon 20 group should be around 520. And this would allow sufficient time for the Ptoon 12 group (540–520 B.C.)[29] gradually to develop into the Ptoon 20 group.[30] It will be seen that several kouroi are transitional between the two groups (cf. e.g. nos. 158, 159 bis).

The year 480–479 was a crucial one in Greek art. After the Persian sack of their Akropolis,[31] the Athenians buried their broken statues in pits; all sculptures, therefore, found in the so-called Persian debris should date not later than 480–479 B.C. Unfortunately the well-preserved kouros Akropolis 698[32] (no. 190)—which is slightly more developed than the kouroi of the Ptoon 20 group (cf. p. 247)—cannot with certainty be connected with this debris.[33] The excellent preservation of its surface indicates that it was buried soon after its erection, and the Persian destruction would furnish a reason for such a burial. A comparison between it and the Tyrannicides at Naples—of which the originals, probably in bronze, are known to have been erected in the archonship of Adeimantos, 477–476 B.C.[34]—suggests that Akropolis 698 is slightly earlier in date.[35] Renderings which are still

[25] Cf. Pomtow, *Rh. Mus.* LI, 1896, p. 329, LII, 1897, pp. 10 ff.; Payne in Payne and Young, *Acropolis*, pp. 63 ff.; Schefold, *Museum Helveticum*, III, 1946, pp. 61 f., 87 f.; Jacoby, *Frag. griech. Historiker*, III, B, Supplement, I, pp. 149 ff.

[26] II, 180.

[27] Weickert, *Typen der archaischen Architektur*, pp. 146 ff.

[28] I was able to re-examine these fragmentary kouroi in the summer of 1938 during the rearrangement of the museum, and to study them in a good light while they stood on the floor—with the kind help of P. de La Coste-Messelière; and again in recent years, when, however, they had been replaced on their lofty platform.

[29] Cf. pp. 114 ff.

[30] I have accordingly moved up the beginning of the Ptoon 20 group to 520 (instead of 515, as in the first edition), and ended the Ptoon 12 in 520.

[31] Cf. Herodotos VIII.53 (480 B.C.) and IX.13 (479 B.C.).

[32] Payne in Payne and Young, *Acropolis*, p. 44, mentions the possibility that the head now mounted on Akropolis 698 may not originally have belonged to the statue—on account of the extensive chipping round the edges. But there are similar stains on the neck above and below the break; and, though the edges do not meet, the contours undoubtedly fit (cf. Wolters, *Ath. Mitt.* XIII, 1888, p. 226 f.). There can, therefore, be no question that the head belongs to the body; cf. Schuchhardt in Schrader, *Die archaischen Marmorbildwerke der Akropolis*, p. 192 f.

[33] On this subject cf. Kavvadias, *Δελτ. Ἀρχ.* 1888, p. 103 f.; Schrader, *Auswahl archaischer Marmorskulpturen*, p. 55 f.; Furtwängler, *Meisterwerke*, p. 40 f., note 2; Homann-Wedeking, *Ath. Mitt.*, LX/LXI, 1935/6, p. 212.

[34] Olympiad 75.4; *Marm. Par.* lines 70–71, ep. LIV.

[35] So also Payne in Payne and Young, *Acropolis*, p. 44, note 3, and Schuchhardt, op. cit. p. 194. For a contrary view cf. Homann-Wedeking, loc. cit. Of course we must make allowance for the fact that Akropolis 698 is a Greek original and is therefore more sensitively modelled than the Roman copies of the Tyrannicides. But the newly discovered torso of Aristogeiton (*A.J.A.* XLIV, 1940, p. 396 f., fig. 28), though superior in execution to the Naples one, is so close to it in construction that we obtain confidence that the copies in this case reproduce in all essentials the anatomical structure of the originals.

tentative in Akropolis 698 are modelled with ease in the Tyrannicides; the structure of their athletic bodies is accentuated and perfectly understood; for instance, the skeleton of the thorax with the muscular covering in action is rendered as never in archaic art. But if Akropolis 698 is earlier than 477 B.C., the Ptoon 20 group, which is earlier than Akropolis 698, should antecede that date by some years. It follows that the lower limit of the Ptoon 20 group is probably a little before 480.

Hence we may tentatively date the Ptoon 20 group about 520-485 B.C.

This assignment is borne out by other evidence.

The torso from Cyprus (no. 179), which is an early member of the Ptoon 20 group (cf. p. 128), was found in the dromos of a tomb with a silver coin of Idalion 'dating before 500 B.C.'[36] and with a fragment of a black-figured Attic amphora datable about 520 or 530.[37]

On a coin of Poseidonia datable[38] about 525-515 the nude male figure has four transverse divisions of the rectus abdominis above the navel; on coins of Kaulonia of about 530 three such divisions occur; and on coins of Poseidonia of about 515-505, there are sometimes three, sometimes two divisions.[39] On the other hand, on the coins of Poseidonia datable after 510, two divisions are regularly shown. As the kouroi of our Ptoon 20 group for the first time show this rendering of two instead of three transverse divisions above the navel, the placing of the upper limit of this group a little before 510 is hereby substantiated.

If, as seems likely, the electrum stater with the head of Athena wearing a winged helmet[40] is rightly interpreted as issued at the time of the Ionian Revolt, perhaps by Priene, it could be dated within the narrow limits of 499 to 494. The rows of spiral curls round the forehead and at the nape of the neck, the elongated eyes, the round, firm chin, and the general shape of the head present certain similarities with the Barracco head and the Ptoon 20 kouros (nos. 188, 155).

The damareteion of Syracuse struck in commemoration of the victory of Gelon of Syracuse over the Carthaginians at Himera in 480 B.C., may be dated immediately after that event.[41] The renderings of hair, neck, and features conform in a general way with the latest examples of the Ptoon 20 group.

The temple of Aphaia at Aegina, the pedimental sculptures of which are related to the later examples of the Ptoon 20 group, is 'the most perfectly developed of the late archaic temples in European Hellas' (Dinsmoor), and so must belong towards the end of the archaic period. It has been suggested that the eastern pediment of this temple—which is more advanced in style than the western—was a substitution for an earlier one destroyed by Nikodromos *c.*487-485.[42] But, as has been pointed out,[43] the destruction was more probably caused by a bolt of lightning. Hence it cannot be dated.

The Nike in the Akropolis Museum, no. 690,[44] has recently been identified as the crowning feature of a column dedicated as a thankoffering after the battle of Marathon.[45] Since the monument

[36] Pryce, *Catalogue*, I, I, p. 155. Mr. Pryce wrote me in May 1938: 'Mr. E. S. G. Robinson has re-examined the coin and repeats that he would prefer before and not after 500, adding, "recent evidence suggests that we have underdated Cypriot issues".'

[37] On this subject Beazley wrote me (1939): 'The fragment found "with" the kouros from Marion seems to be from an ordinary Attic neck-amphora of the canonical late type, but this is not one of the latest and may be *about* 520 or perhaps even 530.'

[38] The dates here given are those tentatively suggested by E. S. G. Robinson.

[39] Cf. *Catalogue of Greek Coins in the British Museum*, XXIII, Italy, p. 265, no. 3 (three divisions) and 8 (two divisions).

[40] Jameson, *Revue numismatique* 4e série, XV, 1911, pp. 60 ff.; P. Gardner, *History of Ancient Coinage*, p. 98. Cf. also Baldwin, *The Electrum Coinage of Lampsakos*, 1914, pp. 26 ff., pl. II (Priene pl. II, 11).

[41] Schwabacher, *Das Demareteion*, *Opus nobile*, 7, p. 14 f.

[42] H. Thiersch, *Äginetische Studien*, II.

[43] Welter, *Arch. Anz.* 1938, cols. 1-6.

[44] Payne and Young, *Acropolis*, pl. 120, 1-2; Langlotz in Schrader, *Akropolis*, pls. 91-2, pp. 122 ff.

[45] Raubitschek, *A.J.A.* XLIV, 1940, pp. 53 ff.; and *Dedications*, no. 13; Hampe, *Die Antike*, XV, 1939, pp. 168 ff.

was destroyed by the Persians, it must have been erected in the decade 490-480. The date 490 previously proposed on stylistic grounds[46]—for instance, on the resemblance of the drapery to that of the Athena from the western pediment of the temple of Aegina—has thus been substantiated.

According to Pausanias (I, 16, 3), the bronze statue of Apollo Philesios by Kanachos of Sikyon[47] was transferred by Xerxes from the temple at Didyma to Ekbatana in Persia (494 B.C.). From Pliny's description of it (XXXIV, 75), a Roman marble relief found at Didyma and representations on Roman coins of Didyma have been identified as reproducing this statue.[48] To judge by these generalized copies, the statue must have belonged to the Ptoon 20 group. A date for this group before 494 B.C. is here again indicated.

Unfortunately comparisons with Attic vase paintings are limited in scope, for frontal figures are not often depicted there, and many of our criteria are based on the front view of the human figure. We can nevertheless make a few helpful observations. In black-figured and red-figured vases until about 515 the serratus magnus is not indicated[49] and there are three transverse divisions of the rectus abdominis above the navel;[50] the clavicles, if indicated, are straight, or form a single curve.[51] In works of the late sixth century, the serratus magnus is rendered first by a series of straight lines, then by a set of single curves, and finally—by the end of the sixth century and the beginning of the fifth—by a series of double curves to show the interlacement with the digitations of the external oblique muscle;[52] the rectus abdominis now has two transverse divisions above the navel, first without, then with indication of their attachment to the lower arch of the thorax;[53] and the clavicles are drawn as a double curve.[54] In other words, the development which we observe in the kouroi is observable also in contemporary vase paintings. At least to a limited extent; the economy of line necessitated by the technique of vase painting and its two-dimensional quality prevent some changes from being followed. The renderings of the eye, the mouth, and especially the ear do not correspond to those observable in sculpture. For instance, the antitragus is not depicted in Athenian vase painting, even in the latest period.[55]

The moulded Athenian vases in the form of human heads occasionally have painted scenes which can be dated independently. For instance, the head vase in New York[56] with pictures by the Brygos Painter may be dated 490-480 B.C.[57] from the style of its painted reclining satyrs. In the structure of its features, especially of the mouth, the head resembles the 'polos' kore from the Akropolis, no. 696,[58] and several kouroi of the Ptoon 20 group (cf. e.g. nos. 155, 162).

[46] Brunn-Bruckmann, *Denkmäler*, no. 526A; *Jahrbuch*, XXXV, 1920, pp. 97 ff.

[47] Lippold, Pauly-Wissowa, *R.E.*, X, 2 (1919), s.v. Kanachos, and *Griechische Plastik*, p. 86 f.

[48] Cf. E. Simon, 'Beobachtungen zum Apollon Philesios', in *Charites*, 1957, pp. 38 ff., and the references there cited.

[49] It is not always easy in this early period to distinguish the straight lines intended for the serratus magnus from those intended for ribs; for instance those on Oltos's spear-thrower (Richter and Hall, *Red-figured Athenian Vases in the Metropolitan Museum*, p. 7, fig. 2) are probably ribs, owing to their position; the same applies to Psiax's archer on p. 8, fig. 8.

[50] Cf. e.g. Beazley, *Vases in Poland*, pl. 3 (Goluchow Painter, *c.*530 B.C.).

[51] Pfuhl, *Malerei und Zeichmung der Griechen*, III, pl. 88, no. 315 (Andokides Painter).

[52] Cf. e.g. Richter and Hall, op. cit. p. 10, fig. 10, p. 7, fig. 3, pls. 16, 17; Beazley, *Vases in Poland*, pl. 5 (Euthymides).

[53] Richter and Hall, op. cit. p. 10, fig. 10; p. 7. 7, fig. 3, pl. 16.

[54] Ibid. pl. 38; Pfuhl, *Malerei und Zeichnung der Griechen*, III, pl. 106.

[55] The same abbreviated renderings especially of ears may be observed on small bronze statuettes of all periods, and of course on coins. The successive anatomical changes in vase-paintings are illustrated by drawings in my *Red-figured Vases, A Survey*, revised edition, 1958.

[56] Richter and Hall, op. cit. no. 43, pls. 43, 178.

[57] Beazley, *Journal of Hellenic Studies*, XLIX, 1929, pp. 56 ff., fig. 9.

[58] Payne and Young, *Acropolis*, p. 39 f., pls. 82, 83; Langlotz in Schrader, *Akropolis*, no. 20, pl. 29. Dated by Payne in the early fifth century before the Euthydikos kore; by Langlotz 'um 500'.

Anatomical Analysis

The anatomical shapes are now well understood and are used to form a co-ordinated whole. Though the stance remains strictly frontal, as time goes on the differentiation of the flanks is correctly observed; the left flank advances in sympathy with the advanced leg, as it already had occasionally in the Anavysos-Ptoon 12 group, but now for the first time dips instead of rising. In other words, the weight is placed on the receding leg and its hip is raised. At the back, the buttocks, instead of being represented at the same height, as hitherto, occasionally rise or fall in accordance with the hips.

STRUCTURE IN GENERAL. Back and front of thorax fully developed.

HEAD. *Skull.* Spherical.

Ear. In correct position (for an exception cf. no. 175) and well shaped. Tragus and antitragus marked.

Eye. Set horizontally. Upper eyelid arches over eyeball. Recess at inner corner indicated and occasionally the lachrymal caruncle.

Mouth. Lips curve upward only in earlier examples. Upper lip protrudes markedly over lower, and both lips are well shaped.

Hair. Short or rolled up at back; only occasionally still hangs down back; divided into wavy strands which generally radiate from a centre at top of skull.

NECK. Sterno-mastoids and throat modelled. Attachment of former to sternum and clavicles now generally indicated; there is therefore no longer a continuous groove above clavicles (for an exception cf. no. 179). Swelling of trapezium on outline of shoulder indicated for the first time.

TORSO, FRONT. Clavicles assume their characteristic *S*-shaped curve and disappear beneath deltoid. Lower boundary of thorax forms semicircular arch at correct distance below pectorals. At lower end of sternum there is sometimes observable a small, raised plane caused by the projection of the xiphoid appendage (cf. nos. 155–6, 159, 166). Serratus magnus occasionally marked in earlier examples, regularly in later ones. Two transverse divisions of rectus abdominis above navel, the third (top) division now being incorporated into the semicircular arch of thorax; lower boundary of rectus abdominis sometimes indicated by grooves, one on each side of abdomen. Bulge of external oblique over iliac crest is well developed. Groove over linea alba sometimes continued for a short distance below navel. Navel generally modelled in the form of a knob with a fold of skin above it. Lower boundary of abdomen forms semicircular arch (except in a few early examples; cf. nos. 162, 174, 175, 179, 181). Pubes often marked as a stylized raised plane, with upper edge in the form of two concave curves rising to a central point.[59]

TORSO, BACK. Construction well understood.

ARM. In earlier examples hands are still joined to body by supports, but action of arms becomes gradually freer, with hands holding attributes. Metacarpal bones generally indicated.

LEG. Construction well understood. Toes do not recede along one line, second toe projecting further than the big toe; small toe short and turned inward. Toes and nails point forward. Joints of toes strongly articulated and metatarsal bones indicated.

FOOT PLINTH. Hexagonal (no. 165) or rectangular (see under no. 161 bis).

[59] For parallels on vases cf. C. M. Robertson, *J.H.S.* LVIII, 1938, p. 49. For earlier examples cf. nos. 82, 106.

Kouroi Nos. 155-189

155 : Figs. 450-457

ATHENS, NATIONAL MUSEUM, no. 20. From the Ptoan Sanctuary.

Statue, from head to back of right knee. Small sliver at fracture of right arm restored, as well as fairly broad sliver at fracture of neck.

Parian marble.
Height 1.03 m.
Torso found in 1885 in temple of Ptoan Apollo; head in 1886 at the foot of the hill on which temple stood.
Holleaux, *B.C.H.* x, 1886, pp. 269 ff., pl. vi (torso).
Holleaux, *B.C.H.* xi, 1887, pp. 275 ff., pls. xiii, xiv (head and statue); p. 287 (inscription).
Budde, *Die attischen Kuroi* (Diss. 1939), p. 29 ff.
Buschor, *Fr. J.*, pp. 122 f., figs. 139-141.
Deonna, no. 31.

Inscription: On left thigh: *Πυθιας ὀκραιφ[ιευςμε] | και ἀσχριον ἀν[ε]θ̣[εκεν]*, on right thigh: *φι* . . . . | *Πτοι[. . . . ἀργυ]ροτοχσοι*, 'Pythias of Akraiphia and Aischrion dedicated me to the Ptoan . . . of the silver bow' (two hexameters). For the singular verb cf. *I.G.* I^2, 627.

GENERAL STRUCTURE. Seen in profile, greatest protrusion of back level with that of chest. Vertebral column forms *S*-shaped curve.
HEAD. Features sharply cut.
Skull. Spherical.
Ear. Small and set sloping. Tragus and antitragus marked.
Eye. Groove marks fold in upper eyelid; inner recess shown as small loop; lachrymal caruncle not discernible.
Mouth. Lips well shaped; curve upward at outer corners ending in a point; upper lip protrudes markedly over lower.
Hair. In front, above forehead and temples, double row of small spirals, arranged symmetrically to right and left of centre. Wavy strands radiate from centre at top of skull. Rolled up at back round fillet, leaving neck clear. Fillet outlines round shape of skull at back.
NECK. Part of neck restored. No sterno-mastoids visible. No continuous groove above clavicles. Slight indication of bulge of trapezium.
TORSO, FRONT. Clavicles curve backward; attached too high on shoulders. Fleshy breasts. Median line marked by groove from lower end of sternum to a little below navel. Thorax well developed; lower boundary approaches shape of semicircle. At lower end of sternum small, raised plane caused by projection of xiphoid appendage. Two transverse divisions above navel in rectus abdominis. Navel marked as knob surrounded by circular groove. External oblique swells over iliac crest, but flanks not as developed as in no. 144. Left flank advances in sympathy with advanced leg, and for the first time dips instead of rising. Lower boundary of abdomen approaches form of semicircular arch.
TORSO, BACK. Well developed. Erector spinae indicated.
ARM. Held away from body. Traces of round supports on thighs.
LEG. Buttocks about level. Depression over great trochanter indicated.

156 : Figs. 458-460

THEBES, MUSEUM, no. 7. From Eutresis.

Torso from neck to below left knee.

White marble, fine grained, with slightly bluish veins, perhaps Boeotian.
Height 1.22 m.
Found at Eutresis during excavations 1924-6.
Goldman, *Excavations at Eutresis*, pp. 270 ff., figs. 329-32.
Karouzos, *'Οδηγός*, p. 15, no. 7, fig. 7.

GENERAL STRUCTURE. Seen in profile, greatest protrusion of back level with that of chest. Vertebral column makes *S*-shaped curve.
NECK. Slight indication of swelling of trapezium.
TORSO, FRONT. Clavicles travel upward to shoulders and form double curve. Median line marked by depression from lower end of sternum to a little below navel. Thorax well developed; lower boundary formed by semicircular arch. At lower end of sternum small, raised plane caused by projection of xiphoid appendage. Rectus abdominis has two transverse divisions above navel. Navel shown by knob, with fold of flesh above it. Bulge of external oblique over iliac crest is well developed. Right hip lower than left. Lower boundary of abdomen descends towards genitals, forming shallow curve. Pubes indicated by raised plane, with upper edge formed by two concave curves rising to a central point. Penis carved separately and is missing.
TORSO, BACK. Well developed. Wide groove for spinal furrow. Shoulder-blades and erector spinae modelled.

ARM. Trace of support for left hand on left external oblique muscle.
LEG. Buttocks level. Depression over great trochanter modelled. Muscles on thighs modelled. Inner vastus well developed.

157 : Figs. 467-469

ATHENS, NATIONAL MUSEUM, no. 7381. From the Ptoan Sanctuary.

Statuette, from head to above ankles. The left lower leg and perhaps the right forearm are somewhat out of position. An early member of this group.

Bronze.
Height 15.5 cm.
Found in 1885 in the Ptoan Sanctuary.
Holleaux, *B.C.H.* x, 1886, pp. 190 ff., pl. IX.
Papaspiridi, *Guide*, p. 186 f., no. 7381.
Deonna, p. 270, no. 83.
I.G. VII.2730.

Inscription: On front of left leg: *Εὐϝειτιας ἀνεθεκε*; on front of right leg: *το Πτοιεο*[ς], 'Eueitias dedicated it. Property of the Ptoan.'
GENERAL STRUCTURE. Well-developed thorax. Broad shoulders. Greatest protrusion of back, seen in profile, level with that of chest. Vertebral column forms *S*-shaped curve.
HEAD. *Skull.* Spherical.
Ear. Modelled in different planes, but generalized. Tragus indicated, but no antitragus.
Eye. Horizontal. Recess at inner corner.
Mouth. Horizontal.
Hair. On skull, indicated by incised lines travelling obliquely downward on either side of median line; at back, falls down shoulders in mass divided vertically and horizontally into beaded tresses with ends forming curving line. On each side in front fall two tresses. Above forehead and temples curls arranged symmetrically to right and left of centre. Thick, notched fillet encircles hair.
NECK. Sterno-mastoids not indicated. Outline of shoulders hidden by hair. Groove marks lower boundary of neck (perhaps intended for clavicles).
TORSO, FRONT. Lower boundary of thorax forms thick, rounded arch immediately below pectorals. Median line marked from top of sternum to navel. Two transverse divisions of rectus abdominis modelled above navel. Navel marked as button. At flanks external oblique bulges over iliac crest. Flanks about level. Short groins.
TORSO, BACK. Spinal furrow marked by groove. Shoulder-blades hidden by hair. Erector spinae not indicated.
ARM. Separated from body and brought forward.
Hand. Held attribute.
LEG. Buttocks level. Depression over great trochanter modelled. Inner vastus bulges over patella and descends markedly lower than outer. Anterior border of shin curves inward.

158 : Figs. 470-473

NEW YORK, COLLECTION OF WALTER C. BAKER.

Statuette, from head to plinth. A very early member, it would seem, of this group, transitional between Ptoan 12 and Ptoan 20.

Bronze.
Height 15.2 cm.
Provenance not known. Formerly in the collection of Mr. Matoussian, Paris.
D. von Bothmer, *Catalogue of Antiquities from the Collection of W. C. Baker, shown in an exhibition at the Century Association, New York*, 1950, no. 49A.
Buschor, *Alt. St.*, IV, p. 71, figs. 301-303.

GENERAL STRUCTURE. Well developed thorax. Broad shoulders. Greatest protrusion of back, seen in profile, level with that of chest. Vertebral column forms *S*-shaped curve.
HEAD. *Skull.* Domed.
Ear. Modelled in different planes, but generalized.
Eye. About horizontal. Curving lids. Recess at inner corner.
Mouth. Light curve upward at inner corners. Upper lip protrudes over lower.
Hair. On skull, indicated by incised lines travelling obliquely downward on either side of median line; at back, falls down in mass divided vertically and horizontally into beaded tresses, with ends forming curving line. Incised line at back perhaps marks fillet.
NECK. Generalized. Hollow marks lower boundary.
TORSO, FRONT. Lower boundary of thorax forms thick, rounded arch immediately below pectorals, covering uppermost (i.e. third) transverse division of rectus abdominis. Median line marked from top of sternum to navel. Navel shown as button surrounded by circular groove. At flanks external oblique bulges over iliac crest. Flanks about level.
TORSO, BACK. Spinal furrow marked by groove. Shoulder-blades hidden by hair. Erector spinae not indicated.
ARM. Separated from body; right lowered, left bent at elbow and extended.

Hand. Right holds attribute, left held open.
LEG. Depression over great trochanter indicated. Buttocks about level. Patella rounded. Inner vastus descends lower than outer. Anterior border of shin curves inward. Inner malleolus higher than outer.
Foot. Second toe projects further than big toe.
PLINTH. Rectangular; cast in one piece with statuette.

159 : Figs. 461-463

LONDON, BRITISH MUSEUM, no. B 475. From Anaphe (?).

Statue, from head to knees.

Parian marble.
Height 1.01 m.
'From the collections of the sixth Viscount Strangford. Acquired by British Museum in 1864; stated in that year to have come from Lemnos but more generally believed to have been found in Anaphe' (Pryce).
Pryce, *Catalogue*, B 475, p. 204 f., pl. XLIII.
Deonna, no. 161.

GENERAL STRUCTURE. Seen in profile, greatest protrusion level with that of chest. Vertebral column forms strongly pronounced *S*-shaped curve.
HEAD. *Skull.* Developed at top and back.
Ear. Small and set strongly sloping towards line of jaw; modelled in different planes. Both tragus and antitragus marked.
Eye. Recess at inner corner with indication of caruncle. Eyeball does not protrude.
Mouth. Lips horizontal and well shaped, forming Cupid's bow; lower lip has vertebral depression at middle. Upper lip protrudes slightly over lower.
Hair. On skull, mass differentiated into shallow, circular waves over which wavy strands radiate from crown; at back, strands are twisted round fillet and so assume a horizontal direction and are divided into a series of separate rolls (cf. no. 184). In front, hair is arranged in two rows of spiral curls, symmetrically to right and left of centre, and at sides, in three rows; the curls protrude directly under fillet. Holes (two above left ear, one above right, one in centre front, and one at back, the last with bronze peg preserved) indicate former presence of another fillet or wreath, presumably of bronze.
NECK. Sterno-mastoid muscles modelled with attachment to sternal notch. Hair no longer covers back of neck. Swelling of trapezium indicated.
TORSO, FRONT. Clavicles have double curve and ends are covered by shoulder. Median line indicated by a shallow groove from bottom of sternum to below navel. Horizontal divisions of sternum marked. At its lower end is a small, raised plane caused by projection of xiphoid appendage. Thorax well developed; lower boundary approaches shape of semicircle and is placed just underneath pectorals. Nipples placed correctly. In rectus abdominis, two transverse divisions above navel indicated by shallow grooves. Navel indicated as small irregular flat plane with slight fold above it. Five digitations of serratus magnus indicated, with digitations of external oblique interlinked. External oblique descends over iliac crest, but this bulge at flanks not much developed. Flanks about level. Lower boundary of abdomen approaches form of semicircular arch.
TORSO, BACK. Spinal furrow, shoulder-blades, and erector spinae modelled in different planes.
ARM. Was held away from body, for there is no trace of supports.
LEG. Slight indication of depression over great trochanter. Buttocks about level. Inner vastus descends much lower than outer and is well developed. Patella rounded; rests on pads of fat.

159 bis : Figs. 478-480

Statue, found with others of different periods at the Piraeus in July 1959. Figs. 478-480 reproduce it from photographs taken shortly after its discovery, before cleaning, and are here published with the kind permission of Mr. Papadimitriou. Left leg broken off and reattached; otherwise practically intact. It has not yet been decided whether these statues will be exhibited in the National Museum, Athens, or in the Piraeus Museum. I was able to examine the kouros and to discuss it with Mr. Karouzos in April 1960. It was then still lying horizontally on its back in the process of being cleaned. An interesting feature is the iron armature that was left inside the body, arms, and legs. Like no. 158, this kouros seems to be transitional between Ptoon 12 and Ptoon 20 groups.

Bronze. Cast hollow, except hands and wrists which are solid.
Height 1.92 m.
Εἴκονες, no. 198, August 10-16, 1959, p. 18.
Illustrated London News, August 29, 1959, pp. 130-1.
Orlandos, *Ἔργον τῆς Ἀρχαιολ. Ἑταιρείας*, 1959-1960, pp. 161 ff.

GENERAL STRUCTURE. Body well developed. Right instead of left leg advanced.
HEAD. *Skull.* Spherical.
Ear. Modelled in different planes, with tragus and antitragus marked.
Eye. Placed horizontally. Upper eyelid arches over eyeball. Recess at inner corner indicated.
Mouth. Finely modelled lips; lower one broad.
Chin. Prominent.

Hair. Descends to shoulders. Two thick tresses are brought forward on each side. Over forehead and temples are large spiral curls arranged symmetrically to right and left of centre; and in front of each ear are three short corkscrew tresses. Simple fillet surrounds hair.

NECK. Sterno-mastoid muscles and throat between indicated by modelling. Apparently no indication of swelling of trapezium.

TORSO, FRONT. Clavicles curve backward. Median line marked by depression from lower end of sternum to below navel. Chest well developed. Pectorals placed rather high. Lower boundary of thorax forms rounded arch. Nipples marked by knobs surrounded by a circle and are separately worked. Two transverse divisions shown above navel in rectus abdominis. Navel marked by knob inside a depression. No indication of digitations of serratus magnus. External oblique bulges over iliac crest. Pubes indicated as raised plane of which upper boundary forms concave curve.

ARM. Separated from sides and extended. The left hand evidently held a bow, of which a bit is preserved; the right perhaps a phiale. The statue must, therefore, have represented an Apollo. The fingers are finely modelled, with ends slightly bent backward; metacarpal bones indicated.

LEG. Slight indication of depression over great trochanter. Vastus internus descends well below vastus externus. Inner malleolus higher than outer.

FOOT. Well shaped, long, and slender. Joints of toes articulated and metatarsal bones indicated. Toes do not recede along one line, second toe projecting further than big toe; small toe turned inward. The soles are omitted but a flat rim runs along the contours. The iron armature evidently passed through the feet and was secured with molten lead, portions of which remain.

160 : Figs. 464-466

ATHENS, AKROPOLIS MUSEUM, no. 692. From the Akropolis.

Torso, from neck to knees.

Parian marble.
Height 87 cm.
Found in 1864, SE. of Parthenon. Right arm added in 1900.
Dickins, *Catalogue*, p. 254 f., no. 692 (ill.).
Payne and Young, *Acropolis*, p. 46, pl. 108, 1-3.
Schuchhardt in Schrader, *Akropolis*, p. 195 f., no. 300, pls. 118, 119.

GENERAL STRUCTURE. Greatest protrusion of back, seen in profile, corresponds to that of chest. Vertebral column forms *S*-shaped curve. Gentle curves of body.

NECK. Swelling of trapezium indicated.

TORSO, FRONT. Clavicles swing backward in double curve. Median line suggested by modelled depression. Lower boundary of thorax forms flat arch under pectorals, which are placed rather high. Slight indication of serratus magnus. Two transverse divisions of rectus abdominis modelled above navel. Navel marked by knob with fold of flesh above it. External oblique bulges over iliac crest. Left flank is not advanced, but dips slightly, conforming with action of advanced left leg. Lower boundary of abdomen forms deep curve.

TORSO, BACK. Construction feeble. Spinal furrow and erector spinae modelled, but shoulder-blades not separately indicated.

ARM. Bent and held away from body. No trace of supports.

LEG. Right buttock lower instead of higher than left. Indication of depression over great trochanter. Inner vastus descends lower than outer.

161 : Figs. 481-482

ATHENS, NATIONAL MUSEUM, no. 3370. From near Athens.

Torso, from middle of chest to bottom of buttocks. Large fracture in front with deep hole.

Parian marble.
Height 67 cm.
Found near Athens in 1914.
Homann-Wedeking, *Ath. Mitt.* 60/61, 1935/6, pp. 201 ff., pls. 71-5.

GENERAL STRUCTURE. Vertebral column *S*-shaped.

TORSO, FRONT. Median line marked by groove which descends a little below navel. Lower boundary of thorax (partly missing) formed semicircular arch. Two transverse divisions of rectus abdominis modelled above navel. Navel marked by knob in modelled depression, with fold of flesh above it. Digitations of serratus magnus represented interlocked with digitations of the external oblique. External oblique bulges markedly over iliac crest. Left flank dips, conforming with advanced leg. Lower boundary of abdomen approaches form of semicircle. Pubes indicated by raised, stylized plane, with upper edge formed by two concave curves rising to a central point.

TORSO, BACK. Broad groove for spinal furrow. Erector spinae modelled.

LEG. Right buttock higher than left. Depression over great trochanter modelled.

161 bis: Figs. 483-484

ATHENS, KERAMEIKOS MUSEUM. Found by Mr. Threpsiades in the Themistoklean wall in 1953. An early member of this group.

Middle portion of a torso and pieces of a right and of a left leg found near it and perhaps belonging to it. (The fragment of a left leg is not included in figs. 483, 484.)

Marble.
Height of torso, about life-size; of piece of leg c.31 cm.
From the Kerameikos, Athens.
Courbin, *B.C.H.* LXXVIII, 1954, p. 106, fig. 11.

TORSO, FRONT. External oblique swells over iliac crest, but flanks not much developed. Lower boundary of rectus abdominis marked by curving groove above lower boundary of abdomen; the latter descends with slightly curving sides towards genitals. Pubes was painted (traces remain).
TORSO, BACK. Spinal furrow and lumbar region modelled.
LEG. Depression over great trochanter indicated. In the right leg inner vastus descends lower and is more developed than outer; in the left leg shin bone curves inward. Buttocks level.

In the same excavations came to light two bases, evidently of kouroi. One, *c.*22.5 cm. high, with a hexagonal plinth inserted, has a bilingual inscription, in Greek and Carian, stating that the monument was erected to the Carian Tymnes and was the work of Aristokles (perhaps the same Aristokles who carved the stele of Aristion). The other base, *c.*31.5 cm. high, has a rectangular plinth inserted, on which are traces of two feet, the left advanced.

Here too belongs the torso, from neck to beginning of thighs, AKROPOLIS 4075 (Buschor and Hamann, *Olympia*, text, p. 28, figs. 4, 5).

162 : Figs. 474-477

ATHENS, NATIONAL MUSEUM, no. 6445. From the Akropolis.

Statuette, from head to feet.

Bronze.
Height 27.3 cm.
Found in 1888 between Parthenon and Akropolis Museum.
De Ridder, *B.C.H.* XVIII, 1894, pp. 44 ff., pls. V-VI.
De Ridder, *Catalogue des bronzes trouvés sur l'Acropole d'Athènes*, p. 268 f., no. 740, pls. III, IV.
Buschor, *Fr. J.*, pp. 95 f., figs. 105, 106.

GENERAL STRUCTURE. Leans slightly forward, as if starting to walk. (This was indicated after cement below soles of feet was removed, in 1938, and statuette was remounted.[60]) Viewed in profile, greatest protrusion level with that of chest. Vertebral column forms *S*-shaped curve.
HEAD. *Skull.* Spherical.
Ear. Slants somewhat towards line of jaw. Tragus and antitragus indicated (latter clearly visible on right ear).
Eye. Horizontal. Inner recess and lachrymal caruncle indicated. Iris and pupil incised.
Mouth. Lips more or less horizontal.
Hair. Short. Finely incised strands radiate from centre at top of skull. No fillet.
NECK. Sterno-mastoids lightly modelled. Swelling of trapezium indicated.
TORSO, FRONT. Clavicles travel upward and lose themselves in shoulders. Median line from bottom of sternum to a little below navel veers towards right flank. Nipples inlaid. Lower boundary of thorax forms semicircular arch. Two transverse divisions of rectus abdominis modelled above navel. Navel modelled, with fold of flesh above it. External oblique, swelling over iliac crest, well developed. Left flank higher and more advanced than right. Lower boundary of abdomen descends towards genitals, with fairly straight sides.
TORSO, BACK. Well developed. Spinal furrow, shoulder-blades, and erector spinae modelled.
ARM. Bent at elbow and held away from body.
Hand. Loosely clasped; probably held something.
LEG. Well shaped. Left buttock slightly lower than right. Depression over great trochanter modelled. Inner vastus well developed and descends much lower than outer. Inner malleolus higher than outer.
Foot. Second toe projects slightly further than big toe and little toe slants inward. Joints of toes strongly articulated.

[60] Mr. Young's photographs reproduced in figs. 474-476 show the statuette before the remounting; fig. 477 shows it as now set up.

163 : Figs. 490-491

PARIS, LOUVRE, no. MND 890. From Attica (?).

Head, with part of neck. Remains of meniskos. Surface battered.

Island marble.
Height *c.* 21 cm.
Perhaps from Attica. Acquired by the Louvre in 1910.
Michon, *Mon. Piot.* XIX, 1911, pp. 171 ff., fig. 1, pl. XIV.
Louvre, *Catalogue sommaire*, 1922, p. 42, no. 3015.

HEAD. *Skull.* Spherical.
Ear. In correct position and modelled in different planes. Tragus marked. Antitragus not preserved.
Eye. Set horizontally. Upper eyelid arches over eyeball. Recess at inner corner indicated, but (as far as visible now) no caruncle.
Mouth. Lips placed horizontally.

Hair. Short, ending at nape of neck in two rows of spiral curls. Similar spiral curls round forehead and temples. On skull, mass left more or less smooth.
NECK. Upper ends of sterno-mastoids modelled; more developed on right side than on left; therefore head may have been turned towards left.

164 : Figs. 485-488

KANSAS CITY, WILLIAM ROCKHILL GALLERY OF ART.

Head and part of neck.

Marble.
Height 19 cm.
Provenance not known, but thought to be Athens.
Guide to the Collection, 3rd. ed., p. 18.
Sieveking, *Pantheon*, 1939, p. 36.
Arias, *Istituto d'Archeologia e Storia d'Arte*, I, 1952, p. 245, fig. 5.

HEAD. *Skull.* Rounded. Has hole for meniskos.
Ear. Well shaped and modelled in the round. Both tragus and antitragus indicated. Slants towards line of jaw.
Eye. Upper eyelid arches over eyeball. Line of demarcation was probably accentuated in colour. Eyeball protrudes.
Mouth. Lips full and well shaped.
Hair. Radiates from crown in wavy strands; falls down at back to top of shoulder and is then looped up in *krobylos* fashion. Fillet encircles head. Over forehead and temples the strands terminate in spiral curls, arranged symmetrically to right and left of centre.

165 : Figs. 489, 492-493[61]

ATHENS, NATIONAL MUSEUM, no. 3938.

Statue, from head to base. Inscribed on base: Ἀριστοδικο 'of Aristodikos'.

Parian marble.
Height from top of head to bottom of feet 1.95 m.; height of base 28·7 cm.
Found in 1944, in the Mesogeia, near Mt. Olympus, Attica.
Buschor, *Fr. J.*, p. 114 f., figs. 131, 132.
C. Karouzos, *Atlantis* XXVIII, 1955, pp. 44 ff. (a definite publication to follow shortly).

GENERAL STRUCTURE. Seen in profile, greatest protrusion of back level with that of chest. Vertebral column forms *S*-shaped curve.
HEAD. *Skull.* Spherical.
Ear. Modelled in different planes; small lobe; tragus and antitragus marked. Upper end of helix (external rim) descends into concha in marked curve.
Eye. Set horizontally. Inner recess and lachrymal caruncle both indicated. Surface of iris injured.
Mouth. Lips horizontal and meet at outer corners.
Hair. Surface of skull picked, evidently to simulate hair. Above forehead and temples, triple row of spiral curls, arranged symmetrically to right and left of centre. At back, double row of similar curls.
NECK. Sterno-mastoid muscles modelled, with slight indication of throat between. Swelling of trapezium on line of shoulder indicated.
TORSO, FRONT. Clavicles travel upward in double curve to shoulders. Median line modelled from sternal notch to below navel, veering slightly towards right flank. Right nipple indicated (left one broken off). Lower boundary of thorax forms semicircular arch. Two horizontal divisions of rectus abdominis modelled above navel. Navel indicated as a modelled knob with fold of skin above. Flanks about level; left one a little more advanced than right. Serratus magnus not indicated. Lower boundary of abdomen approaches form of semicircular arch. Bulge of external oblique over iliac crest indicated, but flanks not well developed. Pubes indicated by raised, stylized plane, with upper edge formed by two concave curves rising to a central point.
TORSO, BACK. Spinal furrow, shoulder blades, and erector spinae modelled. Three top vertebrae of spinal column between shoulder-blades indicated by three protuberances.
ARM. Held away from body, bent at elbow, and connected with thigh by semi-cylindrical support. Elbow indicated by modelled projection. Forearm correctly semi-pronated. Hands missing.
LEG. Left buttock slightly lower and slightly more advanced than right. Depression over great trochanter modelled. Inner vastus well developed and descends much lower than outer. Inner malleolus higher than outer.
Foot. Second toe projects slightly further than big toe and little toe slants inward. Metatarsal bones only slightly indicated.
FOOT-PLINTH. Worked in one piece with statue. Hexagonal; outline follows roughly that of soles. Let into base.
BASE. Rectangular, with depression on upper face for insertion of plinth. Interstices between base and plinth wide in places. Lead that was poured into interstices partly preserved. Sides and upper surface of base smoothed with claw chisel and drove (some marks of which remain on sides).

[61] The back view of the statue will be published in C. Karouzos' *Aristodikos*.

166 : Figs. 500-503

DELPHI, MUSEUM, inv. nos. 1874, 4821, 4828, 4827, 4822. Parts of kouroi from East pediment of Temple of Apollo at Delphi.

Of the three standing kouroi in the east pediment of the Temple of Apollo at Delphi, one is tolerably well preserved; of the others only a few small pieces remain. We select for description here the best-preserved figure, and a fragment of each of the other two. All are of Parian marble and were found in 1894 in a fill NE. of the temple.

For a discussion of the date cf. p. 129 f.

Nos. 1874, 4821, 4828. Statue from middle of head to below left knee, with fragment of drapery. (Piece of left knee, no. 4828, almost certainly belongs to this statue.) Figs. 500, 501.

Parian marble.
Height 99 cm. (without knee); height of fragment of knee 24 cm.; height of whole statue computed to have been about 1.75-1.80 m.
De La Coste-Messelière, *F.d.D.* IV, fasc. 3, pp. 44 ff., no. 7 (XXIX-XXXI), fig. 15, pl. hors-texte VI.

NECK. Slight indication of swelling of trapezium on left side.

TORSO, FRONT. Clavicles travel upward and backward, disappearing into shoulders; only slightly curved; no continuous groove above them. Groove indicating median line travels from lower end of sternum to navel. Well-developed thorax; lower boundary indicated by narrow, grooved arch. At lower end of sternum small, raised plane caused by projection of xiphoid appendage. No transverse divisions of rectus abdominis marked above navel. External oblique bulges over iliac crest; left side (i.e. that of forward leg) is further forward than right, so that pelvis is slightly turned to (spectator's) left. Lower boundary of abdomen approaches form of semicircular arch. Navel marked by knob with a fold of skin above it. Penis was attached separately.

TORSO, BACK. Left unfinished.

ARM. Completely free from body.

No. 4827. Right knee belonging to a second kouros. Fig. 503.

Parian marble.
Height 21 cm.
De La Coste-Messelière, *F.d.D.* IV, fasc. 3, p. 47, no. 8, XXXII, pl. hors-texte VII.

Inner vastus descends much lower and is more developed than outer. Patella mostly missing.

No. 4822. Fragment of torso, from below shoulder to above waist, belonging to a third kouros. Fig. 502.

Height 38 cm.
De La Coste-Messelière, *F.d.D.* IV, fasc. 3, p. 47 f., no. 9 (XXXIV), fig. 16, pl. hors-texte, VII.

Left side is executed with care; right side was turned to pediment wall and not finished. Was intended to be seen in three-quarter view.

Serratus magnus marked by series of ridges digitating from underneath the latissimus dorsi.

167 : Fig. 504

CHALKIS, MUSEUM, no. 54. From Euboea.

Torso, from neck to above knees. Piece in middle of body and under left breast restored.

Island marble.
Height 80 cm.
Found at Metochi, about 20 km. west of Kyme on Euboea.
Homann-Wedeking, *Ath. Mitt.* 60/61, 1935/6, pp. 204 ff., pl. 76.

GENERAL STRUCTURE. Seen in profile, greatest protrusion of back level with that of chest. Vertebral column forms *S*-shaped curve.

NECK. Indication of bulge of trapezium.

TORSO, FRONT. Clavicles have backward curve. Lower boundary of thorax obliterated. No divisions of rectus abdominis above navel discernible, but its lower boundary is marked by groove. External oblique swells over iliac crest, but flanks not much developed. Left flank partly missing, but enough preserved to show that it dipped slightly. Lower boundary of abdomen approaches form of semicircular arch.

TORSO, BACK. Well developed. Spinal furrow, shoulder-blades, and erector spinae modelled.

ARM. No trace of supports on thighs; arms were therefore held away from body.

LEG. Buttocks about level. Depression over great trochanter modelled.

168 : Figs. 494-496

CHALKIS, MUSEUM, no. 3. From Eretria.

Torso, from bottom of neck to middle of thighs. Back finished; therefore not from pediment group.

Island marble.
Height 77 cm.
Found at Eretria, on site of temple of Apollo Daphnephoros.
Buschor and Hamann, *Olympia*, p. 37, figs. 2, 3.

GENERAL STRUCTURE. Advanced modelling. Greatest protrusion of back, seen in profile, level with that of chest. Vertebral column forms *S*-shaped curve.

NECK. Bulge of trapezium indicated.
TORSO, FRONT. Clavicles form backward curve. Median line marked by groove from lower end of sternum to a little below navel. Lower boundary of thorax forms semicircular arch. Five digitations of serratus magnus indicated. Rectus abdominis has two transverse divisions above navel. Navel modelled. Lower boundary of abdomen forms semicircular arch. Pubes indicated by raised stylized plane, with upper edge in the form of two shallow, concave curves rising to a central point. Bulge of external oblique over iliac crest well developed. Left flank dips slightly and is a little further advanced than right.
TORSO, BACK. Powerful back. Spinal furrow, shoulder-blades, and erector spinae modelled, latter with considerable depth.
LEG. Enough preserved to show that left buttock was lower than right. Depression over great trochanter modelled.

169 : Figs. 497-499

FLORENCE, MUSEO ARCHEOLOGICO. From Greece (?).

Torso, from neck to knees.

Marble.
Height 66.5 cm.
Acquired by Professore Milani from a private collector at Osimo (Ancona), cf. no. 70.
Minto, *Critica d'Arte*, VIII, 1943, pp. 12 ff.

GENERAL STRUCTURE. Greatest protrusion of back, seen in profile, level with that of chest. Vertebral column forms *S*-shaped curve.
HAIR. Fell down back in beaded tresses, each ending in a pointed member.
NECK. Swelling of trapezium indicated.
TORSO, FRONT. Attempt made to indicate backward curve of clavicles, which protrude all the way to deltoid. Lower boundary of thorax forms semicircular arch. Median line marked from lower end of sternum to a little below navel. No transverse divisions of rectus abdominis indicated above navel, but its lower boundary marked by two curving grooves, one on each side of the abdomen. Navel marked by knob with fold above. Protrusion at flanks indicates swelling of external oblique above iliac crest. Lower boundary of abdomen descends towards genitals, forming semicircle. Penis was carved separately and is missing.
TORSO, BACK. Spinal furrow, shoulder-blades, and erector spinae modelled.
ARM. Hand was attached to thigh by support, of which traces remain.
LEG. Depression over great trochanter indicated by modelled shape. Inner vastus descends markedly below outer, and is strongly developed.

170 : Figs. 507-508

BERLIN, STAATLICHE MUSEEN, no. 536.

Head and part of neck. Nose, mouth, and chin damaged.

Parian marble.
Height 22 cm.
Purchased at Trieste, in 1877.
Brunn, *Ath. Mitt.* VIII, 1883, p. 91 f., pl. VI, 1, 2.
Blümel, *Kat.*, A15.
Deonna, no. 159.

HEAD. *Skull.* Spherical.
Ear. In correct position. Tragus and antitragus indicated.
Eye. Upper eyelid arches round eyeball; eyeball protrudes slightly; inner recess indicated.
Mouth. Lips prominent but undeveloped.
Hair. Hair radiates in wavy strands from crown and is rolled over fillet behind. Over forehead and temples it is arranged in three rows of spiral curls, symmetrically to right and left of centre.

171 : Figs. 509-510

COPENHAGEN, NY CARLSBERG GLYPTOTHEK, no. 12.

Head and neck. Nose, lips, chin, and part of left ear are missing (formerly restored in plaster).

Island marble.
Height 18.5 cm.
Acquired in Rome in 1899. Provenance not known.
F. Poulsen, *Einzelaufnahmen*, nos. 3763, 3764 (figured with restorations).
F. Poulsen, *Catalogue*, no. 12. *Billedtavler*, pl. II.

HEAD. *Skull.* Spherical. Hole for meniskos.
Ear. Slants towards line of jaw. Modelled in different planes. Tragus and antitragus both indicated.
Eye. Elongated and placed more or less horizontally. Prominent lids.
Hair. Mass is differentiated on skull into shallow circular waves, then brought down at back, looped up, and tied in the so-called *krobylos* fashion. In front, above forehead and temples, are two rows of holes in which metal curls must once have been inserted.
NECK. Sterno-mastoids and throat modelled. Cut off smooth at bottom in modern times.

172 : Figs. 505-506

NEW YORK, METROPOLITAN MUSEUM OF ART, no. 19.192.11.

Head and neck. Surface encrusted. Most of nose, parts of lips and of both ears missing.

Marble.
Height 24.8 cm.
Said to be from mainland Greece or the Islands.
Richter, *Cat. of Gk. Sc.*, no. 3 (where previous publications are listed).

HEAD. *Skull.* Spherical.
Ear. Slants towards jaw. Well formed, with indication of tragus and antitragus.
Eye. Placed horizontally. Heavy-lidded. Recess at inner corner marked.
Mouth. Lips curve slightly upward.
Hair. Short. Carved in smooth, cap-like mass (individual locks were perhaps indicated in colour); in front of each ear a single curl projects from mass.
NECK. Sterno-mastoids and throat lightly modelled.

173 : Figs. 511-514

NEW YORK, METROPOLITAN MUSEUM, no. 07.286.92.

Statuette, from head to foot-plinth.

Bronze.
Height 10.4 cm.
Provenance not known.
Richter, *Greek, Etruscan and Roman Bronzes in the Metropolitan Museum*, no. 17.

GENERAL STRUCTURE. Viewed in profile, greatest protrusion of back level with that of chest. Vertebral column curved.
HEAD. *Skull.* Domed.
Ear. Vertical; structure generalized.
Eye. Horizontal. Recess at inner corner indicated.
Mouth. Lips curve up slightly.
Hair. Short; mass divided into notched tresses radiating from crown. In front, flat roll with vertical incisions. No fillet.
NECK. Sterno-mastoids not indicated. Slight indication of swelling of trapezium.
TORSO, FRONT. Clavicles have backward curve. Median line descends to genitals. Lower boundary of thorax approaches shape of semicircle. Nipples marked by circular grooves. Two transverse divisions lightly indicated above navel in rectus abdominis. External oblique bulges over iliac crest at flanks. Left flank dips slightly. Lower boundary of abdomen approaches form of semicircular arch.
TORSO, BACK. Shallow, broad groove marks spinal furrow. Shoulder-blades generalized. Erector spinae not indicated.
ARM. Held away from body; right bent and extended with hand clenched; left bent and holds rounded object (fruit?) in front of body.
LEG. Buttocks level. Depression over great trochanter indicated. Inner vastus marked by protrusion. Anterior border of shin forms inward curve. Inner malleolus higher than outer.
Foot. Protrusion of big toe and second toe about the same.
FOOT-PLINTH. Rectangular; has two holes for attachment, one behind left foot near corner, the other in front of right foot.

174 : Fig. 521, 524

DELOS, MUSEUM, A 4084. From Delos.

Torso, from neck to above waist.

Island marble.
Height 50 cm.
Found in Delos 1885-6.
Deonna, no. 92.

GENERAL STRUCTURE. Forms rounded. Viewed in profile, greatest protrusion of back level with that of chest.
HAIR. Falls down behind in mass reaching to shoulders.
NECK. Attachment of sterno-mastoids above clavicles. Slight indication of swelling of trapezium.
TORSO, FRONT. Clavicles *S*-shaped. Median line marked by depression. Thorax well constructed, with semicircular arch at lower boundary. Two transverse divisions in rectus abdominis above navel.
TORSO, BACK. Broad groove for spinal furrow. Shoulder-blades modelled.
ARM. Separated from body from below armpit. The piece of the right arm reaching to below elbow has recently been added by Mr. Marcadé.

175 : Figs. 515-517

BERLIN, STAATLICHE MUSEEN, no. 7383. From Naxos.

Statuette, from head to plinth. Surface was covered with an encrustation, which was removed in part shortly before 1889, the rest in 1929.

Bronze.
Height 18.5 cm.
From Naxos. Acquired by Berlin in 1878.
Neugebauer, *Katalog der statuarischen Bronzen im Antiquarium*, I, no. 192, fig. 30, pl. 31.
Buschor, *Fr. J.* pp. 118 ff., figs. 136-138.
Deonna, p. 270 f., no. 86.

I.G. XII.5.42.
S.G.D.I. 5420.

Along edge of upper side of plinth incised inscription: *Δειναγο | ρ̣ης μ' ἀνεθεκεν ἑ | κηβολοι | 'Απολλονι δ̣ε̣κατ | ην* [*η* and *ν* boustrophedon], 'Deinagores dedicated me to far-darting Apollo as a tithe'.

GENERAL STRUCTURE. Torso well developed. Viewed in profile, greatest protrusion of back level with that of chest. Vertebral column forms *S*-shaped curve.
HEAD. *Skull.* Spherical.
Ear. Summarily modelled in different planes, and placed high.
Eye. Horizontal. Recess at inner corner indicated.
Mouth. Horizontal.
Hair. Falls down back in mass ending in horizontal line; mass divided into notched tresses which radiate from horizontal, median line across vertex; on each side of front fall three tresses; over forehead and temples, thick roll with vertical incisions. Simple fillet encircles head.
NECK. Sterno-mastoids modelled. Swelling of trapezium on line of shoulder hidden by hair.
TORSO, FRONT. Course of clavicles hidden by hair. Median line descends to a little below navel. Lower boundary of thorax forms semicircular arch. Two transverse divisions of rectus abdominis above navel. Navel marked as knob with fold of flesh over it. At flanks external oblique bulges over iliac crest. Lower boundary of abdomen descends with slightly curving sides towards genitals. Pubes indicated as raised plane with outwardly convex upper edge.
TORSO, BACK. Spinal furrow, shoulder-blades, and erector spinae modelled.
ARM. Separated from body; bent at elbow; one hand holds a pomegranate or aryballos;[62] attribute of other missing.
LEG. Depression over great trochanter modelled. Inner vastus descends lower and is much more developed than outer. Shin curves inward. Inner malleolus higher than outer.
Foot. Protrusion of second toe and big toe about equal, and little toe curves inward. Joints of toes articulated.
FOOT-PLINTH. Rectangular, hollow, with thick walls. Tangs on soles of statuette pass into plinth and are fastened with iron bolts.

176 : Figs. 518-520

VATHY, MUSEUM. From Samos.

Torso, from below neck to knees.

Coarse-grained bluish marble.
Height 1.05 m.
Found in the Heraion, Samos.
Buschor, *Alt. St.* I, p. 54, figs. 204-6.
Wiegand, *Ath. Mitt.* XXV, 1900, p. 153 f., no. 6 (ill.).

GENERAL STRUCTURE. Fleshy forms. Viewed in profile, greatest protrusion of back level with that of chest. Vertebral column forms *S*-shaped curve. Right instead of left leg advanced.
TORSO, FRONT. Lower boundary of thorax lightly modelled as semicircular arch. Median line marked by depression from lower end of sternum to a little below navel. Two transverse divisions of rectus abdominis above navel. Navel indicated by knob with fold of flesh over it. Protrusion at flanks indicates swelling of external oblique over iliac crest. Left hip higher than right. Lower boundary of abdomen forms semicircular arch. Pubes indicated by stylized plane, with upper edge in the form of two concave curves rising to a central point. Penis was made as separate piece and is missing.
TORSO, BACK. Much injured; details obliterated.
ARM. Left hung down close to side, right separated and joined to body by support. Perhaps represented as pouring a libation (Buschor).
LEG. Buttocks about level. Depression over great trochanter indicated. Inner vastus well developed.

177 : Figs. 525-526

HERAKLION, MUSEUM, no. 37.

Fragment of torso, from below waist to thighs.

Parian marble.
Height 24 cm. (a little less than life size).
Found at Gortyna, Crete, in pronaos of temple of Apollo.
Savignoni, *Mon. Linc.* XVIII, 1907, cols. 248 ff., fig. 30.

On right thigh remains of attachment for right hand. Pubes indicated by raised, stylized plane, with upper edge in the form of two concave curves rising to a central point. Slight depression to indicate great trochanter.

178 : Figs. 522-523

OLBIA, NIKOLAEV HISTORICAL-ARCHAEOLOGICAL MUSEUM. From Olbia.

Torso, from below neck to above waist.

Marble, probably Island.
Height 17.1 cm., approximately $\frac{1}{3}$ life size.
Found near the village Parutino (the ancient Olbia) 'in an ancient grave'.

[62] Cf. discussion on attributes by Neugebauer, loc. cit.

Pharmakovsky, *Leningrad State Academy for the History of Material Culture, Communications*, 1, pp. 165 ff., fig. 23-6 (in Russian).

GENERAL STRUCTURE. Viewed in profile, greatest protrusion of back level with that of chest.
NECK. Swelling of trapezium indicated.
TORSO, FRONT. Fleshy. Clavicles not clear. Well-developed thorax; its lower boundary forms semicircle below pectorals.
TORSO, BACK. Deep depression marks vertebral column. Shoulder-blades modelled.
ARM. Left arm brought back and was evidently bent at elbow.

179 : Figs. 527-529

LONDON, BRITISH MUSEUM, B 325. From Cyprus.

Torso, from neck to knees.

Marble, perhaps Parian.
Height 72 cm.
From Marion, Cyprus. Found in the dromos of a tomb (see p. 131). Must have been a tomb statue. Acquired by London in 1887.
Pryce, *Catalogue*, B 325, p. 155 f., pl. XXXIV.
Hermann, 'Gräberfeld von Marion,' 48. *Winckelmannsprogramm*, p. 22.
Deonna, no. 141.

GENERAL STRUCTURE. Poor anatomical construction, but softness of flesh successfully suggested. Seen in profile, greatest protrusion of back level with that of chest. Vertebral column makes *S*-shaped curve. Left leg placed only slightly forward of right.
HAIR. Was short. No trace of it visible behind.
NECK. Slight indication of swelling of trapezium.
TORSO, FRONT. Clavicles curve upward and backward and are covered on shoulders; continuous groove above them. Median line not marked. Nipples placed correctly. Flat chest. Lower boundary of thorax formed by small arch placed below pectorals. Two transverse divisions of rectus abdominis faintly indicated above navel. Navel marked by elongated knob with fold of flesh above it. Protrusion indicates external oblique swelling over iliac crest. Lower boundary of abdomen descends with straight, modelled sides towards genitals.
TORSO, BACK. Spinal furrow modelled. Shoulders rounded; lower boundary of shoulder-blades indicated by shallow, curving grooves. Slight indication of erector spinae. Protrusion at back perhaps to indicate posterior part of iliac crest; construction misunderstood.
ARM. Traces of support for hand placed very high; arm must have been considerably bent.
LEG. Buttocks undeveloped and at same height. Slight indication of depression over great trochanter. Thigh muscles on sides slightly modelled. Inner vastus descends much lower and is more developed than outer.

180 : Figs. 530-532

NICOSIA, CYPRUS MUSEUM, no. 1939, vii-14/1.

Statue, from head to knees.

Limestone.
Height 53 cm.
Found in Cyprus.
Dikaios, *Guide to the Cyprus Museum*, 2nd. ed., 1953, p. 85, pl. XX, 1.

GENERAL STRUCTURE. Well developed.
HEAD. *Skull*. Spherical. Face rounded. Surface disintegrated. Wears fillet.
Ear. Small and set sloping. Tragus and antitragus indicated.
Mouth. Lips thin and straight.
Chin. Prominent.
Hair. Short. Arranged above fillet in ridges right and left of central parting, and below fillet, both front and back, in corkscrew curls.
NECK. Broad. Little detail; throat and sterno-mastoid muscles hardly marked.
TORSO, FRONT. Clavicles only slightly modelled. Lower boundary of thorax arched. Two transverse divisions indicated above navel in rectus abdominis. Flanks undeveloped. Lower boundary of abdomen descends with fairly straight sides towards genitals.
TORSO, BACK. Flat, and summarily worked, with indication only of vertebral column by groove. Buttocks about level.
ARMS. Lowered and attached to body at armpit and at hand to above wrist. Forearm turned inward in semi-pronated position.
HAND. Clenched. Each held something. Object in left hand carved in stone and partly preserved (thong of an aryballos?).

Here also belongs the little head, 14 cm. high, from Cyrene, no. 14,007, carved with great precision in Parian marble (E. Paribeni, *Catalogo delle sculture di Cirene*, no. 13, pls. 18, 19).

181 : Figs. 533-540

PARIS, LOUVRE. From off Piombino.

Statue, from head to feet. Eyeballs were inlaid separately and are missing. Eyebrows, lips, and nipples inlaid in copper.

Bronze.
Height 1.15 m.
Said to have been found in the sea near Piombino (ancient Populonia), in 1812. Purchased by the Louvre in 1835.
Raoul-Rochette, *Annali*, v, 1833, pp. 193 ff.
Mon. dell' Inst. I, 1829-33, pls. LVIII, LIX.
Longpérier, *Notice des bronzes antiques du Louvre*, 1868, no. 69.
De Ridder, *Les bronzes antiques du Louvre*, I, no. 2.
Charbonneaux, *La sculpture grecque au Musée du Louvre*, pls. V-VI.
Buschor, *Fr. J.*, pp. 155 f., figs. 179, 180.
Deonna, p. 274, no. 102.
Löwy, *Inschriften griechischer Bildhauer*, no. 515.
I.G. XIV, 2274.

Inscription:[63] On left foot, encrusted in silver, in 3 lines: [ ]ος | 'Αθαναια[ι] | δεκαταν, '. . . os dedicated it to Athena as a tithe.'

GENERAL STRUCTURE. Plastic conception of form. Head goes approximately seven times into total height. Seen in profile, greatest protrusion of back higher than that of chest. Vertebral column forms *S*-shaped curve.
HEAD. *Skull.* High and well developed.
Ear. Modelled, with tragus and antitragus indicated.
Eye. Hollow; eyelids modelled; recess at inner corner indicated.
Nose. Small. Nostrils seen from underneath *M*-shaped.
Mouth. Lips modelled and meet at corners.
Chin. Strong.
Hair. Long; tied with little bow at back, then brought up to pass over fillet with ends hanging down. On top engraved wavy lines radiate from crown over circular, horizontal waves. Double row of spiral curls round forehead and temples, arranged symmetrically to right and left of centre.
NECK. Sterno-mastoids modelled with their attachment to sternum, as well as throat between. Slight indication of swelling of trapezium.
TORSO, FRONT. Clavicles slope upwards and backwards. Nipples inlaid in copper. Median line indicated by shallow depression from bottom of sternum to navel. No indication of serratus magnus. Well-developed chest. Lower boundary of thorax approaches shape of semicircle. Rectus abdominis has two transverse divisions above navel. Navel indicated by knob, which slopes downward and backward and has thin fold of flesh above. External oblique bulges over iliac crest. Flank of advanced leg higher instead of lower than right leg. Lower boundary of abdomen descends with fairly straight sides towards genitals, forming approximately a right angle.
TORSO, BACK. Spinal furrow marked by shallow depression. Shoulder-blades and erector spinae modelled.
ARM. Detached from body; bent at elbow and brought forward; right arm more advanced than left, with palm of hand directed upward to hold something, and forearm, therefore, in supine position; left hand also held something, and is directed towards body, with forearm in correct semi-pronated position.
LEG. Depression over great trochanter indicated. Vastus internus developed and extends beneath vastus externus. Anterior border of shin rounded and curves inward. Inner malleolus higher than outer.
Foot. Joints of toes strongly articulated and metatarsal bones indicated. Ends of toes do not recede along one line, protrusion of second toe and big toe being about equal, and small toe short and turned inward; toes and nails point forward.

[63] In 1842, when the interior of the statue was cleaned out, there emerged, mixed with dried mud, four inscribed, broken pieces of lead, of which one has since been lost. The inscription, written in letters not earlier than the first century B.C., has been read '[M]enodo [tos of Tyre and] ...phon of Rhodes made it.' Recently a suggestion has been made that it might refer to a repair of the statue before the latter was shipped and the ship sank (Dow, *Hesperia*, X, 1941, pp. 357 ff.). Another possibility is that the pieces were inserted through the eye-holes at some time during the thirty years between the discovery and the cleaning of the statue.

182 : Figs. 547-549

AGRIGENTO, MUSEO CIVICO. From Agrigento.

Statue, from head to above right ankle.

Marble.
Height 1.04 m.
Found at Agrigento, near the river Akragas, beneath the church of S. Biagio. Right lower leg found later, in 1898, in same vicinity (fractures fit, cf. Herrmann loc. cit.).
Hauser in Arndt, *Einzelaufnahmen*, Serie III, p. 32, nos. 759-61.
Herrmann, ibid. Serie IV, Nachträge, p. 67, zu 759.

GENERAL STRUCTURE. Seen in profile, greatest protrusion of back level with that of chest. Vertebral column makes bold, *S*-shaped curve. Right instead of left leg advanced.
HEAD. *Skull.* Domed.
Ear. Carved in the round, with indication of tragus and antitragus.
Eye. Horizontal. Recess at inner corner marked.
Mouth. Horizontal. Full under lip.
Hair. Rolled in front and behind round fillet; on skull radiates from crown in straight ridges.
NECK. Sterno-mastoids modelled; attachment to sternum indicated. Swelling of trapezium developed.
TORSO, FRONT. Clavicles form *S*-shaped curve. Thorax well developed; its lower boundary approaches form of semicircle. Median line shown as groove from sternum to a little below navel, swerving slightly to

left. In rectus abdominis two transverse divisions modelled above navel. Navel indicated by knob with fold of flesh over it. External oblique bulges strongly over iliac crest. Left flank higher than right. Lower boundary of abdomen forms deep curve.
TORSO, BACK. Spinal furrow, shoulder-blades, and erector spinae modelled.
ARM. Held away from body. Well rounded.
LEG. Left buttock higher than right. Depression over great trochanter modelled. Lower vastus well developed.

183 : Figs. 550-552

SYRACUSE, MUSEUM. From Leontinoi.

Torso, from neck to above right knee.

Parian marble.
Height 1.03 m.
From Leontinoi; said to have been found in 1902.
Orsi, *Mon. Linc.* XVIII, 1907, cols. 169 ff., pl. VI.

GENERAL STRUCTURE. Seen in profile, greatest protrusion of back level with that of chest. Vertebral column *S*-shaped.
NECK. Swelling of trapezium indicated.
TORSO, FRONT. Clavicles have double curve and ends are covered by shoulder. Median line descends to a little below navel. Lower boundary of thorax forms semicircular arch. Rectus abdominis has two modelled transverse divisions above navel; its lower boundary marked by two curving grooves, one on each side of the abdomen. Navel indicated by knob with fold of flesh above it. Bulge of external oblique over iliac crest well developed. Left flank dips, conforming with advanced leg. Lower boundary of abdomen approaches form of semicircle. Penis was carved separately and is missing.
TORSO, BACK. Well developed. Wide, deep groove forms spinal furrow. Shoulder-blades and erector spinae modelled.
ARM. Was held away from body; no trace of attachment for hand to side.
LEG. Right buttock slightly higher than left. Depression over great trochanter indicated.

184 : Figs. 556-558

CATANIA, MUSEO COMUNALE. From Leontinoi.

Head and part of neck. Has been conjectured to belong to the kouros no. 183, since it is of the same period and marble and was also found at Leontini (see below).

Island marble.
Height 25 cm.
Found at Leontinoi. Formerly in the Biscari Collection.
Libertini, *Museo Biscari*, no. 1, p. 3 f., pls. I-II, pl. A. Plate A shows an attempted reconstruction with the Leontinoi kouros. Unfortunately the bottom fracture of the Biscari head was sawn smooth for mounting and a piece of neck has had to be restored in plaster; this restoration appears to be somewhat too long, so it is difficult to judge the effect as a whole.

HEAD. *Skull*. Spherical.
Ear. Slants towards line of jaw. Modelled in several planes. Both tragus and antitragus indicated.
Eye. Horizontal. Recess at inner corner.
Mouth. Lips well shaped and curve up slightly at corners.
Chin. Strong.
Hair. On skull, mass differentiated into shallow, circular waves over which wavy strands radiate from crown. At back strands are twisted round fillet in a series of separate rolls (cf. no. 159); over forehead and temples are three rows of spiral curls, arranged symmetrically to right and left of centre.

185 : Figs. 544-546

SYRACUSE, MUSEUM. From Grammichele.

Torso, from below neck to bottom of buttocks.

Parian marble.
Height 48.5 cm.
From Grammichele.
Orsi, *Mon. Linc.* XVIII, 1907, cols. 129 ff., pl. III.

GENERAL STRUCTURE. Greatest protrusion of back, seen in profile, level with that of chest. Vertebral column forms *S*-shaped curve.
TORSO, FRONT. Lower boundary of thorax forms flat arch under pectorals, which are placed rather high. Median line marked by depression from lower end of sternum to navel. Two transverse divisions in rectus abdominis above navel. Navel marked by knob with fold of flesh above it. External oblique bulges markedly over iliac crest. Left flank dips slightly, conforming with advancing leg. Lower boundary of abdomen approaches form of semicircle.
TORSO, BACK. Wide, deep groove forms spinal furrow. Shoulder-blades and erector spinae indicated by modelled forms.
ARM. Was held away from body; no trace of attachment to side.
LEG. Depression over great trochanter shown.

186 : Figs. 541-543

SYRACUSE, MUSEUM. From Megara Hyblaia.

Upper part of small torso, from neck to below navel.

Parian marble.
Height 25.5 cm.
Found in 1889 in the cemetery of Megara Hyblaia.
Orsi, *Mon. Linc.* I, 1890, cols. 789 ff., pl. VI, 7, 8.

GENERAL STRUCTURE. Seen in profile, greatest protrusion of back about level with that of chest.
NECK. Swelling of trapezium indicated.
TORSO, FRONT. Clavicles have double curve. Lower boundary of thorax approaches semicircular arch.
TORSO, BACK. Wide, deep groove forms spinal furrow. Shoulder-blades modelled.
ARM. Both arms were held away from body.

187 : Figs. 553-555

POTENZA, MUSEO ARCHEOLOGICO.

Torso from neck to below buttocks.

Parian marble.
Height 85 cm.
Probably from the temple of Apollo Lykeios at Metapontum.
Valente, *Not. d. Sc.*, 1941, p. 257, fig. 15 (on p. 260).
M. Sestieri Bertarelli, *Museo Archeologico di Potenza*, 1957 (*Itinerari*, no. 96), p. 9, pls. 47, 48.

GENERAL STRUCTURE. Greatest protrusion of back, seen in profile, level with that of chest. Vertebral column forms *S*-shaped curve.
TORSO, FRONT. Battered. Details not visible. Flanks developed. Lower boundary of abdomen descends to genitals in deep arch.
TORSO, BACK. Spinal furrow indicated by deep groove. Shoulder-blades modelled. Right buttock higher than left. Depression caused by great trochanter indicated.
ARM. Right arm was brought forward and joined to body at side, where trace of attachment remains.

188 : Figs. 560-563

ROME, BARRACCO MUSEUM, no. 80.

Head and part of neck. Bust and lower part of neck restored. Iris was inlaid separately and is missing. As the youth wore drapery (see below), he cannot have been a kouros in the strict sense.

Parian marble.
Height from crown to chin 25.5 cm.
Acquired in Rome.
Barracco and Helbig, *La Collection Barracco*, p. 32, pl. XXIX.
Helbig, *Führer*[3], I, p. 612, no. 1088.
Buschor, *Fr. J.*, p. 153 f., fig. 178.
Pietrangeli, *Guida, Museo Barracco*, p. 42, no. 80, pl. IX, I.

HEAD. *Skull.* Spherical.
Ear. Slants slightly towards line of jaw. Carved in several planes. Both tragus and antitragus indicated.
Eye. Narrow. Placed horizontally. Recess at inner corner and lachrymal caruncle indicated.
Mouth. Lips well shaped and curve up very slightly at corners.
Hair. On skull, mass differentiated into shallow, circular waves over which wavy strands radiate from crown; at back strands terminate in three rows of spiral curls, arranged symmetrically to right and left of centre; three similar rows, strongly protruding, are carved above forehead and temples. Behind these curls simple fillet passes from ear to ear.
NECK. At back, just above break, are two horizontal ridges; the youth, therefore, evidently wore a mantle (or a cuirass?).[64]

189 : Fig. 559

MARZABOTTO, MUSEUM.

Head.

Parian marble.
Height 16.7.
Found at Marzabotto in 1952.
Arias, *Istituto d'Archeologia e Storia d'Arte*, I, 1952, pp. 242 ff.

HEAD. *Skull.* Spherical.
Ear. Well developed. Tragus and antitragus both indicated. Slants towards line of jaw.
Eye. Upper lid arches over eyeball. Line of demarcation probably was accentuated in colour.
Mouth. Lips full and meet at corners.
Hair. Worn short, reaching at back only to neck. Rendered over whole surface by globules which terminate behind in a curved line.

Here should belong, as a late member, the torso, said to be from Southern Italy, height 66·5 cm., now in the collection of G. Ortiz, PARIS; cf. Schefold, *Meisterwerke griechischer Kunst*, no. 234b.

[64] Cf. Helbig, loc. cit.

EPILOGUE

(*c.* 485-460 B.C.)

Here our study of Greek kouroi properly ends. The sculptor had now achieved mastery of the anatomical structure—and what follows is the opening of a new era. He was in possession of a full repertory of anatomical forms. Such details as the serratus magnus, the swelling of the trapezium, the lachrymal caruncle—which in the preceding period he had only tentatively indicated—he now regularly featured. The naturalistic rendering of head and figure, attained after an intensive study of almost two centuries, now became constant (cf. nos. 190 ff.). Artists were ready for the new problem, equally important in the development of sculpture, of adapting these forms to action and movement. Though various attitudes suggesting movement had been tried before—especially in pedimental sculptures—these movements were comparatively simple in conception and did not affect the complicated distribution of weight of the standing figure. The sculptures ranging in date from just before 480 B.C. to about 460 show the artist's preoccupation with this problem of balance.

He now abandoned the strictly frontal attitude of the figure and the more or less symmetrical construction. The head is turned; the weight of the figure is boldly poised on one leg—which entails a slant of the pelvis downward and a swing backward on the side of the flexed leg. This turn of the pelvis is at first accompanied by strictly frontal shoulders (cf. e.g. the Akropolis Museum 698 (no. 190); the 'Blond Boy' (no. 191); the torso from Miletos in the Louvre (no. 192); the torso Cordier in the Louvre (no. 193); the torso in the Ashmolean Museum (no. 194); the torso from Cyrene[1]; the bronze torso in Florence (no. 195); a torso in Boston (no. 196); the so-called Amelung torso;[2] and a torso in Ancona[3]—the last three presumably Roman copies.[4] Presently the upper part of the body is also made to rotate (cf. e.g. the Omphalos statue (no. 197) of about 460 B.C., figs. 446-7), in an opposite direction from that of the pelvis. The distance between shoulder and pelvis on the side of the standing leg is now shorter than on the side of the flexed leg. The knee of the standing leg is higher than that of the flexed leg. These changes entail a sideward curve of the median line in front and of the vertebral column behind. The lines of the eyes, shoulders, hips, knees are no longer horizontal, but incline upward and downward in alternating rhythm. The various parts of the body are in proportional relation to one another, forming a balanced whole. This play of proportion in course of time led to the Canon of Polykleitos, which took the place of the interrelated patterns of the early age.[5] And this feeling for the interrelation of parts to one another and to the whole remained a characteristic of Greek art throughout its history.

[1] E. Paribeni, *Catalogo della Sculture di Cirene*, no. 16, pls. 24-26.

[2] Langlotz, *Bildhauerschulen*, p. 132, pl. 79.

[3] In the Museo Nazionale della Marche; Marconi-Serra, *Itinerari*, no. 37, p. 64, left.

[4] As heads probably of kouroi of *c.*485 to 460 B.C. may be cited among others, those from Cyrene (Chamoux, Cyrène, pp. 360 ff., pl. XXIV; E. Paribeni, op cit., no. 14, pls. 20, 21); from Cyprus (Dikaios, *Guide to the Cyprus Museum*, p. 86, pedestal 27, pl. XX, 2); from Thessaly, in the Museum of Halmyros (Brommer, *Ath. Mitt.* LXV, 1940, p. 105, pls. 63-5); in the Conservatori Museum (E. Paribeni, *Boll. d'Arte*, III, 1948, pp. 193 ff.); in the Museo Giovio of Como (Arias, *Rivista d'Archeologia e Storia d'Arte*, N.S.I., 1952, p. 247, fig. 7); and the bronze head in Athens (Papaspiridi, *Guide*, pp. 196 f., fig. 38).

[5] One may surmise that in this representation of complicated movement the sculptor often preferred to model his figure in clay and then cast it in bronze—especially as hollow casting had by now become general. He could thereby pursue his naturalistic aims with greater ease than by carving directly into stone. As a result, bronze statues came into high favour in the fifth century (cf. p. 9 and Wace, *An Approach to Greek Sculpture*, pp. 16 ff.).

Kouroi Nos. 190-197

190 : Figs. 564-569

ATHENS, AKROPOLIS MUSEUM, no. 698. 'Kritios boy.'

Statue, from head to above left ankle. Head broken from body and reattached.

Parian marble.
Height 86 cm.
Body found 1865/6 south-east of Parthenon; head in 1888 between Museum and south wall. Must belong together, for fractures fit (cf. Schuchhardt, loc. cit.).
Payne and Young, *Acropolis*, p. 44 f., pls. 109-12.
Schuchhardt, in Schrader, *Akropolis*, no. 299, pls. 120-3.

GENERAL STRUCTURE. Weight rests on left leg; right instead of left leg advanced. Seen in profile, greatest protrusion of back level with that of chest.
HEAD. *Skull.* Spherical. Well developed top and back. At apex remains of a bronze rod that served as a meniskos.
Ear. Modelled in different planes with tragus and antitragus correctly indicated.
Eye. Inner recess and caruncle both indicated. Eyeballs were inserted separately and are missing.
Mouth. Upper lip forms two flat curves. Lower lip broad and strongly curving.
Hair. Radiates from crown in wavy ridges. At forehead and temples tresses are separately looped over fillet; a few stray curls carved at neck and in front of ears.
Chin. Strong.
TORSO. Clavicles, trapezium, serratus magnus, thorax, rectus abdominis, flanks, shoulder-blades, spiral furrow, erector spinae, depression over great trochanter, all delicately modelled in naturalistic manner. Left flank higher than right, and left buttock correspondingly higher than right. Navel marked by knob, with fold of skin above it. No indication of pubes.
LEG. Inner vastus much higher than outer.
ARM. Both arms were attached to sides by supports oval in section.

191 : Figs. 570-574

ATHENS, AKROPOLIS MUSEUM, no. 689. 'Blond boy.'

Head and neck, evidently of a kouros. A fragment of a torso (figs. 572-574) probably belongs to the same statue, and perhaps also the fragment of a foot.

Head. Figs. 570, 571.

Marble, apparently Pentelic.
Height 25 cm.
Found in 1887 north-east of Museum.
Payne and Young, *Acropolis*, p. 45, pls. 113-5.
Schuchhardt, in Schrader, *Akropolis*, no. 302, pls. 125, 126.

Turned slightly to right shoulder. At apex is a hole 1.2 cm. in diam., 3.1 cm. deep, for meniskos.
Ear. Finely modelled, with tragus and antitragus correctly indicated.
Eye. Heavy-lidded. Inner recess and caruncle both indicated.
Mouth. Upper lip forms two curves. Lower lip broad and strongly curving.
Hair. Radiates from crown in wavy ridges, terminating in front in two rows of unsymmetrical curls. Behind ears start two plaits, which are wound round head, disappearing beneath hair in front. At temples, in front of each ear, hair is brushed back.

Fragment of torso, from below waist to buttocks (no inv. no.). Figs. 572-574.

Pantelic marble.
Height 34 cm.
Found in 1886 at north wall.
Wolters, *Ath. Mitt.* XII, 1887, p. 266.
Bieber, *Ath. Mitt.* XXXVII, 1912, pp. 151 ff., pls. IX, X.
Schuchhardt, op. cit., p. 198, pl. 127.
Payne, op. cit., p. 46.

Weight on left leg; right instead of left leg advanced.
TORSO, FRONT. Sensitive, soft modelling. Swelling of external oblique over iliac crest well developed. Lower boundary of abdomen forms semicircular arch. Pubes indicated as raised, stylized plane, with upper edge rising to a central point. Penis worked separately and mostly missing. Left flank higher than right. Depression of great trochanter modelled.
TORSO, BACK. Erector spinae modelled. Left buttock higher than right.
LEG. No trace of supports on hips. Arms were, therefore, held away from body, as shown also by position of right shoulder.

Fragment of right foot; inv. no. 424*a*.

Height 15.3 cm.
Schuchhardt, op. cit. p. 198, fig. 188.

192 : Figs. 579-581

PARIS, LOUVRE, no. MND 2792. From Miletos.

Torso of a colossal statue, from below neck to above left knee.

Island marble (Parian?).
Height 1.32 m.
Found in the theatre of Miletos during excavations by O. Rayet and A. Thomas and given to the Louvre in 1873 by Gustave and Edmond de Rothschild. Perhaps came from the sanctuary of Apollo that was destroyed by the Persians in 494 B.C.
Rayet and Thomas, *Milet et le golf lamique*, pl. 20, r.
L. Curtius, Brunn-Bruckmann, *Denkmäler*, text to pls. 601-4, pp. 12 ff.
Charbonneaux, *Mon. Piot*, XLV, 1951, pp. 47 ff., pl. VI.
Catalogue des marbres antiques, Musée du Louvre, p. 151, no. 2792.
Kunze and Schleif, III. *Olympia Bericht*, 1938/39, p. 130.

GENERAL STRUCTURE. Seen in profile, greatest protrusion of back level with that of chest. Vertebral column forms *S*-shaped curve.
Powerfully modelled. Clavicles, trapezium, serratus magnus, thorax, rectus abdominis, flanks, lower boundary of abdomen, shoulder-blades, spinal furrow, erector spinae, depression over great trochanter all modelled in naturalistic manner. Right flank and buttock higher than left. Navel represented as a knob inside a depression, with a fold of skin above it. Pubes rendered as a raised, stylized plane, with upper edge rising to a central point.

193 : Figs. 575-576

PARIS, LOUVRE, no. MND 862. From Paros.

Torso, from bottom of neck to top of thighs. Much battered, especially in front.

Parian marble.
Height 73.5 cm.
From Paros. Gift of Ch. Cordier.
Charbonneaux, *Mon. Piot*, XLV, 1951, p. 50, figs. 8, 9.

GENERAL STRUCTURE. Seen in profile, greatest protrusion of back level with that of chest. Weight of figure on right leg, with left leg advanced.
Modelled throughout in naturalistic manner. Vertebral column forms *S*-shaped curve. Right flank somewhat higher than left, and right buttock correspondingly higher than left. Navel represented as a knob with a fold of skin above it.

194 : Figs. 577-578

OXFORD, ASHMOLEAN MUSEUM.

Torso, from bottom of neck to below buttocks. Front battered.

Island marble.
Height 82 cm.
From the Arundel Collection. Presented by the Dowager Countess of Pomfret, 1755. Perhaps from Paros.
Michaelis, *Ancient Marbles in Great Britain*, p. 554, no. 52.
Charbonneaux, *Mon Piot*, XLV, 1951, p. 49, figs. 10, 11.

GENERAL STRUCTURE. Greatest protrusion of back, seen in profile, level with that of chest. Vertebral column forms strong curve. Weight of figure on the right leg, with left leg a little advanced.
Torso modelled throughout in naturalistic manner. Right flank somewhat higher than left, and right buttock correspondingly higher than left.
No marks of attachments on sides of body.

195 : Figs. 585-588

FLORENCE, MUSEO ARCHEOLOGICO.

Torso, from neck to middle of thighs.

Bronze.
Height 94 cm.
Found in Livorno.
Furtwängler, *Meisterwerke*, p. 676.
Amelung, *Führer durch die Antiken in Florenz*, no. 269.
Langlotz, *Bildhauerschulen*, p. 53.

GENERAL STRUCTURE. Viewed in profile, greatest protrusion of back level with that of chest. Weight on right leg, and left leg slightly advanced; nevertheless left hip is placed higher than right.
NECK. Sterno-mastoids and throat indicated.
TORSO. Clavicles, trapezium, serratus magnus, thorax, rectus abdominis, flanks, and back modelled in naturalistic manner. Navel indicated as a knob inside a depression. Hair of pubes rendered as a stylized, raised plane, with rows of spiral curls; upper edge forms two shallow curves rising to a central point. Nipples and penis were inlaid separately and are missing.

196 : Figs. 582-584

BOSTON, MUSEUM OF FINE ARTS, no. 22.593.

Torso, from neck to below knees.

Marble (Pentelic?)
Height 58 cm.
Bought in Rome.
L. D. Caskey, *Catalogue of Greek and Roman Sculptures*, no. 14.

GENERAL STRUCTURE. Highest protrusion of back, seen in profile, level with that of chest. Weight on right leg, with left leg advanced and placed slightly sidewise; that is, the stance of the 'Kritios boy', no. 190, is reversed.
TORSO. Modelled throughout in naturalistic manner. Both arms were lowered, for on the left thigh is part of a support that connected with the arm, and on the right thigh is a fracture where there evidently was another support; it is somewhat lower than the support

on the left side, so the left arm must have been bent more sharply at the elbow than the right. There is also a fracture of a large support on the lower right leg, such as occurs on Roman copies rather than Greek originals. The shape of the support on the left hip (directed upward) is also not like those that regularly appear on Greek originals of this period (cf. e.g. nos. 155, 190), and resembles rather those current on Roman copies. Noteworthy also is the rendering of the navel as a simple, somewhat mechanical depression, instead of, as is usual in this period, as a modelled knob inside a depression (cf. e.g. nos. 190, 192). It would seem, therefore, that the torso is a Roman copy of excellent workmanship rather than a Greek original.

197 : Figs. 589-591

ATHENS, NATIONAL MUSEUM, no. 45. The 'Omphalos Apollo'.

The name is derived from the fact that the statue was once thought to belong to a plinth, found at the same time, on which there is an omphalos; but the traces of feet on this plinth do not correspond to the legs of the statue.

Statue, from head to ankles.

Marble.

Height 1.75 m.

Found in the theatre of Dionysos, Athens, in 1862.

Staïs, *Marbres et bronzes*, p. 23.

Kastriotes, *Glypta*, no. 45.

Papaspiridi, *Guide*, p. 34, no. 45.

The statue is an excellent Roman copy, of which a number of replicas exist (cf. A. H. Smith, *Catalogue of Scupture, British Museum*, no. 209).

GENERAL STRUCTURE. Frontal position has been abandoned. Head, shoulders, and hips turn sidewise to right or left. Weight rests on right leg, with left leg advanced and placed sidewise. Right hip higher than left and right buttock correspondingly higher than left. Vertebral column forms *S*-shaped curve.

HEAD. *Skull.* Spherical.

Hair. Long; radiates from vertex of skull, and is then dressed in two braids, starting on sides, brought round head, and knotted in front; variegated locks hang over forehead and temples.

Head and body modelled throughout in naturalistic manner.

Left arm bent and brought sidewise; probably held something that connected with the small support on the left hip.

ILLUSTRATIONS

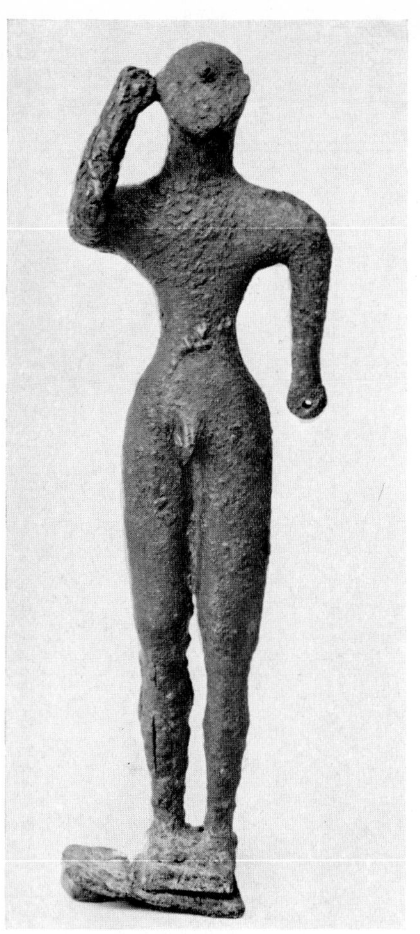

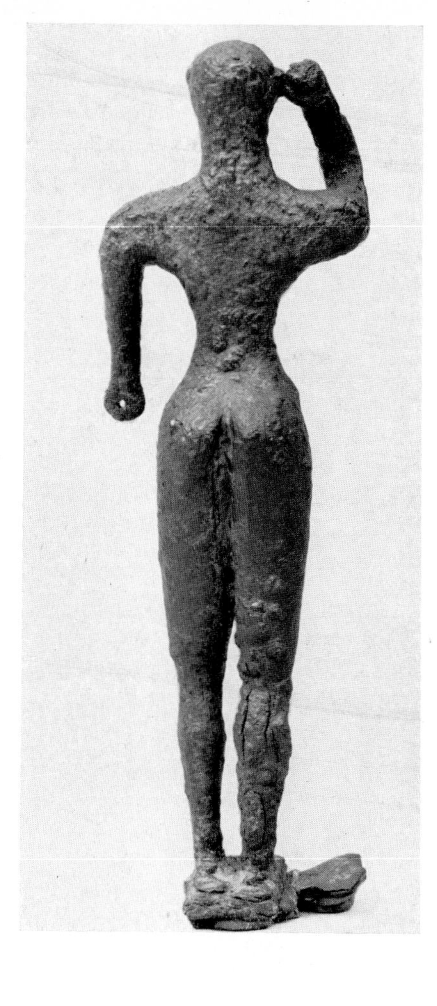

Figs. 3-5 (New York)

Figs. 6-8 (Olympia)

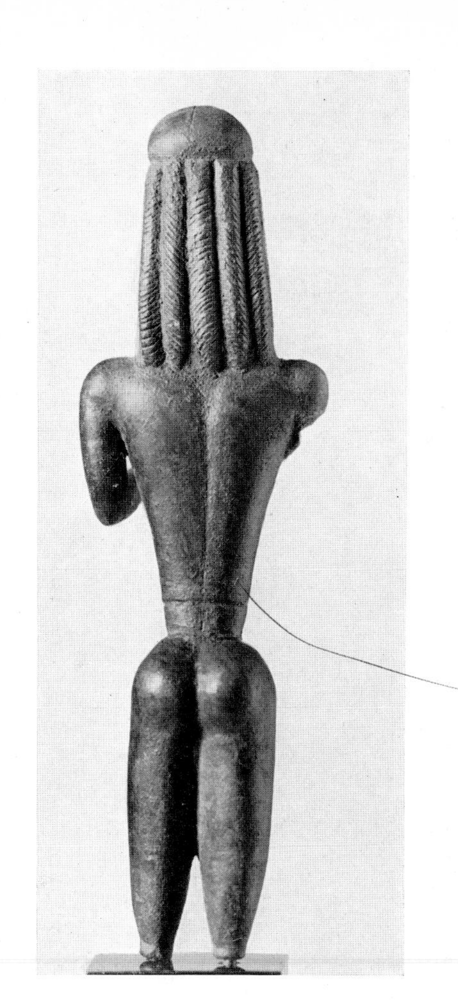

Figs. 9-11 (Boston)

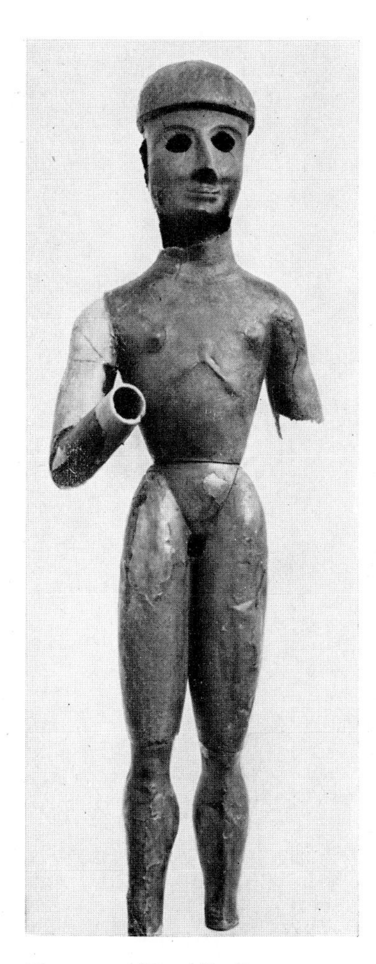

Figs. 12-13 (Heraklion)

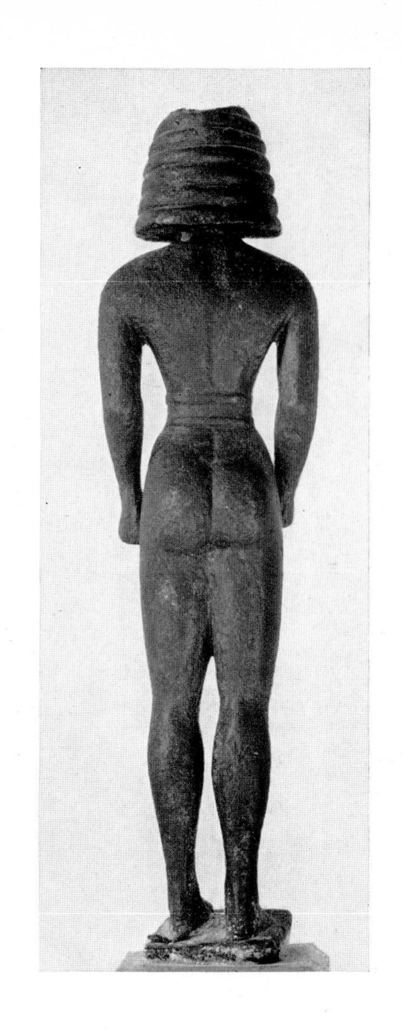

Figs. 14-16 (Delphi)

Figs. 17-19 (from Samos)

Figs. 20–21 (Delos)

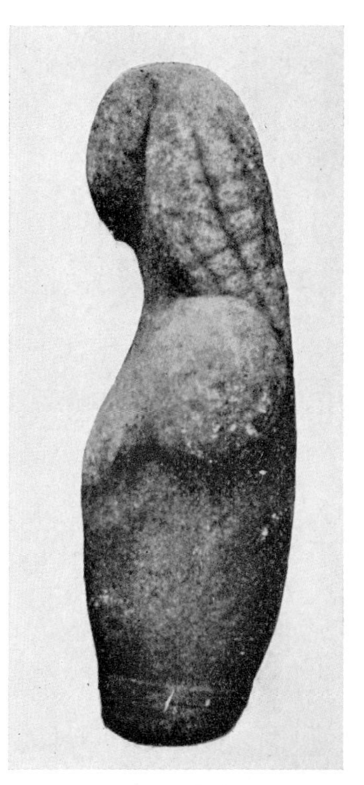

Figs. 22–24 (Delos)

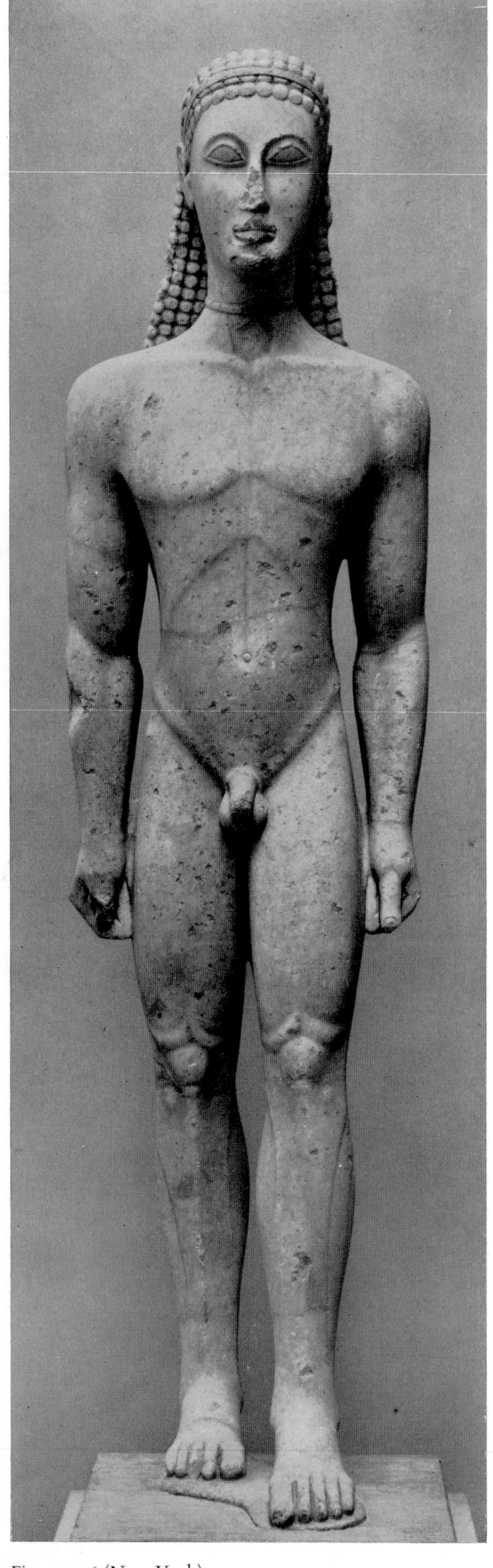

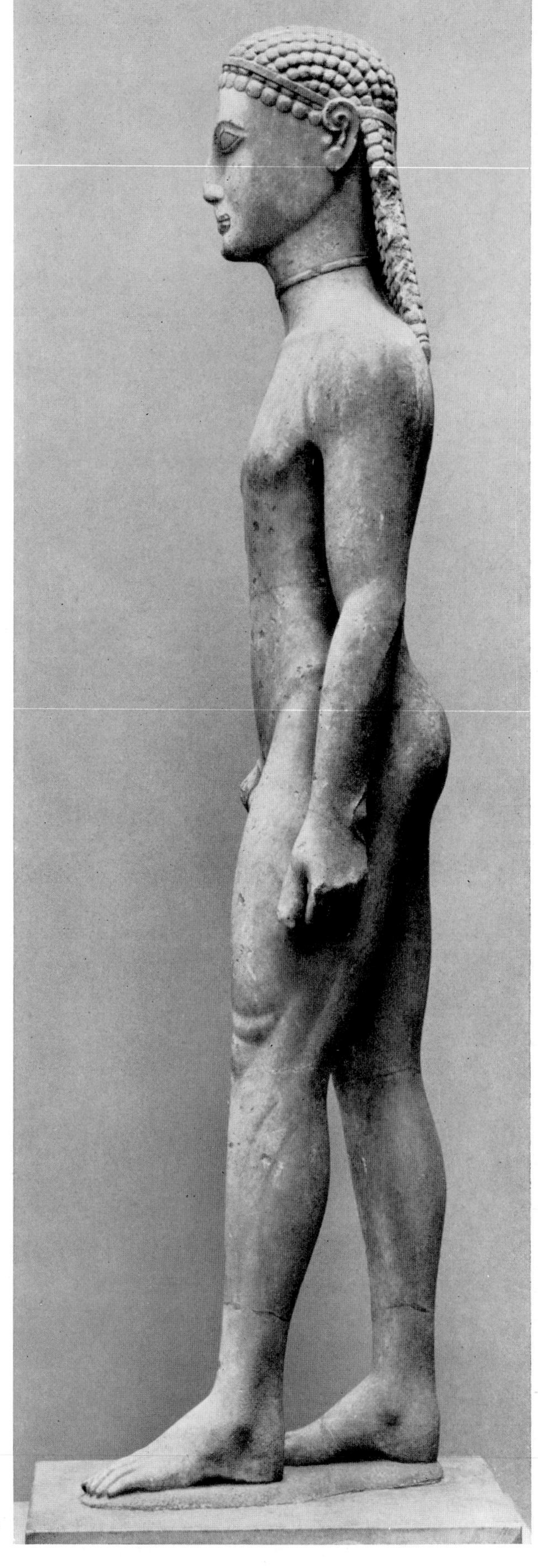

Figs. 25-26 (New York)

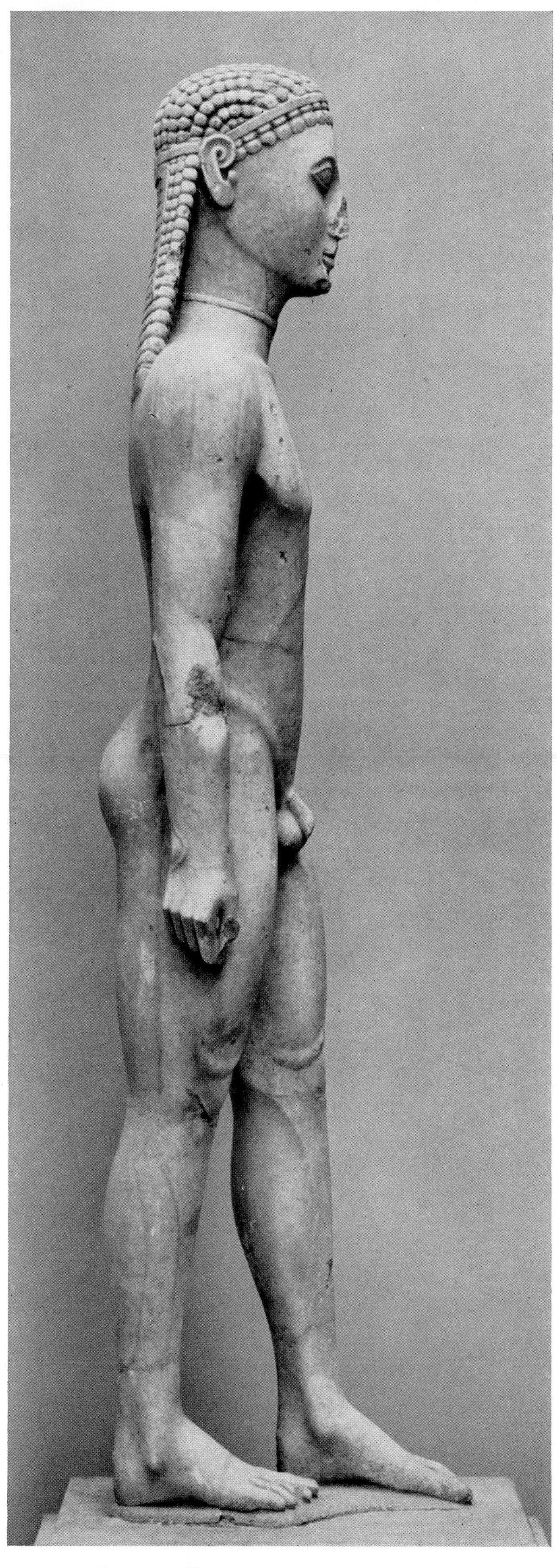

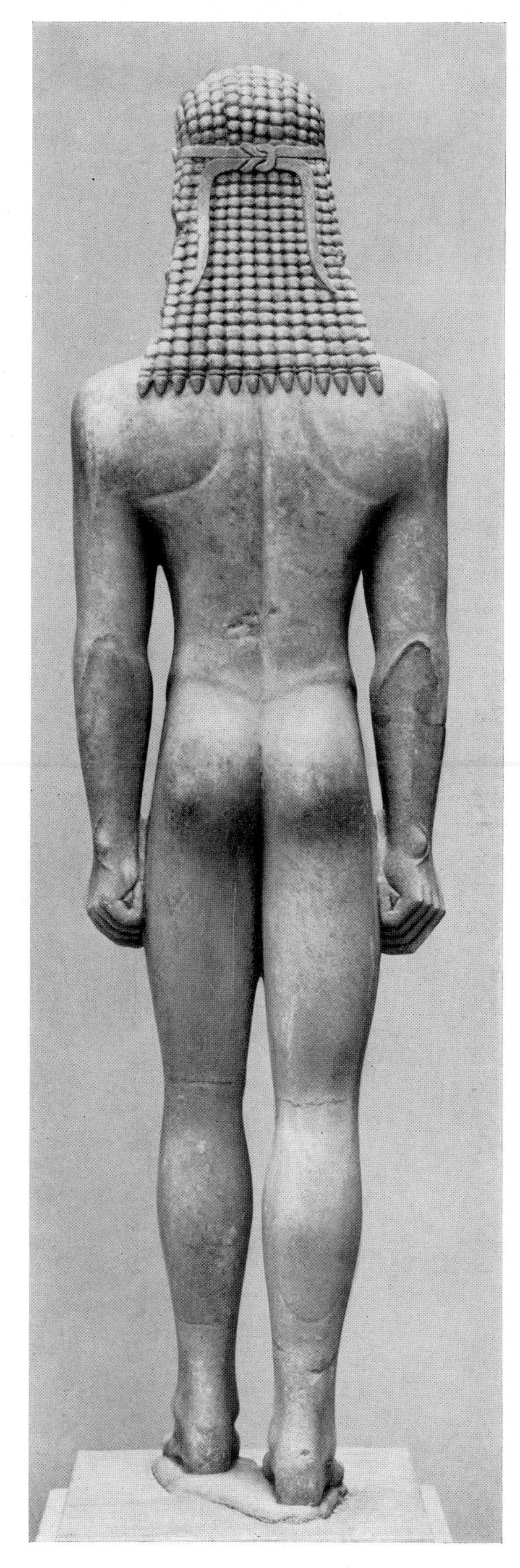

Figs. 27-28 (New York)

Figs. 29-30 (New York)

Figs. 31-32 (New York)

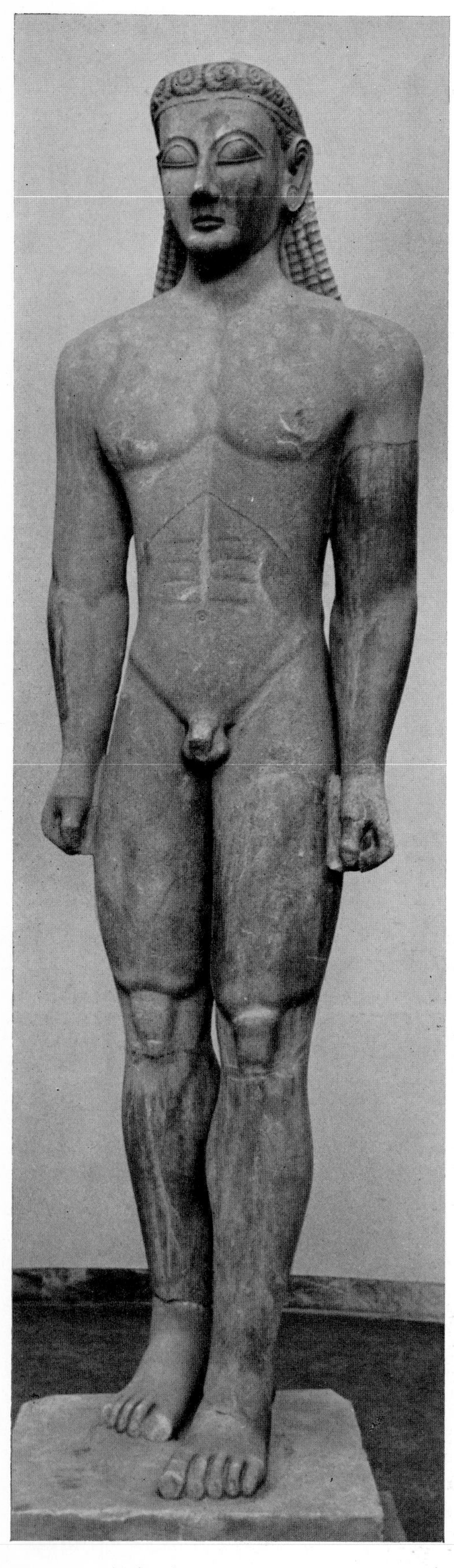

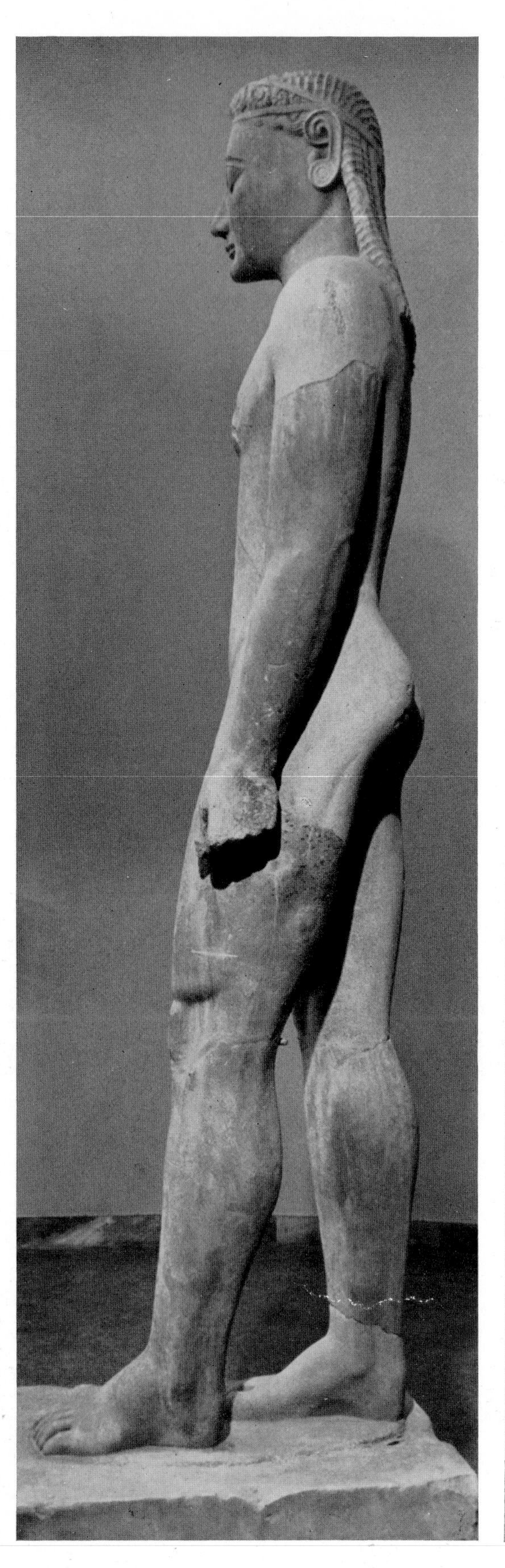

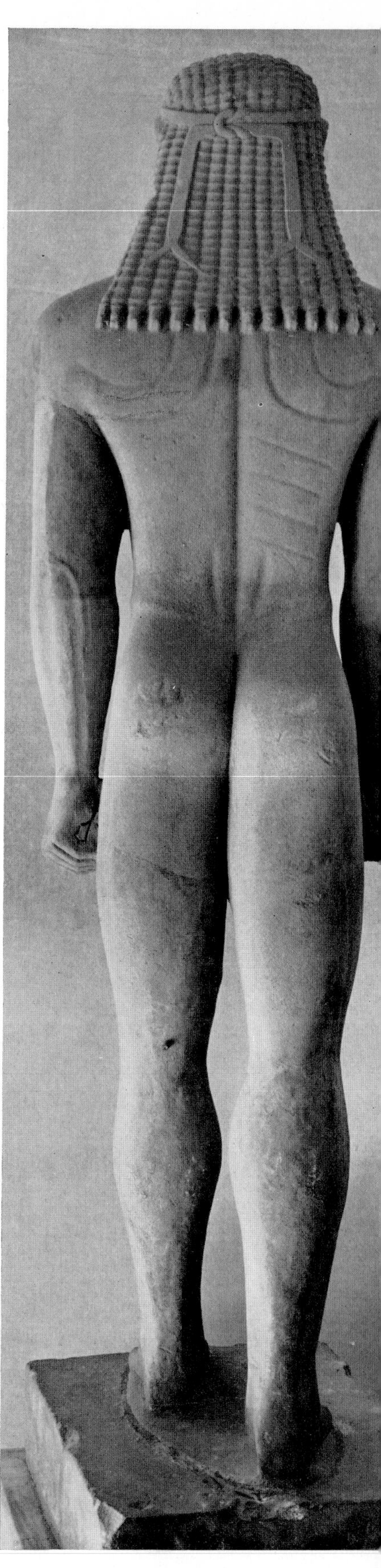

Figs. 33-35 (Athens)

Figs. 36-37 (Athens)

Figs. 38-39 (Athens)

Figs. 40-41 (Athens)

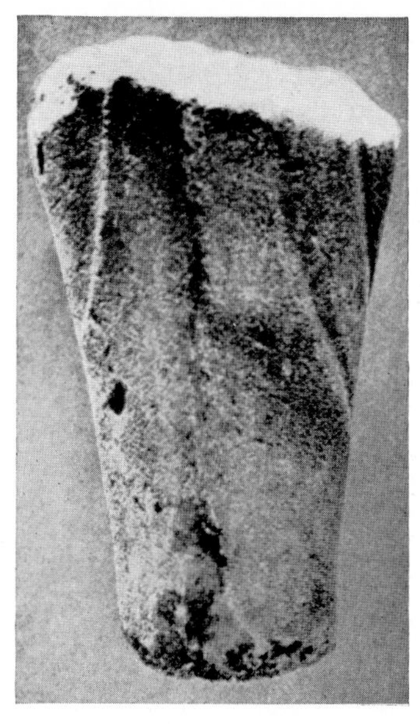
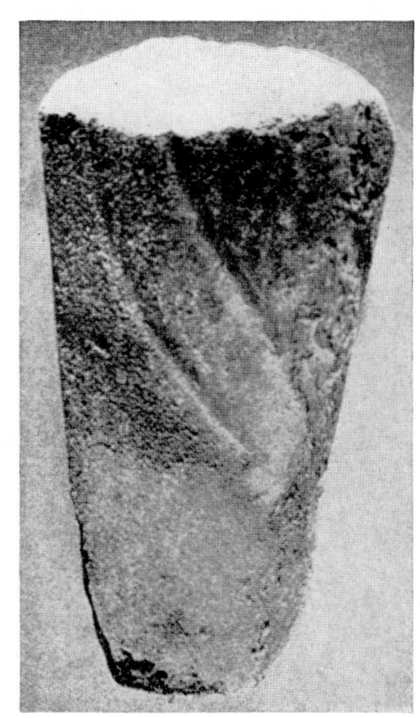
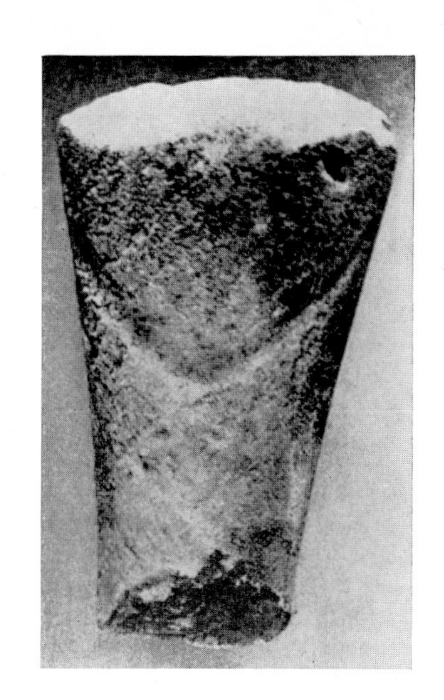

Figs. 42-44 (Athens) 4

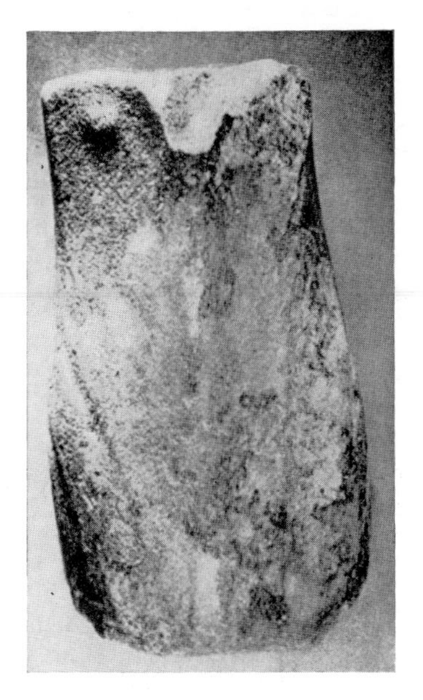
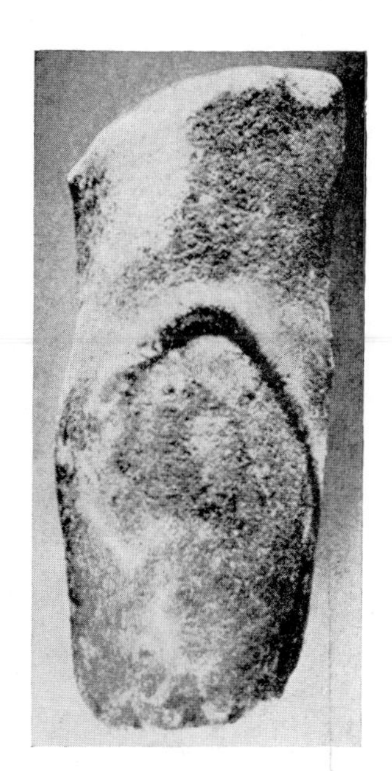

Figs. 45-47 (Athens) 4

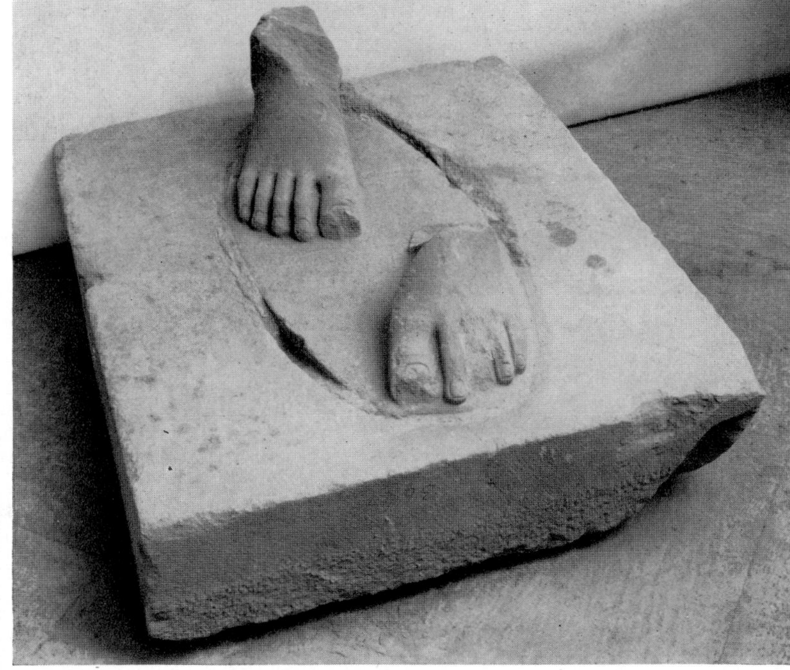
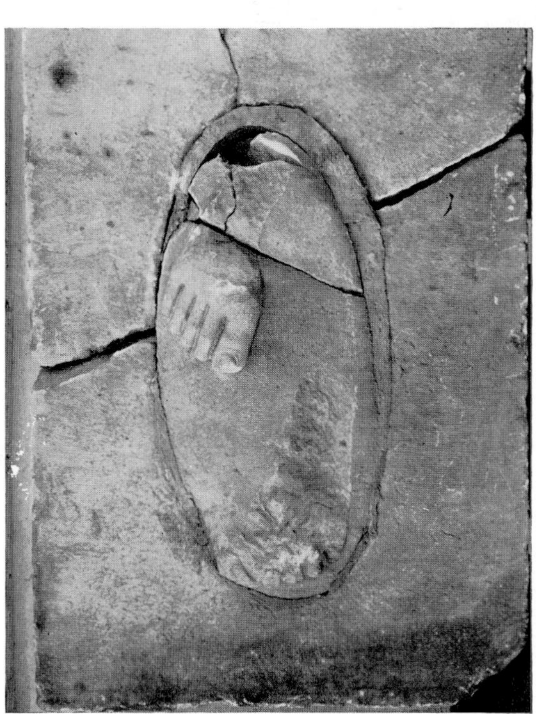

Figs. 48-49 (Athens) 5

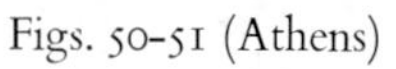

Figs. 50–51 (Athens)

6

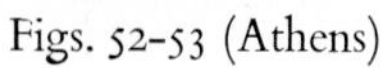

Figs. 52–53 (Athens)

6

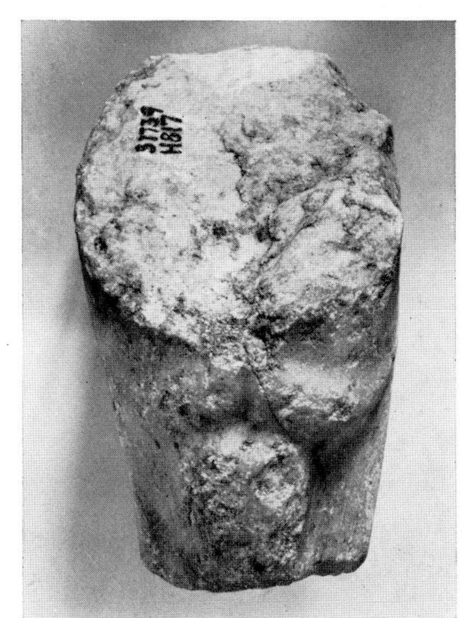

54–56 (Athens)

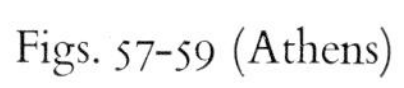

Figs. 57–59 (Athens)

7

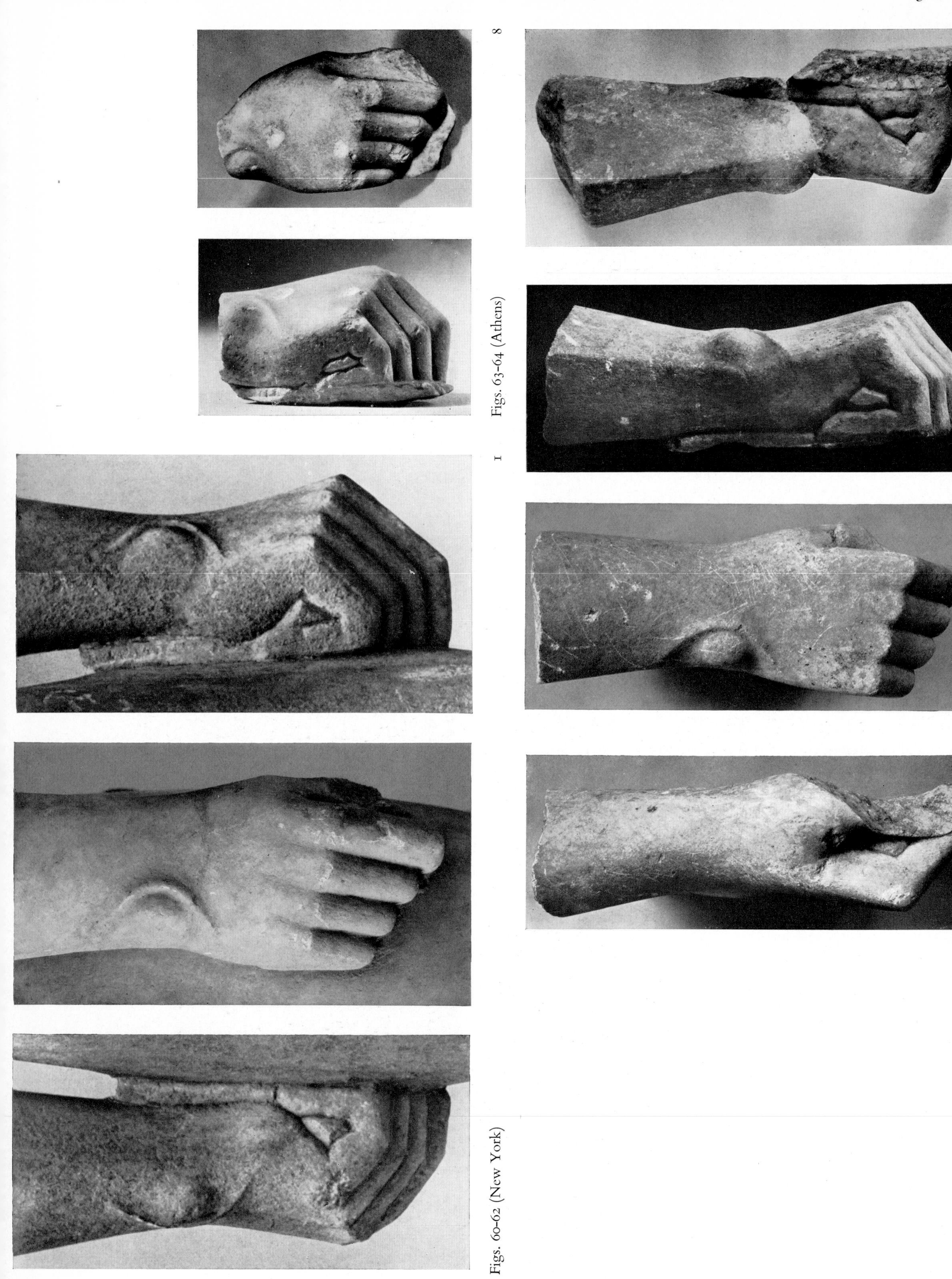

Figs. 63–64 (Athens)

8

1

Figs. 60–62 (New York)

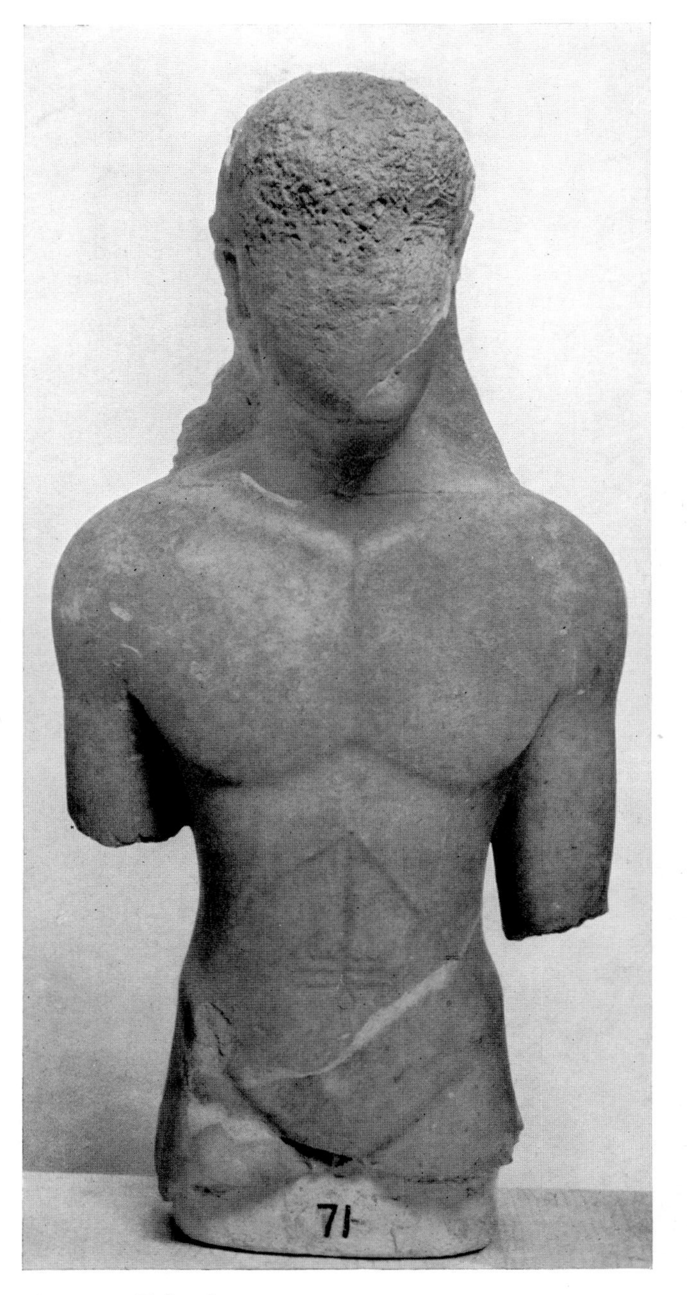

Figs. 69-71 (Athens)

Figs. 72-73 (Athens)

10

Figs. 74-75 (Athens)

10

Figs. 76-77 (Athens)

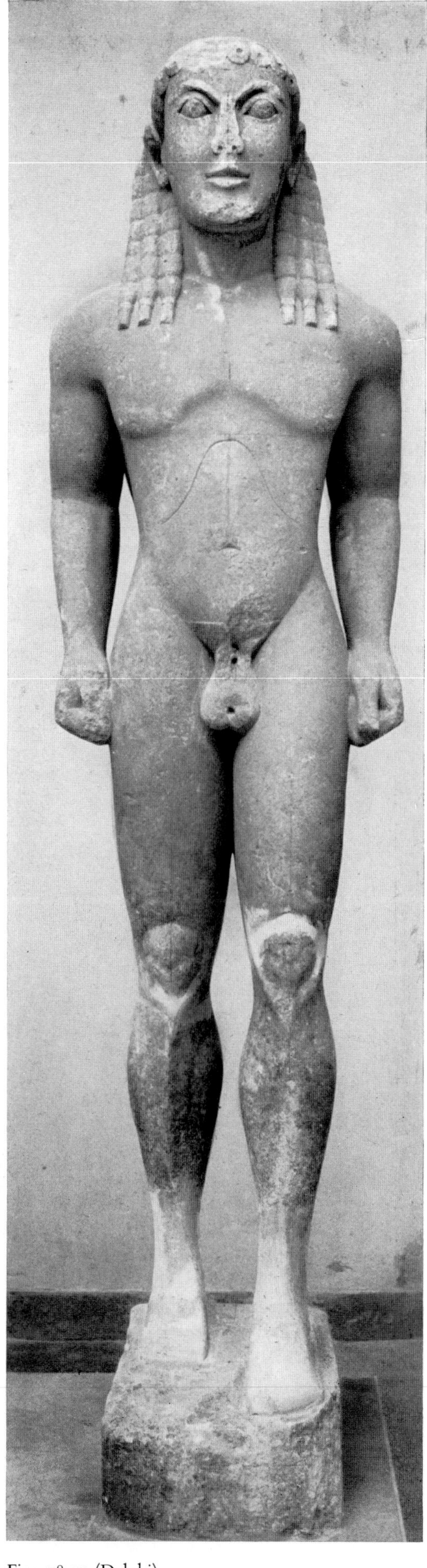

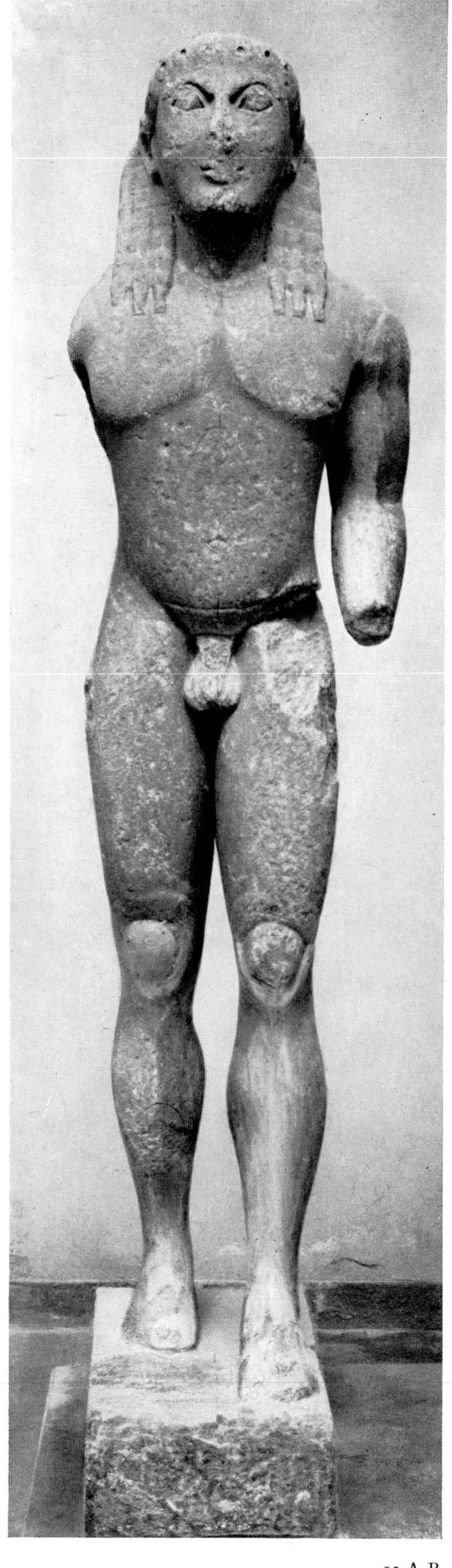

Figs. 78-79 (Delphi)

12 A-B

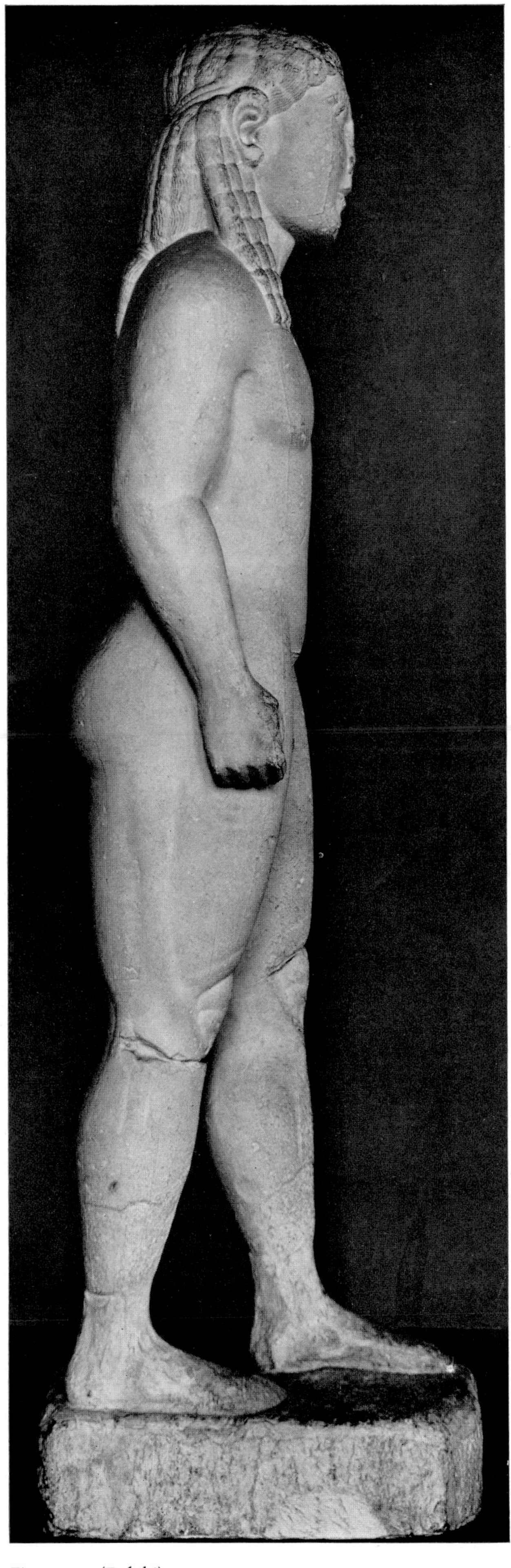

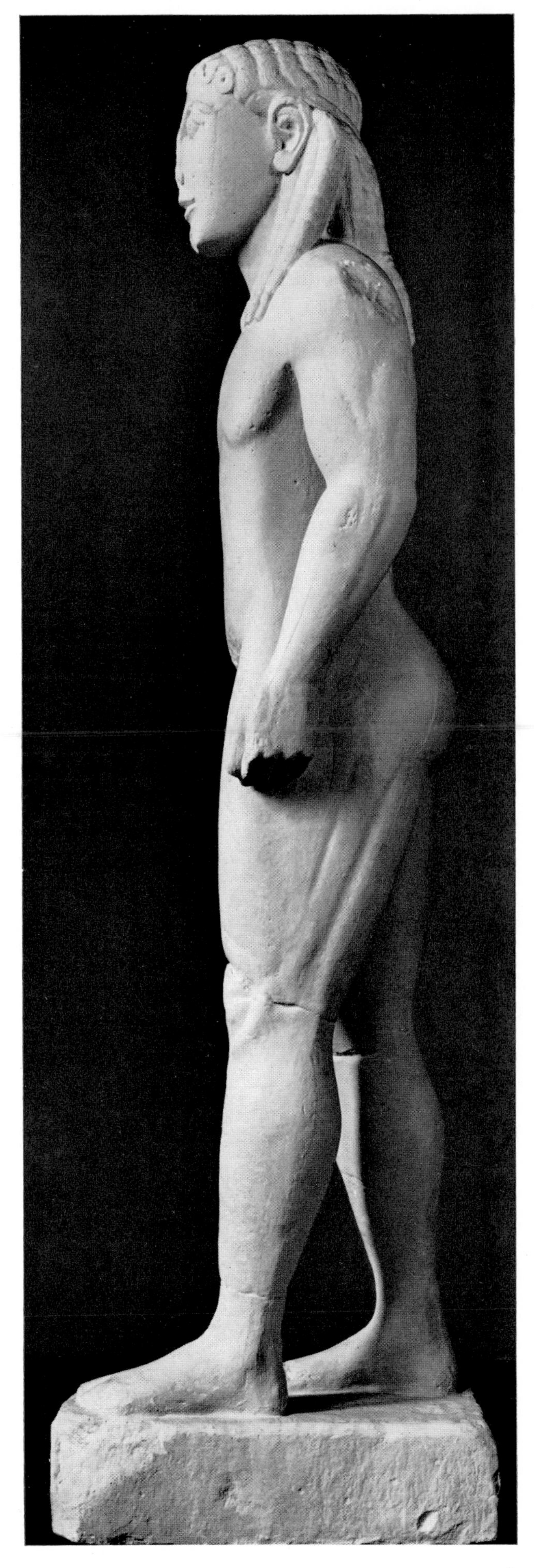

Figs. 80-81 (Delphi)

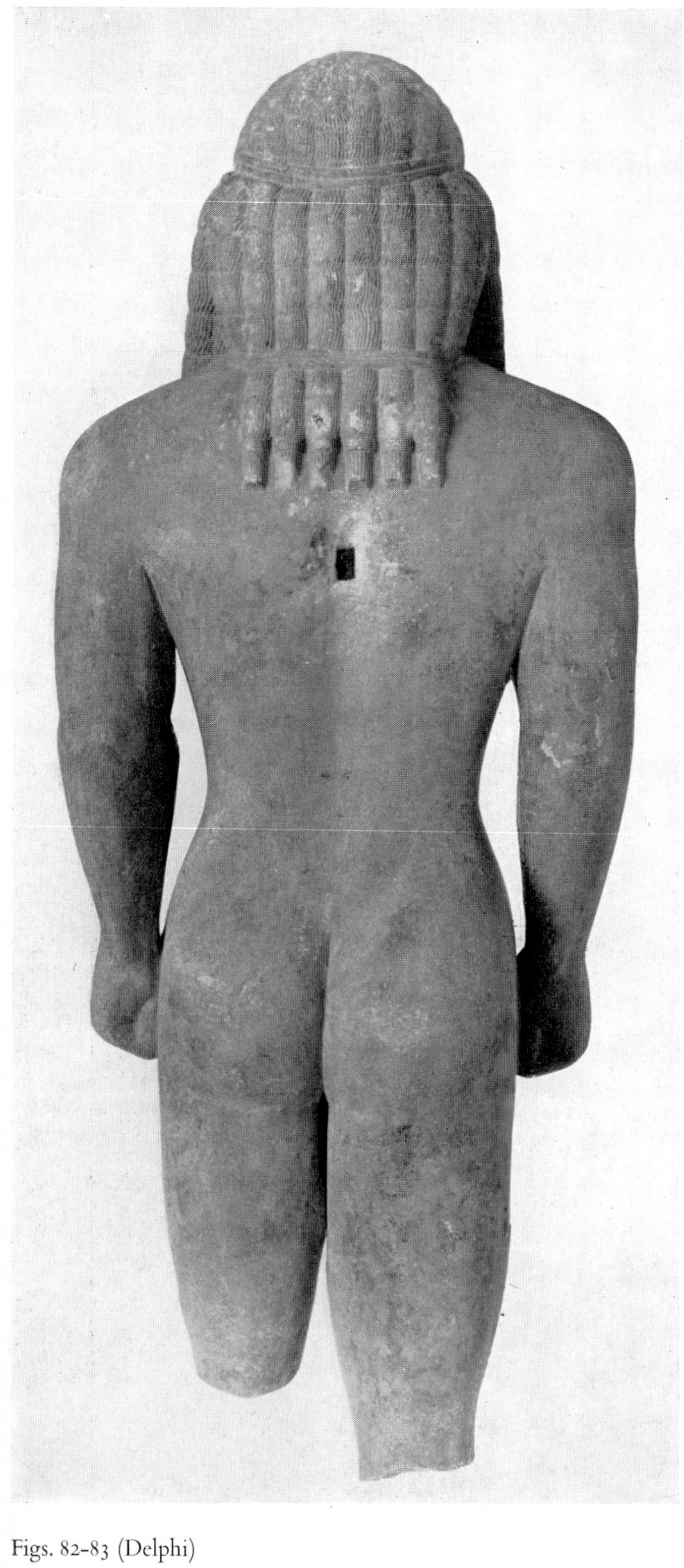

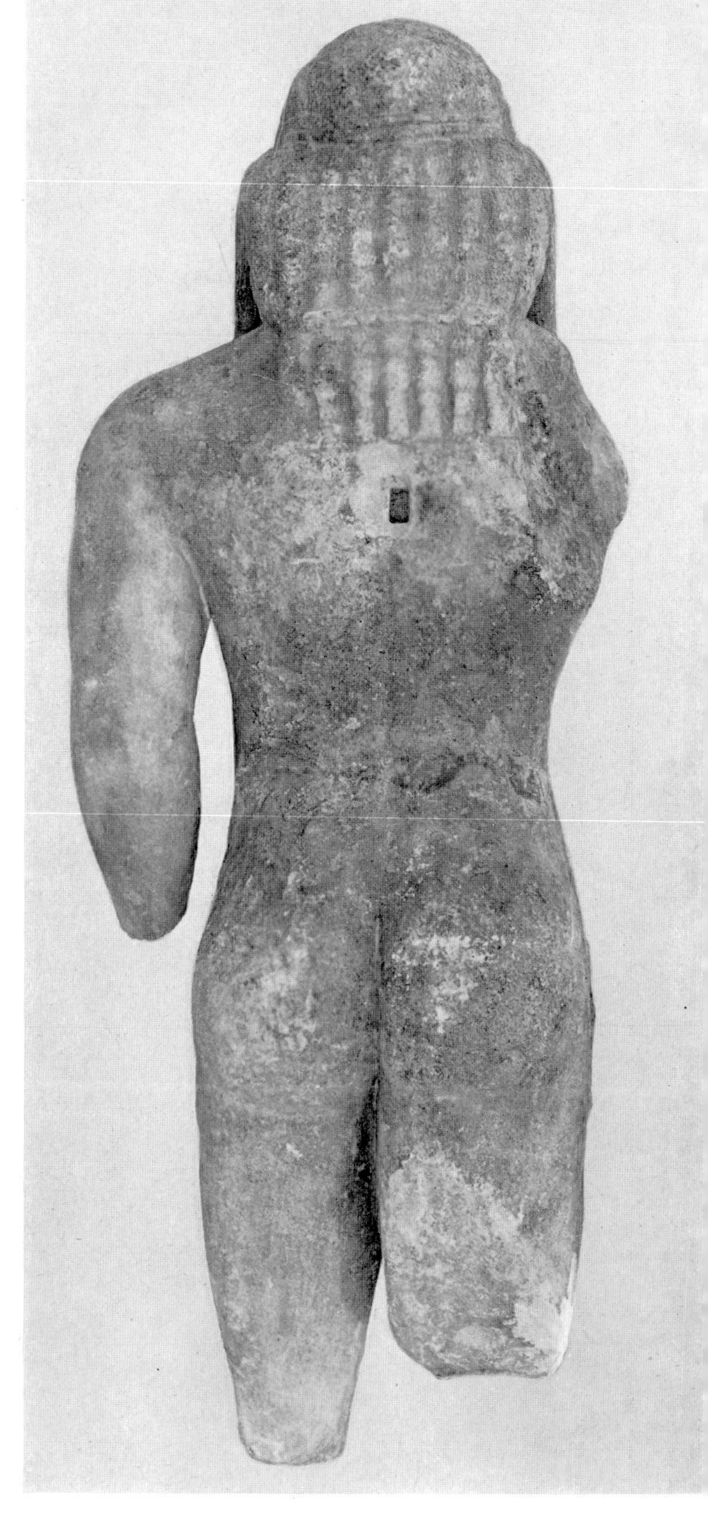

Figs. 82-83 (Delphi)

4-86 (Thasos)

Figs. 87-88 (Delos)

15

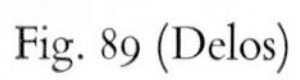

Fig. 89 (Delos)

15

Fig. 90 (London)

Figs. 91-92 (Delphi) 12B

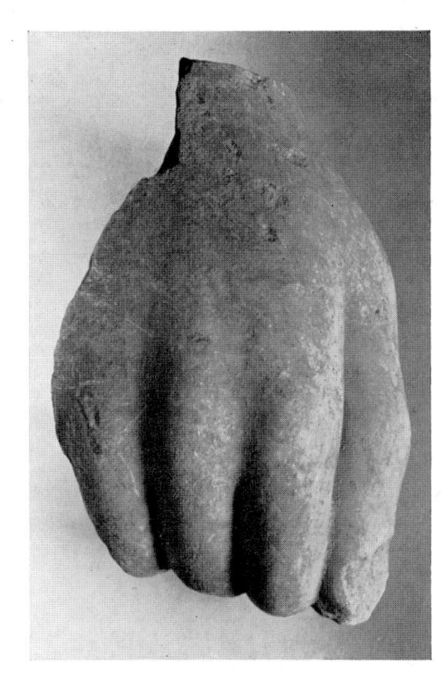

Fig. 93 (Samos) 25

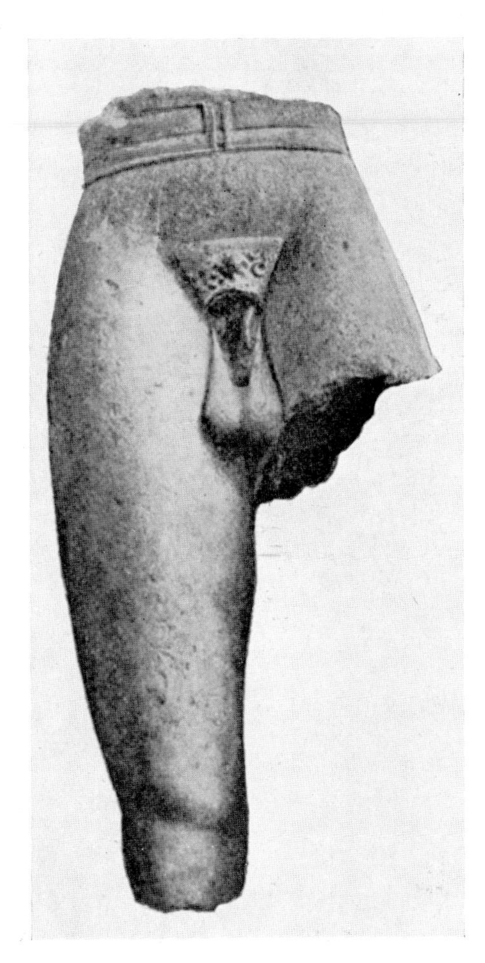

Figs. 94-95 (Delos) 17

Fig. 96 (Samos) 24

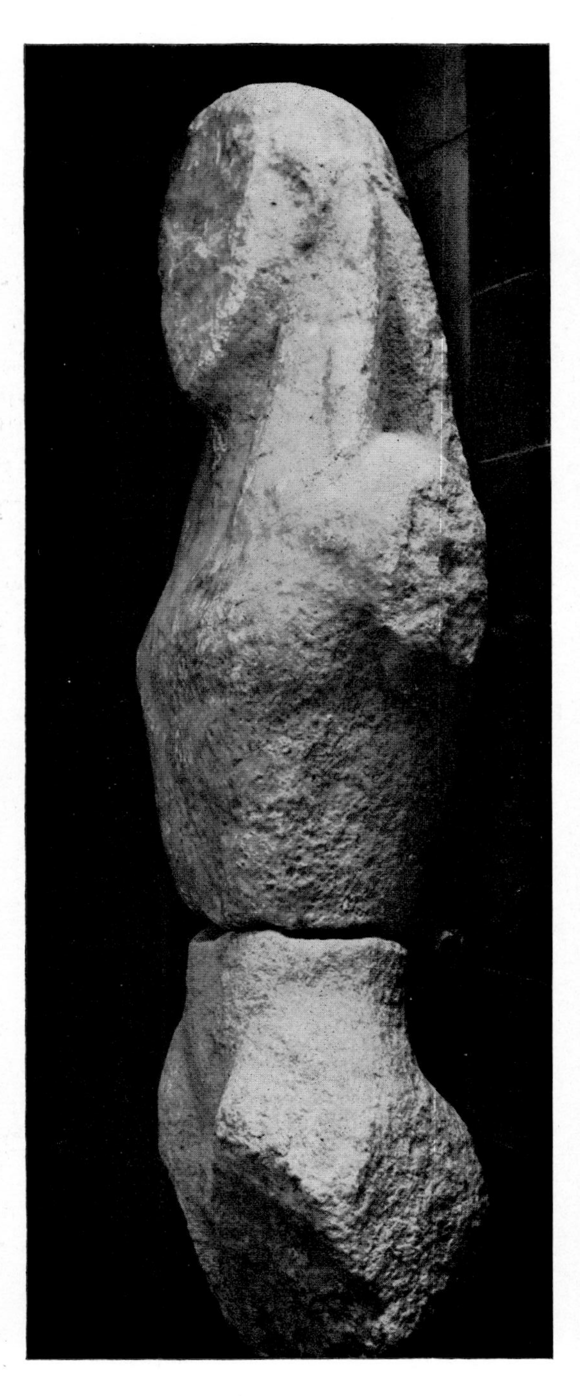

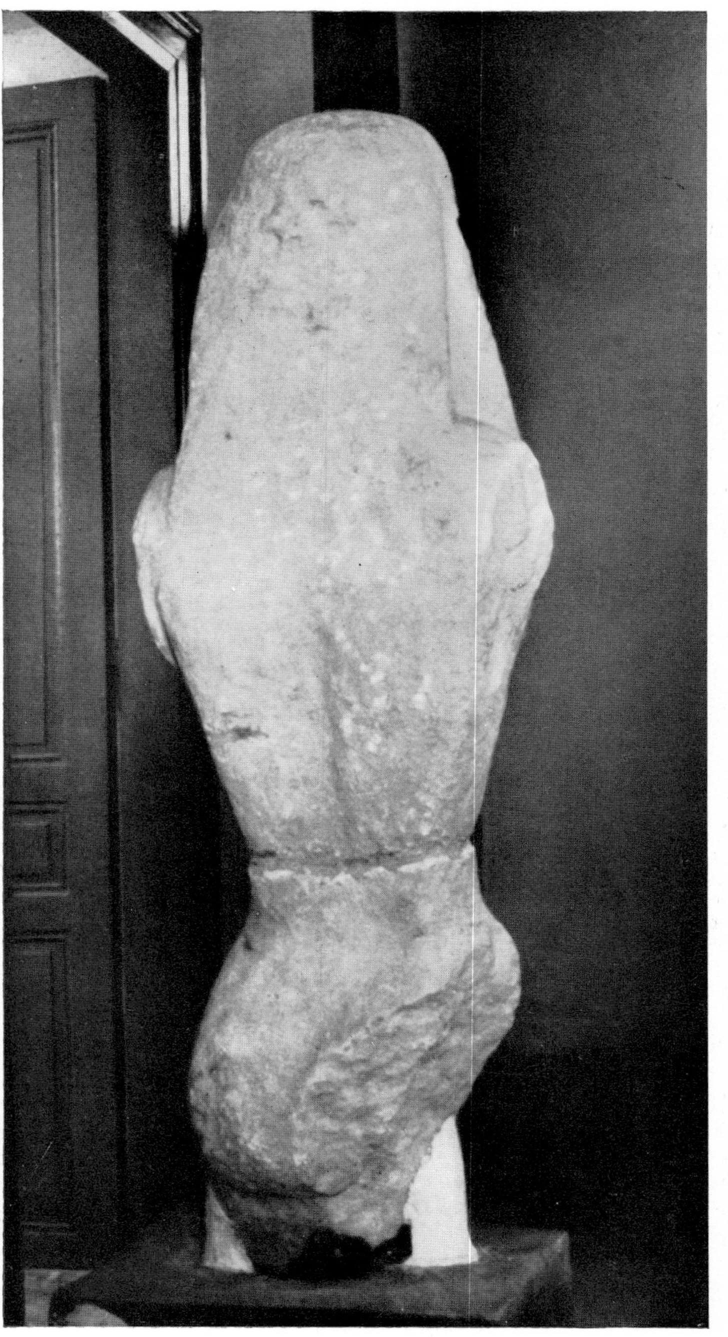

Figs. 97-99 (Santorin)

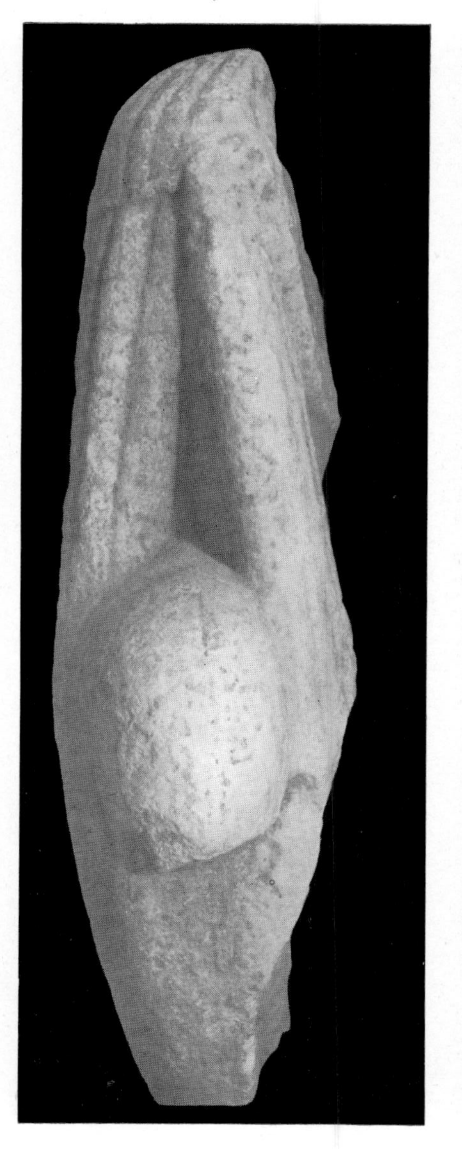

Figs. 100–102 (Santorin)

Figs. 103-104 (Leyden) 19

Fig. 105 (Leyden) 19

Fig. 106 (Thasos) 14

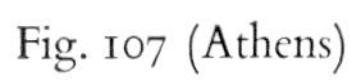

Fig. 107 (Athens) 20

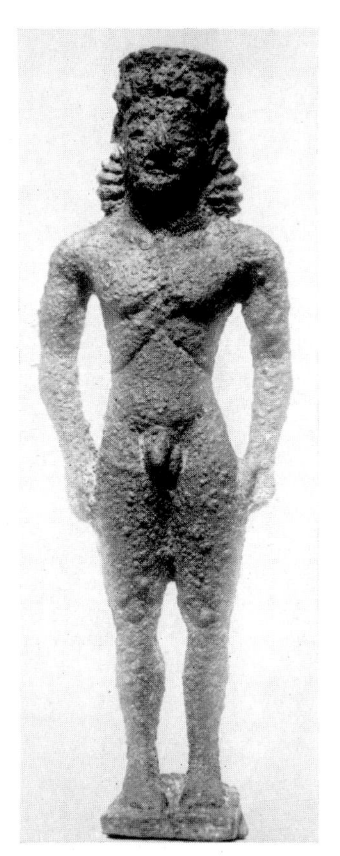

Fig. 110 (Athens) 20

Figs. 108-109 (Palermo) 30 bis

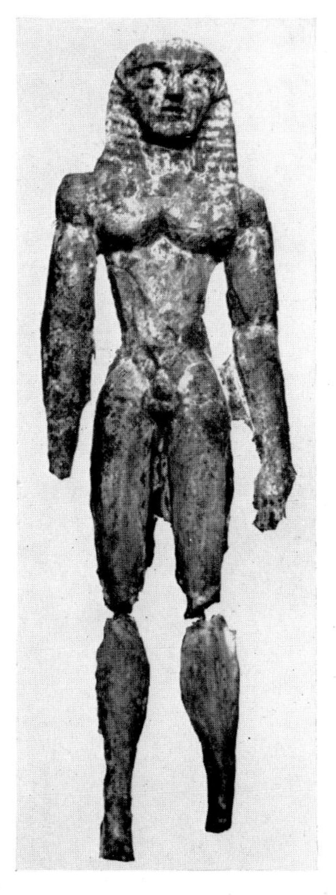

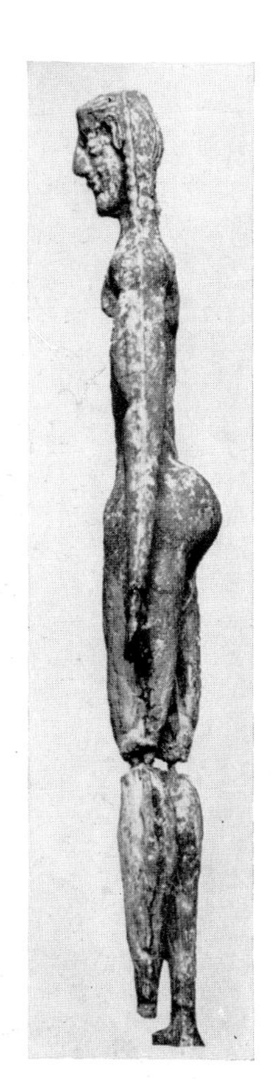

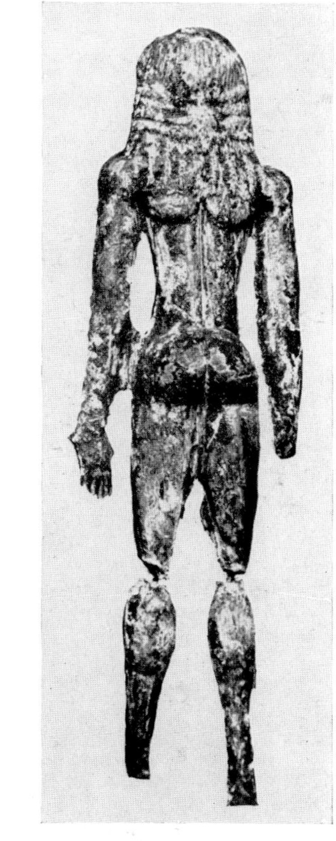

Figs. 111-113 (Florence) 21

Figs. 114-116 (Athens)

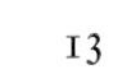

13

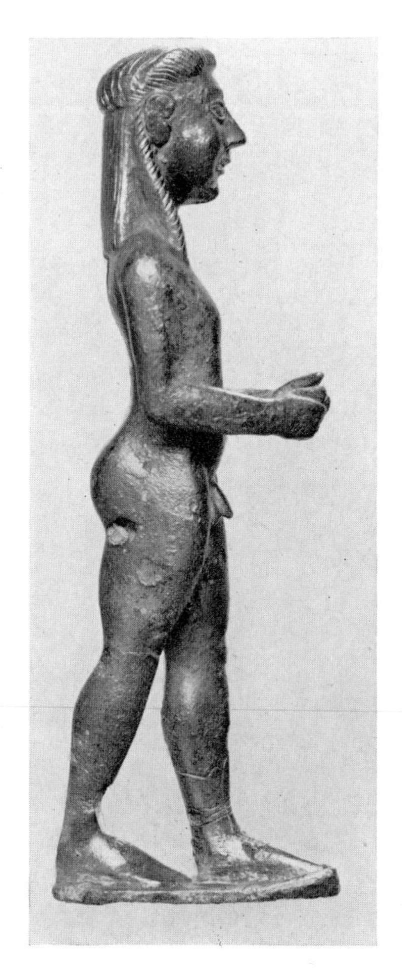

Figs. 117-119 (Samos)

22

Figs. 120-122 (Samos) 23

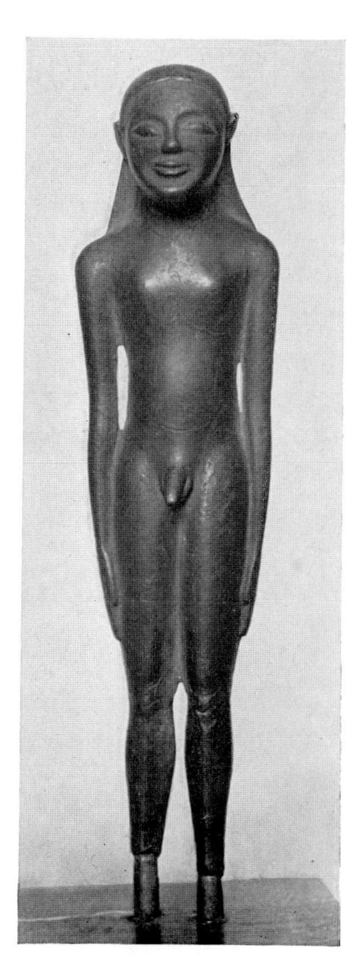

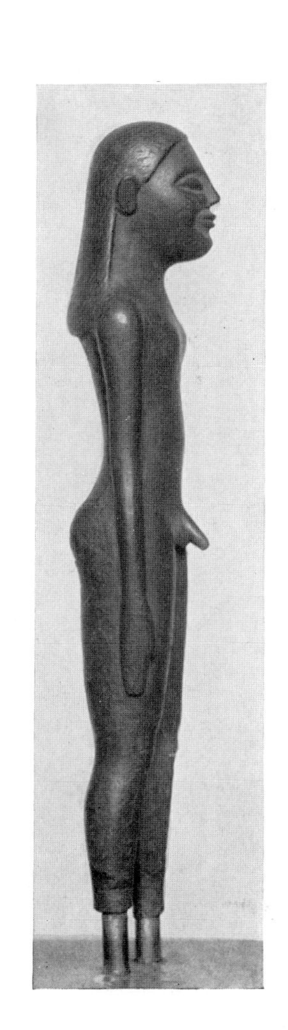

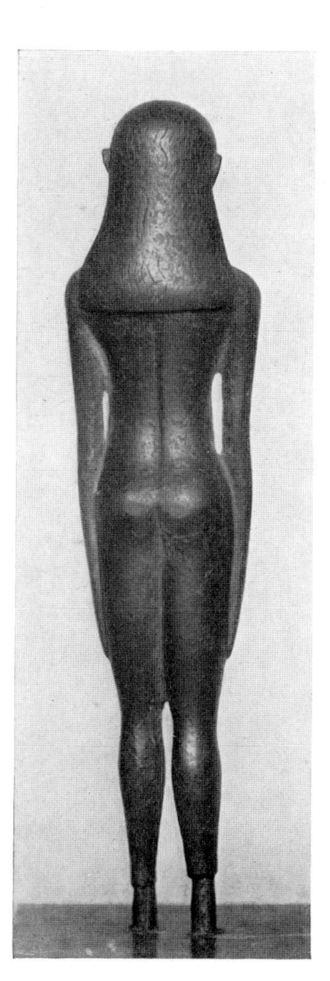

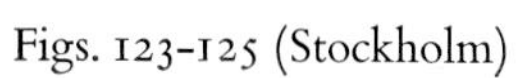

Figs. 123-125 (Stockholm) 26

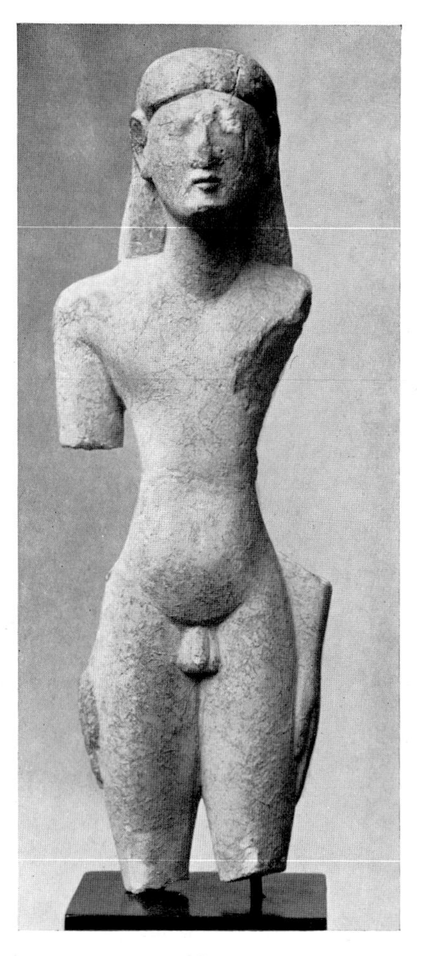

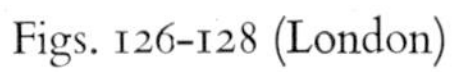

Figs. 126-128 (London)

27

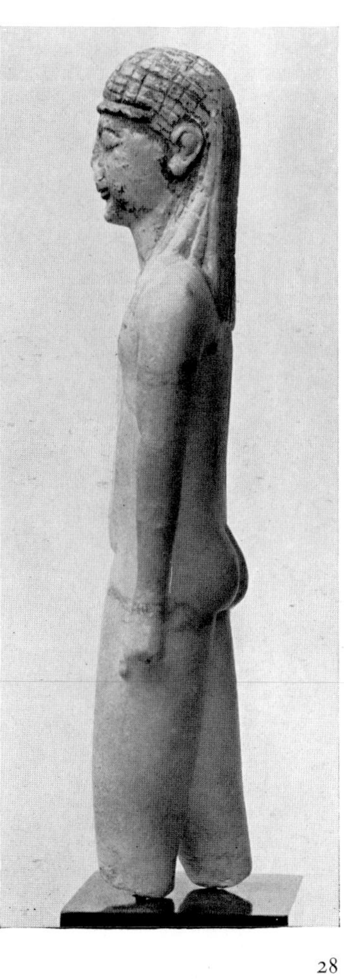

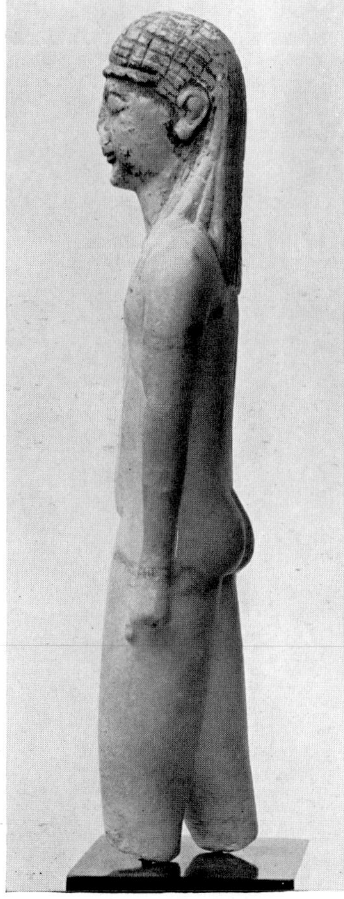

Figs. 129-130 (London)

28

Fig. 131 (London)

29

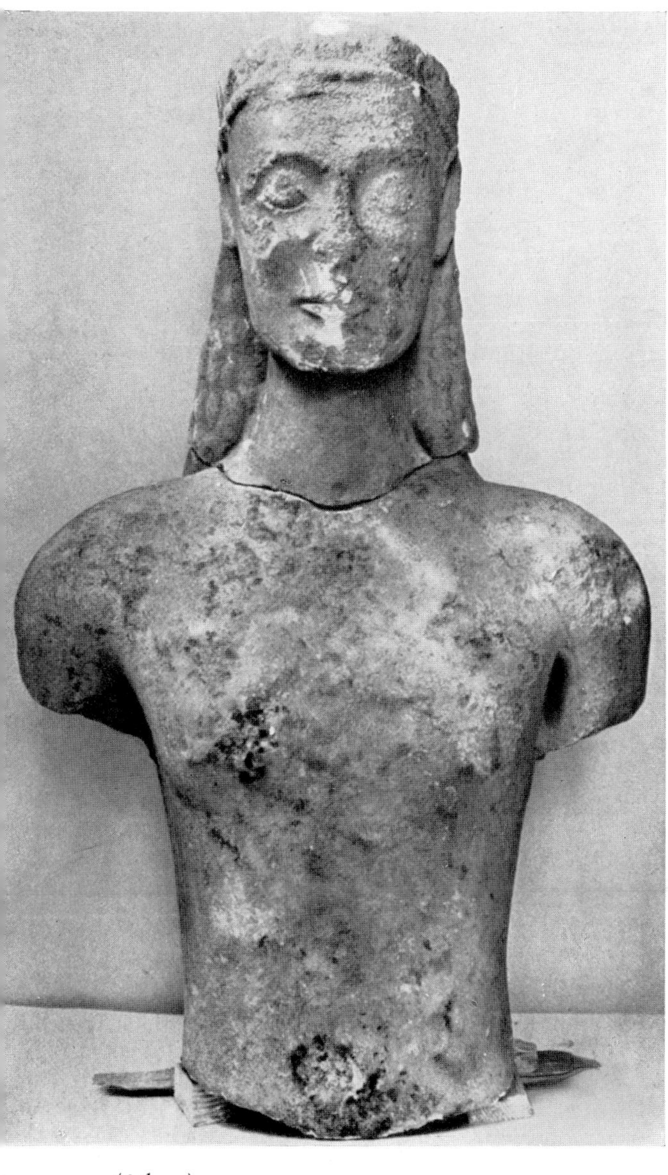

Figs. 132-133 (Athens)

Figs. 134-135 (Athens)

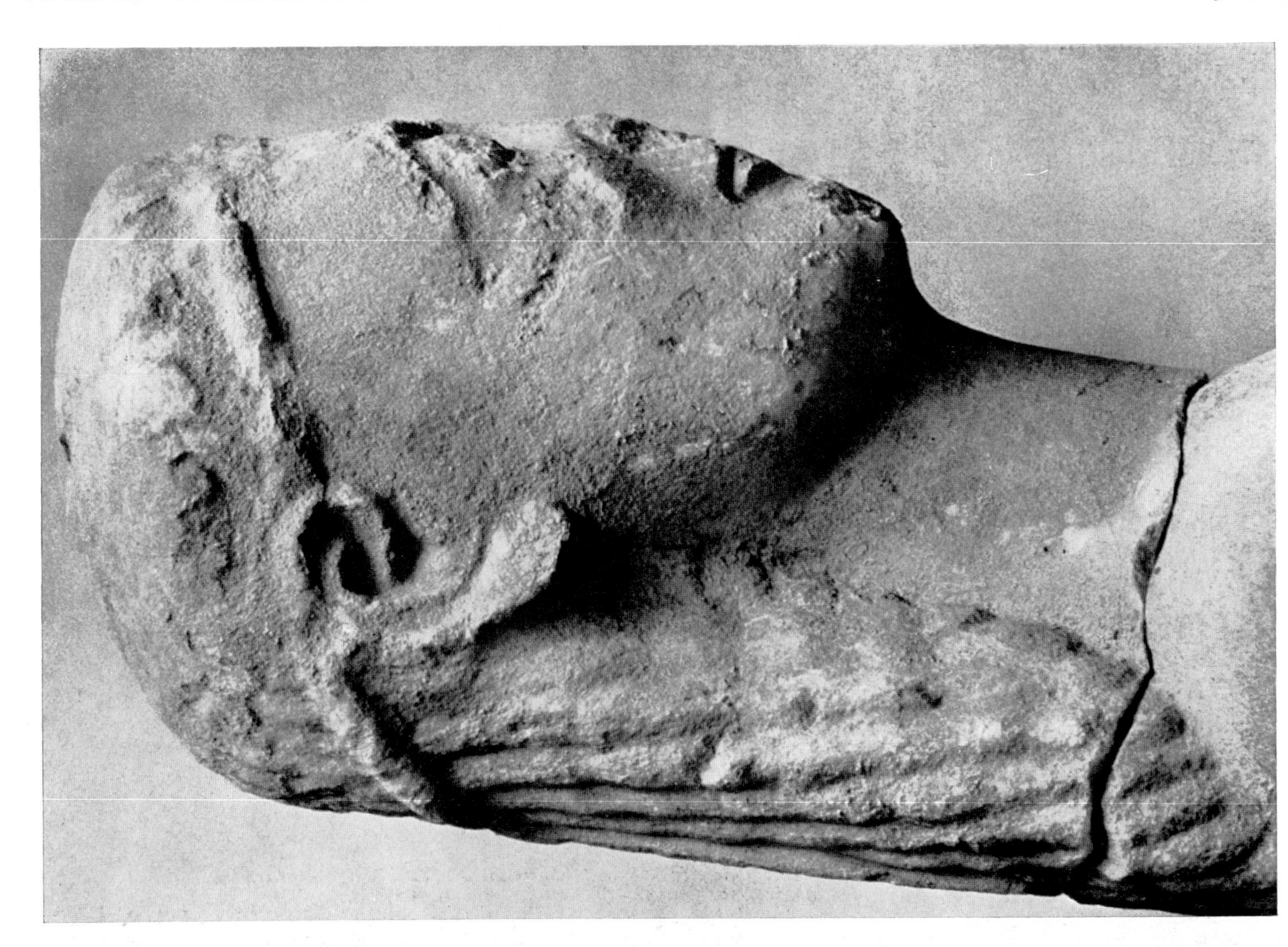

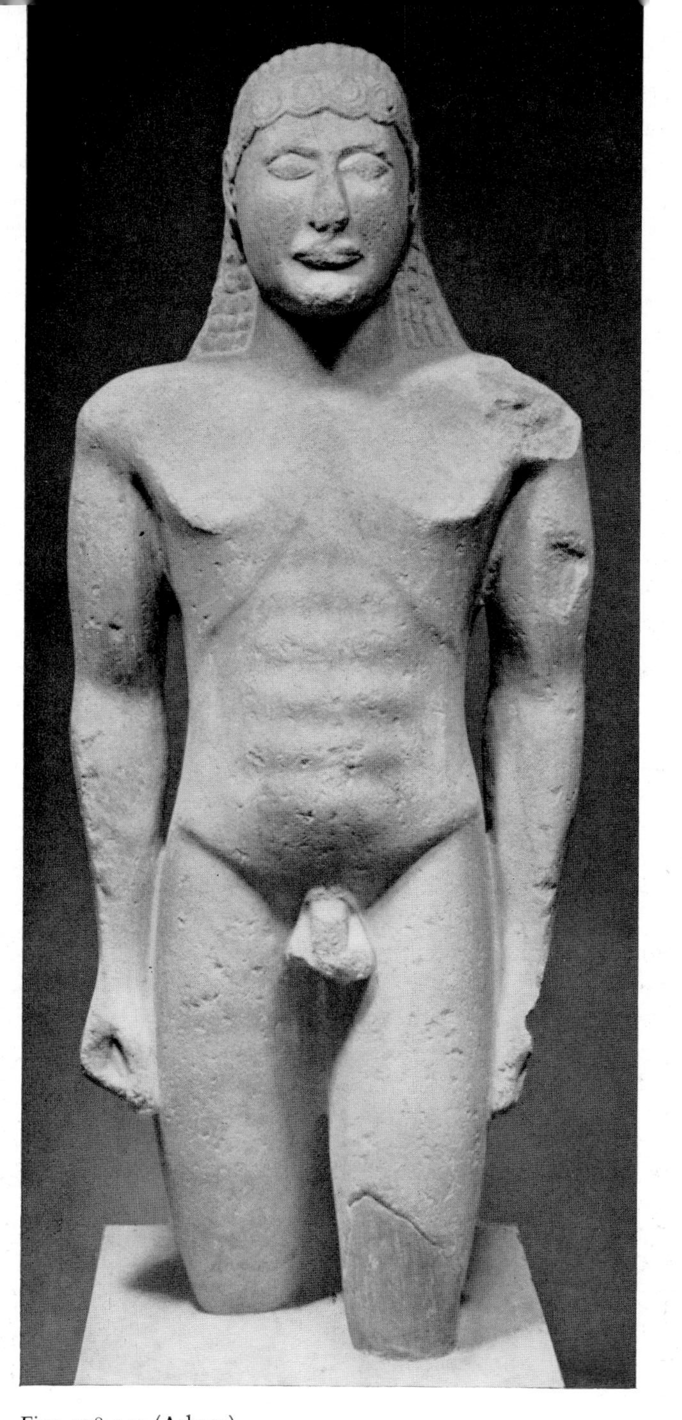

Figs. 138-140 (Athens)

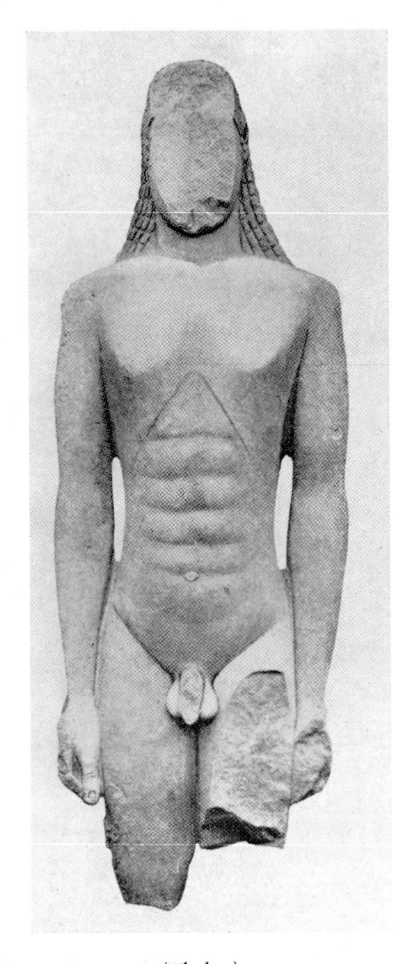

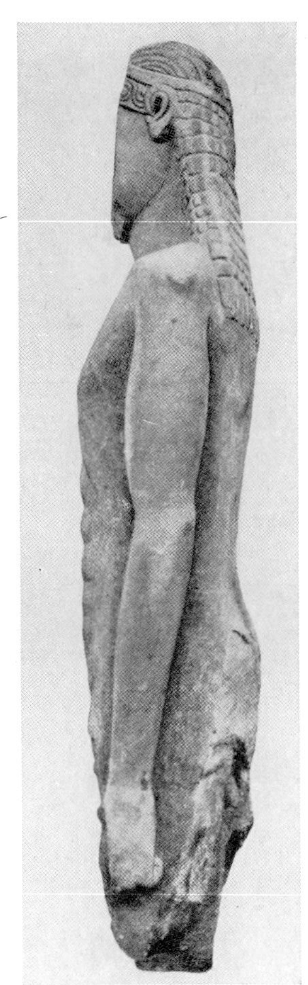

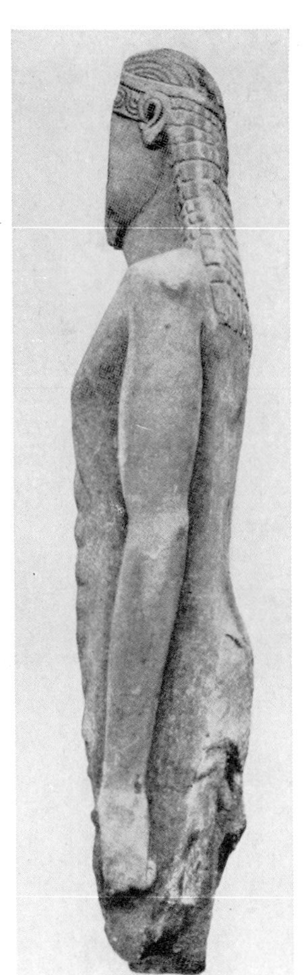

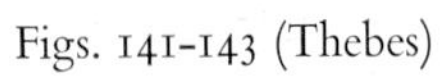

Figs. 141-143 (Thebes)

34

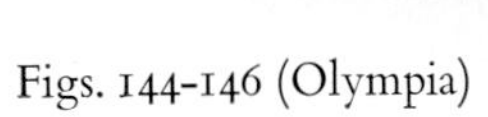

Figs. 144-146 (Olympia)

41

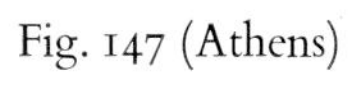

Fig. 147 (Athens) 38

Fig. 148 (Thebes) 36

ig. 149 (Thebes) 37

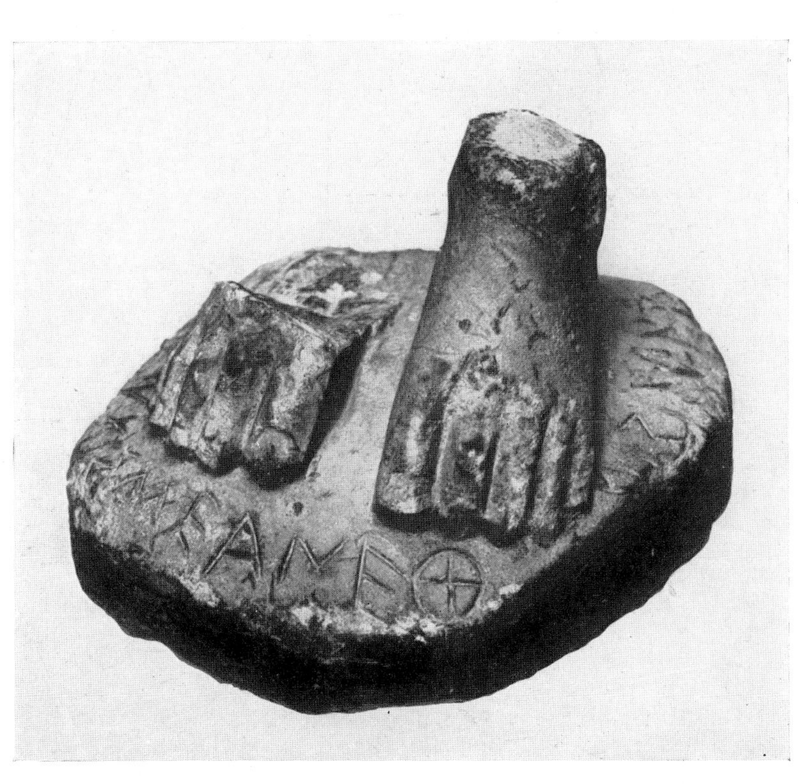

Fig. 150 (London) 57

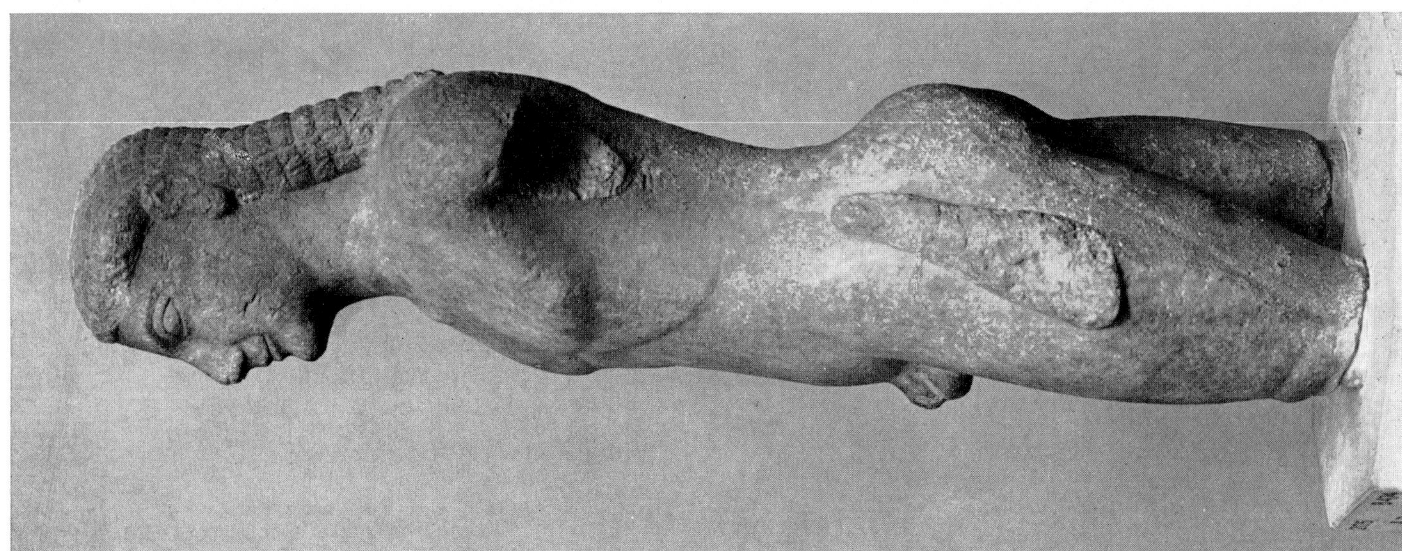

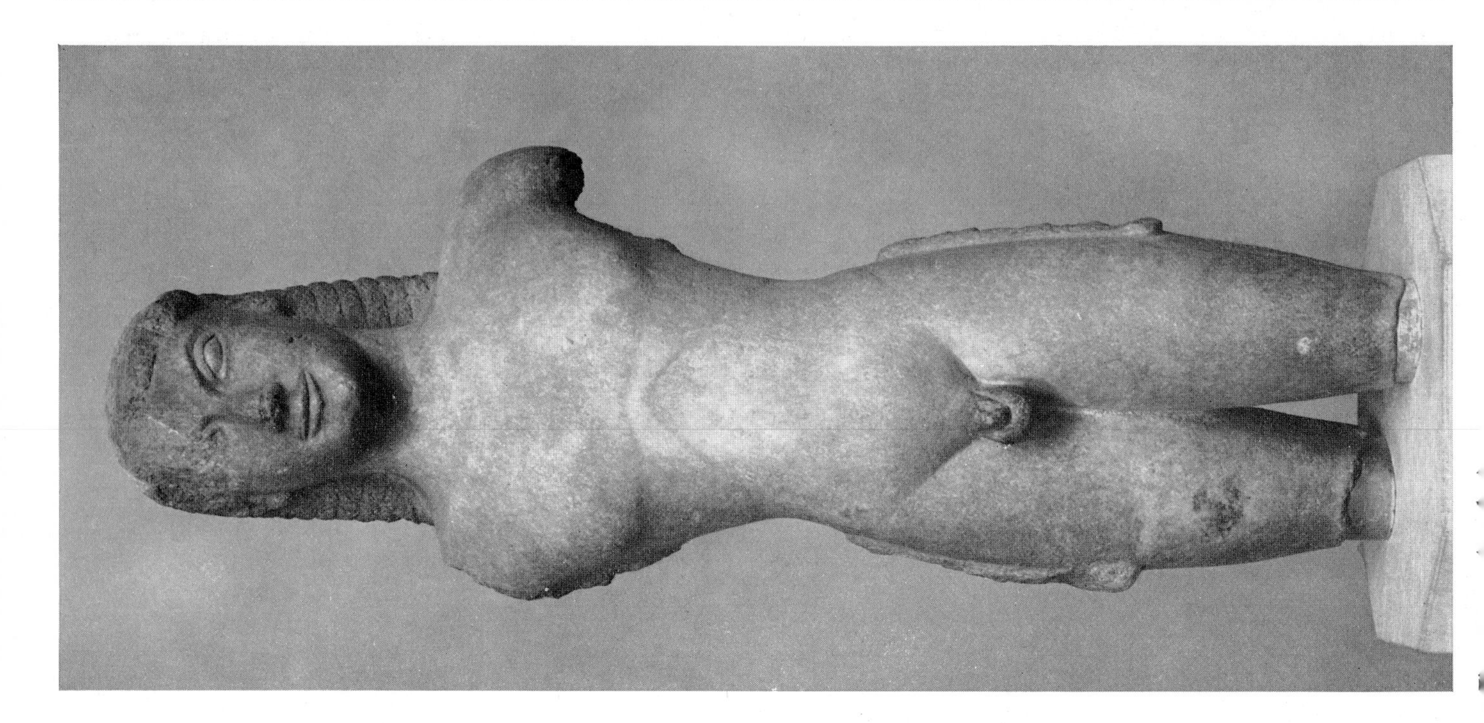

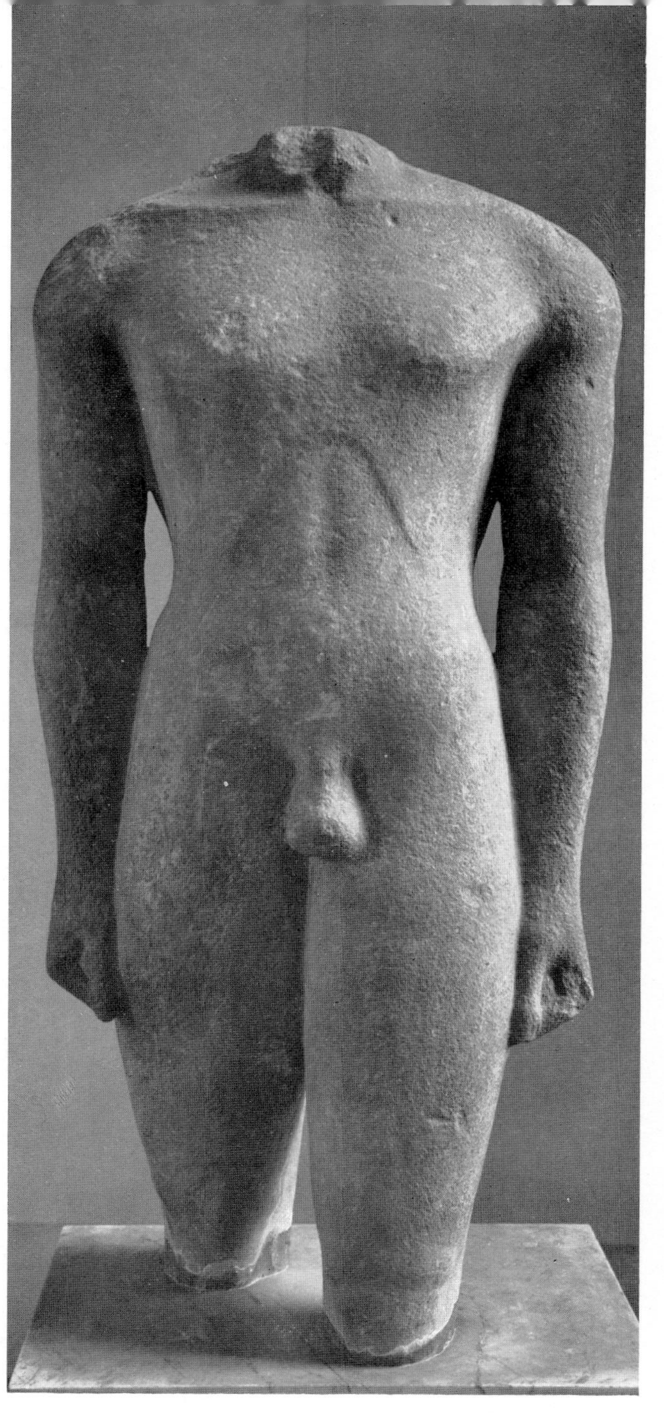

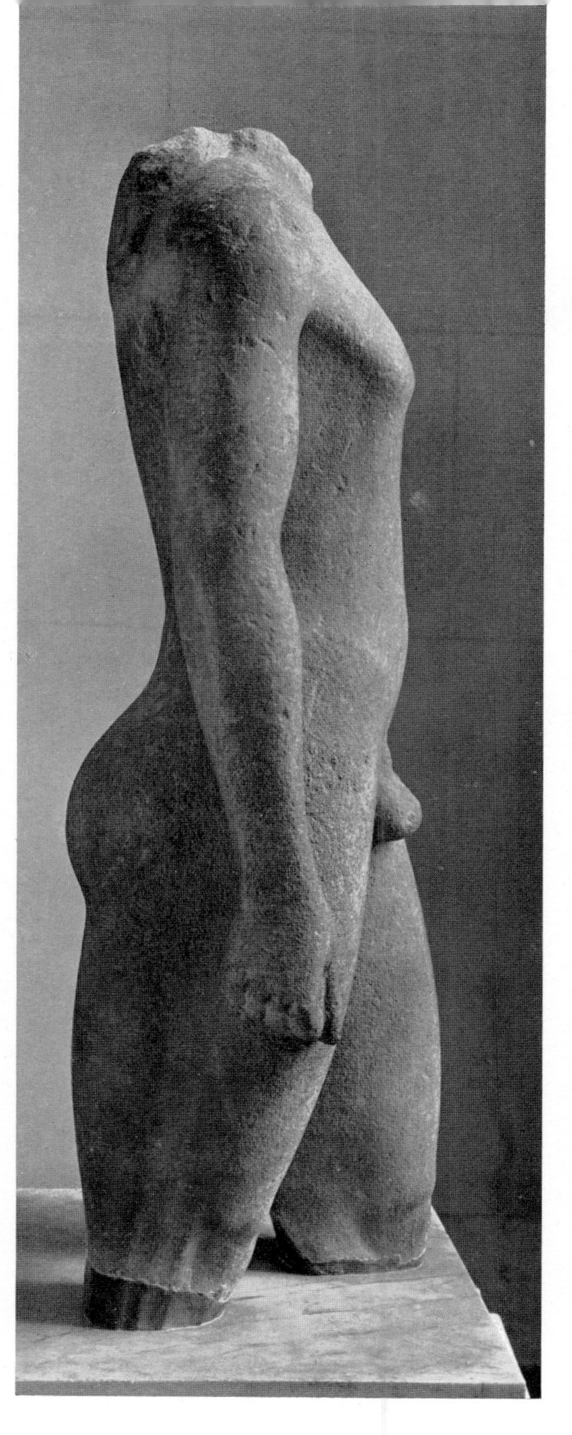

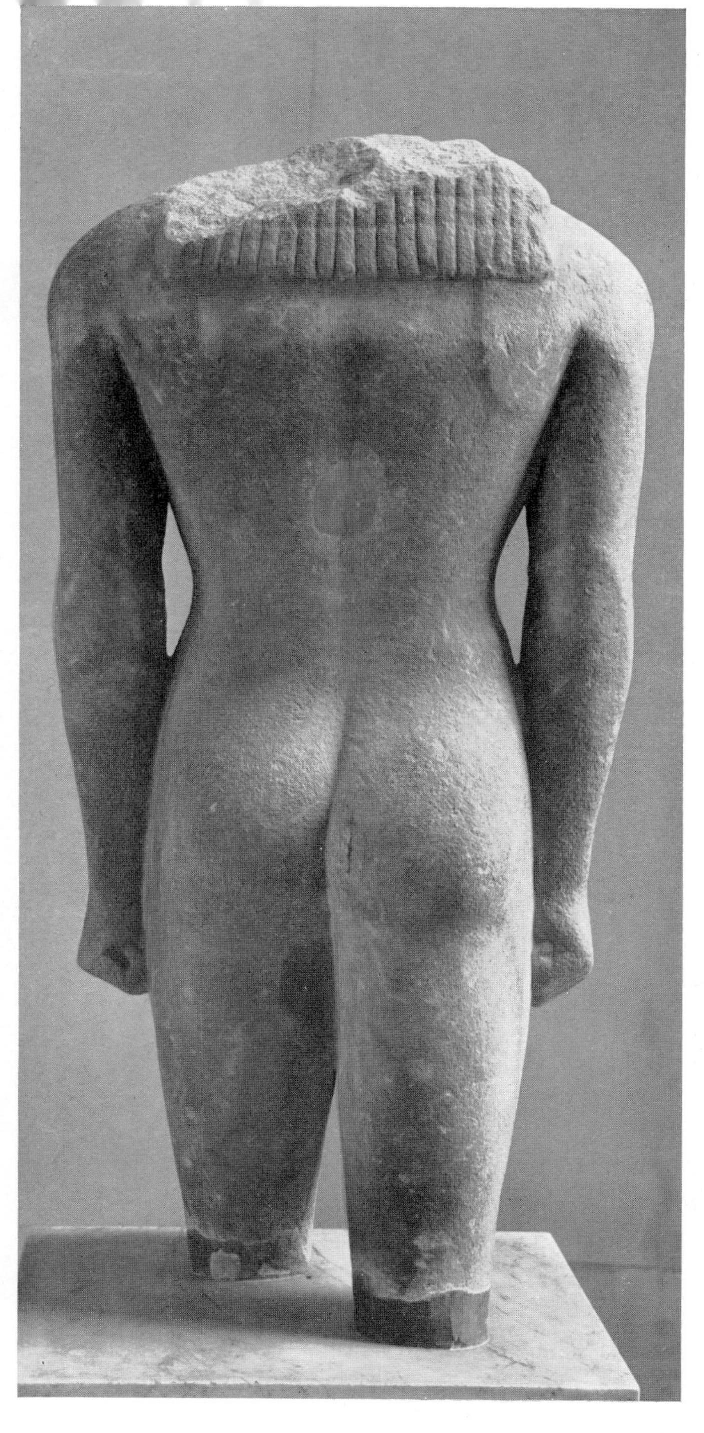

Figs. 154-156 (Paris)

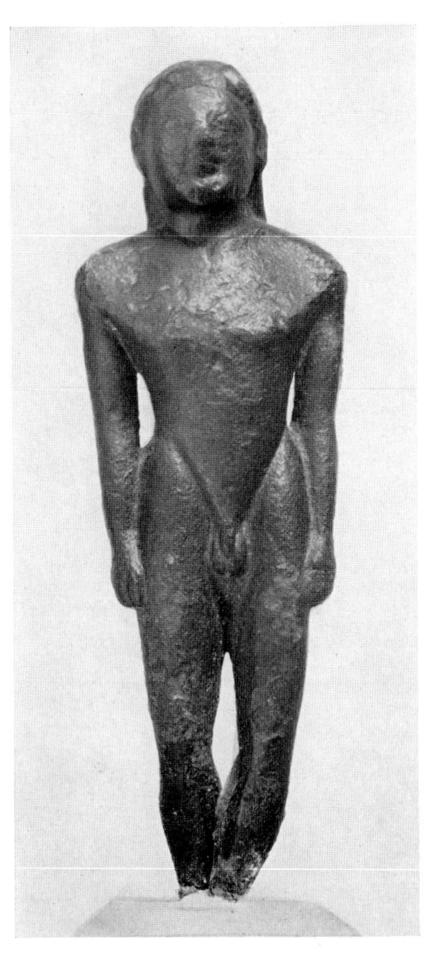

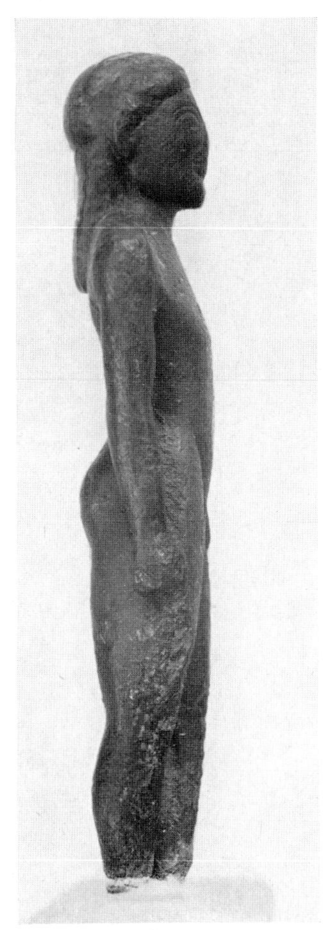

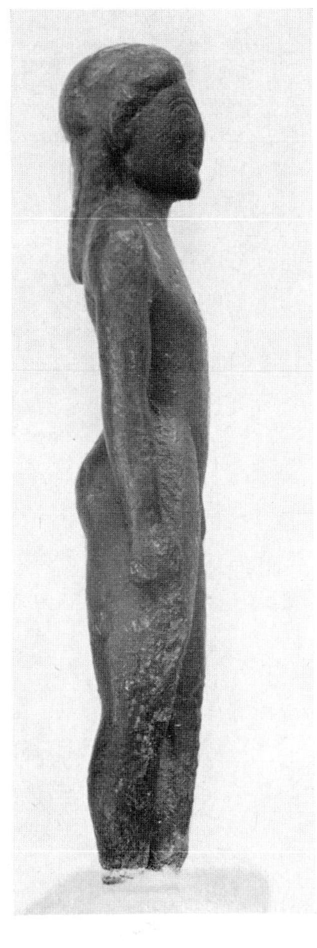

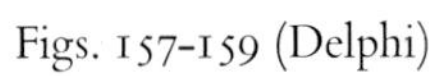

Figs. 157-159 (Delphi)

42

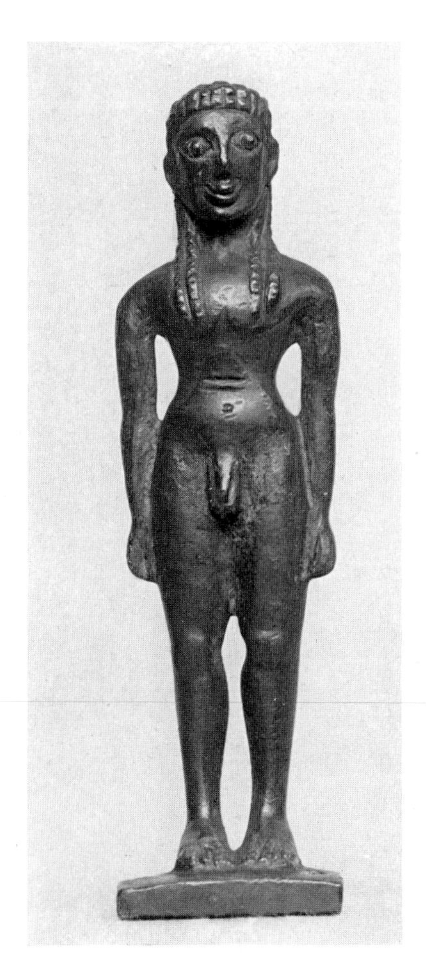

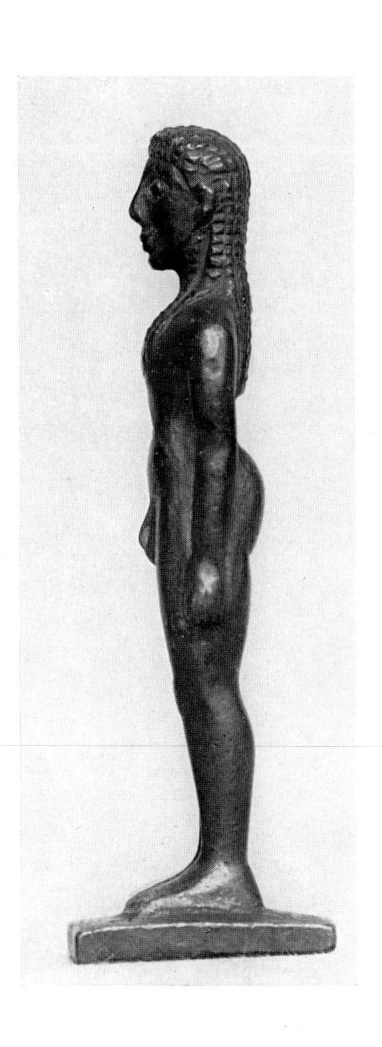

Figs. 160-162 (London)

43

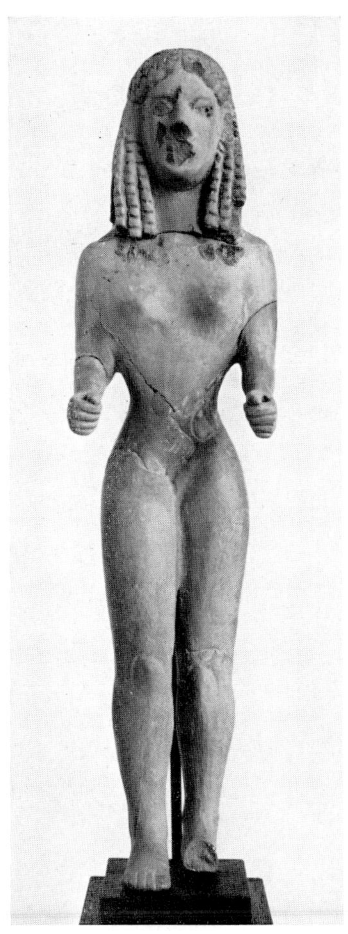

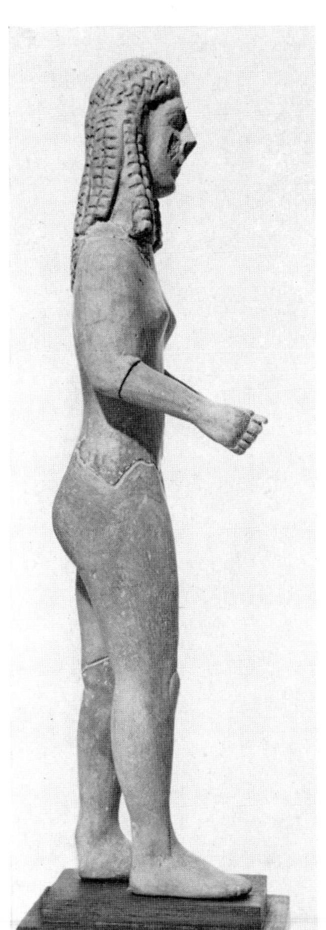

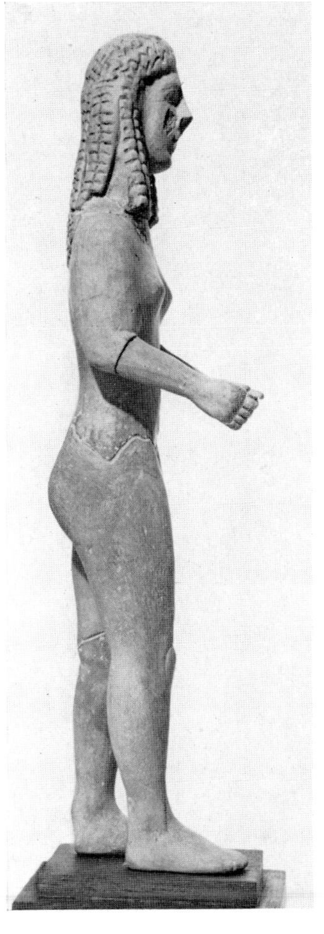

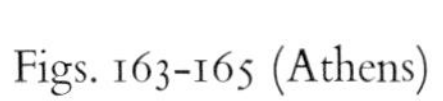

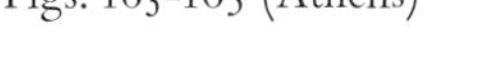

Figs. 163-165 (Athens) 44

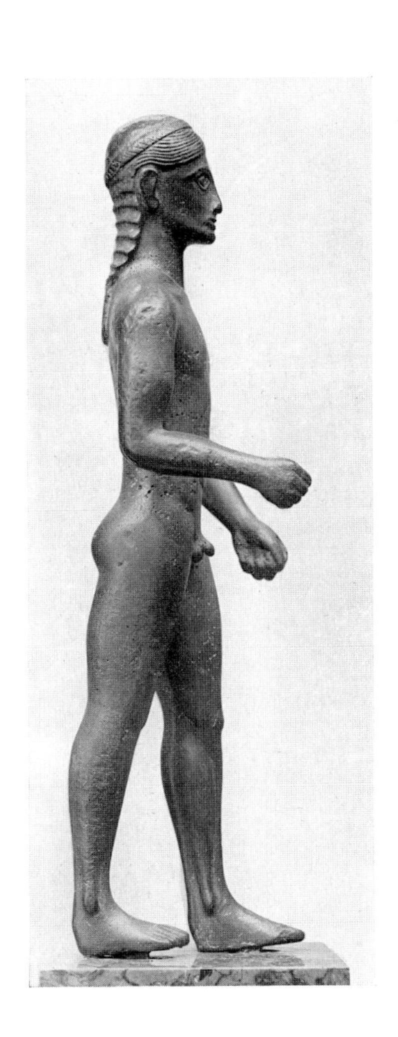

Figs. 166-168 (Berlin) 45

Figs. 169-171 (Delphi)

46

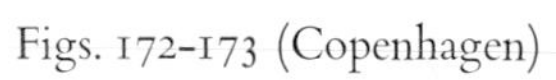

Figs. 172-173 (Copenhagen)

50

Figs. 174-175 (Delos)

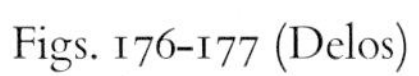

Figs. 176-177 (Delos)

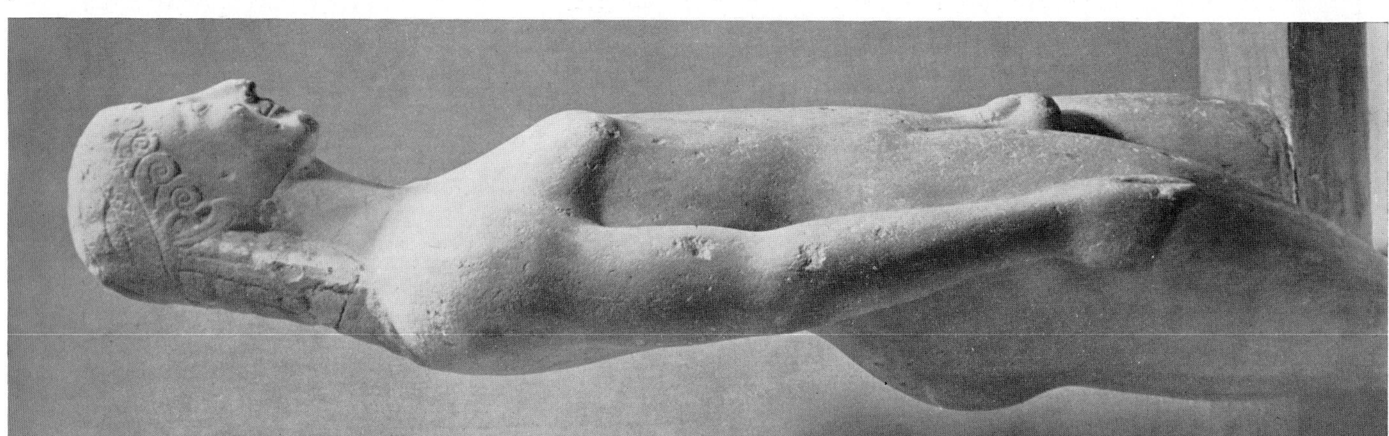
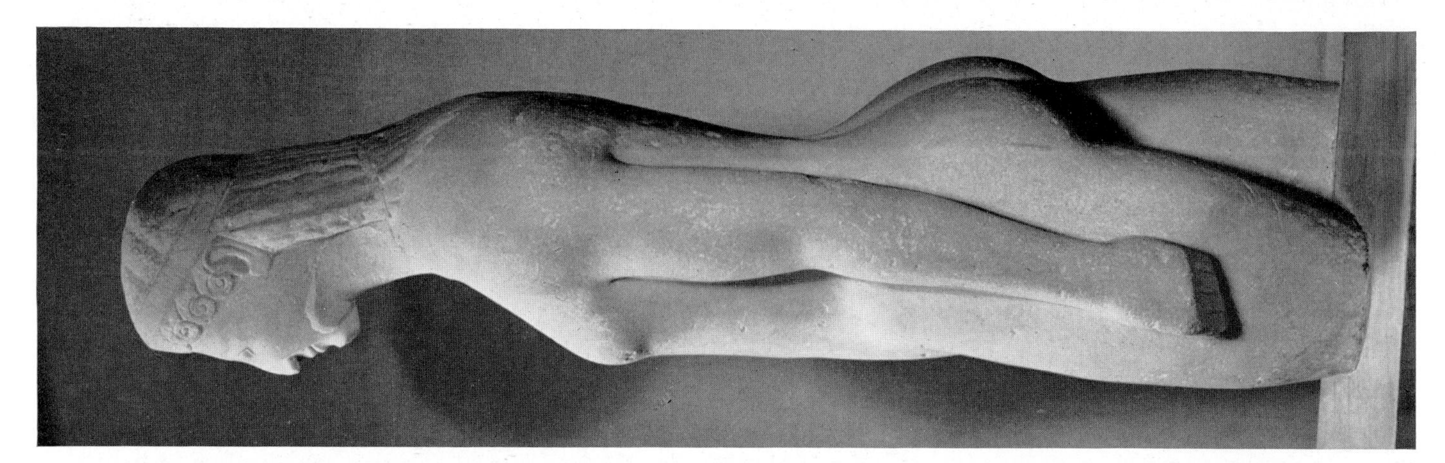

Figs. 182-183 (Athens)

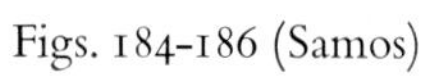

Figs. 184-186 (Samos)

51

Figs. 187-189 (Samos)

52

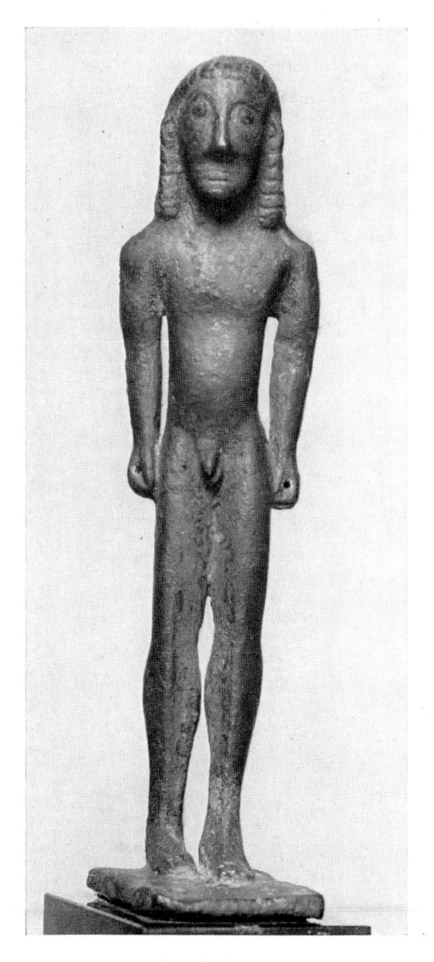

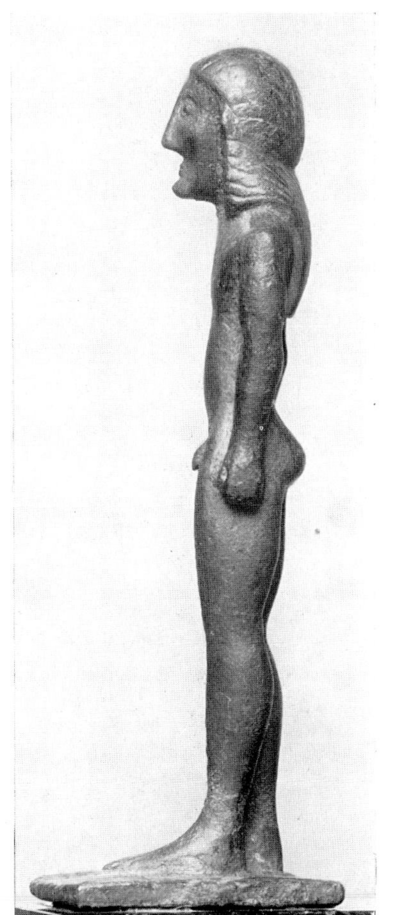

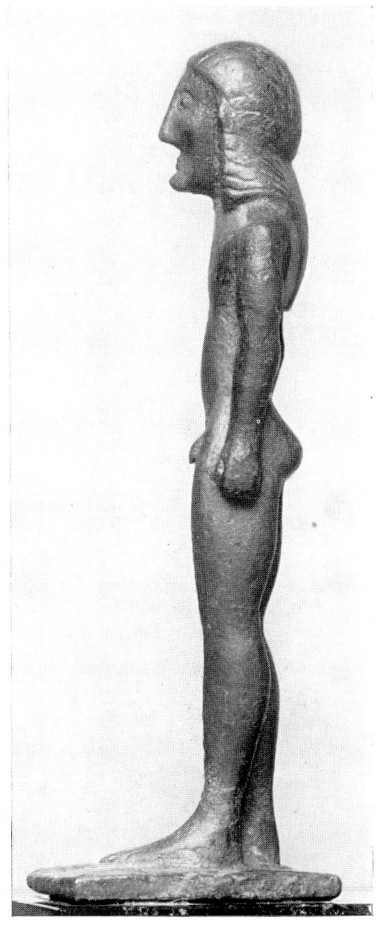

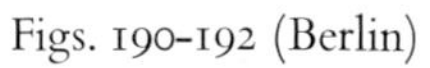

Figs. 190-192 (Berlin)

53

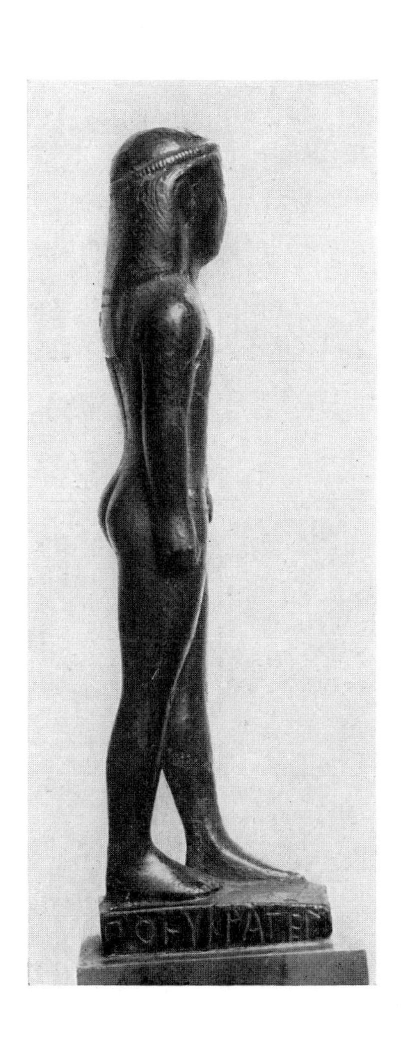

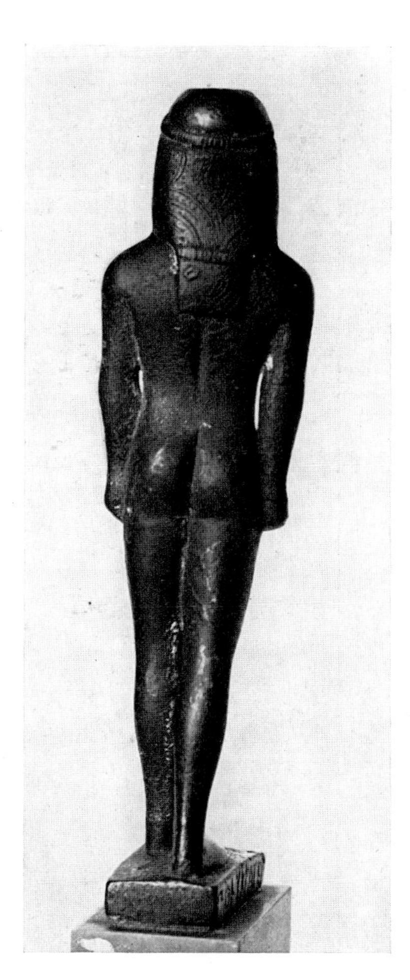

Figs. 193-195 (Leningrad)

54

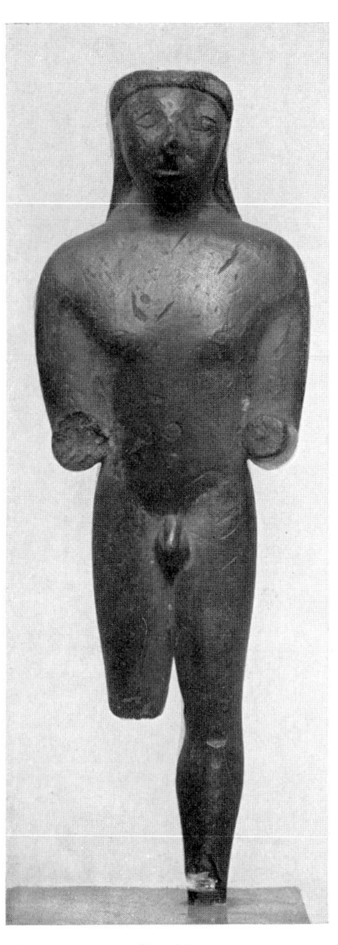

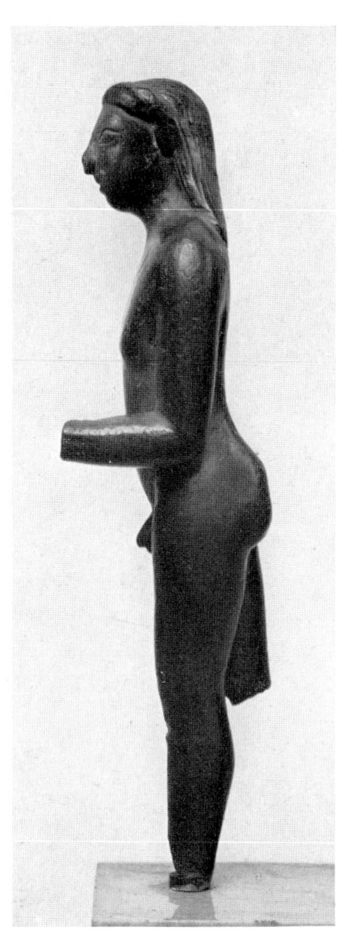

Figs. 196-197 (Paris) 55

Figs. 198-199 (Leipzig) 58

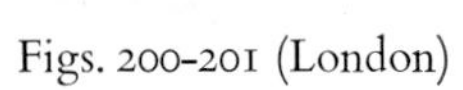

Figs. 200-201 (London) 56

202-203 (Oxford) 62

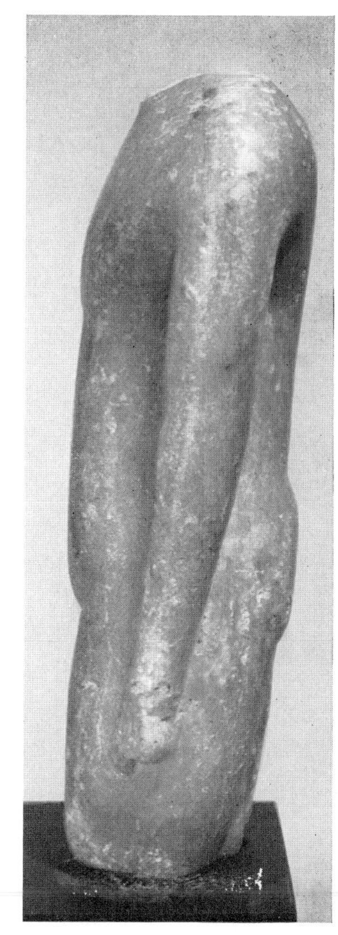

Figs. 204-205 (Cairo) 61

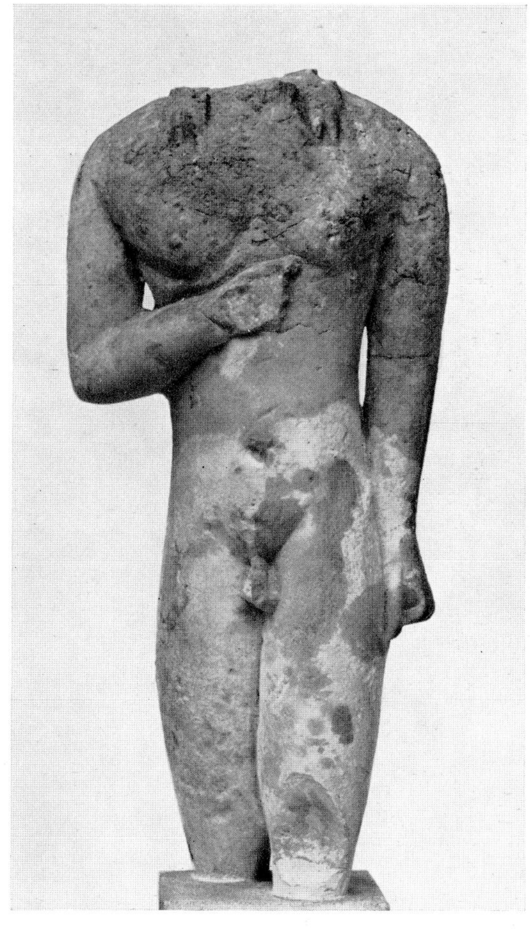

Fig. 206 (London) 59

Fig. 207 (London) 60

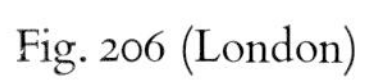

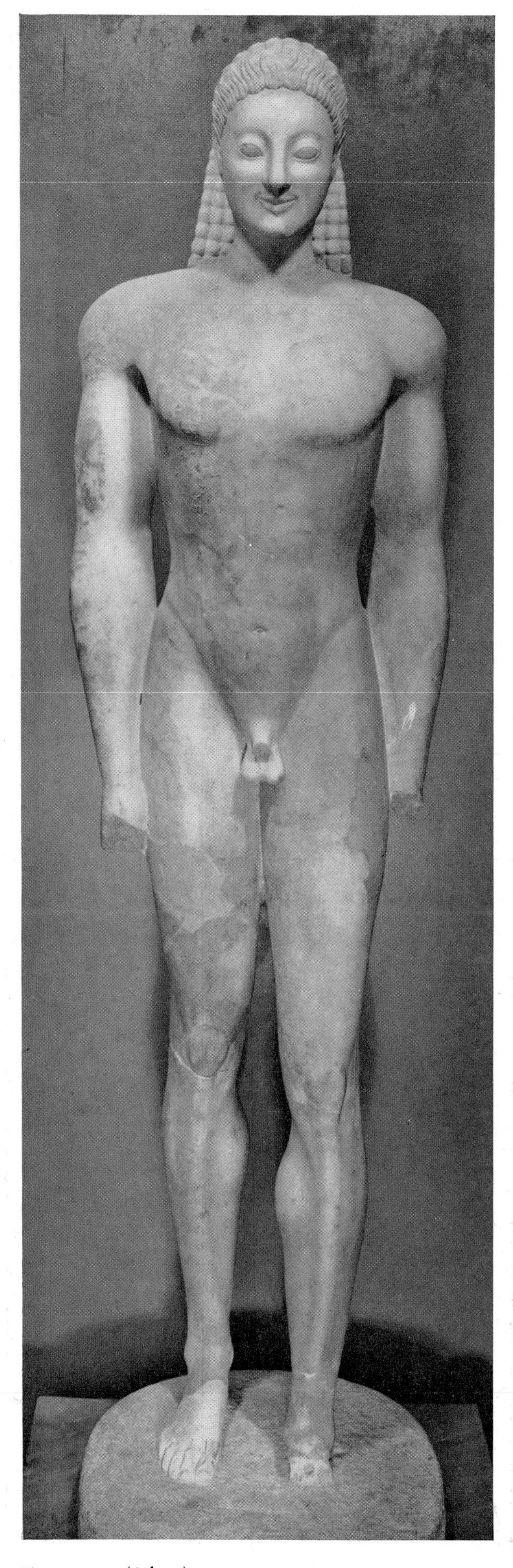

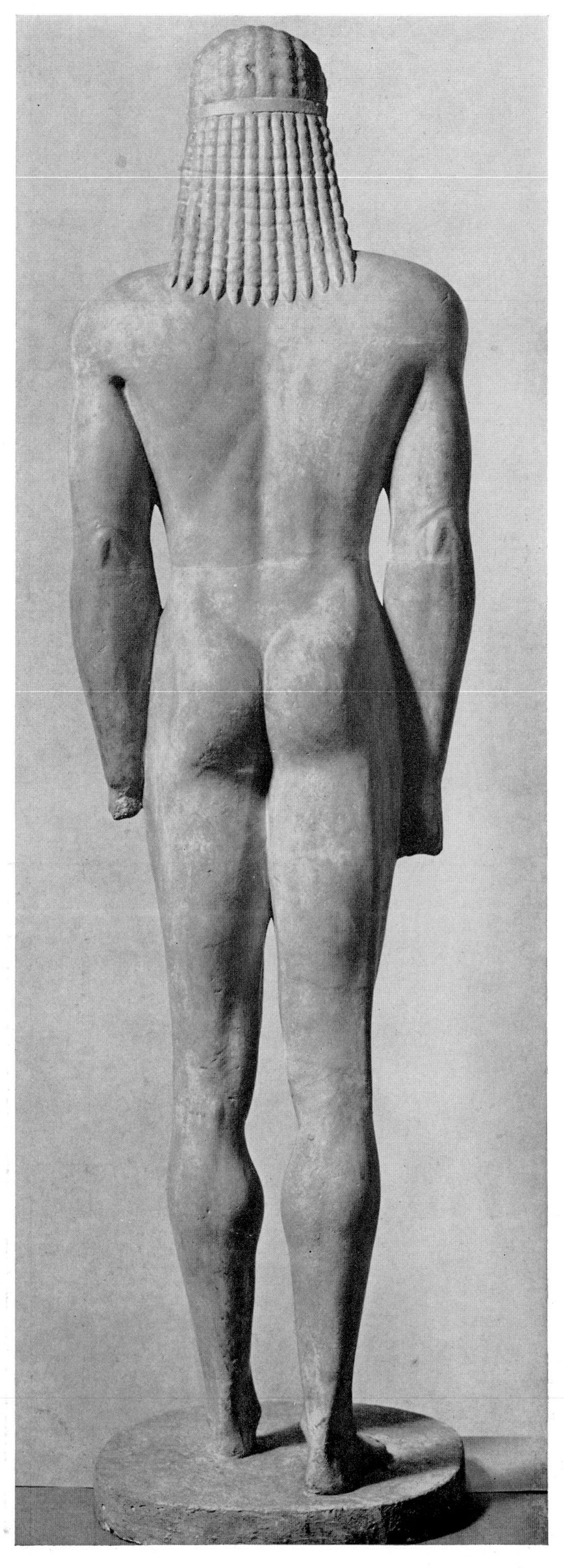

Figs. 208-209 (Athens)

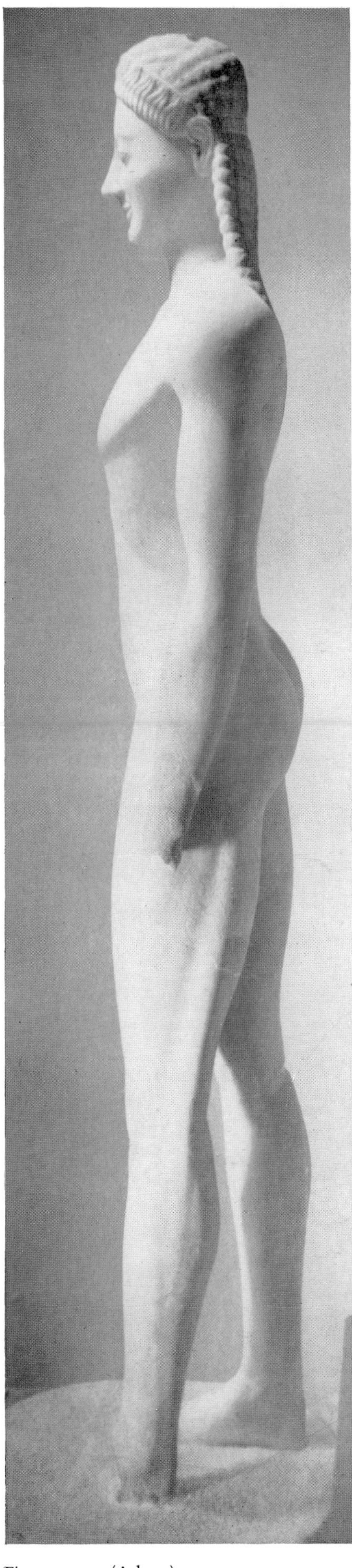

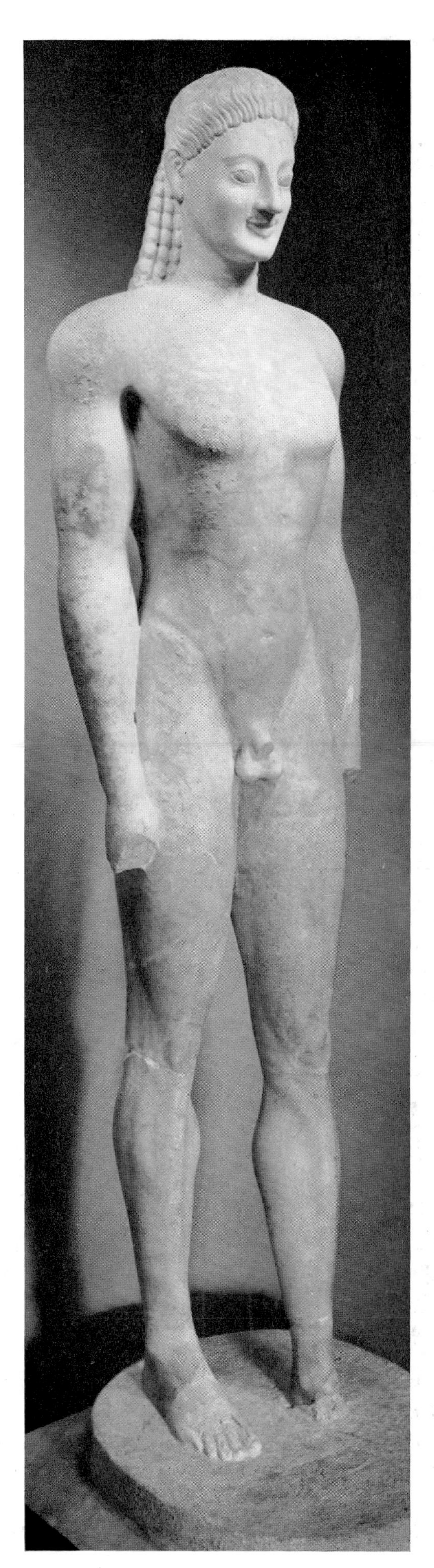

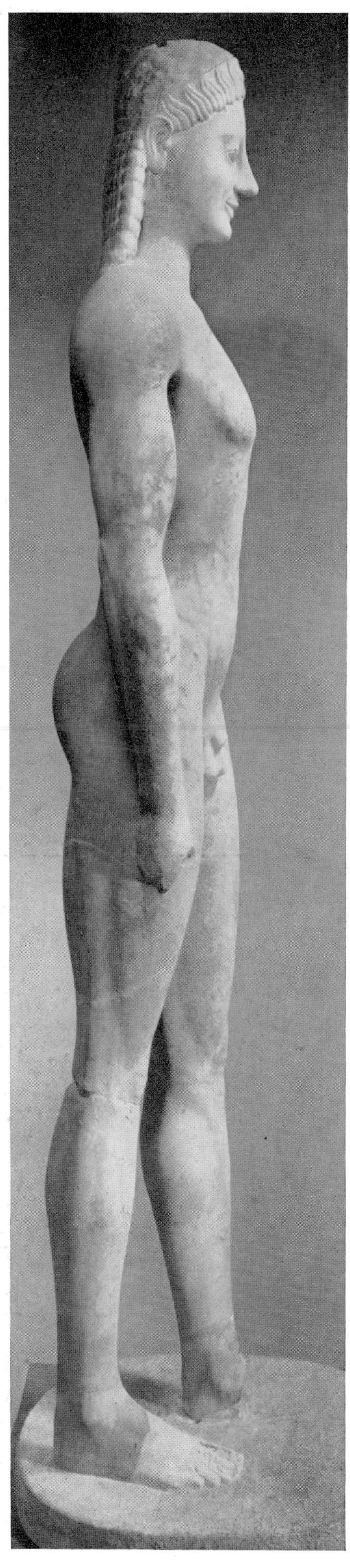

Figs. 210-212 (Athens)

Figs. 213-214 (Athens)

Figs. 215-216 (Athens)

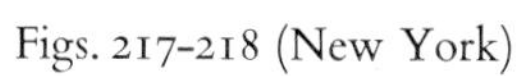
Figs. 217-218 (New York)

64

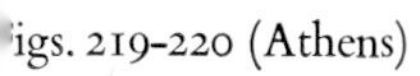
igs. 219-220 (Athens)

Figs. 221-222 (Paris)

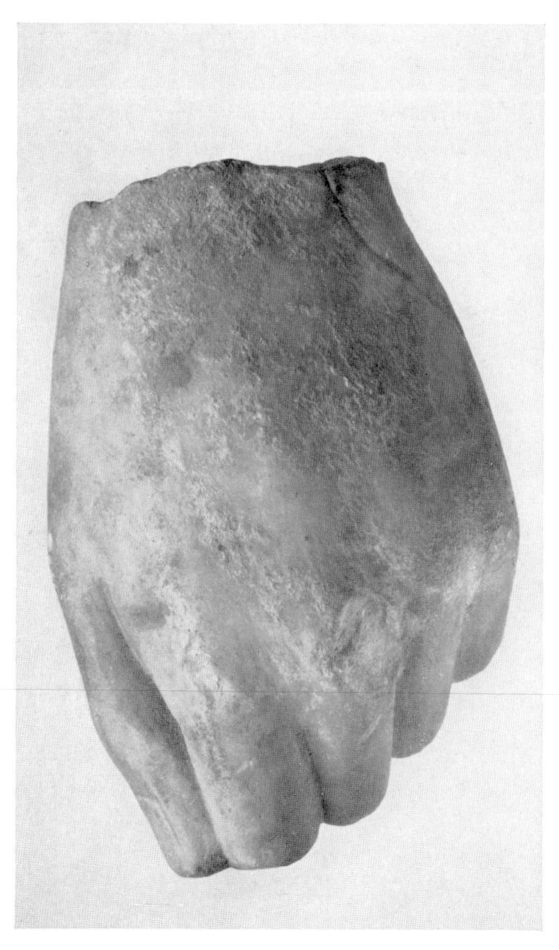

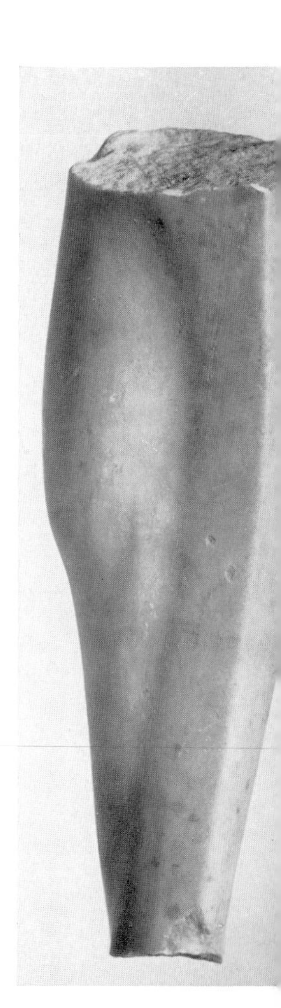

Figs. 223-225 (Paris)

Figs. 226-227 (London)

67

Figs. 228-229 (Athens)

68

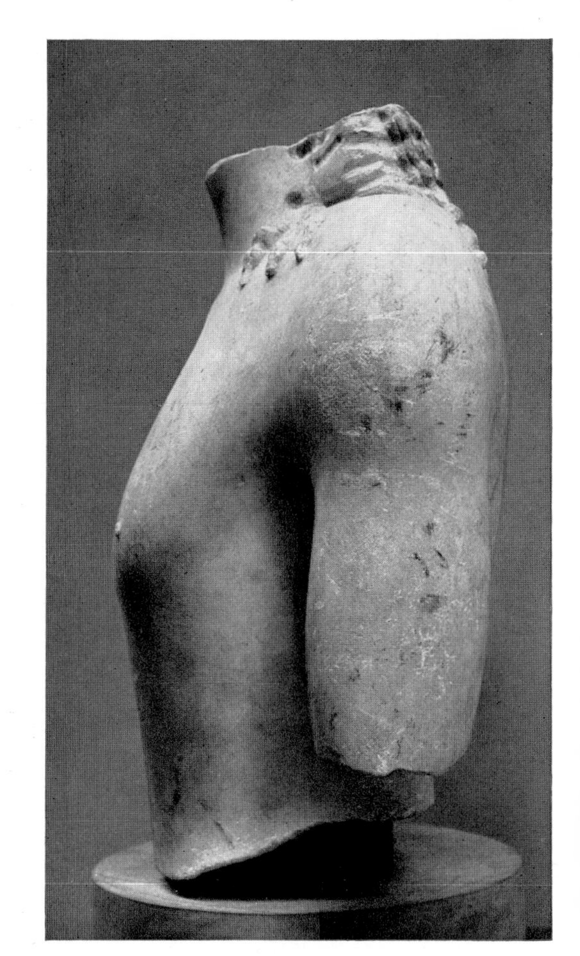

Figs. 230-231 (Boston)

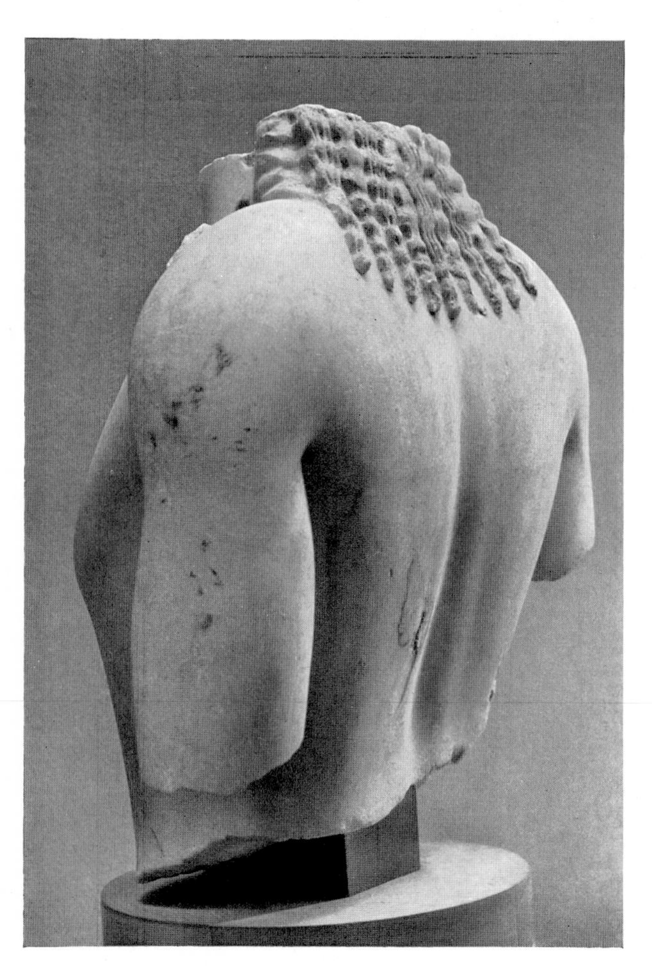

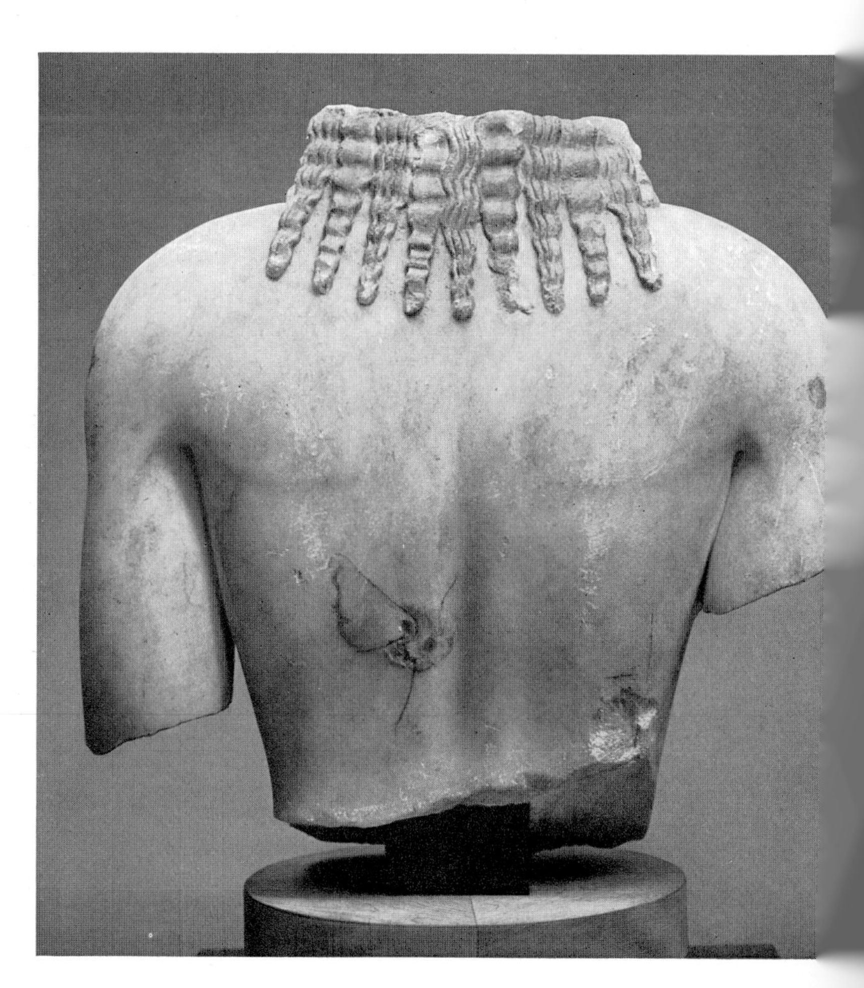

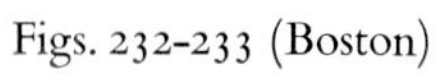

Figs. 232-233 (Boston)

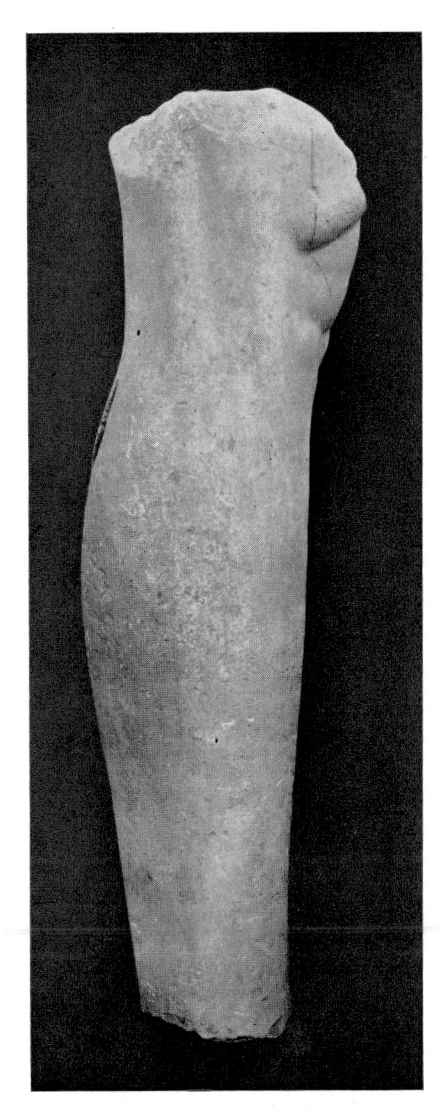

Figs. 234-235 (from Samos) 78

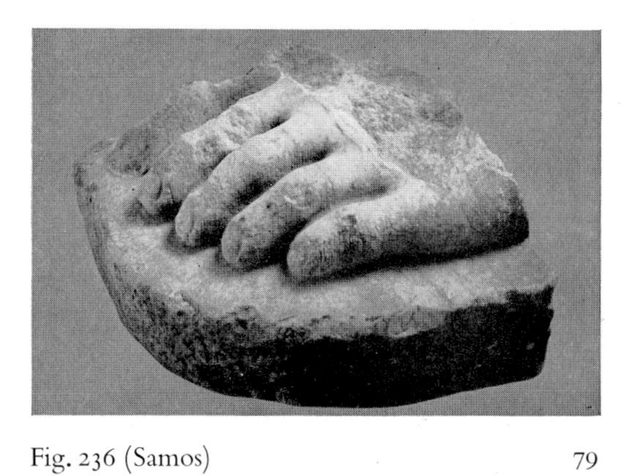

Fig. 236 (Samos) 79

Fig. 237 (Samos) 80

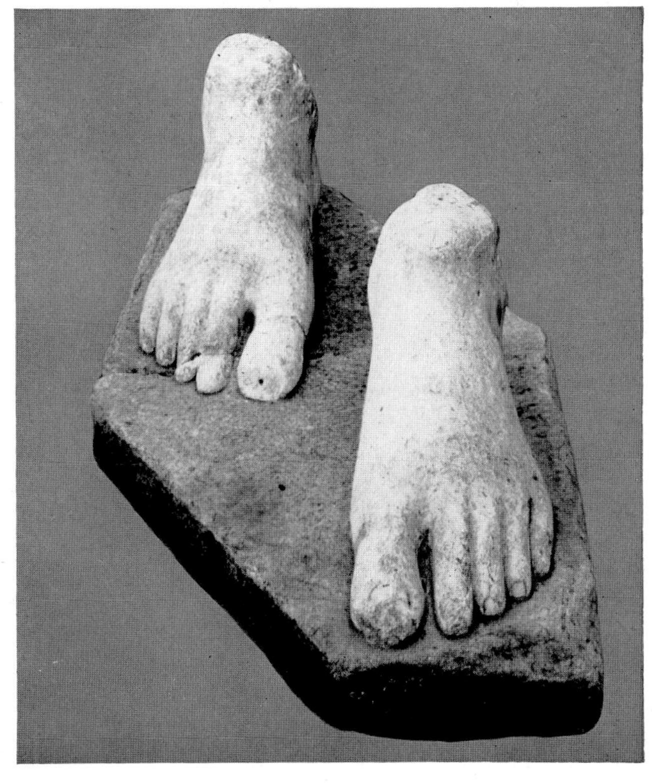

Fig. 238 (Samos) 80

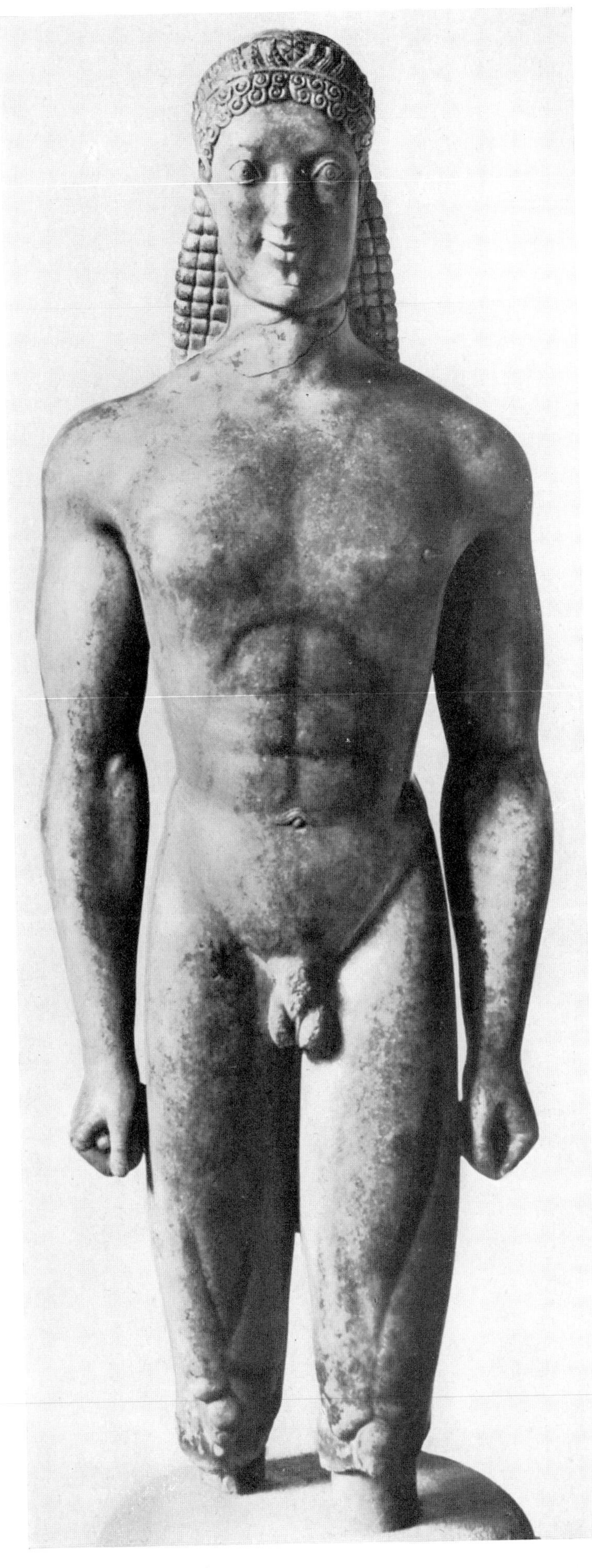

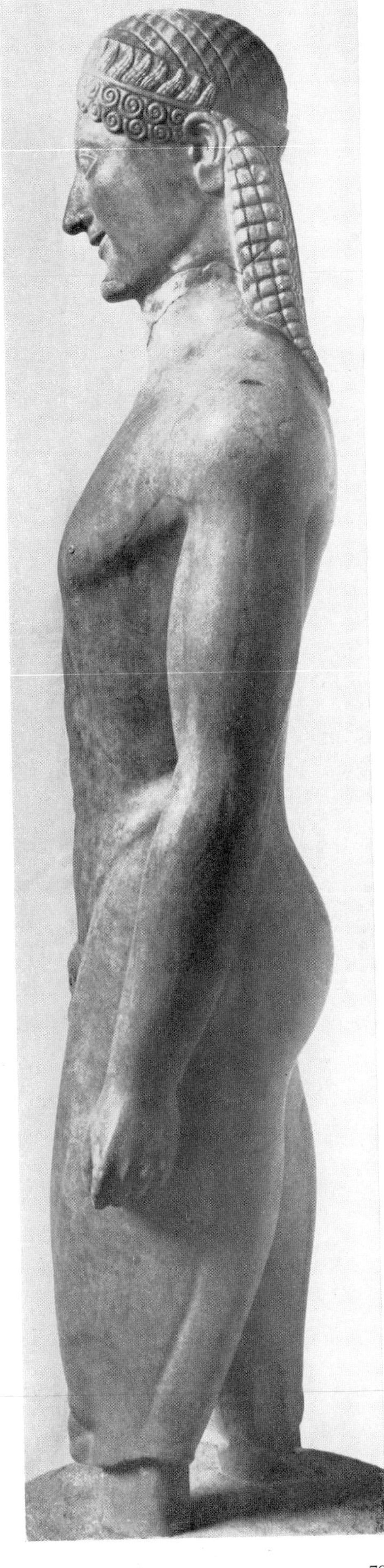

Figs. 239-240 (Florence)

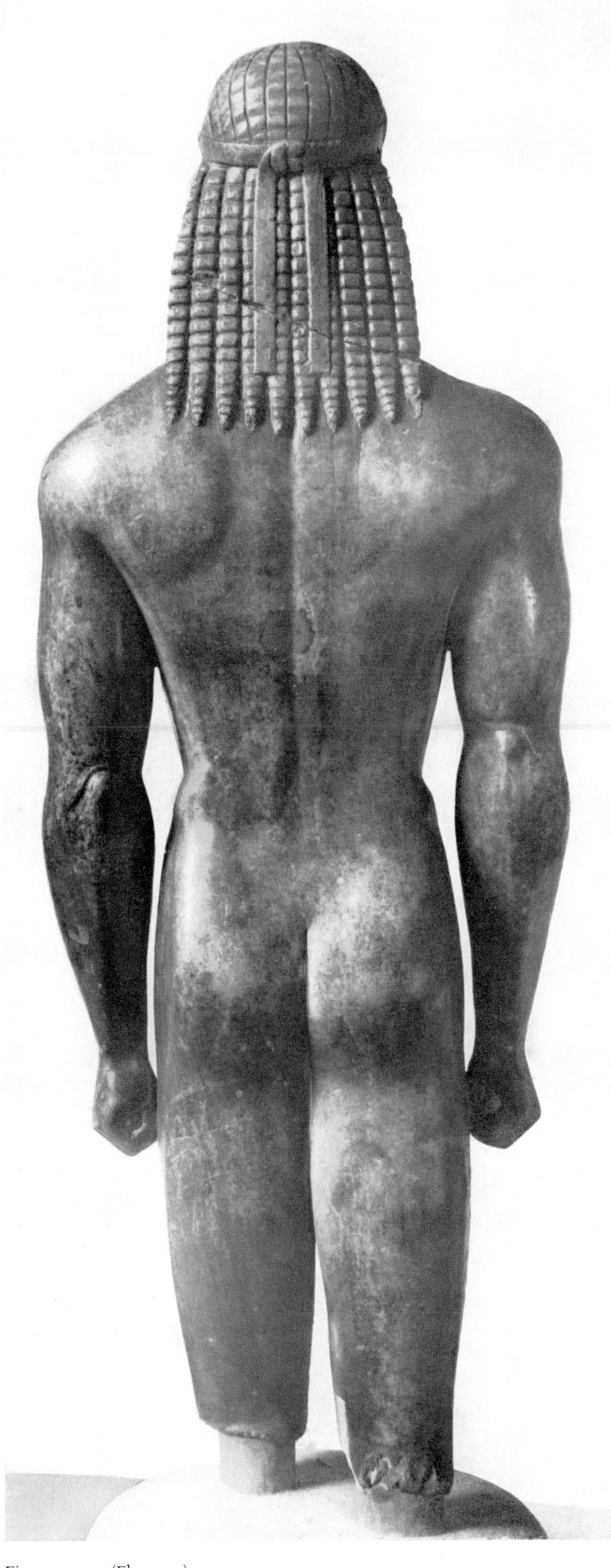

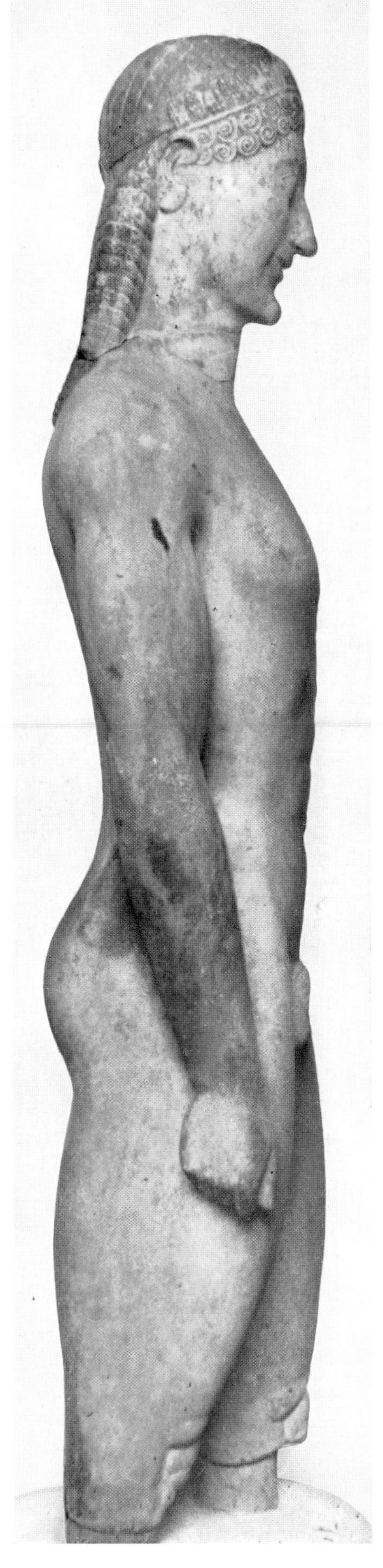

Figs. 241-242 (Florence)

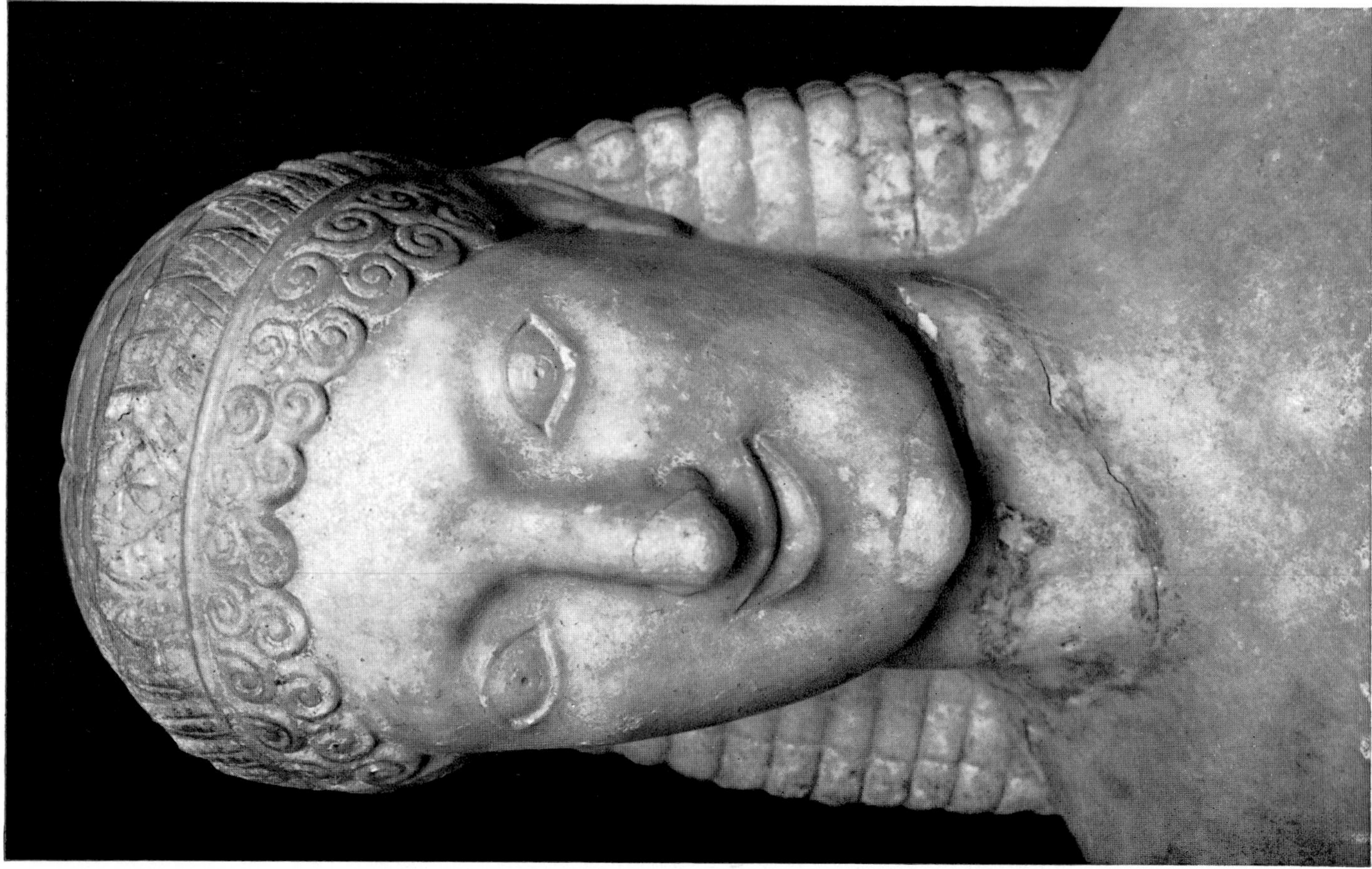

Figs. 245-246 (Munich)

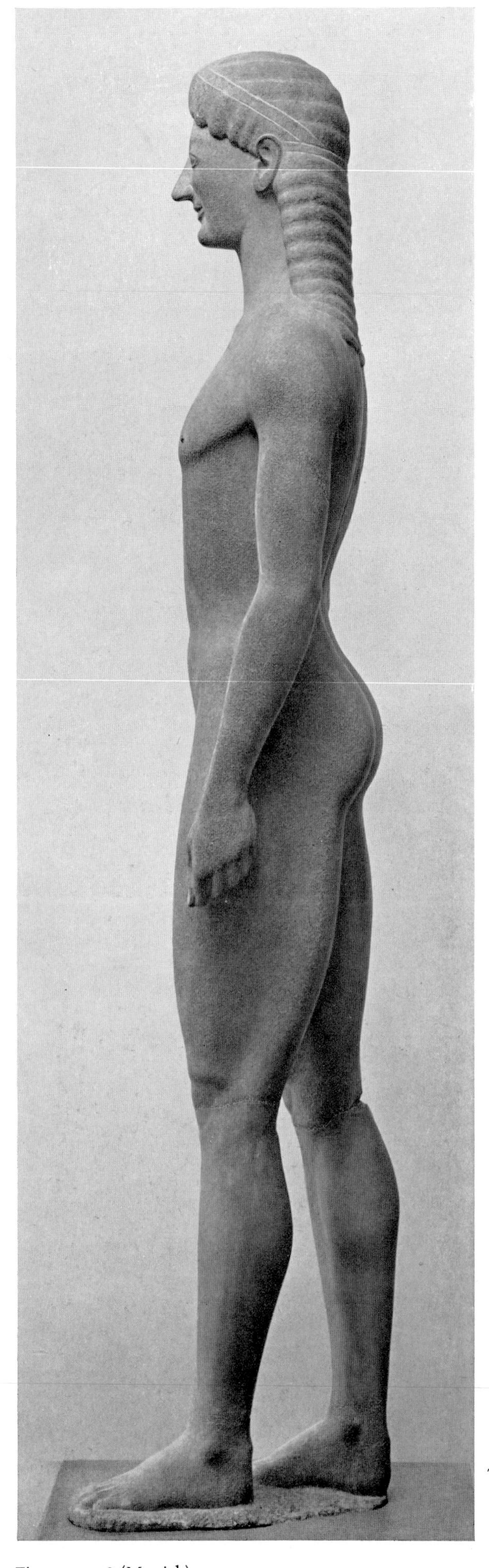

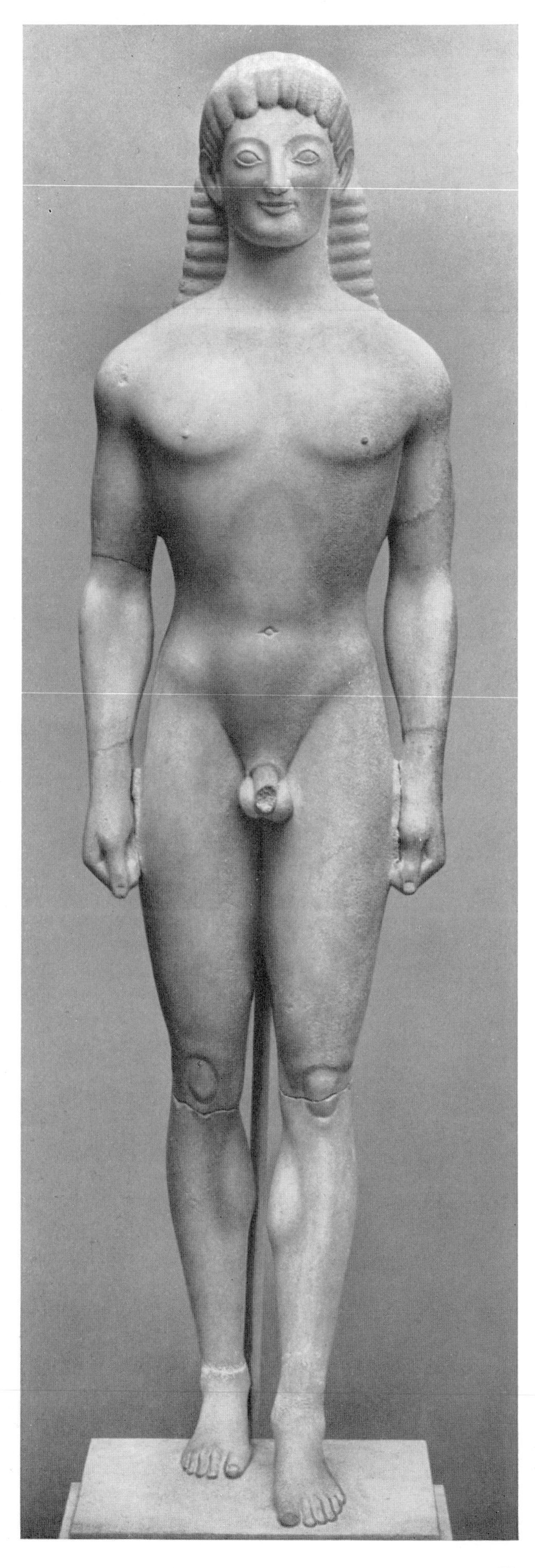

Figs. 247-248 (Munich)

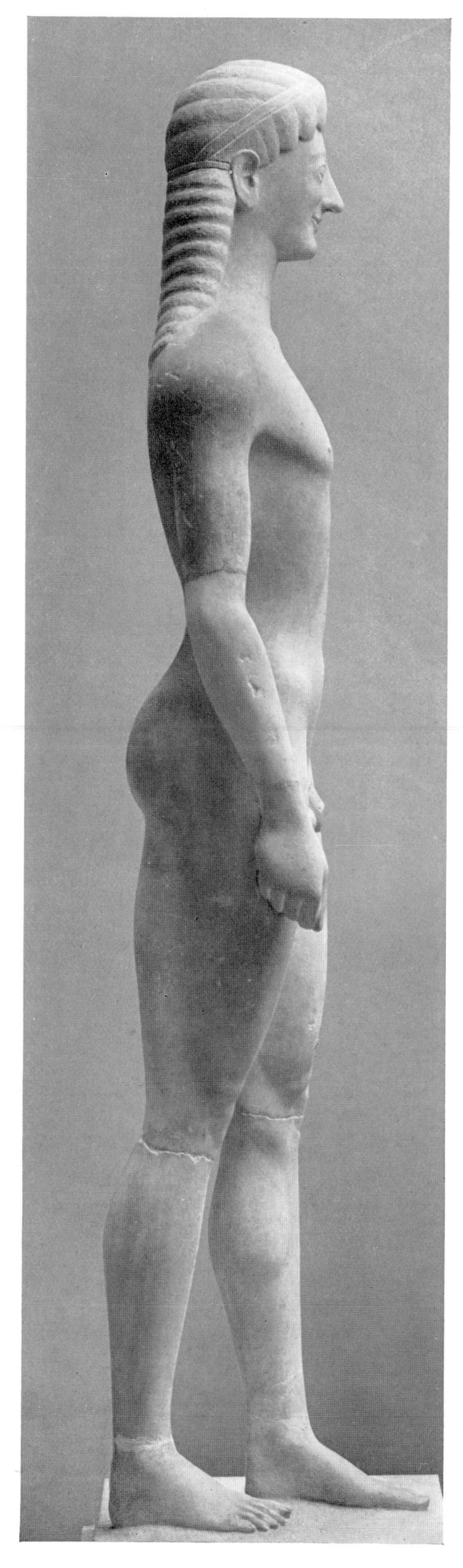

Figs. 249-250 (Munich)

Figs. 251-252 (Munich)

Fig. 253 (Athens) 72

Fig. 254 (Thebes) 75

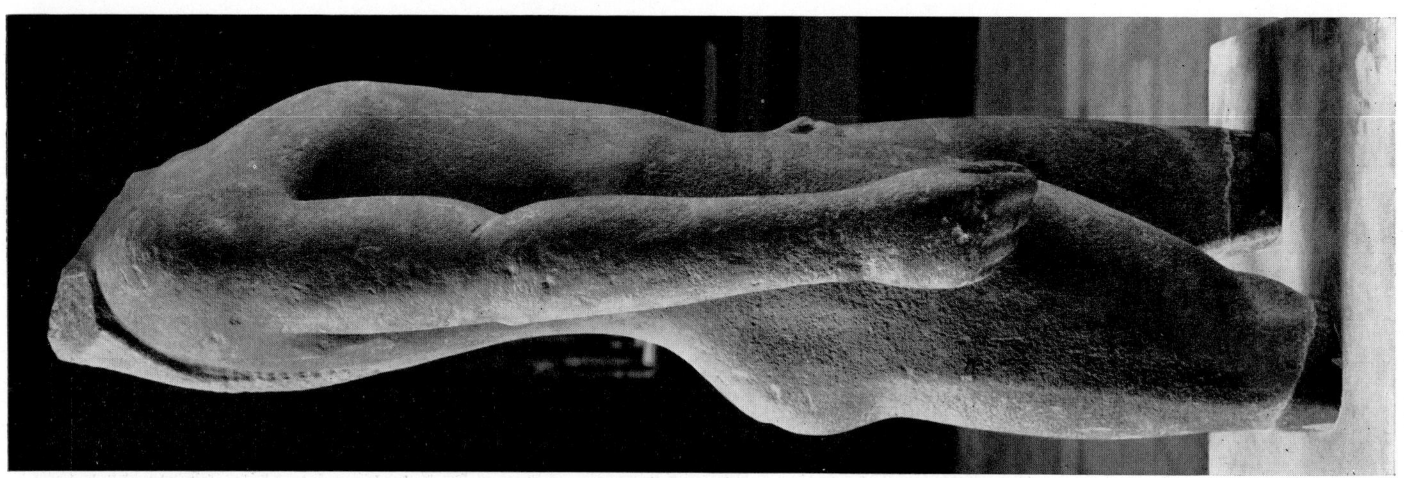

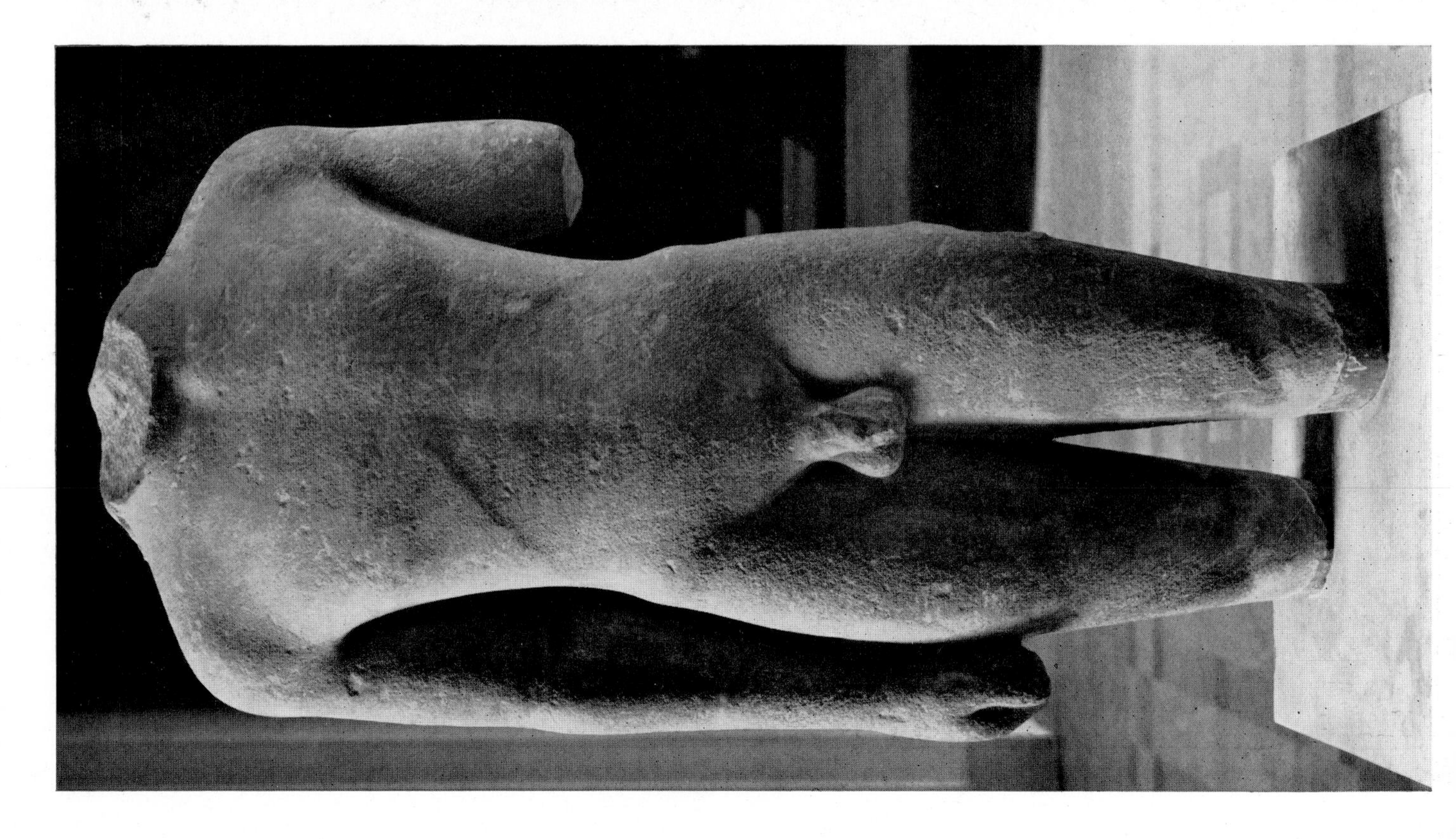

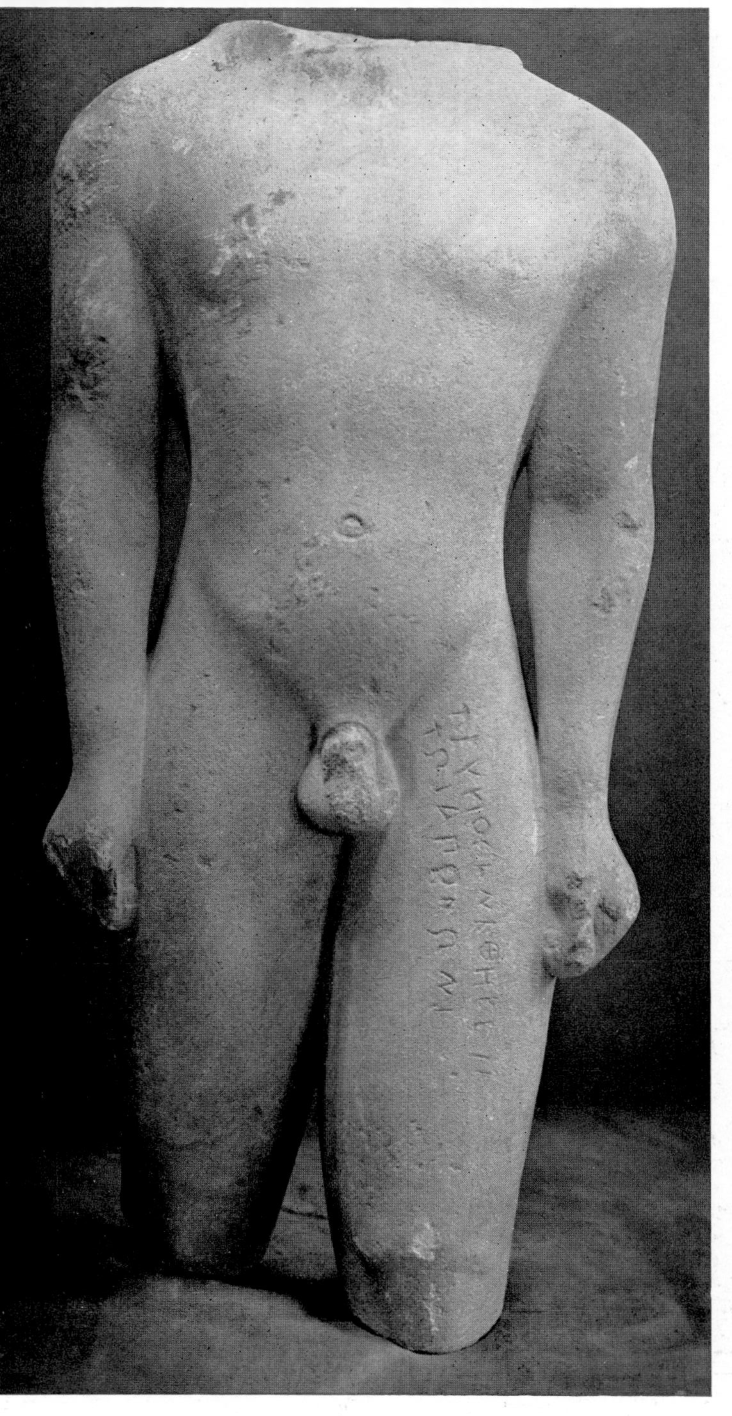

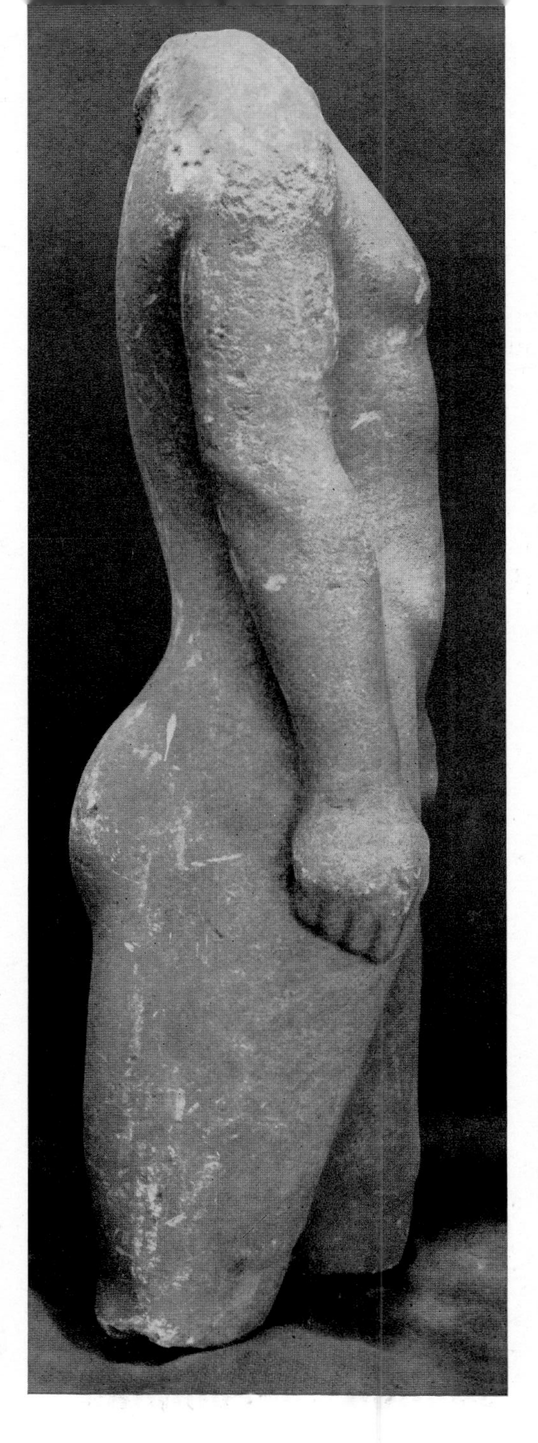

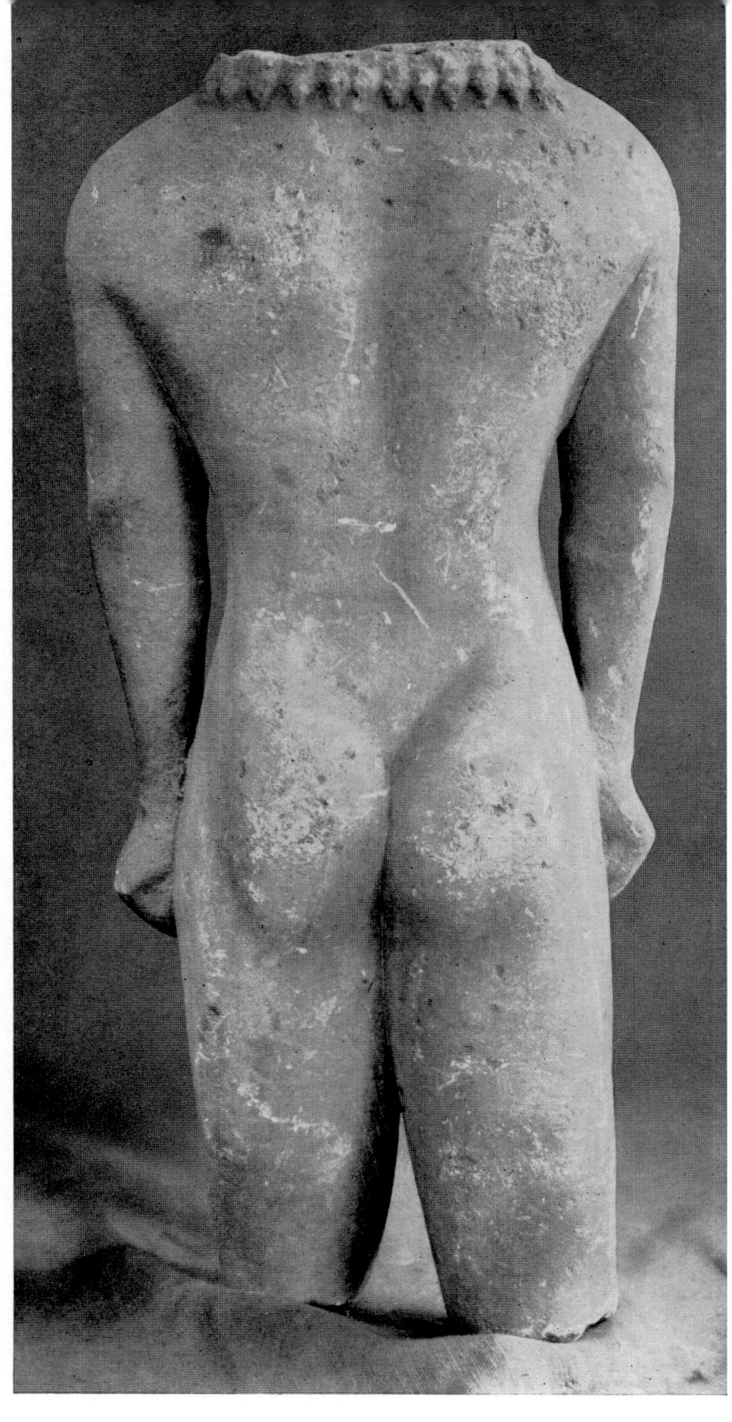

Figs. 258-260 (Samos)

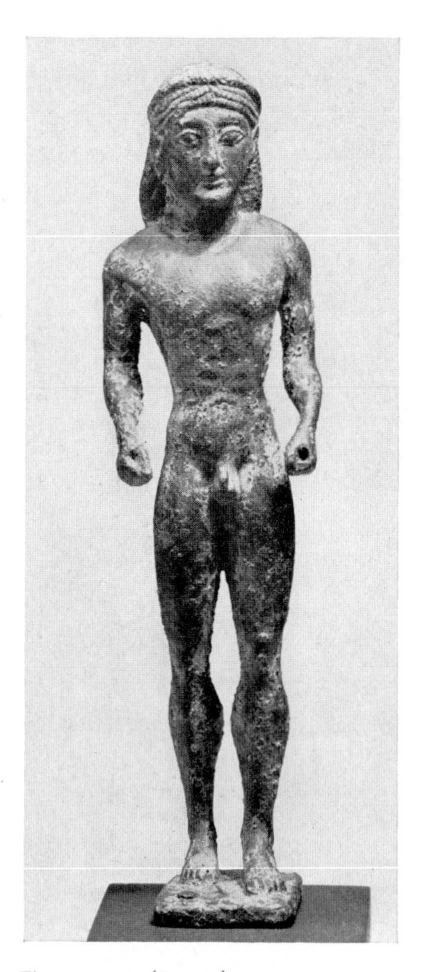

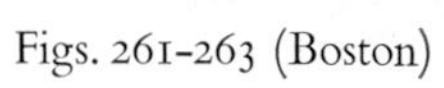

Figs. 261-263 (Boston) 76

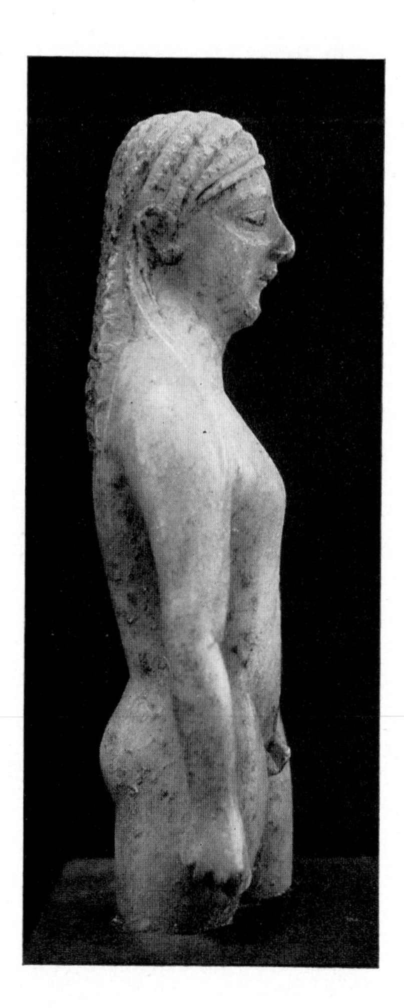

Figs. 264-266 (Moscow) 82

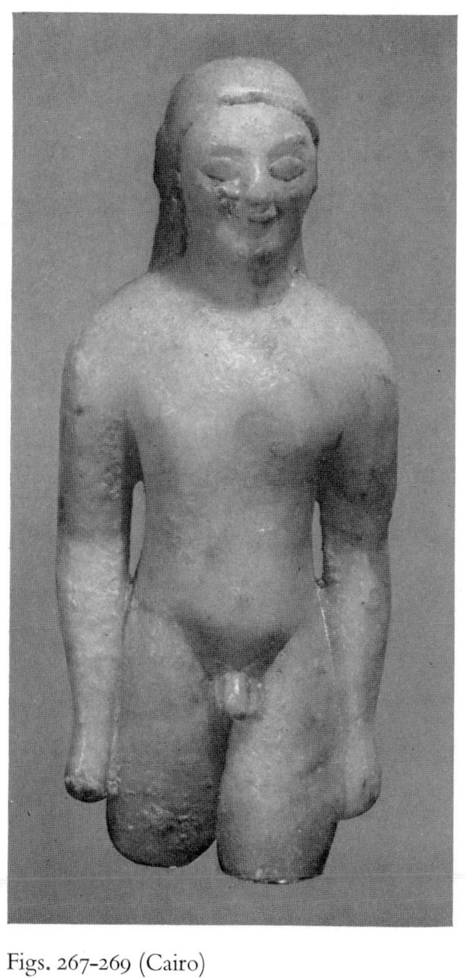

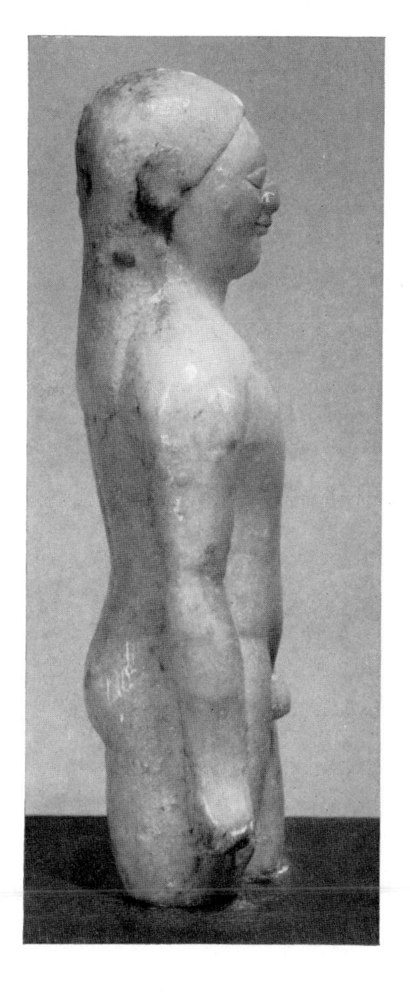

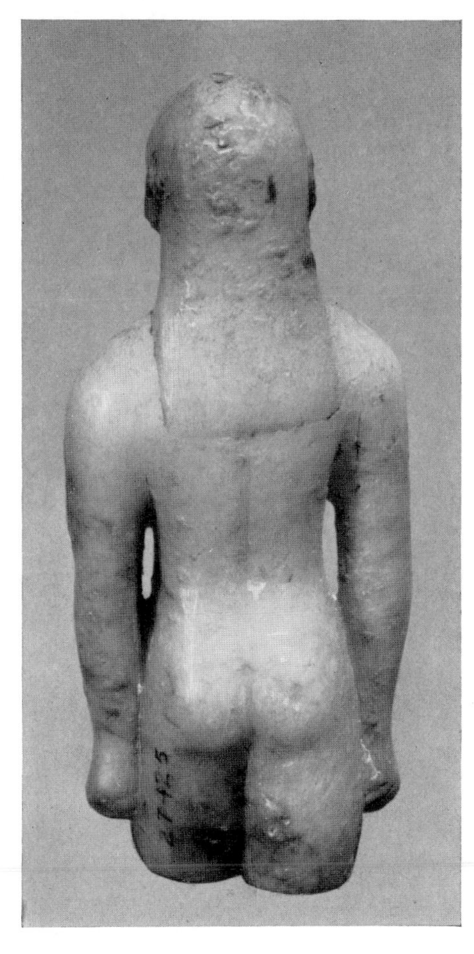

Figs. 267-269 (Cairo) 81

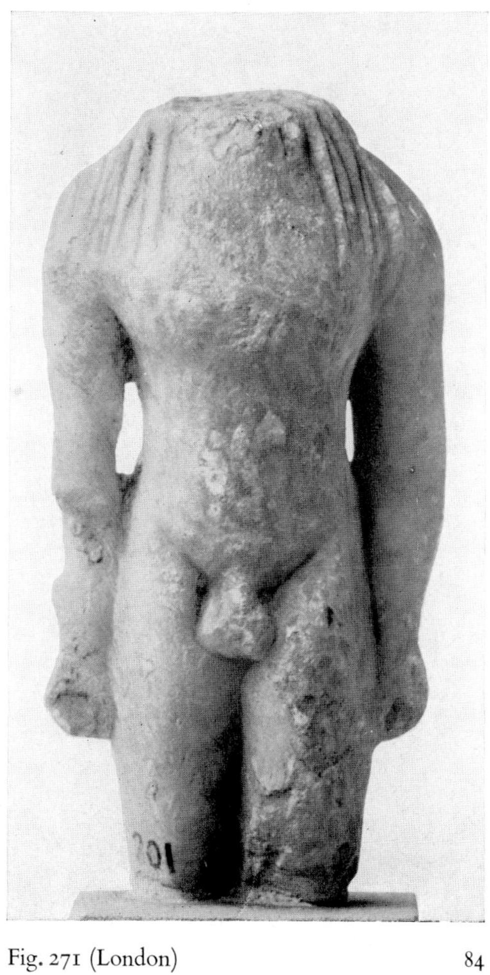

270 (London) 83

Fig. 271 (London) 84

Fig. 272 (Boston) 85

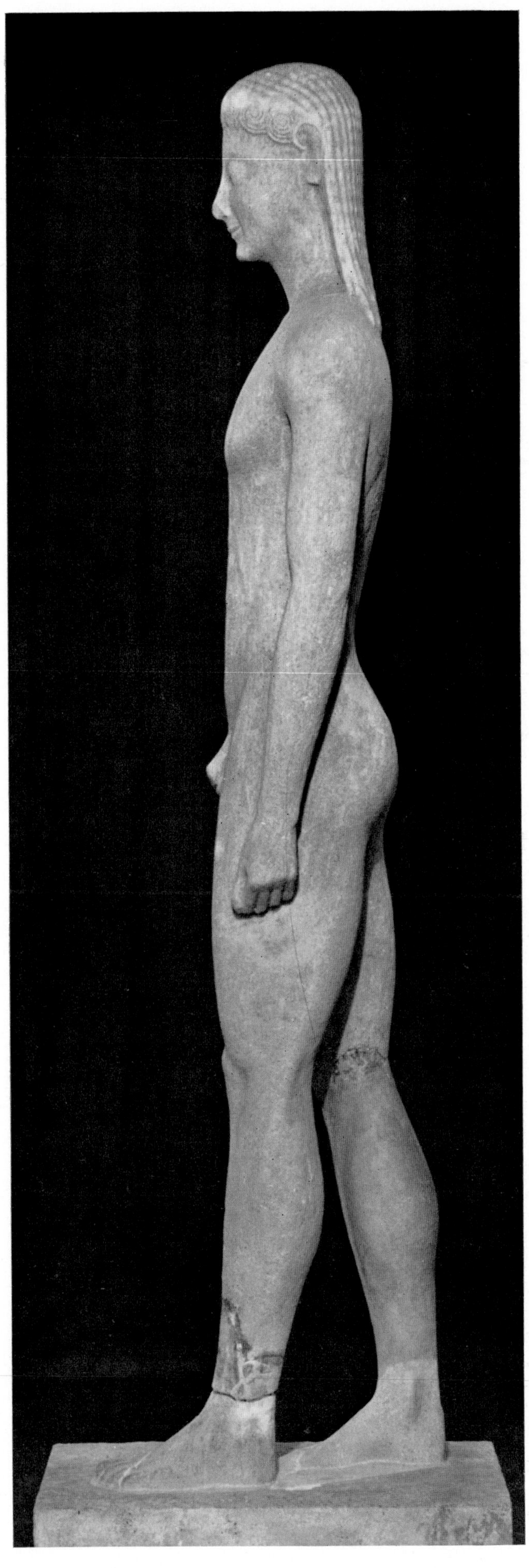

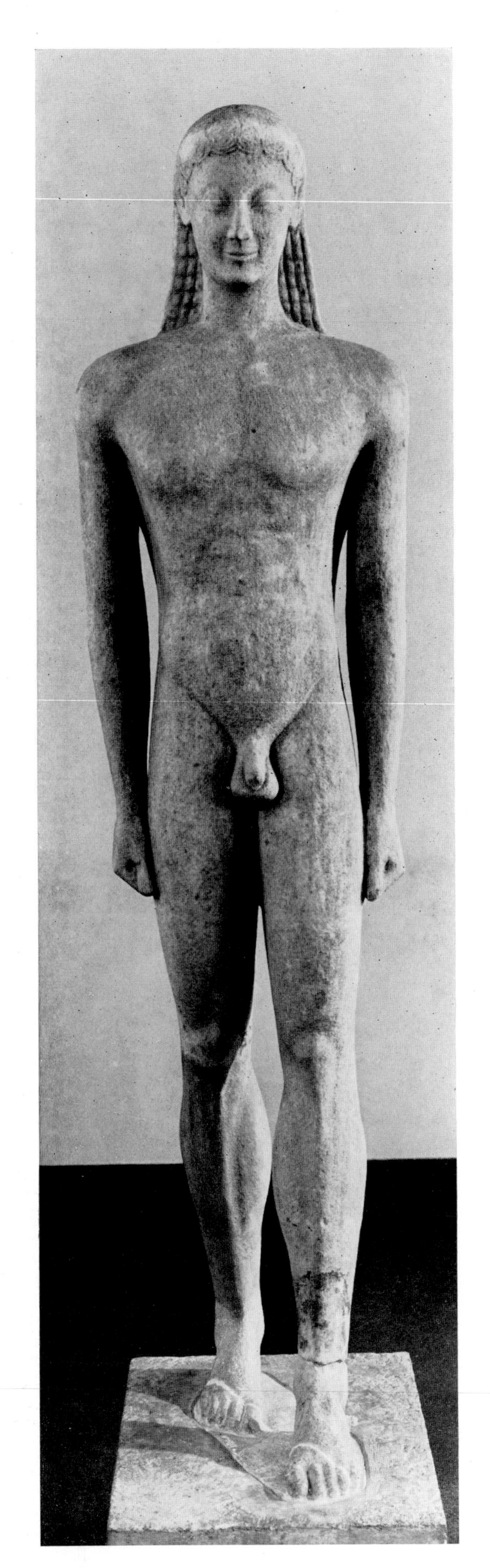

Figs. 273-274 (Athens)

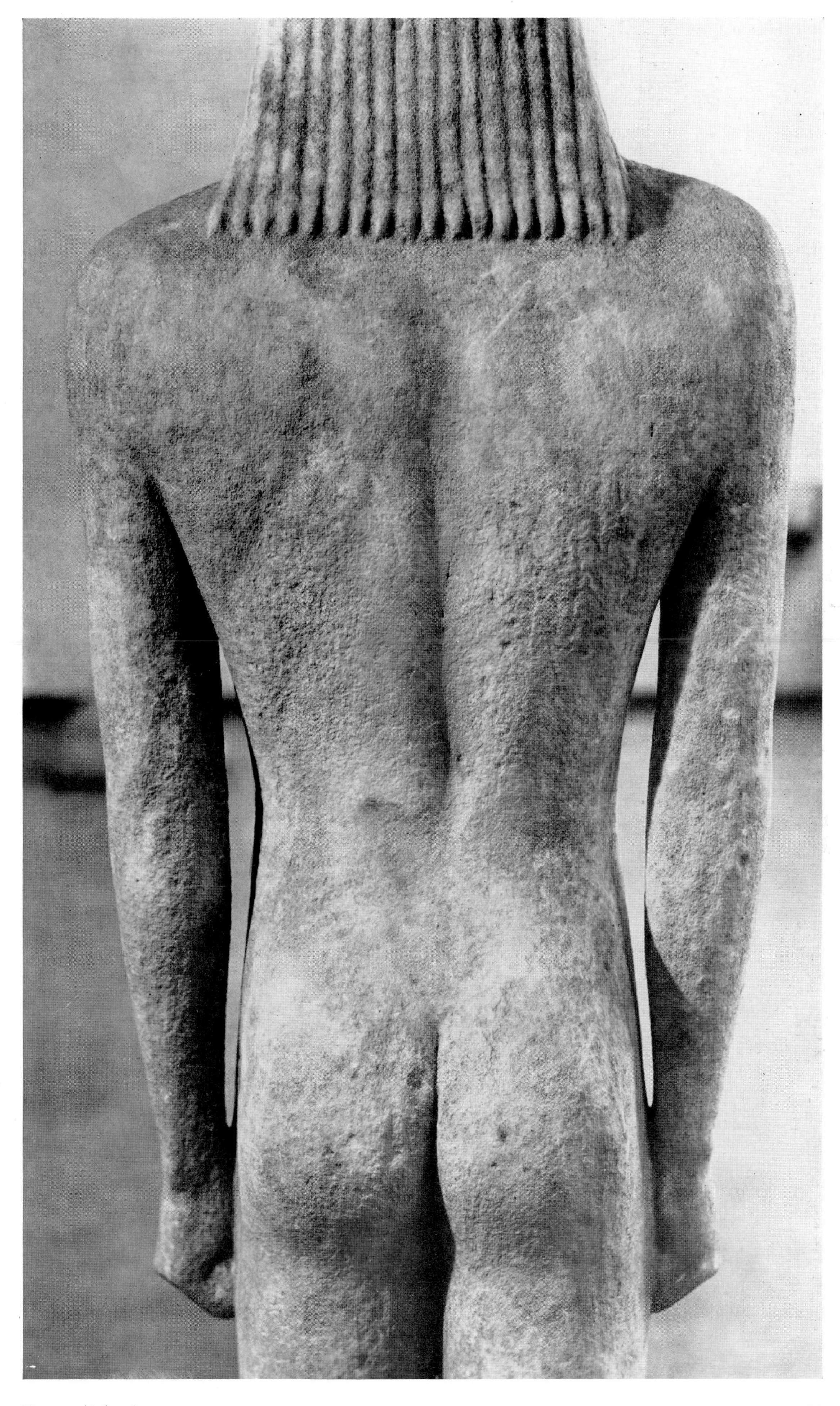

Fig. 275 (Athens)

Figs. 276-278 (Athens)

Fig. 279 (Athens)

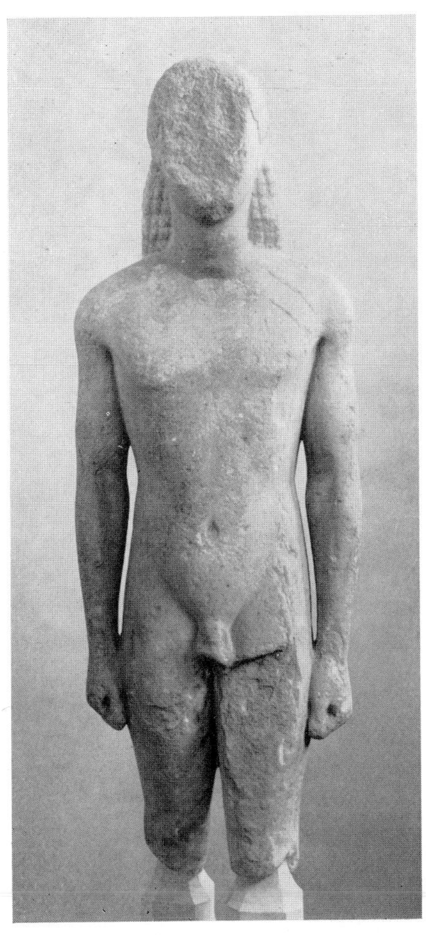

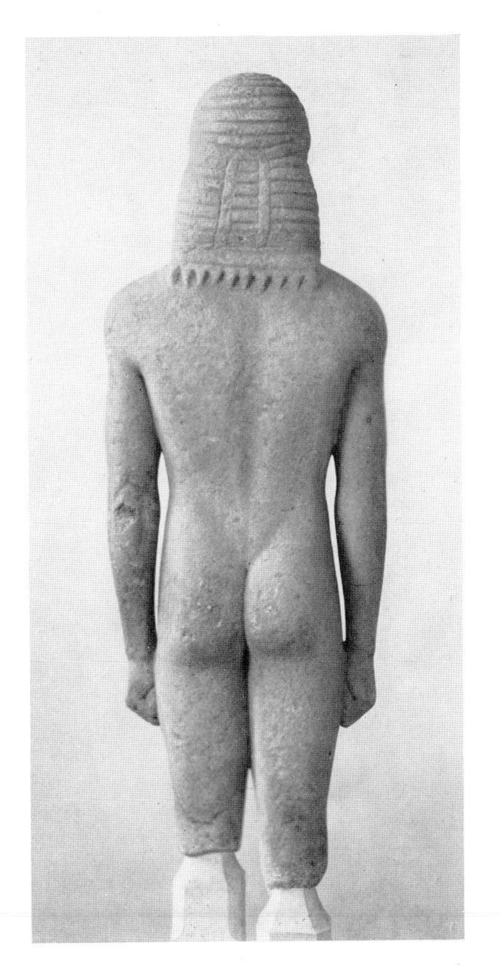

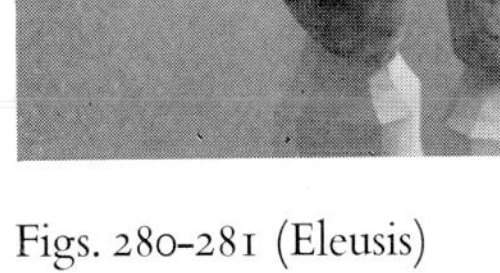

Figs. 280-281 (Eleusis)

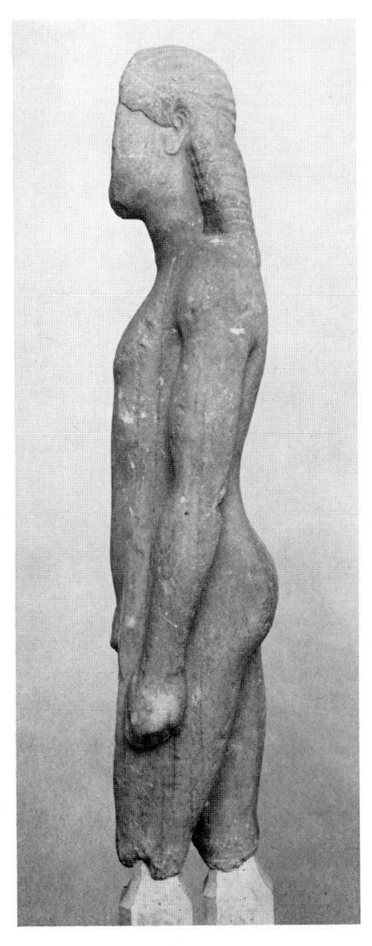

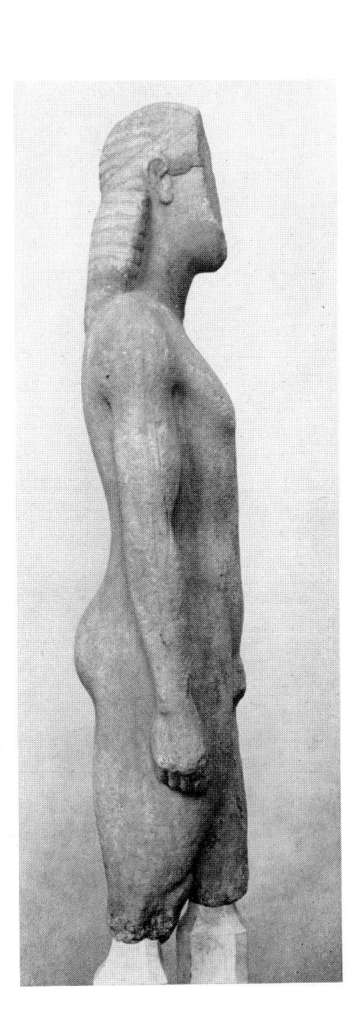

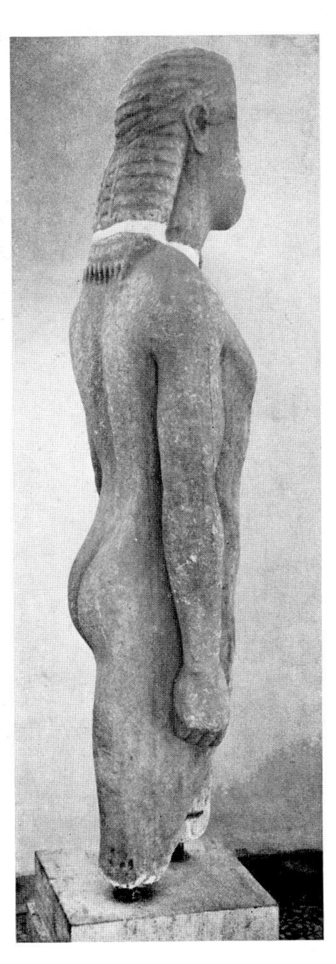

Figs. 282-284 (Eleusis)

87

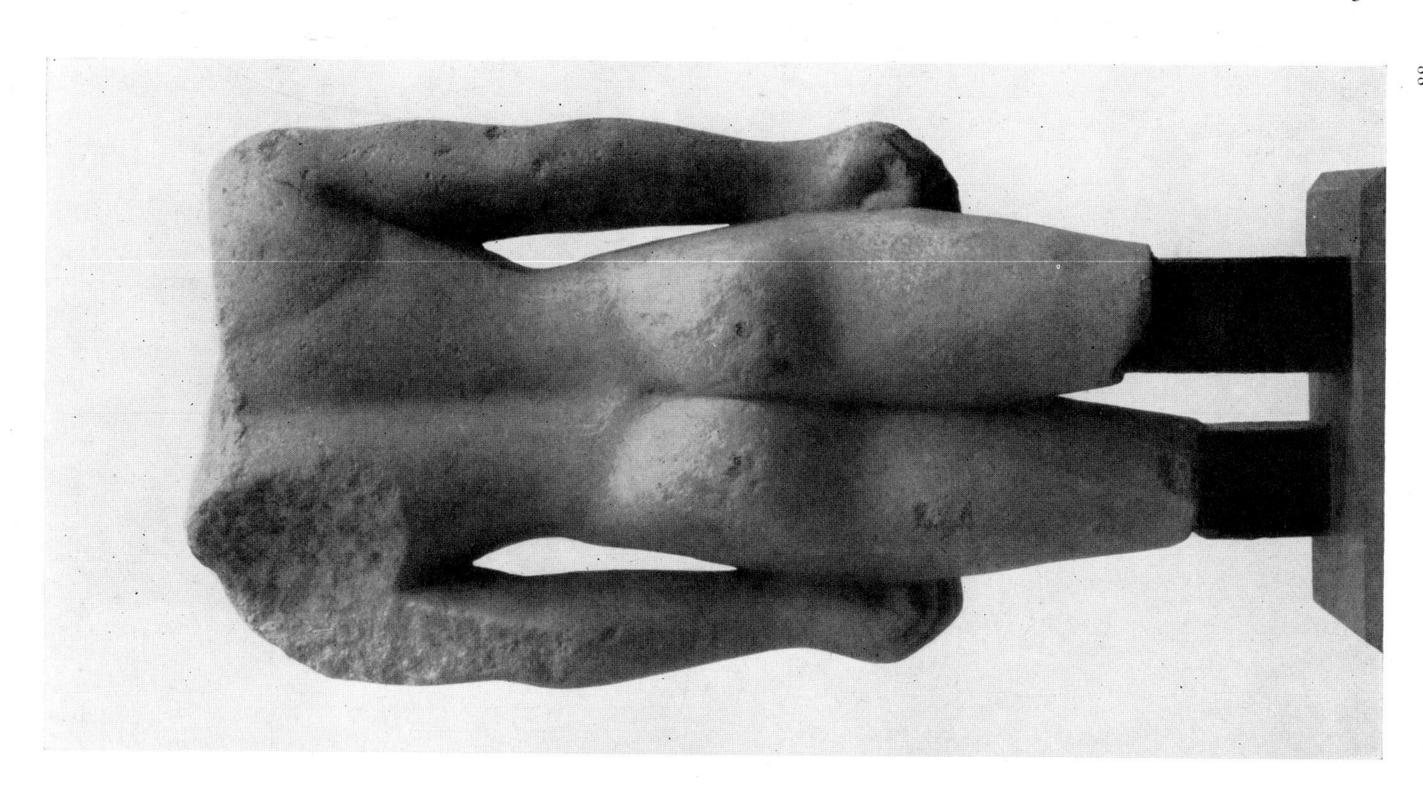

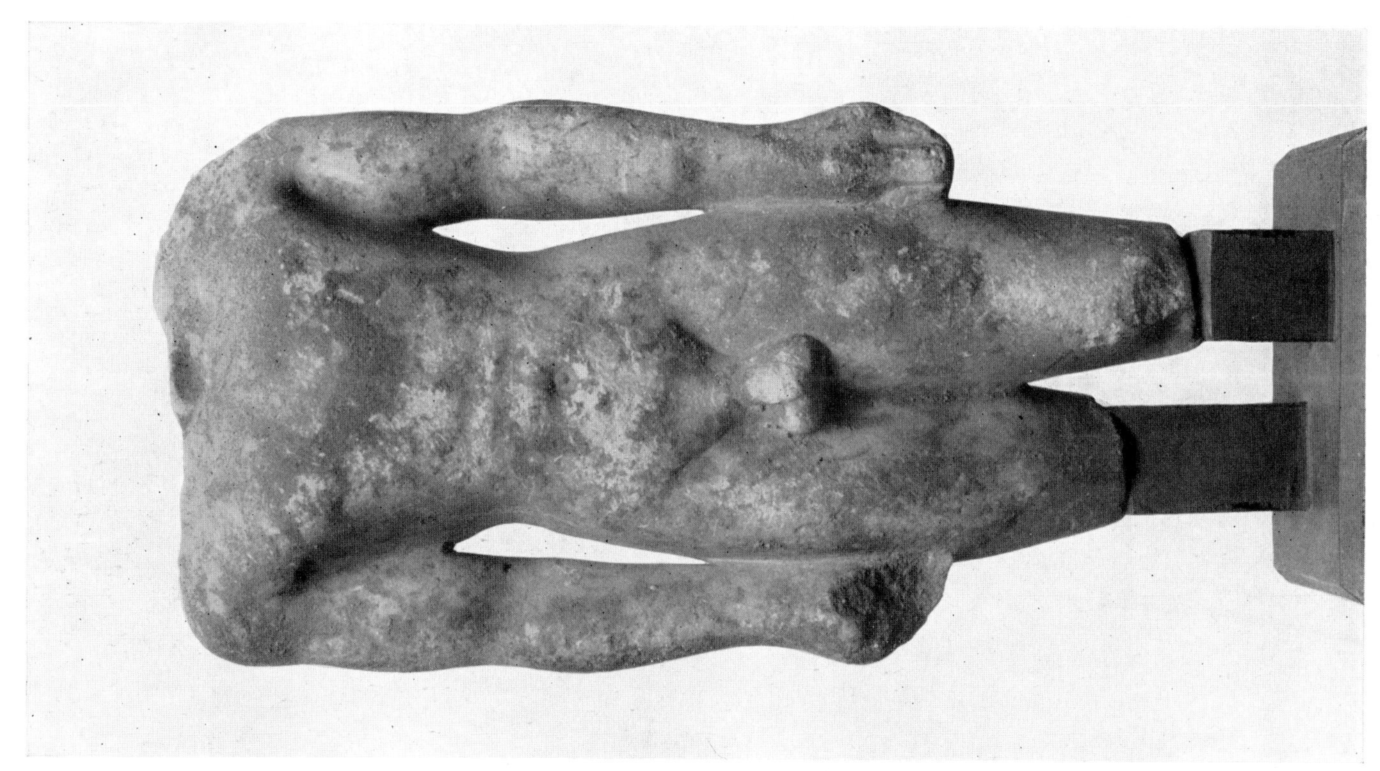

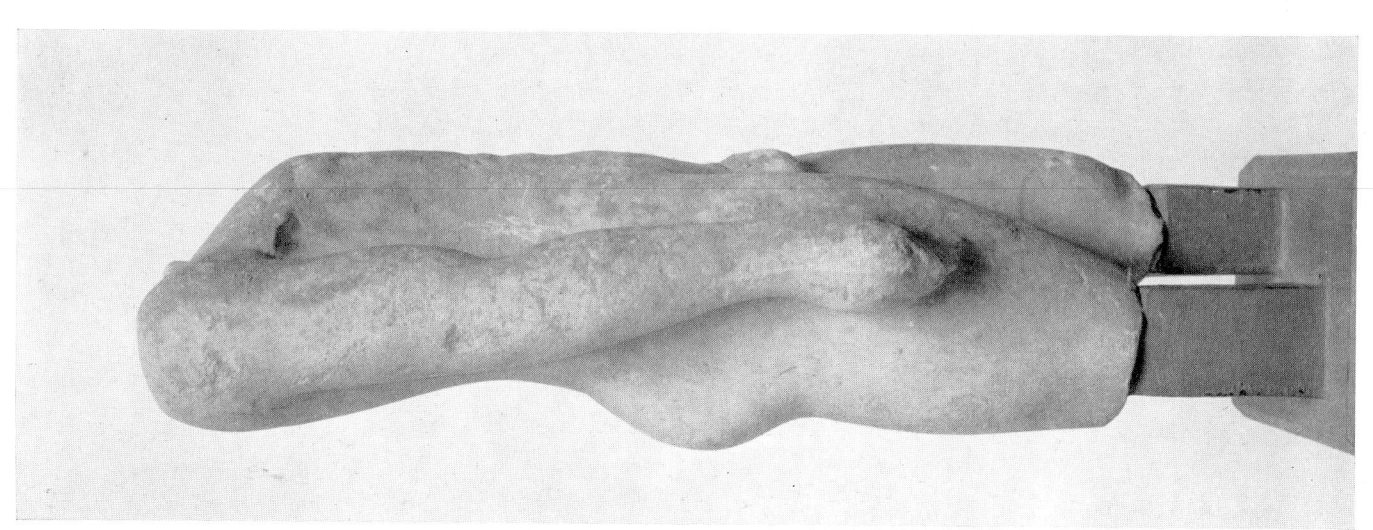

Figs. 285-287 (Athens)

Figs. 288–290 (Geneva)

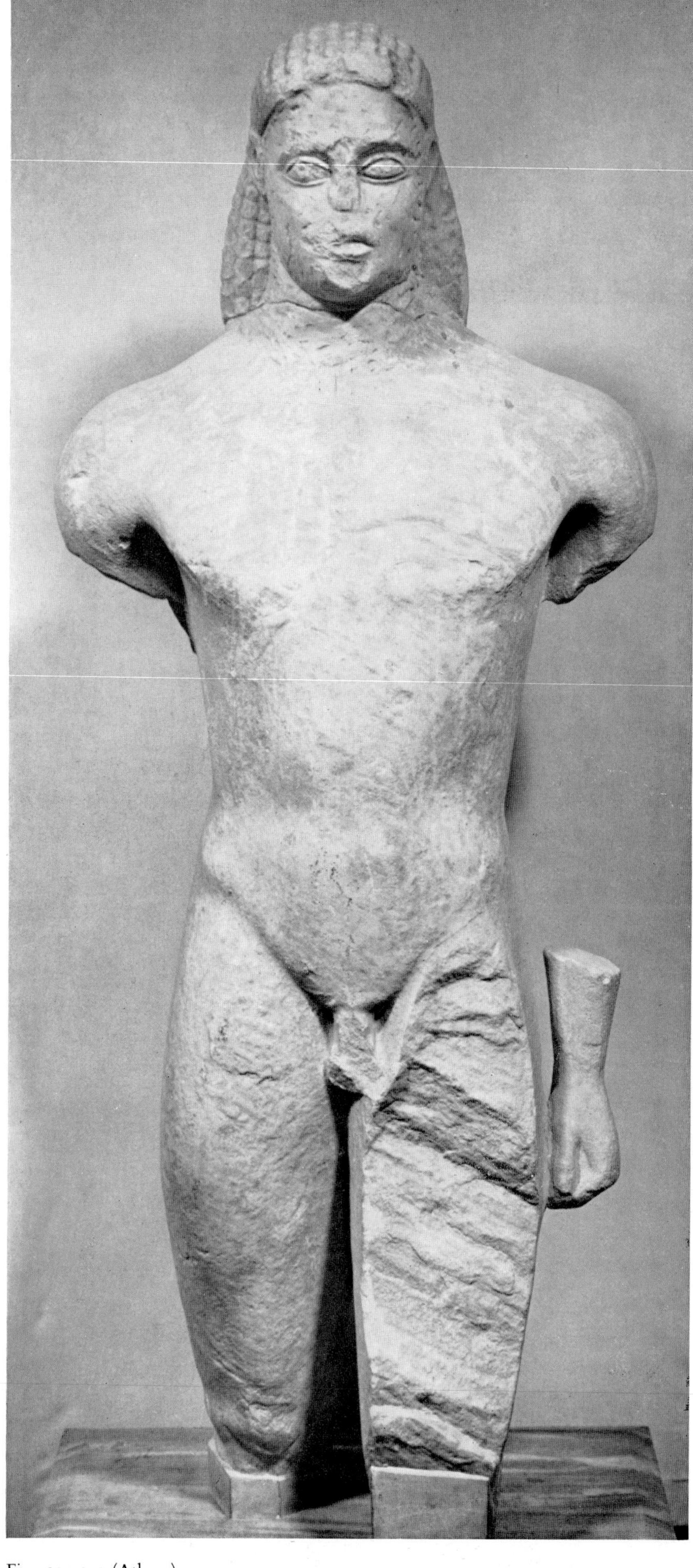

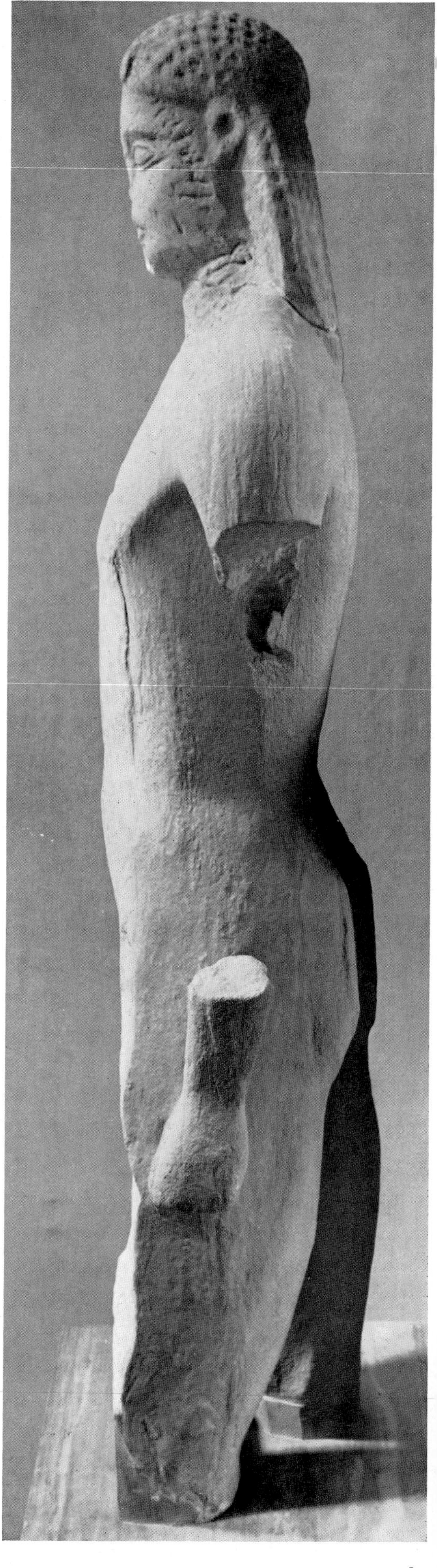

Figs. 291-292 (Athens)

Figs. 293-294 (Athens)

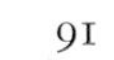

91

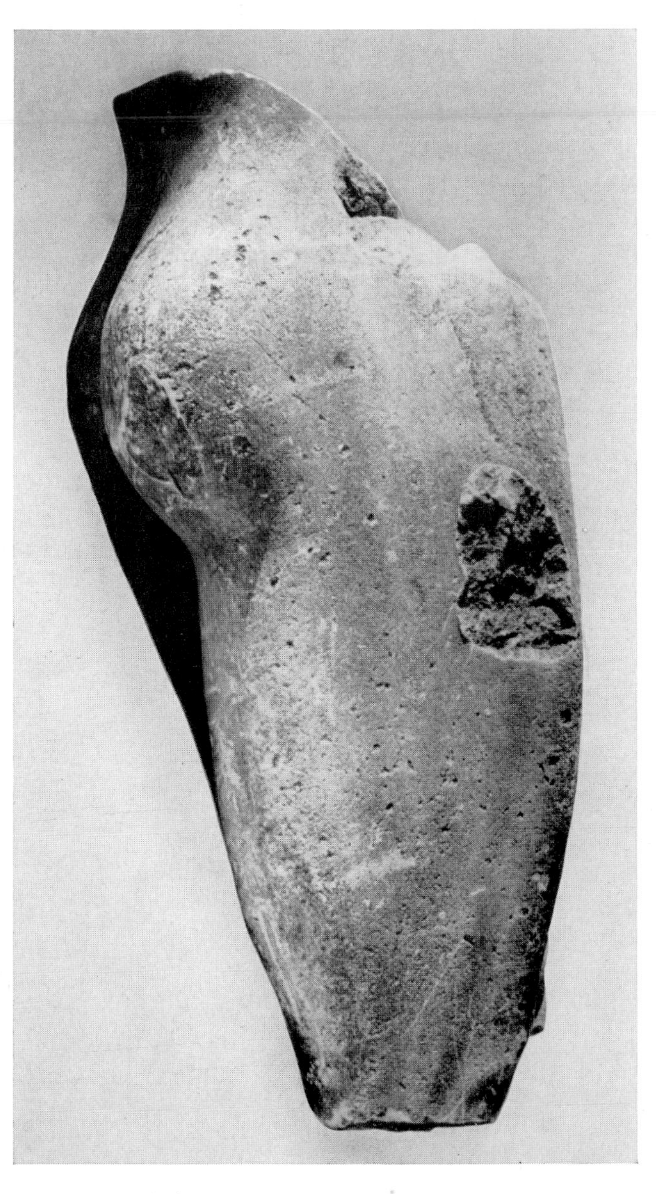

Figs. 295-296 (Athens)

91

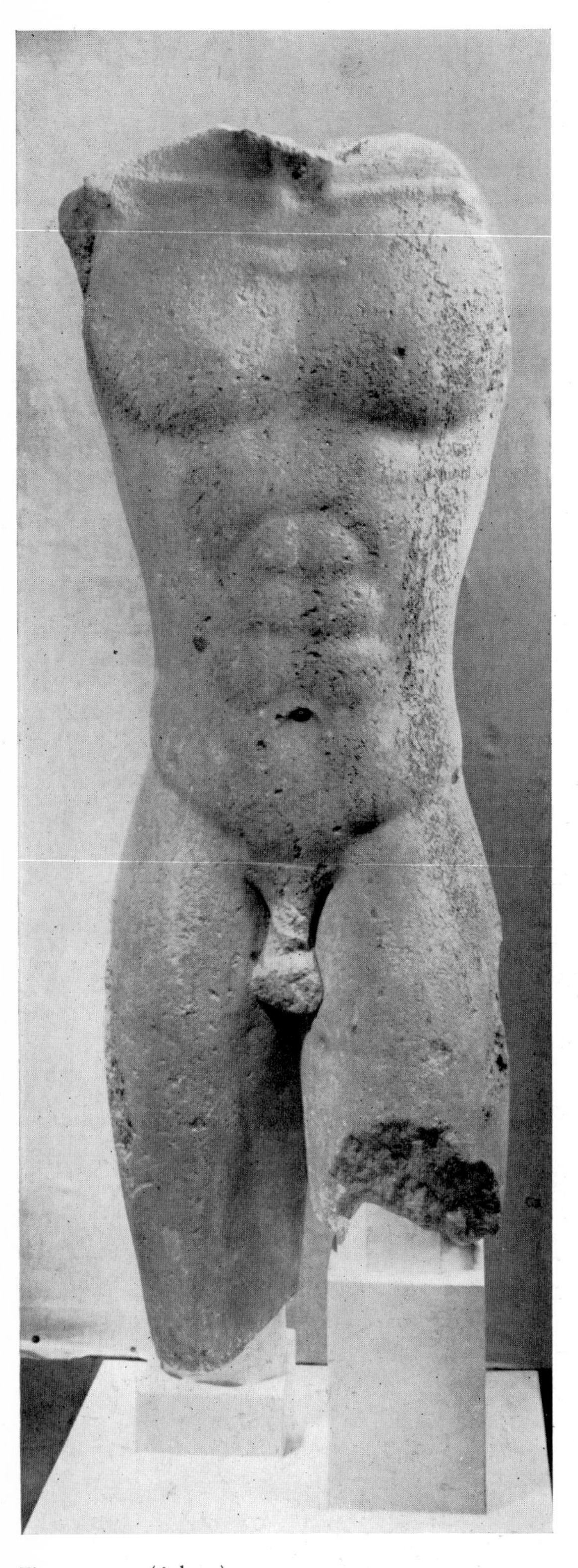

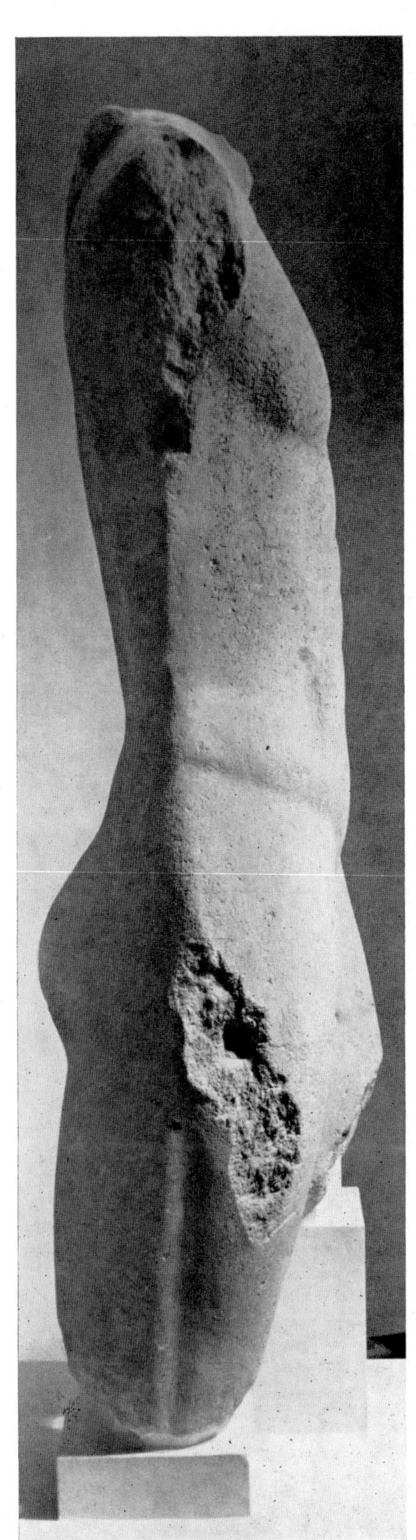

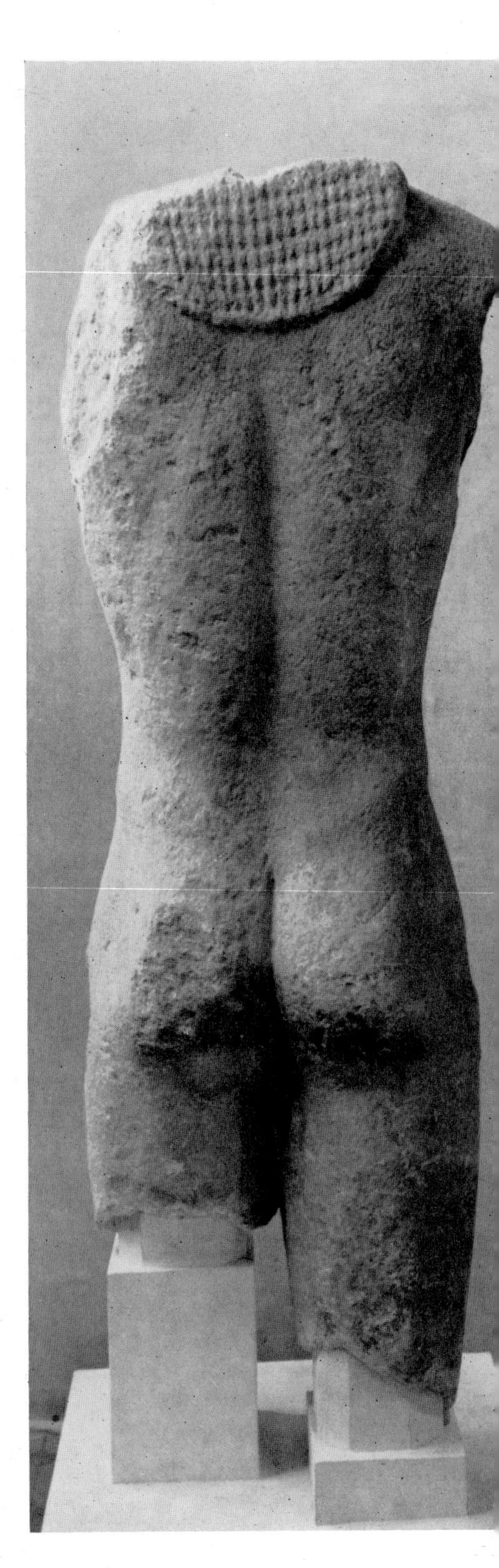

Figs. 297-299 (Athens)

300-301 (Eleusis)

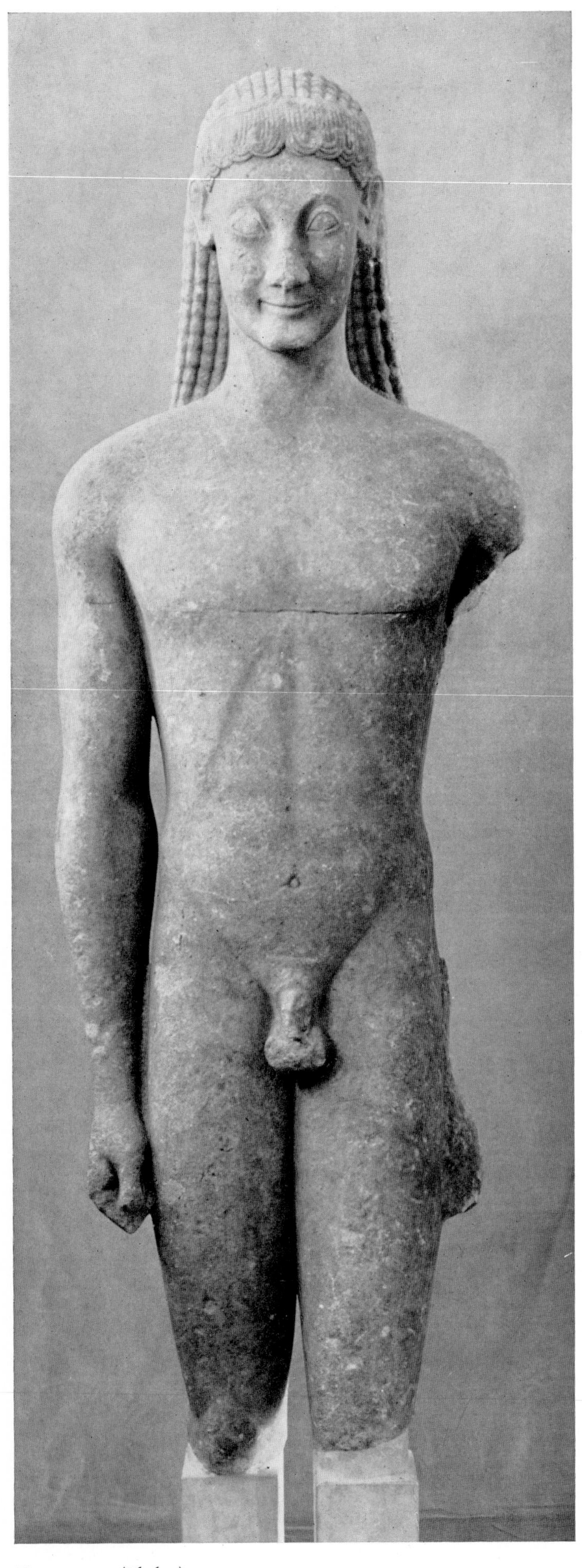

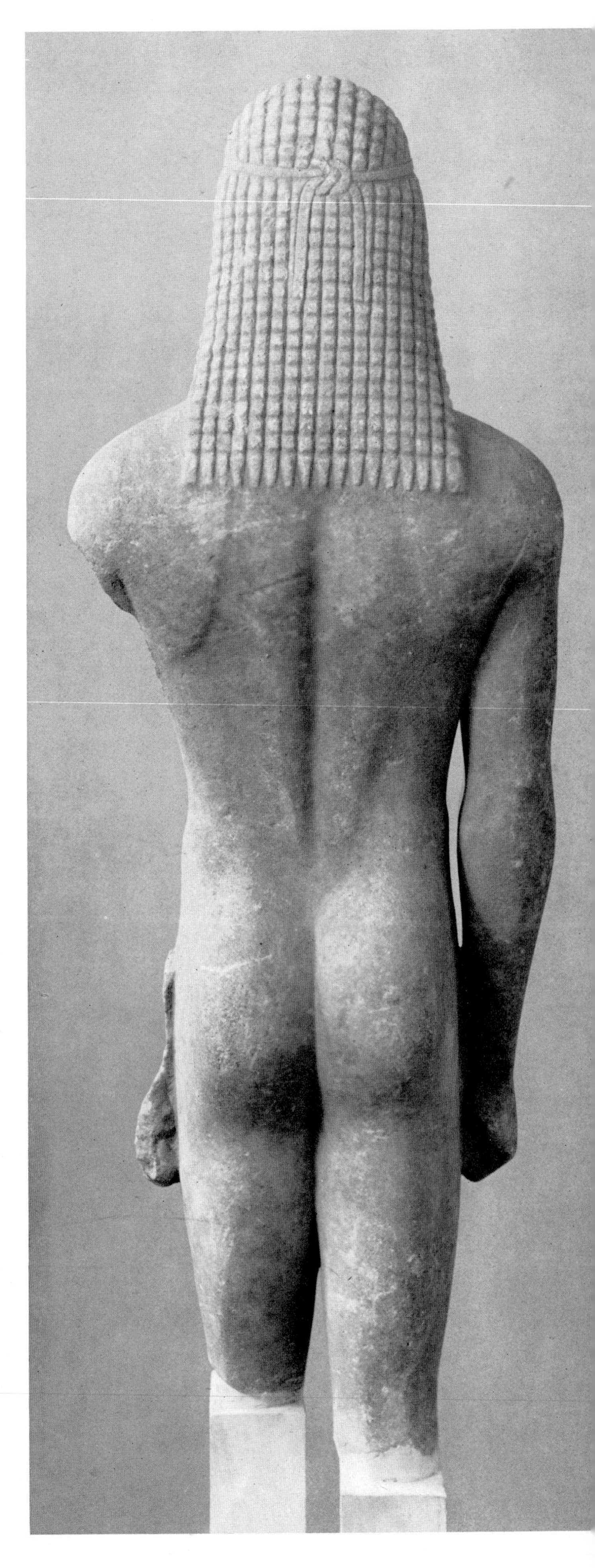

Figs. 302-303 (Thebes)

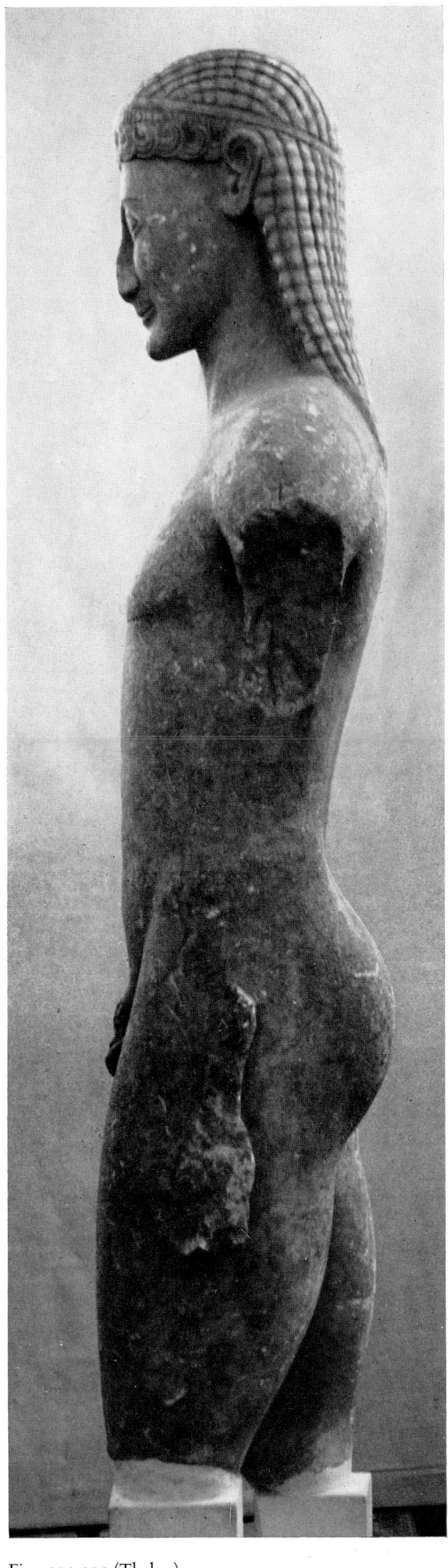

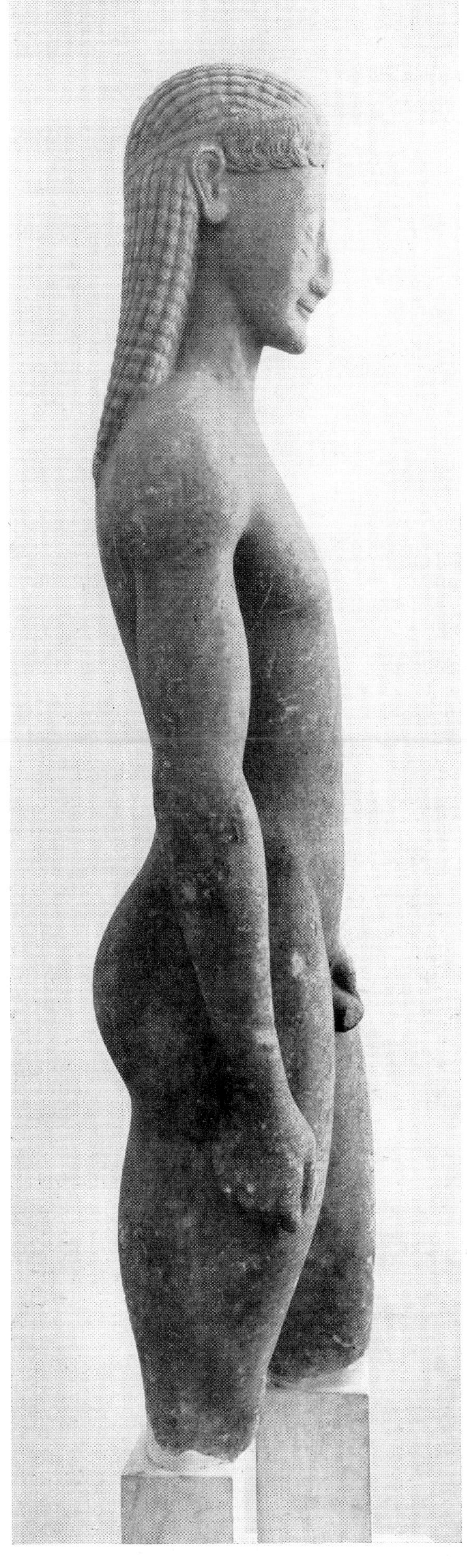

Figs. 304-305 (Thebes)

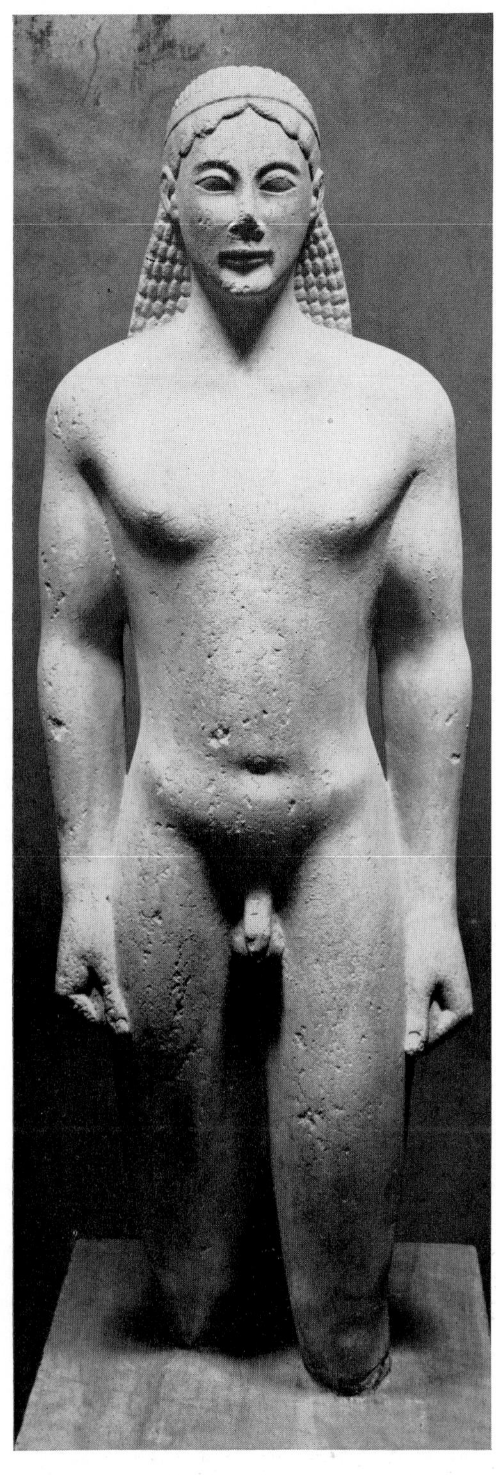

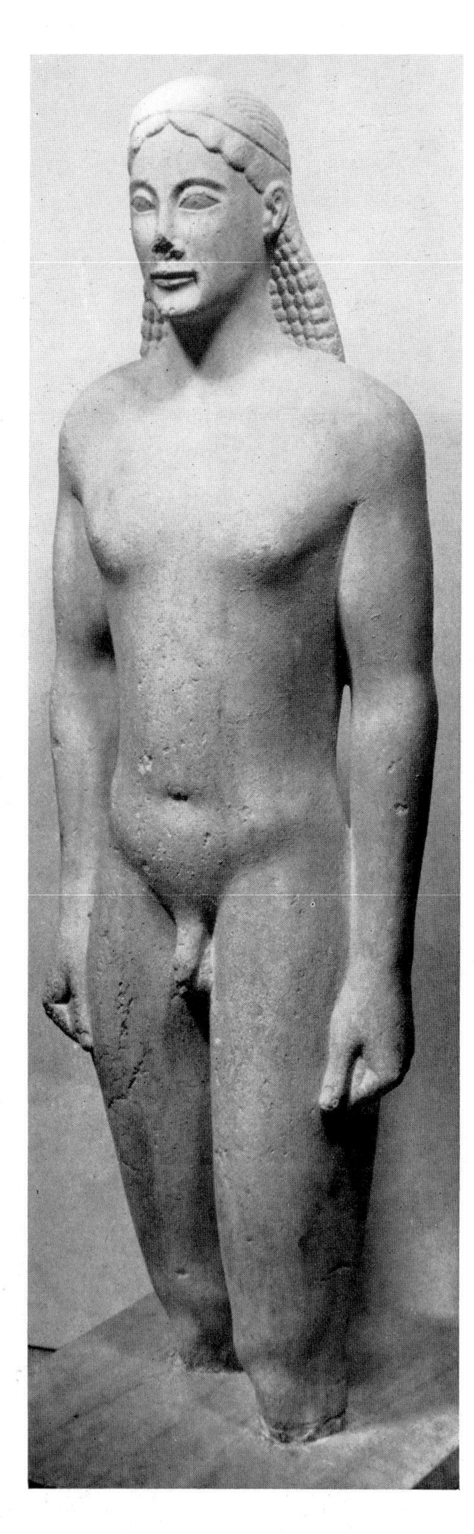

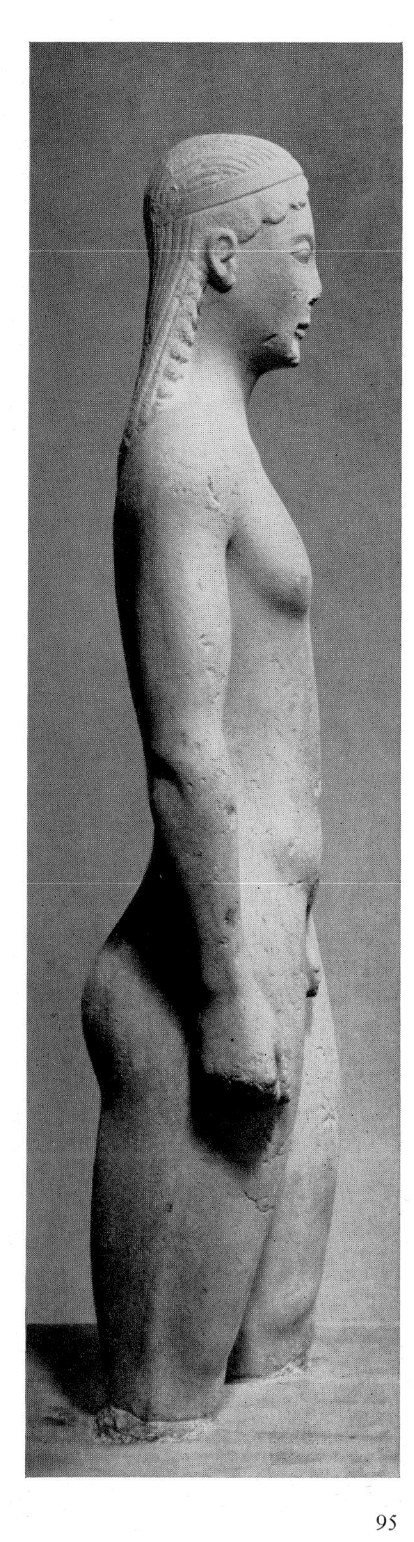

Figs. 306-308 (Athens)

Fig. 309 (Athens) 95

igs. 310-311 (Athens)

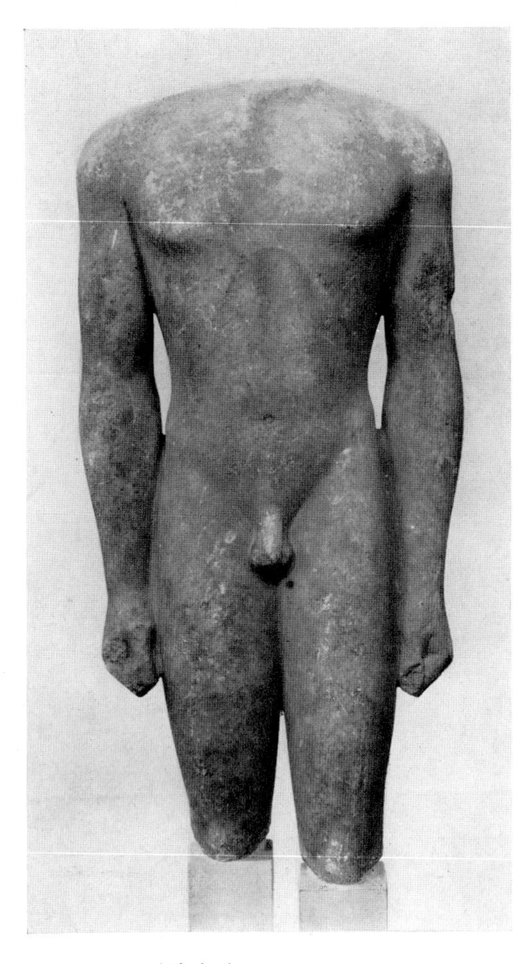

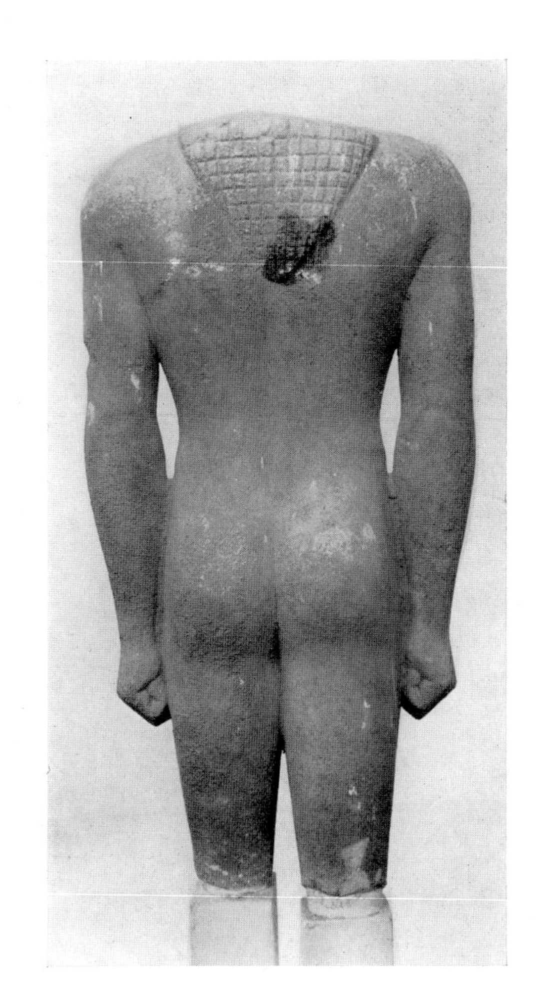

Figs. 312-313 (Thebes) 96

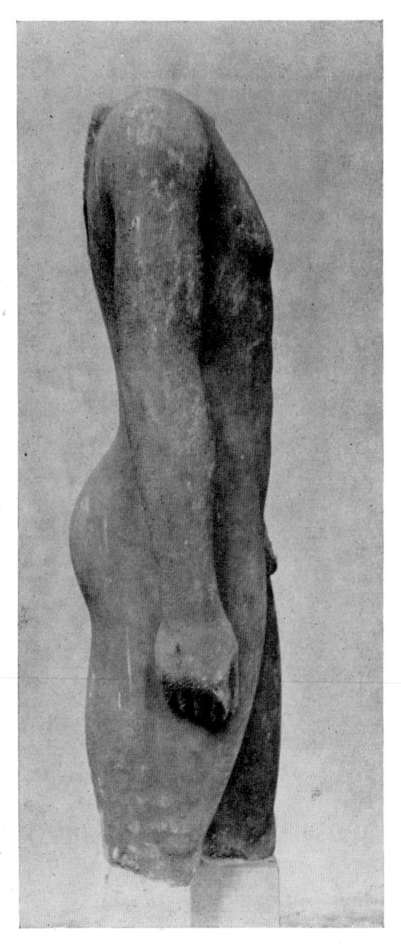

Fig. 314 (Thebes) 96

Fig. 315 (Thebes) 97

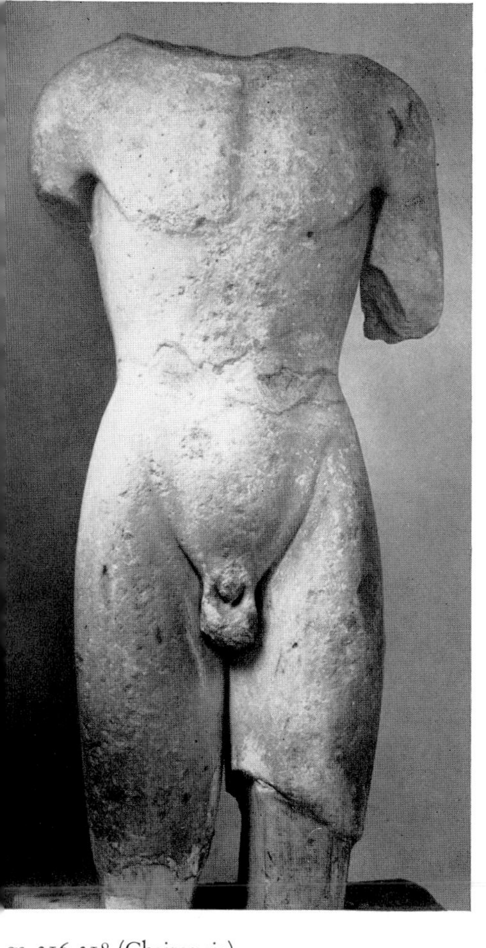

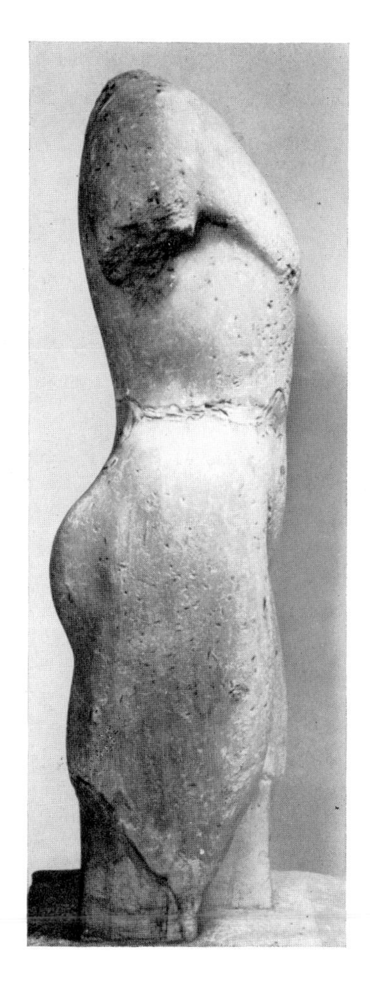

gs. 316–318 (Chaironeia)

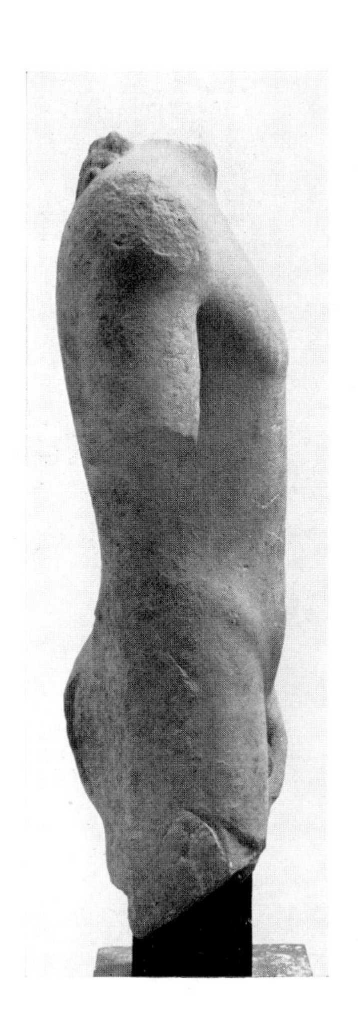

igs. 319–321 (Athens)

Figs. 322-323 (Athens)

Figs. 324-325 (Chalkis)

Figs. 326-327 (Berlin)

Figs. 328-329 (Copenhagen)

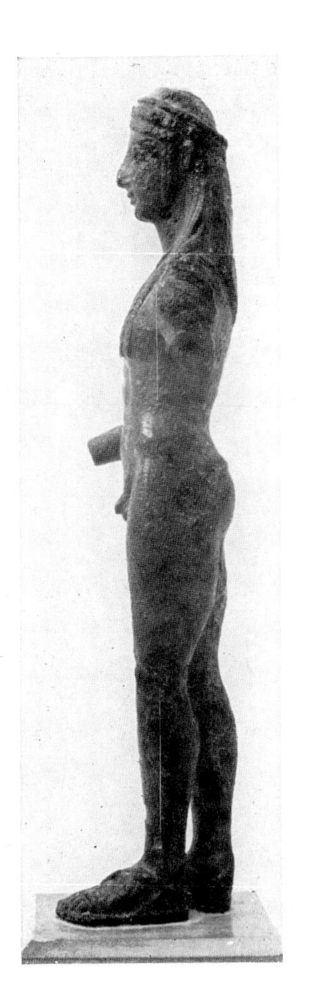

Figs. 330-333 (Delphi) 106

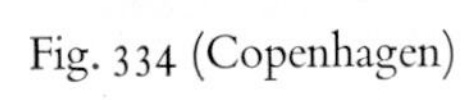

Fig. 334 (Copenhagen) 109

Fig. 335 (Delphi) 105

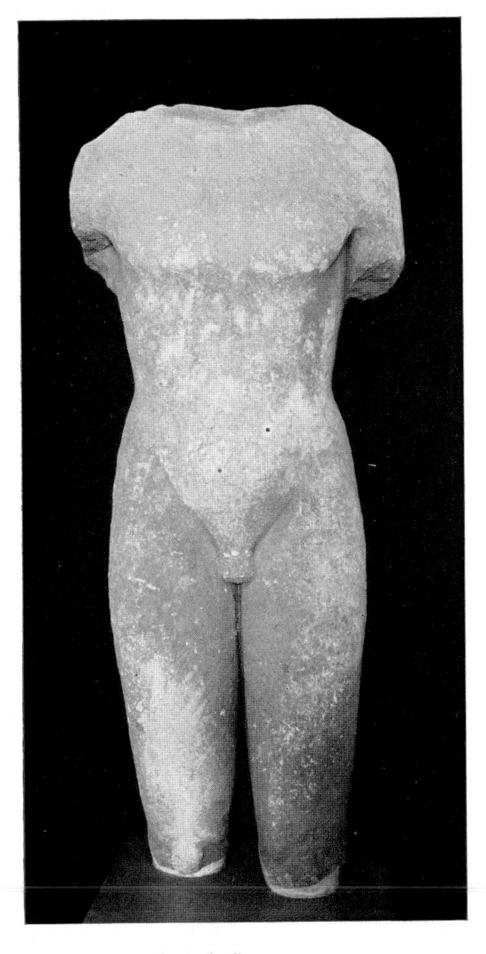

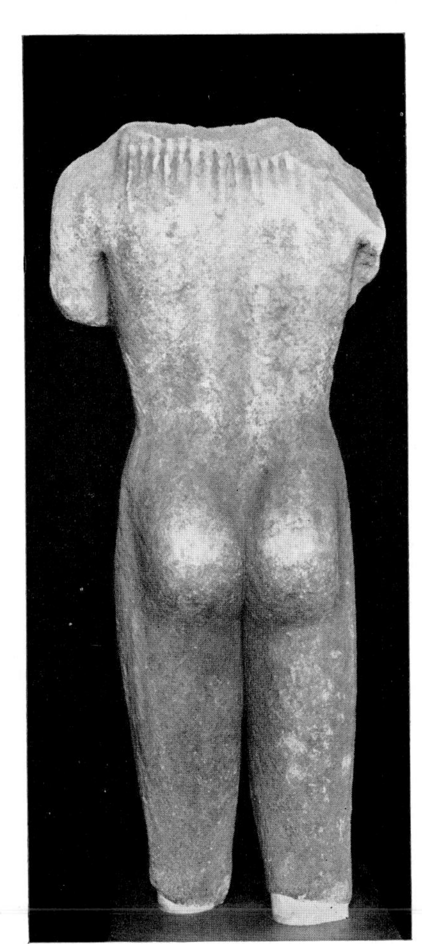

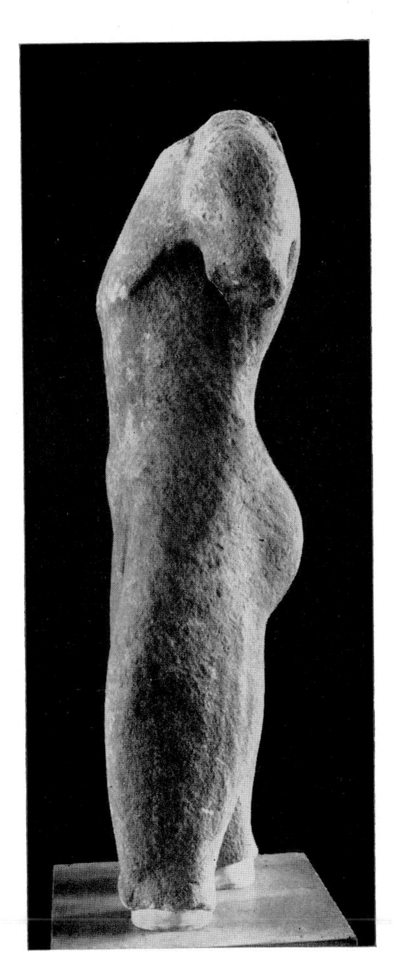

Figs. 336–338 (Istanbul) 108

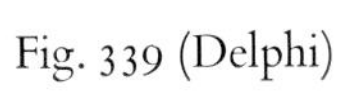

Fig. 339 (Delphi) 103

Fig. 340 (Delphi) 104

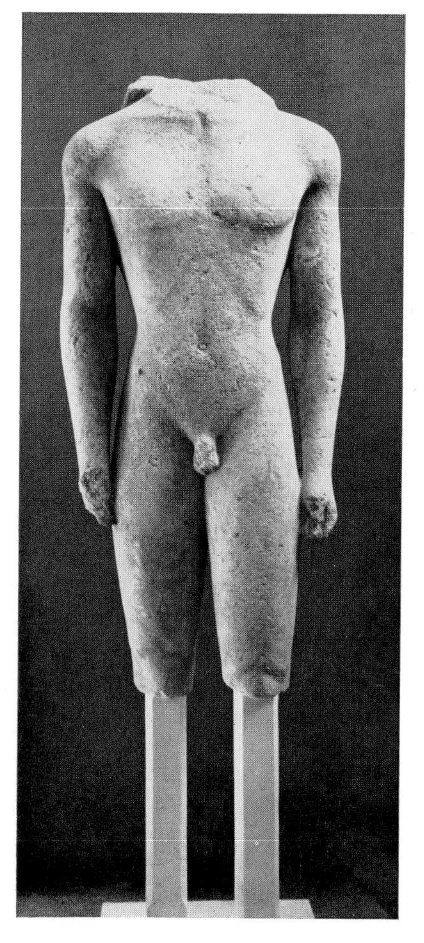

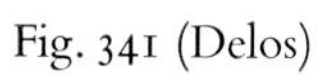

Fig. 341 (Delos) 110

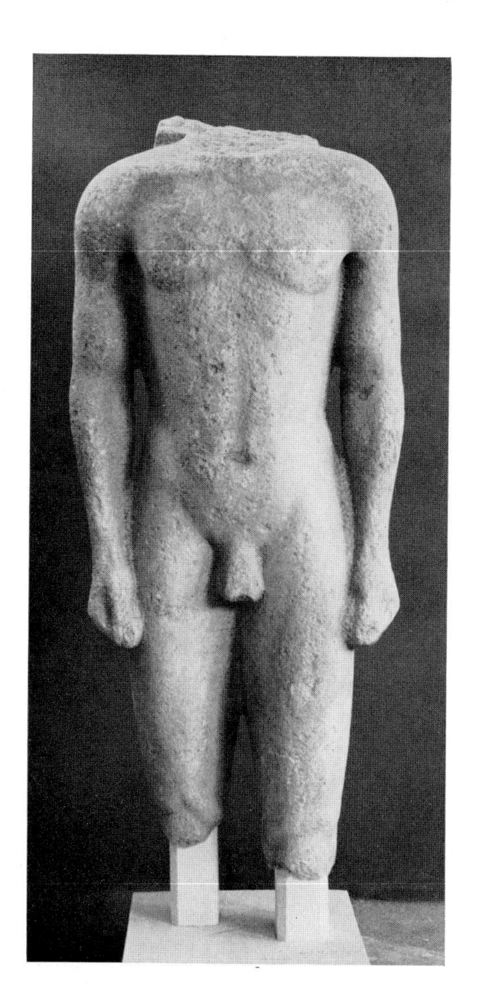

Fig. 342 (Delos) 111

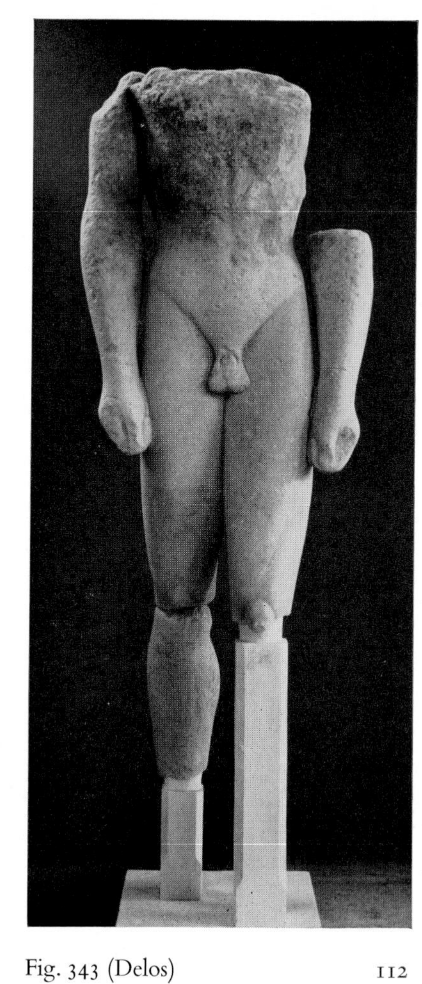

Fig. 343 (Delos) 112

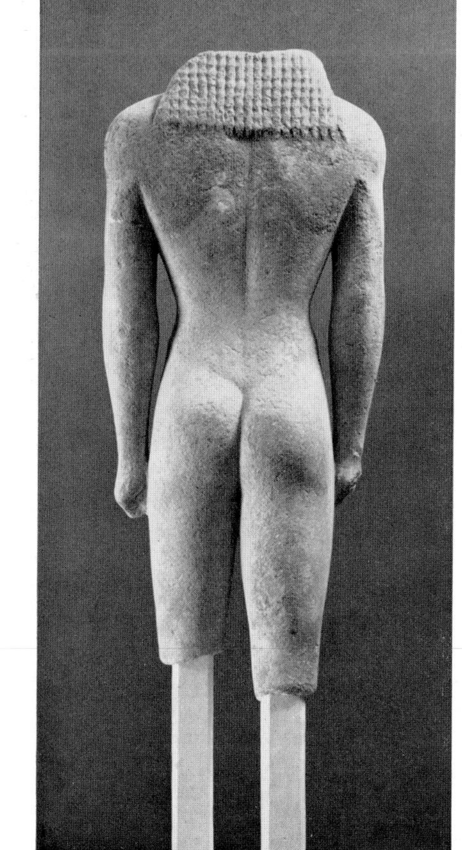

Fig. 344 (Delos) 110

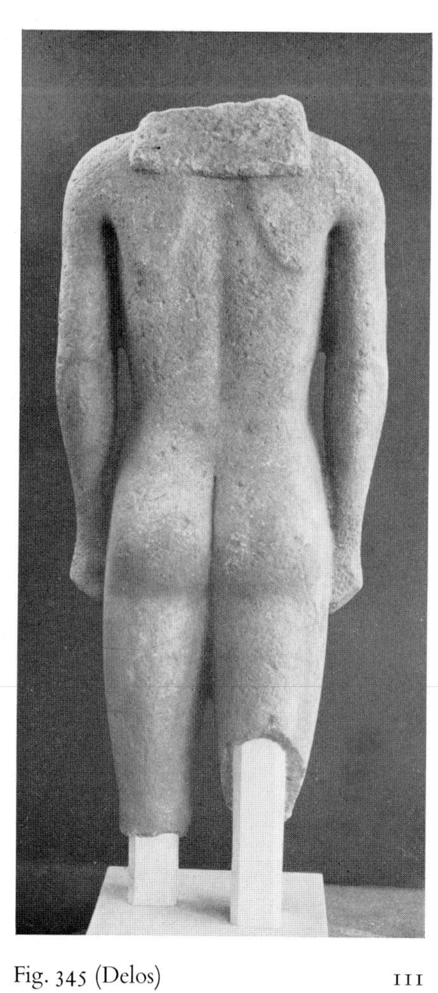

Fig. 345 (Delos) 111

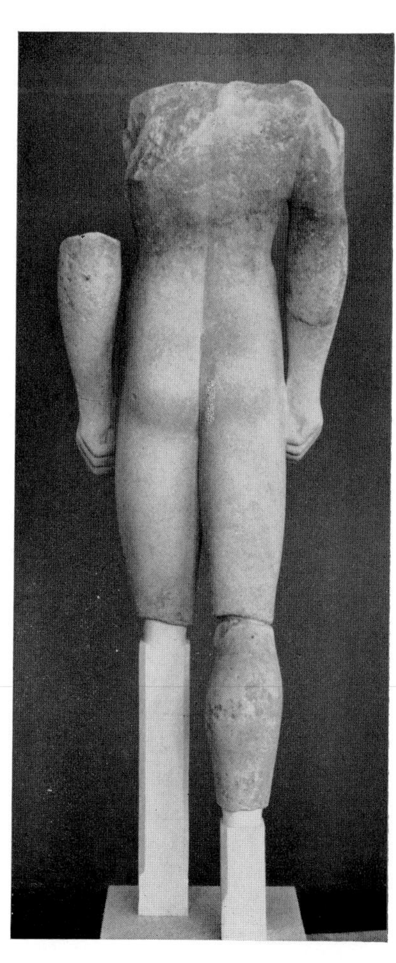

Fig. 346 (Delos) 112

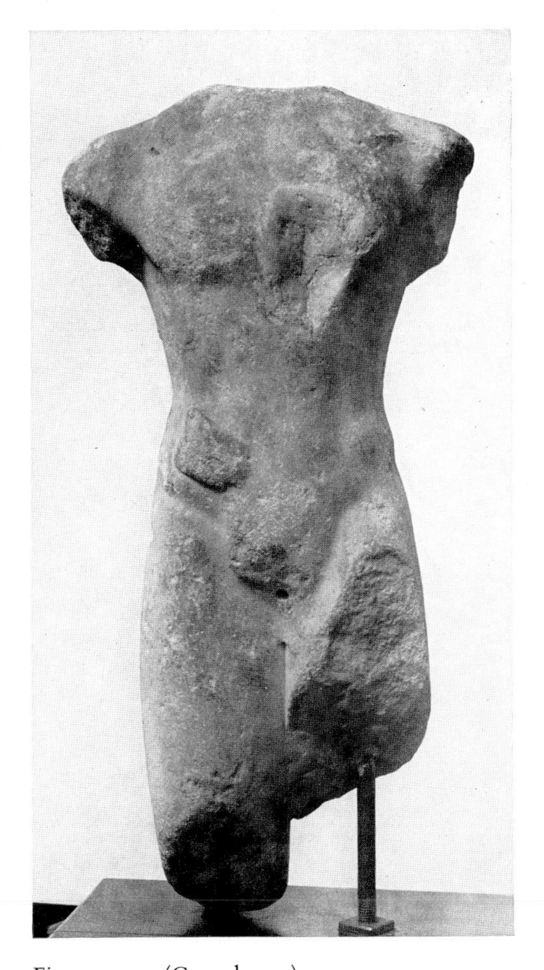

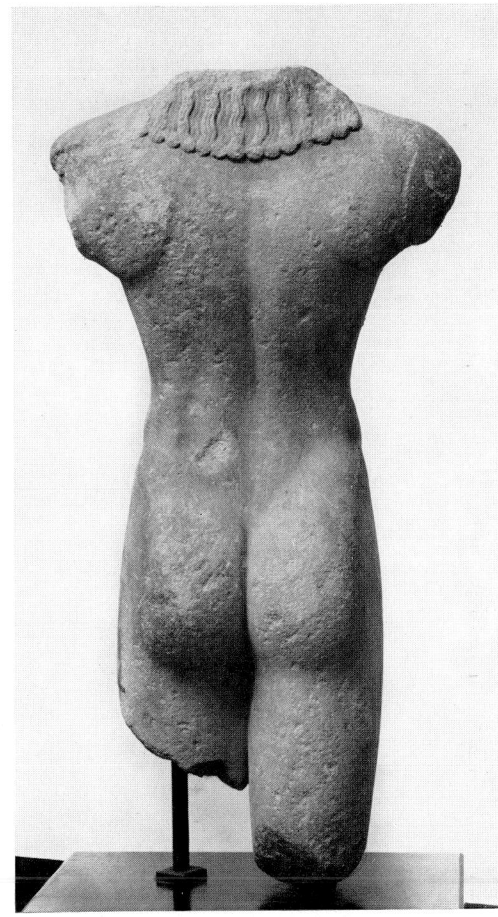

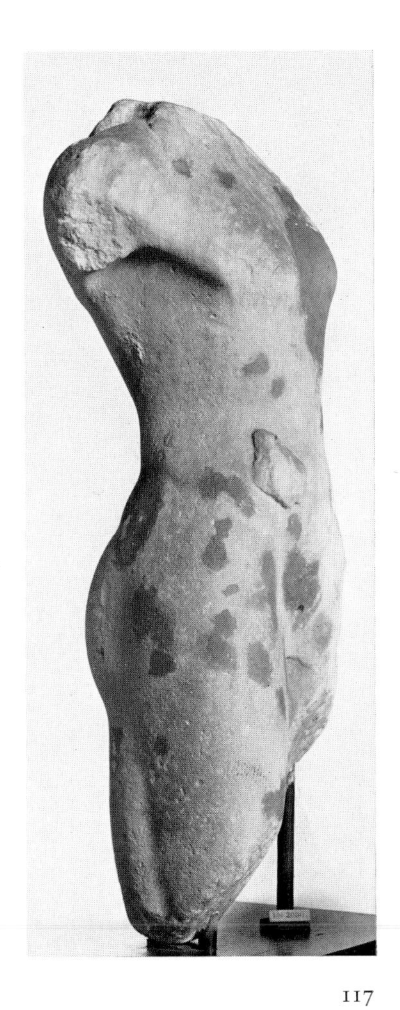

Figs. 347-349 (Copenhagen) 117

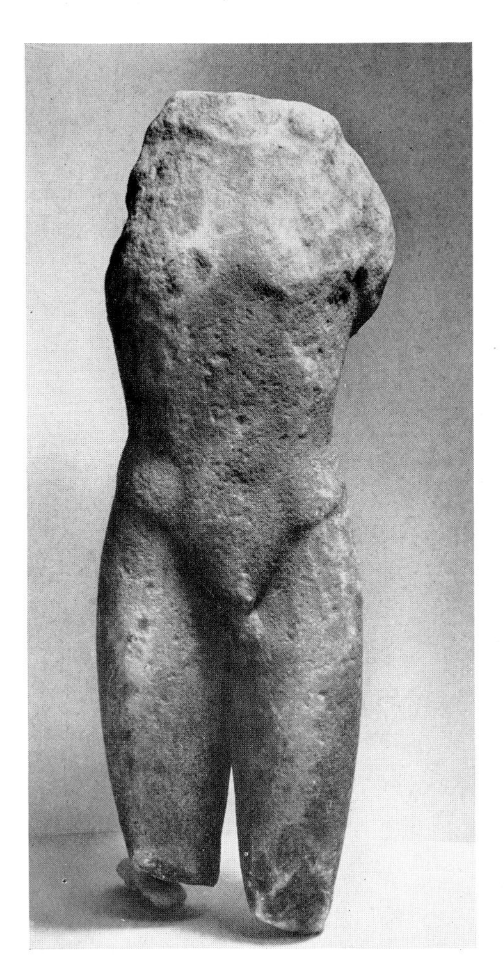

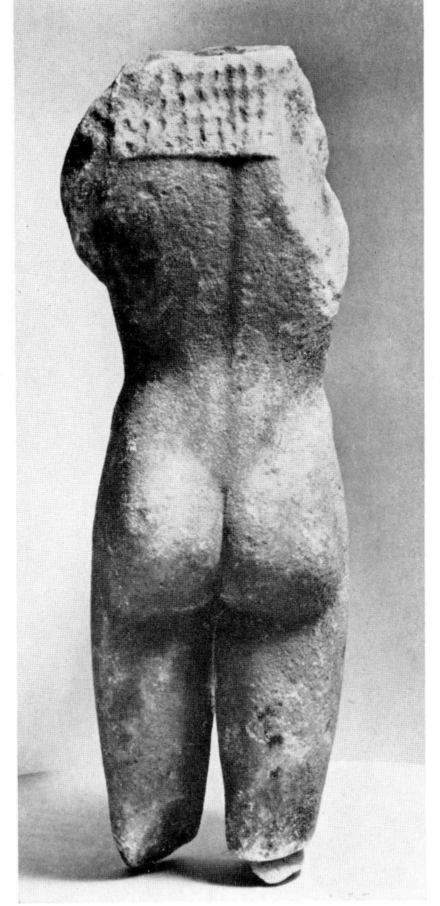

Figs. 350-351 (Paros) 118

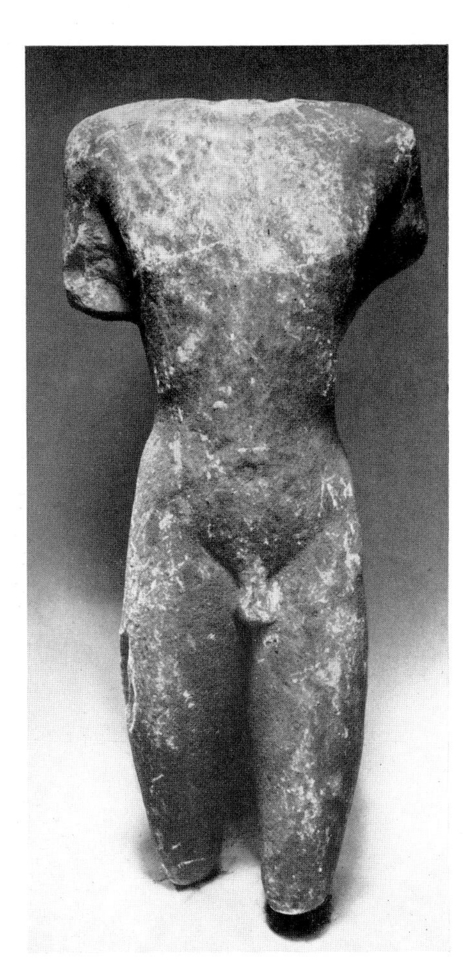

Figs. 352 (Andros) 119

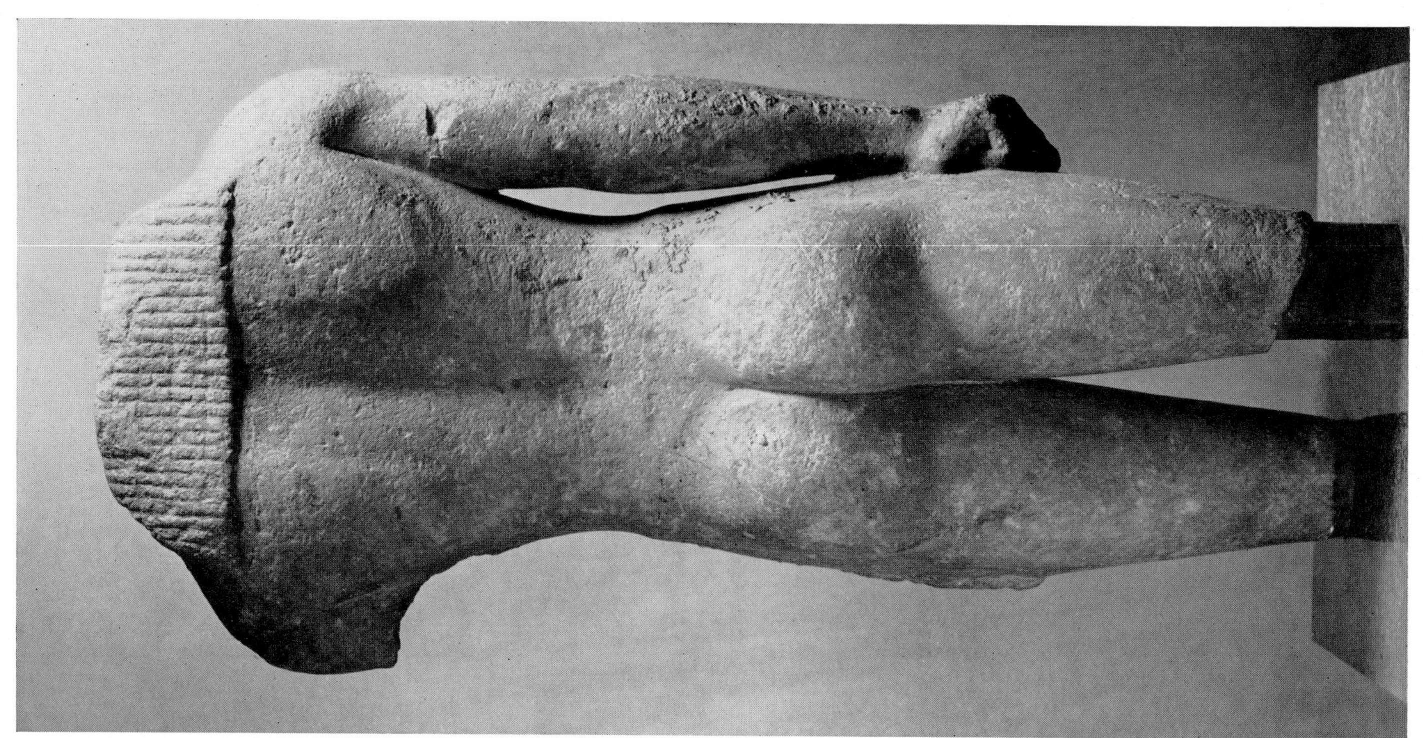

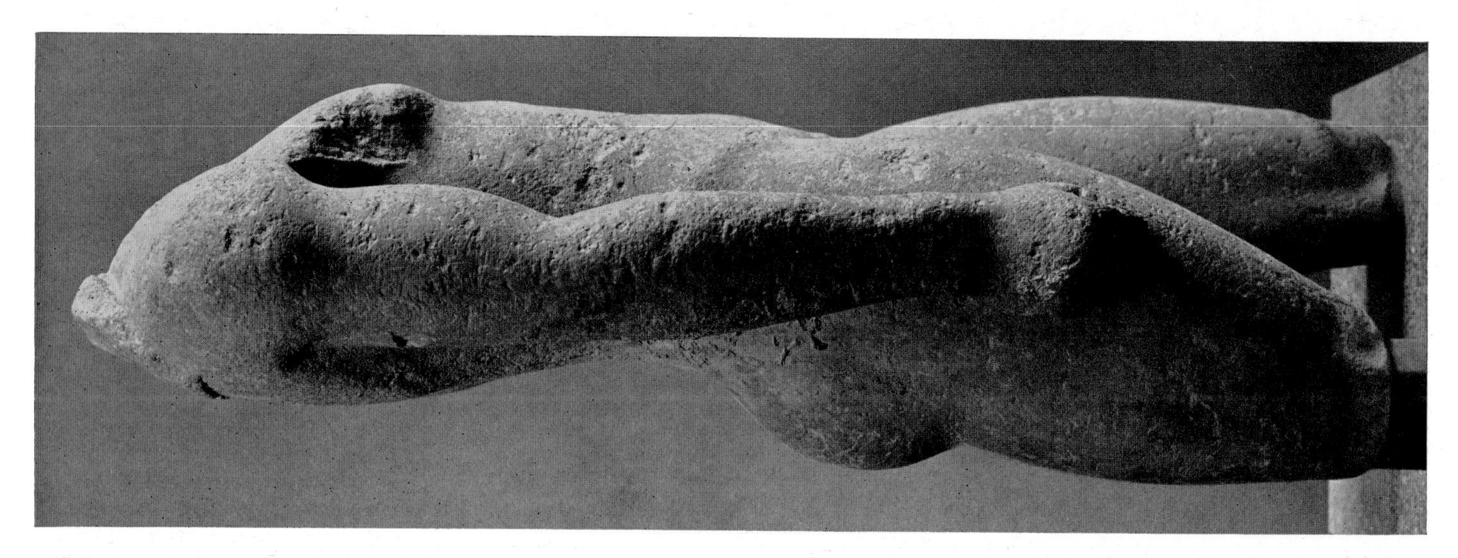

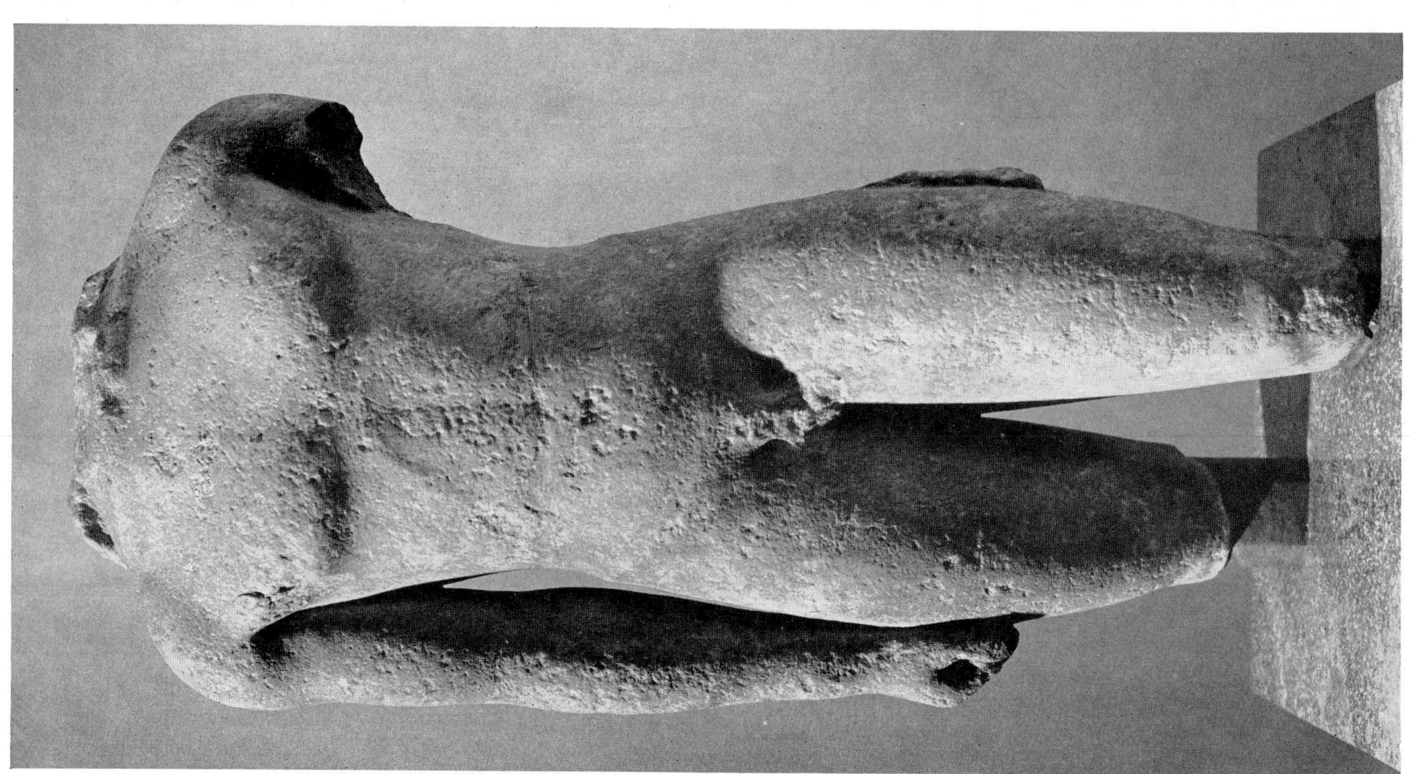

Figs. 356–358 (Paris)

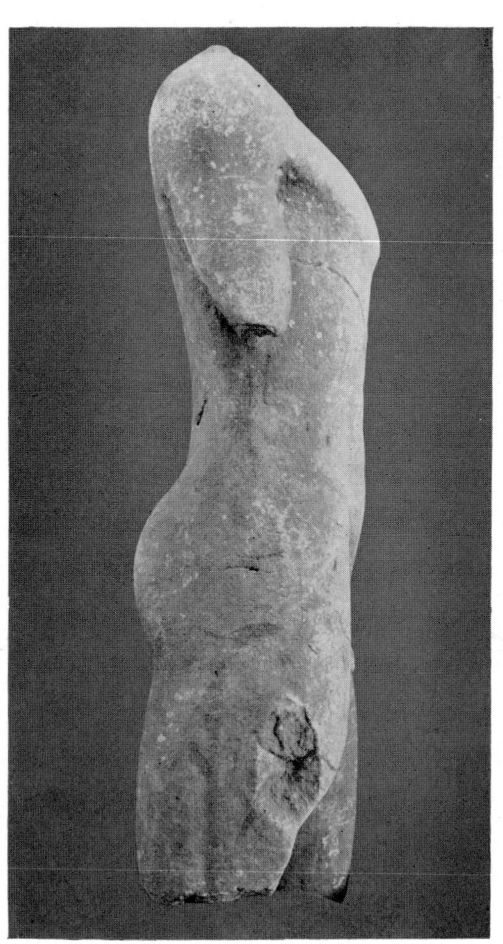

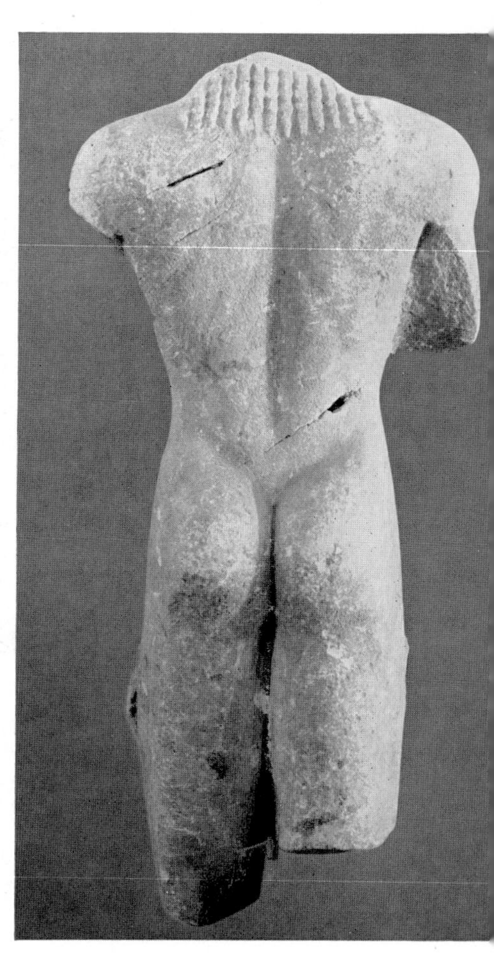

Figs. 359-361 (Samos)

Fig. 362 (Santorin) 114

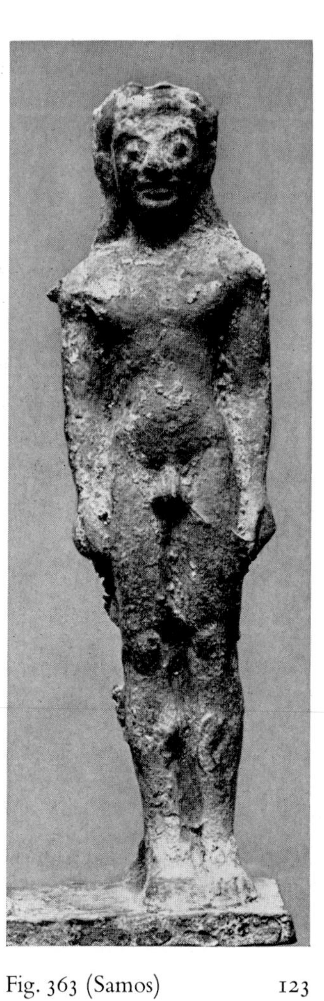

Fig. 363 (Samos) 123

Fig. 364 (New York) Cf. p. 93

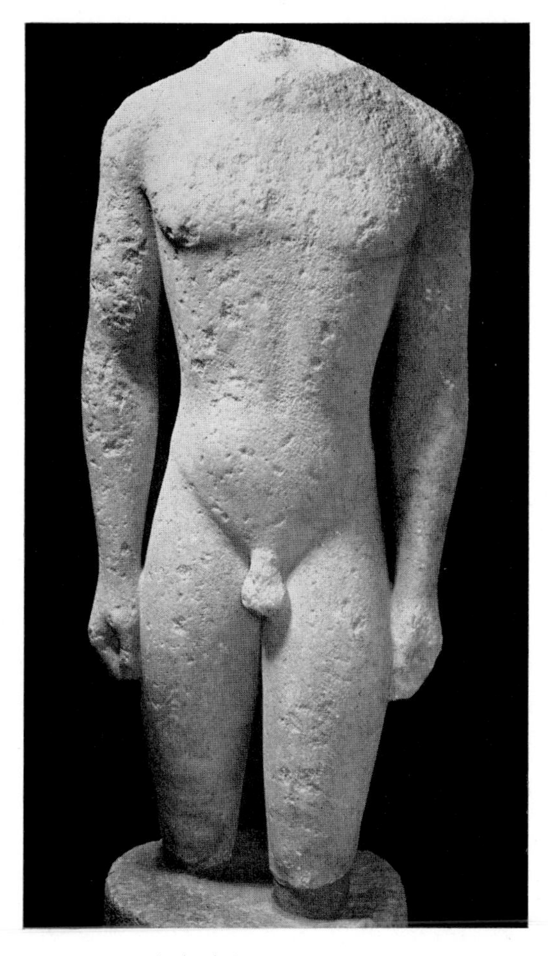

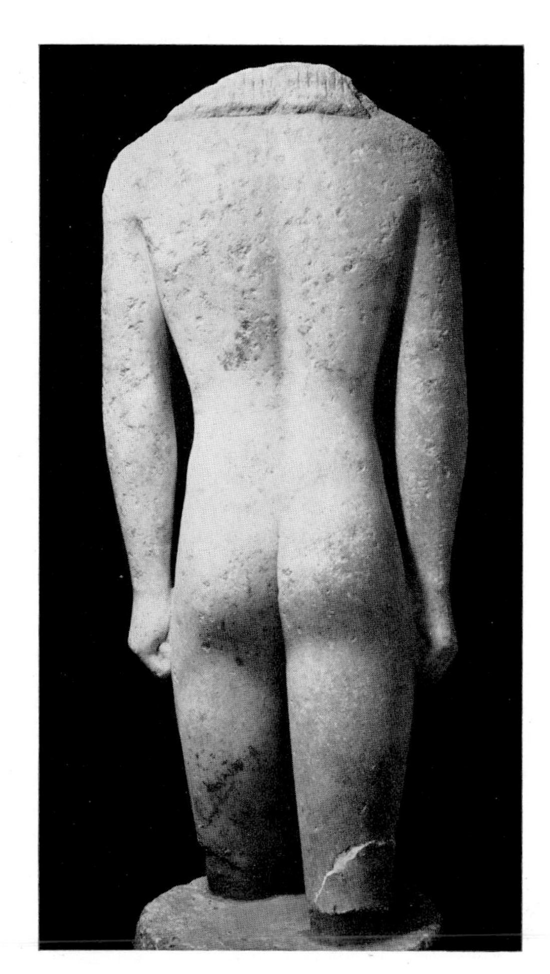

Figs. 365–366 (Rhodes)

124

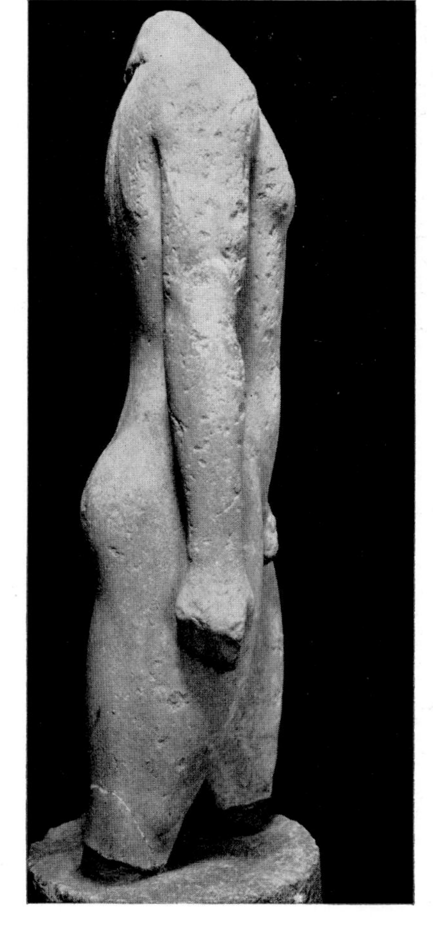

Figs. 367–368 (Rhodes)

124

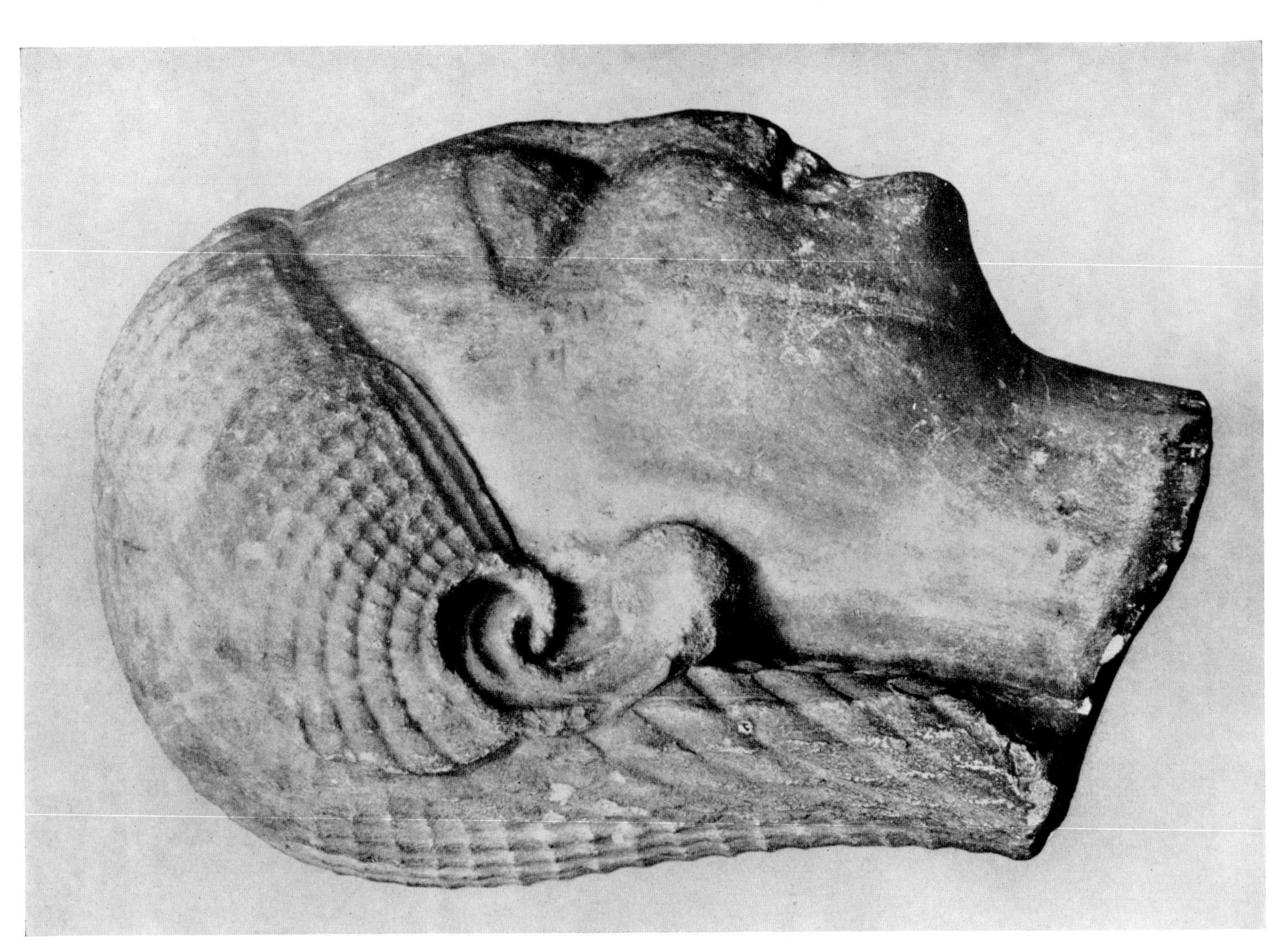

Figs. 371-372 (London)

Figs. 373-374 (Rhodes) 125

Fig. 375 (Rhodes) 125

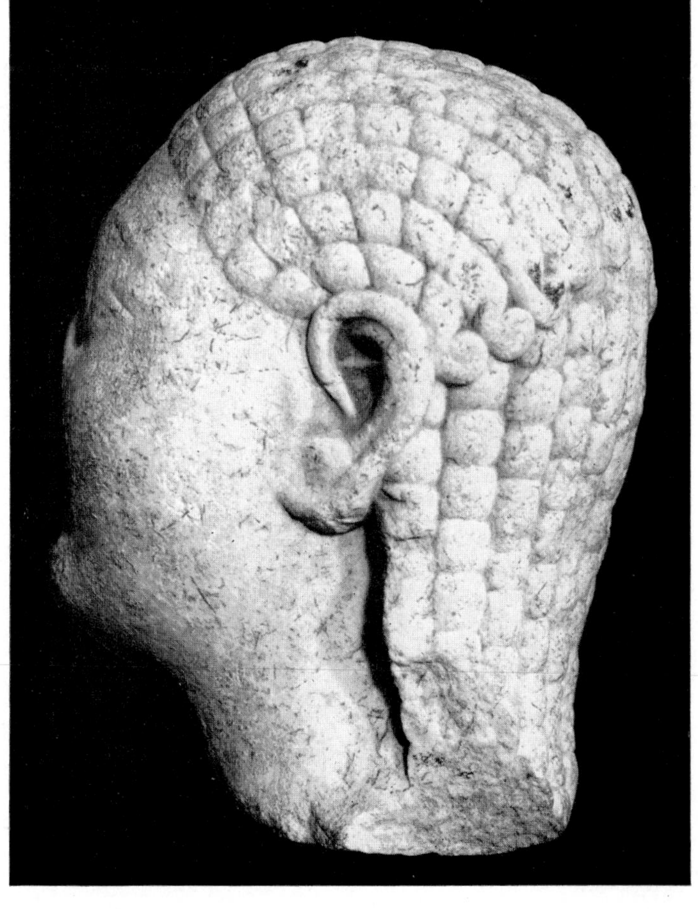

Fig. 376 (Rhodes) 126

Figs. 377-378 (Samos) 122

Figs. 379-380 (London) 129

Figs. 381-382 (Smyrna) 130

Fig. 383 (Smyrna) 130

Fig. 384 (Smyrna)  131

Figs. 385-386 (Smyrna) 132

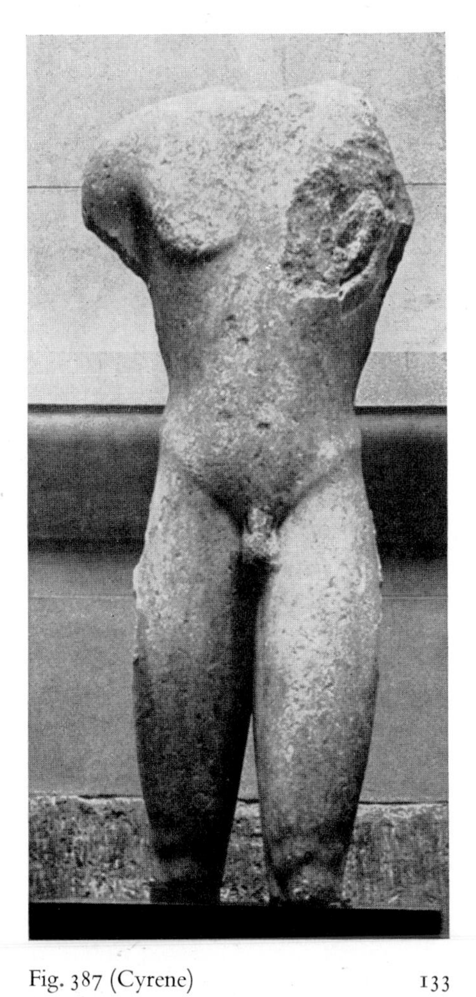

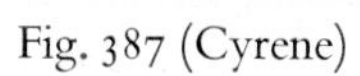

Fig. 387 (Cyrene) 133

Fig. 388 (Syracuse) 134

Figs. 389-390 (Syracuse) 134

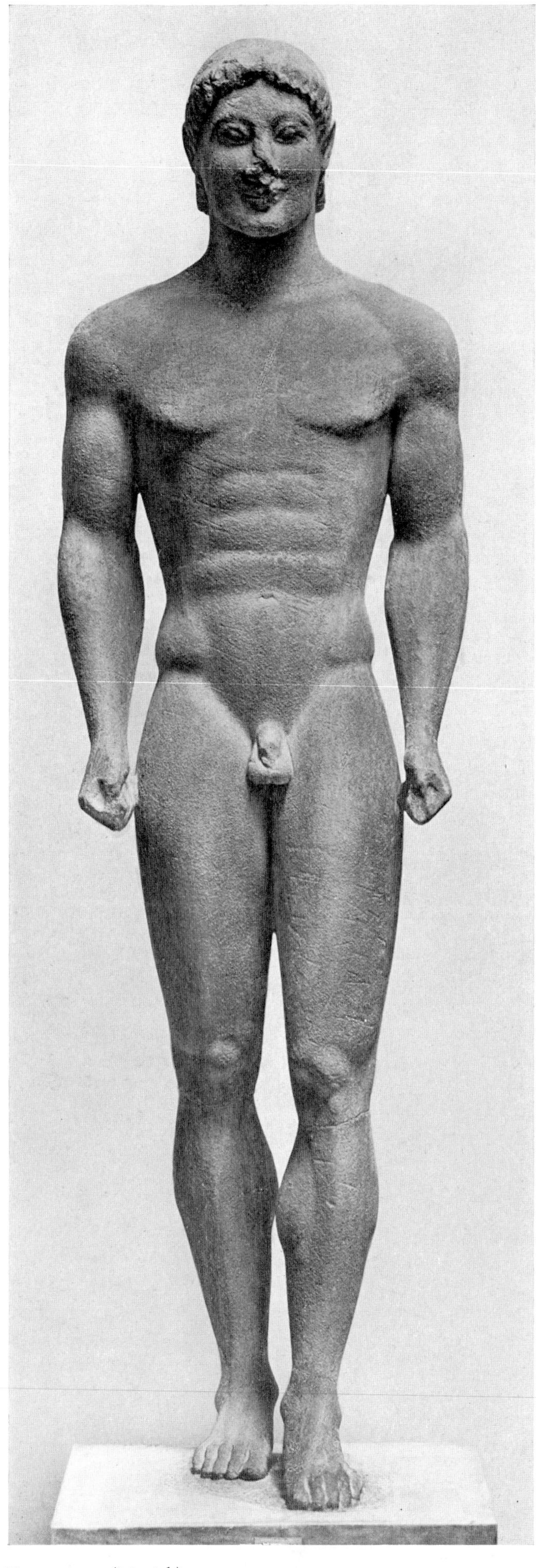

Figs. 391-392 (Munich)

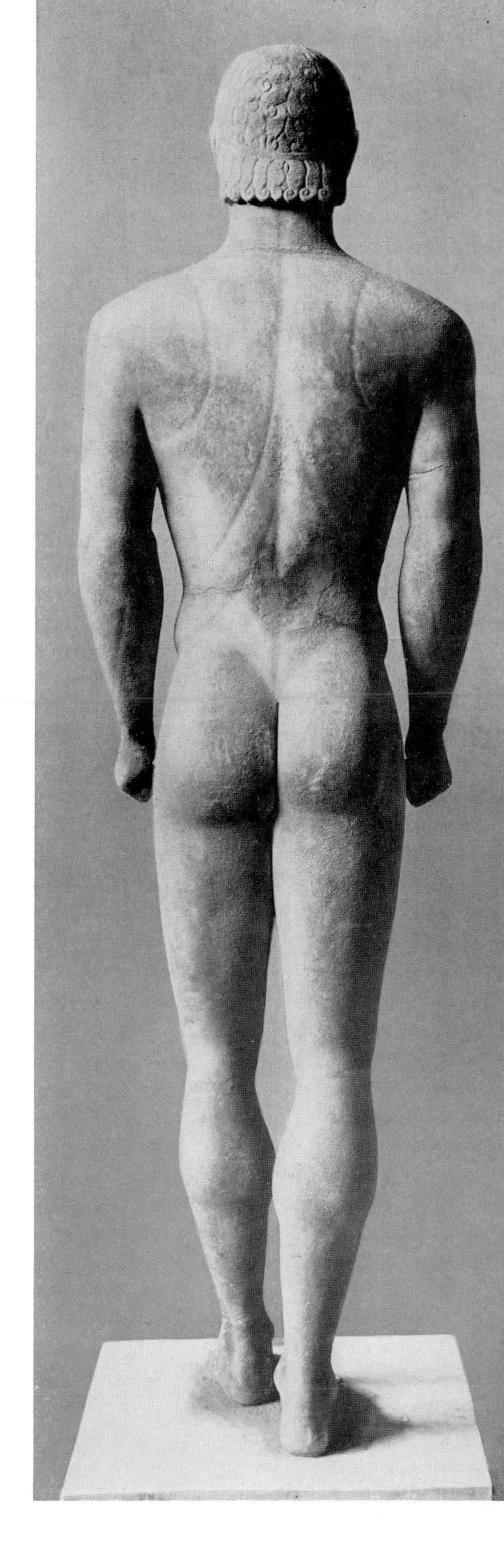

Figs. 393-394 (Munich)

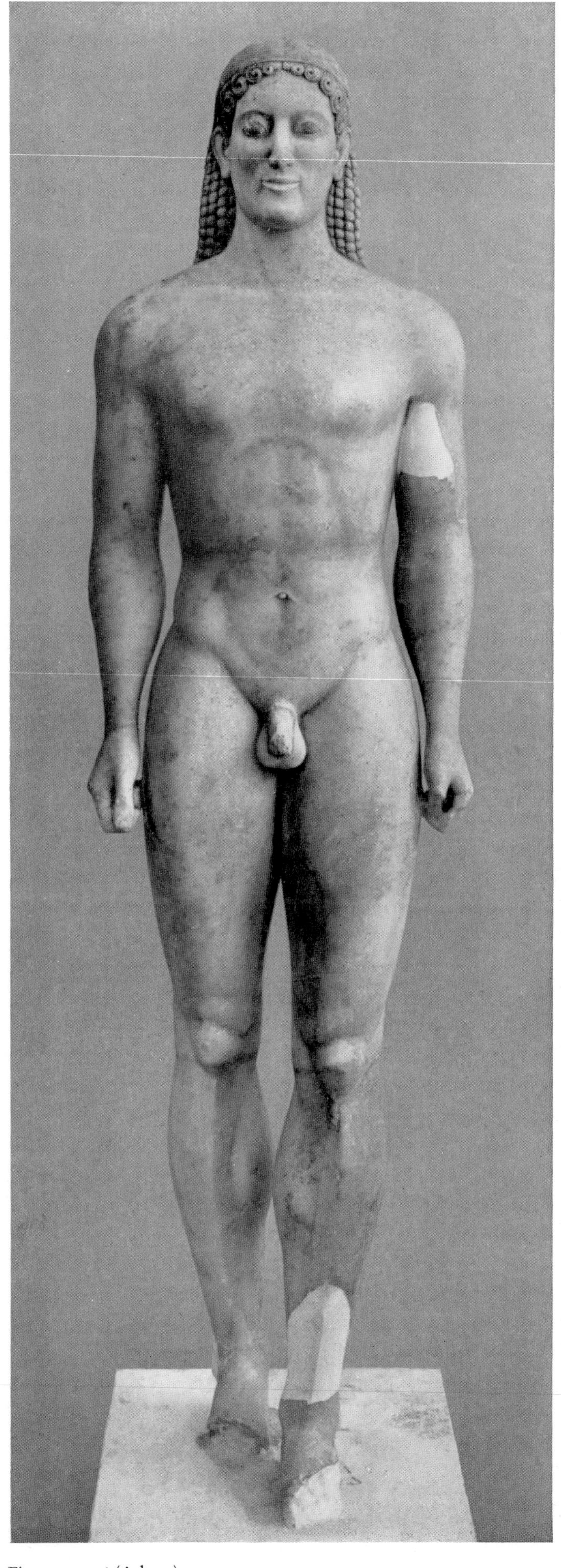

Figs. 395-396 (Athens)

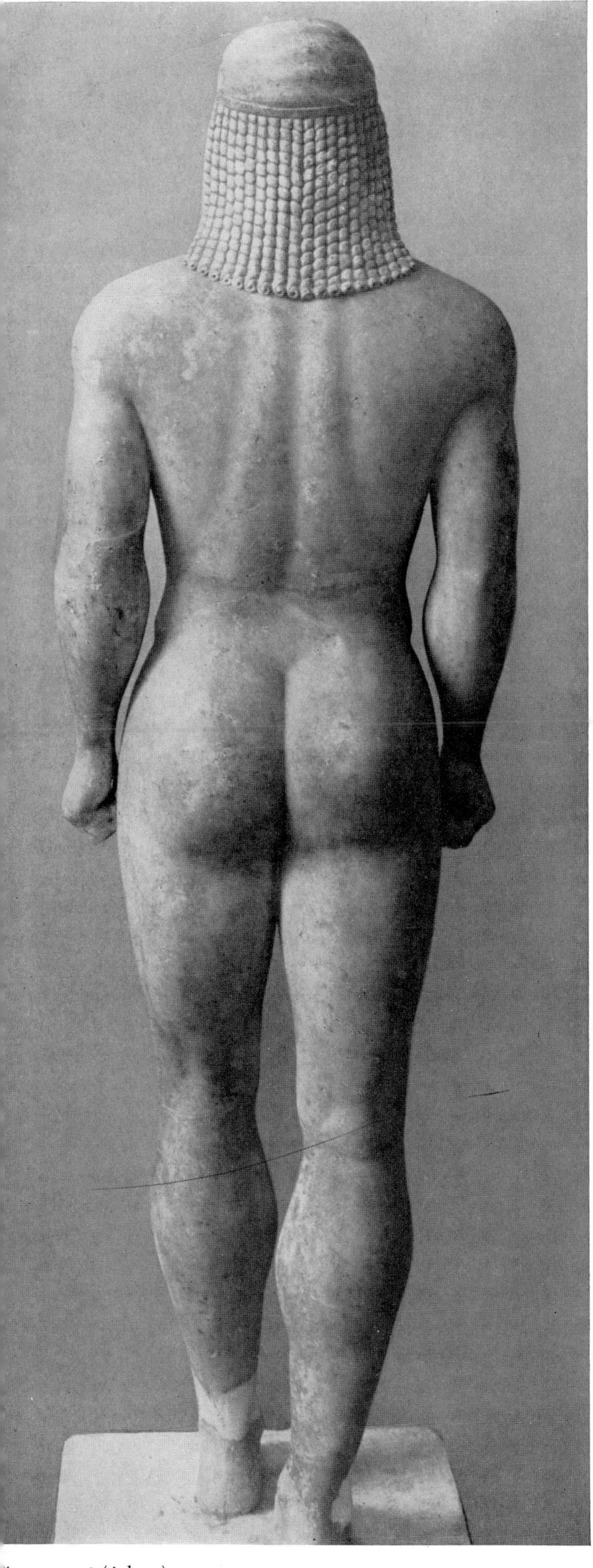

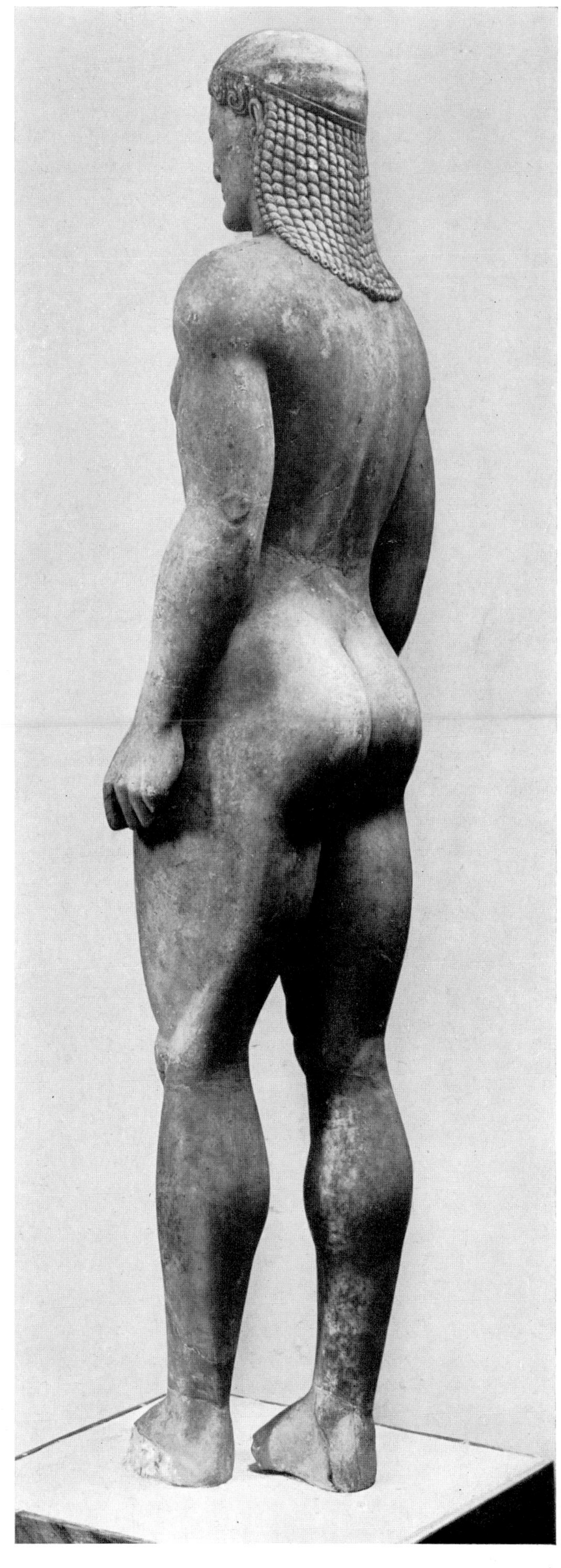

igs. 397-398 (Athens)

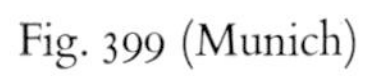

Fig. 399 (Munich) 135

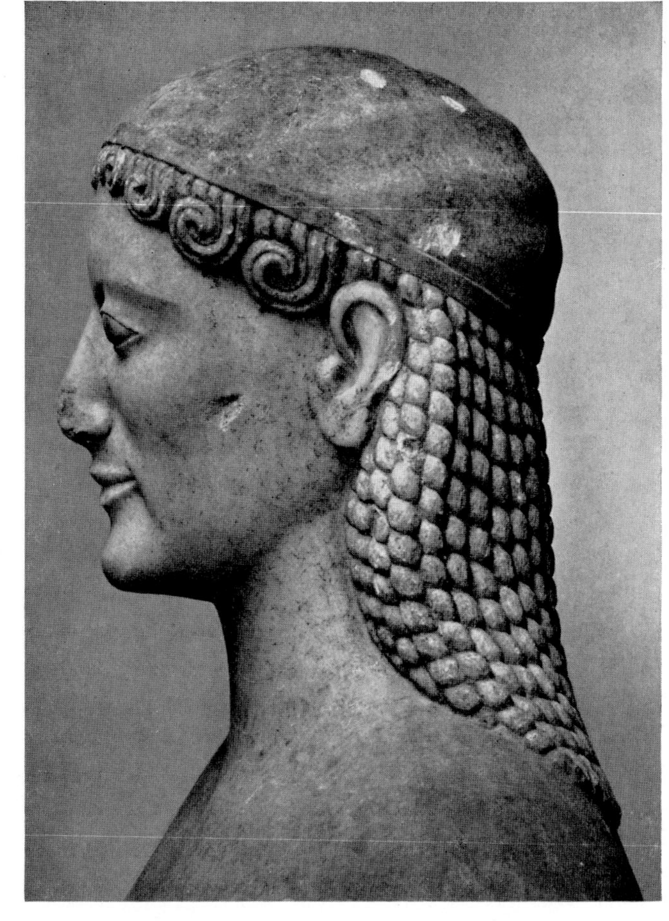

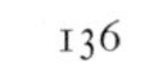

Fig. 400 (Athens) 136

Fig. 401 (Athens) 13

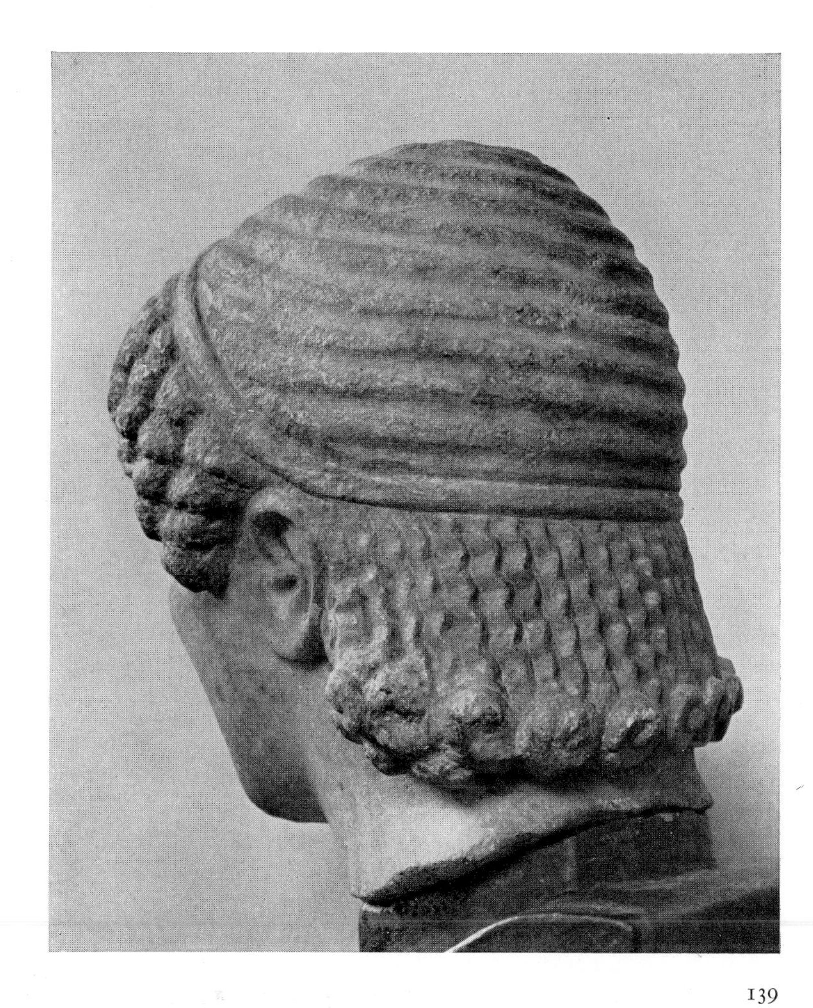

Figs. 402-403 (Athens)

Figs. 404-405 (Paris)

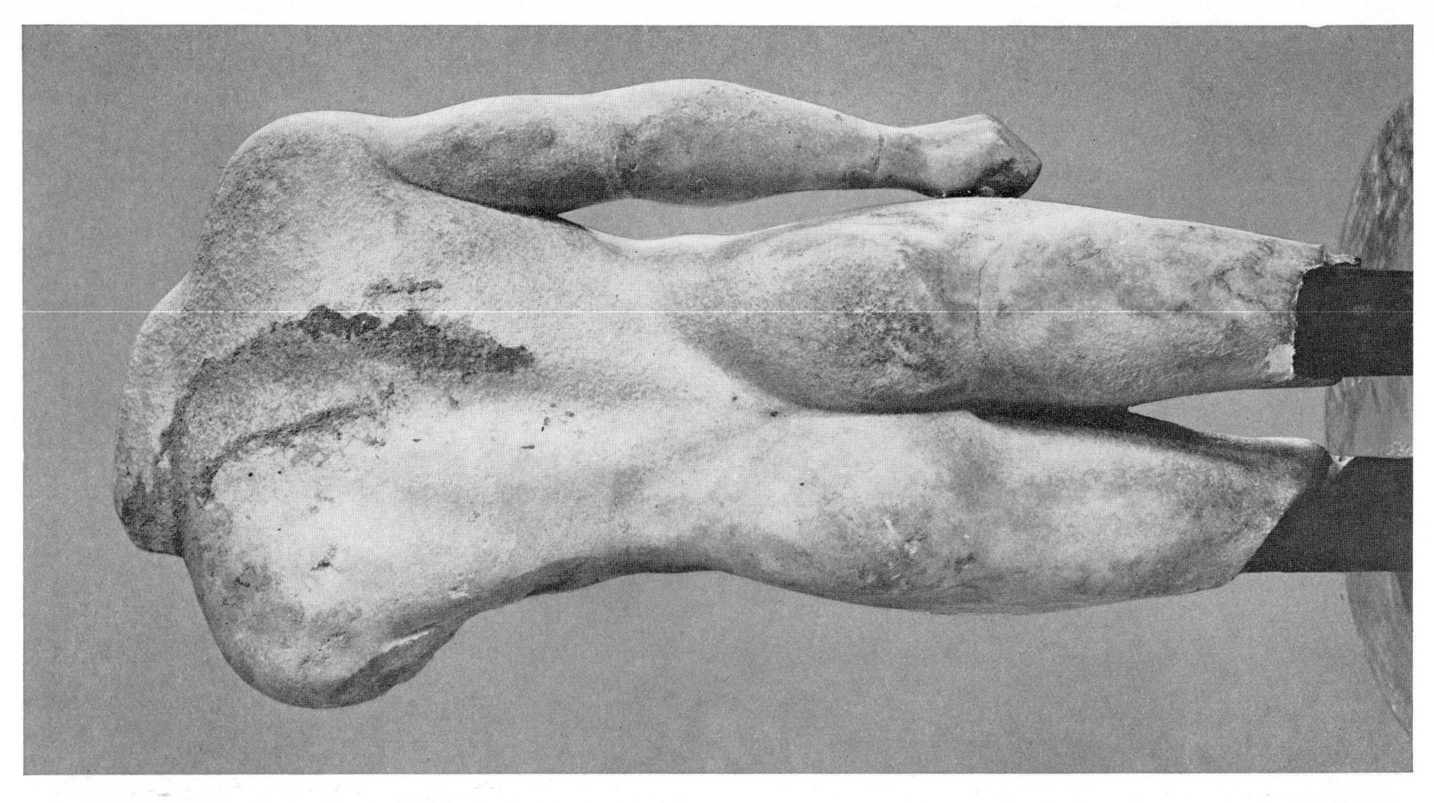
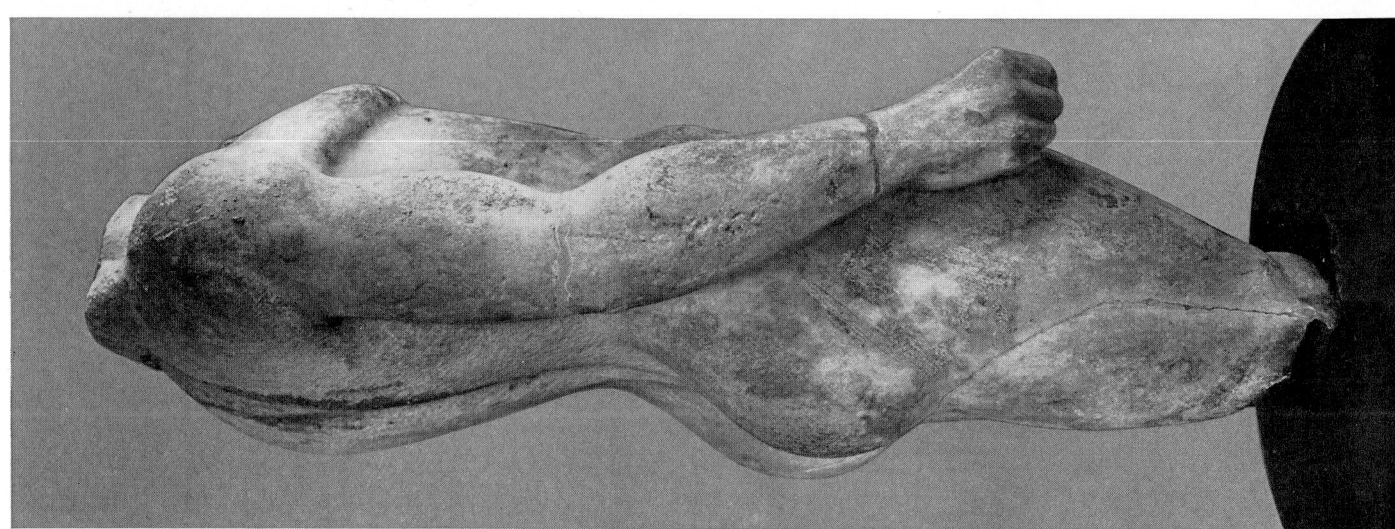
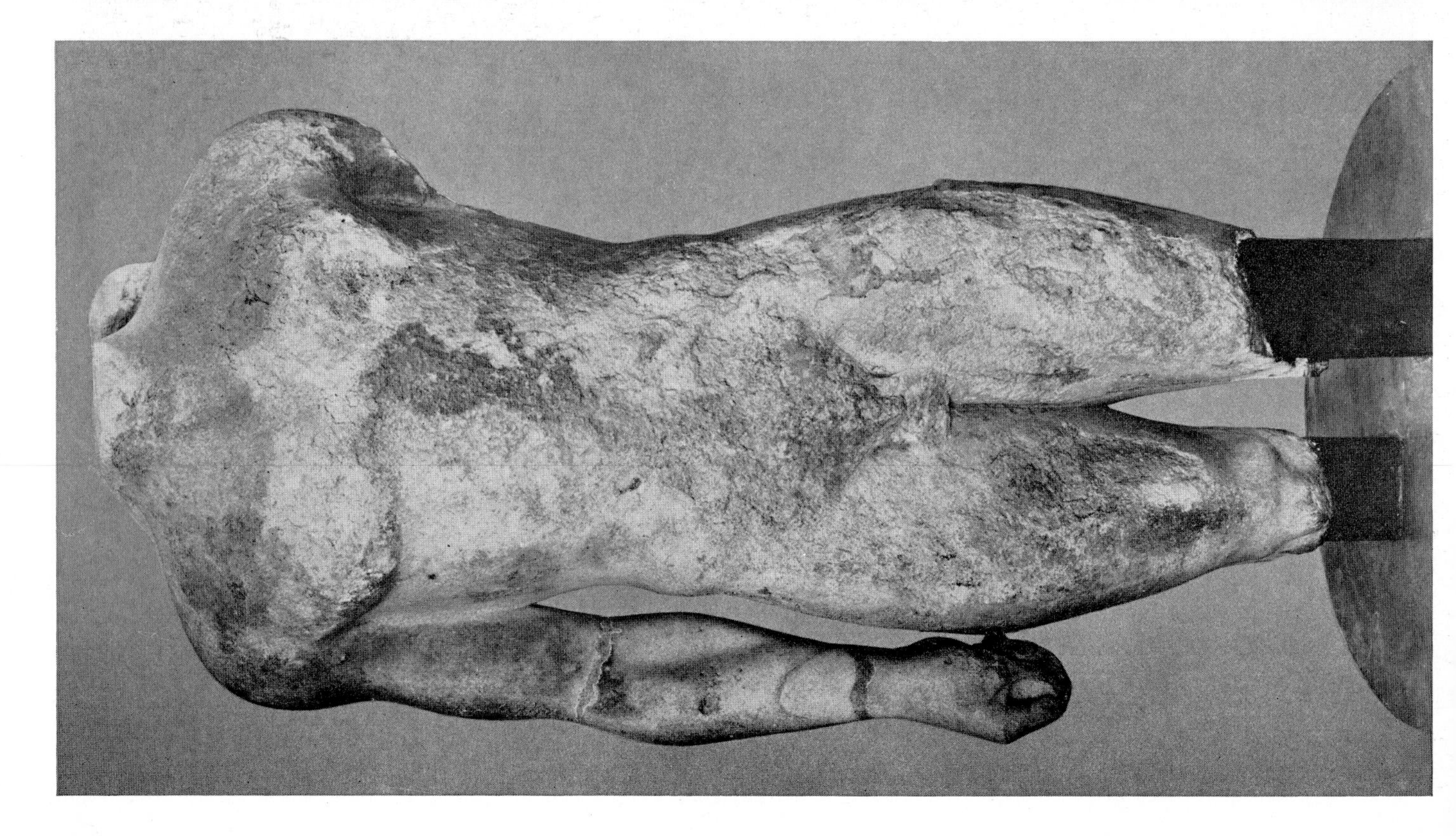

Figs. 409-410 (Copenhagen)

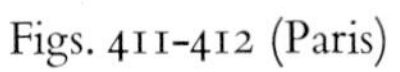

Figs. 411-412 (Paris)

142

Figs. 413-414 (Boston)

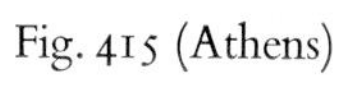

Fig. 415 (Athens) 140

Fig. 416 (Chalkis) 148

Figs. 417-418 (Chalkis) 148

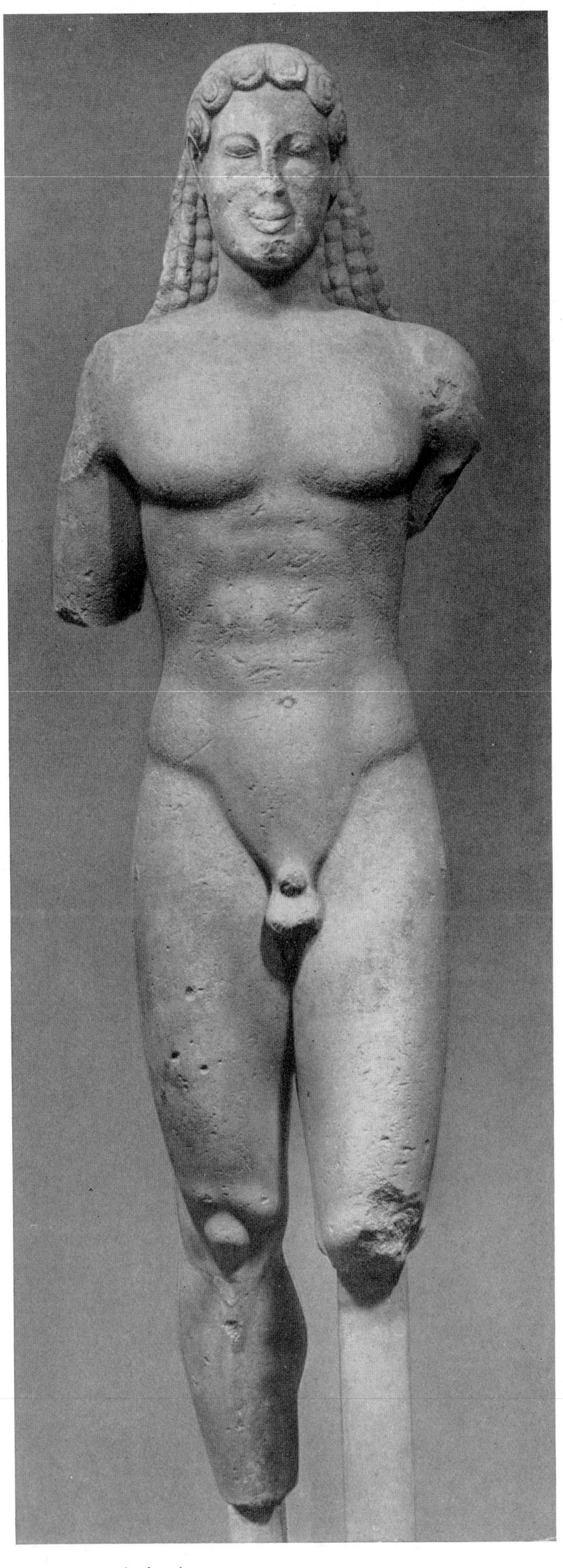

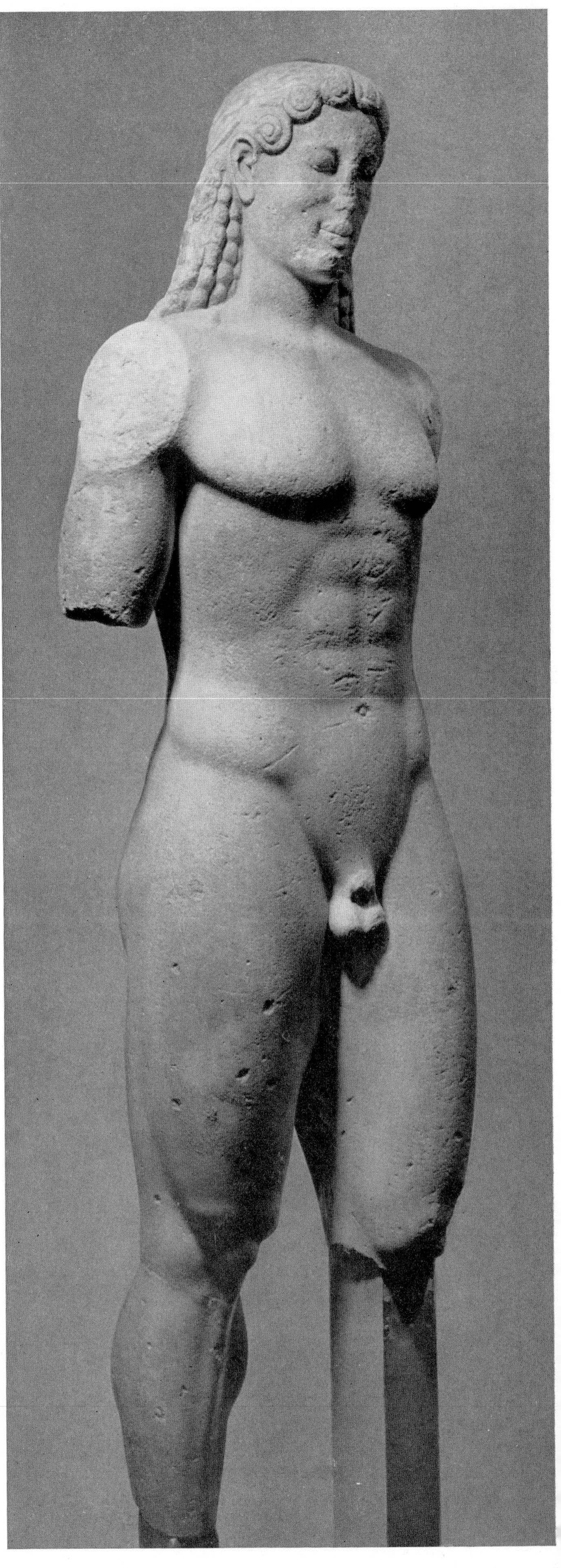

Figs. 419-420 (Athens)

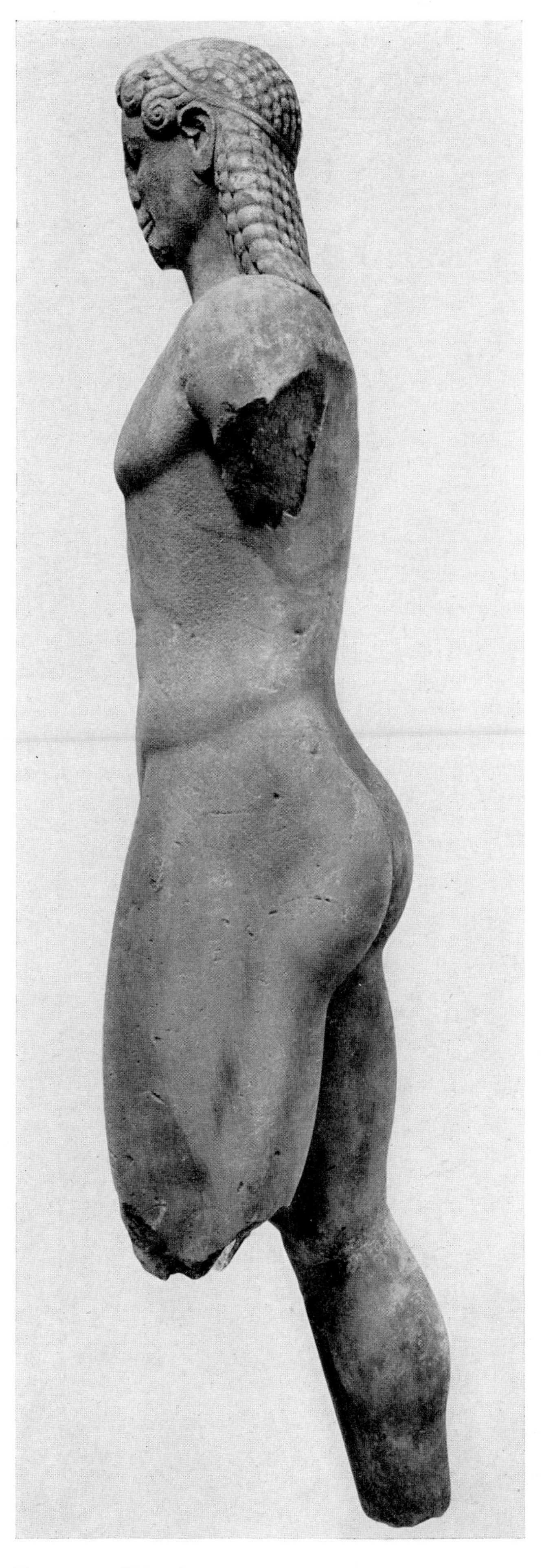

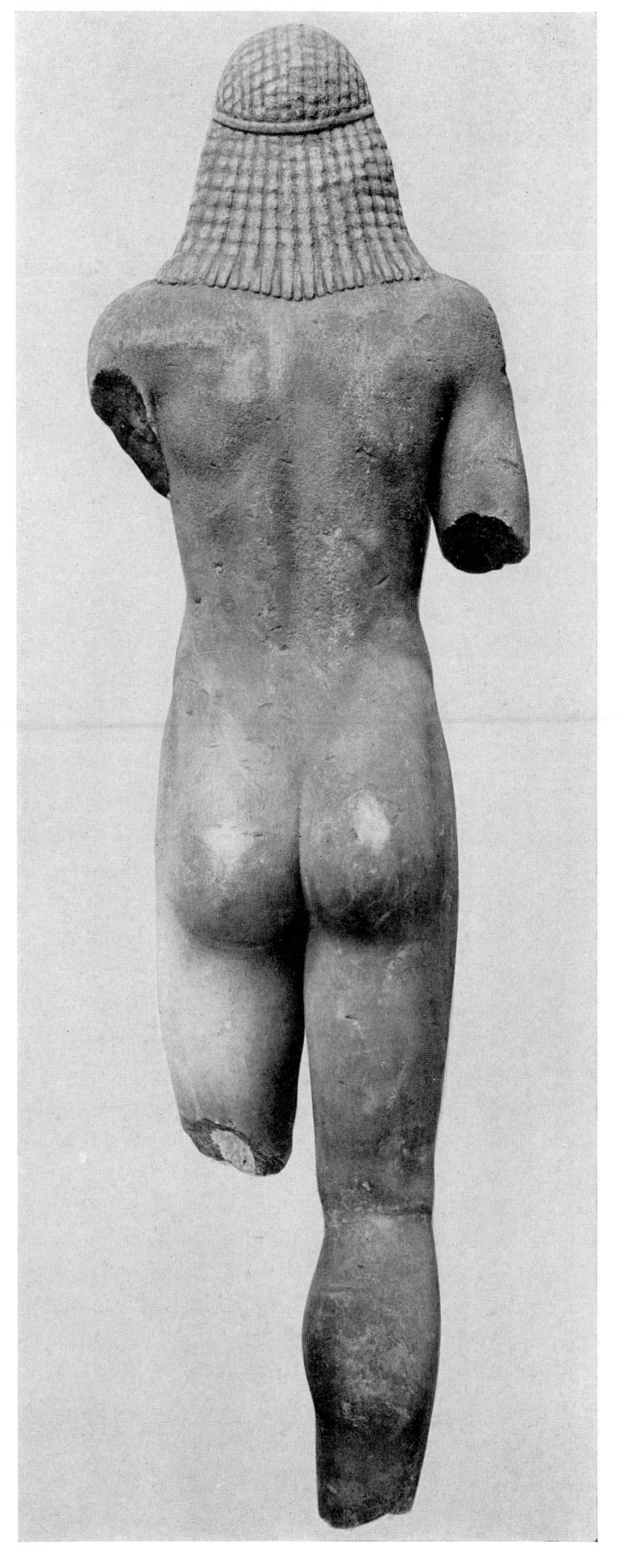

Figs. 421-422 (Athens)

Figs. 423-424 (Athens)

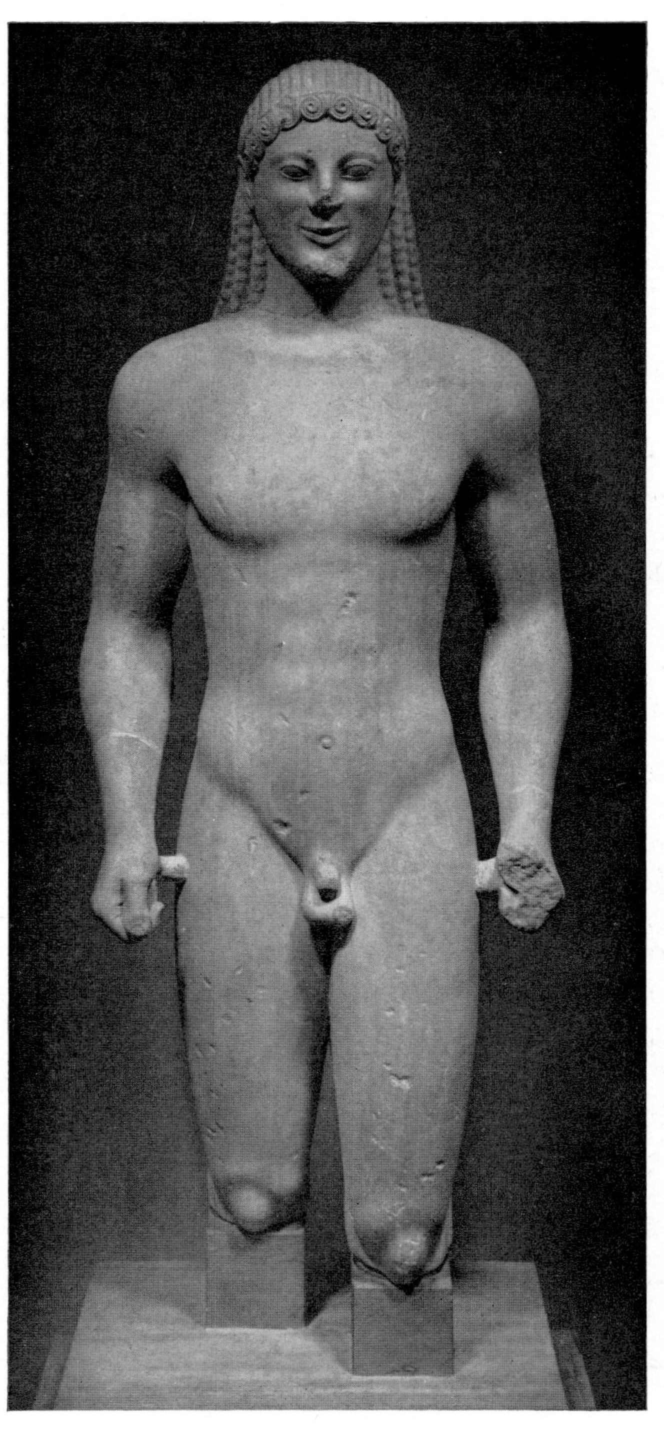

Figs. 425-427 (Athens)

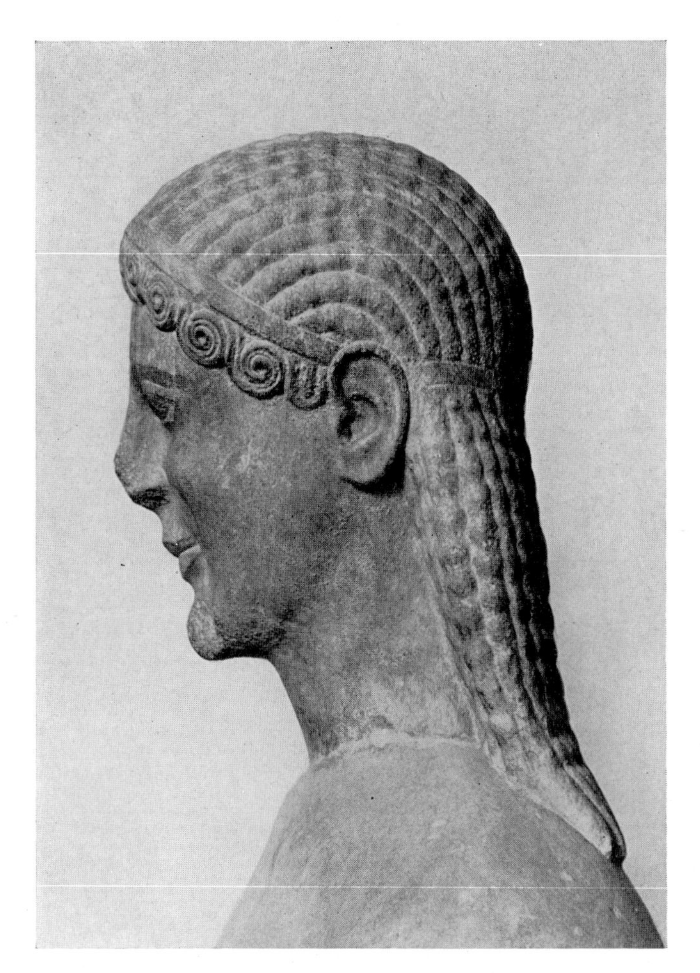

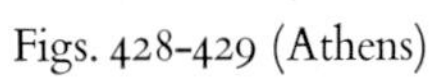

Figs. 428-429 (Athens)

Figs. 430-431 (Thebes)

Figs. 432-433 (Athens) 147

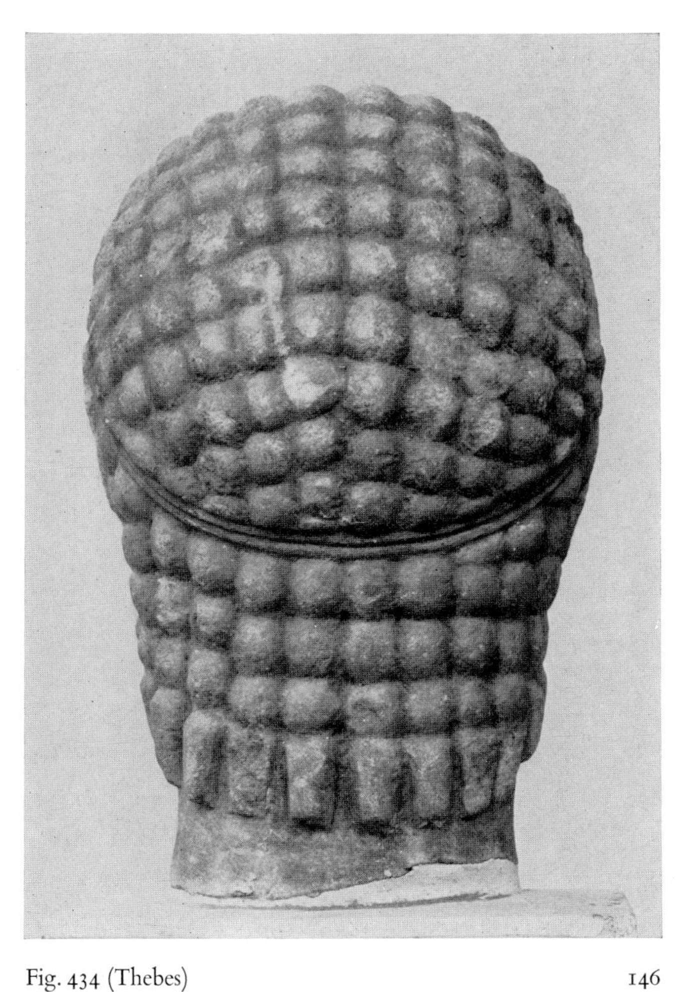

Fig. 434 (Thebes) 146

Fig. 435 (Athens) 147

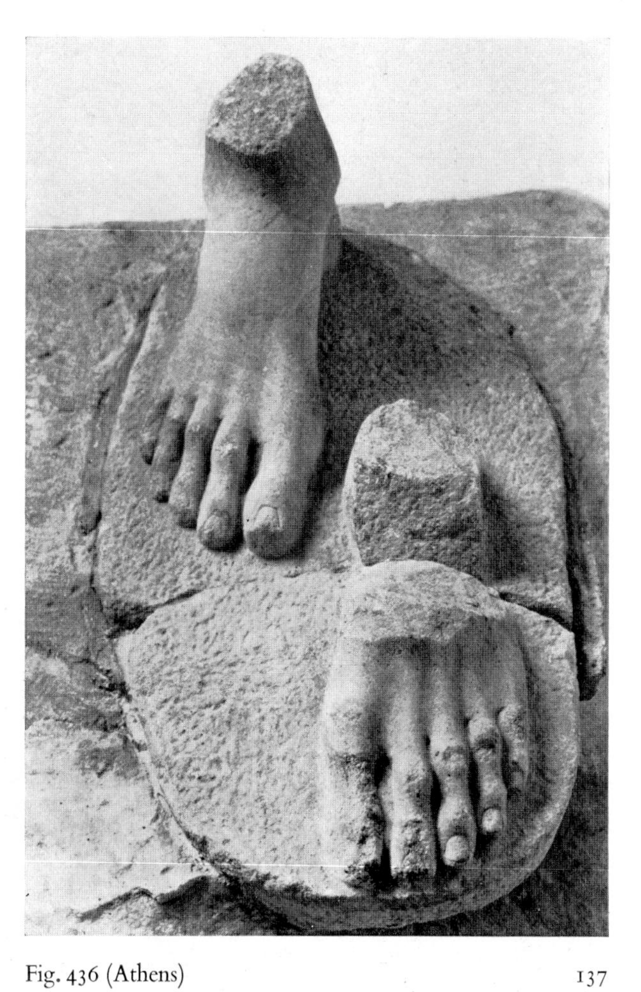

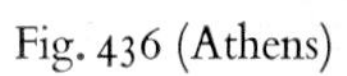

Fig. 436 (Athens) 137

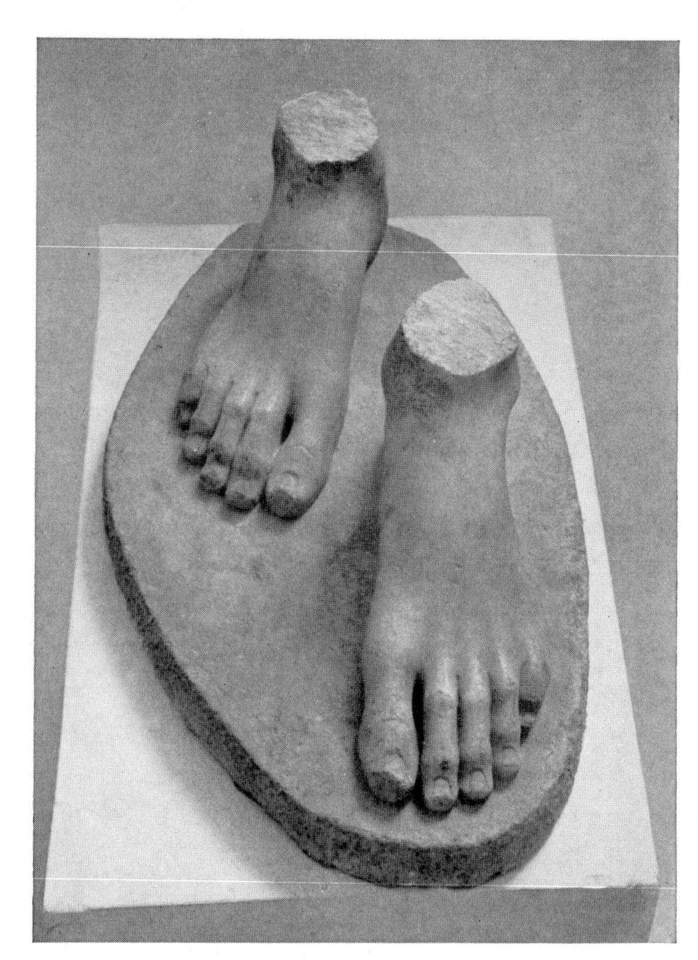

Fig. 437 (Athens) 145

Figs. 438–439 (Athens) 150

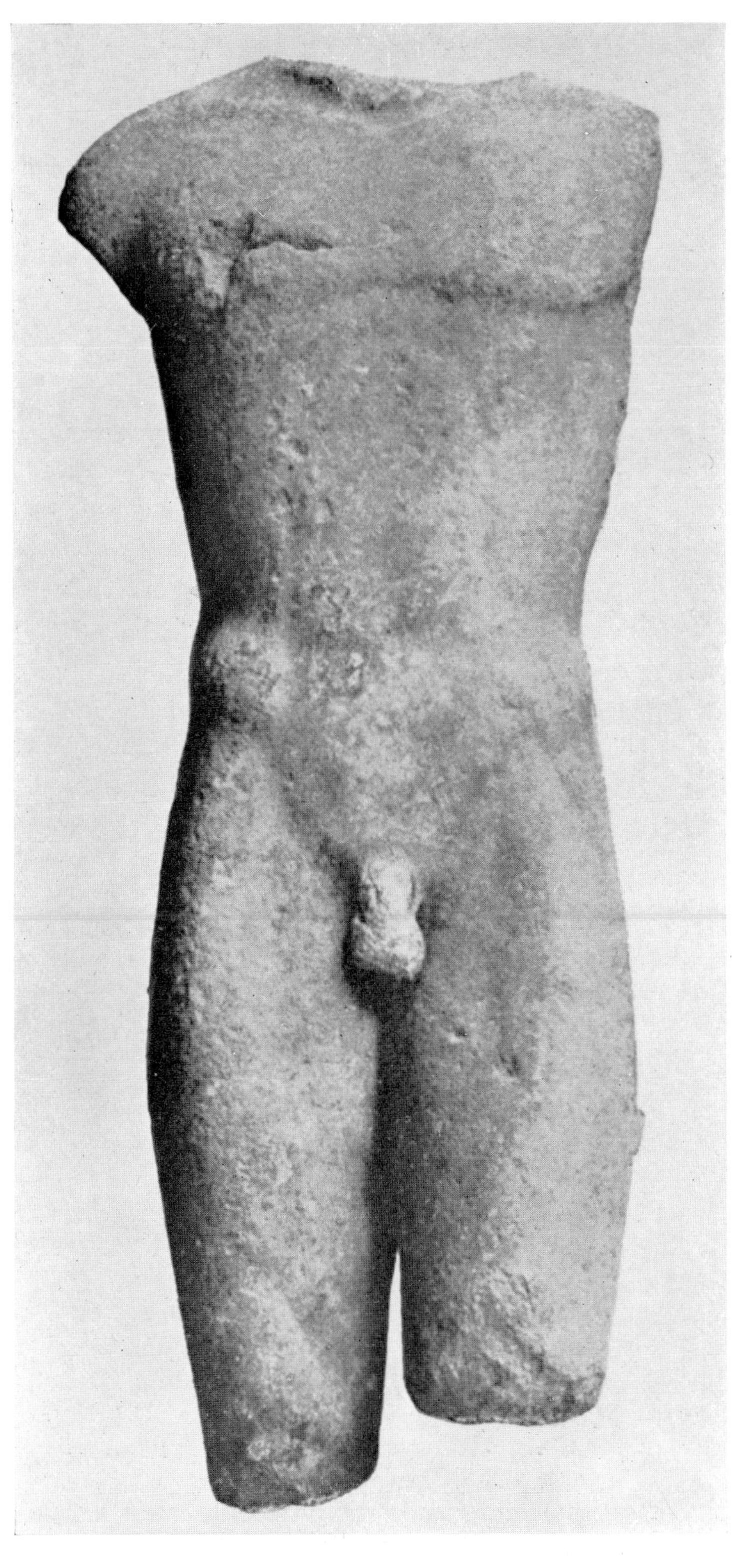

Fig. 440 (Delphi) 149

Fig. 441 (Samos) 153

Fig. 442 (Athens) 137

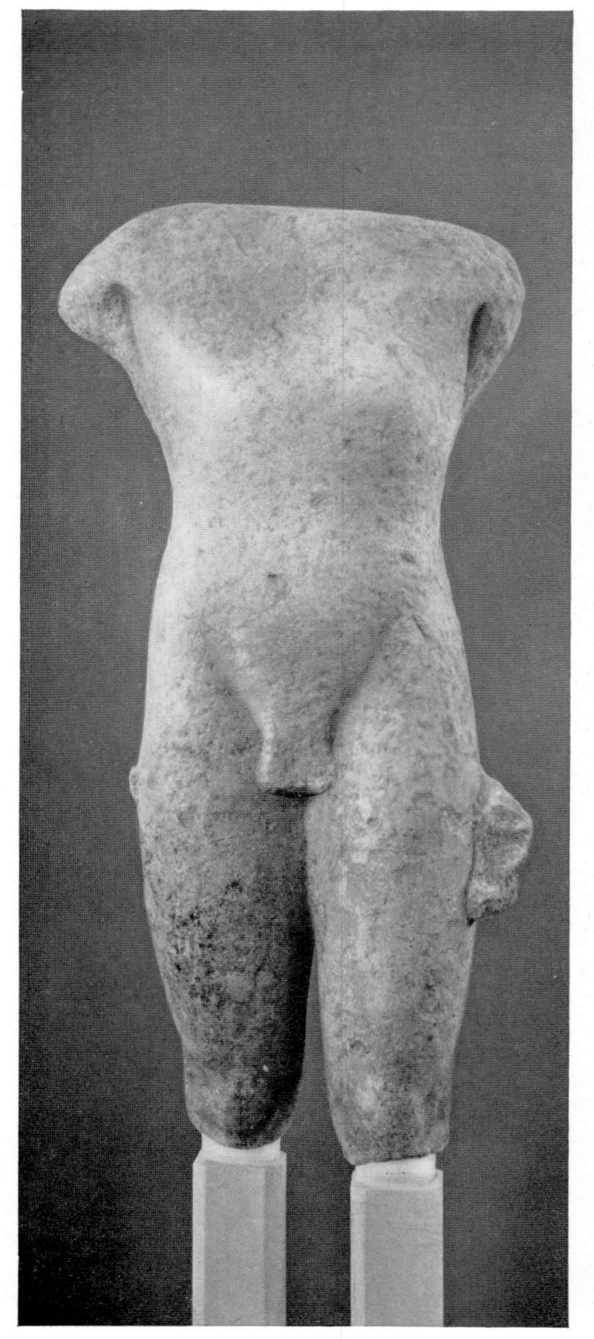

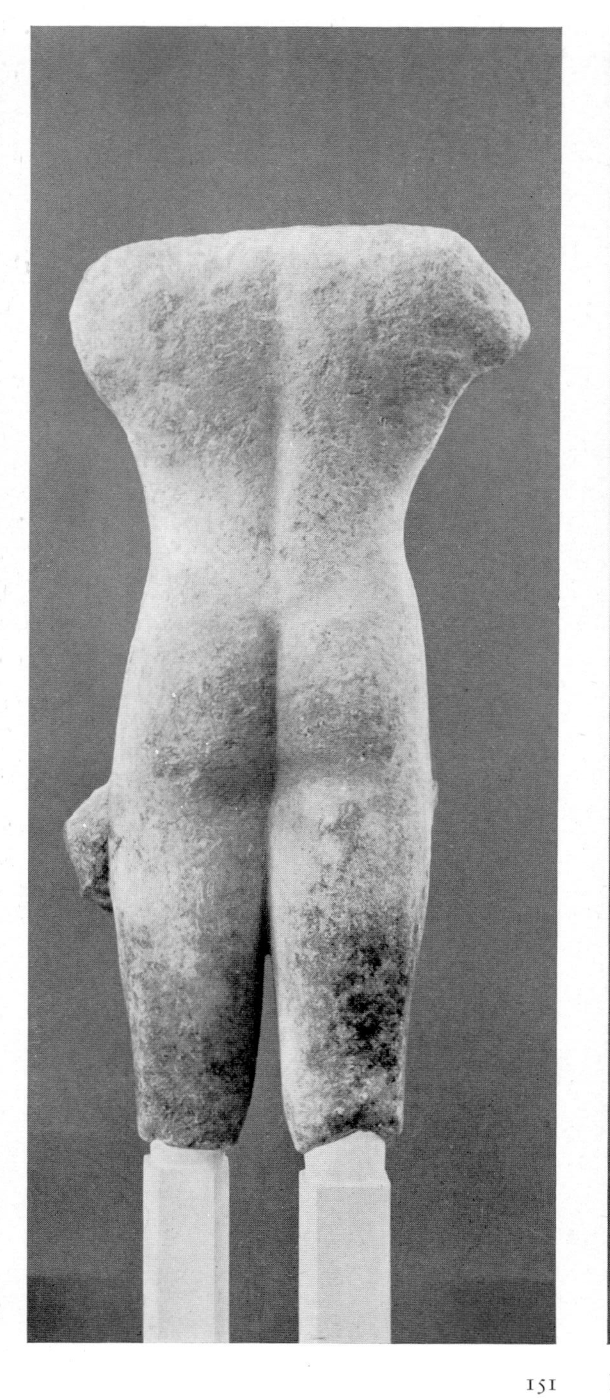

Figs. 443-444 (Delos)

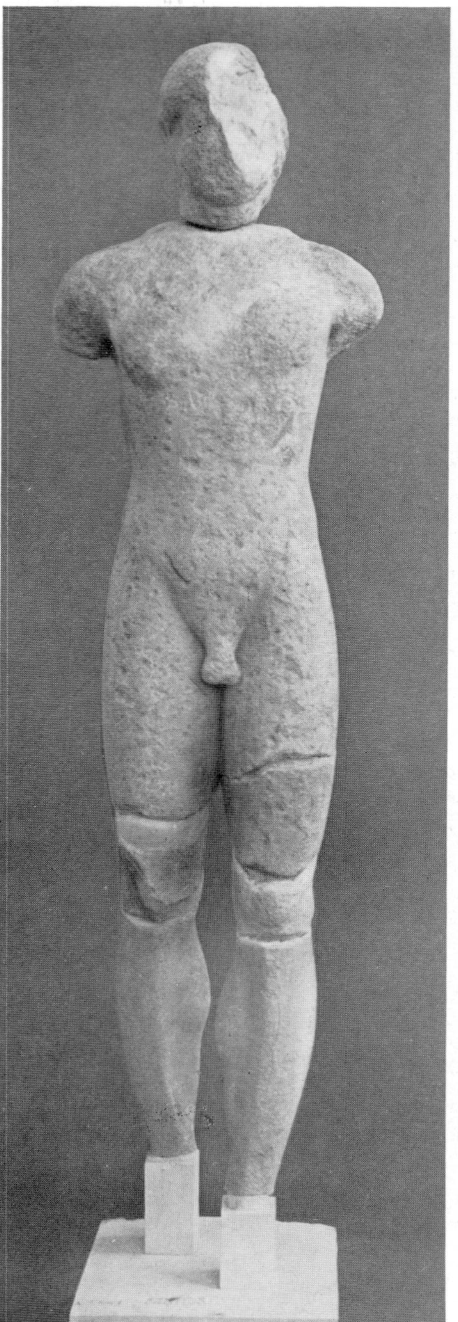

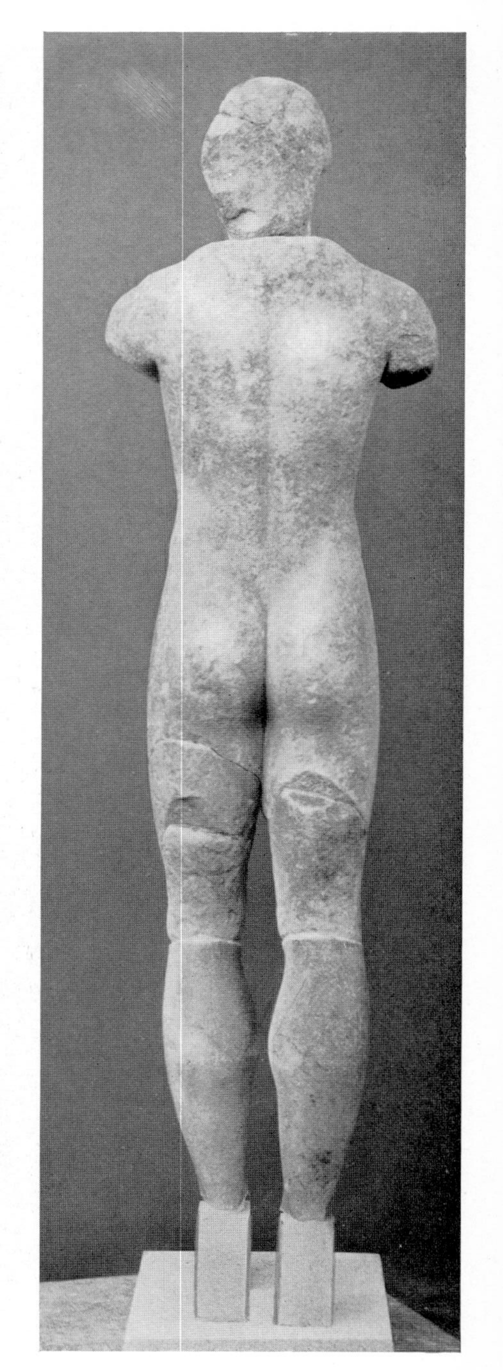

Figs. 445-446 (Delos)

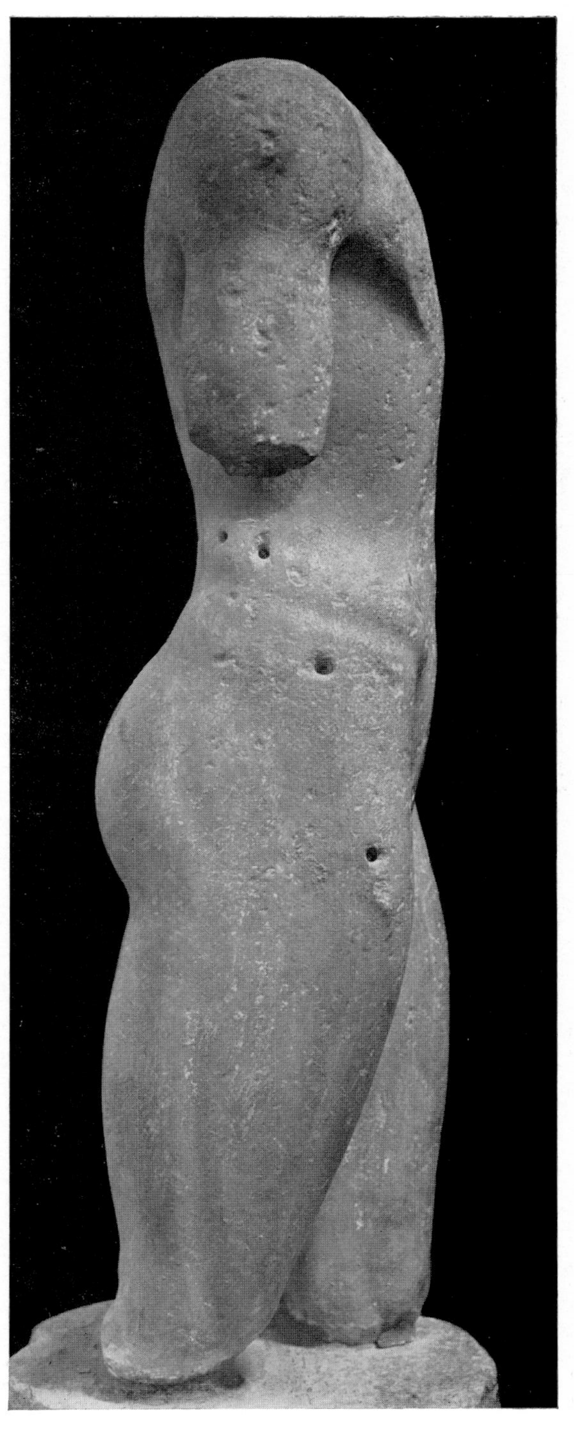

Figs. 447-449 (Rhodes)

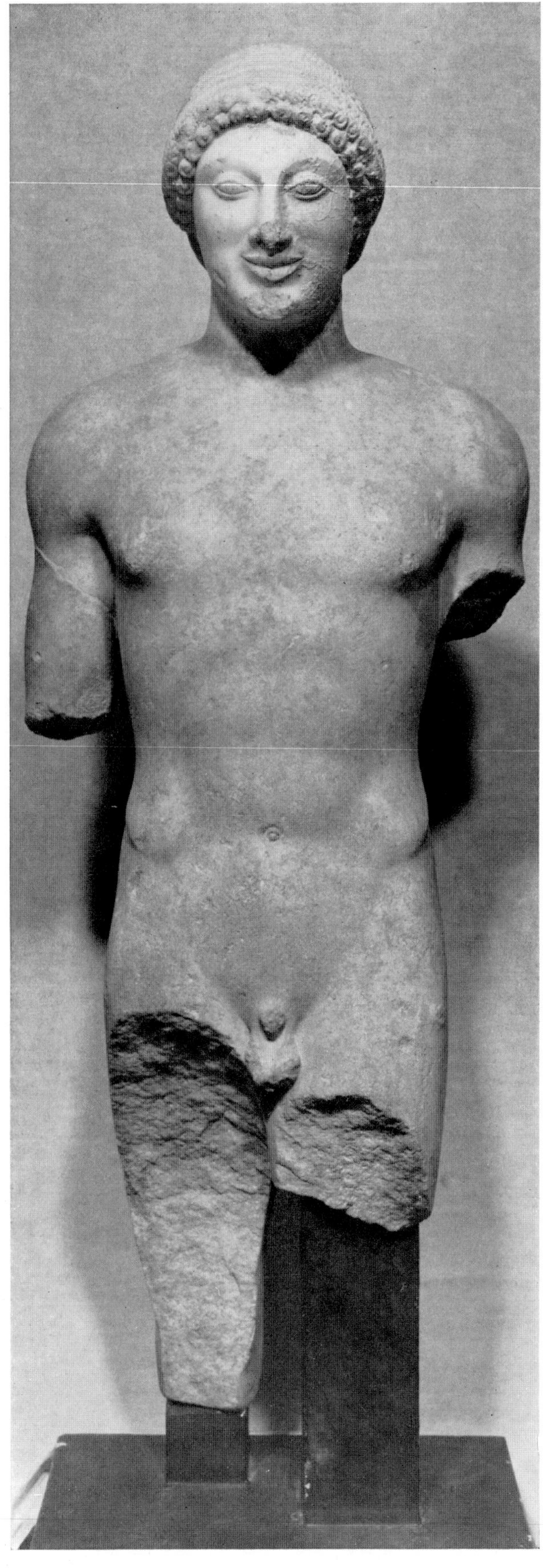

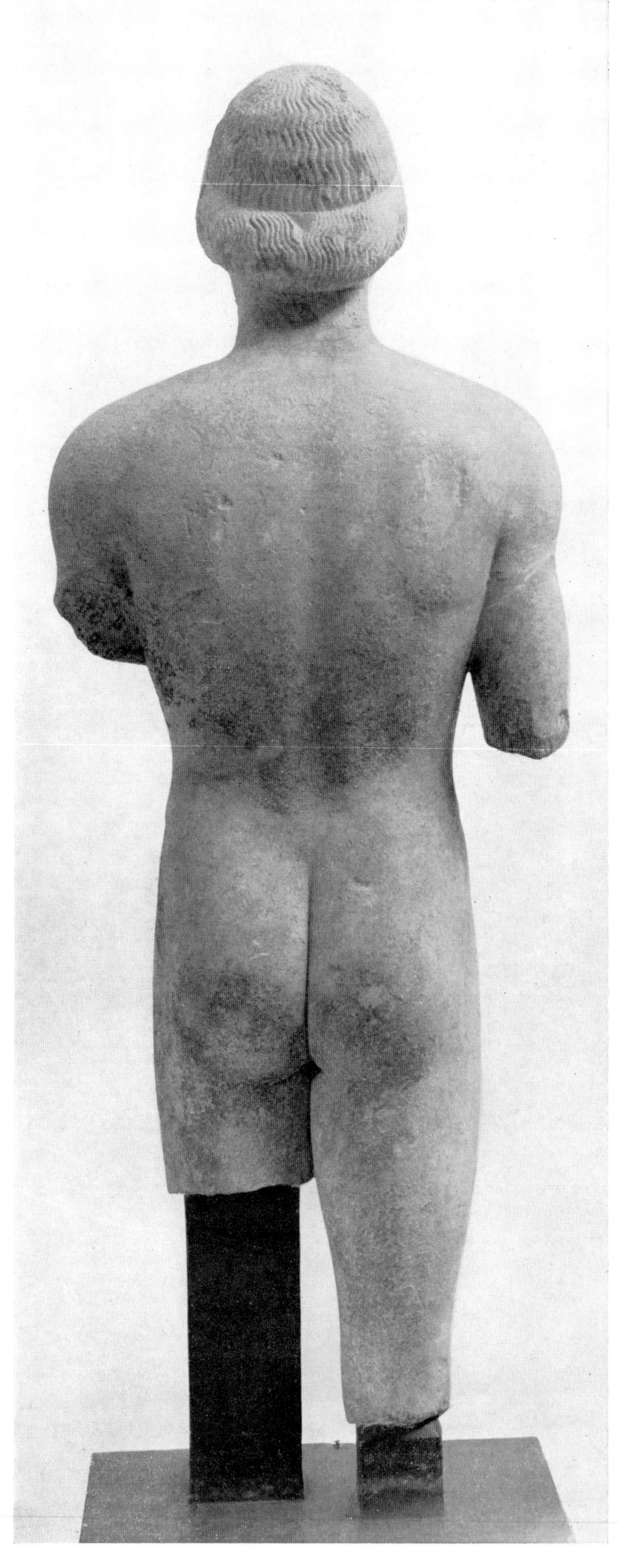

Figs. 450-451 (Athens)

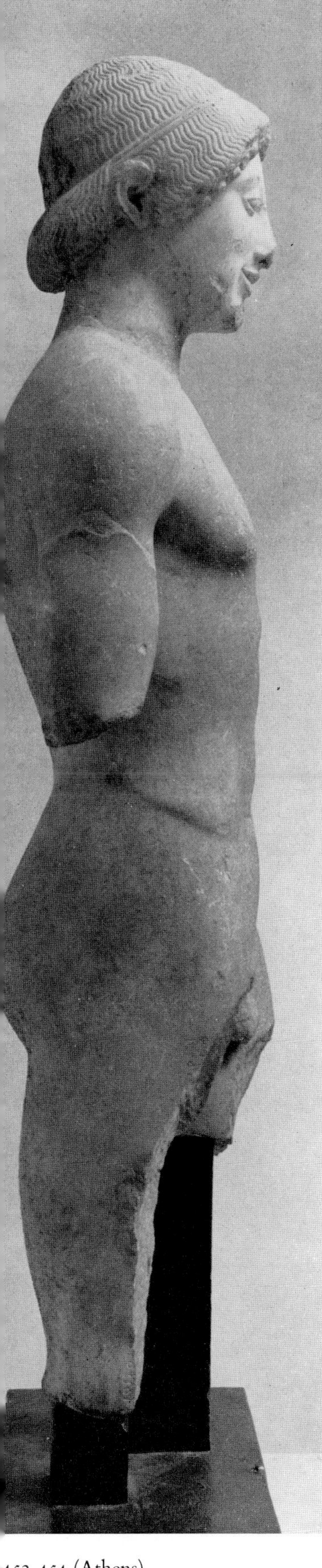
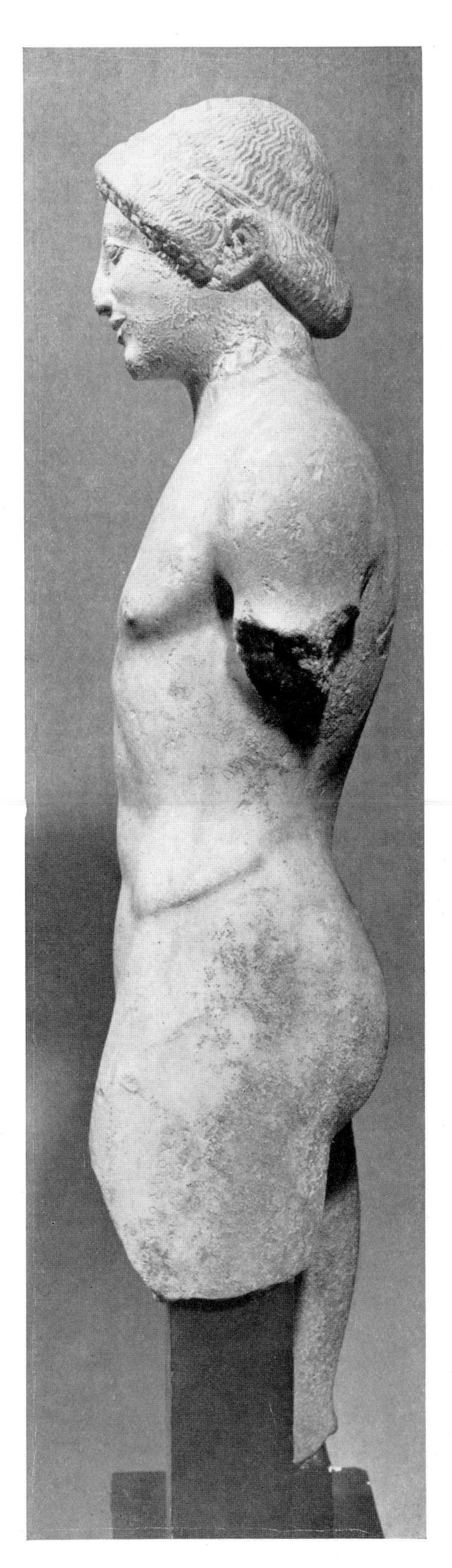
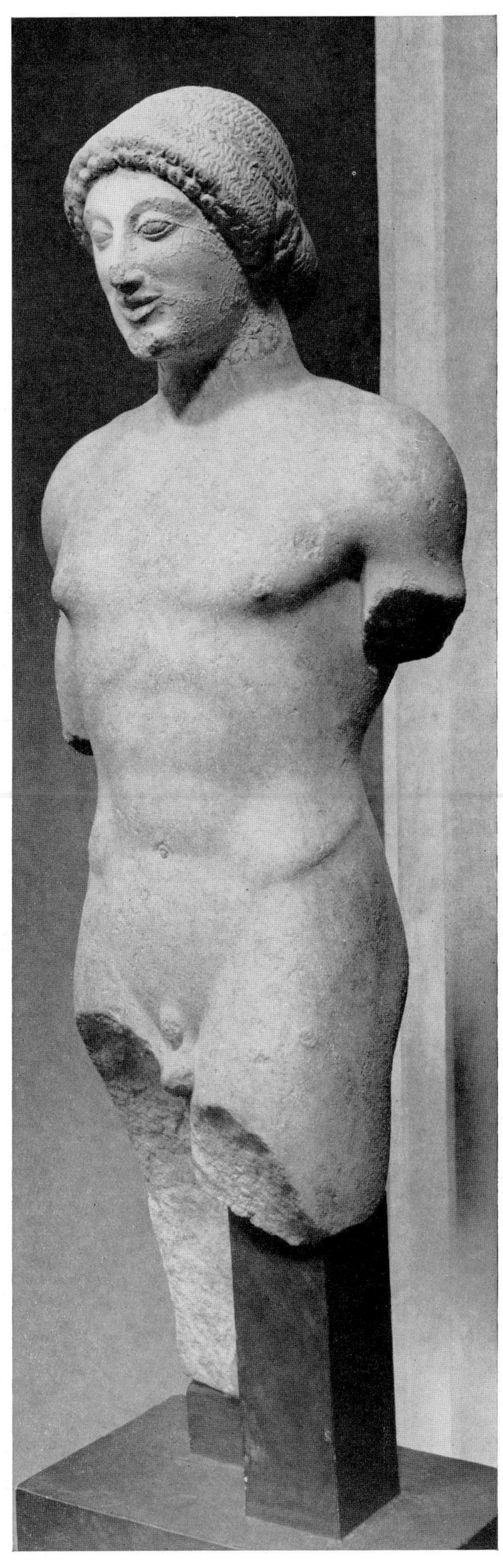

452–454 (Athens)

Figs. 455-457 (Athens)

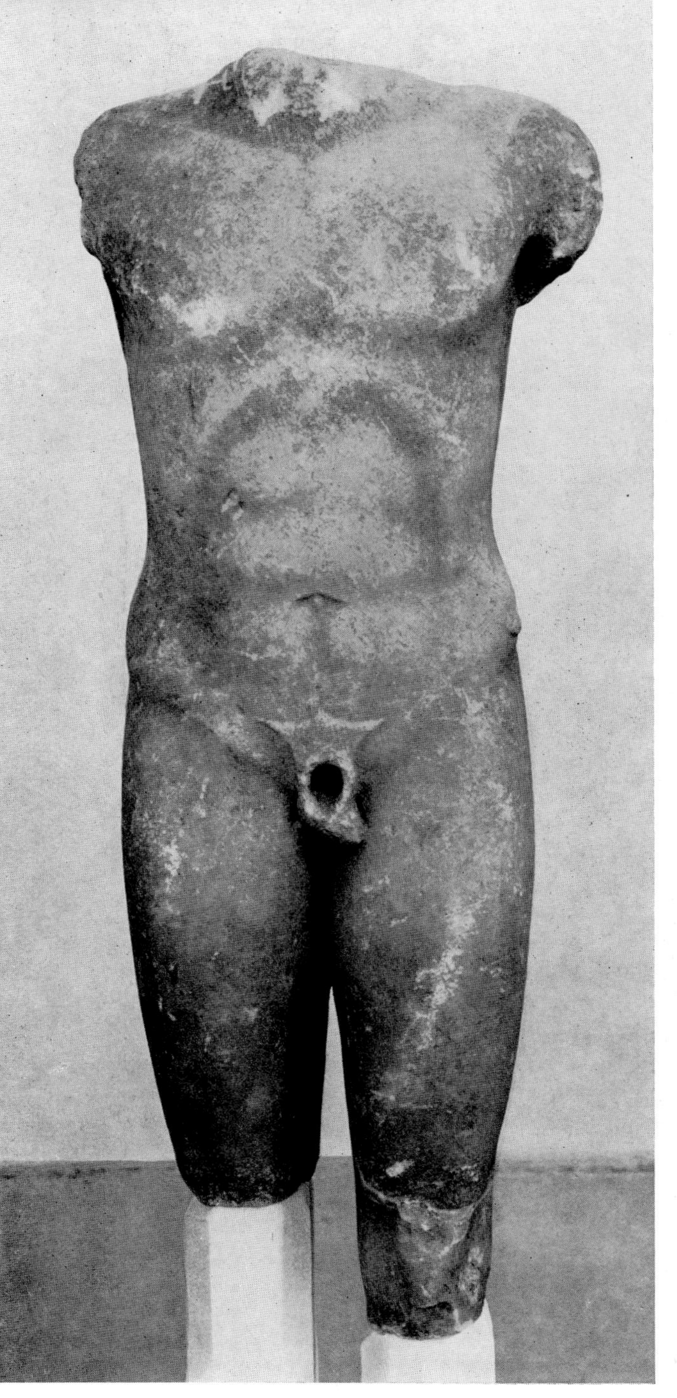
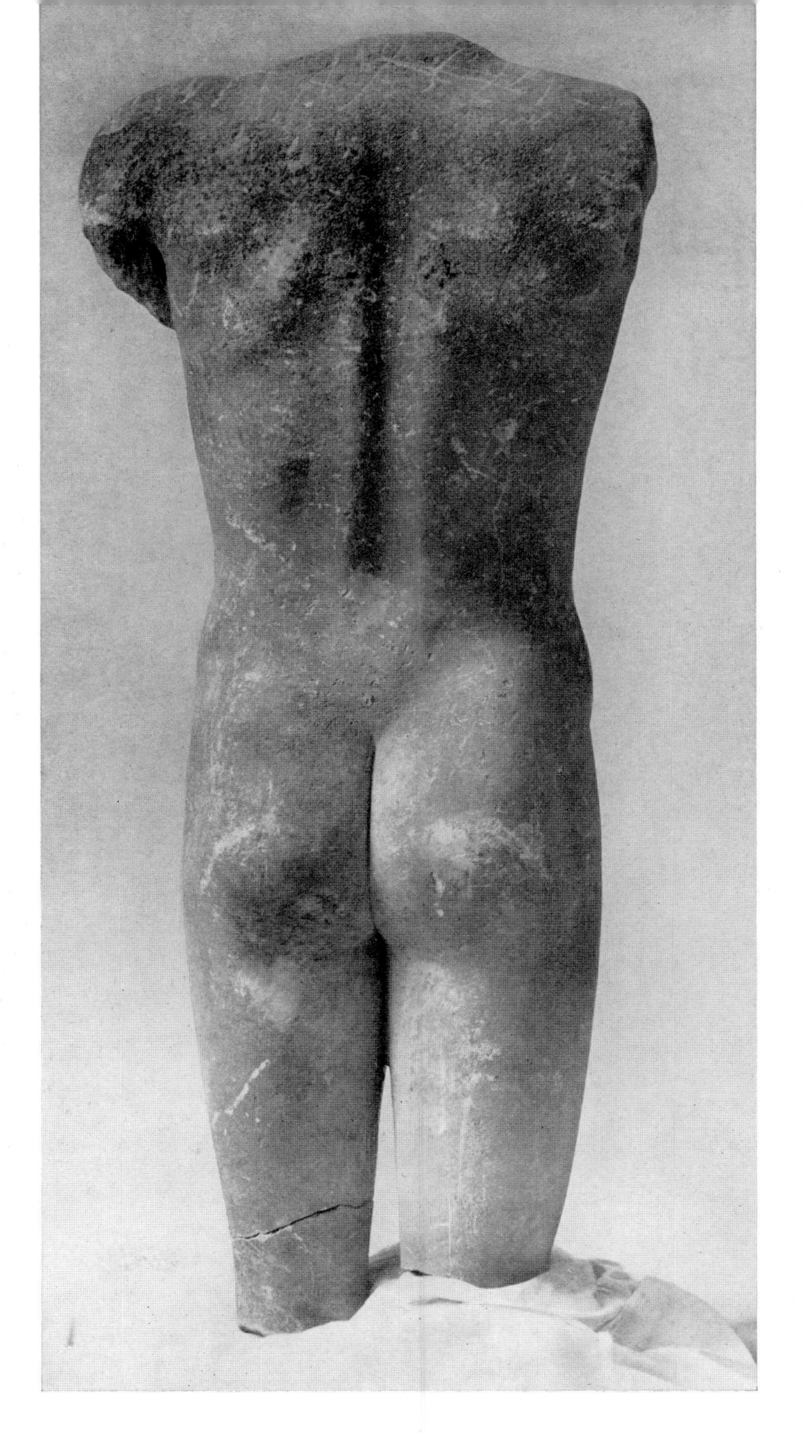
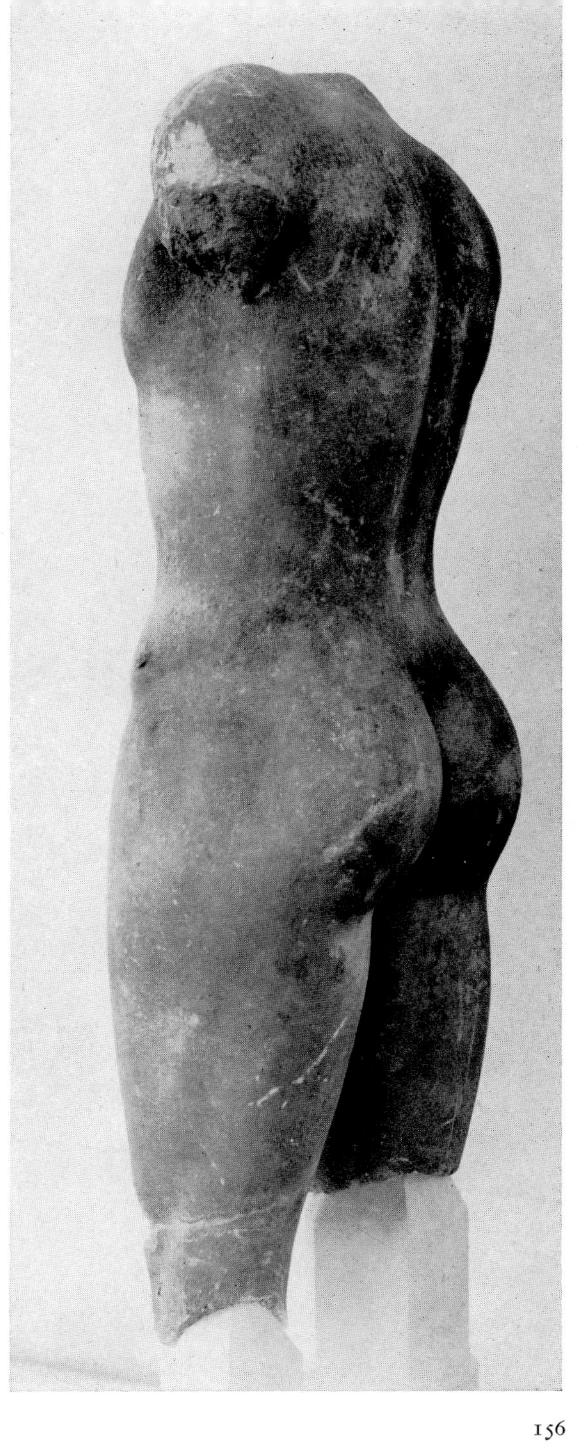

Figs. 458-460 (Thebes)

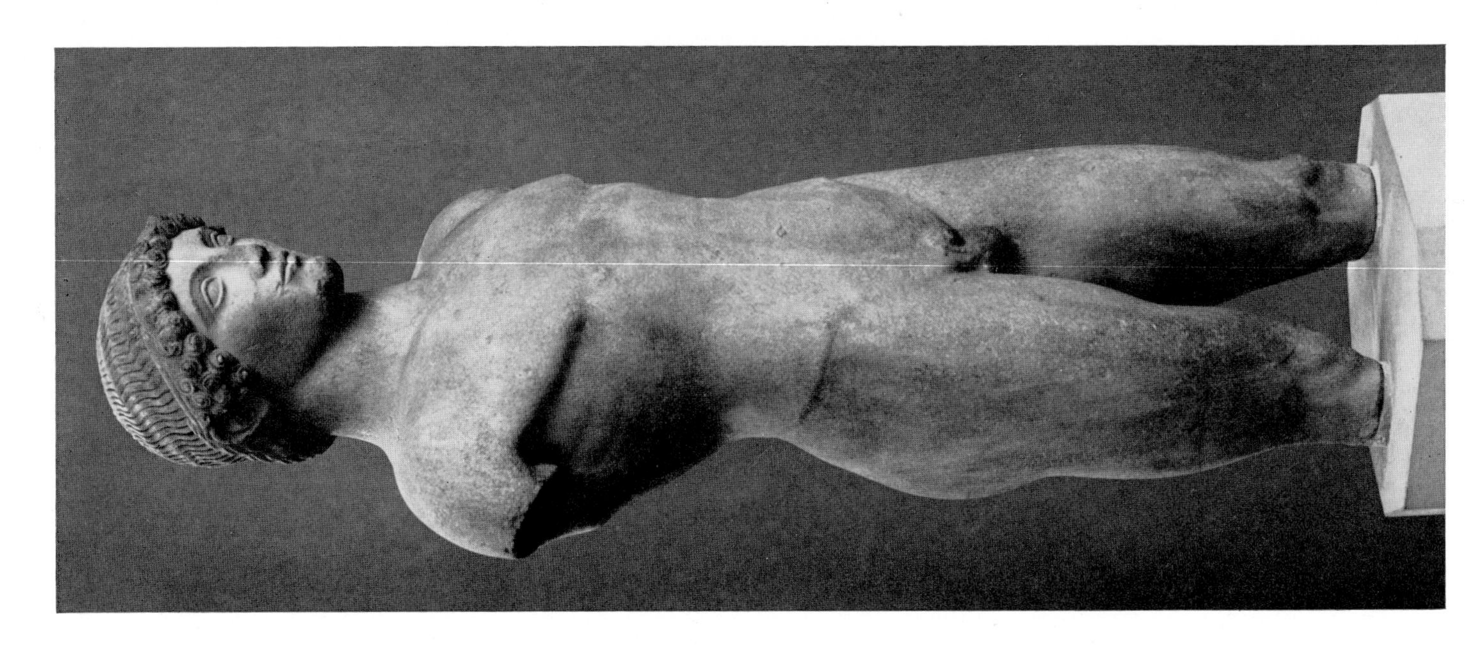

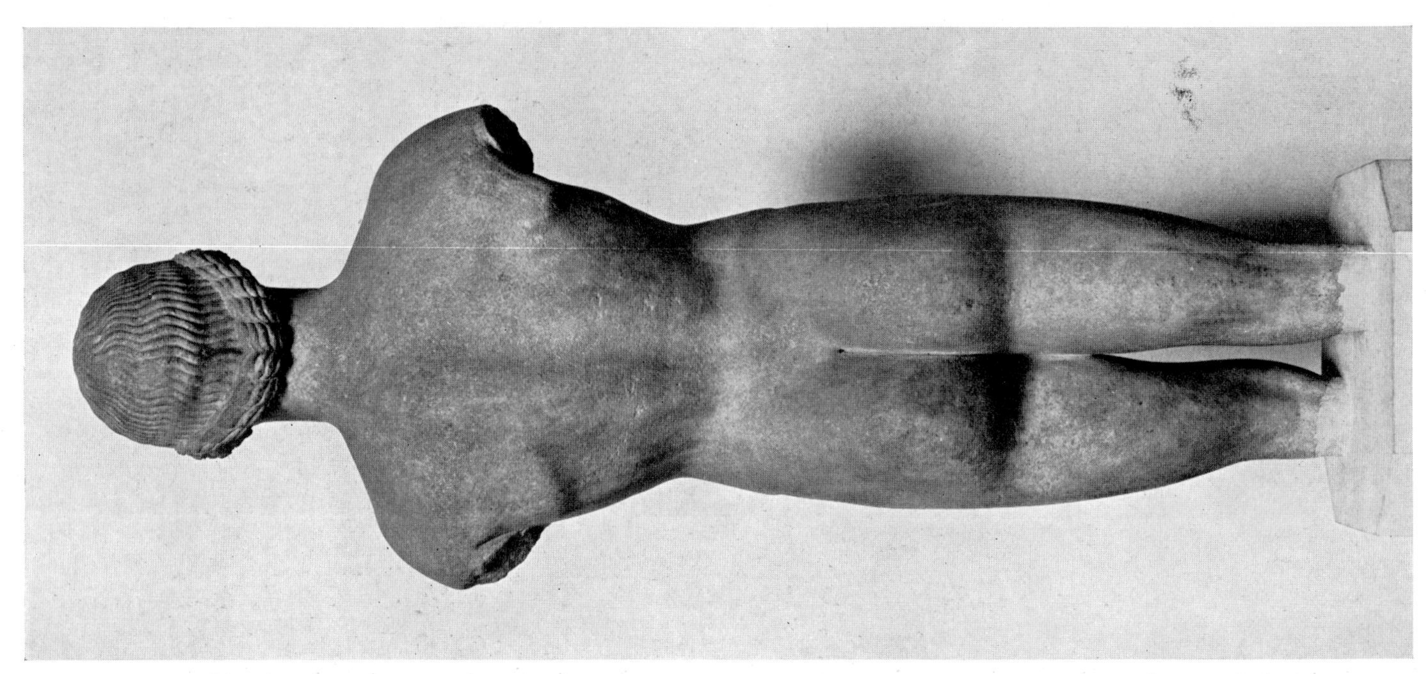

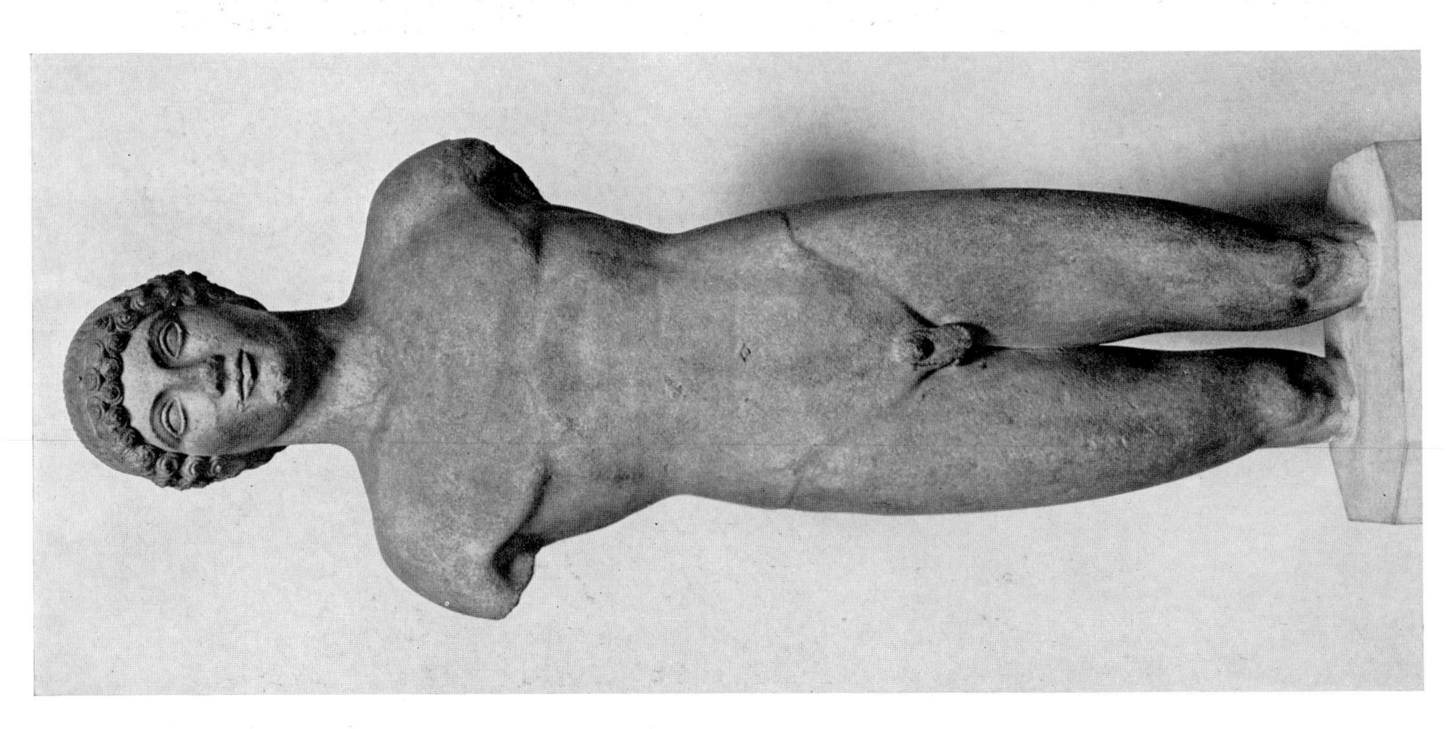

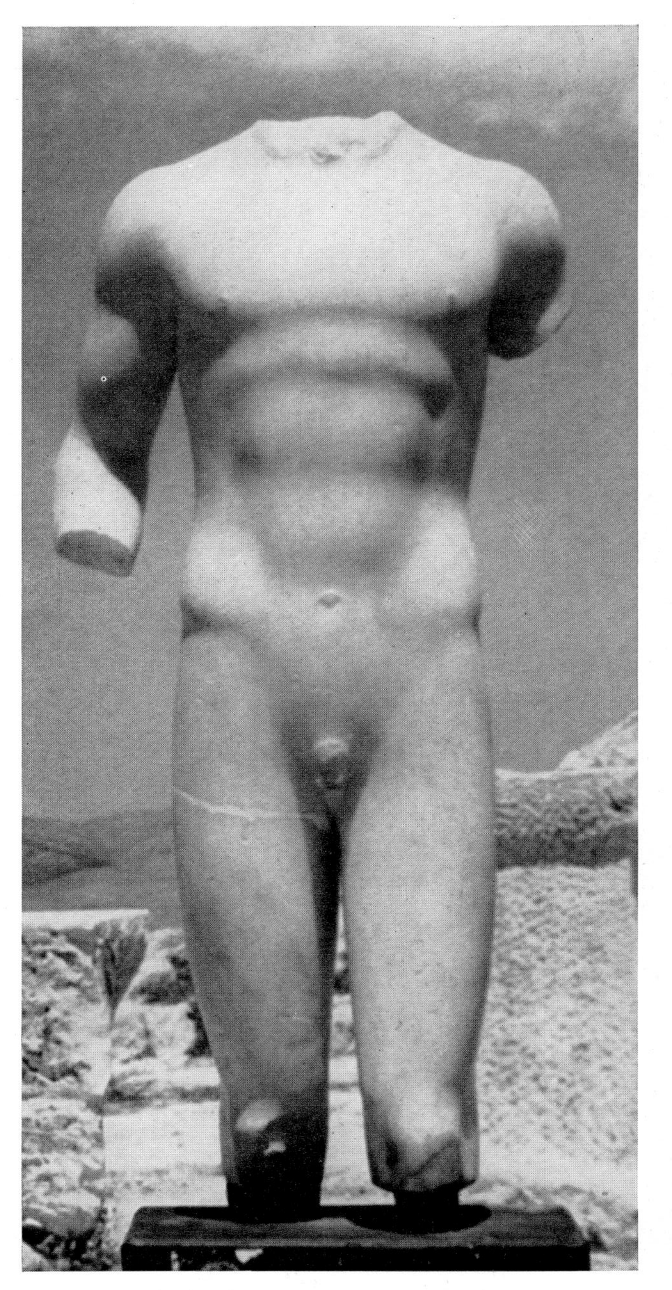

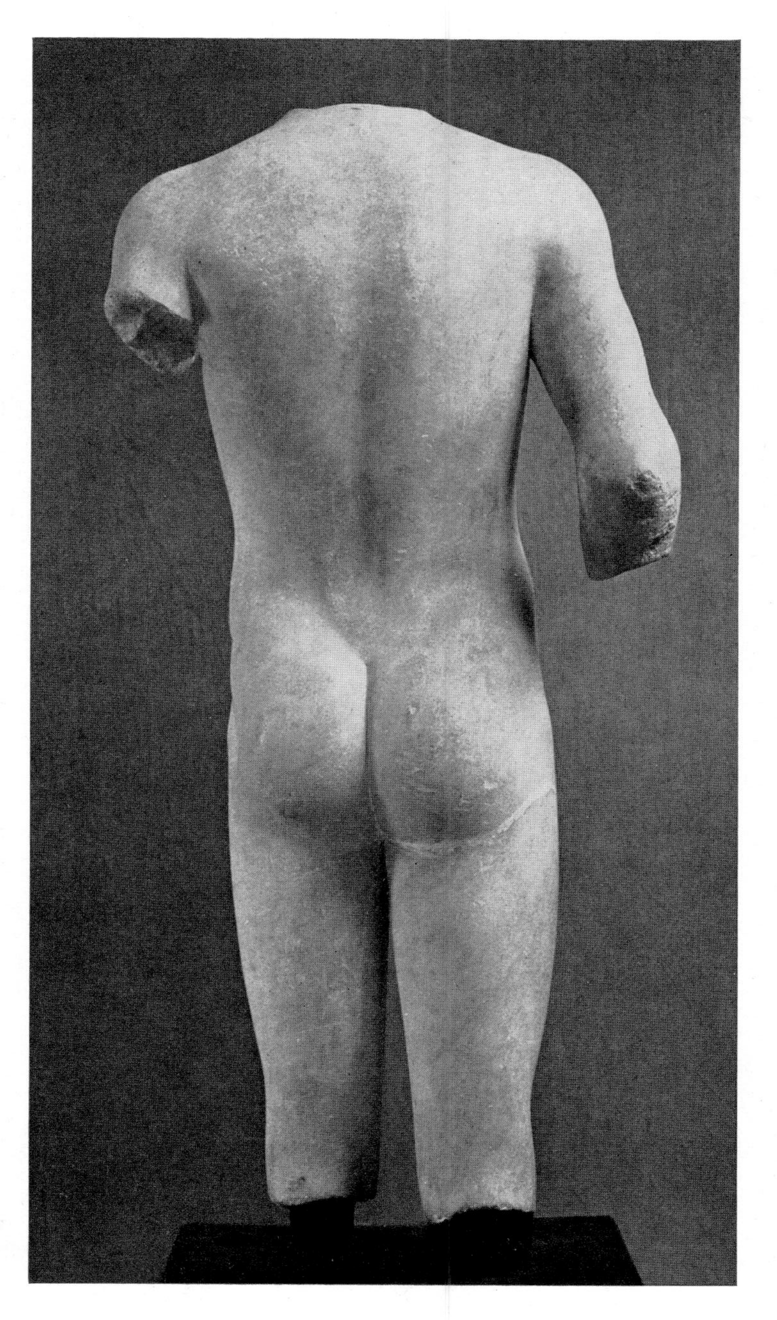

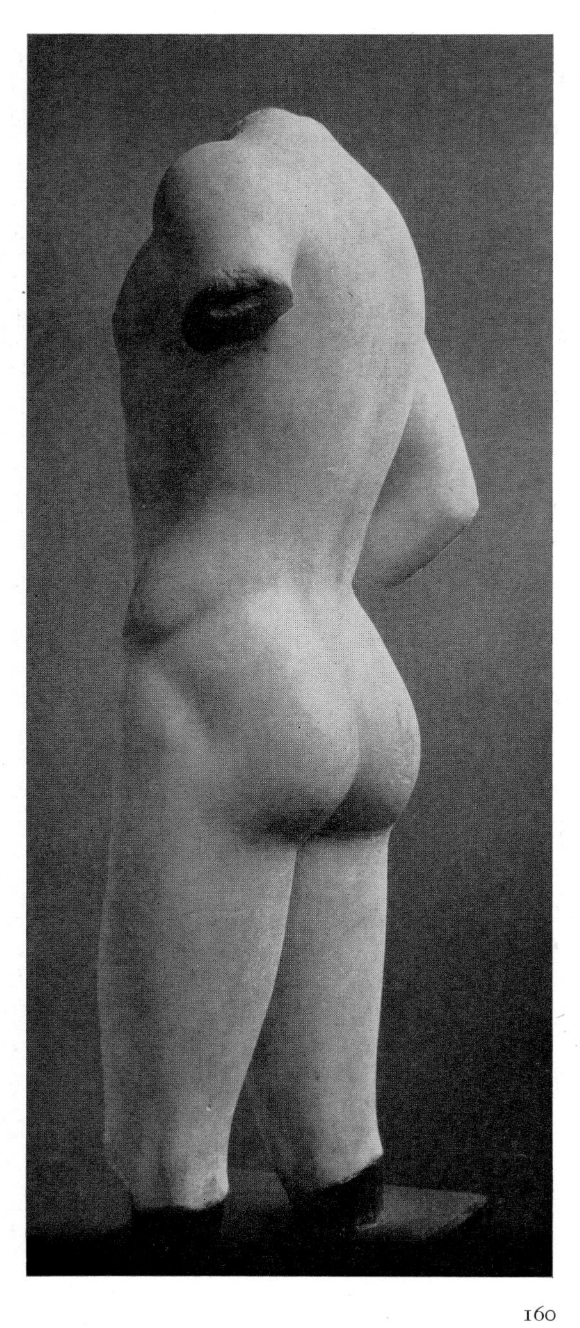

Figs. 464-466 (Athens)

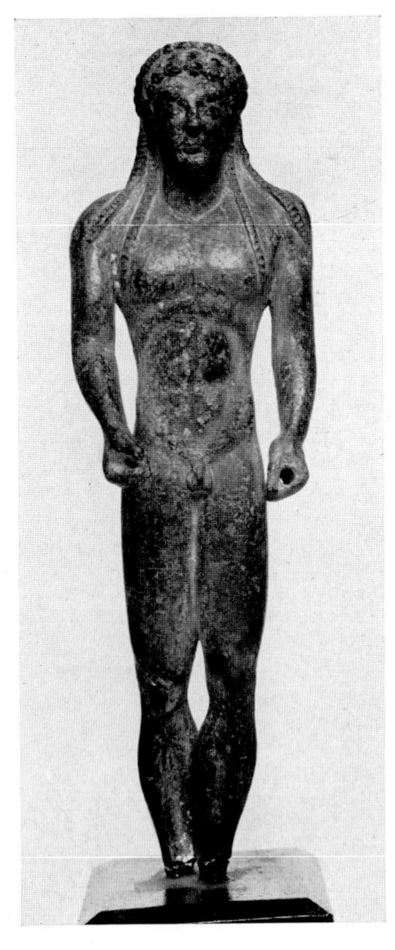

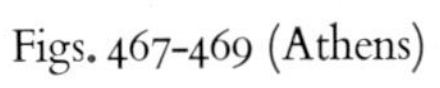
Figs. 467-469 (Athens)

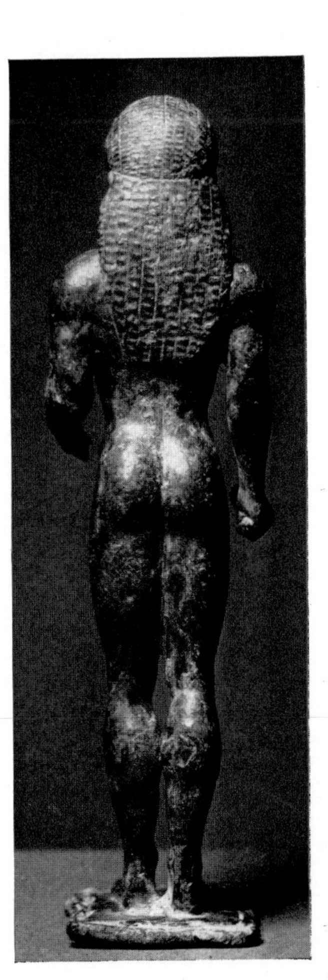

Figs. 470-473 (New York)

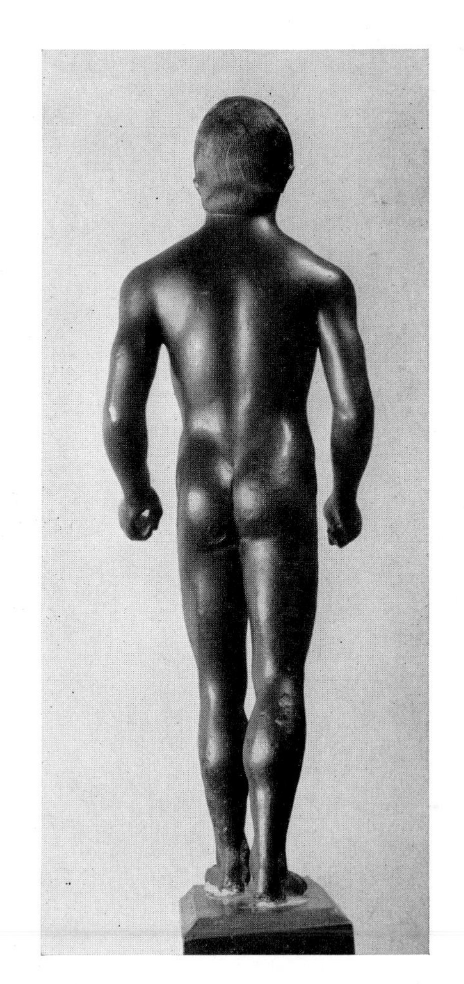

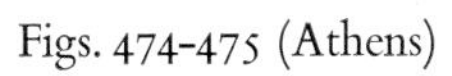

Figs. 474–475 (Athens) 162

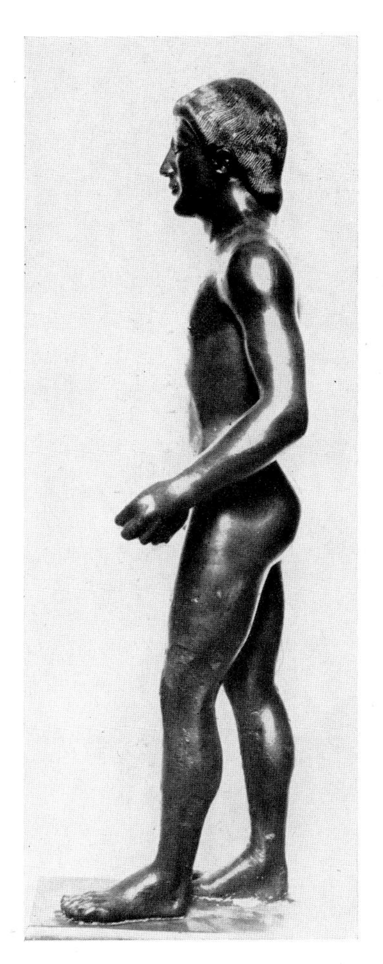

I

Figs. 476–477 (Athens) 162

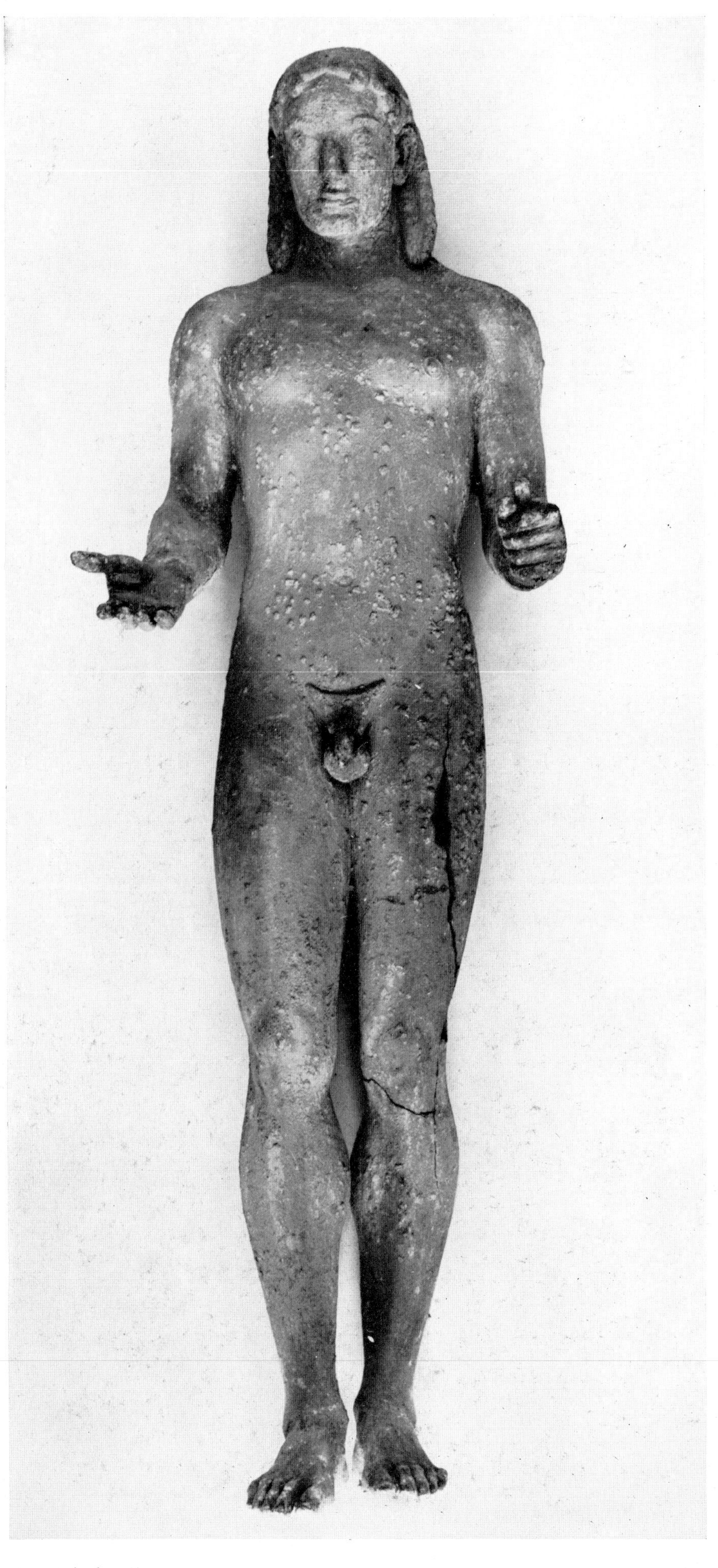

Fig. 478 (Athens?)

Fig. 479 (Athens?)

Fig. 480 (Athens?)

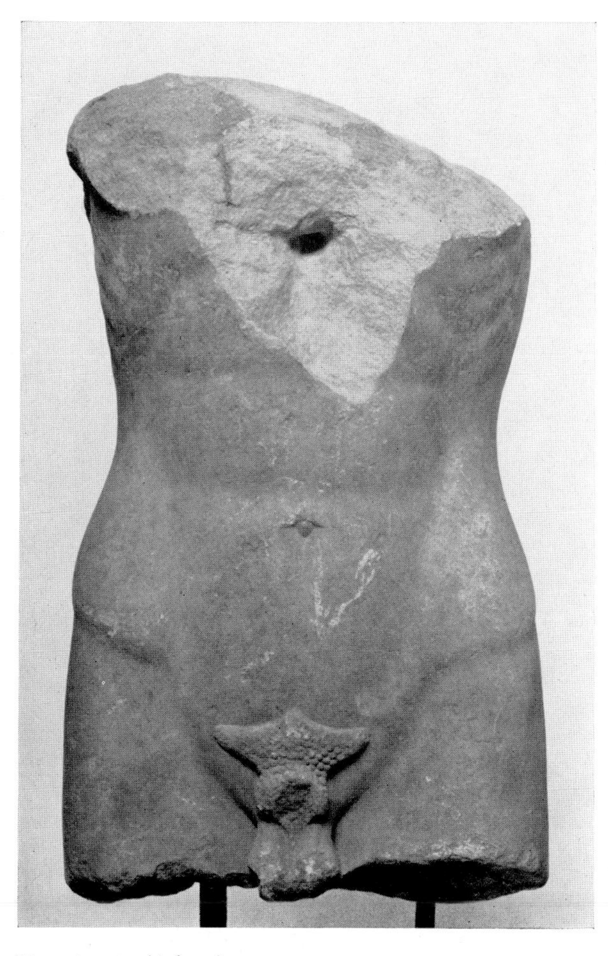

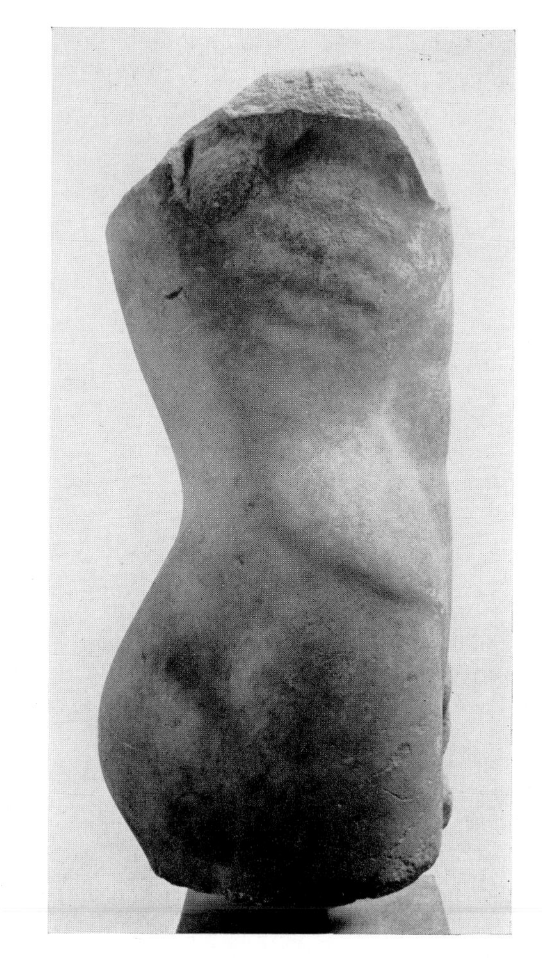

Figs. 481-482 (Athens)

161

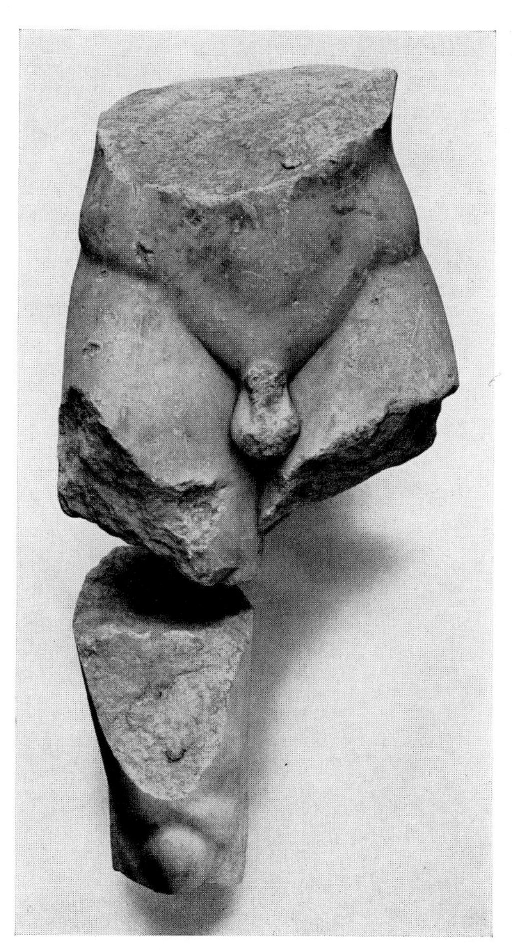

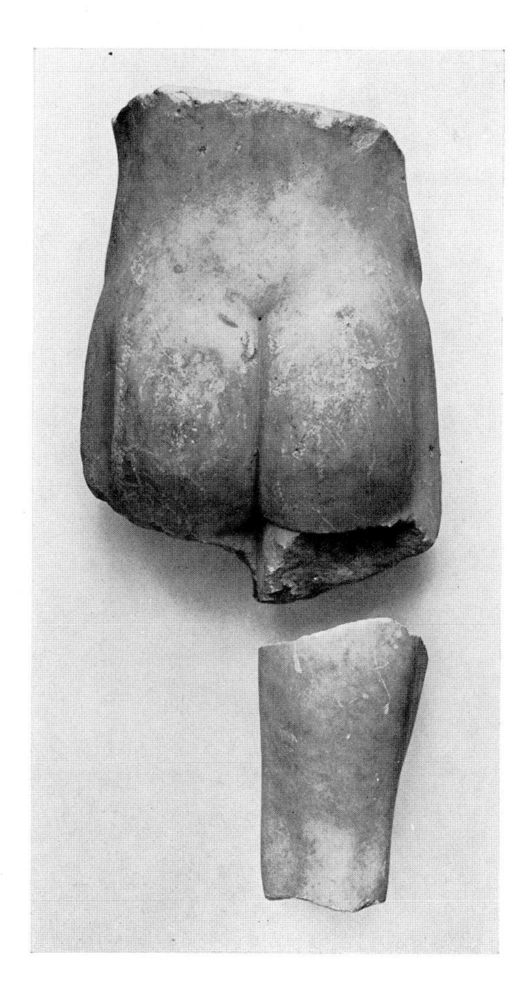

Figs. 483-484 (Athens)

161 bis

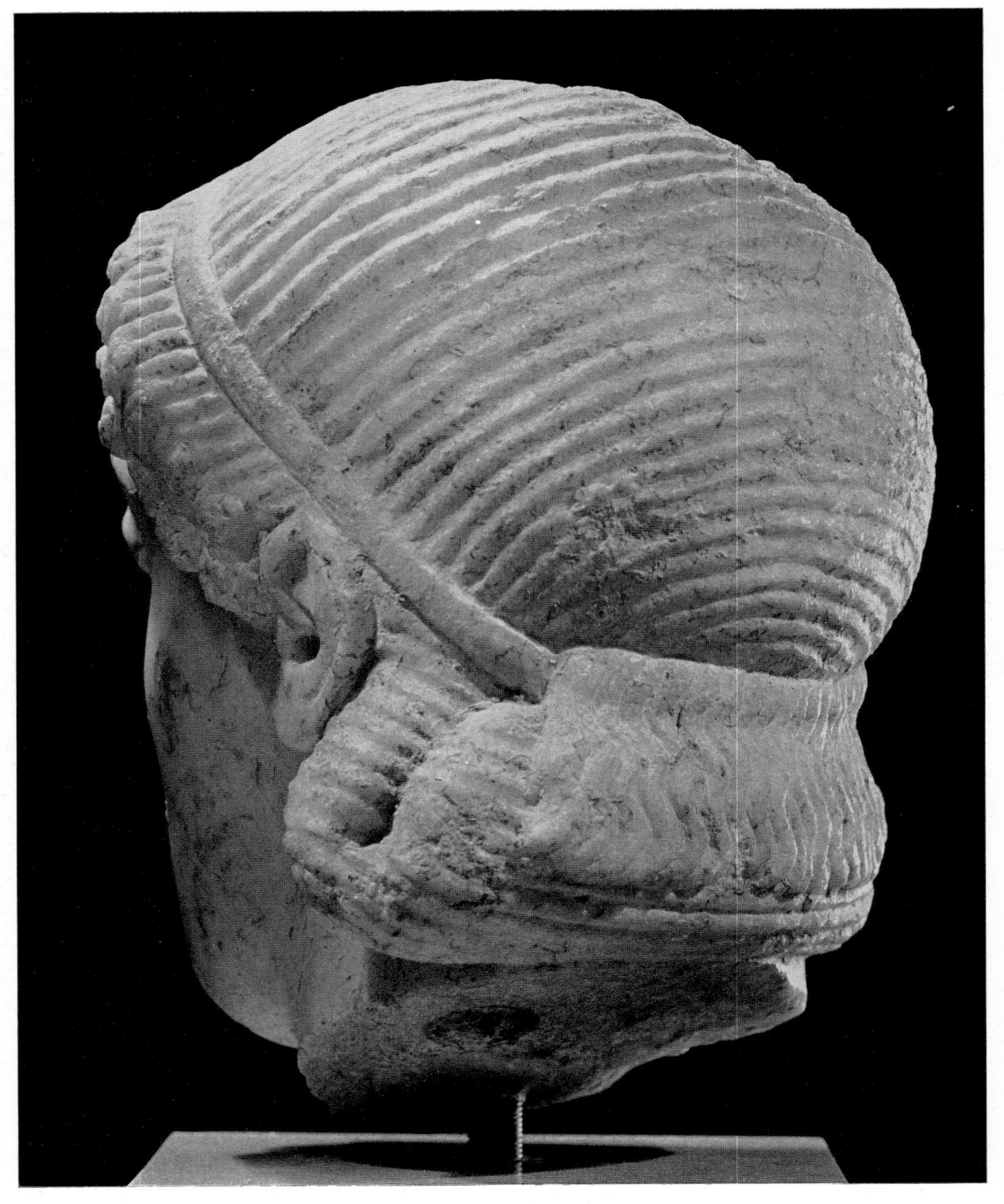

Figs. 485-486 (Kansas City)

Figs. 487-488 (Kansas City)

Fig. 489 (Athens) 165

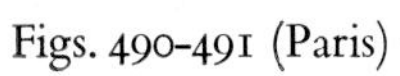

Figs. 490-491 (Paris) 163

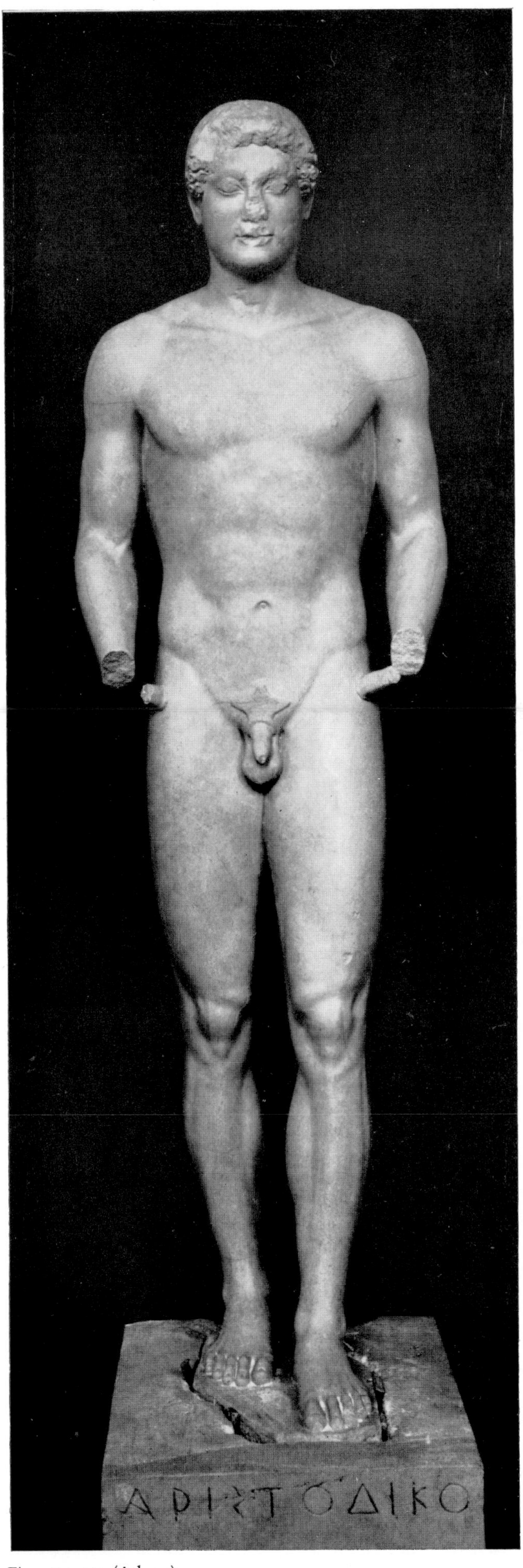

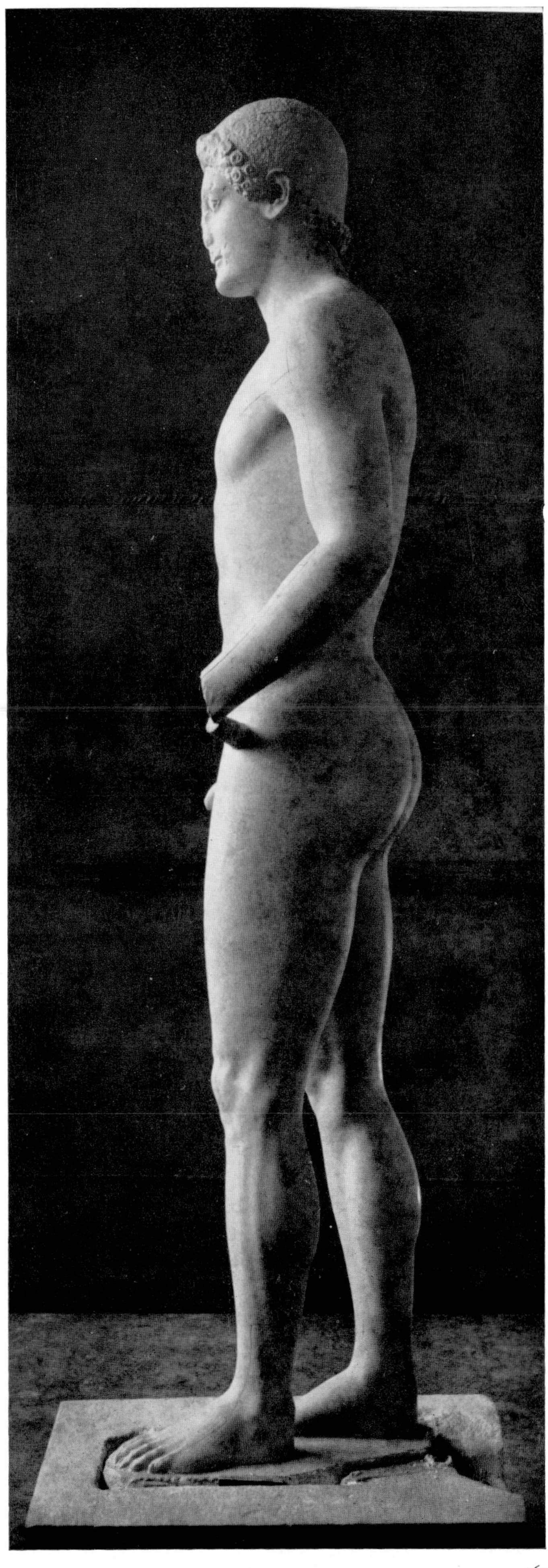

Figs. 492-493 (Athens)

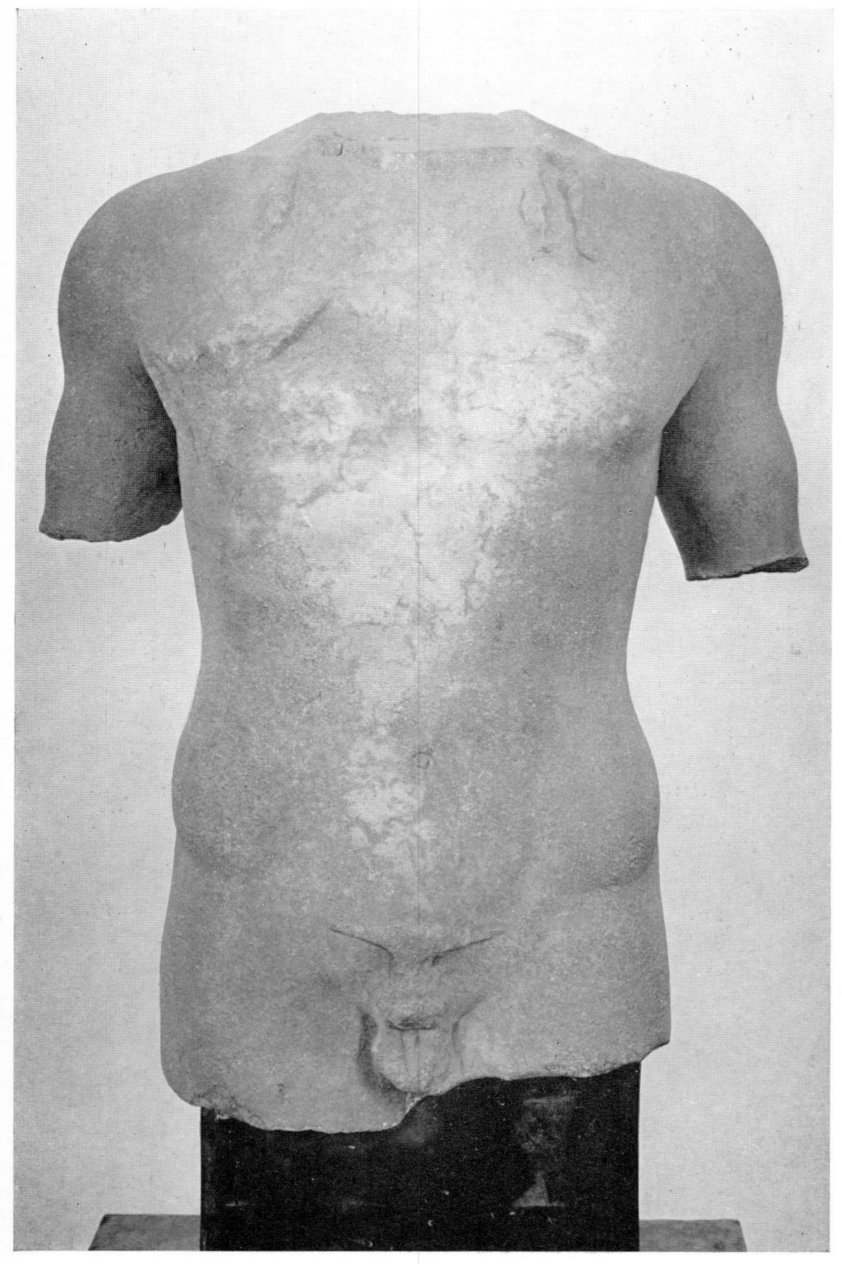

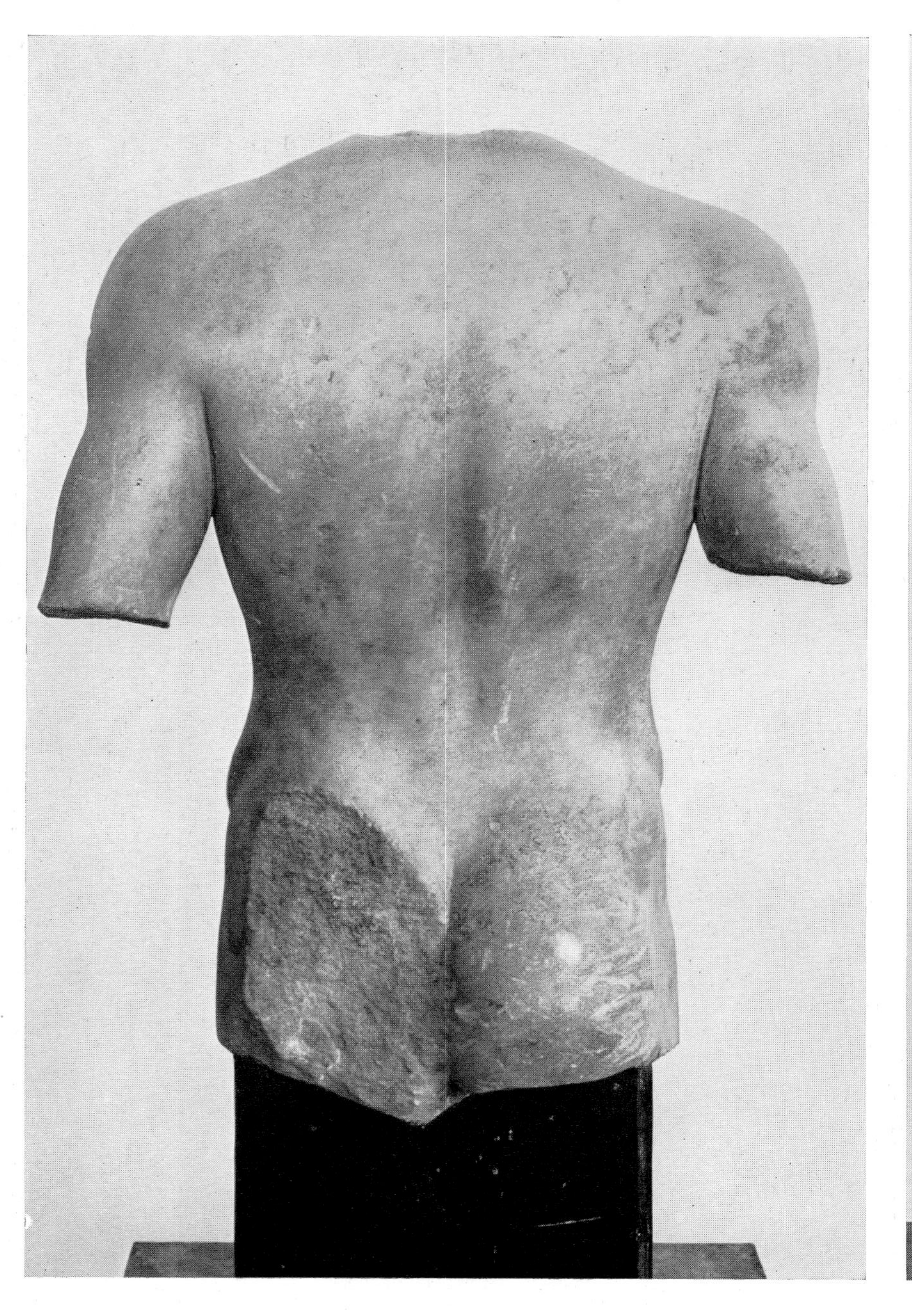

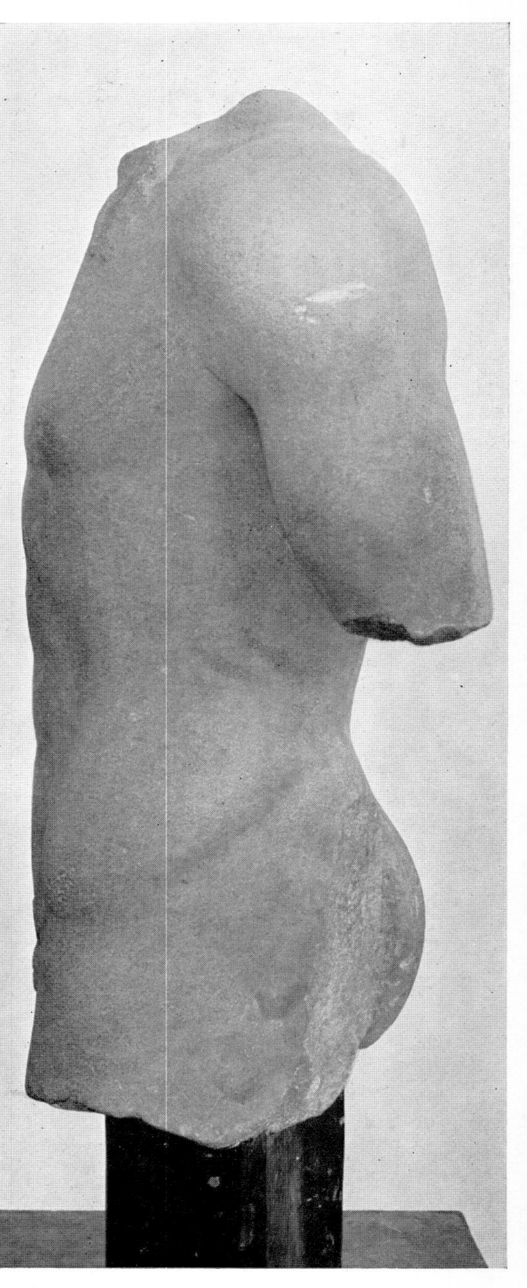

Figs. 494-496 (Chalkis)

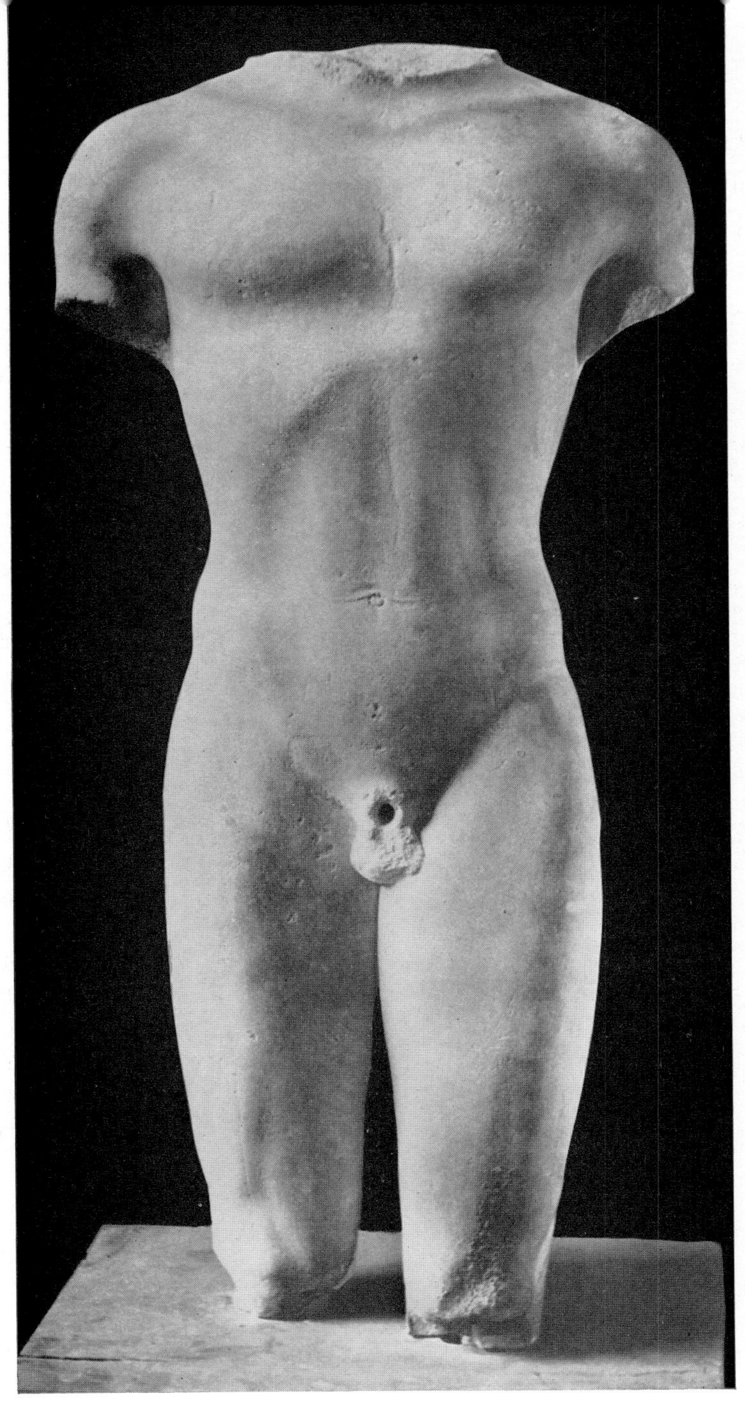

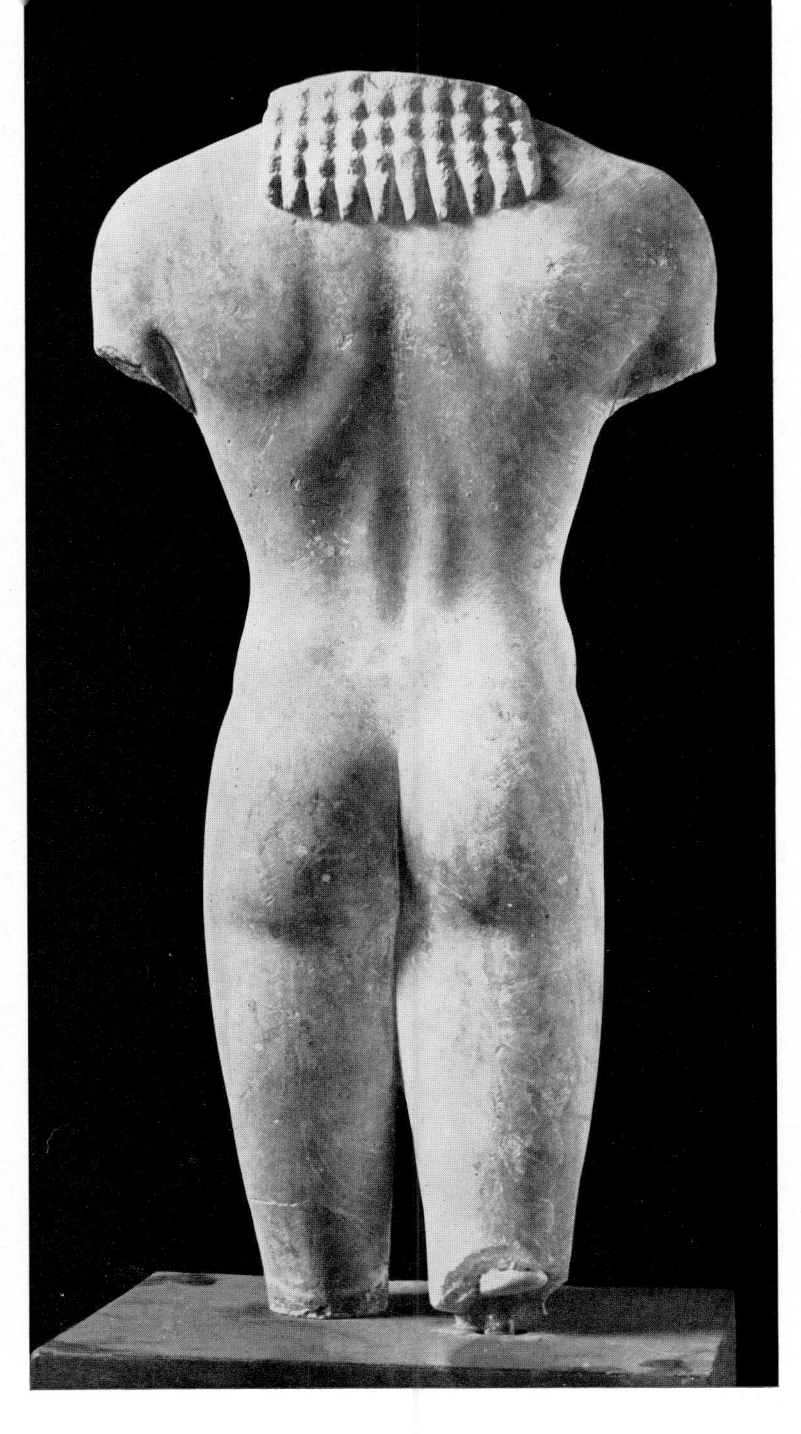

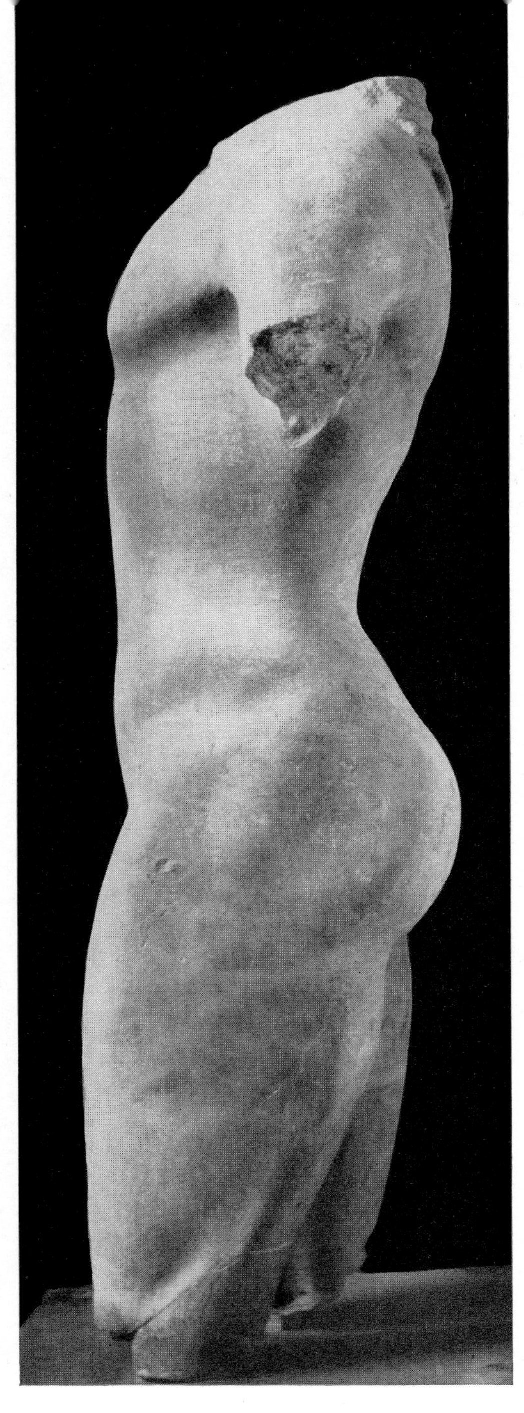

Figs. 497-499 (Florence)

Figs. 500-503 (Delphi)

166

166

166

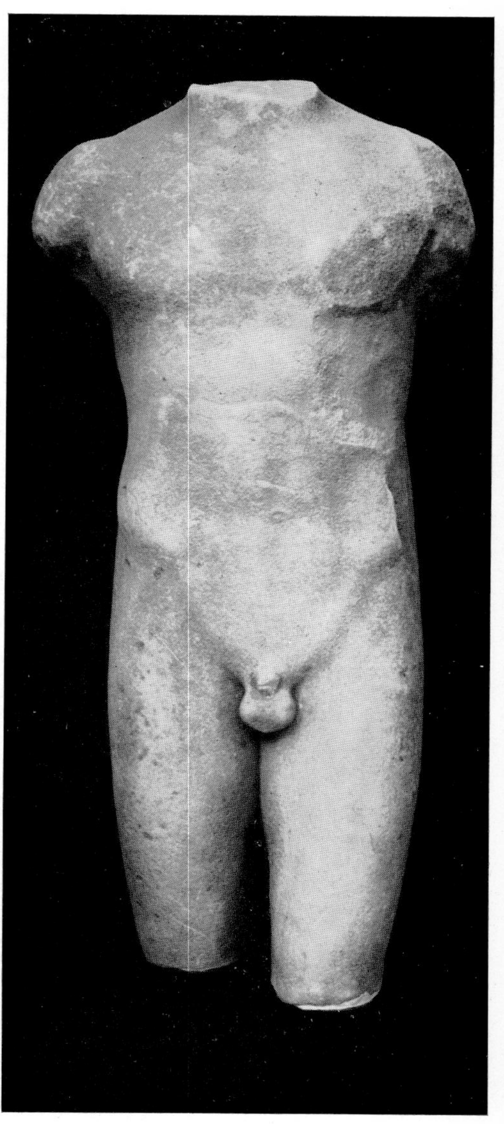

Fig. 504 (Chalkis)

167

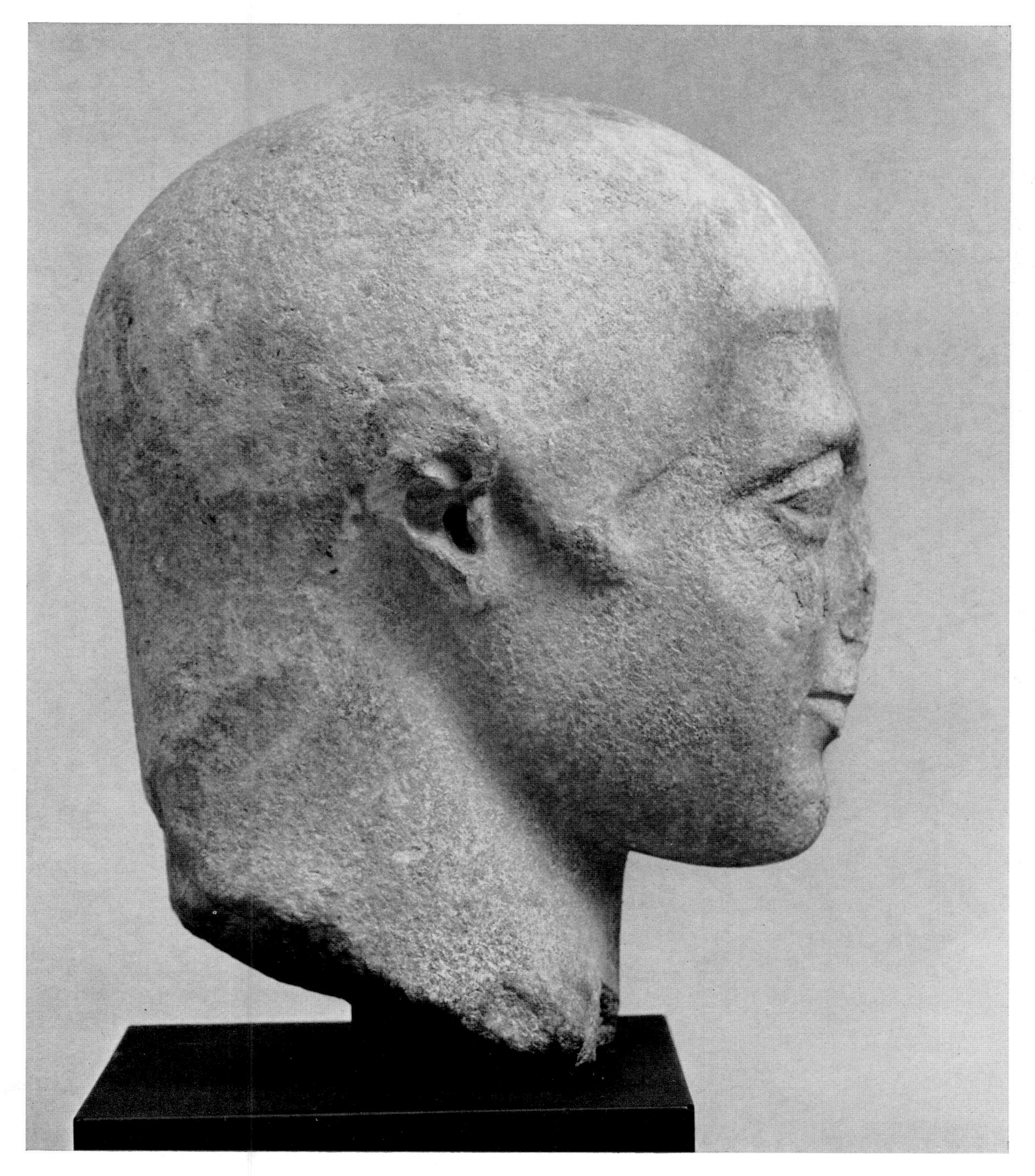

Figs. 505-506 (New York)

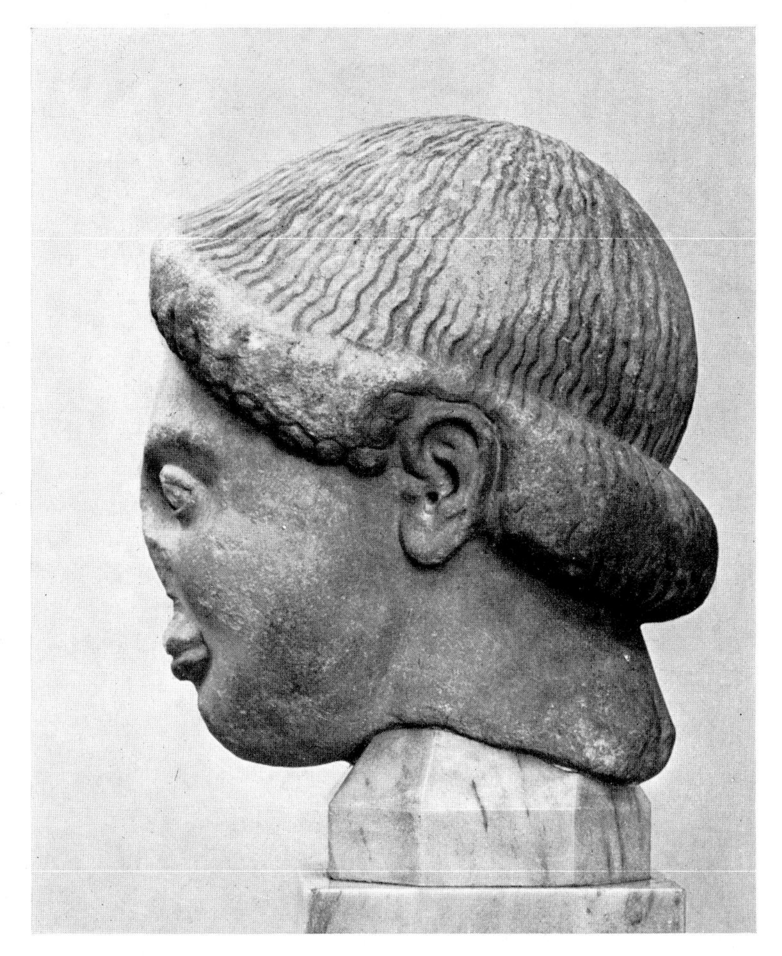

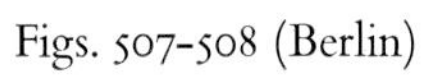

Figs. 507–508 (Berlin)

Figs. 509–510 (Copenhagen)

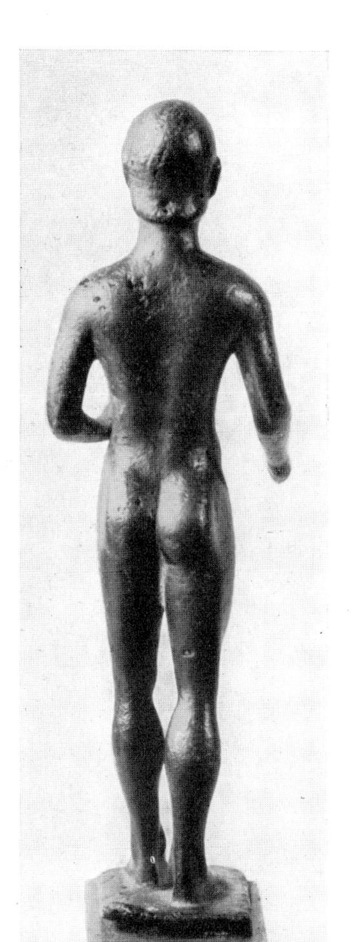

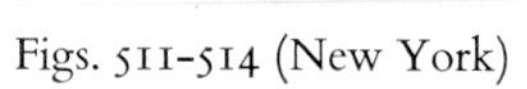

Figs. 511-514 (New York)

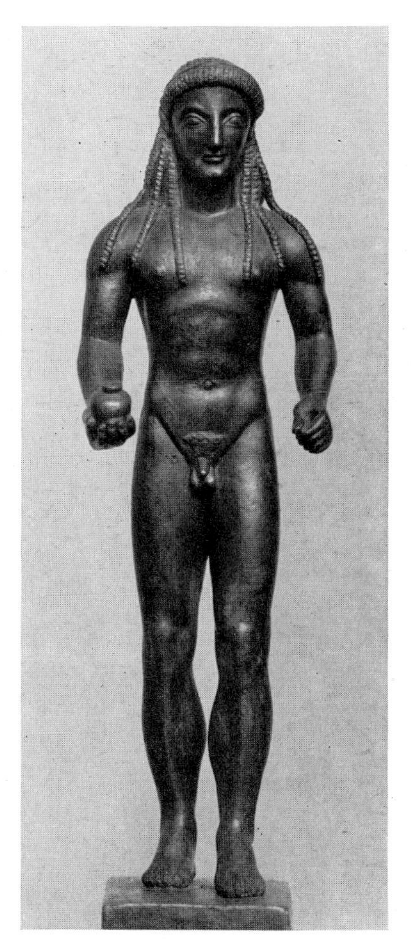

Figs. 515-517 (Berlin)

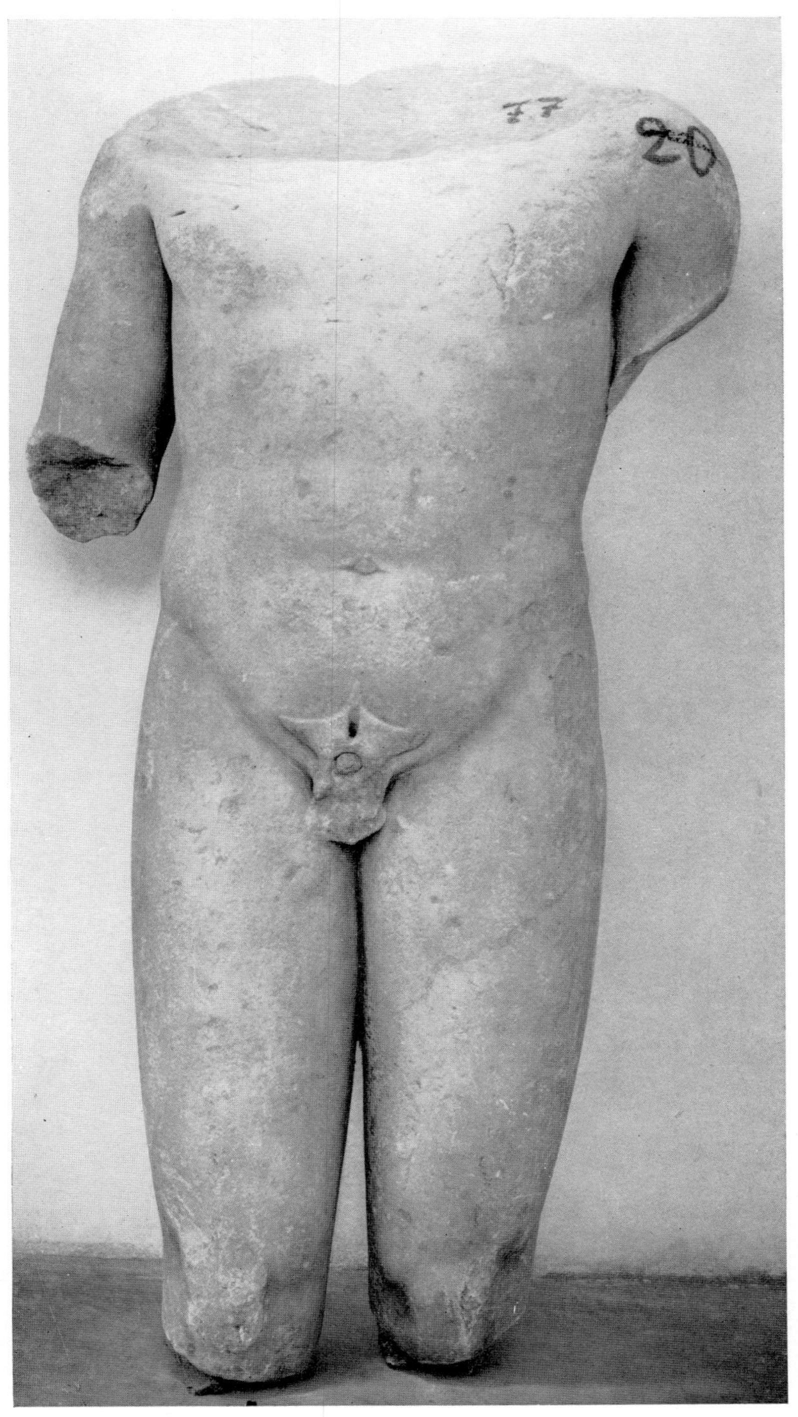

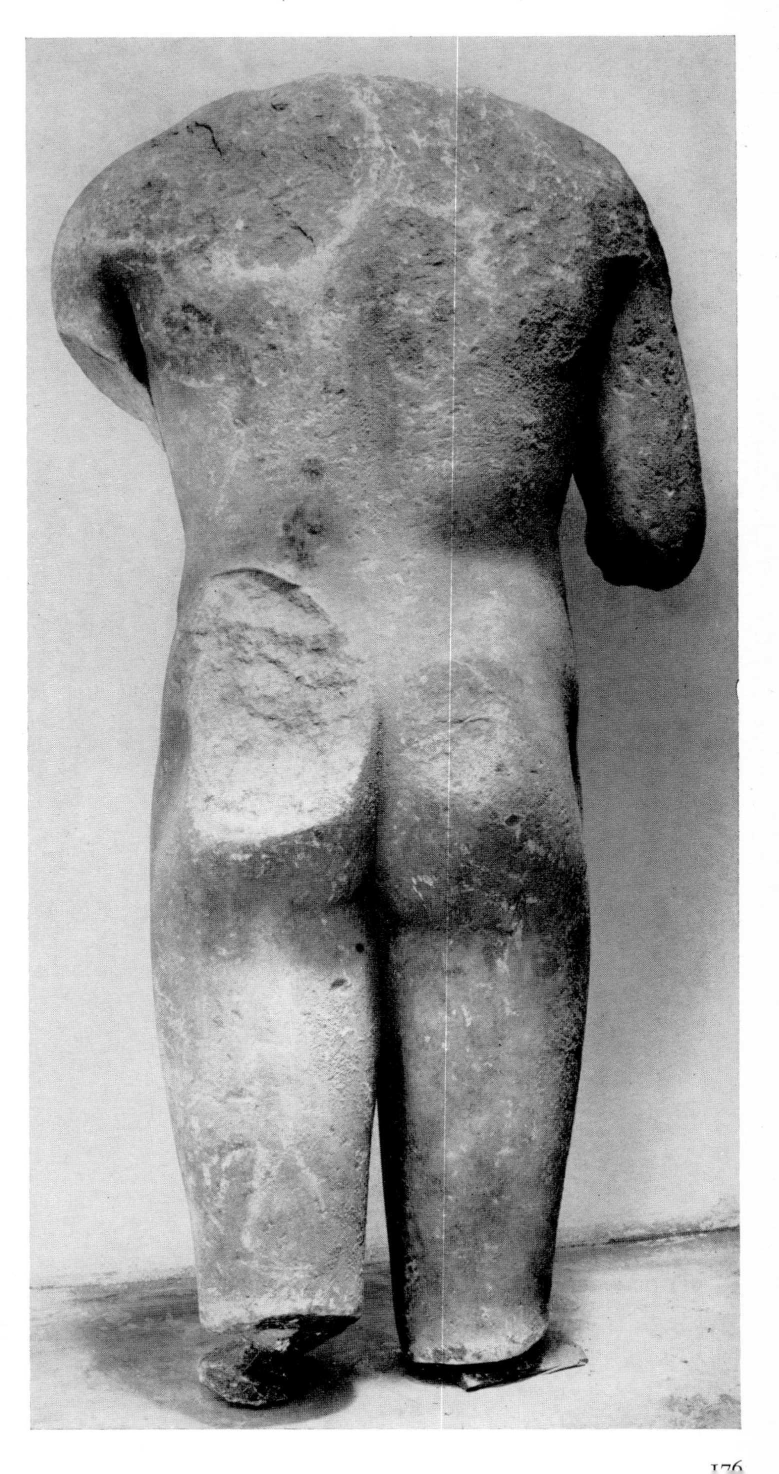

Figs. 518–520 (Samos)

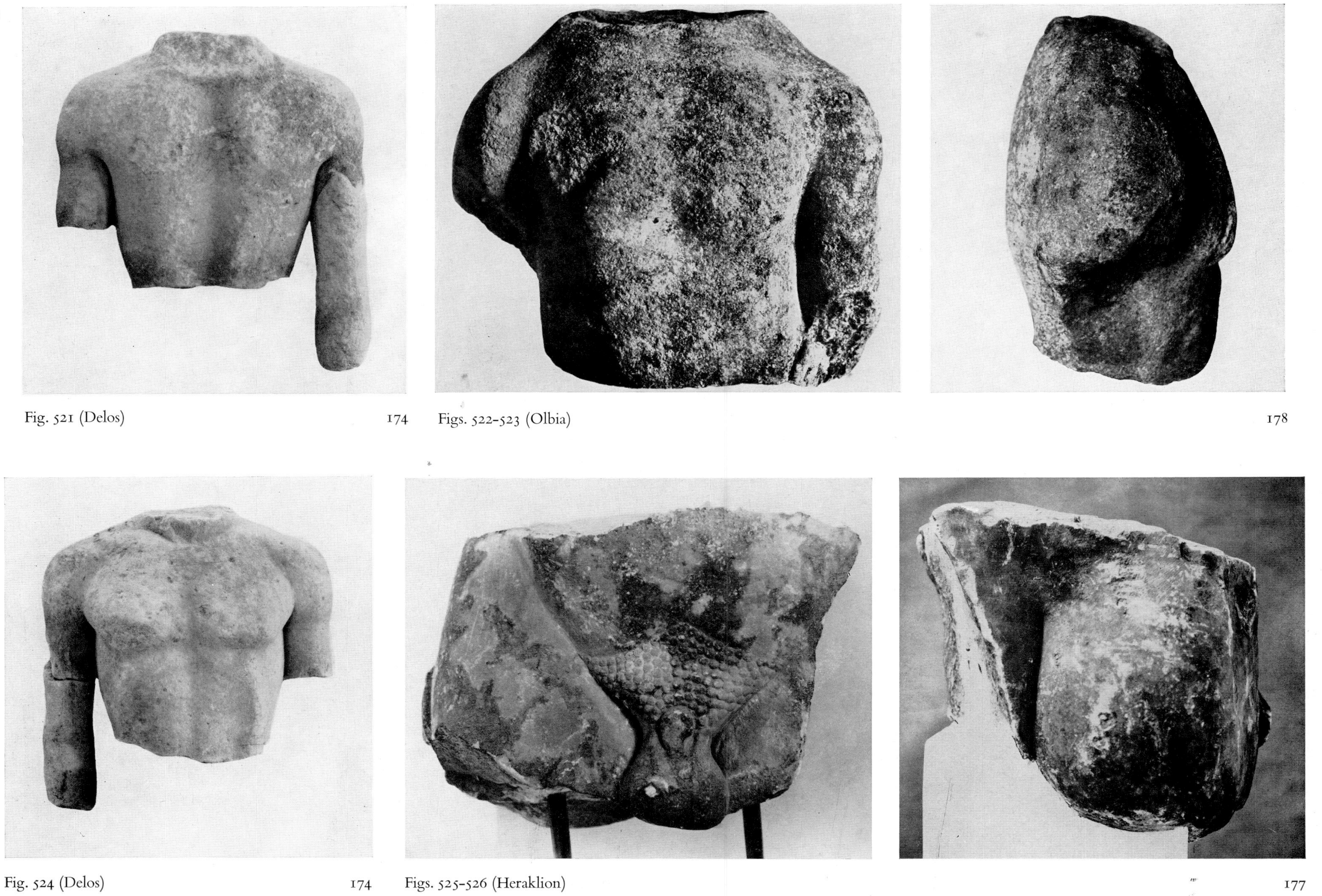

Fig. 521 (Delos) 174

Figs. 522-523 (Olbia) 178

Fig. 524 (Delos) 174

Figs. 525-526 (Heraklion) 177

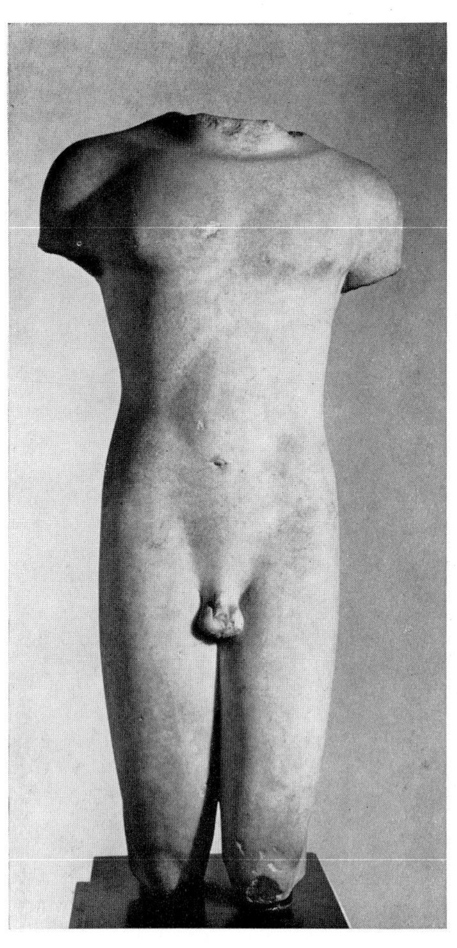
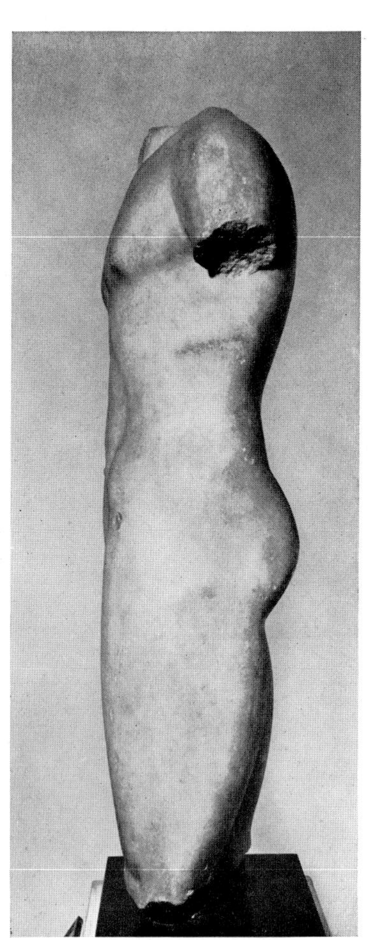
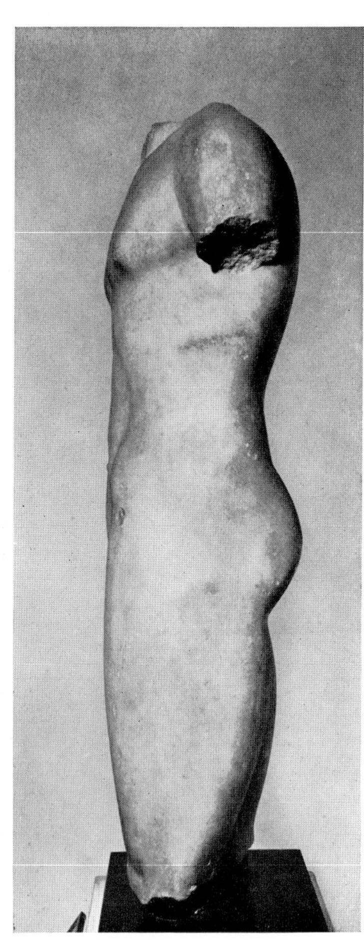
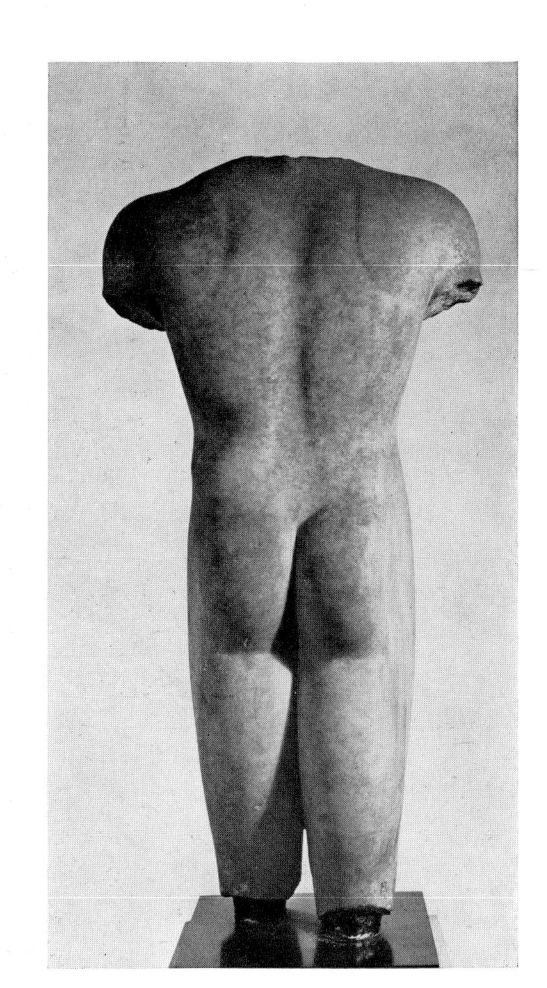

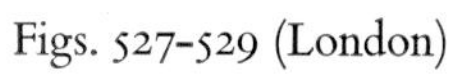
Figs. 527-529 (London)

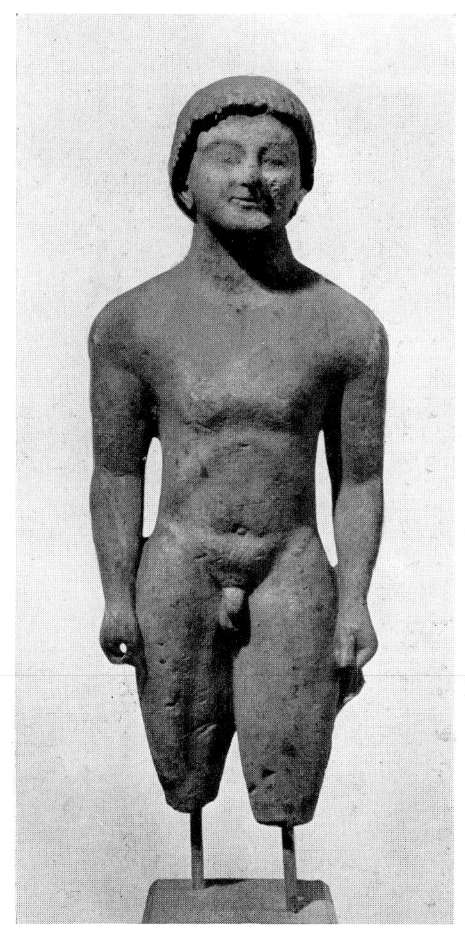
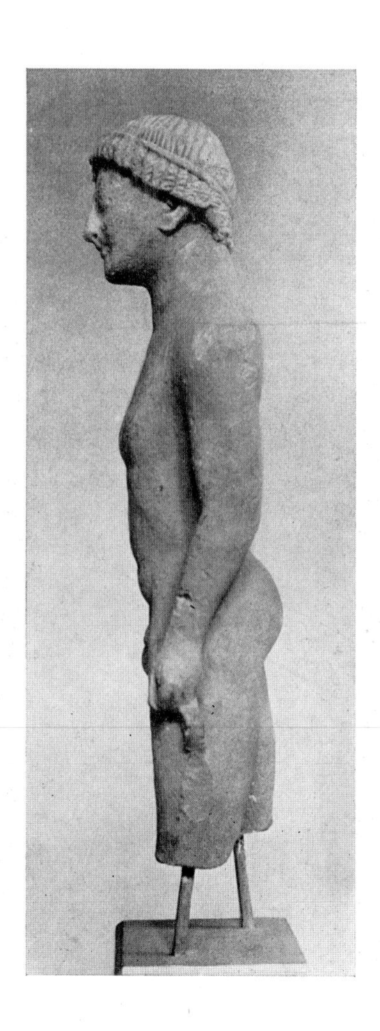
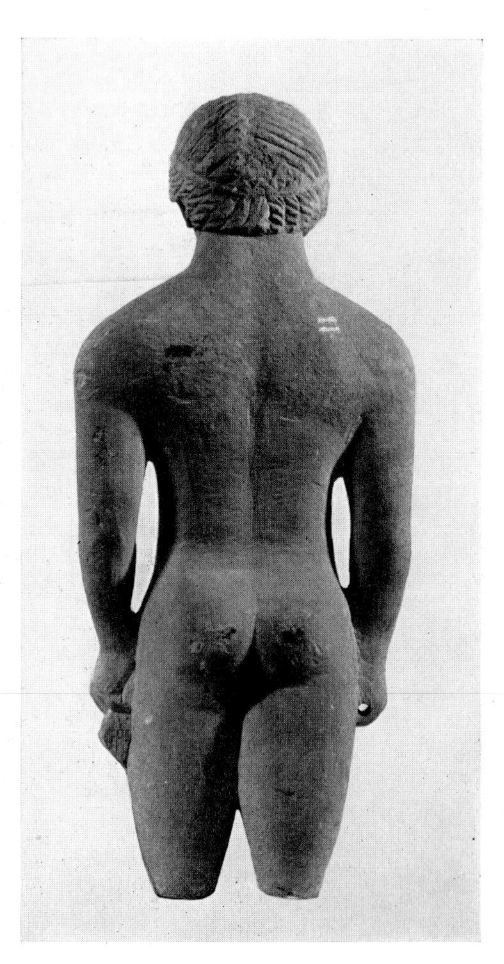

Figs. 530-532 (Nicosia)

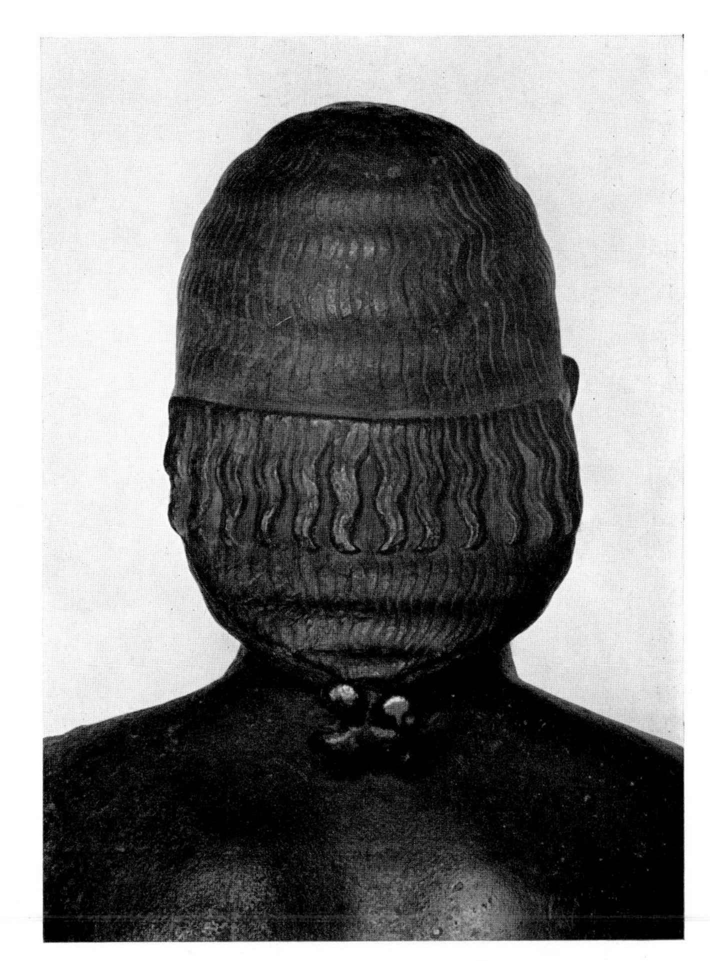

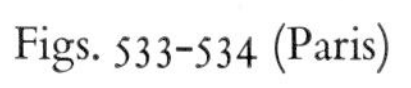

Figs. 533-534 (Paris)

Figs. 535-536 (Paris)

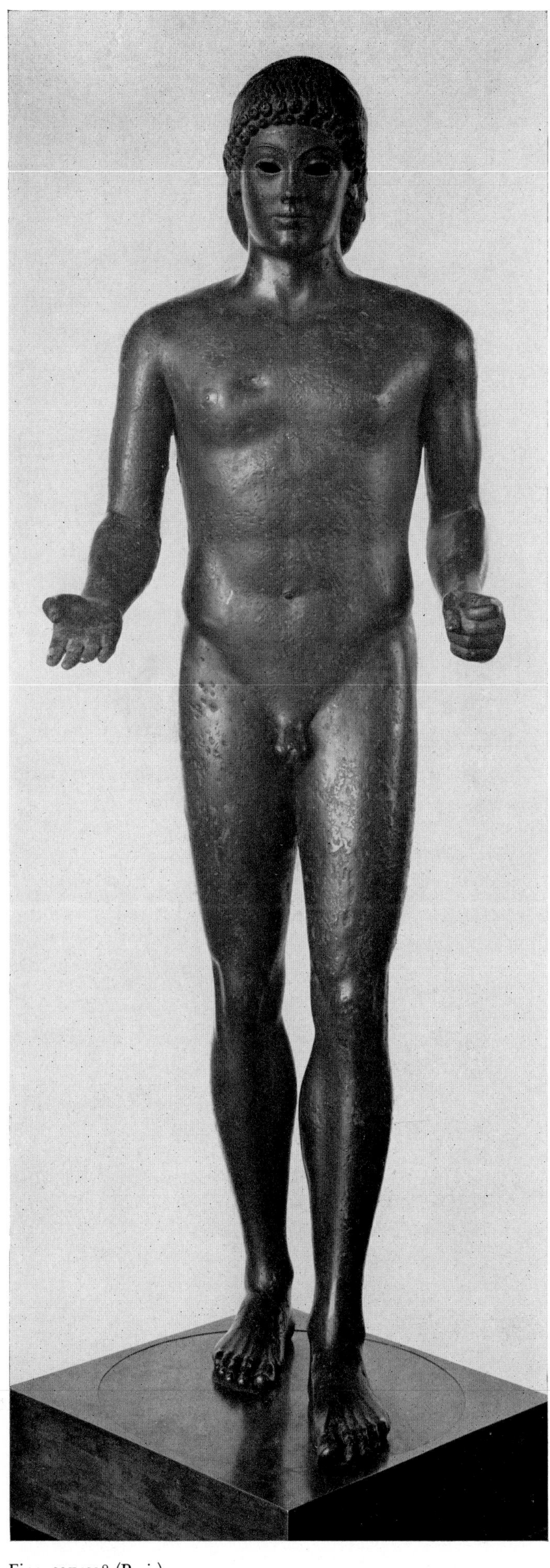

Figs. 537-538 (Paris)

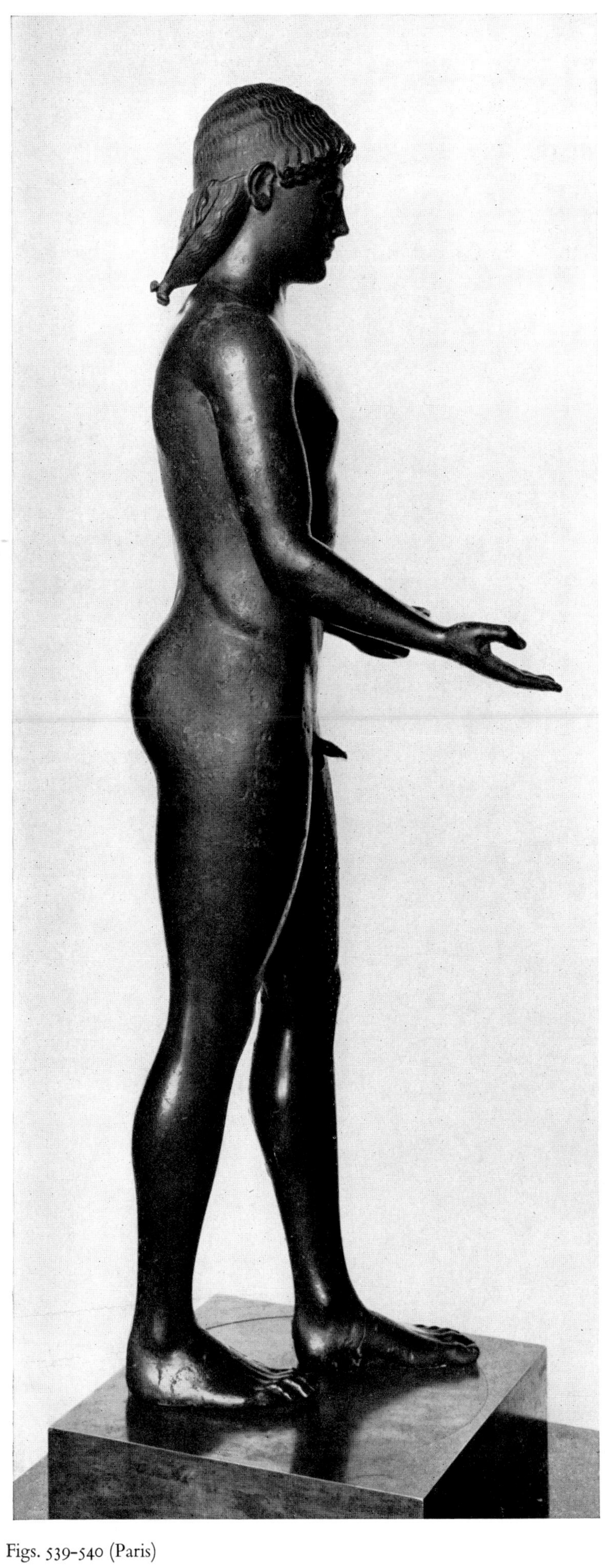

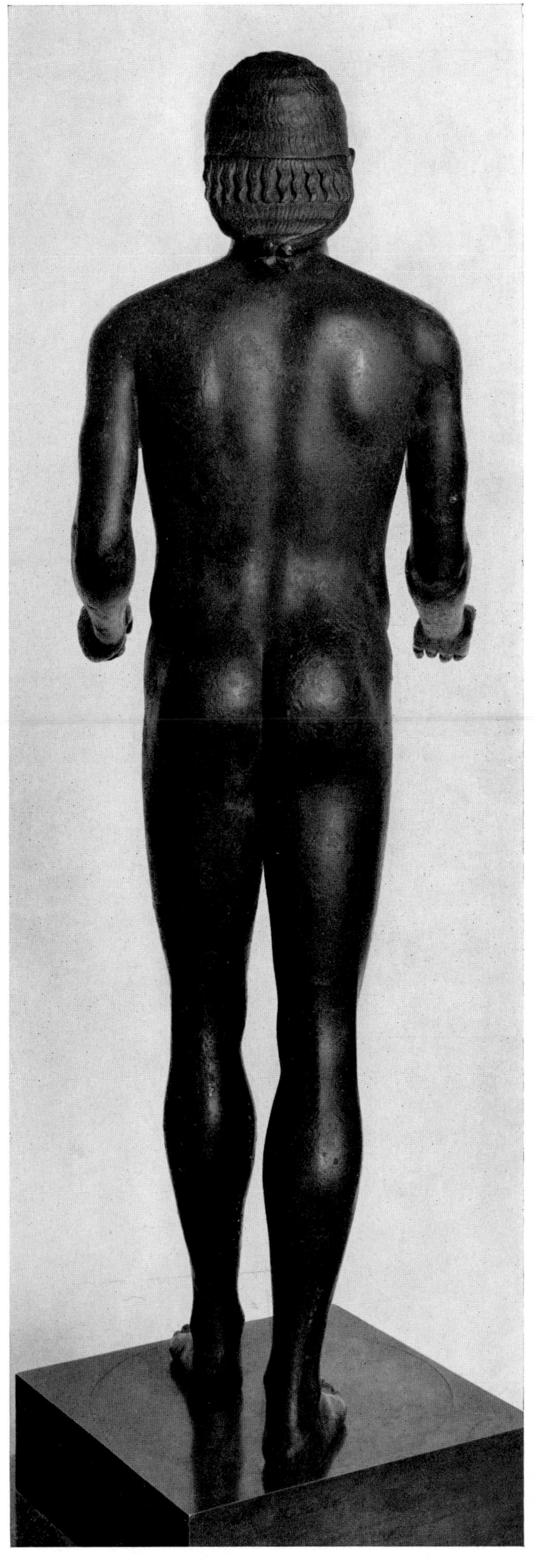

Figs. 539–540 (Paris)

186

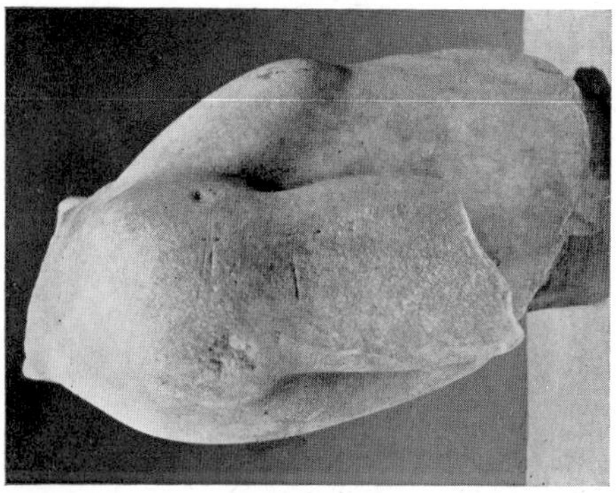

185

Figs. 541-543 (Syracuse)

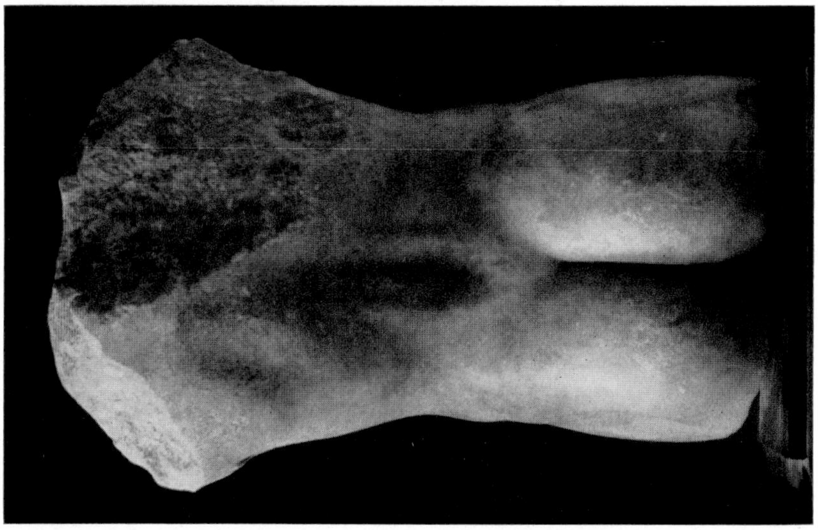

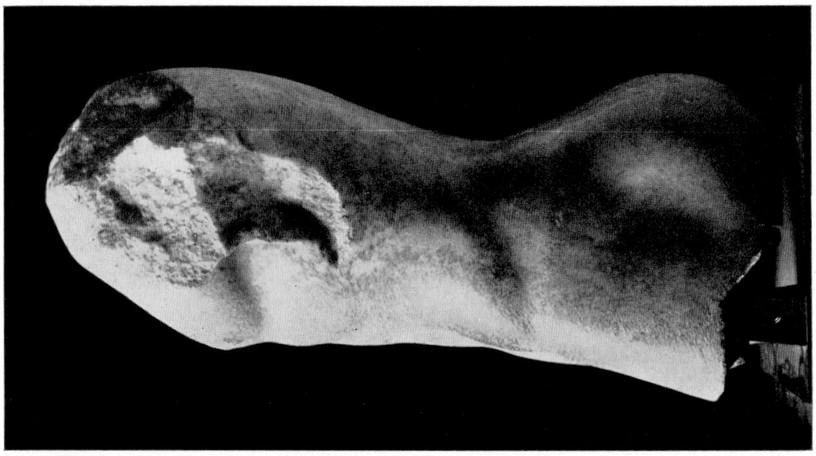

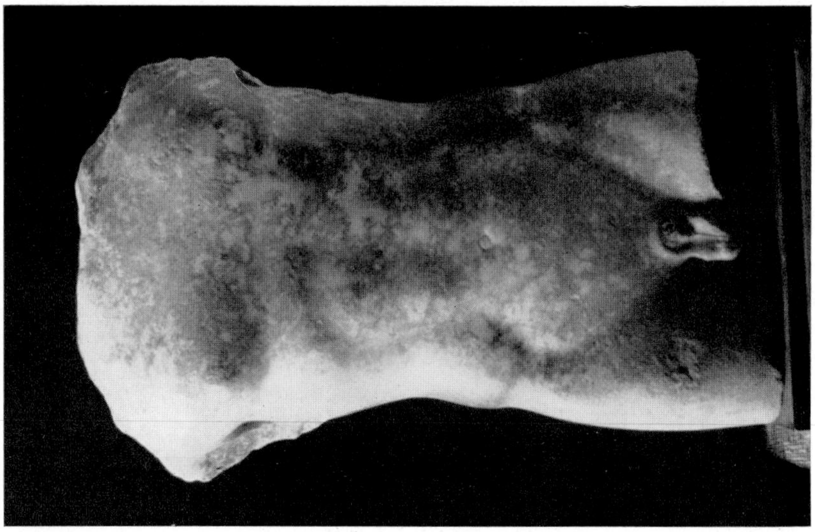

Figs. 544-546 (Syracuse)

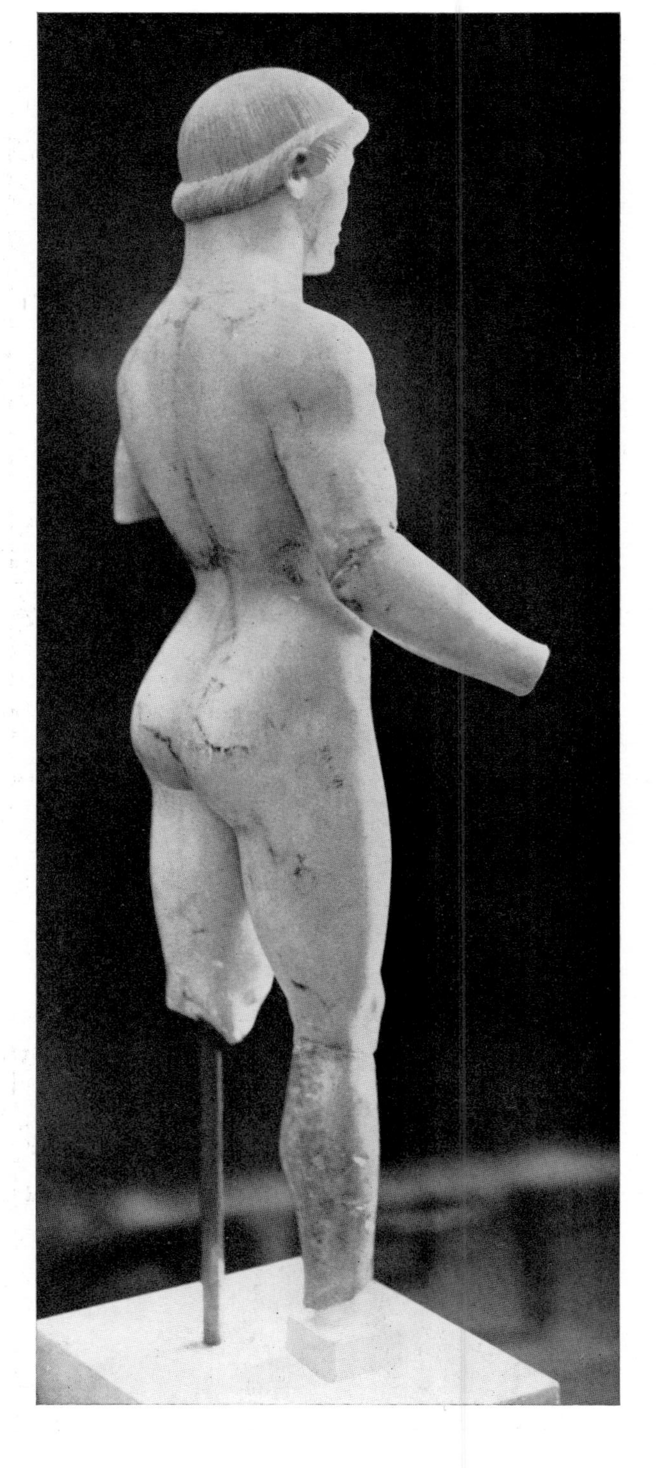

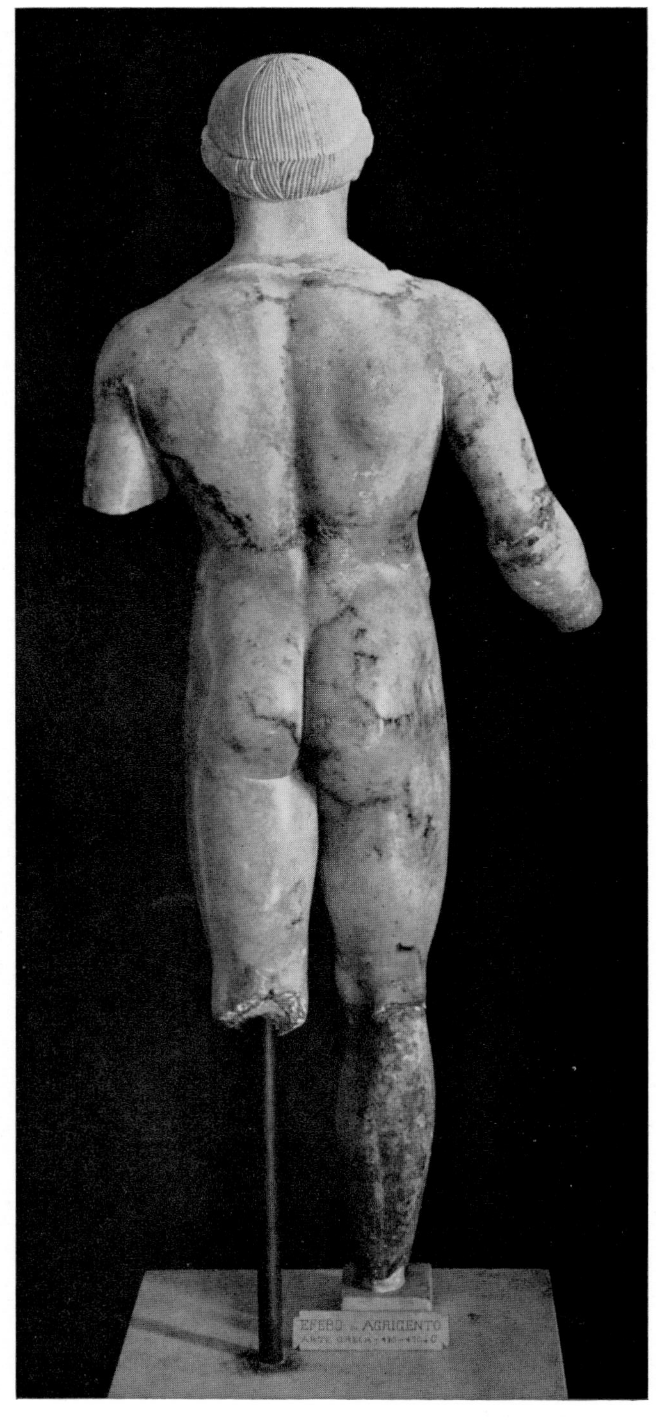

Figs. 547-549 (Agrigento)

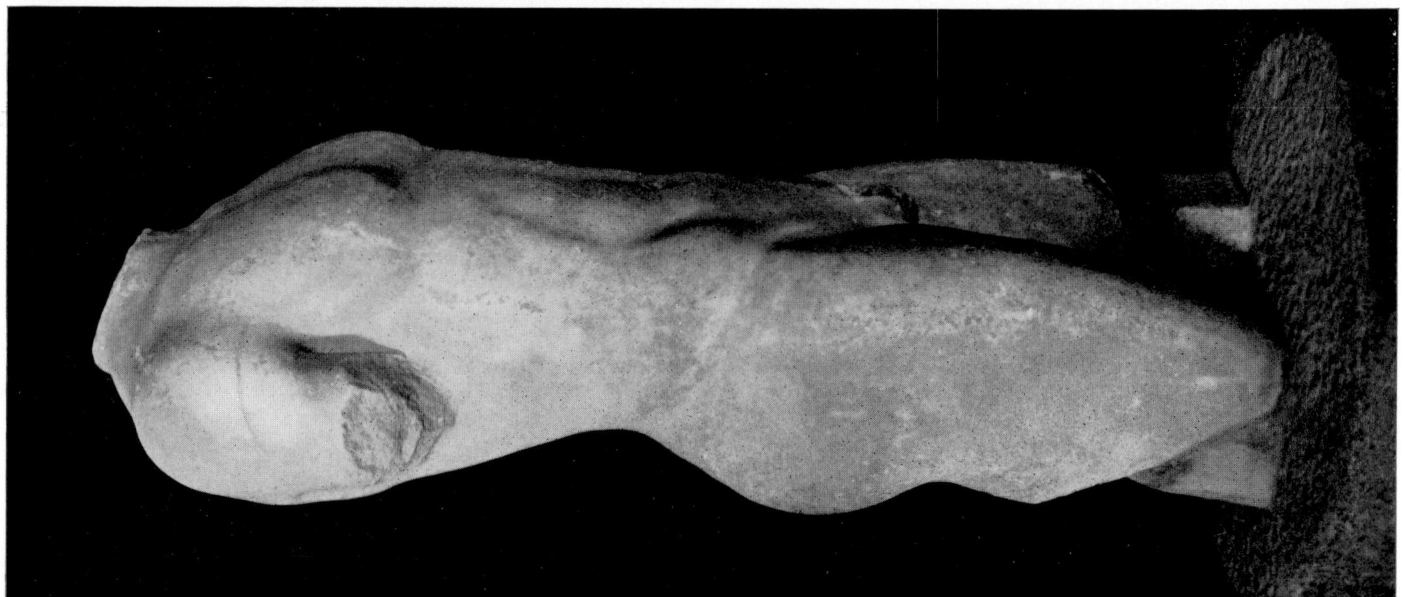

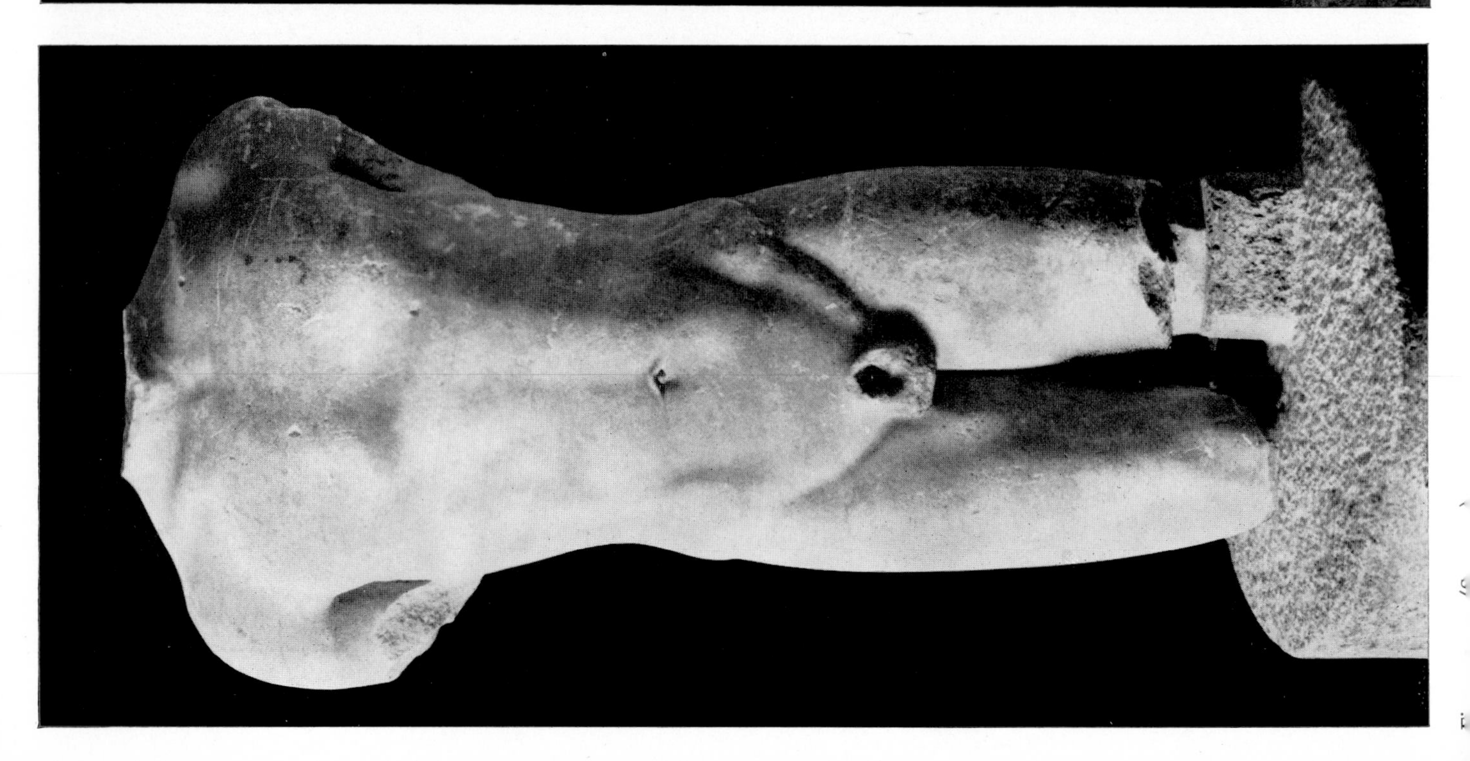

Figs. 553–555 (Potenza)

Figs. 556–557 (Catania) 184

Fig. 558 (Catania) 184

Fig. 559 (Marzabotto) 189

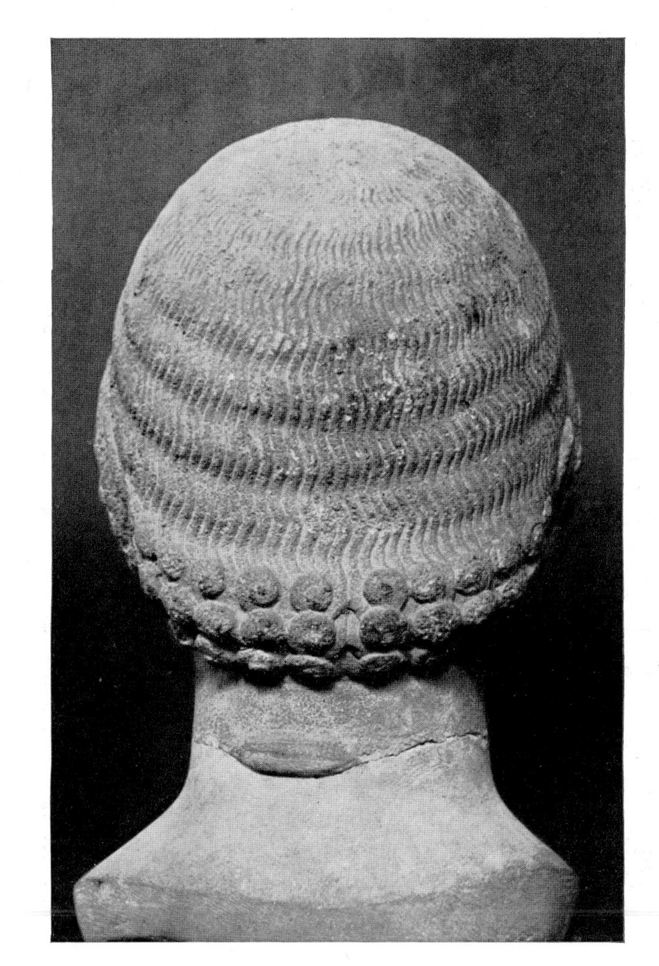

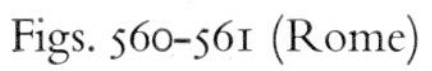

Figs. 560–561 (Rome) 188

Figs. 562–563 (Rome) 188

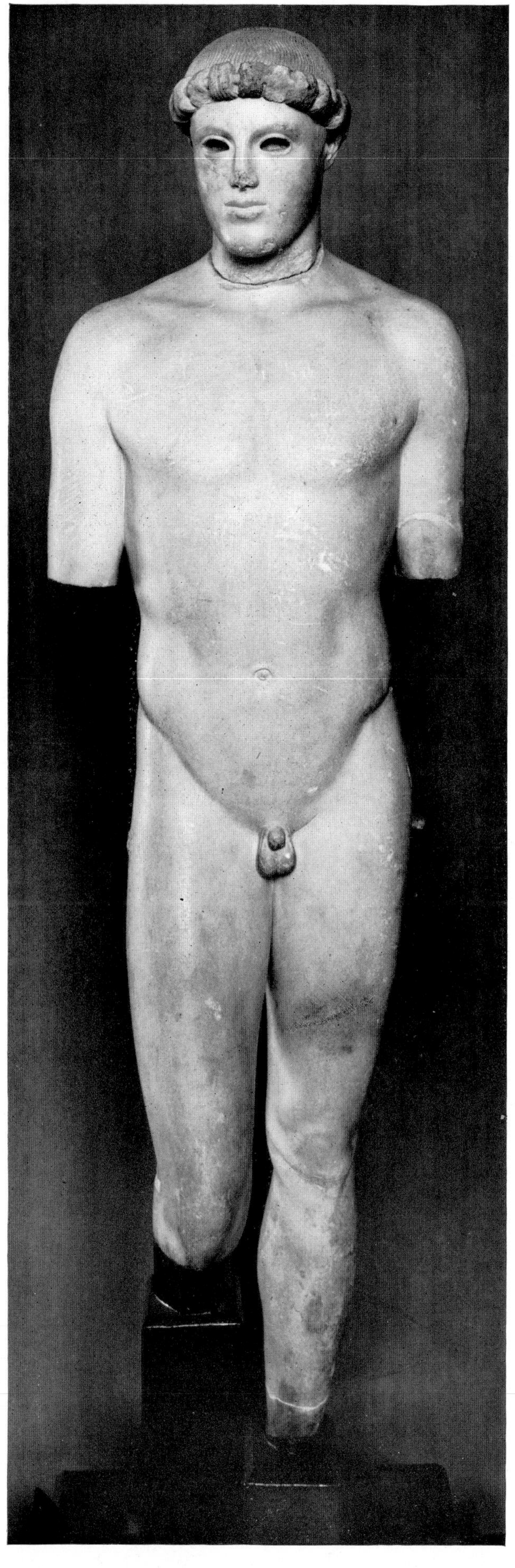

Figs. 564-565 (Athens)

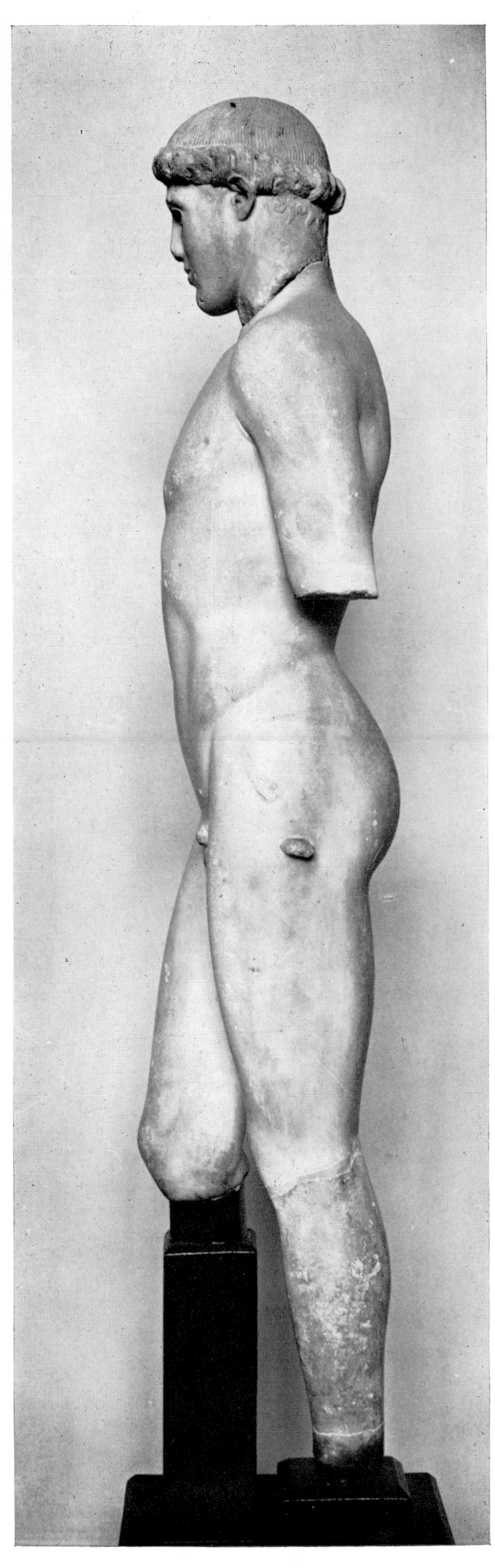

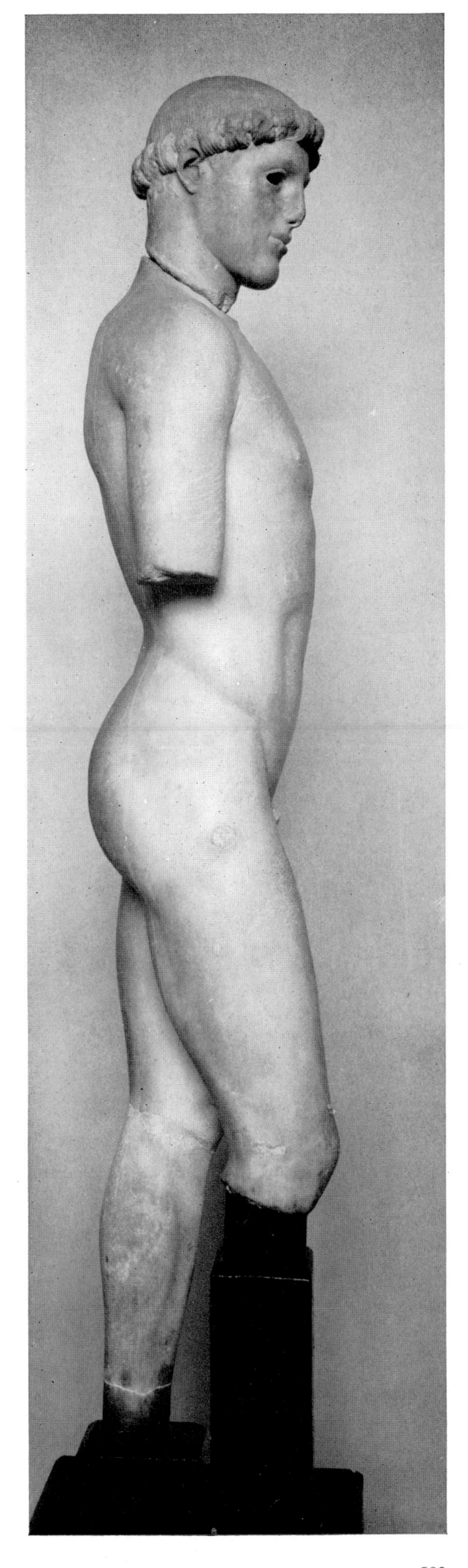

Figs. 566-567 (Athens)

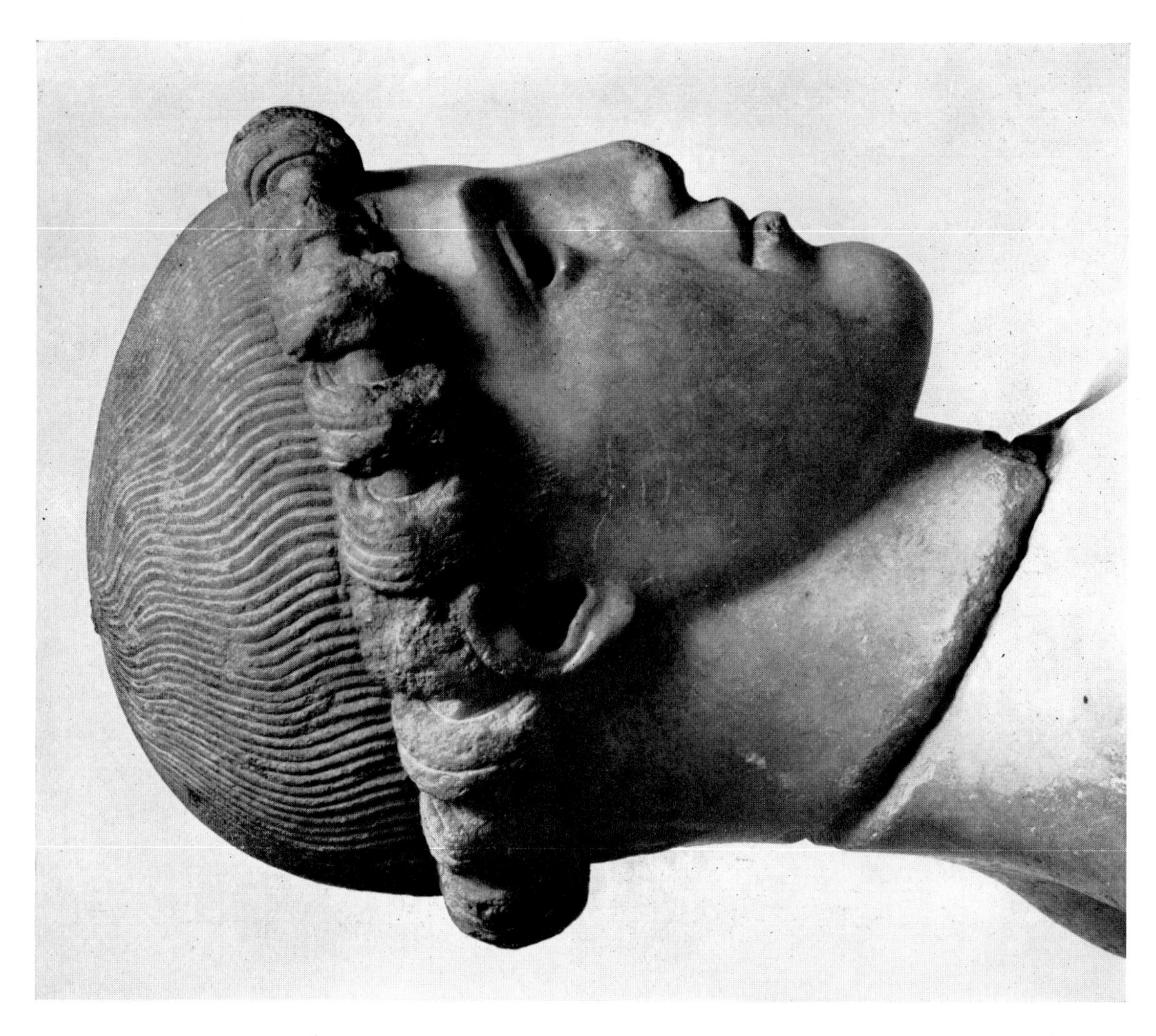

Figs. 568-569 (Athens)

Figs. 570–571 (Athens)

Fig. 572 (Athens) 191

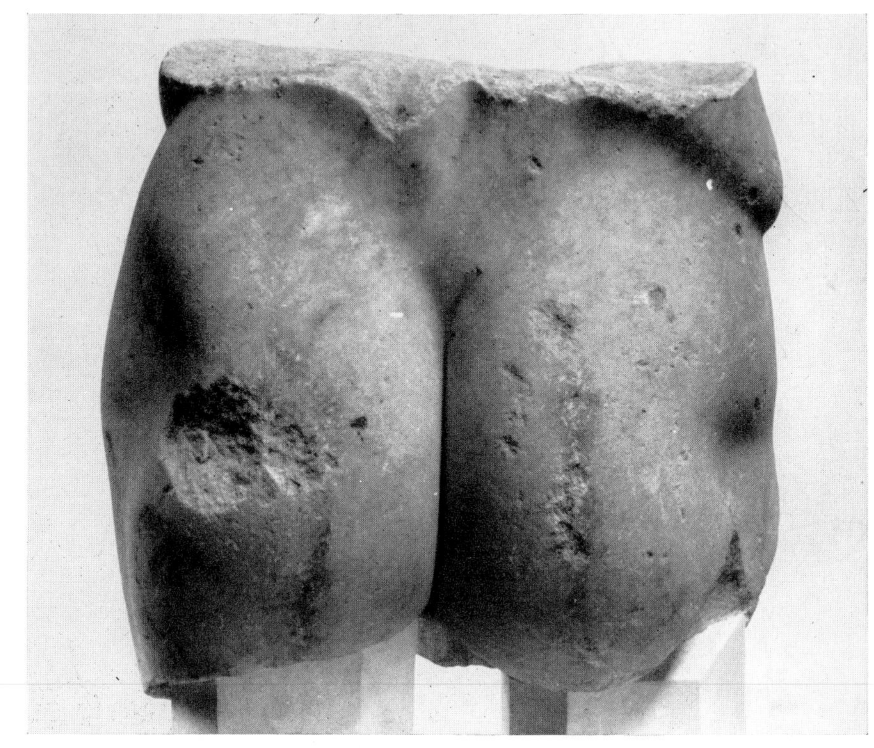

Figs. 573-574 (Athens) 191

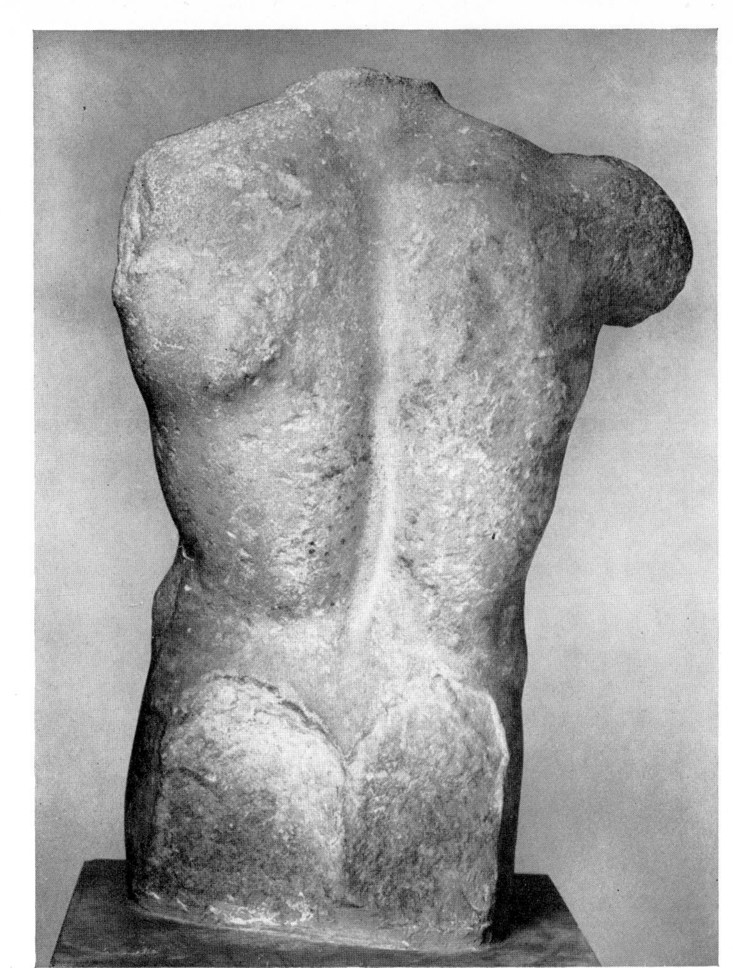

Figs. 575-576 (Paris)

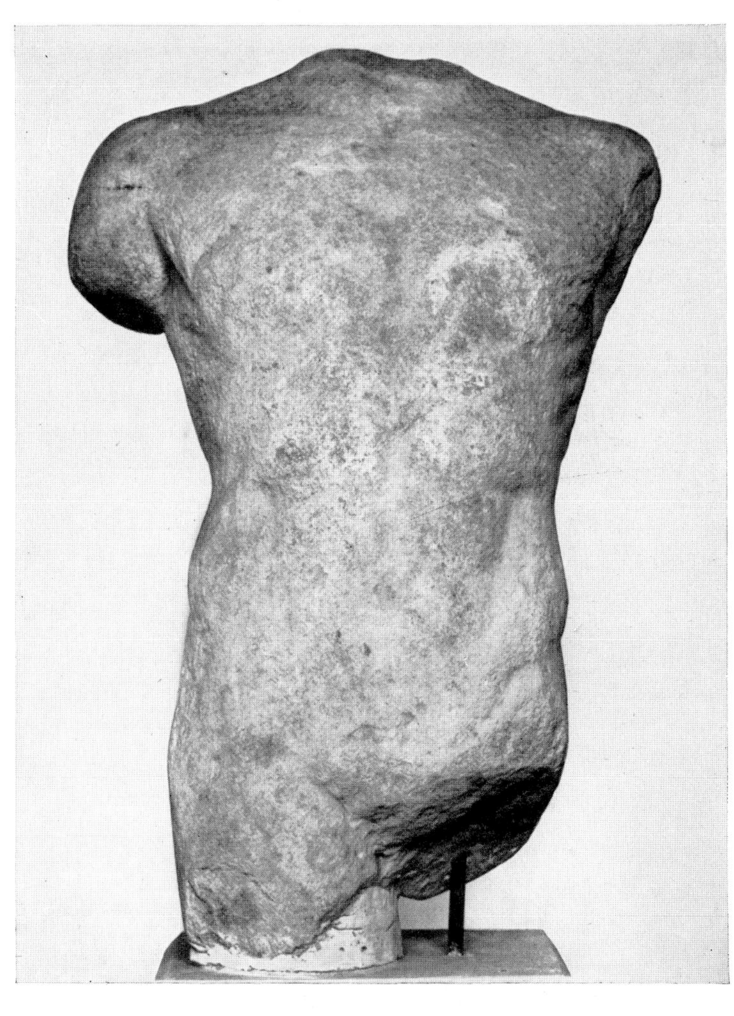
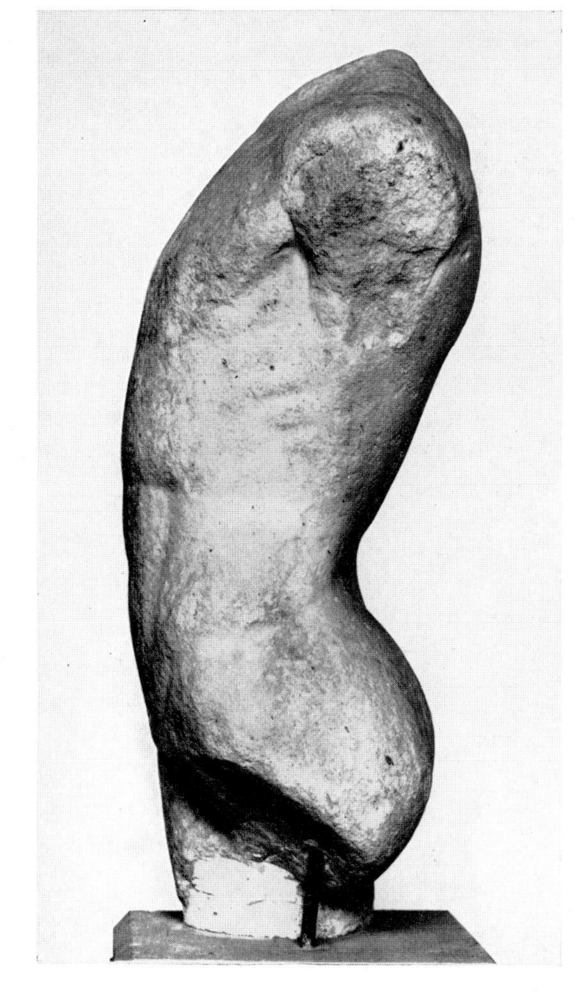

Figs. 577-578 (Oxford)

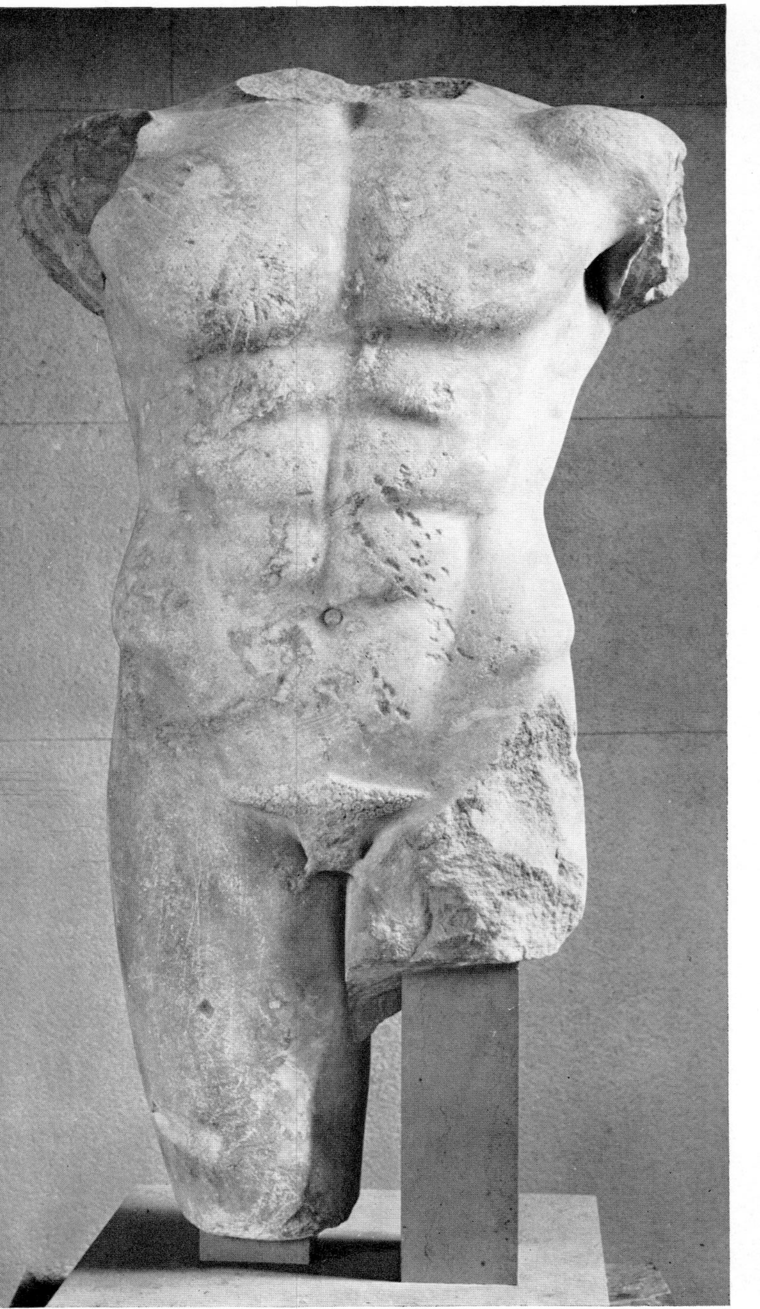

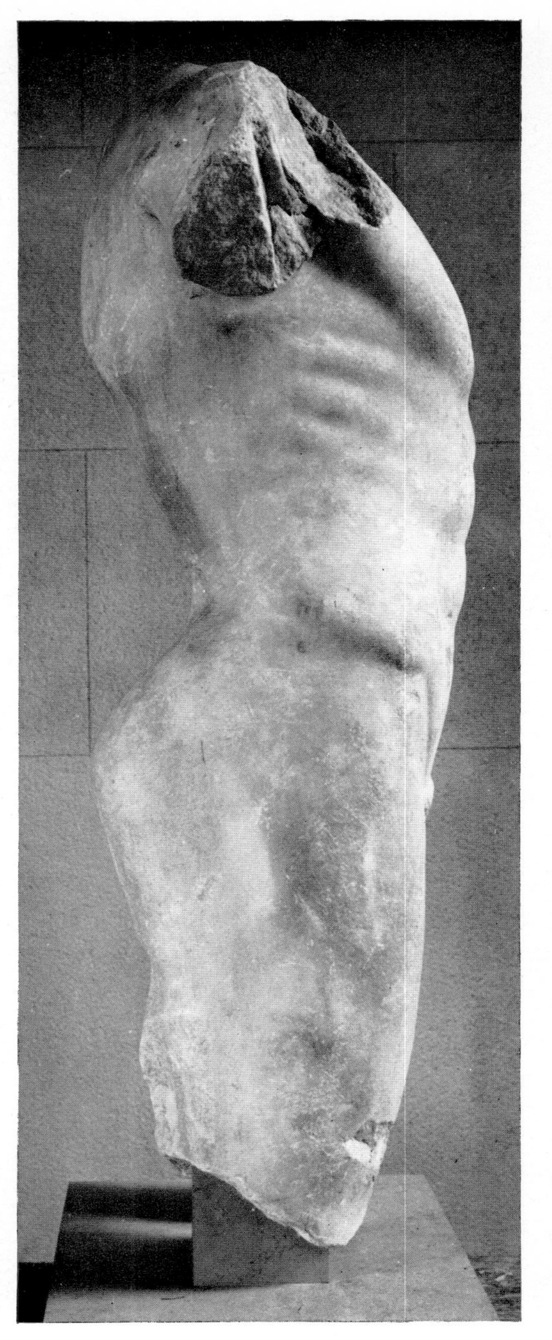

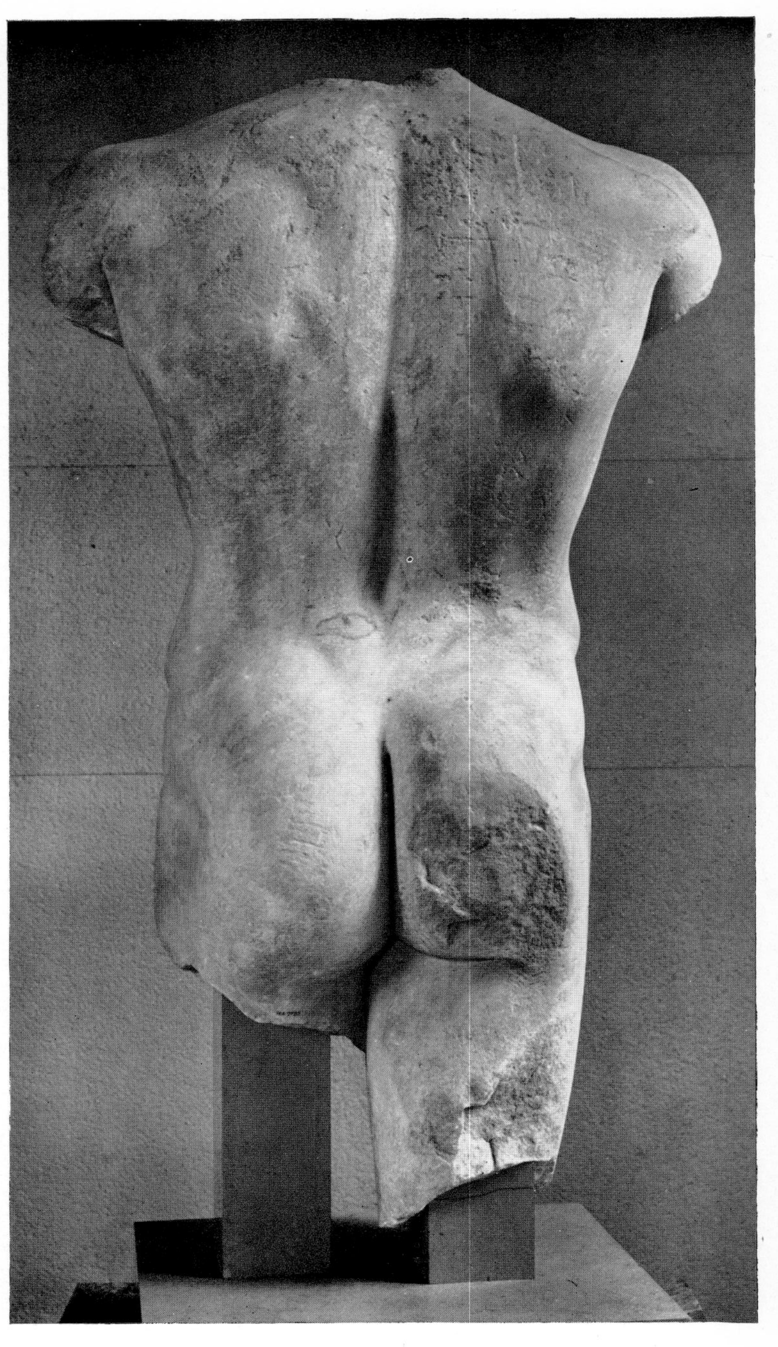

Figs. 579–581 (Paris)

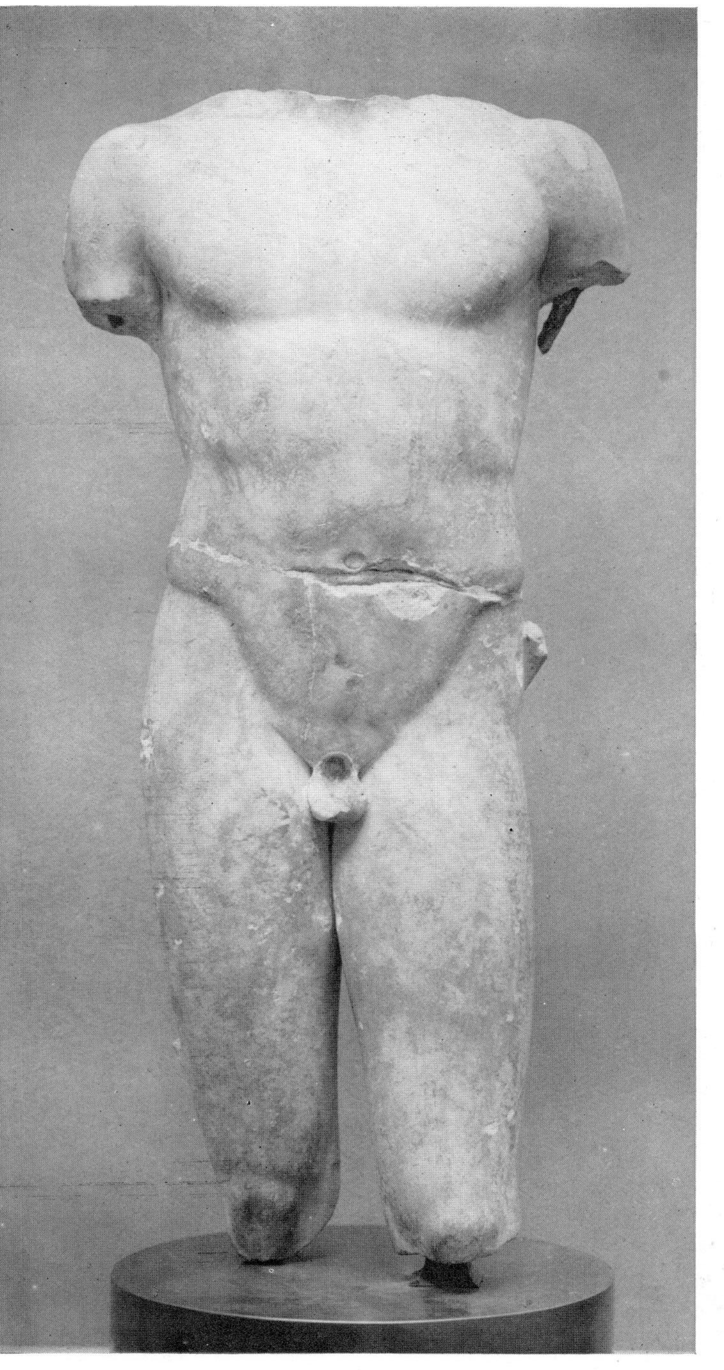

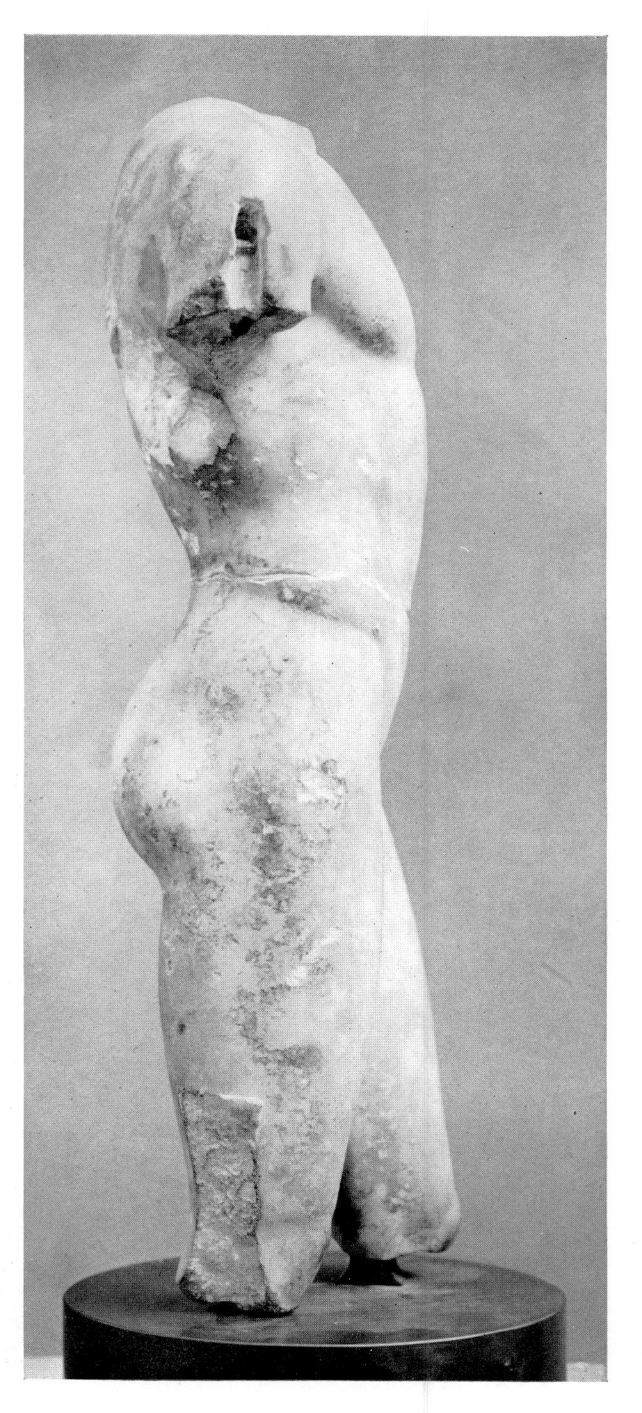

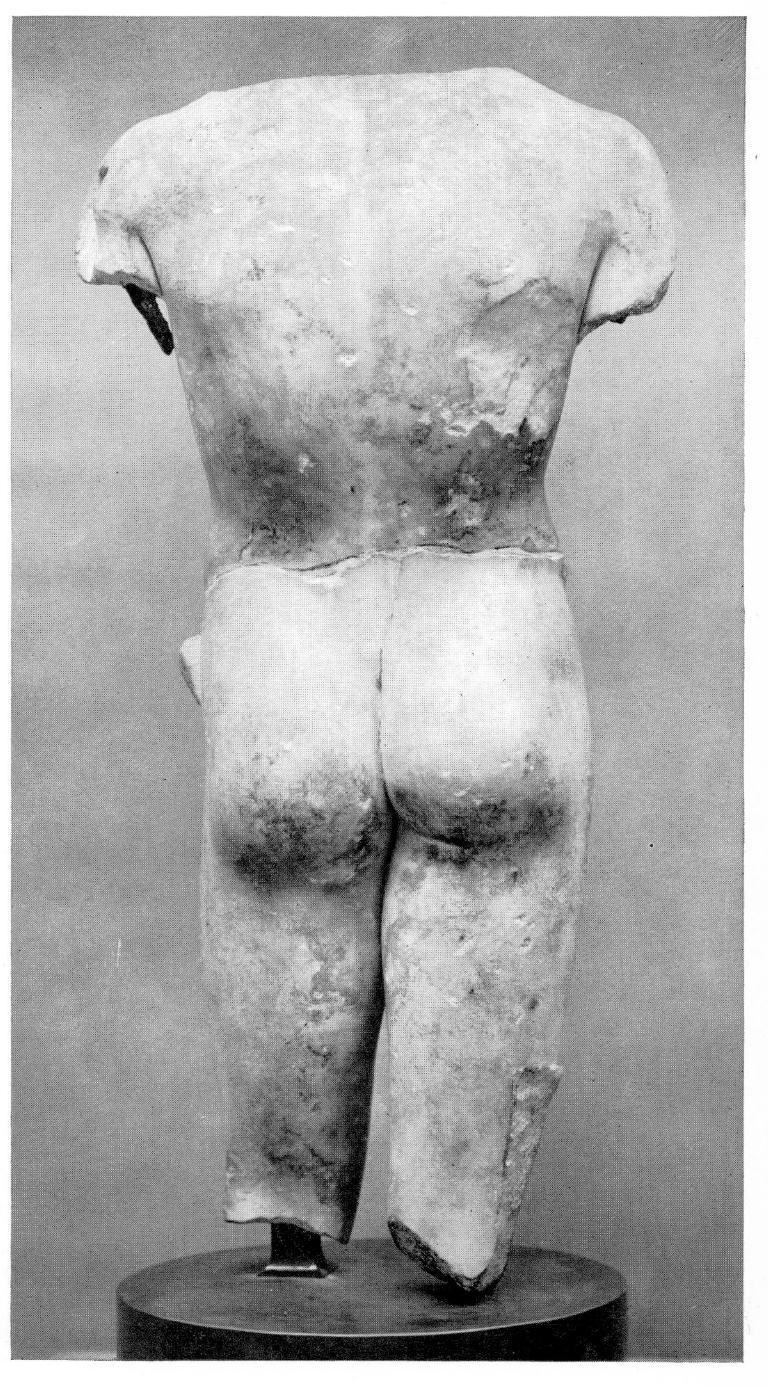

Figs. 582–584 (Boston)

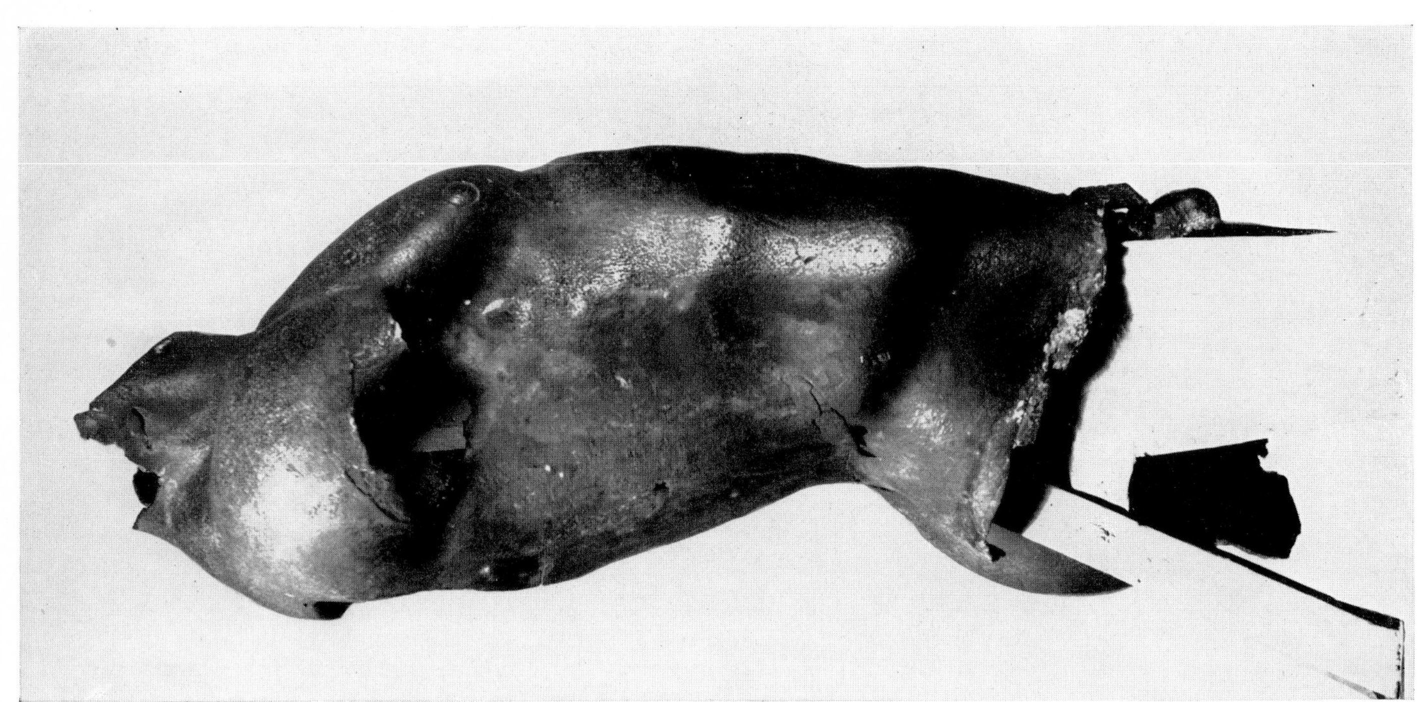

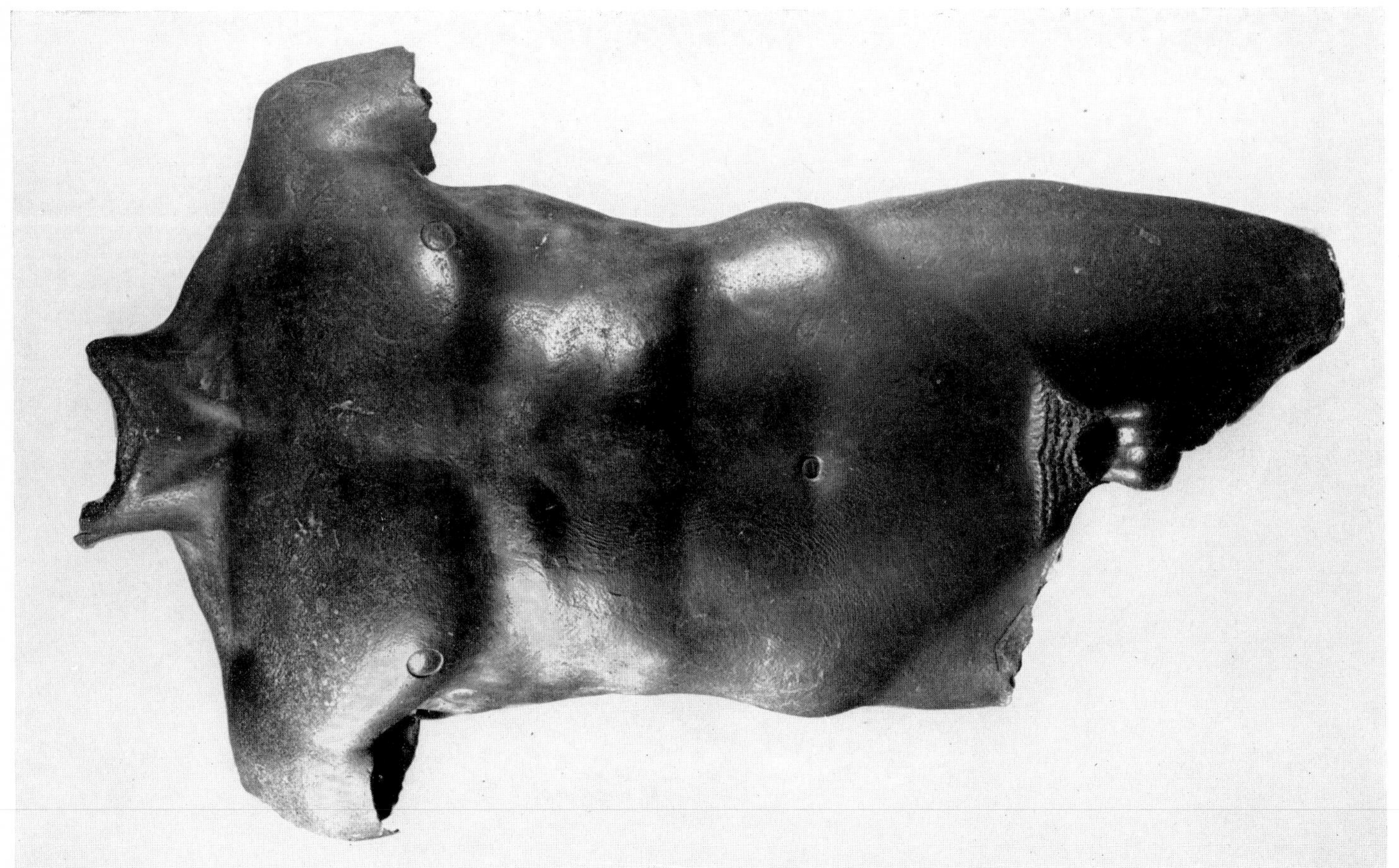

Figs. 585-586 (Florence)

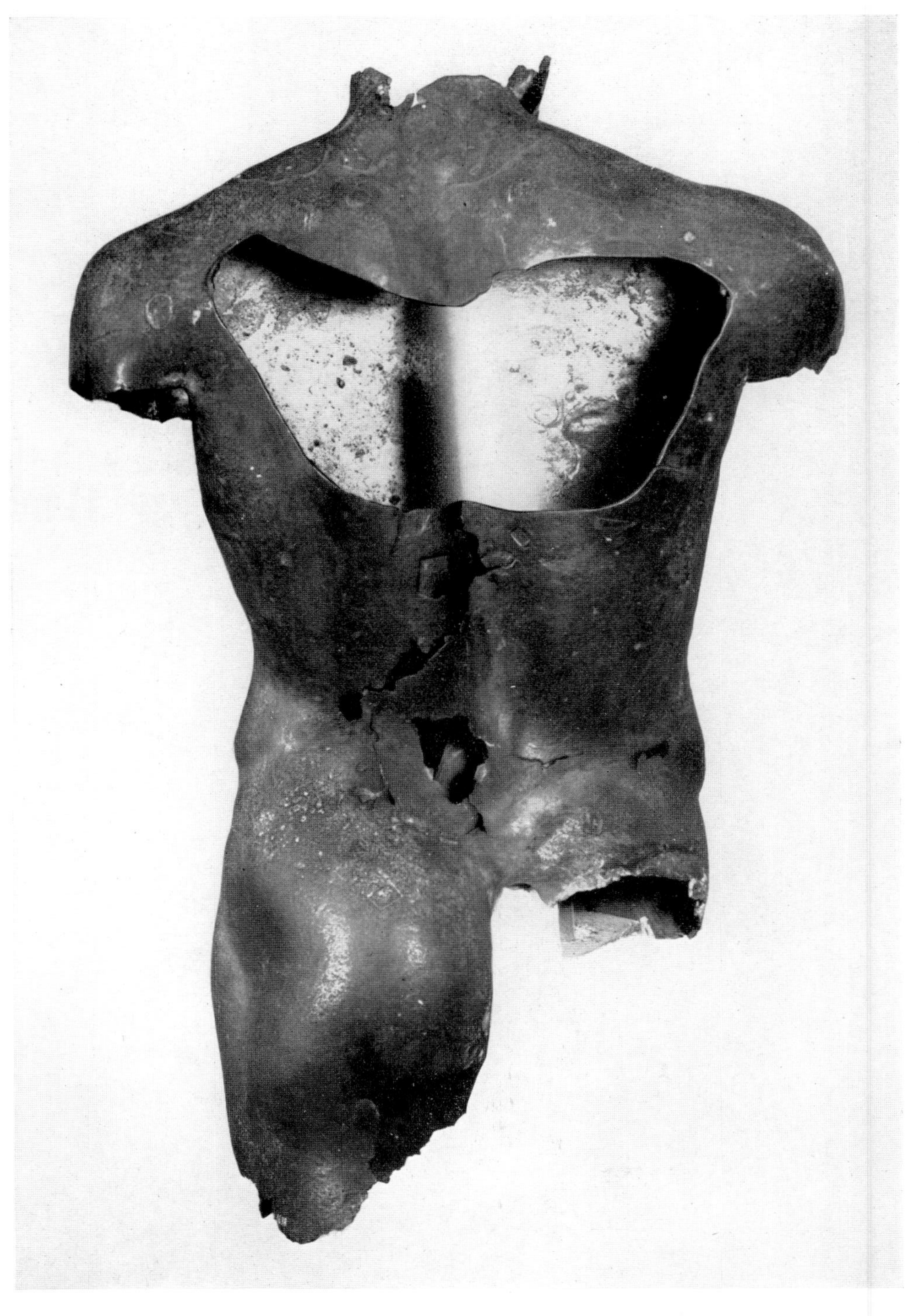

Figs. 587–588 (Florence)

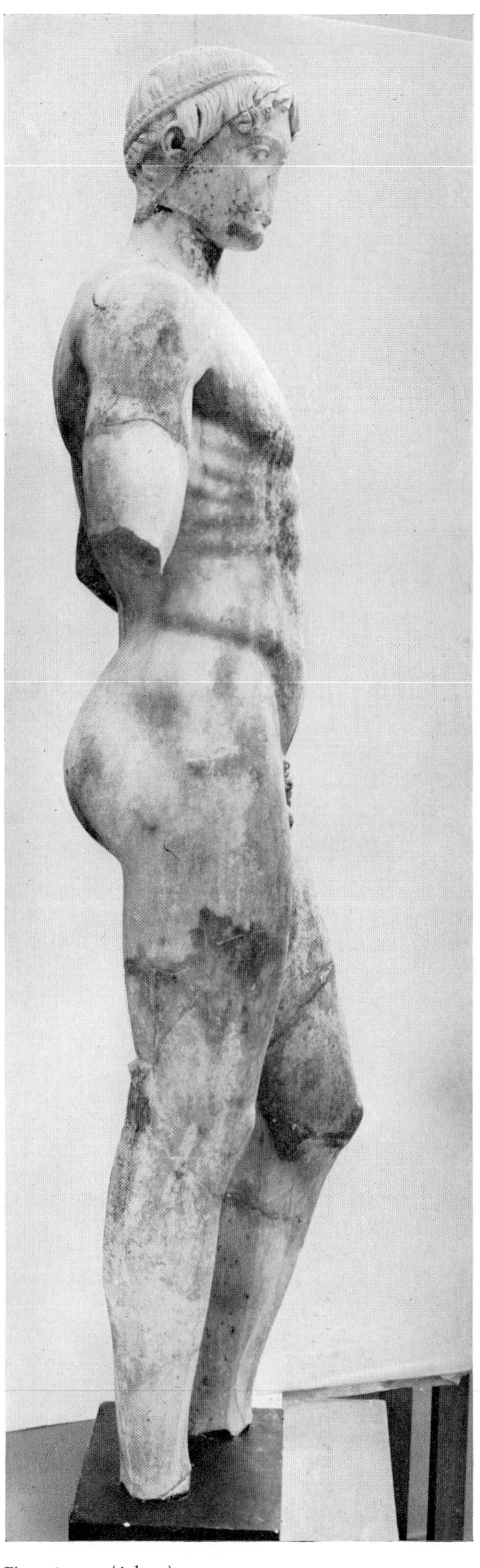

Figs. 589-590 (Athens)

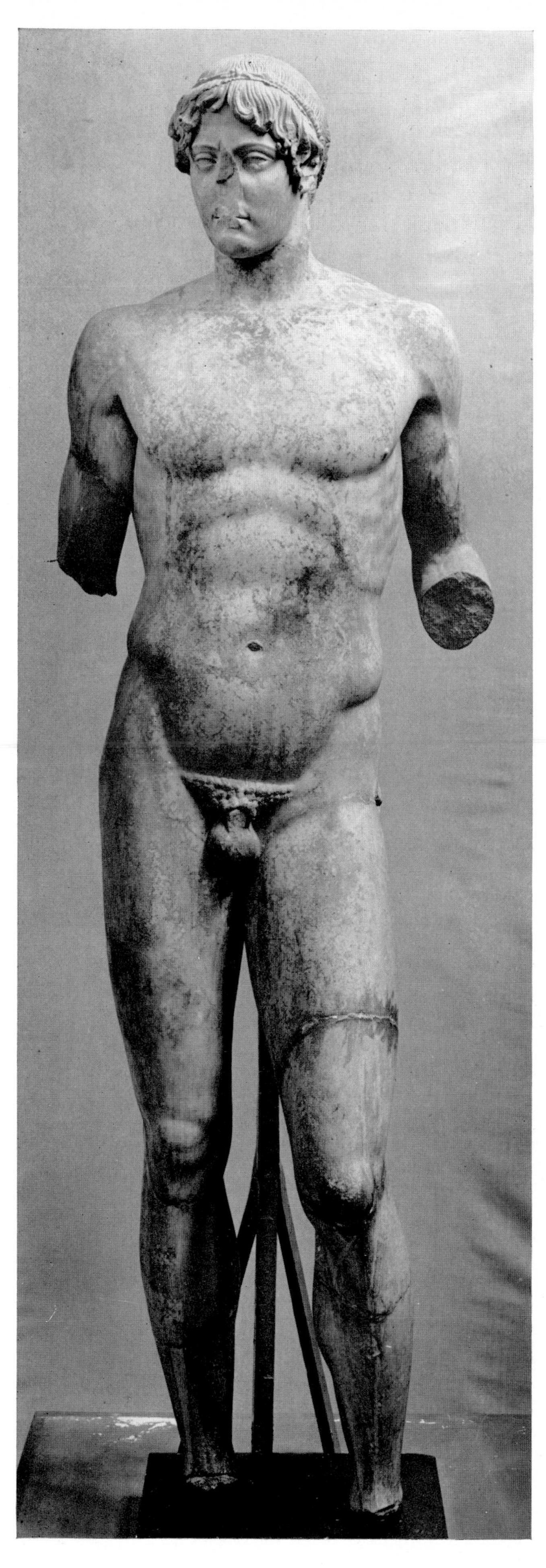

Fig. 591 (Athens)

Detail from Fig. 9

Detail from Fig. 564

LIST OF ILLUSTRATIONS

MUSEUM INDEX

LIST OF KOUROI WITH INSCRIPTIONS

CONCORDANCE

GENERAL INDEX

LIST OF ILLUSTRATIONS

Unless otherwise stated the material of the sculptures is marble.

Where no photographer is mentioned the photograph was sent by the institution without the name of the photographer.

The number put in square brackets after the figure numbers is the catalogue number.

THE SOUNION GROUP

THE ORCHOMENOS-THERA GROUP

THE TENEA-VOLOMANDRA GROUP

THE MELOS GROUP

THE ANAVYSOS-PTOON 12 GROUP

THE PTOON 20 GROUP

EPILOGUE

MUSEUM INDEX

INDEX OF KOUROI WITH INSCRIPTIONS

CONCORDANCE OF NUMBERS IN SECOND AND FIRST EDITIONS

2nd ed.	*1st ed.*	*2nd ed.*	*1st ed.*	*2nd ed.*	*1st ed.*	*2nd ed.*	*1st ed.*
1	1	50	—	100	84	150	126
2	2	51	41	101	85	151	127
3	3	52	42	102	86	152	128
4	4	53	—	103	87	153	129
5	5	54	43	104	88	154	130
6	6	55	44	105	89	155	131
7	—	56	45	106	90	156	132
8	7	57	46	107	91	157	133
9	8	58	47	108	92	158	—
10	9	59	48	109	93	159	134
11	10	60	49	110	94	159 bis	—
12	11	61	50	111	95	160	135
13	—	62	—	112	96	161	136
14	12	63	51	113	97	161 bis	—
15	13	64	52	114	98	162	137
16	14	65	53	115	99	163	138
17	15	66	54	116	100	164	—
18	16	67	55	117	101	165	—
19	—	68	—	118	102	166	139
20	—	69	56	119	103	167	140
21	—	70	61	120	104	168	141
22	17	71	—	121	105	169	154
23	18	72	57	122	106	170	142
24	19	73	58	123	107	171	—
25	20	74	59	124	110	172	—
26	21	75	60	125	108	173	143
27	22	76	62	126	109	174	144
28	23	77	63	127	111	175	145
29	24	78	64	128	112	176	146
30	25	79	65	129	—	177	—
30 bis	—	80	66	130	—	178	156
31	26	81	67	131	—	179	147
32	—	82	68	132	—	180	—
33	27	83	69	133	—	181	148
34	28	84	70	134	—	182	149
35	29	85	71	135	113	183	150
36	30	86	72	136	114	184	151
37	31	87	73	137	115	185	152
38	32	88	74	138	116	186	153
39	33	89	75	139	117	187	—
40	34	90	—	140	—	188	155
41	35	91	76	141	—	189	—
42	36	92	77	142	118	190	—
43	37	93	—	143	119	191	—
44	—	94	78	144	120	192	—
45	—	95	79	145	121	193	—
46	—	96	80	146	122	194	—
47	38	97	81	147	123	195	—
48	39	98	82	148	124	196	—
49	40	99	83	149	125	197	—

GENERAL INDEX

References to the kouroi themselves are not included in this general index as they are given in the museum index; nor are the places in which the kouroi were found included when these are given in the table of contents